First Edition

REASON IN THE BALANCE
An Inquiry Approach to Critical Thinking

Bailin & Battersby

McGraw-Hill Ryerson
Connect. Learn. Succeed.

The McGraw·Hill Companies

McGraw-Hill Ryerson
Connect. Learn. Succeed.

Reason in the Balance: An Inquiry Approach to Critical Thinking
First Edition

ISBN-13: 978-0-07-007341-8
ISBN-10: 0-07-007341-4

1 2 3 4 5 6 7 8 9 10 TCP 1 9 8 7 6 5 4 3 2 1 0

Printed and bound in Canada

Care has been taken to trace ownership of copyright material contained in this text; however, the
publisher will welcome any information that enables them to rectify any reference or credit for
subsequent editions.

Vice President, Editor in Chief: *Joanna Cotton*
Sponsoring Editor: *Karen Krahn*
Marketing Manager: *Margaret Janzen*
Developmental Editor: *My Editor Inc.*
Permissions Editor: *My Editor Inc.*
Editorial Associate: *Marina Seguin*
Supervising Editor: *Graeme Powell*
Copy Editor: *Elspeth McFadden*
Production Coordinator: *Emily Hickey*
Cover Design: *Michelle Losier*
Cover Image: *David Fischer/Getty Images*
Page Layout: *Laserwords Private Limited*
Printer: *Transcontinental Printing Group*

Library and Archives Canada Cataloguing in Publication

Bailin, Sharon, 1948-
     Reason in the balance : an inquiry approach to critical thinking / Sharon Bailin, Mark Battersby.
Includes bibliographical references and index.

ISBN 978-0-07-007341-8

     1. Critical thinking—Textbooks. I. Battersby, Mark II. Title.

BC177.B33 2010   160   C2010-904754-0

We would like to dedicate this book to our favourite critical thinkers, present and future, our grandchildren:

Heath Ailey Bailin

and

Sylvanna Baugh, Zahara Baugh, Tavish Allen, Angus Fisher, Mark Fisher,

Rylan Metcalf, Willow Allen, and the little one to come

Meet the Authors

Sharon Bailin

Sharon Bailin is a Professor Emeritus in the Faculty of Education at Simon Fraser University. She has written extensively on critical thinking and on creativity, focusing particularly on the creative dimensions to critical thinking and on critical thinking as inquiry. Bailin is the author of the award-winning book *Achieving Extraordinary Ends: An Essay on Creativity*. She is also one of the originators of a conception of critical thinking which has formed the foundation of a major curriculum project for K–12 schools both in North America and internationally. Bailin's work on critical thinking and on creativity has been presented in Italy, Hong Kong, Singapore, Israel, Mexico, Chile, the Netherlands, and England. Bailin is a Past President of the Philosophy of Education Society (of North America) and of the Association for Informal Logic and Critical Thinking. In addition to these academic pursuits, she also has a background in theatre and the arts.

Mark Battersby

Mark Battersby is a Professor of Philosophy at Capilano University, where he has taught courses in critical thinking since 1978. He has also taught critical thinking at the University of British Columbia, Simon Fraser University, and Stanford University. Battersby is the founder of the British Columbia Association for Critical Thinking Research and Instruction, and he has written and presented extensively on the subject of critical thinking and informal logic. He also led a provincial curriculum reform project focusing on learning outcomes in higher education. In addition to informal logic and argumentation theory, his research interests include philosophy of science, statistics, and democratic participation. His book on critical thinking about statistical and scientific information, *Is that a Fact?*, was published in 2009.

Brief Contents

Preface   x

Section I: The Nature of Inquiry

Chapter 1:
The Nature and Value of Inquiry   1

Chapter 2:
Introducing Guidelines for Inquiry   19

Section II: Arguments

Chapter 3:
Arguments and Their Structure   39

Chapter 4:
Inductive Arguments and Fallacies   58

Chapter 5:
Key Argument Types   81

Chapter 6:
Credible Sources and Appeals to Experts   100

Section III: Conducting an Inquiry

Chapter 7:
Identifying the Issue   119

Chapter 8:
Understanding the Case: Reasons and Context   138

Chapter 9:
Evaluating the Arguments   156

Chapter 10:
Making a Judgment and Making a Case   174

Chapter 11:
Dialogue and the Spirit of Inquiry   192

Section IV: Inquiry in Specific Areas

Chapter 12:
Inquiry in the Natural Sciences   211

Chapter 13:
Inquiry in the Social Sciences   237

Chapter 14:
Inquiry in the Arts   263

Chapter 15:
Inquiry in Philosophy: Ethics   291

Chapter 16:
Inquiry into the Extraordinary   306

Glossary   336

Photo Credits   341

Index   342

Contents

Preface   x

Section I: The Nature of Inquiry

Chapter 1:
The Nature and Value of Inquiry   1

Opening Dialogues: *Mystery Meatloaf*   1

What Is Inquiry?   4
   The Focus on an Issue   4
   A Careful Examination of the Issue   4
   A Reasoned Judgment   5

Dialogue: *Cruelty to Chickens?*   6

Occasions for Inquiry   10
   Feature: *Stun-gun inquiry costs at $3.7 million*   11

The Nature of Inquiry   11

Inquiry and Dialogue   13

The Value of Inquiry   13
   Feature: *"What Is Enlightenment ?"*   14

The Spirit of Inquiry   14
   Feature: *Socrates*   15

Check Your Understanding   16

Exercises   16

Chapter 2:
Introducing Guidelines for Inquiry   19

Opening Dialogue: *The Great Film Debate*   19

Guidelines for Inquiry   20
   What Is the Issue?   20
   What Kinds of Claims or Judgments Are at Issue?   21
   What Are the Relevant Reasons and Arguments on Various Sides of the Issue?   22
   What Is the Context of the Issue?   24
   How Do We Comparatively Evaluate the Various Reasons and Arguments to Reach a Reasoned Judgment?   25
   Feature: *The Sweet Hereafter*   27

Guidelines for Inquiry: Application   28

Dialogue: *Those Dangerous Dogs*   28
   What Is the Issue?   29
   What Kinds of Claims or Judgments Are at Issue?   29

What Are the Relevant Reasons and Arguments on Various Sides of the Issue?   30
What Is the Context of the Issue?   31
   Feature: *Vicious Dog Attack Angers Sask. Mom*   32
How Do We Comparatively Evaluate the Various Reasons and Arguments to Reach a Reasoned Judgment?   32
   Feature: *City May Redefine "Vicious"*   34
Applying the Guidelines for Inquiry   35

Check Your Understanding   36

Exercises   36

Section II: Arguments

Chapter 3:
Arguments and Their Structure   39

Opening Dialogue: *Raising the Minimum Wage I*   39
   Argument and Inquiry   40

The Structure of Arguments   41
   Standardizing Arguments   41
   Standardizing and the Principle of Charity   41
   Diagramming Arguments: Linked and Convergent   42
   Sub-arguments   44

Two Types of Arguments: Deductive and Inductive   45

A Brief Introduction to Formal Logic   50
   Necessary and Sufficient Conditions   50

Unstated Premises and Assumptions   53
   Dubious Assumptions   54

Check Your Understanding   55

Exercises   55

Chapter 4:
Inductive Arguments and Fallacies   58

Opening Dialogue: *Raising the Minimum Wage II*   58
   Feature: *B.C.'s $8 Minimum Wage Turns Eight*   60

Inductive Arguments   61
   Prima Facie   61
   Feature: *Truth and Credibility*   62

Fallacies   62
   Feature: *Similar Fact Evidence*   63
   Informal Fallacies   64
   Fallacies of Illusory Support   64

Feature: *Environmental Guru's Inconvenient Truth: His Diesel Bus Belched 20 Tonnes of CO$_2$*   66

Fallacies of Unacceptability   75

Check Your Understanding   79

Exercises   79

Chapter 5:
Key Argument Types   81

Opening Dialogue: *Legalizing Marijuana I*   81

Reductio   82

Analogical Arguments   83
Precedent Analogies   83
Causal Analogies   84

Evaluating Analogies   85

Argument and Explanation   88
The Difference Between Arguments and Explanations   89
Reason Explanations   89
Causal Explanations   90

Evaluating Particular Causal Explanations   91
1. Did the Claimed Cause Occur Before the Effect?   91
2. Is There a Credible Causal Link?   91
3. Are There Other Plausible Alternative Explanations that Fit the Facts? Can They Be Eliminated?   92
4. Which Is the Simplest Explanation?   93
Feature: *William of Occam*   93

Evaluating General Causal Explanations   93
Correlation   93
Feature: *The Pickle Fallacy*   94
From Correlation to Causality   94

Evaluating Reason Explanations   95

Check Your Understanding   96

Exercises   96

Chapter 6:
Credible Sources and Appeals to Experts   100

Opening Dialogue: *Legalizing Marijuana II*   100

Evaluating the Credibility of Sources   103
Guiding Questions for Evaluating Sources   104

Fallacy: Improper Appeal to Authority   108
Feature: *Fallacious Appeal to Expertise: An Example*   108

Finding Credible and Useful Sources   109

Using the Web   110
Guiding Questions for Evaluating Websites   112
Feature: *Example of an Abstract*   112
Feature: *Wikipedia and Appeals to Authority*   113
Misleading or Untrustworthy Sites   113
Feature: *Misleading Websites*   114
Using Footnotes to Check Credibility   114

Using Books   116

Check Your Understanding   116

Exercises   116

Section III: Conducting an Inquiry

Chapter 7:
Identifying the Issue   119

Opening Dialogue: *War?*   119

What Is the Issue?   121
Feature: *Atomic Bombings of Hiroshima and Nagasaki*   121

What Is an Issue?   122
Characteristics of an Issue   122

Problems with Language   124
Lack of Clarity   124
Loaded Language   125

Types of Judgments   126
Feature: *Canada and the First Atomic Bombs*   127
Feature: *Scientists and Responsibility*   127
Factual Judgments   128
Evaluative Judgments   129
Distinguishing Between Factual and Evaluative Judgments   131
Interpretive Judgments   133

Check Your Understanding   134

Exercises   135

Chapter 8:
Understanding the Case: Reasons and Context   138

Opening Dialogue: *Capital Punishment*   138

Relevant Reasons and Arguments on Various Sides of the Issue   139

Context of the Issue   140
State of Practice   140
History of the Debate   141
Intellectual, Social, Political, and Historical Contexts   141

Mapping the Contexts   142
Laying Out the Current Debate   142
Laying Out the Context   145
Feature: *The Death Penalty in Canada: Twenty Years of Abolition*   146
Feature: *No More Clemency Appeals for Canadians on Death Row in U.S.: Tories*   147
Feature: *Liberal and Conservative versus liberal and conservative*   152
Mapping the Context: Capital Punishment   153

Check Your Understanding   153

Exercises   154

Chapter 9:

Evaluating the Arguments   156

Opening Dialogue: *Capital Punishment II*   156

Evaluating the Main Reasons and Arguments   157
Evaluating the Pro Arguments   158
Evaluating the Con Arguments   165
Feature: *Wrongfully Convicted: High-profile Cases Where the Courts Got It Wrong: Steven Truscott*   166

Identifying and Evaluating Additional Arguments   168

Evaluating Individual Arguments: Summing Up   169

Check Your Understanding   172

Exercises   172

Chapter 10:

Making a Judgment and Making a Case   174

Opening Dialogue: *Capital Punishment III*   174

Reaching a Reasoned Judgment   175

Weighing Competing Considerations   177
Dealing with Differences in Weighting   179

Apportioning Judgment   180

Evaluating a Given Case   182
Fallacies of Judgment   182

Making a Reasonable Case   183

Check Your Understanding   190

Exercises   190

Chapter 11:

Dialogue and the Spirit of Inquiry   192

Opening Dialogue: *Hate Speech*   192
Feature: *The Law and Hate Speech*   194

Achieving the Spirit of Inquiry   197

Dialogue: *Post Mortem*   198

Obstacles to the Spirit of Inquiry   199

Overcoming the Obstacles to Inquiry   201
Know Your Initial Views and Biases   201
Monitor Your Process of Inquiry and Dialogue   201
Evaluate Your Own Views   202

Conducting a Dialogue   203
Respectful Treatment   204
Meaningful Participation   204
Productive Interaction   204
Feature: *Political Debate in Canada*   205

Responding to Fallacies   205
Ad Hominem and Straw Person   206
Post Hoc (False Causal Claim)   206
Popularity   207
Faulty Analogy   207
Problematic Premise   207
Irrelevant Reason   207
Anecdotal Evidence and Hasty Conclusion   208

Check Your Understanding   208

Exercises   209

Section IV: Inquiry in Specific Areas

Chapter 12:

Inquiry in the Natural Sciences   211

Opening Dialogue: *I Hate Science!*   211
Feature: *Technology in Science*   213

The Basics of Scientific Reasoning: Arguments and Evaluation   214
Feature: *Dialogue in Science*   215

Argument to the Best Explanation in the Natural Sciences   215
The Process of Inquiry in the Natural Sciences: An Example   219

Reasoned Judgment and Scientific Inquiry   221
Causal Explanations   221
Testability   221
Feature: *Early Experiments*   222
Fruitfulness   222
Peer Review   223

Dialogue: *Evolution*   223
Feature: *Charles Darwin,*   224
Feature: *The Creation*   225

Science and Statistics   228

Dialogue: *And I Really Hate Statistics!*   228
Feature: *Early Medical Statisticians*   229
Inquiry and Statistics: An Example   231

Scientific Inquiry: A Final Note   232

Check Your Understanding   233

Exercises   233

Chapter 13:

Inquiry in the Social Sciences   237

Opening Dialogue: *Video Violence*   237
Feature: *Games List in Family Media Guide*   238

Assessing Scientific Claims in the Social Sciences: An Example   239

Evaluation of Claims Based on Statistical Inference   240
Observational Studies   240
Experimental Studies   241
Feature: *Effect size*   245
Evaluating Causal Claims in Statistical Research   245
Considerations for Evaluating Causal Claims in the Social Sciences   247

Studying Human Nature   248

Dialogue: *Human Nature: Nasty or Nice?*   248
Feature: *Rousseau and Hobbes on Human Nature*   252
Feature: *Darwin on Generosity*   253
Feature: *Darwin on Group Selection*   254
Further Reflections on the Study of Human Behaviour   258

Check Your Understanding   260

Exercises   260

Chapter 14:
Inquiry in the Arts   263
. . . .

Opening Dialogue: *Guernica*   263

**Applying the Guiding Questions to Inquiry about
Works of Art   265**
Observation   266
Interpretation   268
Feature: *"The Meat Dress"*   278

The Nature of Inquiry in the Arts   279

A Public Art Controversy   280

Dialogue: Tilted Arc   281
Feature: *Public Art*   284
Feature: *Olympic Public Art to Light Up Vancouver*   287

Check Your Understanding   287

Exercises   288

Chapter 15:
Inquiry in Philosophy: Ethics   291
. . . .

Opening *Dialogue: It's All Relative*   291
Feature: *B.C. Religious Leaders Charged with
Polygamy*   292

Ethical Inquiry   293
Inquiry on Ethical Relativism   293
Feature: *Moral Progress*   295
Inquiry into Polygamy   298

Check Your Understanding   304

Exercises   304

Chapter 16:
Inquiry into the Extraordinary   306
. . . .

Opening Dialogue: *The Secret*   306
Feature: *Do Americans Believe in the Paranormal?*   308
Feature: *Bigfoot and Other Beasts*   309
Prima Facie Evaluation   310
Evaluation of Scientific Claims and Causal
Reasoning   313
Comparative Evaluation   317
Feature: *W. K. Clifford, "The Ethics of Belief"*   321
Conspiracy Theories   321

Dialogue: 9/11 Conspiracy?   321
Feature: *Is Elvis Alive?*   330

Check Your Understanding   332

Exercises   333

Glossary   336

Photo Credits   341

Index   342

Preface

Professor: Today I'd like to continue our discussion of fallacies, beginning with the fallacy of ad hominem. There are two kinds of ad hominem fallacies. The most notorious is the abusive ad hominem, which consists of using a malicious denigration of a person to reject his or her argument or position.

Student: Sir, I have a question. It may be a little off topic, but it's something that's been bothering me for a while.

Professor: Of course—go ahead.

Student: When I saw this course on critical thinking in the calendar, I thought, "Great! This will really help me to think about all those issues out there—like what we ought to do about global warming or the economic crisis. It might even help me make decisions like whether I should buy a car or take the bus."

Professor: Well, it can do all those things, though perhaps indirectly ... Or at least provide a necessary condition—

Student: Intending no disrespect sir, but I just don't see it. You've got these guys debating about global warming: one of them has a bunch of arguments claiming one thing and another has this evidence claiming the opposite, and then they argue with each other, and then a third guy chimes in, and I'm not even sure if they're all arguing about the same thing! So finding a few logical mistakes may be useful. But I don't see how that helps me figure out what to believe.

Professor: Knowing whether the various participants in the debate are reliable sources or whether there are errors in their reasoning are important aspects in evaluating their arguments.

Student: Sure, I see that all that stuff's important, but I don't see how it gets me to the point of figuring out what's the best view.

This dialogue may have a ring of familiarity about it. It certainly does for us. And we take seriously the issue that it raises: How can we teach critical thinking in such a way as to provide students with the understanding and skills to be able to make reasoned judgments in real life contexts? This was the issue that motivated us to develop a new approach, and it is the issue that prompted us to write this text.

We began our quest for a better approach by looking at the actual practice of critical thinking and what it involves. We concluded that coming to a reasoned judgment on complex issues is at the heart of the kind of critical thinking which actually takes place both in the disciplines and in everyday life. Yet students tend to have very little instruction in how to go about the inquiry process and in understanding the criteria used to make such reasoned judgments. It is the goal of our text to address this problem.

Thus, unlike most texts in the area, which have as their central focus the analysis and critique of individual arguments, *Reason in the Balance* focuses more broadly on the practice of inquiry. By inquiry we intend **critical** inquiry, the process of carefully examining an issue in order to come to a reasoned judgment. The notion of reasoned judgment is crucial here: we are not referring to inquiry as simply the process of gathering information, but rather as the process of coming to a reasoned judgment based on a critical evaluation of relevant reasons. The analysis and critique of individual arguments certainly have an important role to play and are given due emphasis in the text; however, our book goes beyond this dimension to focus on the various aspects that go into the practice of inquiry, including identifying issues, identifying the relevant contexts, understanding the competing cases, and making a comparative judgment among them.

Distinctive Features of the Text

This inquiry orientation gives rise to certain distinctive features of the text:

- emphasis on the dialectical dimension of critical thinking
- inclusion of inquiry in specific contexts
- attention to the dialogical aspect of inquiry
- emphasis on the spirit of inquiry

Emphasis on the Dialectical Dimension of Critical Thinking

Arriving at reasoned judgments is a dialectical process that takes place in contexts of disagreement, debate, or challenge. It involves the adjudication among various positions offered in the context of such debate. Our text puts significant emphasis on this dialectical dimension. This takes several forms:

Emphasis on the Current Debate

The text focuses not just on evaluating particular arguments, but more broadly on making a comparative assessment of the relative strengths and weaknesses of the competing views in the debate. This involves knowing the various positions, the evidence and arguments mustered in their favour, the criticism and objections which have been levelled against them, the responses to the criticisms and objections, and alternative arguments and views.

Attention to the History of the Debate

When an issue is controversial or has been contested, discussion and debate will likely have gone on over a period of time. The text gives due attention to learning about the history of the debate in order to understand the issue, the various positions which are contesting for acceptance, and where the burden of proof lies.

Attention to Relevant Aspects of the Context of the Debate

Certain aspects of the context surrounding a debate, including the intellectual, political, social, historical, and disciplinary contexts, are usually relevant in understanding some positions and the assumptions behind them. We explore in the text in what ways a consideration of various aspects of context is relevant in arriving at a reasoned judgment.

Inclusion of Inquiry in Specific Contexts

With our focus broadening from argument evaluation to inquiry, the range of material treated has broadened as well. Thus, the text goes beyond a focus on individual arguments found in media, politics, and everyday interactions to treat inquiry which takes place in a variety of different contexts, both disciplinary and everyday. There are chapters on inquiry in the natural sciences, in the social sciences, and in the arts, as well as a chapter on inquiry into extraordinary claims. These chapters use detailed examples to demonstrate the common structure of inquiry across these areas as well as the types of judgments and criteria which are distinctive to each. While instructors may choose to use only some of these chapters, the wide range of topics is supplied in order to provide ample opportunity for the application of the strategies and criteria of inquiry in a diversity of areas.

Attention to the Dialogical Aspect of Inquiry

In actual contexts, inquiries are conducted not only in written form, but very often in the form of dialogues among individuals or groups of individuals. Even when there is not an actual dialogue with people talking face to face, inquiries involve a number of views or positions in conversation with each other and thus can be seen to exhibit the characteristics of a dialogue. This dialogical aspect is one which is given attention in our text through the extensive use of dialogues with an ongoing cast of characters to exemplify the topics under discussion. Your students will identify with the characters in these dialogues, providing a very accessible and engaging narrative entry point for them. The dialogues also serve to model the process of inquiry which the students are learning. In addition, the text encourages the creation and use of dialogues in and out of class as a way to conduct and represent inquiries.

Emphasis on the Spirit of Inquiry

Reason in the Balance puts considerable emphasis on the attitudes or habits of mind necessary for inquiry, such as open-mindedness, fair-mindedness, and the awareness of one's own biases and irrational tendencies. We also emphasize the attitudes required for conducting a civil, respectful, and productive inquiry dialogue.

Online Learning Centre

The text's Online Learning Centre (www.mcgrawhill.ca/olc/bailin) holds the weblinks and other material to assist students with the chapter exercises. The following ancillaries are available to instructors:

- Instructor's Manual
- PowerPoint lecture slides

Acknowledgments

We must begin by thanking Lisa Rahn, former Acquisitions Editor at McGraw-Hill Ryerson, for her strong belief in and commitment to this project right from the moment the prospectus first landed on her desk, and for her unflagging support, constant encouragement, and sound advice as the project proceeded.

Our deepest gratitude to our Development Editor, Katherine Goodes, for guiding the book, and us, through the editorial and publication processes with such consummate skill. Her tireless efforts, commitment, and advice and support have been key to the successful completion of this project.

We would like to express our thanks to the personnel at McGraw-Hill Ryerson, Karen Krahn, Sponsoring Editor; Katherine Goodes, Developmental Editor; Megan Jones, Permissions Editor; Graeme Powell, Supervising Editor; Emily Hickey, Production Coordinator, and Elspeth McFadden, Copy Editor, for giving shape and form to our ideas and turning them into a concrete reality.

A special note of thanks must go to the students in Mark's critical thinking courses at Capilano University in 2009 and 2010 for giving this material a "test run" and for their feedback and comments, which have been enormously useful in our revision process.

Thanks to our colleagues in the field of critical thinking, whose ideas and clarity of thought have provided inspiration, and whose feedback has been a source of clarification and insight. As well, our thanks go out to the following reviewers, whose insightful comments, challenges, criticisms, and suggestions have resulted in *Reason in the Balance* being a much improved work:

- Alan Belk, University of Guelph
- Leslie Burkholder, University of British Columbia
- Karen Chandler, George Brown College
- Darcy Cutler, Douglas College
- Mano Daniel, Douglas College
- Jacqueline Davies, Queen's University
- Eugene Earnshaw, Seneca College
- Anthony Fabiano, Algoma University College
- Mark Gardiner, Mount Royal College
- Antoine Goulem, Seneca College
- Hans V. Hansen, University of Windsor
- Alison Horton, Mohawk College
- Jonathan Katz, Kwantlen University College
- Ken Kirkwood, University of Western Ontario
- Jean Lachapelle, Champlain Regional College
- Colleen Mahy, George Brown College
- Veronique Mandal, St. Clair College
- Mark Mercer, St. Mary's University
- Andreea Mihali, Wilfrid Laurier University
- Mary Richardson, Athabasca University
- Jonathan Salem-Wiseman, Humber College
- Maria Vasilodimitrakis, Seneca College
- Patrick Walsh, University of Winnipeg
- Joanne Wotypka, Athabasca University

It would not be possible to even begin to put into words the extent of our appreciation to the two individuals who, more than any others, made this project possible— our spouses, Diana Davidson and Adam Horvath. We would like to express special thanks to Mark's wife, Diana Davidson, for seeing that we could and should write a text, and for encouraging us to do so. And the roles of both Diana and Adam as idea sources, sounding boards, manuscript reviewers, and logistical advisors played an important role in the quality of the book's content. But most important to the successful completion of the book was the unfailing support of both through the demands and challenges of the writing process and their enthusiastic encouragement of the project.

No list of acknowledgements would be complete without each of us expressing our heartfelt thanks to each other. This has been a stimulating, productive, supportive, and synergistic collaboration, in which the resulting whole is greater than either Bailin or Battersby contributions would have been on their own.

Mark Battersby & Sharon Bailin
Vancouver, September 2010

Chapter 1
The Nature and Value of Inquiry

Learning Objectives

After reading this chapter, you should be able to:

- explain the characteristics of inquiry
- identify situations which are occasions for inquiry
- understand the nature of inquiry and its relationship to dialogue
- appreciate why inquiry is of value
- identify the features which constitute the spirit of inquiry

Mystery Meatloaf

It's lunch time. Five classmates have assembled in the cafeteria and are surveying the lunch choices. Present are Phil Gold, Sophia Onassis, Ravi Singh, Ahmed Ali, and Nancy McGregor.

Phil: Ah ... mystery meatloaf—my favourite. I'll have a big piece with lots of gravy—and a double order of fries.

Nancy: Gross!

Phil: Yeah, I guess you're right—double fries is a bit much.

Nancy: No ... I mean—MEAT! RED meat, yet! How can you eat that stuff?

Phil: So what's the big deal?

Ravi: Haven't you heard? Our Nancy's become a vegetarian.

Ahmed: No way! Not one of those granola-munching hippies?

Nancy: I just don't see how you can possibly bring yourself to eat another living creature. It's cruel ... and inhumane!

Ravi: But animals eat other animals. It's just natural.

Ahmed: And besides, meat tastes so good. Just think of biting into a big, juicy, pink steak ... mmm.

Nancy: Ugh!

Phil: Everyone eats meat—at least all normal people. It's just some dumb cow.

Sophia: I've heard that animals used for meat are kept in horrible conditions.

Ravi: So now you believe everything you hear? That's not like you, Sophia. It's all a load of propaganda from those animal rights loonies.

Nancy: You guys are just a bunch of … cannibals!

Ahmed: Well, isn't she on her high horse, dictating to us what we should and shouldn't eat!

Nancy: Come on, Sophia—let's move to another table. I can't sit with these … insensitive boors!

Phil: Fine! Now at least we can eat in peace. Bring on the meatloaf …

You have likely been involved in scenes like this, possibly quite often. They are, unfortunately, fairly typical. There is a disagreement over an issue about which people feel strongly. The disagreement escalates into name-calling and high emotions, and ends in misunderstanding.

But this conversation could go in a very different direction.

Mystery Meatloaf—Take II

Phil: Ah … mystery meatloaf—my favourite. I'll have a big piece with lots of gravy—and a double order of fries.

Nancy: I'll have the vegetarian lasagna please, with a side of yam fries.

Ahmed: What, no meatloaf today?

Ravi: Haven't you heard? Our Nancy's become a vegetarian.

Ahmed: No way! Why did you do something like that?

Nancy: It just finally got to me that I was eating an animal, another living creature, and that didn't seem right.

Ravi: But animals eat other animals. It's just natural.

Ahmed: And besides, it tastes so good.

Phil: Anyway, it's just a dumb cow, isn't it? It doesn't have thoughts or feelings like a person, does it?

Ravi: I'm pretty sure that animals feel pain. My dog sure howls when he gets his tail caught in the door.

Phil: Well, what about fish? They're not too with it.

Nancy: Some of my vegetarian friends do eat fish. I've been struggling with that one.

Sophia: I've heard that animals used for meat are kept in horrible conditions.

Ravi: I wonder if that's true or whether it's mostly propaganda from the animal rights folks?

Sophia: I haven't really checked that out …

Ahmed: And there are some animals that live quite well. There are those free-range chickens who get to roam around and have lots of grain to eat and lead a normal chicken life—in fact, probably better than most. Until it's time to hop into the pot, that is. So, is it OK to eat those free-range chicks?

Nancy: It's still killing other living creatures for our own selfish purposes. Why should we think that human beings have a right to do that?

Phil: It bothers me, though, when folks get so worked up about how we treat animals—especially cute ones with big eyes—and ignore all the people getting mistreated and even killed all over the world. Isn't that more important?

Sophia: Like the way all those movie stars and famous people protest about the seal hunt but don't take any action about all the genocides happening around the world.

Ahmed: Wow—we've sure come up with a lot of questions. Not many answers, though.

Sophia: I wonder…maybe there's some way to go about trying to answer some of the questions. We can't be the first people to think about these issues. So we could have a look to see what ideas and information are out there.

Nancy: I'm sure there's information about the conditions in which animals are kept.

Ravi: And there must be research about whether different animals can feel pain, or even have other feelings.

Phil: And I'll bet other folks have thought about the moral issues about the treatment and rights of animals.

Ravi: Though I don't expect that they'll all agree.

Phil: No, but that would at least give us some ideas to consider.

Ravi: And evaluate.

Sophia: I think it's worth a try. I don't know if we'll end up agreeing. Maybe we will. But even if we don't, at least we'll be able to think about the issues in a more informed way. And we'll be able to understand where the others are coming from.

Nancy: Now that would be progress!

The two versions of these scenes begin in the same place, with the issue of Nancy's vegetarianism. It's an issue about which many of the classmates have definite opinions and, in some cases, quite strong emotional reactions. The two versions of the scene quickly go off in different directions, however.

List some ways in which the two scenes are different.

What Do You Think ?

In the first scene, the students' emotional reactions have full reign from the outset. The students are not willing to find out more about the views of those with whom they disagree nor are they prepared to give other ideas serious consideration. Instead, they engage in put-downs and name-calling. They cannot find any way to get past their initial disagreement—in fact, it escalates into a nasty breakdown in communication. In the end, there are no winners. No one has gained in terms of an understanding of the issue or of each other's opinions, and everyone has lost in terms of hurt feelings and possibly ruptured friendships.

The second scene begins in the same place, with the students holding differing views about vegetarianism. But a crucial difference is that the students are open to finding out about the views of the other students with whom they disagree. They offer reasons for their positions, explore the ideas of the others, and engage in a genuine dialogue. The students also have strong emotional commitments to their initial positions, and this may be entirely appropriate. The difference in the second scene is that they are not so wedded to these positions that they are unwilling to listen; instead, they show respect for the others' views and are open to hearing and considering their ideas. The students show a willingness to grapple with the issue to the point of seeking out additional information and ideas and giving them serious, critical consideration. They are beginning to engage in the process of **inquiry.**

The situation which is portrayed in the second scene is, of course, an ideal. It is, however, an ideal which is worth aspiring toward since, in the process of inquiry, there is the potential for many gains. The students may acquire new knowledge and understanding, both about the issue itself and about other related issues and questions. They will be in a position to think about the issue more critically and make a more informed and thoughtful judgment. They will have found a way to understand the basis for their disagreement, to resolve their disagreement in a reasonable way, and to interact in a civil and respectful manner, even when they continue to disagree. In addition, by engaging in this type of joint inquiry, they may experience the satisfaction of working and learning together in a community.

> **Inquiry** is the process of carefully examining an issue in order to come to a reasoned judgment.

What Is Inquiry?

We said that the students are beginning in the second dialogue to engage in the process of inquiry. But what, exactly, do we mean by inquiry? We use the term "inquiry" to refer specifically to *critical* inquiry, which is the process of carefully examining an issue in order to come to a reasoned judgment. Let's look at this definition more closely.

The Focus on an Issue

> An **issue** is a challenge, controversy, or difference in point of view that can be the focus for inquiry.

The first thing to note is that inquiry focuses on an **issue.** This might involve a political controversy, an ethical decision, a scientific debate, a puzzle or problem in some specific subject area, or a decision to be made or problem to be resolved in daily life. The key factor is that there is some challenge, controversy, or range in points of view.

The first dialogue we read did revolve around an issue, namely whether a person should eat meat, but the dialogue displayed none of the other features of inquiry.

A Careful Examination of the Issue

> Inquiry involves an active pursuit of knowledge and understanding.

The second aspect to note is that inquiry involves a careful examination of the issue. When we're engaged in inquiry, we don't just accept our existing views without question, as the students do in the first dialogue. Neither do we simply accept what others say or what we read. Instead, we investigate to find out for ourselves what the best position or action is. Inquiry involves an active pursuit of knowledge and understanding.

In the second dialogue, we can see that the participants are beginning to engage in this process by questioning some of the ideas they began with. They show a willingness to investigate and inquire. For example, Ahmed asks Nancy her reasons for becoming a vegetarian; Phil starts to question whether animals have feelings; Ravi and Sophia recognize the need to investigate the conditions in which animals are kept; and Nancy and Phil start to raise questions about the moral issues involved in eating meat. The participants also realize that there are resources they can seek out to investigate these questions and issues; thus, they do not need to be content with their own unreflective views or to rely uncritically on the views of others. They are in a position to inquire.

A Reasoned Judgment

The third and most important aspect of inquiry noted in the definition is that it involves coming to a judgment . The investigation is not just a matter of gathering information from various sources. Rather, it has a purpose: to come to (or try to come to) a judgment about the issue. Actual inquiries will not always result in a judgment that is agreed upon by all. They may end instead in reasonable and respectful disagreement; and this may be entirely appropriate. Indeed, for some inquiries—in philosophy, for example—there is little or no expectation of a resolution; rather, the aim is to come to a reasoned position. Nonetheless, the important point here is that inquiry is not just an exercise in data-gathering. It also involves evaluation and aims toward a judgment. In the second dialogue, the participants are setting about gathering information, but they will still need to evaluate the information and arguments which they find in order to try to come to some judgment about the issue of vegetarianism.

> A **reasoned judgment** is a judgment based on a critical evaluation of relevant information and arguments.

The idea that the judgment is a **reasoned judgment** is central here. The judgment aimed at in inquiry is not arbitrary; it is not just a matter of unreflective opinion, nor is it based uncritically on what others say. Rather, coming to a reasoned judgment involves **critical evaluation.** The practice of critical evaluation is also central to inquiry. We need to evaluate the information and arguments we find because not all opinions are equally valid. Some opinions are better justified than others; some views can be supported with better reasons than others.

> A **critical evaluation** is an assessment of the reasons and arguments on various sides of an issue.

The critical evaluation involved in reaching a reasoned judgment is not just a matter of evaluating individual arguments and pieces of information. It involves, in addition, comparing the arguments in terms of their strengths and weaknesses, and deciding how much weight to assign to each in order to see what, on balance, is the best view to hold.

Critical evaluation is based on **criteria** which identify the relevant considerations providing the basis for making a judgment. We make judgments on the basis of criteria all the time although we may not always be explicitly aware of the criteria we are using. But we can usually come up with them if we think about it.

> **Criteria** specify the relevant considerations that provide the basis for making a judgment.

If you were thinking about buying a car, what are some criteria which you might use to decide which car to buy?

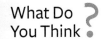

What Do You Think

Some of the criteria which people would commonly use in contemplating a car purchase would be affordability, fuel efficiency, comfort, reliability, and pleasing appearance. Some of these criteria, such as fuel efficiency, are specific to the subject of purchasing a car, while others, such as affordability and a pleasing appearance, would apply to other types of purchases as well.

Criteria often specify the degree to which an object—in this case, a car—must fulfill a certain consideration. For example, affordability is a consideration for most people when buying a car, but a more precise criterion for purchase might be "costs less than $30,000."

When we use the term more loosely, we can talk about criteria being traded off. For example, we might pay more (less affordability) for a car that was extremely fuel-efficient (more fuel efficiency).

Keep in Mind

Features of Inquiry
- the focus on an issue
- a careful examination of the issue
- a reasoned judgment

It is important to recognize that the criteria for making a reasoned judgment must refer to considerations which are publicly available for all to consider. Some public considerations for making the decision whether to eat meat would include nutritional value, impact of meat production on the environment, the treatment of animals raised for meat, and the morality of humans killing animals for food.

Personal preferences, although they may provide an individual with a reason to do something, cannot supply the criteria for a reasoned judgment in the public realm, as they would not necessarily be agreed to by someone else. For example, the fact that Ravi likes meat may provide him with a reason for eating it, but would not constitute a reason for Nancy.

Many criteria are specific to particular areas. The criteria for making political decisions would include bringing more benefits than harms to those affected, cost effectiveness, and respect for the rights of the individuals involved. Criteria for evaluating a mystery novel would include coherence of plot, amount of suspense, and believability of the characters. Criteria for evaluating scientific claims would include ability to explain the evidence and relationship with existing theory.

Critical evaluation is at the heart of inquiry.

Coming to a reasoned judgment on complex issues also involves the evaluation of numerous arguments. Such an evaluation calls for criteria for assessing reasoning: the reasons offered must be relevant to the conclusions, and there should not be any logical errors or weaknesses (fallacies). These criteria are not specific to particular areas but apply in just about any area in which reasoning takes place.

Apply Your Understanding Exercises 1, 2, 3

Critical evaluation is at the heart of inquiry. If in the second dialogue the students go about seeking out information and arguments and then proceed to evaluate what they have found according to appropriate criteria, they will be engaging in the process of inquiry. Let's see what this might look like.

Cruelty to Chickens?

Our group of classmates has reconvened in the local café after doing some research on their questions about eating meat.

Sophia: Well, after a trip to the library and a session on the internet, I can see that I was right about one thing: we aren't the first people to think about these issues.

Nancy: You can say that again. I found all kinds of information about the conditions of animals raised for meat.

Ravi: And there's certainly been a lot written about whether animals have feelings.

Phil: That's nothing! Do you know that there are folks who spend their lives thinking about whether it's morally OK for people to eat animals?

Ravi: So where do we start?

Ahmed: Why don't we start with how they treat animals raised for meat? That seems to me to be pretty important and quite straightforward.

Nancy: Well … I came across a very disturbing item on that score. There's this video I saw on the web about how a certain fast food chain treats (or should I say, mistreats) the chickens it uses for those tasty morsels we all enjoy so much. There's some heartbreaking footage of chickens living all jammed together in horrible unhygienic conditions, suffering with broken bones, hung upside down, tortured by having their beaks cut off, unable to stand up because they've been forced to put on so much weight. It's just terrible! According to Pamela Anderson, who narrates the video, chickens are as intelligent as dogs and cats. And when they live in natural surroundings, they form friendships and lasting bonds with other birds, they love their young, and they enjoy a full life.

Ahmed: What was the website you found that on?

Nancy: The website for PETA—People for the Ethical Treatment of Animals.

Ravi: That's a well-known animal rights group—not exactly an unbiased source of information.

Ahmed: Why do you say that?

Ravi: Because they clearly have an agenda—to promote animal rights and criticize how animals are treated. So I'd have to wonder if they're giving a fair account of all the information. Of course, what they say might be true, but I'd want some additional support from other sources before giving up my chicken treats.

Sophia: That video sounds like sensationalism to me. It's set up to play on people's emotions, and they may not stop to think critically about what they're seeing and hearing.

Phil: Pamela Anderson—you've got to be kidding! I'm not sure I'd rely on her as my source of information. Just because she's a famous star does not make her an expert on the behaviour of chickens.

Sophia: Even if what they say on the video is true (and we won't know that until we do some more research), we still wouldn't know how widespread these practices are. Maybe this is an isolated case. I read several articles that said that there are laws in many parts of the world that regulate the treatment of animals and that conditions are improving. In Canada, although there are general laws about animal cruelty that also apply to farm animals, there are no laws specifically governing the on-farm care of animals. There are only voluntary codes.[1]

Ahmed: Something else that's bothering me is the way that Pamela Anderson describes chickens' lives in natural surroundings—forming friendships, loving their young, leading a full life. Give me a break! She's assuming that chickens are just like humans, but one of the main questions here is whether they are. I mean, how do we really know what the good life is for a chicken?

Ravi: Yeah … life's not necessarily a picnic even for the chickens wandering around in a farm yard, what with the foxes and all.

Phil: I found a website that's very critical of PETA, claiming that they kill a lot of animals, that they use scare tactics to try to forcibly dictate to the public how they should act, and that they even support eco-terrorism.

Nancy: What was the website?

Phil: It's called "PETA kills animals".

Nancy: I think that the name says it all. It doesn't exactly sound like an unbiased source of information either.

Ahmed: From what you say, it seems like they're just attacking the PETA folks with emotionally charged accusations without offering any real support for their claims.

Ravi: And anyway, I don't see how any of the claims from the "PETA kills animals" website are relevant to the issue of how animals raised for meat are treated.

Sophia: I agree, Ravi. Well, I came across a really interesting article on animal welfare and factory farming, published by the Food and Agriculture Organization of the United Nations, written by a university professor who appears to have some expertise on the subject.[2]

Phil: Now he sounds like a more neutral and reliable source.

Ahmed: Well, it does sound like he has more expertise than Pamela Anderson. But why should we think that he's a neutral source? Couldn't the Food and Agriculture Organization of the U.N. have an agenda as well?

Sophia: I suppose it's possible. But he doesn't just make unsubstantiated claims. He analyzes the arguments on all sides and provides lots of research to support his arguments. And based on this, he argues that the situation is really more varied than many of the animal rights activists claim. There's actually very little research about how animals are treated on factory farms, and what little there is shows a wide range of values and practices. He argues that we shouldn't condemn factory farms as a whole; instead, we need to address issues of animal welfare directly, ensuring animals freedom from hunger, from thirst, from discomfort, from fear, and from disease.

Nancy: But does he consider the possibility that the real solution to the problem is to stop eating animals?

Sophia: Actually … no, he doesn't. He says that he accepts the fact that vegetarianism hasn't really caught on and doesn't seem likely to, so he's looking for the best solution given the assumption that people will continue to eat meat.

Ahmed: I found some articles that agree with that point of view, arguing that meat is an important source of protein and will continue to be throughout the world. So the key is to find ways of raising animals more humanely. And they point out that this is starting to happen.

Nancy: I'd want to see some evidence before believing that.

Sophia: Well, folks, we've found lots of information and different arguments—but where does all of this leave us in thinking about our question?

Phil: It seems to me that we don't have a clear and simple answer to the question of how animals raised for meat are treated. We've come across claims and arguments from various sources, some biased and some not. But we'll need to do more research to check up on the accuracy of some of the claims and to find out how widespread any mistreatment might be.

Ravi: I think that this discussion has shown us that we need to think more carefully about what animal welfare might mean. And wouldn't our earlier question about whether animals have feelings be important here?

Ahmed: It does seem that it's at least possible to raise animals in a more humane way, so animals raised for meat don't have to be kept in horrible conditions.

Nancy: But I still don't think that it's right to eat them, no matter how they're kept.

Sophia: The issue of the treatment of animals raised for meat is obviously more complex than we'd realized. I don't think that we can expect to resolve it in one sitting. We have made some progress, though. But Nancy's right—even if we do figure that one out, that still leaves us with the moral issue of whether people even have a right to eat animals.

Phil: And I do have a lot of material on that! But that will have to wait. I have to get to class …

At this point in the process, the students have actively sought out information from books and from the internet in order to investigate their issue. But they realize that they cannot just accept everything they have heard or read, especially since much of the information and many of the arguments conflict. They need to evaluate what they have found.

What Do You Think ?

Describe any problems that you see in the material which the students have found.

One aspect of the evaluation involves examining the sources of the information they have come across in order to determine to what extent they can be relied upon. The students quickly recognize that both PETA and "PETA kills animals" are organizations with strong agendas and so may uncritically promote one perspective. Thus they must be aware of the likelihood of **bias** in the information presented and exercise caution about accepting it uncritically. The Food and Agriculture Organization of the United Nations, on the other hand, appears to be a much more neutral and less biased source in that it is an extremely well-respected international organization which does not have an explicit mandate to promote one point of view. This judgment is supported by the fact that the arguments presented on its website are backed up by research and a consideration of various sides of the issue. The students realize that a university professor who works on issues of agricultural production has more relevant expertise with respect to issues of animal treatment on factory farms than a media star.

The students also begin to evaluate the claims and findings in the material which they have found, recognizing the need for evidence to substantiate claims, as well as the need for corroboration (additional support) for findings. They recognize that they should not generalize from the one possible case of the mistreatment of animals raised for meat to all factory farms. More evidence and research are required in order to know what the situation is on a larger scale.

In addition, the students start to evaluate the reasoning and argumentation offered in the various articles which they have found. Argumentation is the process of offering arguments, or reasons, in support of a conclusion. The students begin to recognize some **fallacies** (common types of weak arguments that have considerable persuasive power) and see how they weaken the force of the arguments. For example, Ravi notices that the claims made on the "PETA kills animals" website are irrelevant to the issue of the treatment of animals raised for meat, and Ahmed notices how emotionally charged labels are used on the same website to substitute for arguments. Ahmed also notices that Pamela Anderson's claims about the lives of chickens in natural surroundings assume that chickens are a lot like humans, but this is one of the issues which is in contention in the debate. (This is the fallacy of begging the question which we'll learn more about in Chapter 4.)

One central aspect of evaluation that the students recognize is the need to look at both (or many) sides of a debate and not just critique arguments on one side. Thus they realize the importance of finding **counter-examples** to some of the claims (that chicken life in the wild is idyllic, for example, or that all factory farms mistreat animals), and they look at arguments both for and against factory farming.

The students also realize the importance of examining the assumptions which underlie various views and of being clear about the meaning of various terms in the debate. In this regard, Ravi observes that, in order to make a judgment about the treatment of animals raised for meat, it will be necessary to be clearer about what could be meant by animal welfare and to understand what is being assumed about animal well-being by the various arguers.

In addition to evaluating the information and arguments which they have discovered, the students are beginning to engage in another important aspect of inquiry: they are formulating their own arguments on some of the issues.

Finally, the students continue to keep in mind the main issue that interests them—the morality of consuming meat. They are aware that they need to think about how their deliberations about animal treatment fit into the debate about the larger issue. If they plan to pursue this inquiry further, they need to bring in a fuller range of information and arguments and then begin the process of comparing the various positions and weighing their strengths and weaknesses in order to come to a reasoned judgment on the issue of meat consumption.

In this dialogue, we have seen how the students are beginning to evaluate claims and arguments in order to investigate the issue and try to come to a reasoned judgment. We have begun looking at some of the criteria used, including the reliability and expertise of

Bias refers to the tendency to favour one perspective uncritically.

A **fallacy** is a common type of weak argument that has considerable persuasive power.

A **counter-example** is an example or instance which is an exception to a claim.

Apply Your Understanding Exercises 4, 5, 6

sources, the evidence for and corroboration of claims, the strength of argument and reasoning, and the consideration of all sides of the issue. This examination of the evaluation of claims and arguments has been only a brief introduction, in order for you to get a sense of the main features of an inquiry. In coming chapters, we will be examining in much greater details the kinds of criteria which are used to evaluate claims, information, and arguments, both in general and in specific areas.

Occasions for Inquiry

We have discussed what inquiry is. But when and in what situations can inquiry take place? Read the following scenarios and try to decide which of them are occasions for inquiry.

What Do You Think ?

Which of the following are occasions for inquiry?

1. Ravi Singh has an assignment for history class to write an essay about the causes of World War II.

2. Dr. Sunita Singh is working on an astrophysics problem concerning how certain galaxies were formed.

3. Mona Gold is trying to decide whether she should let her children eat sugary treats.

4. Omar Ali and Diego Alvarez are trying to resolve their disagreement over whether to spray the hedge that runs between their properties with pesticides.

5. City Councillors Agatha Chong, Theo Onassis, and Daimon McGregor are deliberating over the issue of what to do about pit bull attacks.

6. Nancy McGregor and Juanita Alvarez are debating over whether it's OK to copy and share their DVDs.

7. Sophia Onassis and Phil Gold are arguing about capital punishment.

8. Camillia Bell and her colleagues are choosing the artworks for a new exhibition at their art gallery.

9. Several students are having a discussion about whether there's such a thing as free will.

Which of these are occasions for inquiry? If you answered "all of them," then you are correct. Inquiry involves examining an issue in order to come to a reasoned judgment. All the scenarios present issues where there is some controversy, a puzzle, a challenge, or differences in point of view which can be examined in a reasoned manner. Not all differences in point of view provide occasions for inquiry, however. Have a look at the following scenarios:

1. Juanita is trying to convince Phil that broccoli is really tasty.

2. Lester and Stephen disagree about whether the music is too loud at the local disco.

3. Ahmed wants to go the beach, but Ravi would prefer to go to a movie.

Occasions for inquiry are situations where there is some controversy, a puzzle, a challenge, or differences in point of view which can be examined in a reasoned manner.

Although the participants in these scenarios disagree about some matter, these are not disagreements that can be examined in a reasoned manner. Rather, they are matters of personal preference. In the end, the participants may negotiate a course of action or agree to disagree. Inquiry would not be helpful in these instances.

You may have noticed that the cases in Situations 1–9 are different from each other in certain ways. For one thing, the kinds of issues they deal with are different: they include a puzzle in history, a research problem in astronomy, a practical health-related decision, a

Inquiries sometimes take place as formal processes to investigate issues of public concern, as, for example, in the case of legal or medical inquiries:

From UPI.com

Stun-gun inquiry costs at $3.7 million [3]

An investigation into the stun-gun death of a Polish immigrant at Vancouver International Airport has cost taxpayers $3.7 million, officials said. A public panel, known as the Braidwood Commission, is investigating the use of stun guns in general and the specific use of a stun gun against Robert Dziekanski, the *Vancouver Sun* reported Monday. Royal Canadian Mounted Police shocked Dziekanski five times with a stun gun at the airport in October 2007, the *Sun* reported. Despite their costs, such inquiries usually result in enormous public awareness of complicated issues and guarantee the attention of key decision makers, said Herman Bakvis, a University of Victoria public administration professor. "Really, the Canadian public as a whole is getting excellent value out of that particular inquiry," Bakvis said.

neighbourhood disagreement, a political decision, an ethical dilemma, a political/ethical debate, an evaluation in the arts, and a problem in philosophy. As you can see, the issues which can be the impetus for inquiry span a variety of types: puzzles, problems, decisions, dilemmas, debates, disagreements, or evaluations. They can also take place in a variety of areas, including scientific and academic disciplines as well as social and practical contexts. Inquiries may also take different forms. An inquiry may be conducted as a casual conversation, a written piece of research, or a formal decision-making process.

There are differences as well in terms of the participants involved. An inquiry may involve two individuals or several, or it can even be (and often is) conducted by just one person inquiring on his or her own. The inquirers may be friends, relatives, acquaintances, or strangers. They may be undertaking the inquiry in an amicable manner, or they may begin with bitter disagreement. But whatever their starting points and initial stances, once they've undertaken an inquiry, the task of the participants is to engage in the process of genuinely examining and evaluating various views in order to come to a reasoned judgment.

Apply Your Understanding Exercises 7, 8

The Nature of Inquiry

At this point, we shall look more closely at the nature of inquiry and see in greater detail what it means to inquire. As we saw earlier in the chapter, the students who were arguing over the issue of vegetarianism discovered that there was a way to look into the issue more deeply and critically in order to try to come to a reasoned judgment. What they discovered, however, is that there did not seem to be one clear and straightforward answer to their questions. Instead, they found evidence, arguments, and reasons supporting a diversity of views. This is not surprising given that the issues which are the starting points for inquiry involve some type of controversy, puzzle, or challenge to understanding. This means that inquiry takes place in the context of ongoing discussions or debates.

Inquiry takes place in the context of ongoing discussions or debates.

One implication of this aspect of inquiry is that it is not enough to evaluate only the reasons or arguments which support one position or view. Rather, we must look at all or at least many sides of an issue, evaluate the reasons and arguments supporting different positions, and weigh the relative strengths of each (much as the students were beginning to do in the "Cruelty to Chickens?" dialogue). The judgments we come up with in the process of inquiry are based on a process of evaluation which is comparative.

It is important to recognize that these debates which form the context for inquiry do not suddenly arise out of nowhere full-blown. When an issue is contested or controversial, discussion and debate will likely have gone on over a period of time. Many ideas which were once taken as fact—that atoms are the smallest particle of matter, for example, or that Christopher Columbus discovered North America, or that women do not have the intelligence to

The judgments we come up with in the process of inquiry are based on a process of evaluation which is comparative.

exercise the vote—have since been overthrown in the light of new evidence and arguments. There have been ongoing historical conversations which have led to the current ideas on various issues. With respect to issues that are currently controversial, the debates are ongoing.

An implication of this aspect of inquiry is that it is important to have knowledge about the history of the debate on an issue. This knowledge is vital in order to understand the argumentation which led to current views and thus to be able to make the kind of comparative judgment which inquiry requires. (We will be looking at this in more detail in Chapters 9 and 10.)

The recognition that the state of our knowledge is continually evolving is also crucial when engaging in the process of inquiry. Views in the disciplines and in society in general are constantly compared, tested, revised, and sometimes even rejected (as the examples above demonstrate); and this takes place through on ongoing process of inquiry. Inquiry is the process by which knowledge is gained and through which it evolves.

Because what we know is always changing, we can't ever be certain that we have the truth. Thus our judgments always need to be provisional. New information might come to light or new arguments might be offered which could give us good reasons to modify or change our views. This can happen at the level of the society, as, for example, when societies which had previously practised slavery started to view it as immoral. It can happen at the level of academic disciplines, as, for example, when astronomers rejected the geocentric model of the universe (the theory that the earth is at the centre) in favour of the heliocentric model (the theory that the sun is at the centre). And it can, and should, happen at the individual level. We each, in our own inquiries, need to try to make a reasoned judgment; but we also need to recognize that our judgment could be wrong. We need to recognize that we are fallible (thus the name for the recognition of this provisionality is **fallibilism**). This recognition should instill in us a degree of humility and an openness to seriously considering views which differ from our own.

Fallibilism is the recognition that any claim to knowledge could be mistaken.

Although all our knowledge is fallible, there are differences with respect to the degree of certainty which has been obtained and which is likely to be obtained with respect to different questions. Some issues, such as whether blood circulates through the body, are well settled. Others, such as how the universe began or whether euthanasia is ethical, remain the subject of ongoing inquiry. Still others—such as the philosophical issue "What is justice?"—have gone on for millennia and are not likely ever to reach resolution. Even with some issues that seem settled, however, there is still always the possibility of revision.

Some of the difference in degrees of certainty and the likelihood of revision relates to the particular area of inquiry in which the issue arises. Because of the methods of inquiry, the physical sciences have attained a level of agreement among experts in the field which has not been possible with respect to most issues in the humanities. (We will be looking at these differences in Part IV.) Nonetheless, the degree of certainty that can be obtained is not always an important criterion of how significant an issue is. Many issues in the humanities—in ethics, for example—are highly significant to the lives of human beings but are often not issues where we can obtain a high degree of certainty and agreement.

Although we aim for a constant improvement in our state of knowledge, it is also important to recognize that, historically, bodies of knowledge have not always evolved in a linear and progressive way. For example, some older cultures had what we would now consider to be a more progressive view of the role of women than did later European cultures.[4] Individuals also sometimes take up positions which are less well justified than the position they held previously. Thus the importance of critical evaluation becomes paramount.

An implication of the recognition that we are fallible is that we need to consider carefully how much confidence to place in any one of our judgments. How good are our reasons for any particular judgment? How much of the relevant information do we possess? Are our reasons good enough to make a confident judgment or only a tentative judgment? Or does the lack of compelling evidence on any side of an issue warrant that we suspend making a judgment?

The fact that inquiry is ongoing and evolving can be a cause for celebration rather than concern. Inquiry is an enterprise which involves creativity and imagination as much as it does logic and reasoning; the two aspects are, in fact, very closely intertwined. Inquiry involves the evaluation of information, reasons, and arguments; but it also involves thinking of alternatives and objections, imagining counter-examples, and constructing one's own view. Inquiry is the means by which knowledge advances. It is alive and exciting, and each of us can become an active participant in this process rather than merely a passive spectator.

Apply Your Understanding
Exercise 9

Inquiry and Dialogue

You will have noticed that we have used a number of dialogues in this chapter. We will continue to do so throughout the text, and you will also be engaged in the process of writing dialogues. There is a reason for this. As we mentioned above, there will be debate around the kinds of issues which are subjects of inquiry. A variety of positions or views exist on such issues. Thus inquiries don't just involve critiquing one view or one side of a debate; rather, they involve examining views and positions on both, or many, sides of an issue. In this way, an inquiry has the characteristics of a dialogue, with a number of views or positions in conversation with each other.

Real-life inquiries are often conducted as dialogues between two or more people. But even when people are inquiring on their own as individuals, they have to consider the views on various sides of the issue, and thus need to conduct a kind of "inner" dialogue. For these reasons, we believe that dialogues are an excellent way of representing the inquiry process.

Not all dialogues between people are inquiry dialogues. Sometimes people just have conversations to chat, to exchange news or gossip, to discuss their lives. And sometimes what might look like an inquiry dialogue is really just a confrontation of views, with no real effort to inquire and find the best position. The first "Mystery Meatloaf" dialogue is of this type. The kind of dialogue involved in inquiry is distinctive since its goal is to come to a reasoned judgment.

An inquiry has the characteristics of a dialogue, with a number of views or positions in conversation with each other.

The Value of Inquiry

This idea that the state of our knowledge is always changing might be a cause for concern for some people: "If what we believe today may change tomorrow," they might wonder, "then what's the point of inquiring?" The point is that inquiry allows us to come up with the best judgment we can, given the information which is currently available. We can try to base our beliefs and actions on the very best reasons possible. (This is called **justification.**) And having good reasons for holding a view is much better than having bad reasons, or no reasons!

Believing something because I have good reasons for the belief is vastly preferable to believing something uncritically, just because someone with power has told me to believe it or because that's what the people around me believe. People used to believe, for example, that smoking was an appealing and harmless activity; but scientific research has given us excellent reasons to believe that smoking causes cancer. This understanding has likely saved millions of lives. Human societies are also arguably much better off since people have generally come to realize that there are no defensible justifications for some human beings to enslave others. Despite its uncertainties, inquiry is still the most reliable method (some would say the only method) for seeking the truth—even though we can't ever be completely certain that we've found it.

Trying to find the truth is not the only aim of inquiry. A central goal of inquiry is to have a better understanding of the world—an understanding that should enable us to live richer

Justification means having good reasons for one's belief or action.

The well-known philosopher, Immanuel Kant, wrote about the importance of autonomy in his essay, "What Is Enlightenment?" (1784)

"What Is Enlightenment ?" (1784)

Enlightenment is man's emergence from his self-imposed immaturity. Immaturity is the inability to use one's understanding without guidance from another.

This immaturity is self-imposed when its cause lies not in lack of understanding, but in lack of resolve and courage to use it without guidance from another. ... Nothing is required for this enlightenment, however, except freedom; and the freedom in question is the least harmful of all, namely, the freedom to use reason publicly in all matters ...

and more effective lives. We wish not only to understand the nature of the phenomena, but also how scholars, artists, and scientists make sense of the world. We need to know how inquirers establish their theories and claims and how they weave what they are learning into the great tapestry of knowledge.

Autonomous means self-directed, not forced.

Inquiry also provides a means for being more **autonomous** and self-directed. As thoughtful citizens as well as responsible individuals, we need a means for thinking critically about the complex issues which we face. Otherwise, we are in danger of falling prey to the manipulation of marketers, the rhetoric of politicians, or the innumerable bad arguments which barrage us daily. The ability to make judgments on the basis of reasons is central to our notion of what it means to be a mature, independent, and responsible human being.

Engaging in a dialogue focused on inquiry is also valuable as a way of "civilizing the discourse." An inquiry dialogue is a particular way of conducting a conversation which focuses on reasoning, is respectful of the views of the other participants, and gives these views serious and careful consideration. Thus we saw that in the second dialogue the students were able to conduct a less fractious and more profitable discussion than in the first dialogue. At times, inquiry will lead to a resolution of a disagreement. At other times, however, the participants may continue to disagree; but even so, inquiry is of value. The process of inquiring may allow us to become clearer about our own reasons as well as those of the other participants. It may also help us to better understand any underlying bases for disagreement.

Inquiry allows us to interact in a more civil and respectful manner, even when we disagree. Treating the views of others with respectful consideration does not mean that we necessarily agree with these views. At the end of an inquiry, we still may disagree with the other person's views, perhaps even disagree passionately. Yet respect for other persons is a basic moral principle, and the freedom to one's beliefs is a central norm of a democratic society. Participating in inquiry with others allows us to learn together and to build a more productive and enriching community.

Keep in Mind ☑

THE SPIRIT OF INQUIRY

- open-mindedness
- fair-mindedness
- curiosity
- concern for truth and accuracy
- admiration for human intellectual achievements
- willingness to follow arguments and reasoning wherever they lead
- desire to act on the basis of reason
- acceptance of uncertainty

The Spirit of Inquiry

As we have seen throughout this chapter, inquiry is a very particular sort of enterprise with particular aims and characteristics. The primary aim of inquiry is to find out what is the best view or position to hold on an issue. Inquiry is not merely about finding the faults in other people's arguments. It is not about winning. It is not chiefly about convincing others of your own opinions or views. Rather, it is focused on a genuine search for the best-justified position or view. Its aim is to try to arrive at a reasoned judgment. Because of this, inquiry requires of its

Socrates (469–399 BCE)[5]

Socrates was a classical Greek philosopher whose commitment to truth, both in his thought and in his life, have made him a model for all subsequent inquirers. Described as a person of great insight, integrity, and skills in argumentation, he spent his life engaging in discussions with Athenian youth, forcing them to examine their unquestioned views and popular opinions. He refused to accept payment for his teaching. Although he had a loyal following among his students, many of their parents were suspicious of his influence. In the end, Socrates was brought to trial for impiety and corrupting youth and was sentenced to death by poisoning. He accepted the verdict with grace. The speech which he is said to have made at his trial was a defence of the value of the examined life.

participants a certain orientation or attitude which we shall refer to as the spirit of inquiry. At the most general level, the spirit of inquiry involves a commitment to base one's beliefs and actions on inquiry.

The spirit of inquiry is demonstrated in certain attitudes. The first is **open-mindedness.** Because we realize that we are fallible, we must be genuinely open to views which oppose our own, as well as to challenges to our views and to evidence which runs against our views. The spirit of inquiry, in fact, requires that we seek out any possible objections or contrary evidence. And we should be willing to revise our views if better arguments are presented and to concede to the most defensible position.

Open-mindedness refers to the willingness to consider evidence and views that are contrary to our own.

Another dimension of the spirit of inquiry centres on **fair-mindedness.** Fair-mindedness means that we are willing not only to consider opposing views but also to make unbiased and impartial judgments about these views. This requires that we be fair in our portrayal of views with which we disagree, and not mischaracterize them in order to make them easier targets for our criticisms. (This is the fallacy of the straw person which we will be discussing in Chapter 4.)

Fair-mindedness requires us to be as unbiased and impartial as we can when making a judgment.

The respect for reason which is one of the defining characteristics of inquiry shows itself in several ways, including in curiosity, a concern for truth and accuracy, an admiration of what human beings have achieved through their reason, a willingness to follow arguments and reasoning wherever they lead, a desire to act on the basis of reason, and an acceptance of the uncertainty which is a part of inquiry.

A final and central aspect of the spirit of inquiry involves the respectful treatment of other participants in the inquiry. This means avoiding insults and manipulation, and it means taking the views of others seriously. (We shall engage in a fuller discussion of the spirit of inquiry and how to achieve it in Chapter 11.)

Apply Your Understanding
Exercises 10, 11, 12

CHECK YOUR UNDERSTANDING

- *What are the main features of inquiry? Explain each one.*
- *What makes a judgment a reasoned judgment?*
- *What are some of the main aspects you should pay attention to when evaluating a claim or argument?*
- *What kinds of issues can provide occasions for inquiry?*
- *Why do we need to look at many sides of an issue?*
- *What is fallibilism?*
- *Why do our judgments always need to be provisional?*
- *In what ways is an inquiry dialogue different from other kinds of dialogues or conversations?*
- *In what ways is inquiry valuable?*
- *What are some of the characteristics of the spirit of inquiry?*

EXERCISES

1. List three criteria which you would use in deciding on each of the following:
   i) whether to go to a certain band concert
   ii) what kind of jeans to buy
   iii) which film to see
   iv) which candidate to support for student council president
   v) whether to believe someone you hear in an interview who claims that smoking may not cause lung cancer.

2. Make a list of the criteria you would use in deciding which classes to take. Place them in order of priority, with the most important ones first. Explain why each is important and how each figured into your decision about choice of classes this semester.

3. Think about another course that you are taking this semester or have taken recently. Try to come up with a list of the main criteria that are used in that discipline to establish and evaluate claims.

4. The students in the "Mystery Meatloaf" dialogues decided that more research would be needed in order to decide whether factory farming practices involve the mistreatment of animals, and to what extent. Help them out by doing some research on the topic.
   i) Find four independent sources of information to help in the decision.
   ii) Assess the reliability of these sources and defend your assessment.

5. The assignment in Question 5 focuses on the issue of whether chickens are just like humans. You will need to do the following:
   i) Make a list of the ways in which you think chickens are similar to humans and the ways in which you think they are different.
   ii) Detail the kind of information you would need in order to help you address the question in more depth.
   iii) Find three different sources of information which can help you to address the question and list their main arguments.
   iv) In light of your own initial views and the information and arguments you have found, write a short essay which addresses the issue of whether chickens are just like humans.

6. Consider the issue of vegetarianism.
   i) List all the reasons you can think of both for and against vegetarianism.
   ii) Form a group with several classmates and pool your reasons.

iii) Go on the internet to try and find more reasons which you haven't yet considered. Make sure you have listed reasons both for and against.

iv) Present your reasons orally in class in the form of a dialogue, with different students presenting different reasons.

7. For each of the following situations,

  i) State whether they are or are not suitable occasions for inquiry.

  ii) Explain why or why not.

   a) Ravi and Phil disagree about whether tuition fees should be raised at their college.

   b) Winnie likes the mountains, but Ahmed prefers the ocean.

   c) Juanita and Sophia disagree about which of the guys in their class is better looking.

   d) Agatha Chong is trying to decide whether to vote for a certain policy at city council.

   e) Nancy is trying to decide whether to take a new herbal remedy for her sore knee.

   f) Lester is writing an essay for his music appreciation class in which he has to argue whether Mozart or Beethoven made a more significant contribution to Western classical music.

8. Describe three situations in your own life, both in academic work and in daily life, which could be occasions for inquiry. Discuss what makes each one an occasion for inquiry.

9. Think of three examples of views that were previously accepted by society being revised or rejected because of new evidence and arguments. What evidence or arguments contributed to the revision?

10. For each of the mini-dialogues below, identify which aspect of the spirit of inquiry is exemplified or is violated by the participants and explain in what way:

   i) **Nancy:** I understand that animals raised on factory farms are treated horribly.

   Ahmed: But not all animals raised for meat are mistreated. Some are allowed to roam freely and are fed on organic grains.

   Nancy: That's a good point—I hadn't considered that before.

   ii) **Sophia:** You should have a look at the material sent around by Greenpeace. They make some interesting arguments about species extinction.

   Ravi: I never pay attention to what those eco-terrorists have to say.

   iii) **Phil:** I really think that it's wrong for a man to have more than one wife. I don't think that it should be allowed under the law.

   Lester: You can't seriously believe that a man should be put in jail for having more than one wife! But maybe that's not your position. Are you arguing that polygamous marriages should not be recognized by law, or that polygamists should be put in jail? I should be clear about your position before I criticize it.

   iv) **Stephen:** Do you really believe what you said in the argument with Ravi about all rapists deserving to be put on a boat and set adrift in the ocean?

   Ahmed: Of course not—but I won the argument, didn't I?

   v) **Sophia:** I'm making good progress on my economics essay. I'm arguing for heavier taxation for the wealthy. Now I just need to look at the arguments of those who don't favour such increases.

   Phil: Why in the world would you look for arguments against your own position? That doesn't make any sense.

   vi) **Winnie:** I've heard that a number of large companies which make some of those great clothes we love really exploit the workers in third world countries. I'd like to investigate and find out whether that's true before I keep buying their stuff.

   Juanita: Why bother? It sounds like a lot of effort. And anyway, it doesn't really affect my life.

11. Continue the dialogue between Winnie and Juanita in Question 10 vi) above. Juanita is skeptical about whether it's worth the trouble to investigate the issue of the exploitation of workers in the third world by some large companies. Winnie tries to convince her of the value of inquiry.

12. Compare the first two dialogues in the chapter, "Mystery Meatloaf" and "Mystery Meatloaf—Take II".

    i) Working in groups, make a list of the places where the two dialogues go off in different directions.

    ii) For each of these points, discuss in what ways each dialogue demonstrates or fails to demonstrate the characteristics of an inquiry dialogue.

    iii) For each dialogue, discuss how the participants demonstrate or fail to demonstrate a spirit of inquiry.

ENDNOTES

1. Shelagh MacDonald, "How CFHS Helps Farm Animals," *Animal Welfare in Focus* (Spring 2009).

2. David Fraser, "Animal Welfare and the Intensification of Animal Production: An Alternative Interpretation," in *FAO Corporate Document Repository*, http://www.fao.org/docrep/009/a0158e/a0158e00.HTM (accessed Sept. 13, 2009).

3. *UPI.com*, "Stun-Gun Inquiry Costs at 3.7 Million," Aug. 31, 2009, © 2009 United Press International, Inc. All Rights Reserved, http://www.upi.com/Top_News/2009/08/31/Stun-gun-inquiry-costs-at-37-million/UPI-25571251755372/.

4. See, for example, *Women in World History,* "Writers of the Heian Era," http://chnm.gmu.edu/wwh/modules/lesson2/lesson2.php?s=0 (accessed April 23, 2010).

5. *Philosophy Pages*, "Socrates," http://www.philosophypages.com/ph/socr.htm (accessed April 23, 2010); *Bio*, "Socrates Biography," http://www.biography.com/articles/Socrates-9488126 (accessed July 12, 2010).

Chapter 2
Introducing Guidelines for Inquiry

Learning Objectives

After reading this chapter, you should be able to:

- start applying the guiding questions for inquiry, including the following:
  - identifying an issue
  - identifying what kinds of claims or judgments are at issue
  - listing the relevant reasons and arguments on various sides of the issue
  - identifying relevant aspects of context surrounding an issue
- comparatively evaluating the various reasons and arguments in order to reach a reasoned judgment

The Great Film Debate

Sophia and Phil have just finished watching the Academy Awards presentations.

Sophia: Isn't it GREAT about the Oscars and *Slumdog Millionaire* winning the best film award? I'm so excited!

Phil: You mean you really liked that film?

Sophia: I didn't just like it—I LOVED it! It was so … AMAZING!

Phil: I thought it was so cliché—boy from slums gets girl and money—with a little Bollywood thrown in for good measure. I mean … give me a break.

Sophia: But it was so exciting and lively and sad … and funny. I didn't want it to end.

Phil: Now take *X-Men Origins: Wolverine*—THAT was an awesome film! But it won't ever get nominated for an award.

Sophia: *X-Men*—you can't really mean that! I mean, it was OK for a laugh, but really …

Phil: OK, OK … let's stop arguing. I hate arguing. Let's see what's on TV.

Sophia and Phil are having a fairly typical disagreement about films: they exchange opinions, react to each other's views, then move on to something else. Disagreements about films (or music or rock videos) often end at this point, with an agreement to disagree. But they don't have to. These disagreements, like many other kinds of disagreements, problems, and perplexities, can become the object of inquiry. We can explore further, analyze in more detail, evaluate ideas, and perhaps come to a reasoned judgment and to some agreement.

But even if we don't end up agreeing, even if you continue to love *Slumdog* while my loyalty stays with *X-Men*, perhaps we can learn something by the process. We may come to notice aspects of the films that we hadn't noticed before, to become more discriminating about films and what makes them good, and to appreciate these films, and others, in new and enriching ways.

What Do You Think ?

Think about how Sophia and Phil could continue their discussion and begin to inquire about the merit of these films. Make a list of the questions they could ask themselves to aid their inquiry. Make a list of the resources (people, places, and things) they could use to help them with their inquiry.

There are a number of resources that Sophia and Phil could draw on to get their inquiry started. First, they have their own opinions and reactions, and this is a good place to start. They could begin by asking themselves why, exactly, they liked or didn't like each film, and what, in particular, they thought was well or poorly done. Trying to think of actual moments from the films would be very helpful.

But there are other resources they can call upon besides just themselves. Inquiry is often a communal enterprise, so soliciting the opinions of friends and acquaintances about these films (and, in particular, the reasons for their views) can add to the pool of information that can form the basis of the inquiry.

There are additional resources as well. Reviews of most films are readily available, often online. Sophia and Phil can consult the reviews of *Slumdog* and *X-Men* to see what kinds of judgments, and reasons for the judgments, have been offered by both film critics and viewers.

These resources will provide Sophia and Phil with lots of opinions, ideas, and arguments which they can add to their own initial impressions. But that's just the beginning. What our two film buffs require is some way to think about and evaluate all this information. They need some guidelines for structuring their inquiry so that they can come to some reasoned judgment about the two films. It is such guidelines that we offer in this book. The guidelines are outlined in this chapter and elaborated in the rest of the text.

Guidelines for Inquiry

Guiding Questions:

- What is the issue?
- What kinds of claims or judgments are at issue?
- What are the relevant reasons and arguments on various sides of the issue?
- What is the context of the issue?
- How do we comparatively evaluate the various reasons and arguments to reach a reasoned judgment?

What Is the Issue?

Before we can even begin to inquire, we need to be very clear about what the issue, problem, or question is that we are trying to inquire about. This may seem obvious; but when we look more closely, we may discover that there are really several different questions at issue—and it is possible that the answers to the various questions are different, or that the answer to one question does not directly give us the answer to the other questions.

Sophia: You know, it occurs to me that we're actually arguing about a few different issues. First, there's the question of whether *Slumdog Millionaire* should have gotten the Oscar. But we're also arguing about whether *Slumdog Millionaire* is even a good film. But it's not always the best film (or even a good film) that wins the Oscar—sometimes a film might win because people think that it's time that the director received recognition. Or a film might be good, but there might be even better films that year that deserve the award more.

Phil: Or a really good film—like *X-Men*—might not even get nominated!

Sophia: I agree with your point (but not necessarily your example).

Phil: Don't forget that I think that *X-Men* is a better film than *Slumdog Millionaire*—so we also have the question of which film is better.

Sophia: OK—so how about if we focus on these two questions: Which is the better film, *Slumdog Millionaire* or *X-Men Origins: Wolverine*? And should *Slumdog Millionaire* have gotten the Oscar?

Phil: And we have to remember that, even if we decide that *Slumdog Millionaire* is the better film (which I very much doubt), that doesn't tell us whether it should have gotten the Oscar.

Sophia and Phil have gone through a number of steps in order to get their inquiry started. These steps are the following:

1. becoming clear about what, exactly, are the issues which will be the focus of the inquiry
2. separating out the various issues, if there is more than one
3. becoming clear about the relationship among the various issues

In deciding on the issue for their inquiry, Phil and Sophia have wisely decided to narrow their inquiry by focusing on a comparison between the two films and on whether *Slumdog Millionaire* should have gotten the Oscar. In formulating an issue, it is important to focus in and to avoid overly broad characterizations, which will be difficult to deal with in sufficient depth. (We will discuss this in more detail in Chapter 7.)

What Kinds of Claims or Judgments Are at Issue?

Phil: You know, Soph, something's bothering me about this whole process. Isn't the issue of which film is better just a matter of taste? I mean, it's not like asking "Who was the producer of *Slumdog Millionaire*?" or even "What did the critics say about *Slumdog Millionaire*?" There are answers to those questions that we could find out. But all we're going to get here are people's subjective opinions.

Sophia: I'm not so sure about that. Sure, I might just give a first impression or gut reaction to a film. But then again, I might be able to give you some reasons for my reaction and even point out specific moments in the film that I thought were good or not so good. Then maybe my response is more than just a subjective opinion. Maybe it's more like what my art professor calls an aesthetic judgment.

Phil: But still, how do I know if my aesthetic judgment about the film is better than your aesthetic judgment?

Sophia: According to my prof, aesthetic judgments can be evaluated according to criteria just the way that judgments about facts can. But the criteria will be different than for judgments about facts.

Phil: So I guess part of our job will be to find out what kind of criteria are used to evaluate films.

Before we can even begin to inquire, we need to be very clear about what the issue is that we are trying to inquire about.

An important aspect of clarifying the issue is to be clear about exactly what type of judgment is involved in the particular inquiry which we are undertaking. In many cases, what we are looking for is a judgment about the way things are. Does sugar cause hyperactivity? Why are some galaxies curved? Will taking a certain herbal remedy help my cold? These questions call for judgments of fact, or factual judgments.

In our film case, it is not a judgment about facts that is at issue, but rather a judgment about what is valuable or worthwhile; this is an evaluative judgment. Evaluative judgments can be of different kinds. These include judgments about right and wrong (moral judgments—e.g., It wasn't fair for the instructor to give Stephen special treatment. It isn't ethical to copy and share DVDs) and judgments about usefulness and practicality (instrumental judgments—e.g., The best way to get a good grade on the test is to do a lot of practice quizzes).

In the case of evaluating *Slumdog Millionaire* and *X-Men,* we are dealing with an evaluative judgment about what makes something aesthetically good; in other words, an aesthetic judgment. This is a kind of judgment which is common in the arts. Issues such as why a famous painting is considered great, which version of a musical piece is the better interpretation, or whether a certain film should receive an Oscar all call for aesthetic judgments. Another type of evaluative judgment which is common in the arts and which is relevant to the students' discussion of *Slumdog Millionaire* is an interpretive judgment, which focuses on what something means. In an upcoming dialogue, when Sophia states that *Slumdog Millionaire* is about human resilience, she is making an interpretive judgment. Aesthetic and interpretive judgments will be a central focus in Chapter 14, which looks at inquiry in the arts. (We will also come across another type of evaluative judgment, the comparative judgment of value, in Chapter 7.)

> It is important to be clear about the type of judgments involved in our inquiries because different kinds of judgments may be evaluated according to different criteria.

It is important to be clear about the type of judgment (or judgments) involved in our inquiries because different kinds of judgments may be evaluated somewhat differently, according to different criteria. So, one criterion for evaluating films might be originality; but originality would not be what we were looking for in making a judgment about, for example, the truthfulness of testimony at a trial. On the other hand, correspondence with other facts might be important for evaluating the trial testimony, but that's really not relevant for evaluating something fictional like a film.

One of the central tasks when conducting an inquiry is to find out what criteria are relevant for the type of judgment involved in our particular inquiry. Although there may not always be complete unanimity on the importance and weighting of each and every criterion in every case, criteria indicate the considerations which are generally seen as relevant to the evaluation of particular issues. We shall examine in more detail various types of judgments and the criteria by which they are evaluated in Chapter 7.

What Do You Think ?

Make a list of some of the criteria that you might use to evaluate films.

What Are the Relevant Reasons and Arguments on Various Sides of the Issue?

Phil: I've just found this great website. It's called *Rotten Tomatoes;* and it's filled with tons of reviews by both critics and film viewers, as well as all kinds of other information about films. And it's interesting—in looking at some of reviews of the two films—that the reviews are not just one-sided. There are both positive and negative reviews for each film (though more positive ones for *Slumdog Millionaire,* I have to admit). And the reviewers don't just give a "thumbs up" or "thumbs down" to the films, but actually do give all kinds of reasons for their judgments. So there really is an actual debate around these films, not just gut reactions!

Sophia: I thought so.

Phil: So let's see what kinds of things people have actually said about these two films. Wow! Looking at all these reviews is mind-boggling! Maybe we should try and summarize the main points.

Sophia: OK. Mmm . . . I'll skim the comments about *Slumdog Millionaire,* while you have a look at the reviews of *X-Men* . . . Well, I'm sorry to have to tell you this, but the vast majority of the reviews are positive—with an average rating of 8.2 out of 10. There are lots of different reasons people give for their views, but there are a few main points that keep recurring. Most of the reviewers say that the film is both heartbreaking and exhilarating at the same time. They think that the writing is brilliant and the story a complex combination of fairy tale and—I love this!— "gritty realism worthy of Dickens." They comment that the film manages to deliver a perfect mix of thrills and tears, with adventure, suspense, and romance all thrown into the mix. Every review that I read mentions the amazing cinematography, saying that the film is both visually stunning and emotionally resonant. Reviewers love the innovative narrative structure using the game show format to frame flashbacks to key episodes in the hero's life. The acting is another ground for praise by most reviewers. They refer to the acting as uniformly impressive and comment on stellar performances by some of the actors. One major strong point of the film for almost all reviewers is that *Slumdog Millionaire* deals with important human themes such as the nature of moral choices, integrity, and resilience, and it does this in a manner which is highly original, visually arresting, and emotionally compelling. Shall I continue?

Phil: Well . . . don't forget to give the negative comments too.

Sophia: I know, I know—but only 14 of the 210 reviews were negative. Still, if we're going to do a fair-minded inquiry, then we can't just present the reasons that favour our position. So here's a summary of the negative comments. A few reviewers think that the film is superficial and frivolous and that the plot is contrived. A few also think that the film is exploitative, profiting from the suffering of others, showing the worst of Indian society, and exploiting stereotypes of India to give westerners an exotic thrill.

Phil: Now it's my turn. Well, I have to admit that most of the reviews of *X-Men* are not . . . well . . . enthusiastic, to say the least. It got an average rating of 5.1 out of 10. The reviewers do say that it's an exciting movie, packed with action and adventure and mostly good, though not spectacular, special effects. Some of the reviewers think that it has a great opening sequence—set in Canada, by the way—and others really like the natural pathos and humour of Hugh Jackman's portrayal of Wolverine. They also mostly like the "sneering malevolence" and "impressively believable intensity" of Victor Creed's character, though the comments on the other characters are not quite so favourable. Generally, the reviewers see it as having no pretensions to being anything more than a big, loud, effects-driven summer action movie, but think that it's a lot of fun.

Sophia: And the negatives?

Phil: Yes, well . . . there are quite a few of those. The reviews really criticize *X-Men* for having a poorly conceived story and cliché-ridden script that depends on convention and contrivance rather than character development. They find the film blandly predictable and unoriginal, with the continual series of stylized action sequences getting to be old hat after a while. They say that the film is formless, lacking internal cohesion and a balance between story, spectacle, characters, and special effects. Most find it nowhere near as good as the other *X-Men* films, and some see this whole *Origins* series as nothing more than an attempt to keep extending a money-making franchise.

Phil and Sophia have discovered that there are actually a variety of views about both films, and that these views are backed up by reasons and arguments. In laying out the various views and positions, they must include the reasons and evidence which support the positions they are backing as well as any objections to these reasons and responses to the objections, if there are any. It is important that this analysis be fair-minded and that they include

Laying out the various views and positions must include the reasons and evidence which support the positions as well as any objections and responses.

both positive and negative views with respect to both *Slumdog Millionaire* and *X-Men*. (They must be careful not to include only those views with which they agree.) This detailing of the reasons and arguments is a necessary prelude to the step of evaluating the views.

What Is the Context of the Issue?

Issues don't generally exist in a vacuum. There is always a context of information and considerations that relate to the issue. If the issue is at all controversial, there will be a history of argument and debate, of views and opposing views, of ideas and alternatives. In conducting an inquiry, it is important to lay out some of this background and history in order to see what aspects are relevant to making a reasoned judgment.

Phil: One of the things I'm noticing is that the reviewers often compare the films to other films. For example, many reviewers compare *Slumdog Millionaire* to the other films nominated for an Oscar in the same year. And I can see why—if you think that *Slumdog Millionaire* deserved to win, then you would have to think that it was better than the other films that year, so you would have to know something about those other films as well.

Sophia: But they also compare it to the director Danny Boyle's other films—and most think it's at least as good as *Trainspotting, 28 Days Later,* and *Sunshine.* I'm wondering whether that's even relevant to our question of whether *Slumdog Millionaire* deserved the Oscar this year—though maybe it is relevant to deciding how good a film it is.

Phil: The reviewers were all excited by the fact that *Slumdog Millionaire* doesn't fit neatly into one genre, so having some knowledge of a variety of relevant film genres might help us in our inquiry.

Sophia: And you have to admit, Phil, that almost all the reviewers thought that this episode of *X-Men* is not anywhere near as good as the other *X-Men* movies. In fact, most reviewers seem to think that the fact that this *X-Men* film is the first of a new series within a series is significant—that it's just an attempt to capitalize on the popularity of the series and make more money without bothering to make a good film.

Phil: You know, I'm also thinking about what you said earlier about films winning the Oscar for other reasons than their being the best film. That makes me wonder about the whole Academy Awards competition—how it works and what role politics plays. Knowing about that might help us to think about what the relationship is between the quality of a film and its winning an Oscar. Maybe that could also be part of our inquiry.

Sophia: Another issue that's got me thinking is the debate about whether *Slumdog* is exploitative. I don't think that it is. Sure, it shows unpleasant aspects of India, but then those aspects obviously exist. I don't agree that the film either glamorizes the poverty or underplays it. In the end, it's about human resilience and that's a worthwhile theme. And besides, I think that a filmmaker has the right to tell the story as he sees it.

There are various kinds of contexts that may be relevant to the evaluation of an issue. One is what we call the state of practice, which refers to the current situation with respect to the issue. In inquiring about vegetarianism, for example, knowing about the current situation with respect to animal treatment on factory farms would be an important aspect of context to understand. Another aspect of context is the history of the debate which has led to current practice or thinking about the issue. Understanding, for example, how views about the moral status of animals have changed can contribute to an inquiry into vegetarianism. In addition, the roots of many issues can be found in certain ideas or philosophies about human nature, society, reality, and the world in general. Thus understanding something about the intellectual, social, political, and historical contexts surrounding an issue can also be of assistance in understanding and evaluating an issue. (These various aspects of context will be elaborated in detail in Chapter 8.)

In conducting an inquiry, it is important to lay out the history of argument and debate around the issue as well as other aspects of context.

Sophia and Phil have picked out some aspects of context that are relevant to their inquiry. One aspect is the state of practice with respect to the Academy Awards debates. They realize, for example, that the awards are based on comparative judgments; and because of this, information about other nominated films would be important. Even in the case of broader discussions of the quality of a film, there is usually a comparison to other films involved in the judgment, even if only implicitly. So part of deciding whether *Slumdog Millionaire* is a good film would involve deciding how it compares to other examples of its genre, or whether it's as good as or better than other films directed by Boyle. And an aspect of making a judgment about *X-Men Origins: Wolverine* would involve comparing it to previous *X-Men* films. The fact that this film is yet another of a money-making series also raises the issue of how commercial interests may interplay with aesthetic considerations; in this way, the economic context is brought into the discussion.

Looking at the actual Academy Awards competition and how it works could bring up another aspect of context, the political context. This aspect might also be revealed by looking at the political nature of debates, both past and present, surrounding particular films or kinds of films. The heated debate around *Slumdog Millionaire* raises the issue of how, and even whether, political considerations should affect one's aesthetic evaluation of a film. Knowledge of the political forces which surround an issue, as well as the intellectual and social situation in which it is embedded, can help us to better understand an issue and provide information which may prove useful when going on to make our evaluations.

> ## Keep in Mind
>
> **KINDS OF CONTEXTS**
> - state of practice
> - history of the debate
> - intellectual, social, political, and historical contexts

How Do We Comparatively Evaluate the Various Reasons and Arguments to Reach a Reasoned Judgment?

What judgment would you come to about the relative merits of the two films based on the reasons listed above by Sophia and Phil?

What Do You Think?

Phil: So now that we have all these views about the two films, what do we do with them? I mean, it's not like they all agree. That would make things easier.

Sophia: But the majority of reviewers did like *Slumdog Millionaire* better.

Phil: So I guess that decides it. Oh well.

Sophia: Well … I'm not so sure. Can the quality of a movie really be decided by popular opinion? And what if some of the folks deciding don't know anything about films? No … I think we really need to look at the reasons people give for their judgments and not just the numbers.

Phil: But quite a few of the reviewers are experienced film critics who know a lot about films—doesn't that make a difference?

Sophia: Hmm … It does seem that it should, somehow. But how? We can't simply accept what they say just because they're critics. But we may want to pay particular attention to their judgments, and especially their reasons and the criteria they use.

Phil: Great point! We were saying earlier that part of our job is to find out what kinds of criteria are used to evaluate films. And the reviews by the critics would be good sources of criteria.

Sophia: So why don't we try to list the main criteria that are used in the reviews and see how our two films stack up against them? Now we're getting somewhere.

Phil: OK. The quality of acting seems to be an important criterion for all the reviewers. Virtually all of them thought that *Slumdog Millionaire* has really strong performances with real depth of characterization, but they also liked some of the acting in *X-Men*.

Sophia: How about dramatic tension and suspense? Both do reasonably well there, though the predictability of the plot of *X-Men* lessened the dramatic tension for some reviewers.

Phil: Originality? Most reviewers thought that *Slumdog Millionaire* was extremely original on many levels. They thought that *X-Men Origins* was just more-of-the-same after the other *X-Men* films.

Phil: One criterion that most of the reviews use is coherence and focus—whether the plot and structure all hang together and have a point. *Slumdog Millionaire* rates high on structure, but I'm afraid *X-Men* really bombs out on that score.

Sophia: The quality of the cinematography is a criterion that every reviewer refers to when discussing *Slumdog*.

Phil: The reviews are somewhat mixed on that score for *X-Men*—some are positive about the special effects, but others find them disappointing.

Sophia: There's also the point that *Slumdog Millionaire* deals with important human themes and is moving on an emotional level—you really couldn't say that about *X-Men*. I think that that should count for something.

Phil: Well, looking at all of this, it's pretty clear that *Slumdog Millionaire* comes out quite a bit better. *X-Men* does come out with some strong points—mainly that it's action-packed and fun and has a some decent acting.

Sophia: But you have to admit that having a cliché script, a predictable plot, and lack of internal cohesion are pretty serious problems, and you can't make up for that with a few decent performances and some action.

Phil: That's true. You know, now that I look back on *X-Men,* I do remember thinking that all the action sequences and effects were getting a little repetitive.

Sophia: And thinking about *Slumdog Millionaire,* I'm realizing that I hadn't really noticed how all the minute details of the hero's life reflect his moral choices. There's a lot more to that film than I realized. And I liked it!

Phil: Hey, Sophia—why don't we rent *Slumdog Millionaire*? I really want to have another look at it and see what I think now that I know more about it. Though I don't know if I'll like it any better.

Sophia: Well, maybe you can recognize why a film is good, but still not really enjoy it.

Phil: Or realize that a movie isn't the greatest work of art in the world, but still find it a hoot? So how about if we rent *X-Men* too?

Sophia: Great! But you know, we still haven't talked about whether *Slumdog* should have won the Oscar. For that, we'll need to compare *Slumdog* to all the other films that were nominated. Then there's the question of whether the Academy Awards process is even a good way to try and pick the best film … now that would be interesting!

Phil: Stop! Enough inquiry for one day. On to the video store!

Phil and Sophia have been engaging in the final—likely the most crucial, and possibly the most difficult—aspect of the process of inquiry: coming to a reasoned judgment about the issue. This involves evaluating the various reasons in comparison to one another.

Film critics engage in precisely this process of making a reasoned judgment about a film. Here is an example.

The Sweet Hereafter[1]

The Sweet Hereafter is film maker Atom Egoyan's most compelling movie to date. . . . [T]he Canadian director/writer/producer shows the powerful effects of grief and anger on a community devastated by an unspeakable tragedy. . . . This is film making at its most powerful: drama capable of shaking the soul, yet free of even the slightest hint of manipulation, sentimentality, or mawkishness. . . .

The central event of *The Sweet Hereafter* is a school bus accident that results in the death of fourteen children and the injury of many others. On a cold winter's day in the small town of Sam Dent, British Columbia, the driver loses control of the vehicle and it careens off the road onto a frozen lake which gives way beneath the weight. The scene of the bus sinking into the water—a stark, simple shot—is one of the most painfully effective and disturbing sequences in any film this year . . . Since Egoyan eschews linear storytelling by allowing time to be fluid rather than fixed, we don't see the actual accident until midway through the movie . . .

The Sweet Hereafter is based on the novel by Russell Banks, but Egoyan has infused it with his own inimitable style. One of the film maker's more successful innovations is to make explicit comparisons between the situation in Sam Dent (the loss of the children) and the one in the Robert Browning poem, "The Pied Piper of Hamelin." In "The Pied Piper," the lone crippled boy left behind by the Piper forever regretted his exclusion from a land where "everything was strange and new." . . . [I]n *The Sweet Hereafter,* the abandoned one is Nicole [the lone survivor of the crash]. The sweet hereafter is the strange, new land that her schoolmates reach, but which she has not yet attained . . . .

As always, Egoyan has assembled a top-notch cast. Ian Holm paints a powerful and stirring portrait of Mitchell as a haunted, hurting figure whose inner torment touches our hearts. Holm acts with his eyes and face, as well as with his voice and actions. . . . Egoyan has given us a powerful motion picture that resonates on every level. The most amazing thing about *The Sweet Hereafter* is not the style, the acting, or the cinematography (all of which are exceptional), but the way the film successfully juggles so many themes, persuading us to reflect upon them all before the 110 minute running time is up. This is truly a great film . . .

If an issue is at all controversial, there will likely be some good reasons and some problems on each side. The challenge is to weigh the strengths and weaknesses, and to come to an overall judgment that takes these into account. This will often involve an assessment of the relative importance of various criteria and the balancing of various considerations (as, for example, when Sophia recognizes that some good acting and special effects can't make up for a weak and incoherent plot). The overall judgment might involve deciding in support of one side, or it might involve coming to a position which is somewhere between the two. The final judgment might even be different from any of the initial positions. We will look at this process of comparative evaluation, and the details of weighing strengths and weaknesses and balancing considerations, in Chapter 10.

Coming to a reasoned judgment involves evaluating various reasons in comparison to one another.

One important task in doing this type of evaluation will be to discover the criteria which are relevant for the particular inquiry. Some of the criteria may be quite general and applicable in many areas—for example, logical soundness or the relevance of a reason to the argument. Other criteria will be specific to the area of inquiry. Originality, quality of acting, dramatic tension, focus, and coherence are some of the criteria which operate in particular in the realm of film.

What criteria does the critic use to evaluate The Sweet Hereafter *in the review quoted above?*

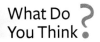

What Do You Think?

At times, evaluating an argument will involve making some judgments about the source of the argument; for example, does the source have sufficient expertise to be relied on as an authority, and, indeed, is this expertise relevant to the issue at hand? This is an issue which Sophia and Phil reflect on when discussing whether film reviewers should be relied on as authorities in judging films.

The importance of arriving at an agreed-upon judgment may vary in different contexts as well. In some cases, as, for example, with legislators having to decide on a law (as in the vicious dog case below), coming to some agreed-upon judgment is vital. In other cases, such as our film case, agreement is not crucial as no decision hangs on the results. Rather, the inquiry can be undertaken simply in order to gain a better understanding.

It must be noted, as Sophia and Phil do, that, in the realm of aesthetics, gaining an understanding of why some work is of value does not necessarily equate with liking the work. Personal preferences may explain why you like or dislike a film (e.g., "I find horror films upsetting") but they don't provide reasons in support of judgments about the work. Nonetheless, you may continue to enjoy a work even if you understand that it "isn't the greatest work of art in the world." There are both subjective and objective aspects to appreciating aesthetic works. It is often the case, however, that gaining some understanding of a work will affect how one sees it, and may open up possibilities for coming to appreciate the work.

Apply Your Understanding Exercises 1, 2

Guidelines for Inquiry: Application

Those Dangerous Dogs

Theo Onassis, along with his fellow city councillors Daimon McGregor and Agatha Chong, are assembled in the Council Chambers at City Hall on Friday morning to discuss a pressing issue.

Onassis: Another pit bull attack. That's the third one this year! We've got to do something. Council has a responsibility to the people to protect them from these attacks.

McGregor: Oh no! There you go again, Onassis, wanting to make another law and take away people's freedoms. Even dogs aren't safe from your rule mongering.

Onassis: So you think it's OK for children, and adults for that matter, to be attacked by pit bulls? Phillip Gold, a good friend of my daughter Sophia, had a close call with a pit bull a few months back, and it was pretty harrowing, I can tell you. Don't you realize that the city has a duty to protect people from just such attacks?

McGregor: I think people have to take responsibility to protect their kids. And I think dog owners have to take responsibility for their dogs. Need I remind the honourable councillor that we already have dog leash laws? So if an unleashed dog attacks someone, then the owner should be fined and sued. But we shouldn't be telling people what kinds of dogs they can have.

Onassis: And what kind of dog do you have, Councillor McGregor? Given your personality, I would assume that you also have a pit bull, or perhaps a Rottweiler.

Chong: Gentlemen, let's not get personal! We have to be careful that we are not overreacting. We need to find out what the facts are. How bad are pit bulls? Are there certain breeds of dogs that tend to attack people, or are there certain people who raise dangerous dogs? We need to look into the issue before we decide what to do.

Political debate and discussion are natural areas for controversy; this makes them natural areas for inquiry. In this case, the councillors are faced with a complex and emotional issue in trying to decide how to deal with the problem of dog attacks. They recognize, however, that it would not be appropriate to rush to a decision based on their initial reactions. It is necessary for them to inquire further into the issue before they can come to a decision which would be reasonable and defensible.

What Do You Think ?

Think about how the councillors might further their debate. Make a list of the questions they could they ask themselves to aid their inquiry. What do they need to know before deciding what to do? Make a list of the resources (people, places, and things) they could use to help them with their inquiry.

In the case of the "great film debate," it made sense for the participants to begin their inquiry by probing their own reactions since people's reactions to art works do have some relevance for aesthetic judgments (but it was also important for the participants in the film discussion to get beyond their subjective reactions and begin to investigate their reasons). The reactions of the councillors are not, however, relevant in the same way to the dog regulation issue. Factors such as whether McGregor loves Rottweilers or Chong her yellow lab, or whether Onassis is understandably upset by reading about a dog attack, will likely be reflected in the perspectives of the councillors; but they do not really help them decide on the proper public policy. What do they need?

Let's use our guiding questions and apply them to this issue.

What Is the Issue?

Chong: Before we go any farther, I think we should clarify the issue. Onassis, you seem to be arguing that pit bulls and perhaps some other dogs should be banned from the city.

Onassis: Absolutely. These dogs are a menace.

McGregor: So now I suppose you'll be arguing that we should also ban people who want to own pit bulls.

Onassis: Of course not. My point is that we do not need to protect their desire to have dangerous dogs.

McGregor: This is daft. This is what leads to gun prohibition. People have perfectly good reasons for wanting to have guns, for hunting and sport, for example; but because guns are used by criminals, people like you claim that no one should have one. People kill people with cars too. The problem is solved by prosecuting misuse, not the whole activity.

Chong: There are at least three questions that are being confused here. The first question is whether there are exceptionally dangerous dogs. The second question is whether the best way to prevent dog attacks is by focusing on the banning of certain breeds or focusing on owner responsibility and training. And the last question is to what extent protecting people from dog attacks is the city's responsibility.

As with the film example, the first step in the inquiry is to become clear about what exactly the issue is. Is the issue whether pit bulls are particularly aggressive dogs? Is the issue whether any species of dog that is vicious should be banned? Is the issue how dog attacks can best be reduced? Or is the issue whether it is even the responsibility of the city to protect people from dog attacks? It is important for the councillors to be clear here because the type of action (or lack of action) they advocate will depend on what the question or problem is that they are trying to resolve. It will also be important for them to try to understand what the relationship is among the various questions; for example, even if the councillors discover that pit bulls are particularly aggressive, that in itself would not answer the question of whether these dogs should be banned. If the councillors decide that the real issue is how dog attacks can best be reduced, then that is an issue that goes well beyond the question of whether one specific breed is vicious. If, on the other hand, the councillors decide that dealing with dog attacks is not the responsibility of the city council, then all the other questions would become irrelevant.

What Kinds of Claims or Judgments Are at Issue?

Chong: To answer any of these questions, we first need some facts. I suggest we adjourn to do some research on this question.

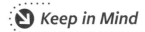

Keep in Mind

GUIDING QUESTIONS
- What is the issue?
- What kinds of claims or judgments are at issue?
- What are the relevant reasons and arguments on various sides of the issue?
- What is the context of the issue?
- How do we comparatively evaluate the various reasons and arguments to reach a reasoned judgment?

It is especially important to be clear about the issue in a decision-making context because the type of action one decides on will depend on the question or problem one is trying to resolve.

Keep in Mind

TYPES OF JUDGMENTS
- factual judgments (describe the way the world is)
- evaluative judgments (express an evaluation or assessment):
  - ethical judgments—about right and wrong
  - instrumental judgments—about usefulness and practicality
  - aesthetic judgments—about what makes something aesthetically good
- interpretive judgments (focus on meaning)

Onassis: I agree that research is in order. There are some facts that we need to know—in particular, whether pit bulls have more violent tendencies than other dogs.

Chong: There might also be some research on the effects of training on the behaviour of certain dogs. And I'd also be interested in seeing what we can find out about the effectiveness of dog-banning legislation.

McGregor: Now wait just a minute! You can go and find out all these facts if you want to. But facts won't answer the main question—whether we as the town council have a responsibility or even a right to legislate about dog ownership. That's a political question, and all the facts in the world won't tell us what's the right thing to do.

Chong: I have to agree with Councillor McGregor that the issue here is ultimately a political one which won't be settled just by facts. But knowing the relevant facts can certainly help us to make a more informed decision. Let's meet again on Monday morning, research in hand. Meeting adjourned.

What this discussion illustrates is that the councillors are dealing with a complex policy question that involves a number of different types of issues. It involves some factual issues about, for example, the violent tendencies of different breeds of dogs. But it also involves some evaluative issues, regarding, for example, the rights of dog owners, the extent of governmental responsibility for protecting its citizens, and the legitimate extent of government intervention in issues such as dog ownership. Instrumental judgments regarding the likely effectiveness of various policies will also be required. Ultimately, the point of the councillors' inquiry will be to make an evaluative judgment about what the city council should do; but they will have to consider many claims, including factual claims, before they get to this final judgment. (We will look in more detail at the various types of judgments and how they can be justified in Chapter 7.)

What Do You Think

Make a list of some of the information that would be helpful for the councillors' decision-making.

What Are the Relevant Reasons and Arguments on Various Sides of the Issue?

Complex policy questions often involve both factual and evaluative judgments.

City Council Chambers, Monday morning.

Chong: Let's see what we've all found out on our vicious dog issue. As I see it, the basic factual question is whether there are certain types of dogs that have a strong tendency to attack humans. And if there are, how great is this tendency; are some dramatically more dangerous than others, or only a little more dangerous? According to a 1996 study conducted by the Canadian Hospitals Injury Reporting and Prevention Program (CHIRPP),[2] German shepherds followed by cocker spaniels, Rottweilers, and golden retrievers were the breeds most commonly involved in biting incidents. That's confirmed by some data I found published in the *Journal of the American Veterinary Medicine Association,* which show that there are certain breeds that appear to be disproportionately involved in fatal dog attacks.[3]

McGregor: Though I've read about cases where the assumption that certain breeds are more dangerous was found to be mistaken. For example, after Kitchener, Ontario, passed a ban on pit bulls, a report by the Ministry of Health showed that pit bulls were responsible for only four percent of dog attacks—they were number eight among breeds, right behind poodles.[4]

Onassis: A report I looked at on dog attack deaths and maimings in Canada and the U.S. found that pit bulls were responsible for about 43 percent of deaths resulting from dog attacks identified in the study. The next highest were Rottweilers at about 21 percent.[5]

McGregor: Well, the research I looked at suggests that there are generally problems with this kind of data. It's difficult to get accurate dog bite statistics because many bites go unreported, unless the person seeks medical care.[6] There are also difficulties with the reporting of breeds involved in attack cases. Most information on dog bites comes from emergency room records and newspaper reports, neither of which can be relied on as accurate sources of information about the breed of dog doing the attacking. In addition, there are difficulties in determining the rate of attack for each breed, because in order to establish the rate, you would also need to know the total number of dogs of that breed which people own.

Onassis: Some of the research I've found suggests that pit bulls and certain other breeds are inherently more dangerous. This is because pit bulls were originally bred for dog fighting, which required strength and aggressiveness.[7] Also, because of their exceptional strength, tenacity, and manner of attacking, pit bull attacks are more likely to result in severe injury.[8]

McGregor: But the statistics also show that any breed of dog may inflict injury. And then there's the question of whether training and care are more important than the dog's breed in predicting whether a dog will be dangerous. Many dog groups claim that no dog or breed is inherently vicious—it all depends on training and environment. These groups point out that dogs that are poorly looked after and poorly trained (for example, dogs left outside on chains all the time) are particularly prone to attack and that any breed can be trained to be aggressive.[9]

Chong: And then there's the problem of whether owners who train their dogs to be vicious tend to own a particular species. It could be a kind of vicious circle where owners interested in cultivating an attack dog are drawn to dogs with a reputation for viciousness and then train them to be so.

Onassis: Many of the articles I've been reading argue that banning certain breeds is effective since it removes from circulation those breeds which are most likely to be involved in serious attacks.

Chong: On the other hand, I've seen articles arguing that the banning of particular breeds is not effective because it doesn't deal with the problem of other dangerous breeds which may be less well known, such as Presa Canarios or Japanese Tosas, or with the problem of dogs trained to be aggressive. In this way, banning pit bulls may give people a false sense of security when the real problem hasn't been dealt with.[10]

McGregor: Another problem that came up is that banning certain breeds is unfair to responsible dog owners. The evidence shows that virtually every breed can be involved in a serious attack, so can just banning some breeds be justified? Many people argue that we should regulate irresponsible owners and dogs with a history of aggressive behaviour rather than one particular breed.[11]

The question of how to deal with dog attacks is a hotly debated issue, with arguments and evidence offered to support a variety of different positions. The councillors will need to be cognizant of this range of views and the evidence and arguments which support them in order to evaluate the various possibilities for action.

What Is the Context of the Issue?

Chong: Thank you all for your research. This is proving to be a very complex issue. Making a decision will require some careful consideration.

We need to be aware of the range of views and the evidence and arguments which support them in order to evaluate various possibilities for action.

Vicious Dog Attack Angers Sask. mom[12]

An Ile-a-la-Crosse woman is calling for tougher animal control bylaws after a stray dog mauled her six-year-old son.

Angella McKay heard her son Shiloh Berscheid screaming outside her home Saturday evening. She ran out and saw that his face was covered in blood.

"The gashes were close to the size of my finger wide," McKay told CBC News. The boy was rushed to the local hospital, and later flown 500 kilometres south to Saskatoon for emergency surgery at the Royal University Hospital. McKay said her son needed roughly 60 stitches to close the cuts, but added that he is recovering well....

RCMP found the dog on Sunday morning, and destroyed it with the owner's permission....

"We need to address the dogs that are still running around, and possibly being a danger to the children," she said.

Onassis: But we shouldn't wait too long. This latest pit bull attack has really got the public upset. And the press is constantly on our case. There are articles on the front page every day calling for us to take immediate action.

Chong: But we can't let those pressures cause us to make a hasty decision. We need to consider all the facts carefully and weigh the pros and cons before deciding what action to take.

McGregor: Speaking of the press, our local rag did feature a very interesting article on the history of dog attacks and people's reactions to them a few days ago. It turns out that in the last few decades, different breeds of dogs, specifically Rottweilers, Doberman pinschers, and German shepherds, have been singled out as "devil dogs" depending on which breeds have been responsible for attacks at that time. If that's true (and I certainly don't always believe everything I read), then that might cast some doubt on some of these claims about the viciousness of pit pulls, or any other breed for that matter.

Chong: We'll keep that in mind when we're considering the various arguments.

A significant point here is that this issue arises in the context of a highly publicized local dog attack. Political decisions often occur in such a context as publicity puts pressure on the politicians to act. But such a highly charged context can also lead to precipitous decision-making without careful consideration of the facts or of the pros and cons of any decision.

A highly charged context can lead to precipitous decision-making without careful consideration of the facts or of the pros and cons of the decision.

Another relevant aspect of context in this case is the history of the issue. An attack by one particular dog is the focus of the councillors' inquiry, but many different breeds have been labelled as vicious over the years. Keeping both these facts in mind should help the councillors keep an appropriately skeptical viewpoint as they evaluate the various arguments.

We can also see how the political/intellectual context plays a role in the views held by the various councillors. Councillor McGregor seems to hold what is known as a **libertarian** view of the world, believing strongly in the priority of human liberty and taking positions that oppose government intervention. He thus opposes any kind of regulation of dog ownership. Councillor Onassis, on the other hand, supports the role of government in regulating behaviour in order to protect citizens from harm.

Someone who holds a **libertarian** view of the world believes strongly in the priority of human liberty and takes positions that oppose government intervention.

How Do We Comparatively Evaluate the Various Reasons and Arguments to Reach a Reasoned Judgment?

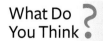

What Do You Think?

What decision would you come to in this situation? How would you deal with the dangerous dog issue based on the reasons and arguments listed above by the councillors?

Chong: Let's see where we are. On our first question, it does appear to be the case that some breeds are more likely to attack than others. The studies that we mentioned before do seem to indicate that the largest number of attacks have been attributed to pit bulls, Rottweilers, and

German shepherds. Now I grant that, without information on the total number of such dogs compared to other breeds, we cannot be certain that these dogs have a higher rate of fatal attacks. But unless we think these kinds of dogs represent a disproportionate part of the dog population, these statistics do support the claim that some breeds are much more likely to be involved in serious attacks on humans than others.

McGregor: But almost all breeds have been involved in fatal attacks. So why pick on just a few? Not only that, but the authors of this study recommend against banning particular breeds because of the impracticality of it. How can we design a law that picks out one particular breed, unless, of course, the dog is a registered pure breed. Any law prohibiting these dogs would be expensive and impossible to enforce.

Onassis: But we do need to do something. I note that some of the research indicates that dog bites are actually a major source of emergency room visits and other medical care. According to Statistics Canada, 656 Canadians were hospitalized in 1993 for dog bites and an average of one Canadian per year died from dog bites between 1991 and 1994.[13] And most of these were children!

McGregor: So, are you suggesting that we ban all dogs? This is the problem with you worrywarts when you get into government. You would have us all wearing seat belts at the dinner table because occasionally someone falls off a chair and gets hurt. Did you notice that while dog bites do represent an important source of injuries that show up in the emergency ward, dog bites are behind baseball as a source of emergency room injuries.[14] Do you want to ban baseball?

Chong: I think McGregor has a point. We need to view the problem of dog bites in the context of other activities which also have some danger, and also recognize that having a dog is something that a very large percentage of people want to do.

Onassis: With all due respect, most of the injuries identified in that study are from people voluntarily doing an activity. I doubt if very many people volunteer to be attacked by a dog. I agree that there should be limits on the government trying to protect people from themselves. People have a right to make choices. But being attacked by someone's off-property Rottweiler is not something a person would choose to do.

McGregor: I'm glad to hear that Councillor Onassis has some concern for our citizens' freedoms. I notice that over half of all fatal attacks occurred on the owner's property. This suggests to me that the owners were at most putting themselves and their family at risk, not others.

Onassis: But most attacks are on children, who can't "volunteer" for the risks their parents involve them in. That's why we have rules that children must be in car seats.

Chong: Gentlemen . . . I think we should move on. Let's see if we can get a resolution here. Let me try to summarize those points that I think we can assert with some degree of confidence after sifting through all the research. 1. Dog attacks constitute a serious problem, and we do need to take some sort of action. 2. We have some reason to believe that certain breeds pose a higher risk for serious attacks, although the data is not unambiguous. 3. Any breed of dog may be involved in an attack and owner behaviour is a crucial determinant of the dog's behaviour. 4. There are problems with breed-specific legislation in terms of practicality and effectiveness in dealing with the real issue, which is dog attacks. 5. We should show some concern for the rights of dog owners and take action that we believe will be effective but at the same time will least infringe on their freedom. Do we have consensus on these points?

Onassis: Very well summarized, Councillor Chong. I agree with all the points.

McGregor: Yes . . . OK.

Chong: Then let me suggest the following. Why not have a much more aggressive policy of leash enforcement? We should target irresponsible owners and dogs that have already

City May Redefine "Vicious"[15]

Pit-bull owners may soon be able to walk their dogs in Vancouver without a muzzle. Owners will also be permitted to take pit bulls to off-leash areas without muzzles if city council approves a staff recommendation to amend the animal-control bylaw on Thursday (July 14). Since 1987, owners have been required to muzzle all vicious dogs in public. Five breeds are currently included in the "vicious dog" definition: pit bull terrier, American pit bull terrier, pit bull, Staffordshire bull terrier, and American Staffordshire terrier, as well as any dog that includes a mix of any of these breeds. Any dog with a propensity to attack or that has already attacked domestic animals or humans without provocation would continue to be defined as "vicious" under the amendment. The minimum fine would increase from $250 to $500 for failing to muzzle or securely confine a vicious dog. However, the definition would be amended to delete references to any breeds.... At the February 17 meeting, representatives of the Canadian Kennel Club, the BC Veterinary Medical Association, and members of a pit-bull-owners group called HugABull criticized a breed-specific ban being considered by the city. HugABull spokesperson Danielle Cross, a resident of Chilliwack, told council that Calgary reduced dog bites by more than two-thirds through effective enforcement and public education, and not with a breed-specific bylaw.

displayed aggressive behaviour. This is the action most of the experts recommend. That won't eliminate all the problems, but it does put responsibility on the owners and provides a fairly straightforward strategy for legal intervention. It also avoids alienating those responsible dog owners who love their Rottweilers, such as Councillor McGregor.

Onassis: It seems to me that that would deal with the problem, and in a sensible and reasonably effective way.

McGregor: And would respect the rights of responsible dog owners. I like it!

Chong: I'll prepare a formal motion for the next meeting. But let's take a straw vote. All in favour?

Onassis, McGregor and Chong: Aye!

The councillors have sifted through a considerable amount of information and research in order to come to a decision on the issue of what to do about dog attacks. The process has presented challenges in that the research does not lead to a clear conclusion in as straightforward a manner as the councillors may have hoped. One difficulty is the problem of gathering accurate data on the rate of dog bites per breed due to the unreliability of information about the breeds involved in attacks. Nonetheless, the councillors realize that a reasonable conclusion can still be drawn on the basis of some of the research that certain breeds are more frequently involved in attacks than others. The research also gives them some reason to believe that training and owner behaviour is at least as important as, if not more important than, breed. This information assists them in refocusing onto the real issue, which is how to prevent dog bites and how to aim their legislation at the behaviour of problematic dogs and owners rather than toward particular breeds. Thus, despite the inconclusiveness of the research, the councillors are able to come up with a reasoned judgment based on a study of systematically collected information and arguments. Making a decision based on such a critical evaluation is far better than basing a decision on personal impressions, which may be biased or uninformed, or on impressions from media reports, which may be one-sided and sensationalistic.

Coming up with a reasoned judgment based on a study of systematically collected information and arguments is better than making a decision based on personal impressions or impressions from media reports.

Because the issue has a normative dimension, the deliberation of the councillors must take into account not only matters of fact, but also ethical issues concerning fairness to owners of unproblematic dogs, the freedom of the dog owners, and the responsibility of governments to protect citizens from themselves and each other. These considerations interact with factual considerations in the making of the final decision.

An important step that enables the Councillors to arrive at a reasoned judgment is Councillor Chong's pointing out that there are many points which can be asserted with some confidence despite the inconclusiveness of the research and conflicts in the arguments. She notes that the councillors can agree on these points despite their differences. This move allows the councillors to arrive at a decision that best accords with the facts they have found out and at the same time satisfies the purpose of their inquiry. In the vicious dog debate, the Councillors manage to arrive at an agreed-upon decision—a consensus— based on this process. In some cases, however, the process may not result in a consensus. In such cases, the agreement of the majority would have to decide the matter.

Highlighting the points on which there is agreement can help participants who disagree arrive at a satisfactory judgment.

Applying the Guidelines for Inquiry

In this chapter, we see examples of two inquiries which are different in a number of ways. They deal with different subjects: the first focuses on the arts, the second on social policy. They involve different participants: the first involves two friends having an amicable discussion, the second a group of individuals making a formal decision. They also have different purposes: the goal of the film discussion is understanding; the purpose of the city council debate is to make a policy decision.

Despite these differences, there are some fundamental similarities. Both cases begin with a problem or disagreement. In both cases, the disagreement is accompanied by emotional reactions and commitments to certain positions (for at least some of the participants). In both cases, the participants go beyond their initial disagreements by engaging in inquiry. And in both cases, the inquiry process involves asking the same guiding questions.

There are, however, differences in how the questions apply in the two cases. First, since the two inquiries focus on issues in different areas, different kinds of claims and judgments are involved. While the film case focuses on aesthetic judgments, the dog regulation case deals with factual as well as ethical controversies. Nonetheless, some factual judgments are also relevant to the film example. Because of the differences in areas and kinds of judgments, the types of reasons offered and the criteria for their evaluation differ as well. Different kinds of contexts play a role in each of the examples. In the film case, other films constitute an important aspect of context, while in the dog case, the political context as well as the history of the issue are central. The process and outcome of the comparative evaluation differ as well, because of the differing purposes of the two inquiries. Since the goal of the film discussion is understanding, it is not necessary that the participants come to an agreement. Since the purpose of the city council debate is to make a decision, the inquiry process must result in some sort of agreed-upon action. (This may be reached by consensus or, if a consensus is not reached, may require majority assent.)

One aspect that is common to both these inquiries, and is central to the process of inquiry in general, is the spirit of inquiry. (See Chapters 1 and 11.) In both our inquiries, the participants have to be willing to go beyond their original commitments and emotional reactions. They have to be open-minded and willing to consider views with which they initially disagree, and they have to be prepared to give such views fair-minded consideration. They also have to be willing to follow the evidence and arguments where they lead and to change their mind when required. In addition, treating other participants with respect even when one disagrees with their views is an important feature of the spirit of inquiry (though one that some of our participants have to work hard to achieve).

The cases presented here represent only two types of inquiries, but inquiries are possible in many other forms and contexts as well. Inquiries may take place in many areas, including science, social science, history, philosophy, ethics, interdisciplinary areas, and everyday life. The nature of the participants may vary, from two people engaged in a dispute, to a group of individuals making a decision, to a single person deliberating on a question. The purposes of inquiries may differ as well: they may include resolving a disagreement, making a decision, deliberating over a perplexity or puzzle, seeking understanding, or doing formal research. We will be meeting examples of these various types of inquiries in the pages to follow.

In this chapter, we have presented an overview of guidelines which can be used to conduct inquiries in a wide variety of areas. In the chapters which follow, each of the aspects will be elaborated in detail. We will also offer examples which show how each of the elements applies in practice. The last section of the book provides a detailed examination of inquiry in particular domains and shows how the guidelines apply in these various areas.

Apply Your
Understanding
Exercises 3, 4, 5

CHECK YOUR UNDERSTANDING

- *What are the five guiding questions for inquiry?*
- *Why is it important to be clear in defining the issue that we are trying to inquire about?*
- *Why is it important to be clear about the type of judgment at issue in our inquiry?*
- *What type of judgment is involved in "The Great Film Debate"?*
- *What types of judgments are involved in the councillors' debate about dangerous dogs?*
- *What aspects of context are important for the Academy Award debate?*
- *What aspects of context are important for the dangerous dog debate?*
- *What are some of the criteria which are relevant to judging films?*
- *What are some of the considerations which are relevant to formulating a policy to deal with dangerous dogs?*
- *What are some of the differences between the two inquiries in this chapter?*
- *What are some of the similarities between the two inquiries in this chapter?*

EXERCISES

1. Find a classmate, friend, or family member with whom you disagree about the issue of whether to ban cellphone use while driving. Then do the following:
   - i) Discuss why each of you has the view you have about the issue.
   - ii) Make a list of the reasons each of you gives for your judgment.
   - iii) Support your judgment with evidence and arguments.
   - iv) Try to figure out what criteria you used to make the judgment and list these as well.

2. Find a review in the newspaper or online of a film you have seen recently.
   Read the review carefully, then do the following:
   - i) List the criteria that the reviewer is using to evaluate the film.
   - ii) Give your evaluation of the film using the same criteria as the reviewer.
   - iii) List any additional criteria that you think are relevant but which the reviewer has missed (if any), and add any additional evaluation according to these criteria.

3. For each of the following dialogues, do the following:
   - i) Identify the issue (hints: be specific; state in the form of a question).
   - ii) Identify what type(s) of claims or judgments are involved in answering the question.
   - iii) Identify the reasons offered on both sides of the issue.

a) Diego Alvarez and his neighbour, Omar Ali, are surveying the hedge that runs between their properties.

Diego: Our privet's not looking so good.

Omar: I'm afraid it's got some kind of insect infestation. I guess we'll need to spray it with a pesticide.

Diego: But aren't pesticides bad for the environment? I've heard that they can kill birds who eat sprayed plants and can even be harmful to people.

Omar: Oh … I think that's an exaggeration. I can't imagine that the small amount that we'll be using could do much harm. And besides, we don't want to let the hedge die, do we?

b) Nancy and Phil have just been watching some TV advertising directed at children.

Nancy: That's really terrible—targeting ads to kids.

Phil: What's so bad about that? It's the kids who are interested in the toys.

Nancy: But it just makes them want whatever they see. The ads manipulate them. They don't know any better.

Phil: Kids are going to want toys anyway. The ads just let them know what's out there.

Nancy: It's just going to turn them into consumers at a young age. And that's exactly what these companies want. I don't think it should be allowed.

Phil: That would be censorship!

c) Juanita and Winnie are looking at the newspaper.

Juanita: Can you pass me the Entertainment section? I want to have a look at my horoscope. I have a test today in class, and I want to know how it's going to go.

Winnie: You don't really believe those things, do you? I mean, they're good for a laugh, but …

Juanita: Why shouldn't I believe them? Usually what they say is right on!

Winnie: That's just because you notice the things that are right and forget everything they say that doesn't happen. Anyway, they're so vague that you can interpret them any way you like.

Juanita: But horoscopes are based on how the stars move and align and all that—it's pretty scientific. Isn't it?

Winnie: I don't think there's any real scientific basis whatsoever to horoscopes.

d) Camillia Bell and Mona Gold are discussing the recent purchase by a local art museum of an art installation work for $500, 000.

Mona: I think it's absolutely shocking!

Camillia: Why do you say that?

Mona: Spending all that money on that thing! It just looks like a pile of rubbish.

Camillia: But it's an important piece by a prominent artist. It's making a profound statement about our consumerist society.

Mona: Maybe you arts folks can see that in it. But spending that kind of taxpayer money on what looks to the rest of us like a pile of rubbish is just not acceptable. The public should have been consulted.

Camillia: You can't leave decisions about art to the general public. People with some expertise should make those choices.

4. Imagine that you are thinking about buying a cellphone and there is a particular cellphone which initially appeals to you. Engage in a process of inquiry in order to decide whether that really is the best cellphone to buy given your circumstances. (This will require doing some research on different kinds of cellphones.) Use the following questions to guide your inquiry:

i) What is the issue I am focusing on? Is there more than one issue; and if so, which is the most important? How can I state the issue clearly?

ii) What kind of judgment or judgments will I need to make? What kinds of claims will I need to consider in order to make the judgment?

iii) What is the context in which I am making this judgment, including my own situation and other surrounding circumstances?

iv) What are the pros and cons of buying this particular cellphone?

v) How can I take all the information I have gathered and make a reasoned judgment about whether I should buy this cellphone?

5. Your instructor will show a film in class. After seeing the film, work in pairs to evaluate the film. In order to do this, follow these guidelines:

i) Answer the five guiding questions for inquiry.

ii) Write an inquiry dialogue using your responses to the guiding questions as a guide. Present your dialogues orally in class.

ENDNOTES

1. James Berardinelli, "The Sweet Hereafter," *Reel Reviews*, http://www.reelviews.net/php_review_template. php?identifier=66 (accessed April 22, 2010).

2. Vanessa, "Preventing Dog Bites: Media Asked for Help by HSC," *Humane Society of Canada website*, Feb. 13, 2005, http://humanesociety.com/news-releases/130.html.

3. Jeffrey J. Sacks, Leslie Sinclair, Julie Gilchrist, Gail C. Golab, and Randall Lockwood, "Breeds of dogs involved in fatal human attacks in the United States between 1979 and 1998," *Journal of the American Veterinary Medicine Association,* 217 (2000): 836–40.

4. Gary Goeree, "Pitbull Attacks Were Never Very High in Kitchener," *DVM*, Sept. 28, 2009, http://www.doglegislationcouncilcanada.org/KWBOH.html.

5. Merritt Clifton, "Dog Attack Deaths and Maimings, US & Canada, September 1982 - January 1, 2008," *Scribd*, Sept. 28, 2009, http://www.scribd.com/doc/11249213/Dog-Attack-Deaths-Maimings-US-Canada-September-1982-to-January-2008.

6. Amy Cheung, "Aggression and Biting in Dogs," *Pets.ca,* http://www.pets.ca/articles/article-dog-aggression.htm (accessed Sept. 28, 2009).

7. Susan Thompson, "Pit Bull Breed Profile," *Rescue Every Dog*, http://www.rescueeverydog.org/pitbull_breed.html (accessed Dec. 26, 2009).

8. *Wikipedia*, "Pit Bull," http://en.wikipedia.org/wiki/Pit_Bull (accessed Dec. 26, 2009).

9. National Companion Animal Coalition, "Reducing the Incidence of Dog Bites and Attacks: Do Breed Bans Work?" *CanadianVeterinarians.net*, http://canadianveterinarians.net/Documents/Resources/Files/59_Public_Do-Breed-Bans-Work.pdf (accessed Dec. 26, 2009).

10. Safia Gray Hussain, "Attacking the Dog-Bite Epidemic: Why Breed-Specific Legislation Won't Solve the Dangerous Dog Dilemma," *Fordham Law Review* 2847 (2006).

11. National Companion Animal Coalition; see note 9 above.

12. "Vicious dog attack angers Sask. Mom," *cbc.ca*, Sept. 22, 2009, http://www.cbc.ca/canada/saskatchewan/story/2009/09/22/sask-dog-attack.html.

13. Cheung; see note 6 above.

14. Harold B. Weiss, Deborah I. Friedman, and Jeffrey Cobban, "Incidence of Dog Bite Injuries Treated in Emergency Departments," *The Journal of the American Medical Association* 279, no.1 (1998): 51–53.

15. Charlie Smith, "City May Redefine 'Vicious'," *Straight.com*, http://www.straight.com/article/city-may-redefine-vicious (accessed April 24, 2010).

Chapter 3
Arguments and Their Structure

Learning Objectives

After reading this chapter, you should be able to:

- identify and standardize the structure of deductive and inductive arguments
- identify the form of some basic valid arguments
- apply the concept of validity when evaluating deductive arguments
- identify unstated premises and assumptions in arguments
- apply the concepts of necessary and sufficient conditions when evaluating deductive arguments

Raising the Minimum Wage I

Daimon McGregor and his daughter Nancy have just been listening to a news report in which a politician has been arguing that the minimum wage should be raised.

McGregor: Now that is a dumb idea if ever I've heard one.

Nancy: You mean raising the minimum wage? Why do you think it's so dumb?

McGregor: Because it is—it's just stupid.

Nancy: What makes you say that?

McGregor: Measures that put undue burdens on business are bad for the economy. Raising the minimum wage would do that. So raising the minimum wage would be bad for the economy. It only makes sense. Raising the minimum wage would hugely increase labour costs for businesses, so they would no longer be able to remain competitive. Their profits would disappear and pretty soon companies would have to shut down because they couldn't afford all the extra wages and everyone would be unemployed.

Nancy: Now wait just a minute, Dad. Paying people a wage that allows them to have enough to eat is hardly an "undue" burden. I guess your view is that it's OK that companies are pulling in huge profits and CEOs are living in mansions and flying around in executive jets while other people starve to death.

McGregor: Now, Nancy, you know that is not my point of view.

Nancy: True, Dad. I'm sorry. But I do think that we need to take measures to help those on the lower end of the economic ladder. So I still think we should raise the minimum wage.

McGregor: This thinking that raising the minimum wage will help the poor is just more of that left-wing logic. Increases in the minimum wage always result in the loss of minimum wage jobs. So you could help the poor more by lowering the minimum wage. Then there would be more jobs and more employment for the poor.

Nancy: You're actually saying that we should lower the minimum wage in order to help the poor? That sounds like a pretty weird argument to me.

McGregor: But it makes sense if you stop using that misguided left-wing logic. It's all a matter of pricing. Everyone knows that the lower the price, the more goods you can sell. The same is true of labour. It's common knowledge that the cheaper the labour, the more workers will be hired.

Nancy: I haven't seen any evidence that that's the case.

McGregor: Well, I haven't seen any evidence that it's not!

Nancy: I don't believe that lowering the minimum wage ever leads to an increase in lower-end jobs. When they introduced a lower minimum wage for young people in B.C., there was no increase in the number of jobs for young people. And besides, there are lots of countries that have no minimum wage but still have widespread unemployment.

McGregor: We shouldn't increase the minimum wage. What we should really do is simply get rid of it, period. That's what's best for the economy; and if it's good for the economy, it will be good for everyone, including the poor.

Nancy: Measures that are good for the economy will help the poor? Well, raising the minimum wage will help the poor. So by your own reasoning, it must be good for the economy.

McGregor: That doesn't sound quite right to me ...

Nancy and her dad continue this dialogue in the next chapter. But for now, we want to look in more detail at their arguments and the relationship of argument to a broader inquiry.

Argument and Inquiry

In this exchange, Daimon McGregor and his daughter Nancy are exchanging a series of arguments on the question of raising the minimum wage. Arguments have also played a central role in all the inquiries we have seen to this point. (The exchange above is not quite at the level of an inquiry, although it could become one with some work and good will on the part of the participants.) Two of our guiding questions for inquiry focus on arguments, in terms of both laying out and evaluating the relevant reasons and arguments on various sides of an issue. Arguments are, in a sense, the building blocks of inquiry. But until this point, we have not really discussed the nature of arguments in any detail. So, before moving on to work through the various aspects of our guidelines for inquiry, we will take some time to focus on the nature, analysis, and evaluation of individual arguments.

The Structure of Arguments

What exactly is an argument? The word "argument" has many meanings, and we will use several of these in the text. The loud and red-faced type of argument is not, you may be relieved to know, the focus of this text, although occasionally the participants in our dialogues may get into that state. The exchange between the two councillors over the dog banning issue came alarmingly close to exhibiting this sense of the word "argument." But in this text, we will generally be concerned with **argument** as a set of claims. The purpose of an argument is to provide reasons to believe a claim. The reasons offered in support of a claim are the **premises.** We will call the claim being supported the **conclusion.** So an argument consists of at least two claims, a premise and a conclusion.

An **argument** is a set of claims, one of which, the **conclusion**, is supported by one or more other claims, called **premises**.

Standardizing Arguments

The first job when reading or hearing an argument is to figure out exactly which of the author's statements is the conclusion or point of the argument and which are the premises. We can then make an outline of the argument which should reveal clearly the structure of the argument. The process of outlining an argument is called **standardizing the argument.**

For example, we can standardize one of McGregor's first arguments above as follows:

The process of outlining an argument to reveal its structure is called **standardizing the argument**.

P 1. Measures that put undue burdens on business are bad for the economy.

P 2. Raising the minimum wage would put an undue burden on business.

M **Conclusion:** Raising the minimum wage would be bad for the economy.

This argument is quite similar to a famous argument used by the great Greek philosopher Aristotle to teach logic:

1. All humans are mortal.

2. Socrates is a human.

Conclusion: Socrates is mortal.

Standardizing and the Principle of Charity

Many arguments are open to a variety of interpretations. When one is interpreting an argument, one should employ the **principle of charity.** The principle of charity states that one should choose the most favourable interpretation of the argument consistent with the actual argument content. This principle of interpretation is really intended to discourage unfairness in argument interpretation. By encouraging us to err in the direction of charity, the principle is intended to discourage us from allowing our initial disagreement with someone to lead us to make an unfair or an inaccurate interpretation of that person's position or argument. The principle of charity is not meant to suggest that, when interpreting an argument, you should always try to interpret it as a good argument. You are not expected to be that charitable when simply standardizing an argument. For example, suppose someone makes this statement: "Canadians are very polite." This sounds like a universal generalization (i.e., "All Canadians are polite"). A charitable revision of this claim would be as follows: "Many, perhaps even most, Canadians are polite." It still might not be true despite its cliché status, but the revision is more likely to express what the speaker intended. If someone had objected to the claim with "What about Guy Earle, a notoriously rude Canadian comic?", the speaker would likely have responded, "Well, I didn't really mean 'All.' I was claiming that politeness is a common attribute of Canadians."

Aristotle (384–322 BCE) was a Greek philosopher, a student of Plato and teacher of Alexander the Great. **Together with Plato and Socrates (Plato's teacher), Aristotle is one of the most important founding figures in Western philosophy. Aristotle is credited with the earliest study of formal logic, and his conception of it was the dominant form of Western logic until the late nineteenth century.**

The **principle of charity** states that one should choose the most favourable interpretation of the argument consistent with the actual argument content.

Remember this argument from the dialogue?

McGregor: Measures that put undue burdens on business are bad for the economy. Raising the minimum wage would do that. So raising the minimum wage would be bad for the economy …

Nancy: Now wait just a minute, Dad. Paying people a wage that allows them to have enough to eat is hardly an "undue" burden. I guess your view is that it's OK that companies are pulling in huge profits and CEOs are living in mansions and flying around in executive jets while other people starve to death.

McGregor: Now, Nancy, you know that is not my point of view.

Nancy's response clearly violates the principle of charity. We doubt she would have made her response if she had standardized her father's argument:

1. Measures that put undue burdens on business are bad for the economy.
2. Raising the minimum wage would put an undue burden on business.

Conclusion: Raising the minimum wage would be bad for the economy.

It is clear that McGregor has said nothing about allowing people to starve to death.

What Do You Think ?

Why do you think we should adopt the principle of charity when interpreting arguments?

Why should we adopt the principle of charity when interpreting arguments?

We should always follow the principle of charity when interpreting or standardizing an argument.

- It is generally the decent thing to do, especially in a dialogue.
- It helps keep a dialogue on a rational track as each person tries to listen sympathetically to the other side through this lens of charitable interpretation.
- It will help us avoid the common fallacy known as straw person (see Chapter 4). You commit the fallacy of straw person when you create and then attack an oversimplified or distorted version of your opponent's argument (as Nancy did). This fallacy is common, because when we disagree with people, we tend to misrepresent their position.

The classic domestic dispute below illustrates this tendency.

S: I really wish you would remember to put your dirty socks in the wash.

H: So, again you are saying I am a complete slob, as if I never help clean the house.

- When you evaluate the most charitable interpretation of someone's argument and can still show that it is weak or fallacious, you have made a more effective criticism of the argument than if you were criticizing an uncharitable version of the argument.

Diagramming Arguments: Linked and Convergent

In addition to outlining the argument, we can standardize arguments by creating diagrams of them. Such diagrams often help us to see which claims are premises supporting the conclusion and which are premises supporting other premises in a sub-argument. They also illustrate the distinction between linked and convergent arguments.

Knowing whether an argument is linked or convergent will help us considerably when we come to evaluate arguments. In a **linked argument,** if any of the premises can be shown to be false or not credible, then the whole force of the argument is defeated. In linked arguments, the premises do not provide direct, independent support for the conclusion, but work together like links of a chain. As with a chain, linked arguments are only as strong as the weakest link (or the weakest premise). Showing that one linked premise is weak or false undermines the whole argument's support for its conclusion.

In a **convergent argument,** each premise independently provides support for the conclusion. Showing that any particular premise is weak, false, or simply not credible does not necessarily weaken the total support for the conclusion. The metaphor here is one of support: a porch could be supported by numerous uprights and the fact that one is weak does not mean that the floor is not adequately supported by the others.

To illustrate, let's take the simple argument above about Socrates (see page 41). It is a linked argument and can be diagrammed as follows:

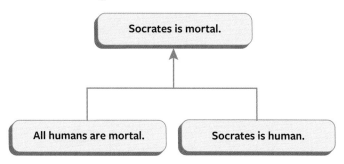

In a **linked argument,** premises do not provide independent support; rather, premises are linked together to provide support.

This diagram shows the two premises working together to provide support for the conclusion.

We can compare this argument to the following convergent argument made by Nancy in the dialogue:

Nancy: You're actually saying that we should lower the minimum wage in order to help the poor? That sounds like a pretty weird argument to me.

McGregor: But it makes sense if you stop using that misguided left-wing logic. It's all a matter of pricing. Everyone knows that the lower the price, the more goods you can sell. The same is true of labour. It's common knowledge that the cheaper the labour, the more workers that will be hired....

Nancy: ... When they introduced a lower minimum wage for young people in B.C., there was no increase in the number of jobs for young people. And besides, there are lots of countries that have no minimum wage but still have widespread unemployment.

We can standardize her argument in this way:

Conclusion: It is not the case that having a lower minimum wage will help the poor.

1. A lower minimum wage did not increase the number of jobs for young people.
2. There are many countries which have no minimum wage but widespread unemployment.

We diagram this convergent argument as follows:

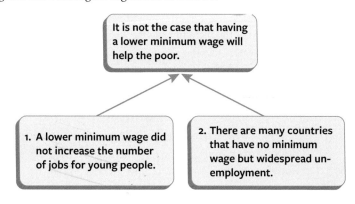

In a **convergent argument,** each premise independently provides support for the conclusion.

Note that the two premises provide independent support—not linked support. The difference is that each premise provides some support for the conclusion independently of the other. In the first argument about Socrates, the two premises were linked together to support the conclusion.

To see the significance of the two different kinds of argument support, let's take McGregor's argument, "We should get rid of the minimum wage to help the poor because allowing the free market to determine the wage rate is best for the economy and what's good for the economy will help the poor."

Here again the premises are linked because neither one provides any independent support for the conclusion but together they do provide some support. But this argument also demonstrates that because the premises are linked, if one premise is weak, the whole argument is weakened. McGregor's premise 1A-b ("What's good for the economy will help the poor") is not a well-supported general claim. An economy's wealth can increase, but most of the increased wealth may go to the middle class and wealthy and not to the poor. Because the argument is linked, the support for the conclusion is no stronger than this weak premise.

Sub-arguments

The support for the premises of an argument are called **sub-arguments.**

Arguments are seldom made up of a straightforward list of premises supporting a conclusion. Premises themselves can and often should be supported. If we look more closely at McGregor's first argument, we can see that it contains **sub-arguments:**

McGregor: Measures that put undue burdens on business are bad for the economy. Raising the minimum wage would do that. So raising the minimum wage would be bad for the economy. It only makes sense. Raising the minimum wage would hugely increase labour costs for businesses. So they would no longer be able to remain competitive. Their profits would disappear.

We can standardize McGregor's argument as follows. Notice that as we standardize, we eliminate the rhetorical expression ("dumb idea") and replace it with the implicit assertion. This is another application of the principle of charity.

Conclusion: Minimum wage should not be raised. (This replaces "Is a dumb idea.")
1. Measures that put undue burdens on business are bad for the economy.
2. Raising the minimum wage would put undue burden on business.
   2.1 When profits disappeared, companies would have to shut down.
       2.1.1 If minimum wage were raised, businesses profits would disappear.
           2.1.1.1 Raising the minimum wage would hugely increase labour costs for businesses.

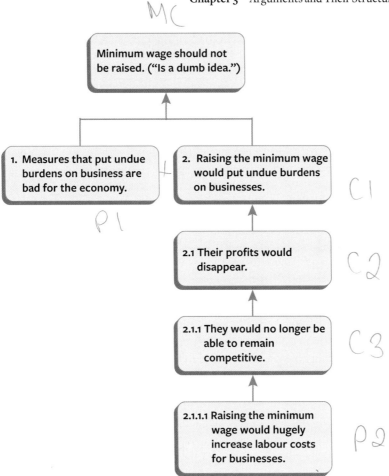

The diagram brings out even more clearly the way sub-arguments work to provide support for premises. As you can see from the standardization of this argument, premises can be supported and even supporting premises can be supported. The support for premises are called sub-arguments. Longer arguments are basically built up of arguments supporting arguments. When we look at a full inquiry, we will see that there will be many arguments, and arguments supporting arguments, and so on. In order to see the structure of longer arguments, we will often have to leave out sub-arguments and focus on just the main premises. But we can always "drill down" into the sub-arguments, if necessary.

Apply Your Understanding Exercise 1

Two Types of Arguments: Deductive and Inductive

Besides linked and convergent, there is another fundamental distinction between types of arguments. That is the distinction between deductive arguments and inductive arguments. The distinction between the two is based on the degree of certainty that the premises are intended to give to the conclusion.

An argument is **deductive** if it is a linked argument and it appears that the author intended the truth of the premises to guarantee the truth of the conclusion. Of course, not every argument that is intended to guarantee the conclusion succeeds. The successful ones, such as the argument above that Socrates is mortal, are called **valid deductive arguments.** Valid deductive arguments are arguments in which if the premises are true, the conclusion *must* be true. This relationship between the premises and the conclusion in

An argument is **deductive** if it is a linked argument and it appears that the author intended the truth of the premises to guarantee the truth of the conclusion.

Valid deductive arguments are arguments in which if the premises are true, the conclusion *must* be true.

A claim X **entails** another claim Y, when if X is true, then Y *must* be true.

In **inductive** arguments, the premises provide support for but do not entail the conclusion.

With **strong inductive arguments,** if the premises are true, then it is *likely* that the conclusion is true.

a valid deductive argument is called **entailment.** A claim X entails another claim Y, when if X is true, then Y *must* be true. For example, the claim that "Bill has a sister, Mary" entails that "Mary has a brother."

Inductive arguments have a weaker relationship between their premises and conclusion. With **strong inductive arguments,** if the premises are true, then it is *likely* that the conclusion is true. In strong inductive arguments with true premises, the premises *do not* entail the conclusion; rather they *provide support for the conclusion*.

When Nancy tries to refute her father's claim that lowering the minimum wage will increase employment, she cites the example of B.C., which introduced a lower minimum wage without any increase in employment. Although this is only one case, this is a good use of historical information to call into question McGregor's generalization. The premise, if true, does provide a good reason to doubt the claim that lowering the minimum wage will always result in increased employment. Nancy's claim that there are many countries without a minimum wage that experience great poverty also supports her point. But neither of these premises *proves* that a lower minimum wage will not benefit the poor (at least sometimes). They just provide *good reasons* not to believe in this claim. Most of the focus of this text will be on inductive arguments like these. The rest of this chapter, however, will look at deductive arguments.

While deductive arguments are not particularly common in everyday argumentation, they are the dominant form of reasoning in mathematics and computer science. They also provide useful examples that illustrate the concept of argument form, and they help explain our ability to identify assumptions.

When describing deductive arguments, we often use a "path" metaphor. In this way of describing an argument, an argument *leads* the reader to its conclusion. This metaphor seems especially apt when describing deduction which leads us, as we say, *inevitably* to the conclusion. We can also see how deductive arguments provide links of a chain that link that conclusion to the premises. In fact, all deductive arguments are linked arguments, although not all linked arguments are deductive. For example, in Chapter 5, we will look at the analogical arguments that marijuana is like alcohol, and since alcohol is legal, marijuana should be legal. This is an example of an argument that is linked but is not deductive.

The argument looks like this:

Conclusion: Marijuana should be legal.
1. Alcohol is legal.
2. Marijuana is like alcohol.

Another example of a linked argument is the main part of McGregor's argument that we cited above:

1. Measures that put undue burdens on business are bad for the economy.
2. Raising the minimum wage would put an undue burden on business.

Conclusion: Raising the minimum wage would be bad for the economy.

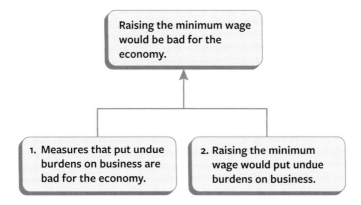

This is an example of a valid deductive argument in that the premises which McGregor offers entail the conclusion. It is important to understand that a set of premises that leads to or entails a conclusion does not prove that the conclusion is true. By saying that an argument is deductively valid, we are only saying that *if the premises are true,* then the conclusion must be true. Ultimately, of course, we are concerned not only with validity but also with having true conclusions. Valid arguments that have true premises and, therefore, true conclusions are called sound. A **sound argument** is a valid argument in which the premises are true. And, of course, in a valid argument, if the premises are true, the conclusion must be true.

A **sound argument** is a valid deductive argument with true premises.

McGregor's premises may not be true; but if they were true, then the conclusion would follow as certainly as the conclusion about Socrates. What this illustrates is that what makes an argument valid is not the content of the argument, not the truth or falsity of the premises, but its underlying form. McGregor's argument actually has the same underlying form as the argument about Socrates' mortality.

Argument Form	Socrates Argument	Minimum Wage Argument
All A's are B.	All humans are mortal.	Anything that puts undue burdens on business is bad for the economy.
X is an A.	Socrates is human.	Raising the minimum wage would put an undue burden on business.
Conclusion: X is a B.	**Conclusion:** Socrates is mortal.	**Conclusion:** Raising the minimum wage would be bad for the economy.

We can see that any argument of this form would be valid. If we substitute categories like "cat" and "furry" for "A" and "B" and real individuals for "X," we can see that if the premises are true, the conclusion must be true. All cats are furry. Toby is a cat. Therefore Toby is furry.

An argument form is a **valid argument form** when, if true statements are substituted into the premises, the conclusion must be true. By parity of reasoning, an argument form is not a valid argument form if the premises could be true, but the conclusion false.

An argument form is a **valid argument form** when, if true statements are substituted into the premises, the conclusion must be true.

What do you think of the following argument by Nancy?

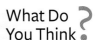

McGregor: Measures that are good for the economy will ultimately help the poor.

Nancy: Measures that are good for the economy will help the poor? Well, raising the minimum wage will help the poor. So by your own reasoning, it must be good for the economy.

Nancy's response is not valid.

Standardizing

1. Measures that are good for the economy will help the poor.
2. Raising the minimum wage will help the poor.

Conclusion: Raising the minimum wage must be good for the economy.

McGregor was justifiably reluctant to accept this reasoning. Why? Because this argument is not valid. Nancy's argument has the following form:

All A's are B.

X is a B.

Conclusion: X is an A.

To see why this form is not valid, look at the following instance of the form:

1. All rabbits are furry.
2. My cat is furry.

Conclusion: My cat is a rabbit.

It is clearly not valid.

What Do
You Think

Do you think that the following argument is valid or invalid?

1. All ravens are birds.
2. All birds are green.

Conclusion: All ravens are green.

Valid! This odd argument should remind us of two key points about valid deductive arguments.

1. The validity of the argument is independent of whether the premises are true.
2. What makes the argument valid is the underlying argument form.

So whether an argument is valid depends on whether it is an instance of a valid argument form, not whether its premises are true or its conclusion true.

Argument Form	Raven Argument
All A's are B.	All ravens are birds.
All B's are C's.	All birds are green.
Conclusion: All A's are C's.	**Conclusion:** All ravens are green.

Validity depends on whether an argument is an instance of a valid argument form, not on whether its conclusion or premises are true.

You might think of valid argument form as a calculator. As the saying goes, "Garbage in, garbage out." The validity of the calculator is not undermined if you type in the wrong numbers and then get a wrong answer. What the calculator guarantees is that *if* you type in the right numbers (and operation signs), you will get the right answer. The same is true of putting claims into a valid argument form.

But not all arguments which look like deductive arguments are valid. The argument below contains two true premises and yet has a false conclusion. This shows that it is not a valid argument. No argument with this same argument form is valid.

1. All crows are birds.
2. All crows are black.

Conclusion: All birds are black.

This argument has this form:

All A's are B.
All A's are C.
Conclusion: All B's are C.

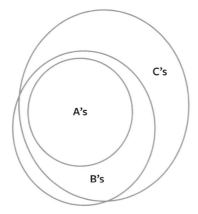

We can illustrate this argument with Euler (pronounced "oiler") circles, an invention by the noted nineteenth century mathematician Leonhard Euler. These diagrams were later improved upon by John Venn, creating the well-known Venn diagrams. Note in the diagram that while A's are inside both B's and C's, there is no guarantee from the premises that all B's are contained in C's.

So far we have been looking at arguments that involve "categorical statements"—claims that an individual or group is a member of some category (e.g., "Socrates is (a member of the category) a human being," or "Cats are (members of the category) furry things"). Many categorical claims involve what are known as universal generalizations or "all" claims. Since most such general claims turn out to be false, it is useful to realize that the refutation of such claims does not require a counter-generalization, but only a counter-example. If you want to deny someone's generalization, you do not need to counter with a generalization of your own. The contradictory (i.e., denial) of a generalization is simply the assertion of some counter-example. The generalization "all swans are white" is refuted by one non-white swan. You do not need to claim that "no swans are white." McGregor made the general claim that "Increases in the minimum wage always result in the loss of minimum wage jobs. So you could help the poor more by lowering the minimum wage. Then there would be more jobs and more employment for the poor." Nancy countered with "I don't believe that lowering the minimum wage ever leads to an increase in lower-end jobs." Nancy's statement is, of course, quite a generalization itself and hard to prove. But importantly, it was unnecessary to make her point. All she needed was a couple of counter-examples to deny her father's claim. Her example of B.C.— where, when they introduced a lower minimum wage for young people, there was no increase in the number of jobs—serves as just such a counter-example. She does not need to assert a counter-generalization. To deny the claim "All pit bulls are

Countering Generalizations

When you are objecting to a generalization, you only need to assert that there are counter-examples ("some cases are different"). You do not need to claim the contrary (i.e., "no cases fit the generalization.")

vicious," we just need a couple of friendly pit bulls ("Some pit bulls are not vicious"). We do not need to counter with "No pit bulls are vicious."

Apply Your
Understanding
Exercise 2

A Brief Introduction to Formal Logic

Late in the nineteenth century, a different approach to studying the forms of deductive argument began to develop. This approach, known as formal logic, came to be the basis of the logic used in computers. This form of logic is often more applicable to arguments in ordinary language than the approach we used standardizing the deductive arguments above; therefore, studying it can help us with everyday reasoning. Let's look at the following argument:

1. If the car runs, then it has gas.
2. It runs.

Conclusion: It has gas.

This argument is obviously valid. If the premises are true, the conclusion must be true.

This argument is a type of argument called Modus Ponens and is a very common type of argument form. It can be symbolized as shown in the following table.

Modus Ponens (MP) Example	Argument Form
If the car runs, then it has gas.	If P, then Q
It runs.	P
Conclusion: It has gas.	Q

Using our test for validity—if the premises are true, the conclusion must be true—we can see that arguments of the form MP, such as the car example above, are clearly valid. Note, of course, that the car could be an electric car. But then premise 1 would not be true and the conclusion would be false. Validity only guarantees a true conclusion if the premises are true.

Let's look at a similar but invalid argument form: the fallacy of affirming the consequent. The "consequent" referred to is the clause that follows the "then."

Fallacy of Affirming the Consequent Example	Argument Form
If the car runs, then it has gas.	If P, then Q
It has gas.	Q
Conclusion: It runs.	P

We can see that the argument is not valid. We all know of occasions in which a car has had gas, but sadly would not run. The error here is to take the necessary condition for the car running, namely gas, and treat it as if it were a sufficient condition.

Necessary and Sufficient Conditions

The concept of validity can also help us understand another set of concepts which are crucial to understanding claims and evaluating arguments: necessary and sufficient conditions.

Take this argument:

1. If there is fire, then there is oxygen.
2. There is a fire.

Conclusion: There is oxygen.

This is another example of the valid argument form Modus Ponens (MP, illustrated above).

> If P, then Q.
>
> P.
>
> **Conclusion:** Q.

One way of understanding this argument is to see that any clause (clauses are sentence-like statements that are part of a larger sentence) in the P position (which is called the *antecedent clause*) states a **sufficient condition** for inferring the truth of the Q clause (known as the *consequent clause*). The claim that "If there is fire, then there is oxygen" states that the existence of fire is a sufficient condition to infer the presence of oxygen.

The claim that "If there is fire, then there is oxygen" also states that oxygen is a **necessary condition** for fire. Clearly oxygen is not *sufficient* for fire since oxygen is everywhere and fortunately we are not in constant conflagration. But we know that fire requires the presence of oxygen, so that when there is fire there must be oxygen. This leads to another valid argument.

To say that X is a **sufficient condition** for Y is to say that if X is present, then Y must also be present.

To say that X is a **necessary condition** for Y is to say that it is impossible to have Y without X.

Modus Tollens (MT) Argument Example	Argument Form
If there is fire, then there is oxygen.	If P, then Q.
There is no oxygen.	Not Q.
Conclusion: There will be no fire.	Not P.

We can easily see why this argument is valid when we note that the second premise claims that a necessary condition for P is not present: No oxygen, then, of course, no fire.

Once we understand that the consequent clause in an "if . . . then" sentence states a necessary condition for the antecedent, we can see that any argument which involves claiming that the consequent condition is not met (e.g., there is no oxygen, or no gas) is a valid argument. This argument form is called Modus Tollens (MT), and you use it every day. Here are a few examples:

- If John was coming to the party, he would be here by now. But he isn't here; therefore, he isn't coming to the party.
- If Mary really loved Bill, she wouldn't date other guys. But she does date other guys; therefore, she doesn't really love Bill.

Modus Tollens (MT) Example	Argument Form
If the car runs, then it has gas.	If P, then Q
It has no gas.	Not Q.
Therefore, it won't run.	Not P.

To further see the significance of necessary and sufficient conditions, consider the following dialogue between Nancy and her father:

Nancy: Dad, can I borrow the car tonight?

McGregor: Only if you clean it first.

Later:

Nancy: OK Dad, the car is clean. Can I have the keys?

McGregor: No, I need the lawn mowed, too.

Nancy: But Dad, you said I could have the car if I cleaned it.

McGregor: No, I did not. What I said was you could have the car only if you cleaned it first. I was specifying a necessary condition for borrowing the car, not a sufficient condition.

Nancy's father is being a bit obnoxious, but he is logically correct. "Only if" is a phrase used to specify a necessary condition; for example, "There is fire, *only if* there is oxygen." There is a world of difference between specifying a necessary condition and a sufficient condition.

In summary, in the sentence form "If P, then Q," P specifies a sufficient condition for Q, while Q specifies a necessary condition for P. We know that whenever something happens, whether it is fire or a running car, all the necessary conditions (including gas or oxygen) must be present. After all, if they are really necessary conditions, you can't have the event without them. And once all the necessary conditions are present, they will be sufficient for the event to occur.

Necessary and sufficient conditions are not just about something being caused. Take the conditions for graduation. At your college or university, you will need a certain number of credits to graduate—let's say 120 credits—plus a certain distribution of these credits—perhaps you must meet a language or math requirement, for example. Each of these conditions must be met before you graduate; each one is a thus a necessary condition. The sufficient condition for graduation is simply meeting all the necessary conditions.

As the car conversation between Nancy and her father shows, when you are making a deal, it is usually quite important to be clear about whether the other person is specifying necessary or sufficient conditions for the deal. We can use this way of looking at arguments to understand what went wrong with Nancy's objection to her dad's position in the following argument.

1. If a policy is good for the economy, then it is good for the poor.
2. Raising the minimum wage is good for the poor.

Conclusion: Raising the minimum wage is good for the economy.

We have seen that this argument is not valid. Nancy has committed the fallacy of affirming the consequent. In other words, Nancy has treated "being good for the poor" as a *sufficient condition* for "being good for the economy," whereas her father was arguing the other way around, that "being good for the economy" was a *sufficient condition* for "being good for the poor." Just a small twist of the argumentative order, and yet this makes the difference between a valid and invalid argument.

Here are some other typical examples of Modus Tollens arguments:

1. If you want Mary to love you, you are going to have to treat her with respect at all times.
2. Well, I do want her to love me, but sometimes she says the stupidest things and I just have to tell her how stupid they are.

Conclusion: I don't think she's going to love you.

1. If you are a vegetarian, then you will be kind to animals.
2. You are not kind to animals.

Conclusion: You must not be a vegetarian.

While these are all familiar valid arguments, there is another argument form that looks quite similar but is not valid.

1. If you are a vegetarian, then you will be kind to animals.
2. You are not a vegetarian.

Conclusion: You will not be kind to animals.

It looks similar to the argument before it but it is not valid. It actually commits the fallacy of denying the antecedent or the "if" clause.

Fallacy of Denying the Antecedent Example	Argument Form
If the car runs, then it has gas.	If P, then Q.
It won't run.	Not P.
Therefore, it has no gas.	Not Q.

Again, we all realize that the absence of gas is one reason (a sufficient reason) why a car might not run, but we cannot infer with certainty from the fact that the car will not run that it does not have gas (e.g., the battery might be dead). And even if all vegetarians are kind to animals, the fact that someone is not a vegetarian is clearly not grounds for asserting that they are generally unkind to animals.

Apply Your Understanding Exercises 3, 4, 5

Unstated Premises and Assumptions

The term "assumption" means literally any claim that is asserted without support; that is, any claim that is just *assumed*. In this sense, any premise in an argument that does not have support from a sub-argument is an assumption. But there is another sense of assumption that we use when we say "I think you are assuming that . . ." In this sense, an **assumption** is an *unstated* but necessary part of an argument. This is the sense of "assumption" that we will use in this text.

An **assumption** is an unstated but necessary part of an argument.

One of the primary ways that we can identify assumptions is by reconstructing (standardizing) a person's argument as a deductive argument and adding a missing premise—the assumption. Take a simple example: "You have to give the money back. You promised."

We standardize as follows:

1. You promised to return the money.
2. . . . .

Conclusion: You have to pay it back.

This is a valid deductive argument if we add the premise "You have to return money that you promised to return." Or, more generally, "You have to keep your promises." How do we know that these are appropriate missing premises? Because either of those claims is sufficient to make the argument valid. For example:

1. You promised to return the money.
2. You have to keep your promises.

Conclusion: You have to pay the money back.

Note that in this case, the assumption is a basic moral generalization or principle. Such basic assumptions often lie behind our moral reasoning and are frequently worth examination. In this case, for instance, the claim that you always have to keep your promises is a good moral principle, but it is not always true. Sometimes, more important factors intervene. A promise to meet someone for dinner can be legitimately overridden by a health crisis in your family.

Assumptions can also be factual. Take the following argument:

Nancy: But I do think that we need to take measures to help those on the lower end of the economic ladder. So I still think we should raise the minimum wage.

In this argument, Nancy seems to be assuming that raising the minimum wage would help those on the lower end of the economic ladder. The argument might be standardized in this way:

> 1. We need to take measures to help those on the lower end of the economic ladder.
> 2. Raising the minimum wage would help those on the lower end of the economic ladder.
> **Conclusion:** We should raise the minimum wage.

How do we know that Nancy is making the assumption in premise 2? Because Premise 2 makes Nancy's argument into a valid deductive argument. So in this case, we could say to Nancy, "You appear to be assuming that raising the minimum wage would help those on the lower end of the economic ladder." We would be justified in ascribing this premise because that claim is necessary for her argument to be a valid deductive argument. It is worth identifying this assumption because, although it is intuitively plausible, it may or may not be true. In fact, McGregor disputes this premise in his response to Nancy's argument:

McGregor: This thinking that raising the minimum wage will help the poor is just more of that left-wing logic. Increases in the minimum wage always result in the loss of minimum wage jobs…

Apply Your Understanding Exercises 6

Dubious Assumptions

Let's have a closer look at one of McGregor's arguments:

McGregor: Increases in the minimum wage always result in the loss of minimum wage jobs. So you could help the poor more by lowering the minimum wage. Then there would be more jobs and more employment for the poor.

What Do You Think ?

What assumption is McGregor making in the preceding argument?

In this argument, McGregor seems to be assuming that lowering the minimum wage will increase the number of minimum wage jobs. Given Nancy's evidence, this looks like a **dubious assumption.** In many cases, assumptions are underlying generalizations that render an argument valid. But some are not true or credible; in these cases, we would call them dubious assumptions. A dubious assumption is a claim that is necessary for the argument but that is itself quite doubtful.

A **dubious assumption** is a claim that is necessary for the argument but that is itself quite doubtful.

Because so few arguments in everyday dialogues and inquiry are, in fact, deductive, we will not devote any more time to this discussion. Most arguments are inductive. In inductive arguments, the premises give us, at best, good reason to believe the conclusion; but they do not entail the conclusion. We will turn to evaluating inductive arguments in the next chapter.

CHECK YOUR UNDERSTANDING

- *What role do arguments play in inquiry?*
- *What is the primary meaning of "argument" used in this text?*
- *Explain the principle of charity.*
- *Give four reasons why we should adopt the principle of charity when interpreting arguments.*
- *Explain the difference between a linked argument and a convergent argument. Give an example of each type from the dialogue.*
- *Explain the difference between a deductive argument and an inductive argument. Give an example of each type from the dialogue.*
- *Explain what a valid deductive argument is.*
- *What constitutes a strong inductive argument?*
- *What is a sound argument?*
- *Explain the difference between a necessary and a sufficient condition.*
- *What is an assumption?*
- *Are all assumptions dubious?*

EXERCISES

1. Standardize or diagram the following arguments (adding missing premises where necessary):

   i) There are several reasons why we should drive cars less and make more use of public transportation. For one thing, it would help to reduce carbon emissions and so would be beneficial to the environment. It would also help to conserve our dwindling reserves of petroleum. And finally, it would help to relieve the traffic congestion that is clogging our roads.

   ii) I don't think that people should eat meat. Animals raised for meat are kept in horrible conditions and we know that animals are capable of suffering. Raising animals for meat consumes a disproportionate amount of the world's resources. And besides, I don't think that human beings have a right to kill other living creatures for their selfish purposes.

   iii) *X-Men Origins* is not a very good film. It has a weak plot, it lacks internal cohesion, and it's repetitive and predictable.

   iv) I am prompted by the large number of recent attacks by pit bulls to move that council ban these dogs. It is well known that pit bulls are inherently dangerous dogs because they were originally bred for dog fighting which required strength and aggressiveness. Because of the pit bull's tenacity and manner of attacking, pit bull attacks are more likely to result in severe injury. City council has a responsibility to protect the public from the dangers posed by these animals.

   v) There are several reasons why a higher minimum wage would not be a good idea. For one thing, it would make it more difficult for businesses to be profitable and thus contribute to the economy. And for another, it rewards those with the lowest skill level and so discourages people from getting more education or training.

2. Give an example of a claim that would counter each of the following generalizations: (example: **Generalization:** Pit bulls are all very dangerous dogs. **Counter:** My friend's pit bull is very gentle.)

   i) Teachers are overpaid for the time they put in.

   ii) Professors are all very reasonable and understanding.

   iii) Documentary films are always so dull.

   iv) Pit bulls don't make good pets.

3. For each of the following deductive arguments, state whether the argument is valid or invalid and explain why:

    i) **Lester:** Is Nancy going to join us?

    Juanita: She has a cold but she said she'll join us if she feels better.

    Lester: Here she is!

    Juanita: I guess she's feeling better.

    ii) **Ahmed:** We should serve some non-meat dishes at our party. I think Wally's a vegetarian.

    Winnie: Why do you think that?

    Ahmed: Well, vegetarians are all granola-munching hippies. And Wally is one of those hippy types.

    iii) **McGregor:** If the government loosens up on controls on business, companies are in a much better position to compete, they'll make more profits, and there will be a trickle-down effect to improve the lot of poor people.

    Nancy: So I guess the poor should be happy with the government's new measures that remove some regulations from corporations?

    McGregor: Definitely! They'll be much better off.

    iv) **Ravi:** If the game lets out at 10, there'll be a lot of traffic on the road and we'll be late for the party.

    Sophia: But the game's supposed to be over at 9:30.

    Ravi: Then we should have no problem getting to the party on time.

    v) **Ahmed:** They say you can't trust anyone over 30.

    Phil: But that salesman is only 28.

    Ahmed: I guess we can trust him then.

    vi) **Nancy:** If everyone stopped driving their cars every second day, that would go a long way toward dealing with the climate change problem.

    Sophia: You'll never get people to give up their cars to that extent.

    Nancy: Then I guess the planet is in trouble.

4. Create ordinary language arguments that have the following forms. Create three arguments for each form:

    i) All A's are B.

    X is an A.

    Therefore X is a B.

    ii) All A's are B.

    All B's are C.

    Therefore all A's are C.

    iii) If P, then Q.

    Q.

    P.

    iv) If P, then Q.

    Not Q.

    Not P.

5. Suppose that, when Nancy asks her dad if she can use the car, he makes one of the following offers:

    i) "You can use the car tonight only if you clean your room."

       OR

    ii) "If you clean the car, you can use it tonight."

   What response should she give to each offer? Explain your answers using the terms "necessary condition" and "sufficient condition."

6. Standardize the following arguments, adding the missing premise or conclusion in each argument that would make the argument valid:

    i) Arnold is a basketball player, so he must be very tall.

    ii) There's a light on in the house. Someone must be home.

    iii) The government should lower taxes on corporations because we rely on corporations for economic growth.

    iv) The higher they fly, the harder they fall. Wally flies high.

    v) Pit bulls are dangerous dogs so we should ban them.

    vi) It's OK to eat meat because animals don't feel pain the way humans do.

    vii) Your dog must be dangerous—after all, it's a pit bull.

    viii) Jason drives a Ferrari. He must have loads of money.

    ix) If the murderer had been driving a Jeep, the police would have found tire tracks near the body. But the police didn't find any vehicles tracks at the crime scene.

Chapter 4
Inductive Arguments and Fallacies

Raising the Minimum Wage II

In the previous chapter, we read a dialogue between Daimon McGregor and his daughter Nancy on the issue of whether the minimum wage should be raised. The dialogue continues below.

McGregor: *Now that is a dumb idea if ever I've heard one.*

Nancy: *You mean raising the minimum wage? Why do you think it's so dumb?*

McGregor: *Because it is—it's just stupid.*

Nancy: *What makes you say that?*

McGregor: *Measures that put undue burdens on business are bad for the economy. Raising the minimum wage would do that. So raising the minimum wage would be bad for the economy. It only makes sense. Raising the minimum wage would hugely increase labour costs for businesses. So they would no longer be able to remain competitive. Their profits would disappear, and pretty soon companies would have to shut down because they couldn't afford all the extra wages and everyone would be unemployed.*

Nancy: *Now wait just a minute, Dad. Paying people a wage that allows them to have enough to eat is hardly an "undue" burden. I guess your view is that it's*

OK that companies are pulling in huge profits and CEOs are living in mansions and flying around in executive jets while other people starve to death.

McGregor: *Now, Nancy, you certainly know that is not my point of view.*

Nancy: *True, Dad. I'm sorry.*

McGregor: *Anyway, this thinking that raising the minimum wage will help the poor is just more of that misguided left-wing logic. Increases in the minimum wage always result in the loss of minimum wage jobs. So you could help the poor more by lowering the minimum wage. Then there would be more jobs and more employment for the poor.*

Nancy: *You're actually saying that we should lower the minimum wage in order to help the poor? That sounds like a pretty weird argument to me.*

McGregor: *But it makes sense if you stop using that misguided left-wing logic. It's all a matter of pricing. Everyone knows that the lower the price, the more goods you can sell. The same is true of labour. It's common knowledge that the cheaper the labour, the more workers that will be hired.*

Nancy: *I haven't seen any evidence that that's the case.*

McGregor: *Well, I haven't seen any evidence that it's not!*

Nancy: *I don't believe that lowering the minimum wage ever leads to an increase in lower-end jobs. When they introduced a lower minimum wage for young people in B.C., there was no increase in the number of jobs for young people. And besides, there are lots of countries that have no minimum wage but still have widespread unemployment.*

McGregor: *We shouldn't increase the minimum wage. What we should really do is simply get rid of it, period. That's what's best for the economy; and if it's good for the economy, it will be good for everyone, including the poor.*

Nancy: *Measures that are good for the economy will help the poor? Well, raising the minimum wage will help the poor. So by your own reasoning, it must be good for the economy.*

McGregor: *That doesn't sound quite right to me . . .*

Nancy: Increasing the minimum wage is just basic decency and long overdue. People who get paid the minimum wage don't have enough to live on. My friend Lester can barely get by on the salary he gets from slinging burgers.

McGregor: Your friend Lester is typical of people on the minimum wage. He lives at home with his parents. I don't see why he needs a lot of money, except for frivolities like beer and movies. So raising the minimum wage will just be helping a bunch of well-off kids have more spending money—hardly a good way to help the poor. And anyway, he's unskilled and lucky to be getting the pay he does. People who are paid the minimum wage get it because that's what they're worth—no skill, low pay. That's only fair.

Nancy: Are you saying that everyone who gets paid the minimum wage is unskilled? And that all unskilled people are being paid fairly? That's just not true. Everyone I know who works for a minimum wage is a student with lots of education and many skills. Lester has tons of education and lots of valuable skills.

McGregor: Besides, hardly anyone is paid the minimum wage. Even unskilled labourers are pulling in fat paycheques. So I don't know what all the fuss is about.

Nancy: But you said before that companies would have to close because they couldn't afford all the extra wages. But if hardly anyone is getting the minimum wage, then there won't be a lot of extra wages!

McGregor: You're getting pretty cheeky since you started taking that critical thinking course. And you're starting to sound like a communist. That's what happens when young people go to one of these liberal universities.

Nancy: A communist? You've got to be kidding. I'm not even going to respond to that. But I certainly don't think that it's fair to pay anyone so little that they barely have enough to eat when others are waltzing around with bulging pockets—no matter what their skill level. The problem is that people who are well paid have no sympathy or understanding of the poor. That's the real reason you're opposed to raising the minimum wage. You just make too much money to really know anything about it.

McGregor: Do you know how much I get paid for all my work on council?

Nancy: I don't know, but you certainly get paid well at your company.

McGregor: I am not paid more than any other executive in my position of responsibility.

Nancy: But it's not fair that you get paid that huge salary, plus all those extra benefits, while lots of hard-working and deserving people hardly get paid enough to survive.

McGregor: If other executives get those benefits, why shouldn't I? And besides, I don't see why you're so concerned about the minimum wage—it's not going to solve the problem of poverty . . .

In this chapter, we focus on inductive arguments, the most common type of argument found in everyday dialogues and inquiries. The premises of an inductive argument do not entail the argument's conclusion. Inductive arguments are common because we can seldom provide arguments where even true premises guarantee the truth of the conclusion. From weather predictions to the issue of whether our favourite director's next movie will be a good one, the best our premises do is to provide good reasons or strong support for the conclusion.

B.C.'s $8 Minimum Wage Turns Eight: Low-Wage Workers Being 'Left Behind,' Says B.C. Federation of Labour[1]

B.C. Federation of Labour activists staged a protest in downtown Vancouver on Sunday in support of an increase in the minimum wage. B.C.'s $8-an-hour minimum wage turned eight Sunday, and the B.C. Federation of Labour says eight is enough . . . "It's absolutely disgraceful," B.C. Federation of Labour president Jim Sinclair said . . . "When the $8-an-hour wage was brought in, it was the highest in Canada. Now we have the lowest wage rate in Canada." While the B.C. Fed activists handed out stickers calling for a $10-an-hour minimum wage, B.C. Chamber of Commerce president John Winter said that the ongoing recession means this is not the time to add costs to struggling businesses . . . Premier Gordon Campbell maintains that the minimum-wage law doesn't need updating because most people in B.C. make more than the minimum wage. Increasing the minimum wage, according to the premier, would mean many corporations would be forced to lay off employees at a time when jobs are scarce . . . But Sinclair said the poor are losing out as the gulf increases between the wealthy and the workers.

Inductive Arguments

The governing concept of inductive arguments is that of support. A **strong inductive argument** is one that, if the premises are true, gives us good reason to believe the conclusion. A **cogent inductive argument** is a strong inductive argument with credible premises. It is the analogue of a sound deductive argument.

> A **strong inductive argument** is one that, if the premises are true, gives us good reason to believe the conclusion.

To understand the criteria of a good inductive argument, we need to remember the key function of an argument. The role of an argument is to provide reasons (evidence, data, principles) that make the conclusion credible (i.e., worthy of reasonable belief) or at least more credible than before the argument was presented. To do that, an argument must have premises that have more credibility than the conclusion so that they can add to the conclusion's credibility.

> A **cogent inductive argument** is a strong inductive argument with credible premises.

The criteria for a cogent inductive argument are these:

- A cogent inductive argument has premises that support the conclusion; that is, it has premises that, if true, make the conclusion more likely or more credible.

- The premises themselves are credible (plausible/acceptable) or, at the very least, the premises are more credible than the conclusion.

One implication of the criteria is that the evaluative procedure for assessing an argument begins with first accepting the premises provisionally and asking this: If these premises are true, would they give good support to the conclusion? Would they provide good reasons to believe the conclusion?

Individual inductive arguments are the usual building blocks of a **case.** Later in this text, when we focus on inquiry leading to a reasoned judgment, we will be concerned with looking at *all* the relevant arguments and evaluating how much support and opposition they provide for a claim. In this chapter, however, we are focusing on *individual* inductive arguments and how to evaluate them.

> A **case** is a collection of arguments (pro and con) marshalled to support a position on an issue.

Judging whether a particular set of premises provides strong support for the conclusion frequently requires more information than that supplied in the particular argument. Nonetheless, we can identify basic criteria for evaluation and a method for argument evaluation that will enable us to make an initial assessment of an argument's strength. There are basically two questions we ask of any argument:

> The *key function* of an argument is to provide reasons (evidence, data, principles) that make the conclusion *credible* (i.e., worthy of reasonable belief) or at least *more credible* than before the argument was presented.

1. Do the premises, if true, give us good reason to believe the conclusion?
2. Are the premises credible?

Even if an argument does give us good reason(s) to believe the conclusion, we still should suspend judgment of the conclusion until we have completed an appropriate inquiry because there may be other arguments and counter-considerations that in the end make the conclusion unworthy of belief. That is why the assessment of arguments usually involves assessing the argument in the context of an inquiry. But we can sometimes make initial or prima facie judgments of an argument's quality before completing our inquiry.

Prima Facie

Prima facie (pronounced "pryma fayshee") is Latin for "on the face" or "first glance." The concept is taken from the legal realm where it is used to describe the requirement that a prosecutor's case must have sufficient preliminary merit (must be a prima facie case) before it can go to court and the defendant be required to reply.

> A **prima facie** judgment is a preliminary judgment made with the knowledge that it is tentative and open to revision in light of subsequent information or other considerations.

A **prima facie** judgment is basically a preliminary judgment. By stating that one is making a prima facie judgment, one is acknowledging the preliminary nature of one's assessment. The idea is that one can often make a reasonable initial evaluation of a claim or

Truth and Credibility

Truth and credibility are distinct but related concepts. When we evaluate arguments and claims, we are, of course, concerned to find the truth, that is, to find true claims, whether they are premises or conclusions. When we say that a claim is credible, we are claiming both that the claim in question is worthy of belief and that it is likely to be true. To assert that a claim is *true* is basically to assert that it correctly describes its object. The assertion that a claim is *credible* refers to the basis for our belief, that is, that there is good evidence for the claim. While we are concerned to pursue truth, what we can usually know is that we have good evidence for a claim and, therefore, can accept that it is likely to be true. Because we are focused on arguments and evidence, we will primarily refer to the credibility of premises and conclusions, meaning that we think that the evidence makes the claim worthy of rational belief. As fallibilists, however, we also recognize that some credible claims will not be true. (A more detailed account of credibility will be presented in subsequent chapters.)

argument while acknowledging that such an assessment is preliminary and open to revision in light of subsequent information or other considerations.

It is often useful to make a prima facie judgment about an argument, especially if the argument is a misleading or fallacious argument. While our prima facie judgments cannot be definitive about the cogency of an argument, we can often make confident judgments about the fallaciousness of an argument. To see why this is so, consider a similar situation. I can make a confident prima facie judgment that $2 + 4 + 7 + 3 + 6 = 4$ is false without having to add up the numbers; but to know that the correct answer is 22, I would have to do the calculation. As we study the fallacies below, we will see that we can judge arguments to be fallacious on initial inspection, although arguments that are not fallacious will require further investigation to assess their worth.

The difference between acknowledging that a judgment is a prima facie judgment and taking a fallibilistic attitude towards all our judgments is one of degree. While we need to recognize that any of our judgments could in principle be wrong, many of them are well substantiated and supported by extensive evidence of our own or our culture. Taking a fallibilistic approach to one's views does not mean that the views are not well supported. A prima facie judgment, on the other hand, admits to being based on initial observation not backed by any extensive investigation. But still, some prima facie judgments can be made with confidence (fallibilistic confidence, of course), such as when errors are obvious on superficial observation.

As stated above, there are two key questions necessary in order to make an assessment of an argument, even a prima facie assessment. The first is the question of the degree of support that premises, if true, give the conclusion. Surprisingly, this support is often little or none. As we will see below, there are many argument types (fallacies) that seem persuasive but actually provide little or no evidence for their conclusion. Later we will address the question of how to assess the credibility of the premises if they do appear to provide some reasonable support for the conclusion.

Fallacies

A fallacy is a common weak (or even terrible) type of argument that nonetheless has considerable persuasive power. Remember McGregor's argument that Lester is typical of people making the minimum wage:

McGregor: Your friend Lester is typical of people on the minimum wage. He lives at home with his parents. I don't see why he needs a lot of money, except for frivolities like beer and movies. So raising the minimum wage will just be helping a bunch of well-off kids have more spending money—hardly a good way to help the poor.

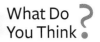

What do you think of McGregor's argument?

This is a good example of fallacious reasoning that results from evidence that is dramatically more persuasive than its evidential worth. McGregor uses one example to overgeneralize about people being paid the minimum wage. Note that we are not saying that a person's experience is of no relevance to understanding the world. The fallacy is taking very limited evidence, often personal experience (subjectively powerful and persuasive as it often is), and treating it as if it strongly supports a generalization.

This kind of argument is known as the fallacy of anecdotal evidence. An anecdote is a story, so the fallacy is one of using a story (one case) to justify a generalization. People are usually persuaded by their experience or the stories they hear about the experiences of others. We all have a tendency to assume that our experiences are typical and are, therefore, an appropriate basis for generalizing.[2] But a moment's thought will show that the people known to McGregor, who is a city councillor and successful businessman, are unlikely to be typical of those earning the minimum wage. McGregor basically uses one case to support a generalization about most people making the minimum wage. Clearly, one case cannot support such a generalization. Nonetheless, we all find it tempting to overgeneralize from our own experiences. The problem with such an argument is that its persuasive power, what we might call its **rhetorical effect**, greatly exceeds its logical worth.

> The **rhetorical effect** of an argument is its persuasive power.

Lawyers and judges talk about the **probative value** of arguments or evidence, which is the legal weight or evidential worth that a piece of evidence should be given when making a finding. Evidence of high probative value includes items such as DNA and finger prints. Items of low probative value include rumours or observations done under poor lighting conditions. Sometimes courts refuse to hear evidence even though it has some probative value because its rhetorical force greatly exceeds its probative value. (See box on "Similar Fact Evidence".)

> In law, **probative value** is the legal weight or evidential worth that a piece of evidence should be given when making a finding.

We can use the idea of probative value to redefine a fallacious argument: A **fallacy** is an argument pattern whose persuasive power greatly exceeds its probative value (i.e., evidential worth).

> A **fallacy** is an argument pattern whose persuasive power greatly exceeds its probative value (i.e., evidential worth).

Because fallacies have two aspects, their logical weakness and their rhetorical effect, we will identify both these qualities when describing the fallacies below. Sometimes the rhetorical effect is just to change the topic and get us off course in the argument. In other fallacies, the effect can be to convince us of a claim for which inadequate evidence has been

Similar Fact Evidence

The law often prohibits the presentation of certain bits of evidence that have probative value because the courts believe that the persuasive power of these pieces of evidence exceeds their probative value. An instance of this is "similar fact evidence" where the accused is charged with a crime similar to one that he has committed before. For example, let's imagine that "Bill" is accused of using a ladder to get to the second story balcony of an apartment and then entering through the unlocked door and stealing a television set. Being caught with the television set would have strong probative value for his guilt (though it would not be conclusive). On the other hand, if it turns out that Bill has been convicted of breaking into the second floor of apartments before,

you might think that this too is relevant evidence. But such "similar fact" evidence is usually not allowed to be presented to the court—not because it is irrelevant, but because it is too persuasive. A jury hearing that the accused has been convicted of a similar crime will be strongly inclined to find this evidence very persuasive. But from a probative point of view, this evidence is very weak because Bill's particular method of crime is very common and could have been used by someone else. The crime he is accused of is not only similar to his past crimes, but similar to crimes committed by many others. Because this evidence carries so much more persuasive power than probative value, the courts generally prohibit the presentation of such evidence.

Rhetorical effect is what enables an argument to be persuasive in excess of its probative value.

presented. Sometimes the effect is more nebulous, such as creating a negative association with a particular point of view. In what follows, we endeavour to help you to identify these rhetorical effects so you can guard against going off topic or being persuaded by considerations of limited or no probative value.

Note that we are not claiming that all of these fallacious moves are necessarily intentional. That is why we do not describe these fallacious rhetorical moves as rhetorical strategies. They can, and perhaps often are, done intentionally. But we have all slid into fallacious reasoning unintentionally. Who has not overgeneralized from a single experience? "That restaurant? I wouldn't go there; the service is terrible. I went there once and had to wait half an hour for the main course to arrive."

INFORMAL FALLACIES

The first criterion for evaluating an inductive argument is that it has premises that support the conclusion. This is why we always start evaluating arguments by assuming that the premises are true and asking whether they then provide reasonable support for the conclusion. A surprising number of arguments fail according to this first criterion. Arguments that fail according to this criterion fall under the category of fallacies of illusory support.

Fallacies of Illusory Support

Arguments commit fallacies of illusory support when, assuming the premises are true, they tend to persuade even though they provide little or no support for the conclusion. The premises may even be completely irrelevant and change the whole focus of the argument, distracting us from the issues involved. When premises provide literally no support for a conclusion, we say that they are **irrelevant.** A premise is irrelevant to a conclusion when its truth or falsity does not influence the truth or falsity of the conclusion.

A premise is **irrelevant** to a conclusion when its truth or falsity does not influence the truth or falsity of the conclusion.

The classic and most generic form of irrelevancy is the red herring. The name is said to come from the English fox hunting practice of dragging a rotten herring across the track of the fox to lead the hounds off the trail. The function of a red herring in argument is to distract the arguers from the claim in question and to focus the argument on some other topic. We have all heard politicians who, when asked awkward questions, come back with some retort which changes the subject. Here is an example:

Reporter: Madam, what has your government done to deal with the pending financial disaster?

Politician: Well, as you know the previous government ignored this problem, and that is why we are in the mess we face now. Had they taken appropriate measures at the right time, we would all be better off. Fortunately, they have been defeated and we are now in charge.

RED HERRING (Changing the focus):

Arguers commit the fallacy of **red herring** when they introduce an irrelevant issue which has the effect of distracting from (or shifting the focus from) the question at hand.

Arguers commit the fallacy of **red herring** when they introduce an irrelevant issue which has the effect of distracting from (or shifting the focus from) the question at hand.

Rhetorical Effect: The red herring fallacy changes the focus of discussion, usually away from a weak part of the proponent's position, distracting the listener away from the issue at hand.

Logical Error: By changing the focus, the reasons and arguments offered apply to a different issue, and so they cannot contribute to finding the truth about the originally identified issue.

Here is another classic red herring:

After a recent protest at the tar sands in Alberta, a Greenpeace spokesperson, Melina Laboucan-Massimo, made the following comment: "There's no way to process . . . oil in a clean way. It's dirty,

dirty oil. It's the bottom of the barrel that we are dealing with here. We definitely need to turn away from tar sands expansion and turn towards investment in clean, renewable energy."

A representative of Shell Oil replied that Shell was "developing an important resource that society needs, and doing it safely, responsibly and in compliance with all laws and regulations."[3]

Why was the reply by Shell Oil a red herring?

What Do You Think?

Many fallacies have subspecies which are also worth identifying since they involve particular rhetorical effects. One of the most effective forms of red herring is the **ad hominem** which shifts the focus of the discussion from an issue or claim to the individual putting forward the argument.

AD HOMINEM (Attacking the proponent of an argument):

Arguers commit the fallacy of ad hominem if they reject a proponent's argument on the basis of critical remarks about the proponent rather than the proponent's argument. The fallacy is an attempt to discredit the proponent's argument or claim by irrelevantly discrediting the proponent. To be clear, not every personal attack is guilty of the ad hominem fallacy. The fallacy is committed only when the remarks about the proponents are used as grounds to dismiss their argument.

Rhetorical Effect: The ad hominem fallacy discredits an argument by attacking the author's background and behaviour and shifts the argument to the author[4] and away from the issues at hand. Such a move often leads to the author defending his or her personal behaviour or background instead of staying focused on the issue at hand. The use of the ad hominem is especially detrimental to conducting a dialogue because not only does it distract from the issue at hand, but also it tends to inflame people's emotions.

Logical Error: If the author has presented evidence and arguments, the author's background or behaviour are largely irrelevant to the logical worth of the argument. When arguments are presented, the issue must be decided on the merits of the argument, not on the qualities of the author.

The situation is different if the proponent is claiming that we should accept the argument because of some fact about that proponent, such as being an expert in the field. In such cases, evaluating the source of the argument can be relevant (as we will see in Chapter 6). What makes ad hominem remarks fallacious is not that facts about the author are always irrelevant, but rather that we usually tend to give such claims too much weight when assessing an argument. Ad hominem fallacies have more persuasive impact than probative value.

Here is an example of an ad hominem fallacy:

We don't even need to listen to her argument; she's such a bleeding heart liberal.

Try to come up with another example of an ad hominem fallacy.

This fallacy comes in a number of forms. The most notorious is the abusive ad hominem. An **abusive ad hominem** consists of using a malicious attack on an author to reject his or her argument or position. It usually results in a complete shift of focus from the issue at hand to the individual who was putting forth the view. Here is an example:

I am not going to listen to an argument from someone who has been divorced three times.

Arguers commit the fallacy of **ad hominem** if they reject a proponent's argument on the basis of critical remarks about the proponent rather than the proponent's argument.

Why learn all these fallacy names? In this chapter, we focus on a small subset of well-identified fallacies—those that we think are the most common. Knowing the names and examples of fallacies helps us identify and resist bad reasoning. In general, having a rich collection of concepts enhances our ability to understand and see what is going on around us. People who have only the concepts of evergreen and deciduous trees will miss the great variety of trees (cedars, hemlock, maple, alder, etc.) that are all around them. People who do not have a good set of fallacy concepts will often miss the misleading nature of arguments to which they are subject.

What Do You Think?

An **abusive ad hominem** is a malicious attack on an author used to reject his or her argument or position.

Environmental Guru's Inconvenient Truth: His Diesel Bus Belched 20 Tonnes of CO_2[5]

Environmental crusader David Suzuki finally got out of his diesel-fuelled, pollution-spewing, greenhouse-gas-emitting bus yesterday and actually pedalled a bicycle during the Victoria leg of his cross-Canada eco-tour. But don't start polishing up the Nobel Prize just yet. Suzuki only biked one measly kilometre—and it was the very last kilometre of his entire 50-city tour to boot. Final tally: 7,204 kilometres by bus, one kilometre by bike. An estimated 20 tonnes of global-warming carbon dioxide belched into the atmosphere. Suzuki, of course, has a comeback for the pollution he's generated on his fossil-fuelled green tour: His foundation is buying "carbon offsets"—planting trees, investing in solar-energy projects and the like—so his road trip is "carbon-neutral." It's becoming a tiresome refrain from the ruling elites of the environmental movement as they seek to explain their own cushy, high-emission lifestyles while preaching to everyone else to change their ways.

What a bunch of hot air. If these people want us to change our lives, shouldn't they be leading by example? Suzuki drove across Canada with an entourage of eight people in a diesel bus that seats more than 30. What's so green about that? He could have done the same tour in two hybrid minivans. But, of course, "He drives across the country in a diesel bus attacking us and then gets on a bike in front of the media for the last kilometre. He's a hypocrite." Yes, he is. But a carbon-neutral one.

A **circumstantial ad hominem** is committed when facts about the background or loyalties of the author are used to dismiss his or her arguments and claims without actual reference to these arguments and claims.

A less inflammatory but highly persuasive form of this fallacy is the **circumstantial ad hominem.** Here the author is not attacked maliciously, but facts about the background or loyalties of the author are still used to dismiss the author's arguments and claims without actual reference to these arguments and claims. For example, the debate about environmental issues often ends up focusing on the behaviour of advocates such as David Suzuki. (See a classic example in the box above.) Note that there is not a single reference to the actual issue and to evidence for global warming.

What Do You Think ?

What is problematic about the argument in the box about Suzuki?

These challenges are totally irrelevant to whether Suzuki has made a good case for human-caused global climate change. Adversaries who attack him on the basis of his "ecologically incorrect lifestyle" are guilty of circumstantial ad hominem.

An Important Qualification. Not all references to an argument's author and his or her character are fallacious. Making negative remarks about a person can only be fallacious if those remarks are used to dismiss the person's argument. If, for example, the person has said, "Trust me, John is a thief," but the person who said that is a notorious liar, then pointing out that the person making this claim is a notorious liar would be appropriate. A critic is justified in raising questions about the author's trustworthiness in any situation where the credibility of a claim rests on the trustworthiness of its author.

What complicates the matter is that with most arguments, one reason we accept a person's argument or premises is our belief that we are not being misled. If we have reasons to think we might be being misled (e.g., the author of the argument has a financial interest in our accepting his argument), then we do have grounds for being skeptical. But be careful. Grounds for skepticism are not grounds for dismissing an argument. If the proponent of an argument has put forth credible reasons to support his case, the case must be evaluated on its merits without regard to the proponent's bias. For example, if a labour union president, in arguing in favour of increasing the minimum wage, gives valid statistics (i.e., statistics from some credible source), his apparent bias does not give us a basis for rejecting his argument or dismissing his conclusion. Nevertheless, one can and should use knowledge of a person's biases to inform the process of evaluation of their arguments.

A critic is justified in raising questions about the author's trustworthiness in any situation where the credibility of a claim rests on the trustworthiness of its author.

GUILT BY ASSOCIATION:

Guilt by association is a fallacy in which a person argues for rejecting a claim because it is a position which is also held by people who are viewed unfavourably. Here is an example from the chapter-opening dialogue:

McGregor: You're getting pretty cheeky since you started taking that critical thinking course. And you're starting to sound like a communist. That's what happens when young people go to one of these liberal universities.

The model for this argument is as follows:

Unpopular or evil people believe P.
Therefore P is false or should be rejected.

We can standardize McGregor's argument in this way:

Nancy's argument for increasing the minimum wage sounds like communist propaganda.
Conclusion: Nancy's position is wrong.

Rhetorical Effect: Guilt by association creates a negative emotional association with a view in question leading to rejection of the view on the basis of this association.

Logical Error: The fact that a view is held by persons who are viewed unfavourably has nothing to do with whether the view is true or credible. No doubt every evil person with a knowledge of arithmetic believes $2 + 2 = 4$. The person's evilness clearly provides no basis for questioning the correctness of this view.

Here is another example of guilt by association. This is from a Canadian responding to a recent study that claims to show that medical marijuana has limited use as a painkiller:

Probably an AMERICAN study paid for by the BUSH administration. . . .[6] (emphasis added by authors).

Describe the rhetorical effect and explain the logical error in this example of guilt by association.

What Do You Think

> **Guilt by association** is a fallacy in which a person argues for rejecting a claim because it is a position which is also held by people who are viewed unfavourably.

STRAW PERSON:

The **straw person** fallacy involves attacking a misdescribed argument or position. Arguers commit the fallacy of straw person when they attribute to a proponent a view the proponent does not hold; they pretend to refute the view the proponents do hold by attacking the misrepresented position.

Rhetorical Effect: The straw person fallacy usually occurs when an arguer summarizes or makes an inference from an opponent's view in such a way as to make it sound totally ludicrous, using, for example, exaggerated generalizations and absurdly black and white contrasts. Once such a description is put forward, the critic then does not even have to argue against the view—the view is already damned. Even if listeners do not know what the other position is, they can be persuaded that the other person holds a ludicrous point of view.

Logical Error: Criticizing a claim or argument that is not the real claim or argument at issue obviously provides no basis for rejecting what is actually being claimed. You can avoid accidentally committing this fallacy by carefully and charitably understanding your opponent's position before criticizing it. In dialogue, you should check with the opponent to see if you have given a correct description of his or her position. When someone who is a critic of a position informs you about an argument, it is often difficult to tell if his or her

> Arguers commit the fallacy of **straw person** when they attribute to a proponent a view the proponent does not hold; they pretend to refute the opposing view by attacking the misrepresented position.

account is fair. A good strategy is to suspect the straw person fallacy if the description of an argument made by the critic makes the argument sound ridiculous.

Example: *The Netherlands has very tolerant drug policies. The Dutch clearly feel that child drug use is of no significance and that the widespread use of heroin will only benefit society.*

The above description of the Dutch attitudes towards heroin based on their stated policy towards soft drugs is a typical example of straw person: the informant accuses a proponent of holding a ridiculous position by making an unwarranted extrapolation from a position that the proponent holds.

In the chapter-opening dialogue, Nancy responds to her father in this way:

Nancy: "I guess your view is that it's OK that companies are pulling in huge profits and CEOs are living in mansions and flying around in executive jets while other people starve to death."

She is committing straw person. Her dad never said anything about people starving people to death, and he is right not to accept this as part of his point of view.

IRRELEVANT STANDARD:

> Arguers commit the fallacy of **irrelevant standard** when they criticize a policy or program for not achieving goals which the program never expected to achieve.

Arguers commit the fallacy of **irrelevant standard** when they criticize a policy or program for not achieving goals which the program never expected to achieve. This is often also a form of straw person—ascribing standards to a proponent that the proponent does not hold.

Examples:

There's no point in studying philosophy—it will never solve all of life's problems. (But of course, no one said it would.)

We shouldn't have gun control legislation—it will never eliminate gun-related crimes. (Obviously, the purpose of gun control is not to eliminate, but to reduce, gun-related crimes.)

McGregor: And besides, I don't see why you're so concerned about the minimum wage—it's not going to solve the problem of poverty. (Neither Nancy nor anyone else thought it would.)

From a blog on the *Toronto Observer* site: *Banning handguns will NOT prevent crime, education of proper USE will.*[7] (But, of course, no one said it would.)

Rhetorical Effect: The effect of the irrelevant standard is to undermine acceptance of a policy on the basis that it cannot achieve some clearly impossible goal. The effectiveness of this strategy is based on the fact that if the ascribed standard were relevant, it would be obvious that the proposed policy could never meet that standard. The rhetorical effect is to make a policy seem hopelessly ineffective.

Logical Error: The problem is that the objection is irrelevant since the standard proposed (usually some absolute one) is an exaggerated one and not the goal claimed for the policy.

TWO WRONGS:

> The **two wrongs fallacy** consists of trying to justify your wrongdoing on the basis that you were wronged, or claiming that you should get away with some wrong because others have gotten away with it.

There are two versions of the **two wrongs fallacy.** One consists of trying to justify a wrong on the basis that you were wronged. "He hit me first" is a frequent example of this fallacy used in the schoolyard. The second form consists of claiming that others have committed the same wrongdoing but have gotten away with it and, therefore, you should get away with it as well. "Johnny came in late last night, and no one made a fuss about that."

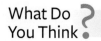

What Do
You Think ?

Explain what is wrong with the preceding arguments.

Rhetorical Effect: The two wrongs fallacy makes listeners focus on the wrongdoing of others or cultivates a sense of grievance to justify an action. It also makes an argument that sounds like an appropriate appeal to justice.

Logical Error: The wrongdoing of others can justify retribution; that is, actions by the state to punish the wrong actions of others. But taking the law into one's own hands, and justifying doing so by using a two wrongs argument, is to claim that revenge is morally legitimate. This is probably not a strictly logical error, but rather an error in moral reasoning.

In the other form of this argument, the claim is that "you shouldn't criticize me, because when THEY did it, you didn't criticize them." Again, this is an apparent appeal to justice (similar cases should be treated in a similar fashion); but the goal is not to have a just punishment, but rather to get away with a wrong because others have gotten away with it.

A CASE OF TU QUOQUE.

She. "How do you like my new Hat?"
Sutherland Highlander. "By Jove, what extraordinary Headgear you women do wear!"

Examples:

You have no right to get mad at me for coming home late. Last night, Billy came in late, and you didn't even notice. (Answer: Well, we should have, but that doesn't mean you should get away with it.)

Why give me a ticket? All those other cars were speeding too. (Answer: I wish I could catch all the speeders, but we do what we can and I caught you. You certainly can't claim you weren't speeding.)

It's OK for me to steal from the Supermarket—they are always ripping us off. (Answer: Victims should have forms of redress, but that does not justify taking the law into their own hands.)

In the international sphere, the question of whether a wrong (e.g., a violent attack) can justify another wrong (retaliation for the attack) is more complicated. Here there is no overarching authority to ensure retribution, so returning wrong for wrong may seem justified. Unsurprisingly, such reasoning can lead to long-term disastrous consequences as in the Israeli–Palestine conflict.

POPULARITY:

There are two forms of the **fallacy of popularity.** One attempts to justify a belief on the basis that most people believe it. The other form attempts to justify an action on the basis that most people do it. This latter form (sometimes called an **improper appeal to common practice**) can be an extension of the fallacy of two wrongs in which the proponent attempts to defend a position by citing the widespread but wrongful acts of others (e.g., cheating on income tax: "but everyone does it").

The **fallacy of popularity** involves attempting to justify a belief on the basis that most people believe it or to justify an action on the basis that most people do it.

Improper appeal to common practice is committed when a proponent attempts to defend a position by merely claiming that a practice is widespread.

Why do you think that justifying beliefs or actions on the basis that they are widely believed or widely practised is problematic?

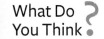

What Do You Think ?

The fact that a practice or belief is widespread has some prima facie relevance. Many of our beliefs are based on common sense. Those who would deny what is commonly believed usually bear the burden of proof. But, of course, a great many popular beliefs are supported by nothing more than unreflective "groupthink."

Another version of this fallacy is the **appeal to tradition.** The fact that a belief or practice has been believed for centuries does not make it true. Too many hallowed beliefs, from the view that the earth was at the centre of the universe to the view that men were superior to women and should be treated accordingly, were widely held traditional views that are now wisely rejected. A great many common practices are common not because they are right, but because people are morally weak or self-indulgent or inheritors of morally dubious traditions. For example, many countries are plagued by a traditional acceptance of widespread corruption. We can see how logically weak the appeal to common practice is when we consider that many of the most egregious forms of oppression, such as racism and sexism, were universally practised at one time and are still widely accepted.

Here is an example of the appeal to tradition fallacy from the dialogue in Chapter 1:

Phil: Everyone eats meat—at least all normal people.

Urban legends are good examples of beliefs that are widely believed but false. They are often circulated on the internet, passed on from one trusting friend to another. There is now a new form of virus (a virus hoax) where people are sent a warning from their friends about bogus viruses. People accept these warnings in part because they can see, from how often they have been forwarded, that they are widely accepted.

The dialogue contains a classic appeal to common practice:

Nancy: But it's not fair that you get paid that huge salary, plus all those extra benefits, while lots of hard-working and deserving people hardly get paid enough to survive.

McGregor: If other executives get those benefits, why shouldn't I?

Rhetorical Effect: The effect of the popularity fallacy is to exploit the natural tendency of people to believe widely accepted claims without questioning, or to feel justified if their behaviour conforms to the behaviour of others. Like hasty generalization below, the appeal to popularity is often the basis of prejudice.

Logical Error: Commonality is only a prima facie basis for belief and can never be the true evidential basis for a claim. What makes a view or claim worthy of belief is that it is true, or at least supported by reasonable evidence, not that it is widely held.

HASTY GENERALIZATION:

Arguers commit the fallacy of **hasty generalization** when they generalize from only a few (or sometimes no) cases. Sometimes cases are provided, but the generalization is still too strong to be supported by the evidence offered.

> Arguers commit the fallacy of **hasty generalization** when they generalize from only a few (or sometimes no) cases.

Rhetorical Effect: This fallacy exploits our natural tendency to generalize from our own limited experience. The ability and tendency of humans to generalize is basically a strength: this ability enables us to learn from past experience. But in the complex and diverse world in which we live, many of our generalizations just don't provide reliable information. Unfortunately, we are too willing to generalize without noticing that we have little or no evidence to support our generalizations.

Logical Error: The error in hasty generalization is ignoring the fact that generalizations require considerable support to be reasonable. A key rule is that the more general a claim, the more substantial the evidence that is required to support it. The error usually results from the failure to recognize how limited our own experience really is in most areas of our lives.

ANECDOTAL EVIDENCE:

> The fallacy of **anecdotal evidence** occurs when an arguer uses an anecdote as strong evidence for a broad generalization.

By far the most common basis for a hasty generalization is a generalization based on an **anecdotal evidence** or individual experience.

What Do You Think ?

What are the limitations of using our own experiences as evidence?

There is, of course, nothing wrong with telling a story that illustrates one's point, or is an example of the kind of evidence needed to support a conclusion. The fallacy occurs when an arguer uses an anecdote as strong evidence for a broad generalization. At best, it is only one case—a very small sample.

In the following dialogue excerpt, notice that both Nancy's and McGregor's arguments about people on the minimum wage are based on their experience with only one such person, Lester.

Nancy: … People who get paid the minimum wage don't have enough to live on. My friend Lester can barely get by on the salary he gets from slinging burgers.

McGregor: Your friend Lester is typical of people on the minimum wage. He lives at home with his parents.

Rhetorical Effect: Experience and stories are extremely vivid and can easily lead us to jump to conclusions. It is rather like judging someone on the basis of your first meeting, or judging a country by a one-week stay in a major city. You may be right, but it is not enough evidence on which to base a strong conviction.

Logical Error: The error of believing anecdotal evidence is that of basing a generalization on only a very few experiences or stories, believing that your experience is reliably "representative" of others.

This is not to say that it is never reasonable to infer tentatively from some experience or from one's reading that a particular claim is likely. But to avoid drawing a hasty conclusion from such evidence, arguers should assert weakly supported claims with appropriate modifiers; some such claims include "it seems to me," "based on the evidence I have," "it is likely that …," "based on my admittedly limited experience …," and "I have a feeling that …" We have myriad ways to indicate uncertainty about our claims, and they should be used when we do not have sufficient evidence to take a more affirmative or confident stance.

Personal experience and stories are not the only source of hasty generalization. Small or biased studies even by professional researchers can also lead to generalizations that are not well supported. In Chapters 12 and 13 on the sciences, we go into more detail about what counts as adequate evidence to support a general claim; but obviously the larger and more carefully done a study is, the less likely it is to result in a hasty generalization.

BEGGING THE QUESTION:

Arguers commit the fallacy of **begging the question** when they use a premise that is identical to their conclusion. Another way to beg the question is just to assume the truth of the claim that is central to the controversy.

Example: *Capital punishment is wrong—it's just legalized murder.*

Sometimes called circular reasoning, some arguments try to make their point by simply restating the conclusion as evidence.[8]

Arguers commit the fallacy of **begging the question** when they use a premise that is identical to their conclusion or assume the truth of the claim that is central to the controversy.

Here is an example from the dialogue:

McGregor: Now that is a dumb idea if ever I've heard one.

Nancy: You mean raising the minimum wage? Why do you think it's so dumb?

McGregor: Because it is. It's just stupid.

What Do You Think?

Explain what the problem is with McGregor's argument.

McGregor starts out his argument with Nancy by simply begging the question: repeating his view that the idea is stupid. Later, of course, he does offer arguments. But his first move is a typical example of begging the question.

Rhetorical Effect: If successful, the fallacy creates the illusion that evidence has been given in support of the conclusion, when, in fact, the premise is merely a statement of the conclusion in slightly different words.

Logical Error: The error involved is ignoring a key criterion for premises. Premises must bring additional reasons to accept the conclusion, by providing supportive claims that are not only different from the conclusion but also more credible.

ARGUMENT FROM IGNORANCE:

A proponent is guilty of the fallacy of **argument from ignorance** when that proponent concludes that his or her position is correct on the basis of a lack of evidence refuting the position.

A proponent is guilty of the fallacy of **argument from ignorance** when that proponent concludes that his or her position is correct on the basis of a lack of evidence refuting the position.

Example: *Since they've never proven that there are no other conscious beings in the universe, there must be something to the claim that there are.*

What Do You Think?

What is wrong with the preceding argument?

Burden of proof (also called **onus**) refers to the responsibility for making the case and the degree of evidence required.

There may or may not be other conscious beings in the universe, but we cannot argue that there are on the basis of our inability to prove that there aren't. A useful concept here is the idea of **burden of proof** (also called **onus**), a concept taken from the English legal tradition. We have all heard of the principle that an accused is innocent until proven guilty. Another way of putting this is to say that the burden of proof is on the prosecution. Without adequate proof, the default view is that the accused is not guilty. Outside the court system, the burden of proof is generally on those who are putting forward the surprising position or who are arguing for a change of view (e.g., those who argue for the existence of sasquatches or for legalizing marijuana bear the burden of proof—without them making a good case for their side, the status quo prevails). But on many issues, there is no clear default view and so no clear burden of proof. In such cases, acting as if one's view were the default view so that lack of evidence against the view proves that it is right is the fallacy of argument from ignorance.

On the issue of the existence of other conscious beings, it is hard to doubt that in a universe of such vastness, there are other planets with intelligent life; but, of course, we do not have any evidence that there are. So all we can say is that we just do not know. In cases like this one, the lack of evidence can only be used to justify claiming uncertainty and ignorance, rather than to defend a point of view.

Here's another example from the dialogue:

McGregor: . . . Everyone knows that the lower the price, the more goods you can sell. The same is true of labour. It's common knowledge that the cheaper the labour, the more workers will be hired.

Nancy: I haven't seen any evidence that that's the case.

McGregor: Well, I haven't seen any evidence that it's not!

Both Nancy and her father commit the fallacy of argument from ignorance—using the lack of evidence for the contrary claim as "proof" of their claim.

Rhetorical Effect: By using the argument from ignorance, a proponent acts as if the burden of proof is on the other side and assumes that the failure of the other point of view to supply evidence justifies the opposing position.

Logical Error: The person making the argument from ignorance acts as if the onus is on the other side of the issue in a situation where there is no clear onus; the only reasonable position to take in the face of a lack of evidence is to admit ignorance.

Note, however, that if there is a clear burden of proof, then "absence of evidence" does justify a negative finding. In the case of intelligent life in the universe, there is no clear onus. The absence of evidence just means that we don't know. In other cases where an appropriate investigation has been made, the failure to find evidence of an effect can be evidence of no effect. In the case of high fibre diets which had been claimed to reduce rates of colon cancer, the result of a large pooled study failed to find any difference in cancer rates between those who consumed high fibre diets and those who did not.[9] The negative results of this study were given as strong evidence that eating a high fibre diet did not reduce colon cancer rates. We will have a more thorough discussion of the complexity of refuting and proving causal claims in science in Chapter 12.

ARGUMENT BY SPECTRE:

Arguers commit the fallacy of **argument by spectre** (often called the "slippery slope fallacy") when they argue against an action on the grounds that the long-run consequences of such an action will be disastrous, without supplying sufficient evidence to show that the supposed consequences are likely to follow.

> Arguers commit the fallacy of **argument by spectre** when they argue against an action on the grounds that the long run consequences of such an action will be disastrous, without supplying sufficient evidence to show that the supposed consequences are likely to follow.

Example: *If they can make us swallow this infringement of personal rights, what's next? A seat belt law for the bedroom, so we won't fall out of bed and hurt ourselves? Boy, when Big Brother watches us, he really watches us, doesn't he?*

McGregor: Raising the minimum wage would hugely increase labour costs for businesses. So they would no longer be able to remain competitive. Their profits would disappear, and pretty soon companies would have to shut down because they couldn't afford all the extra wages, and everyone would be unemployed.

Rhetorical Effect: The effect of spectre arguments or slippery slope arguments is to get an opponent to abandon an action or policy on the basis of fear of an inevitable but terrible outcome. The name "slippery slope" emphasizes the idea that if you make a move in some direction, inevitably you will slide into an unwanted consequence. But the rhetorical effectiveness of this kind of argument is usually achieved through focusing on the feared consequence or spectre. People's fears are easily aroused, so that if a proponent can get the listeners to focus on unlikely but very frightening consequences, the listeners will not think to ask about the likelihood of the frightening outcome.

Logical Error: The claim that one event or decision will inevitably lead to another and another until some disastrous outcome occurs requires considerable evidence. The logical error is the failure to supply credible evidence to support the likelihood of the supposed outcome. The future is uncertain, and people and governments will often change direction. Each stage of the supposed causal chain needs

> The original meaning of "spectre" is "ghost." Spectre is commonly used to refer to a haunting and frightening possibility, for example, the spectre of worldwide starvation.

support and evidence. This fallacy usually involves looking only at the possible negative consequences of an act and not at the actual likelihood of these consequences or the benefits of the act. Reasonable decision-making requires taking both likelihood and consequences into consideration.

EQUIVOCATION:

Equivocation is the deliberate use of ambiguity.

Equivocation in argument occurs when there is a misleading use of a word in two different senses. Equivocation is a fallacy because it involves changing the meaning of a term that is key to the validity or force of the argument.

Let us take the example of this deductive argument:

A feather is light.
What is light cannot be dark.
Therefore, a feather cannot be dark.

The meaning of "light" is obviously different in the two sentences and, therefore, despite the apparent formal validity of the argument, the argument is not valid.

Most troubling cases of equivocation occur in longer arguments, in particular where someone defends a claim by changing the meaning of the term.

Here is an example:

A. *I have realized from working with groups that someone always emerges as a leader.*
B. *That's not my experience. Why, last night the meeting of the club lasted for over an hour and no one took over; we just talked.*
A. *Ah, but in that case, the whole group became the leader.*

A famous example of equivocation is the argument claiming that the theory of evolution is merely a "theory." This issue is discussed in more detail in Chapter 12, but we can give a summary of it here. The argument goes as follows:

Evolution is a theory.
Theories are tentative and uncertain hypotheses.
Conclusion: Evolution is a tentative and uncertain hypothesis.

But "theory" in the first sense just means that evolution is a scientific view like "quantum theory" or "atomic theory." In the second sense, "theory" is used in a more popular sense meaning something slightly more credible than a hunch, as in "That's just your theory." The meanings are profoundly different; and the argument, therefore, commits the fallacy of equivocation.

A famous argument in Canada is over whether Quebec is a nation. Many non-Quebecers have a problem with this idea, thinking of Canada as one nation. But recently, even the prime minister of Canada, Stephen Harper, said that indeed, Quebec is a nation. To most people, "nation" means a state with independent status, such as the nations that have representatives in the United Nations. But in Canada and many other countries, there are nations without such status, such as Aboriginal nations. Since nation is so ambiguous but politically charged, it allows politicians to trade on the ambiguity for their political ends. Consider the following from the CBC report of the November 27, 2006, motion recognizing the Québécois as a nation.

The motion states: "That this House recognize that the Québécois form a nation within a united Canada." The prime minister has said he is using the word nation in a "cultural-sociological" rather than in a legal sense. "I think tonight was an historic night," Harper said after the vote. "Canadians across the country said 'yes' to Quebec, 'yes' to Quebecers, and Quebecers said 'yes' to Canada . . . In politics you take risks—that's what we did—but national unity, national reconciliation are more important than any one party or than any one individual."[10]

The argument might be expressed like this:

There is no need for Quebec to secede from Canada because Quebec has been declared a nation.
Nations are independent.
Conclusion: Quebec is already independent.

This argument is invalid because of equivocation.

Rhetorical Effect: By using the same word in different senses, the arguer creates the impression of making a valid argument. Subtle and not so subtle shifts in meaning are often hard to detect, and this means that such moves can often be persuasive.

Logical Error: Most words have many meanings. Context usually makes it clear which meaning is intended, but using two different senses of a word as if the meaning were constant defeats logical coherence and undermines even apparent formal validity.

Apply Your Understanding Exercise 1

Fallacies of Unacceptability

So far we have focused on the inference quality of an argument; that is, whether the premises if true would provide good prima facie support for the conclusion. We have looked at a whole series of fallacies that involve premises which provide little or no support for the conclusion, but are often persuasive. Now we wish to examine the case where the premises (if true) do provide support for the conclusion. In this case, we need to decide whether the premises are credible or true. Since we want to believe only claims that are true, we naturally want to have true premises. But often all we can know is that the premise is worthy of belief (i.e., credible). A good argument uses the credibility of the premises to support and make the conclusion credible.

We should first distinguish between the **credibility** and the **acceptability** of a premise. A claim is credible if it would be believed by any well-informed and reasonable person. A premise is acceptable to a particular person or audience if they believe it to be true. A premise that is neither credible nor acceptable is called a **problematic premise.**

Whether you or I or anyone believes a premise does not, of course, make it true. Exactly what makes a claim true is a deep philosophical question. But in the case of descriptive claims, what makes a claim true is that it correctly describes the facts of the matter. The claim that St. John's, Newfoundland, is closer to Dublin, Ireland, than it is to Vancouver happens to be true because St. John's *is* closer to Dublin than it is to Vancouver. Some people may not find the claim acceptable, however, because they can't imagine that St. John's could be closer to a city in Europe than to another city in Canada. Nonetheless, the claim is true even if some people don't find it acceptable.

We cannot assume that, because a claim is true, any particular audience will find it acceptable. If you are concerned with reasonable persuasion, as you would be in a dialogue or when presenting a case yourself, you need to consider not only whether *you* think the premises you are putting forward are credible or true, but also whether the audience will find them acceptable.

When evaluating an argument, on the other hand, you must assess whether a claim is acceptable to you. The ideal is to accept only those claims that are credible (believed by reasonable and well-informed people). But, of course, your impression of the acceptability of a claim will be influenced by your biases, experience, and degree of knowledge. Inevitably, your test of acceptability will be "Is this believable to me? Do I believe this?" This

A claim is **credible** if it would be believed by any well-informed and reasonable person.

A premise is **acceptable** to a particular person or audience if they believe it to be true.

A premise that is neither credible nor acceptable is called a **problematic premise.**

is perfectly legitimate since simply to concede to or accept a premise that you do not find believable is to abandon your intellectual autonomy and capacity to make a reasoned judgment. As a consumer of argument and information, you have every right to demand premises that are acceptable to you.

On the other hand, you cannot demand that all premises be proven. Such a demand would lead to an infinite regress of "prove it, prove it." This would leave us with no premises with which to start a dialogue or mount an argument, and, therefore, no basis for reasoned judgment. Since we cannot find all premises unacceptable, what are the criteria for accepting or rejecting a premise? To avoid infinite regress, we must accept that there is a weak onus on those who would reject a premise. This does not mean you need a strong reason to question the premise, but you need some reason.

You have to have some reason to doubt—you cannot just claim that a premise is unacceptable because a premise is unsupported. There will always be unsupported premises. But if a claim seems to you doubtful because of your own experience or something you have read or heard, or because the source has a reputation for deception, then you have a justified basis for questioning the claim. You can make a demand for support for a premise on the basis of prima facie doubt as weak as "I have never heard of that" or "Gee, that is pretty surprising! How do you know that?" or "Bill has a terrible habit of exaggerating; I can't just accept that claim." In doing so, you are not asserting that a claim is false, only that it is not acceptable without additional credible evidence.

> You cannot demand that all premises be proven. You need a reason to challenge a premise.

In addition, if a particular premise provides crucial support for a conclusion—that is, if a premise is central to the argument and if this premise seems even slightly suspect—the audience has a right to demand evidence for it.

Let's look at one of McGregor's arguments:

Premises crucial to an argument bear a greater onus of credibility.

McGregor: And anyway, hardly anyone is paid the minimum wage. Even unskilled labourers are pulling in fat paycheques. So I don't know what all the fuss is about.

Nancy: But you said before that companies would have to close because they couldn't afford all the extra wages! But if hardly anyone is getting the minimum wage, then there won't be a lot of extra wages!

Standardizing:

1. Hardly anyone is paid the minimum wage.
2. Even unskilled labourers are pulling in fat paycheques.

Conclusion: There is no need to raise the minimum wage.

Both premises 1 and 2 are crucial to McGregor's argument and while they might be true, they are far from obviously true. To reach a reasonable decision about raising the minimum wage, we would need to know how many people would be affected; and this cannot be settled by impressions and anecdotal evidence. The premises are problematic because they are crucial and they are far from obviously true.

Finally, we should remember that the point of making an argument is to provide reasons which support the conclusion and have more initial credibility than the conclusion. Premises that are not more credible than the conclusion are also not acceptable. Take this argument, for example:

McGregor: We shouldn't increase the minimum wage. What we should really do is simply get rid of it, period. That's what's best for the economy and if it's good for the economy, it will be good for everyone, including the poor.

McGregor's claims that the minimum wage should be eliminated and that what's good for the economy is good for the poor are more controversial than the claim that the minimum wage should not be raised. The claims, therefore, are not acceptable in this argument. In addition, if McGregor really wishes to persuade his daughter, these claims are obviously bad choices because she is sure to find them even more unacceptable than the position he is trying to defend.

Rhetorical Effect: The effect of using fallacies of unacceptability is a bit like bluffing in poker. People are often fooled by the assertion of an unwarranted claim if it is asserted with misleading confidence.

Logical Error: The error is in providing premises that fail to meet the criteria of acceptability. Premises must be more credible than the conclusion if they are to offer support for the conclusion, and they must be acceptable to the audience if they are to be rationally persuasive.

Criteria for Premise Acceptability

A claim is prima facie **acceptable** if one of these is the case:
- The claim is **credible** or widely known to be true. (e.g., The capital of Canada is Ottawa.)
- The claim is supported by **credible sources.** (e.g., The World Health Organization reported that lung cancer is the most common cause of cancer death in the world.)

- The claim is **offered tentatively** to assess its significance to the argument. If crucial, it **could be supported.** (e.g., I *think* that the polar bear is in danger of extinction; and if it is, that is more evidence of the disastrous effect of global warming.)

A premise is **not acceptable** when one of these is the case:

- It is **not credible:** it is not a belief that a reasonable person would accept without additional support. (e.g., The moon landing was faked.)

- It is **less credible than the conclusion** and, therefore, clearly unacceptable to the audience of the argument. (Consider someone trying to persuade an audience that capital punishment is wrong by using the premise that "Any killing of a human being is wrong." Obviously anyone who accepted this premise would already be opposed to capital punishment and would not need to be persuaded. In addition, this claim is far more controversial than the claim that capital punishment is wrong.)

- It is offered as an **unsupported premise that asserts a claim crucial to the argument and is not obviously credible.** (e.g., Since chickens form lasting bonds and love their young, killing chickens for food is wrong.)

FALSE DILEMMA:

False dilemma is an attempt to force people to consider only two choices, one of which is usually repugnant. If they accept the dilemma, they must choose the other as the conclusion.

A rhetorically powerful fallacy of problematic premise is the **false dilemma.** False dilemma is an attempt to force people to consider only two choices, one of which is usually repugnant. If they accept the dilemma, they must choose the other as the conclusion.

Examples:
You're either part of the solution or part of the problem.

Either you are with us, or you are with the terrorists.[11] (President George W. Bush in 2001 address to the U.S. Congress)

Either we go to Hawaii and have a wonderful time, or we stay home and are miserable.
    The argument form is as follows:

P1 You're either part of the solution or part of the problem.

P2 I don't want to be part of the problem.

Conclusion: I should be part of the solution.

P1. Either we go to Hawaii and have a wonderful time, or we stay home and are miserable.

P2 I don't want to be miserable.

Conclusion: We should go to Hawaii.

Rhetorical Effect: The effect of the false dilemma is to force people to consider only two choices, one of which is usually repugnant; so they must choose the other. Since they have only two choices, they must go along with the least unsatisfactory one.

Apply Your Understanding Exercises 2, 3

Logical Error: The error is in making the assumption that there are only two choices when deciding what to do or believe. This is error is also called black and white thinking; a person accepts without sufficient reflection a very narrow range of alternatives when thinking about what to believe or do.

CHECK YOUR UNDERSTANDING

- *What is a strong inductive argument?*
- *What is a cogent inductive argument?*
- *Why must an argument have premises that have more credibility than the conclusion?*
- *What is a prima facie judgment?*
- *Explain what a fallacy is.*
- *List five fallacies of illusory support. Describe both the logical error and the rhetorical effect of each one.*
- *Under what condition would we consider a claim credible?*
- *Under what condition would we consider a premise acceptable?*
- *What is a problematic premise?*
- *Under what circumstances is a claim prima facie acceptable?*
- *Under what circumstances is a premise problematic?*

EXERCISES

1. For each of the following:

    i) Standardize the argument.

    ii) Identify the fallacy (or fallacies) committed.

    iii) Explain why the argument is fallacious.

    a) Some people think that Rottweilers are dangerous dogs and should be banned. But this is simply not true. Rottweilers are intelligent and hardy dogs and make excellent companions. And as for being dangerous, dog bites are behind baseball as a source of emergency room visits.

    b) In every locality where there are liberal drug policies, there's a huge problem of street crime. More policing is not the answer. The only solution is tougher drug laws.

    c) I just found out that the journalist who writes all those articles about global warming drives an RV. I sure wouldn't pay any attention to his arguments about the greenhouse effect.

    d) Of course, it's OK to take advantage of all those tax loopholes—everyone else does.

    e) Our organization ought to implement affirmative action policies for women. The people who oppose such policies only do so because they're sexists. They can't stand the idea of women in positions of power.

    f) Echinacea is excellent for warding off colds. Everyone should take it on a daily basis. My friend Gina takes echinacea every day and she hardly gets any colds.

    g) I always believe the stories Lee tells me since she's a very reliable source of information. She told me so herself.

    h) I don't support vegetarianism. I'm not one of those granola-munching hippies.

    i) So far as I can see, and going on what businesspeople tell me, people who aren't working don't want to work. There is no real unemployment problem.

    j) You shouldn't believe everything you hear about the treatment of animals raised for meat. It's all a load of propaganda from those animal rights loonies.

    k) It's not right that some folks get so worked up about how we treat animals, when there are people getting mistreated and even killed all over the world.

    l) You can't believe Lester's argument in favour of raising the minimum wage. He's working at a minimum wage job.

m) You can't rely on college students to be punctual workers. I have one working for me, and she's always late.

n) So you think it's OK for children, and adults for that matter, to be attacked by pit bulls?

2. Read the following passage, then do the following:

i) Identify the fallacies in the passage.

ii) Analyze each one in terms of (a) rhetorical effect, and (b) logical error.

It is unreasonable for the Honourable Member of the Opposition to criticize my government's economic policies. We are in our current crisis because of the economic blunders made by his party when it was in power. Their overspending of taxpayer money on wasteful social programs was a case of their leftist ideology substituting for responsible economic restraint. Such flagrant overspending inevitably leads to an excessive tax burden on our corporate sector, a weakening of the economy, and a major economic crisis. The opposition party clearly believes that throwing money at problems in an irresponsible manner will lead to an improvement in our nation, but this is clearly not the road to betterment as the policies of our government have demonstrated.

3. For each of the following, give an example of the fallacy by writing a short dialogue in which the fallacy is committed:

i) ad hominem

ii) anecdotal evidence

iii) straw person

iv) spectre (slippery slope)

v) popularity

vi) problematic premise

vii) red herring

viii) equivocation

ENDNOTES

1. Ian Austin, "$8 Minimum Wage Turns 8," *The Province*, Nov. 2, 2009, http://www.theprovince.com/entertainment/minimum+wage+turns+eight/2171927/2171928.bin?size=620x400

2. Extensive research by Amos Tversky and others on the assumption of representativenss supports this observation. People expect their experience to be representative, just as they expect a sequence of dice rolls to look like a random distribution. (See Tversky et al., *Judgment Under Uncertainty: Biases and Heuristics*, Cambridge: Cambridge University Press, 1982.)

3. CBC.ca, "Greenpeace Occupies Alberta Shell Site," Oct. 3, 2009, http://.cbc.ca/canada/edmonton/story/2009/10/03/edmonton-greenpeace-protest-fort-saskatchewan-shell.html.

4. To avoid endless repetition, we use "author" of an argument and "proponent" as synonyms.

5. Michael Smyth "Environmental Guru's Inconvenient Truth," *The Province*, March 01, 2007.

6. From CCW's blog response to David Wylie, "Medical Marijuana Potency Against Pain Possibly Poppycock," *The Vancouver Sun*, Aug, 13, 2009, http://www.vancouversun.com/health/Medical+marijuana+potency+against+pain+possibly+poppycock/1890541/story.html(accessed Sept. 25, 2009).

7. A citizen, commenting on Rachel Muenz, "How: Solving the Gun Crime Problem," http://www.torontoobserver.ca/2008/12/13/how-solving-the-gun-crime-problem/ (accessed Sept. 25, 2009).

8. Peter Ellerton, "Circular Reasoning," *pactiss.org,* http://pactiss.org/resources/media-articles-cartoons/CircularReasoning.jpg/view (accessed May 1, 2010).

9. Arthur Schatzkin et al., "Dietary Fiber and Whole-grain Consumption in Relation to Colorectal Cancer in the NIH-AARP Diet and Health Study," *Am J Clin Nutr* 85, no. 5 (2007): 1353-60.

10. CBC.ca, "House Passes Motion Recognizing Quebecois as Nation," Nov. 27, 2006, http://www.cbc.ca/canada/story/2006/11/27/nation-vote.html

11. George W. Bush, "Address to a Joint Session of Congress and the American People," http://georgewbush-whitehouse.archives.gov/news/releases/2001/09/20010920-8.html m) You can't rely on college students to be punctual workers. I have one working for me, and she's always late.

Chapter 5
Key Argument Types

Learning Objectives

After reading this chapter, you should be able to:

- identify and use the argumentative strategy of *reductio ad absurdum*
- identify and evaluate analogical arguments
- make use of the distinction between arguments and explanations when assessing claims and arguments
- apply the principle of argument to the best explanation to assess the credibility of explanatory claims

Legalizing Marijuana I

Phil and Stephen have just attended a debate at their college on the legalization of marijuana.

Phil: I really agree with the guy who was arguing that marijuana should be legalized.

Stephen: Why do you say that?

Phil: Anyone can see that keeping it illegal isn't working. It's just like alcohol prohibition. When alcohol was prohibited, all it did was create the conditions for organized crime and make millions of people engage in criminal activity.

Stephen: But marijuana is different. It's a gateway drug—it leads people on to harder drugs. We heard all about it in school last year.

Phil: I really doubt that. What it does do is make people disrespect the law. The problem is that, even though it's illegal, it's still widely used. So it encourages people to think it's OK to do other things that are against the law, like using other illegal drugs.

Stephen: We also learned other good reasons why marijuana is illegal. It's addictive and rots people's brains.

Phil: How do you know that? I bet that idea came from some anti-drug group—it's probably hopelessly biased. Besides, we all know people who use marijuana and seem perfectly sane and competent. Marijuana is actually safer than alcohol. For one thing, it doesn't make people aggressive the way alcohol often does.

Stephen: All you have to do is look at Sophia's cousin Nick to see the negative effects of marijuana. He's bombed all day and never gets anything done. He failed out of high school. He's a mess from the marijuana.

Phil: I'm not so sure—he was pretty messed up with his parents breaking up and his dad going to jail— before he got into marijuana. He just uses it to dull the pain. Of course, he should get some counselling and get it together, but you can't blame the marijuana for his condition. His marijuana use is a sign he has a problem; it's not the cause.

Stephen: I don't think you're right. I talked to my family doctor about Nick, and he said that it's obvious that Nick is suffering from marijuana addiction. The fact is that marijuana is so widely available, it's inevitable that messed-up kids will use it and make their situation worse.

Phil: But you could say the same of alcohol. Lots of messed-up people get drunk. Does that mean we should make alcohol illegal? I don't get why marijuana should be illegal and alcohol legal. They're both recreational drugs that many people like to use. They both have some negative side effects. So how can you justify treating them differently?

Stephen: So you're saying that, since marijuana is a popular recreational drug like alcohol, we should legalize it? And I suppose that since cocaine and meth are popular drugs too, we should legalize them? If people want to use a drug, we should just let them? Maybe they could all be sold in the supermarket? What kind of society would we have then?

Phil: I don't think that follows from what I'm saying. Some drugs are genuinely more dangerous than others. But I do think that we should see drug abuse as a health problem and not a criminal problem. People who use addictive drugs like meth need help.

Stephen: I think people who use addictive drugs are making a really stupid choice. I don't care what their reasons are, they should be held responsible for what they do.

As Stephen and Phil discuss the question of legalizing marijuana, they make many different types of arguments. They use analogies (the situation with marijuana being illegal *is like* prohibition) and causal arguments (marijuana use leads to other drugs), both of which we will discuss in this chapter. They also use appeals to authorities ("We heard all about it [negative effect of marijuana use] in school last year"), which we will discuss in Chapter 6. These are extremely common and important kinds of arguments.

Reductio

Before going on to study these argument types, however, we need to note one other common strategy used in the dialogue, *reductio* argument. It is used by Stephen when he says, "So if people want to use a drug, we should just let them? Maybe they could all be sold in the supermarket? What kind of society would we have then?" *Reductio*, which is short for **reductio ad absurdum** (Latin for "reduction to the absurd") involves showing that a proposed action or principle would lead to an absurd situation and, therefore, should be rejected. Despite its Latin name, it is not a fallacy, but a useful argumentative strategy. When Stephen argues against Phil by raising the idea of all recreational drugs being sold in the supermarket, he is attempting to show that Phil's principle for legalizing marijuana would lead to an absurd situation. Notice that he is not arguing that the decriminalization

Reductio ad absurdum is an argumentative strategy that argues that a particular position should be rejected because accepting it would justify absurd outcomes.

of marijuana would inevitably lead to this outcome. If he were, he would be guilty of the slippery slope or spectre fallacy (see Chapter 4). Rather, he is claiming that if the basis for legalization is respecting people's desire to use a drug, then that means that drugs could and should be sold legally.

The powerful aspect of this argument is that it can lead proponents to abandon their view because they, too, see that their view has an absurd outcome. The danger in using this argument is in committing the fallacy of straw person—making a *reductio* claim that does not really follow from the position being criticized. For example, decriminalization or even legalization of some recreational drugs does not mean that all drugs (or even any drugs) would be sold in the supermarket. In cases like Stephen's argument, the proponent of the *reductio* is guilty of the straw person fallacy (see Chapter 4). But if someone argued, as many libertarians do, that people should be free to do and consume whatever they want as long as it does not hurt anyone else, Stephen would be right to point out that this position does allow for the sale of all recreational drugs. Of course, some people might think that this is satisfactory; therefore, for them, this would not be an absurdity. But for most, this would be an unacceptable outcome and a good argument (a good *reductio*) against the libertarian position.

Here is another typical use of the *reductio* strategy, in this case combined with sarcasm:

Re *"B.C.'s Top Medical Health Officer Calls For Crack-Inhaling Rooms"* (Oct. 20):[1] *As an ER doctor, I sometimes see victims of break-and-enter crimes. These poor souls often have badly lacerated hands, caused when they were forced to break glass to gain entry. Following the harm-reduction strategy to provide safe crack houses, we should also set up safe houses stocked with TVs and stereos with open windows and unlocked doors. Oh heck, maybe we'll put a pile of money on the floor, too. After all, we want to make things as easy as we can for those engaged in criminal behaviour. Hey, maybe we could arrange for police escorts to lead the way when they want to drive home drunk, too.*

We will also see the *reductio* strategy used in the analogical arguments that we study next.

Apply Your Understanding Exercise 1

Analogical Arguments

There are basically two kinds of arguments by analogy: those using precedent analogies and those using causal analogies.

Precedent Analogies

Phil's argument that there is no justification for having alcohol legal while marijuana is illegal is based on the idea that the legalization of alcohol sets a precedent for legalizing other popular recreational drugs. Both justice and logic require that we be consistent in our judgments. For example, if the courts sentence one person to six months for possession of a certain amount of cocaine, then it should also sentence other people who are convicted of the same kind of cocaine possession to six months, unless there is some legally important difference between the cases. While neither the courts nor any of us actually is reliably consistent in our judgments, a reasonable consistency remains a goal of all rational people.

So when someone says, "I don't trust Mary because of her aura," but then challenges others to give concrete evidence for their opinions of why Bill isn't trustworthy, we have a right to object to the inconsistency. Another common example of inconsistency occurs when people use statistics to prove claims; but when the statistics go against their claim, they say, "Oh, you can prove anything with statistics."

> Note that inconsistency is not the same as changing your mind. If new facts come to your attention, or further reflection leads you to think your initial views are wrong, then you should change your mind. Inconsistency is making contradictory judgments without any good reason to do so.

Appeal to precedent is a fundamental principle of legal reasoning. While lawyers debate which earlier case is the appropriate precedent for the case at hand, they do not question the use of precedent as a key determining factor in making a judgment. Citing other cases as precedents is a form of arguing by analogy. The argument goes basically like this:

> In case A, the court decided X.
>
> The case at hand is like case A in relevant ways.
>
> **Conclusion:** The court should also decide X in this case.

> A **precedent analogy** is an argument which attempts to establish a conclusion on the basis that the circumstances of the case at issue are like those of another case.

This is an argument by **precedent analogy,** and it is widely applicable outside the court room situation. Here, too, the proponent attempts to establish a conclusion on the basis that circumstances of the case at issue are like those of another case. Assuming we agree with the conclusion of the other case, we should also accept the conclusion in the case at hand. A crucial part of this argument is that the cases are alike in relevant ways. It would not do, for example, to object that the cases were not analogous because one crime was committed by a tall person and the other by a short person; height is not relevant to the issue.

Let's look at Phil's argument in table form:

Precedent		Issue at Hand
Alcohol is a recreational drug.	**Is like**	Marijuana is a recreational drug.
Alcohol presents some social and health problems.	**Is like**	Marijuana presents some social and health problems.
Alcohol is legal.	**By analogy**	Marijuana should be legal.

What Do You Think ?

Do you think that Phil's analogy constitutes a good argument? Explain why or why not.

We discuss below how to evaluate analogies, but it is important to note that even if Phil's analogy is a good one, it is still a prima facie argument for legalization. It may be that society is inconsistent in legalizing alcohol but keeping marijuana illegal. Someone might argue that legalizing alcohol is unfortunate, given the harm associated with it; but we know from history that we cannot effectively ban it. On the other hand, eliminating the ban on marijuana might mean that its negative effects (e.g., driving when high) would then become more common. This argument sees that appeal to the legal status of alcohol as a kind of two wrongs fallacy: "Legalizing alcohol is wrong, but we can't do much about it; that doesn't mean we should legalize another wrong." That is why the question of whether marijuana should be legalized requires a full inquiry in which Phil's precedent analogy would be one of the considerations.

Causal Analogies

> A **causal analogy** is an argument which suggests that because two phenomena (or entities) share relevant qualities, the causal properties of one will be like the causal properties of the other.

Not all arguments by analogy are precedent arguments. Precedent arguments have conclusions that are evaluative; but other analogical arguments can be factual: for example, causal analogies.

A **causal analogy** is an attempt to understand one phenomenon by comparing it to another. A common form of this argument is the **historical analogy,** where we try to use an understanding of previous events to predict what would happen now if we took similar actions.

> A **historical analogy** is one in which we try to use an understanding of previous events to predict what would happen now if we took similar actions.

The argument is that a current event or situation is like a previous event or situation, so what happened then is likely to happen now, and what worked then is likely to work now.

The argument about the failure of alcohol prohibition is an example of a historical analogy.

Comparable Situation or Event		Issue at Hand
Alcohol was prohibited in the U.S. in the 1920s.	**Is like**	Marijuana is prohibited now.
Alcohol prohibition was ineffective and resulted in increased organized crime.	**By analogy**	**CON1:** Marijuana prohibition will be (in this case, will continue to be) ineffective and result in increased organized crime.
Alcohol prohibition resulted in law-abiding citizens breaking the law and bringing the law into disrespect.	**By analogy**	**CON2:** Marijuana prohibition will result in law-abiding citizens breaking the law and bringing the law into disrespect.

What do you think of Phil's historical analogy as an argument for marijuana legalization?

What Do You Think ?

Not all causal analogies are historical. Many types of analogical reasoning are used in science. To take one well-known example, rats are used for a variety of medical tests, in particular for testing whether a substance is carcinogenic (cancer-causing).

Comparable Situation or Event		Issue at Hand
Rats ingested a significant amount of a chemical for 18 months.	**Is like**	Humans ingested a small amount of a similar substance over a long time.
The experimental rats got cancer.	**By analogy**	Humans exposed to this substance will also get cancer.

Evaluating Analogies

Analogies are tricky to evaluate. Almost anything can be compared to anything else. Things and events can be similar in certain ways but different in others. The question is always whether the two things being compared, called the **analogues,** are comparable in *relevant* ways, that is, in ways that justify the inference from one to the other. Humans are obviously very different from rats; but for some scientific purposes such as testing for carcinogens, they may be comparable.[2] Marijuana and alcohol seem similar from the perspective that they are both widely used social and recreational drugs; but they are different in terms of the historical place they have in this culture, and in their differing behavioural and health effects.

Nonetheless, marijuana and alcohol are similar enough that by researching the behavioural and health problems, we can probably make a reasonable assessment of any analogies that involve them. Things get trickier if we try to compare events or things that are quite different. When lawyers are looking for precedents to support their cases, they look for cases that have extensive similarities. Obviously, the more your case is like another, the stronger your claim that the previous judgment (the precedent) must be followed in this case. The same is true with causal analogies. Rats are apparently quite a good anatomical analogy to humans in certain ways and are, therefore, useful models for a variety of medical tests and experiments. If the health issue involves eyes, however, the rabbit is seen as a better model. And if we are looking at social behaviour, rats would seem too far removed from humans to be of any real explanatory or predictive value.

Because some analogies involve comparables that are very different, we can raise a prima facie objection to them, not on the basis of particular aspects of the comparison but on the basis that there is just too much **analogical distance** to evaluate the analogy. Analogical distance is a metaphor to express the degree of difference between the two things being compared. In the case of historical analogies, events from the distant past have

Two cases that are compared are called **analogues**. The analogue can be either the case at issue or the comparable precedent or event.

For both causal and precedent analogies, the more the case at issue is like the analogue, the stronger the claim that the analogue provides a basis for assessing the case at issue.

Analogical distance is a metaphor to express the degree of difference between the two things being compared.

considerably more analogical distance than more recent events. If, for example, we were looking for a historical analogue to the war in Iraq, the Vietnam war would have less analogical distance than would the Napoleonic wars.

- In the case of causal analogies using animals, the closer an animal is to humans genetically, the less analogical distance is involved.

- In the case of precedent analogies, the more the two issues or events being compared have strongly similar fact patterns, the less the analogical distance.

The concept of analogical distance is useful because a large analogical distance makes the evaluation of the comparison so difficult that we cannot make a reasonable assessment.

To see how to evaluate analogical arguments, let's look at another one. A number of years ago, an interesting analogical argument was made by chemistry professor D.C. Walker of the University of British Columbia when a large nuclear-powered U.S. aircraft carrier planned to anchor in the harbour in Vancouver. There were considerable protests about this plan, and city council decided (ineffectively) to ban the vessel, in part because there were suspicions that the vessel carried nuclear weapons (*Vancouver Sun*, 1989). The professor wrote as follows:

If Vancouver city council's ban on nuclear-powered vessels resulted from a belief that an accident involving such a vessel would be much more environmentally disastrous than one with an oil-fired vessel (or an oil-carrying one), then okay. It might be wrong, but at least the reasoning would be understandable. If, however, any of the aldermen have confused the issue of nuclear bombs with that of nuclear power generation, then they have made fools of themselves and, much worse, fired a death blow at us nuclear-ban lobbyists. Banning nuclear-based generators because of an abhorrence of nuclear bombs is like banning the use of dynamite in road construction because dynamite is the ingredient of conventional bombs, or banning gasoline-powered cars because terrorists throw Molotov cocktails.[3]

> The concept of analogical distance is useful because a large analogical distance makes the evaluation of the comparison so difficult that we cannot make a reasonable assessment.

The analogical arguments are in the last sentence.

Precedent		Issue at Hand
Banning use of dynamite because it is used in bombs	**Is like**	Banning nuclear-based generators because of nuclear bombs
Banning gasoline-powered cars because gas is used in Molotov cocktails	**Is like**	Banning nuclear-powered ships because of nuclear bombs
Both these bannings would be silly	**By analogy**	Both these bannings would be silly

What Do You Think

How effective do you think the professor's analogies are?

Note that the professor was using his analogies to make a *reductio* argument against banning the ship. Both his analogies have obvious weaknesses, however. The issue at hand is the aircraft carrier, a mode of transport like a car; but Molotov cocktails are nothing like nuclear bombs. On the other hand, dynamite is quite a bit like a nuclear bomb—indeed, nuclear bombs are measured in terms of the equivalent amount of dynamite it would take to make a comparable explosion—but dynamite has nothing to do with providing the energy for transport. The question is whether these differences are sufficiently relevant to undermine the analogy. We will leave it to you to decide whether either of these analogies individually or both together make a good case.

But we note that the professor's point was a complaint about guilt by association—namely the association in everyone's mind of nuclear energy with nuclear bombs. We doubt that merely pointing out that this is a misleading association would have carried much weight in the debate. The attempt to demonstrate, through analogical argument, that the association does not support banning the nuclear-powered ship seems more persuasive than merely pointing out that such an association commits the fallacy of guilt by association.

The following are strategies for evaluating analogical arguments:

1. Check to see if there are relevant *comparable* aspects of the items being compared.
2. Extend the analogy to see if it leads to absurd implications (i.e., creates a *reductio* argument).
3. Create alternative analogies that are as good or better, but with different implications.
4. Extract the underlying principle and subject it to criticism.

Here is an exchange of analogies between a columnist and a reader. The columnist, Shelly Fralic, argued against the trend to sympathize with overweight people, including requiring airlines to provide two seats for acutely obese people.[4] Part of her argument was the following:

Maybe we should treat overeaters the way we do smokers. No one feels sorry for smokers these days, because they know the consequences of their addiction and because they have the power to heal themselves. Be fat if you want. But own it. And don't expect special treatment.

A reader responded with a classic example of the second strategy for evaluating an analogy suggested above, a *reductio*:

I agree with Shelly Fralic that we should treat overeaters like we do smokers. We need legislation to ban all saliva-inducing food advertisements on TV, however amusing they may be. Later, we could prohibit eating in public places such as the work place or on the street.
NH, North Vancouver

Fralic's argument can be reconstructed as follows:

Precedent		Issue at Hand
Smokers	**Are like**	Overeaters
We hold smokers responsible for their habits.	**By analogy**	We should hold overeaters responsible for their habits.

NH replied in this way:

Precedent		Issue at Hand
Smokers	**Are like**	Overeaters
We ban advertizing for cigarettes.	**By analogy**	We should ban TV ads for food.
We prohibit smoking in public places.	**By analogy**	We should prohibit eating in public places.
		But this is absurd
	Conclusion	Overeaters should not be treated like smokers.

Which of the two analogies do you think is better? Why?

What Do You Think?

Here is another analogical argument, this one on the issue of capital punishment. It is meant as a response to the well-known objection to capital punishment on the basis that it will inevitably result in some innocent people being executed.

Keep in Mind

STRATEGIES FOR EVALUATING ANALOGICAL ARGUMENTS

1. Check to see if there are relevant *comparable* aspects of the items being compared.
2. Extend the analogy to see if it leads to absurd implications (i.e., creates a *reductio* argument).
3. Create alternative analogies that are as good or better, but with different implications.
4. Extract the underlying principle and subject it to criticism.

All human activities sometimes cost the lives of innocent bystanders, but we still perform these activities. For example, more innocent people are killed by car crashes than by mistaken executions of innocent people, yet we never argue that there ought not to be cars.

What Do
You Think

What do you make of the preceding analogical argument? (To assess it, you will have to look for relevant similarities and dissimilarities between the two positions being compared.)

Precedent		Issue at Hand
Innocent people are killed in car accidents.	**Is like**	Innocent people are killed by mistaken execution.
No one argues that there should not be cars.	**By analogy**	No one should argue that there should not be capital punishment.

Framing refers to the set of concepts that set up an issue and that suggest a certain way of looking at the issue.

This is a tricky analogy because it does something that many analogical arguments do: it changes the **framing** of the issue. The argument invites the reader to see the execution of innocents in the frame of the necessary evils of a social practice, instead of in the frame of a profound violation of an innocent individual's rights. One could respond to this analogy by using the first strategy suggested above, identifying incomparable aspects of the analogy. Such a response might look like this:

Precedent	Are Not Analogous Because	Issue at Hand
In car accidents, (innocent) people are killed **accidentally.**	**Is not like**	In capital punishment, (innocent) people are killed **intentionally** by the state.
Innocent people who are killed accidentally have not had their rights violated.	**Is not like**	Innocent people who are executed have had their rights violated.

Because of the shift in frame induced by the analogy, the critique above may not provide a very persuasively effective reply to the original analogy. The best way to deal with this analogy is to use the fourth strategy above, and extract the underlying principle—in this case, the principles for both sides—and argue about the appropriateness of the principle rather than the analogy. The principle argued by the proponent is that harms resulting from useful social practices are and should be accepted. The principle argued by the opponents is that the state should never risk the profound violation of human rights (such as that involved in the execution of an innocent person). Resolving such a conflict of principles and coming to a reasoned judgment on this topic is complex, and we will not attempt it here. But the argument does illustrate the remarkable power of analogies to shape a controversy. We will return to this challenge in Chapter 10 (where we will address the issues of conflicting principles and weighting, among others).

Apply Your Understanding Exercise 2

Argument and Explanation

One of the most fundamental activities that humans engage in is trying to understand the world. The ability to understand the world enables us both to predict what will happen and to change the world for our purposes. Understanding what is going on involves having adequate explanations. But while some explanations are correct, others are reasonable but wrong, and still others are just plain wrong. Having the wrong explanation for a phenomenon means that we will not be able to make predictions or effect the kind of changes we wish. The great progress in health care, for example, has come from our increased understanding of how the body works. Previously, a poor understanding of the causes of ill health led to practices like bloodletting which were actually harmful. To benefit from our ability to understand, we need to know how to identify credible explanations and what constitutes good evidence for these. But first, we need to clarify an important distinction between arguments and explanations.

The Difference Between Arguments and Explanations

Explanations can often look quite a lot like arguments although they differ in a crucial way. Typically, in an explanation we are looking for why something happened, whereas in an argument we are looking at whether we should believe a particular claim. Explanations are typically about causes while arguments are about beliefs. To further complicate matters, we can make an argument for an explanation. Perhaps an illustration will clarify:

If we are at a party and are looking for Mary, we could ask someone, "Where is Mary?" They might say, "She's gone home." We could ask how the person knows that, and they might answer, "I don't see her anywhere, and earlier I saw her heading for the door." This would be an argument for the claim that Mary has gone.

Standardizing:

1. I don't see her anywhere
2. Earlier I saw her heading for the door.
Conclusion: She's gone home.

We might then ask, "Why did Mary leave the party?" In this case, we are asking for an explanation and are assuming in our question that indeed she has left. The answer could be that "she left because she felt sick." Note that the "because" in this case does not give a reason for believing she left, but rather an explanation of her leaving.

While explanations are not arguments, arguments can and often should be provided to justify belief in a particular explanation. In the case of Mary and the party, an argument could be provided for believing that her feeling sick caused her to leave: "She was looking very pale, and she said she wasn't feeling well and was thinking of going home."

Standardizing the argument looks like this:

1. Mary did not look well.
2. Mary said she wasn't feeling well.
3. Mary said she was thinking of going home.
Conclusion: Mary went home *because* she wasn't feeling well.

The key difference is that in the argument example, we are making a case for the claim that Mary has left, whereas in the explanation example, we assume that she's left and are looking for an explanation. Neither arguments nor explanations yield certainty. Mary may have been sick but went to rest upstairs, so she hasn't even left; or perhaps she left, but really it was because of a fight with John, and her claim of sickness was just to cover up.

There are basically two forms of explanation: **reason explanations** and **causal explanations.**

Reason Explanations

Reason explanations, sometimes called teleological explanations or purpose explanations, are how we usually explain human behaviour. When we understand people's reasons or purposes, we can understand why they are acting in a certain way and can frequently predict what they will do. In pre-scientific societies, people attempted to understand the nature of the world the same way they understood one another—by giving explanations in terms of reasons and purposes. For example, in early Greek civilization, the explanation of

A **reason explanation** is an explanation in terms of the reasons or intentions of the actors in the case.

bad weather was that the gods were angry and needed to be placated. Thanks to the success of science, we now can give causal explanations for a wide range of events. We understand that bad weather in the northwest Pacific coast area is the result of the low pressure system in the Pacific forcing storms from the north down on to the coast—not a result of the anger of the gods.

On the other hand, we still use reason explanations to explain much of the behaviour of humans and even animals. For example, "Why did John go to the store?" The answer "He wanted to get some bread" explains why he went to the store by giving his *reason*. Another example is the question "Why is the dog scratching at the door?" "Because he wants to be taken for a walk" explains the dog's behaviour by giving the *reason* for it.

Causal Explanations

A **causal explanation** is an explanation in terms of antecedent events that made something happen.

When it comes to the physical world, **causal explanations** provide the best and most useful explanations. Why did the pipe burst? Because there was water in it and the water froze. Why does John have ulcers? Not because the gods are out to get him, but probably because he has an infection of *H. pylori* bacteria in his intestines. One advantage of such explanations is that they give us powerful tools for changing the environment. Once we understand that ulcers are usually caused by bacteria, we can treat the condition with antibiotics. Understanding is power.

A causal explanation is an explanation in terms of antecedent events that made something happen. Most causal explanations are physical, as in the following examples:

> *The corrosion caused the pipe to burst.*
> *The wind caused the tree to fall.*
> *Heating water to 100 degrees Celsius at sea level causes it to boil.*

But we also explain people's feelings in terms of causes:

> *Her rejection caused him to be very depressed.*
> *Your kind words made me happy.*

In these cases, an antecedent event is still the cause; but it is not the physical properties of the event which make them causes, but rather their meaning or psychological impact. As we can see from the discussion of the influence of marijuana, physical properties of drugs can be candidates for causes of human behaviour or moods; but so can parental break-up and other psychological events.

How do we decide if a candidate explanation is true or credible? Let's look at a simple but familiar example. You try to print your assignment and nothing happens. Why isn't the printer printing? Is something wrong with the printer? Is the printer turned on? What about the connection to the printer? Your computer? A software problem? Or a hardware problem? What to do?

 What Do You Think *How would you go about determining why your printer wasn't printing the assignment?*

In order to determine why your printer isn't functioning, you would likely attempt to test the various hypotheses we just listed. If your printer has a self-checking capacity, you can print a test page just by using the printer. If that works, it looks like the printer is not the cause of the problem. You've eliminated the "printer hypothesis." Let's check the cable. Connected? If so, then it is probably not the connection that is causing the problem. We could eliminate the particular program as the problem by trying to print from a different program. If that does not work, we could reboot the computer. And so on.

Notice that we look for the cause of the problem by eliminating possible causes. The process is one of generating a hypothesis ("it's the printer"), thinking of ways to test the hypothesis ("print a test page"), and then eliminating false hypotheses ("it's not the printer because it successfully printed a test page"), until we get to one that is not eliminated. We use this process all the time in our lives, and this is also the process used in science. It is an example of **argument to the best explanation.** Eliminating competing hypotheses through tests, as we did with the printer problem, is one of the primary ways to justify an argument to the best explanation. If all but one explanation fails the tests, then we have very good grounds for believing that that is the correct explanation.

Before we look at the criteria for the "best explanation," we should point out that there are typically two focuses for explanations: particular and general.

Particular explanations focus on situations such as "Why did the printer not work?" or "What explains Nick's drug use?" The question is why does this particular person or thing behave that way? **General explanations** address questions such as "How do computers make printers work anyway?" "What causes ulcers?" or "Is marijuana a gateway drug?". This type of question is not directed at an individual or a particular event, but at a more general "why" question. In social sciences, a theory such as the gateway drug theory of marijuana does not claim to explain or predict the behaviour of any particular marijuana user, but rather it claims to provide an explanation for the general tendency of hard drug users to have begun their illicit drug use with marijuana.

Evaluating Particular Causal Explanations

While the evaluation of the explanations provided by particular and general causal claims involve different challenges, we use many of the same criteria for evaluating all proposed explanations.

The following guiding questions are appropriate for evaluating particular causal claims.

1. Did the Claimed Cause Occur Before the Effect?

Causal explanations of an event require that we find an antecedent (earlier) event to explain it. But in many circumstances, it can be difficult to know whether one event did occur before the other. And it is always crucial to the credibility of the causal claim that this be established. Did Nick slide into depression before his marijuana use or after? If he was depressed before he started using marijuana, that means that the marijuana use did not cause his initial depression.[5]

But beware of the post hoc ergo propter hoc fallacy, sometimes called the **post hoc fallacy.** What it describes is the erroneous leap to the conclusion that one event has caused another simply because the one event occurred before the other. This fallacy also shows up when we interpret coincidences as having a causal link. We run into an old friend, and say, "How amazing, and I was just thinking of you yesterday. I guess I have ESP." Superstitions are no doubt perpetuated by our tendency to causally link two unrelated events such as wearing our lucky charm and getting an exceptionally good grade on an exam. The difficulty is that even though these events have the correct temporal relationship of cause and effect, there is no credible causal link that connects the two events.

2. Is There a Credible Causal Link?

We refer to this question all the time. In the first instance, we use it to limit the range of possible causes to be considered. We don't think, "Maybe my printer doesn't work because I skipped breakfast this morning," although we might rightly think, "Maybe I am tired now because I skipped breakfast this morning." In the latter case, we know there is a causal link between not eating and fatigue so it is not merely the sequence of the two events that supports the causal claim.

Argument to the best explanation is a method of reasoning that is used to establish a causal claim. It involves showing that a particular explanation is better than any other hypothesis. This usually involves showing that other hypotheses do not fit all the facts.

Particular explanations focus on the question of why particular persons or things behave in a certain way.

General explanations are not directed at an individual or a particular event, but rather at more general tendencies.

The **post hoc fallacy** is the erroneous leap to the conclusion that one event has caused another from the simple fact that one event occurred before the other.

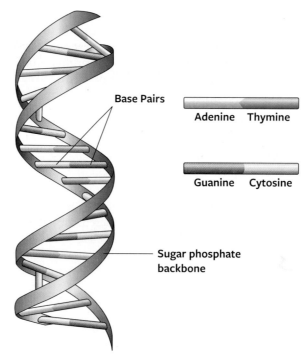

Base Pairs

Adenine   Thymine

Guanine   Cytosine

Sugar phosphate
backbone

**The structure of DNA—DNA is a double helix formed by base pairs
attached to a sugar-phosphate backbone.**

Scientists describe this notion of a causal link in terms of having a model (such as the double helix model of DNA) or theory. Much of science is focused on developing models which are a kind of picture that helps us conceive of how the world works. The double helix model of DNA pictured here is a typical example. Other examples are the model of the atom as a kind of miniature solar system, and the "greenhouse" model of global warming. We will discuss models in more detail in the chapters on the sciences (Chapters 12 and 13). But even in the printer case, we probably have some kind of vague model of how signals are sent to the printer causing it to print, a model which enables us to form a number of hypotheses about why it isn't working.

3. Are There Other Plausible Alternative Explanations that Fit the Facts? Can They Be Eliminated?

Remember the printer problem. We entertained a number of alternative explanations, all of which could explain why the printer failed to print our paper. In that case, we were able to experiment to test various hypotheses and eliminate at least some possible explanations. After printing a test page with the printer disconnected, we knew that the printer worked fine on its own. The explanation that it was a printer defect would now not fit the facts.

But in many cases of particular causal relationships, experimentation is not possible. There are no experiments to help us discover the cause(s) of WWII or why Nick is depressed. If we look at the discussion about Nick's depression in the dialogue, we can see that both Phil's and Stephen's explanations are reasonable. Both drug-induced depression and situation-induced depression seem plausible candidates.[6] Nonetheless, we can still often eliminate some competing explanations by showing that they don't actually fit all the facts. If Nick was depressed *before* he got into drugs, then the idea that it was marijuana that made him depressed (at least initially) just does not fit the facts.

4. Which Is the Simplest Explanation?

Sometimes competing theories, even if they fit the facts, can be eliminated because they are unnecessarily complex or redundant. Attributing the sunny day to my bringing an umbrella is easily dismissed for implausibility. But what about gremlins in the printer? Perhaps this, too, seems absurd; but importantly, there is a useful rule that explains why we would reject the gremlin theory of printer malfunction. This rule also provides a guide for adjudicating between more credible alternative theories. The rule is called **Occam's razor**, and (as applied in contemporary practice) can be stated as "all things being equal, choose the simplest explanation."

Occam's razor, as it is applied in contemporary practice, can be stated as "all things being equal, choose the simplest explanation."

In other words, only consider the less accepted or more complicated theory if the more commonly accepted theory (or simpler theory) does not work to explain the phenomenon. We can reject the theory that your lucky charm explains your doing well on the exam when we have the simpler explanation that you studied hard in preparation.

While we have focused on the criteria for causal explanations, we can apply most of the same criteria for evaluating a reason explanation. For example, John says that he is going to the store to get some bread, but we know that his girlfriend works in the store and we note that she is just coming off shift at this time. His wanting to see his girlfriend would seem to fit more facts. If we notice that, in fact, there is bread in the fridge, then we can pretty well reject his explanation and go with the girlfriend theory. The explanation could also yield a prediction that he will stay away longer than if he was merely picking up bread.

William of Occam (1285–1349) was a Franciscan monk who articulated the principle now known as Occam's razor: *"pluralitas non est ponenda sine neccesitate"* (plurality should not be posited without necessity). Occam's concern was to "cut" away a multiplicity of entities (often angels) that were unnecessary to an explanation. This has often been restated as the principal that we should be "parsimonious" (restrained) in the provision of explanations (or entities) and not provide complex explanations when a simple one will do.

The basis of Occam's razor was already well established in medieval thought, but Occam's clear articulation and frequent usage of the principle resulted in it having become associated with his name.

Evaluating General Causal Explanations

So far, we have only applied the guiding questions for identifying the best explanation to a particular argument. Now we will apply them (and a few additional ones) to general explanatory claims. The key addition is the question of whether there is a well-established correlation. To understand the implications of this question, let's look at the issue of whether marijuana is a gateway drug.

Correlation

Is marijuana a gateway drug? As mentioned above, part of the evidence for this idea was the prevalence of marijuana use in hard drug users. One of the responses to the gateway theory went as follows: since there is a high prevalence of early milk drinking among hard drug users, milk is a gateway drug. This is, of course, another *reductio* argument by analogy. Since it is ridiculous to think that milk is a gateway drug, if the prevalence of early milk usage among hard drug users is like the prevalence of early marijuana use among hard drug users, then clearly the gateway theory is ridiculous.

Does the analogy work? We don't think so. The proponents of the gateway drug theory would almost certainly argue that this is a straw person fallacy. The proponents of the gateway drug theory can (and should) make it clear that their claim is *not* that there is a high rate of early marijuana use among hard drug users (like a high frequency of early milk consumption); their claim is that the *rate* of early marijuana use among hard drug users is *higher* than the rate of early marijuana use in the population at large. This means that the proponents of the gateway theory are claiming that hard drug use and early marijuana use are correlated.

The Pickle Fallacy

Few people realize the deadly, terrifying ability of the pickle to kill or injure a person for life. Pickles are associated with all major diseases of the body. They can be related to most airline tragedies. Auto accidents are often caused by pickles. There is a positive relationship between crime waves and the consumption of pickles. If you don't believe this, consider the evidence:

- 99.9% of all people who die from cancer have eaten pickles.

- 99.7% of all people involved in air or auto accidents have eaten pickles within the 14 days preceding the accident.
- 93.1% of juvenile delinquents come from homes where pickles were served frequently.
- Of all people born in 1860, who later dined on pickles, there has been 100% mortality.
- All pickle eaters born between 1881 and 1901 have wrinkled skin, few if any teeth, brittle bones, and failing eyesight—if the ills of eating pickles have not already caused their deaths.

There is a **correlation** between two things when they *co-vary*.

There is a **positive correlation** between two things if, when one thing increases, so does the other.

There is a **negative correlation** between two things when, as one thing increases, the other decreases.

There is a **correlation** between two things when they *co-vary*. There is a **positive correlation** between two things when, as one thing increases, so does the other. There is, for example, a strong positive correlation between smoking and lung cancer. On the other hand, there is a **negative correlation** between two things when, as one thing increases, the other decreases. An example of a negative correlation is the correlation between exercise and weight gain. The more you exercise, the more likely you are to lose weight.

But here is the crucial point: to establish a correlation between two things, you need to make a comparison between relevant groups. For example, if all we know is that 4% of smokers get lung cancer, we cannot tell whether there is a correlation between smoking and lung cancer. To establish a correlation, we would need to know the rate of lung cancer among non-smokers (which is actually close to .01%).[7]

What Do You Think ?

What makes the pickle fallacy a fallacious form of argument?

Failure to consider relevant comparisons leads to the pickle fallacy—asserting a correlation without making appropriate comparisons. Pickles can only be identified as a health issue if the rate of health problems is higher among pickle eaters than among non-eaters. Without an appropriate comparison, there is no evidence of correlation.

To establish a correlation between two things, you need to make a comparison between relevant groups.

An important note: Correlation is not causality. That two things are correlated (i.e., co-vary) does not prove one is causing the other. Grey hair and the use of reading glasses are undoubtedly correlated, but grey hair does not cause eye problems. The number of doctors in a city and the number of robberies is correlated. This is not because doctors cause crime but because both numbers are a function of city population.

From Correlation to Causality

A correlation is a necessary condition for a general causal claim, but not a sufficient one. To leap from evidence of a correlation to the claim that two things are causally related is the equivalent of the post hoc fallacy reviewed above in relation to particular claims. For general claims, we will use the term **questionable cause fallacy** to identify any argument for a causal explanation that does not provide prima facie adequate evidence for the claim. A general causal claim can, of course, turn out to be false, or simply unjustified, without being fallacious. We continue to save the concept of fallacy for prima facie evaluation and the identification of obvious errors in reasoning. The guiding questions below indicate the questions that we need to consider to evaluate the evidence for a general causal claim.

The **questionable cause fallacy** is committed by any argument for a causal explanation that does not provide prima facie adequate evidence for the claim.

Even if there is a correlation between early marijuana use and the use of hard drugs, that correlation is not enough to show that marijuana is a gateway drug. To justify the gateway theory, it must be shown that there is something about smoking marijuana that *causes* people to turn to harder drugs. How can we tell if this is true? Let's use the relevant guiding questions for assessing a general causal claim:

1. **Is there a correlation between the supposed cause and effect?** As indicated, this seems likely.

2. **Does the cause occur before the effect?** Yes, that is the claim in this case.

3. **Is there a credible causal link?** This is a difficulty for the theory. For marijuana to be a gateway drug, there must be something about the properties of the drug itself that causes people to seek out harder drugs. The analogy here is with addictive drugs. For many drugs, the effect of the drug diminishes with time, causing users to seek more or stronger drugs. But there appears to be no evidence that marijuana has this property. So the evidence for the causal link here is weak.

4. **Are there other plausible alternative explanations that fit the facts? Can they be eliminated?** There are at least two other theories that are competing with the gateway theory. The social theory claims that social factors such as poverty and criminal association lead to both early marijuana use and hard drug use. The psychological theory claims that some individuals just have a tendency to drug usage—all drugs from alcohol to marijuana to cocaine. An article in the *American Journal of Psychiatry* summarizes the argument as follows:

> *Alternatively, abuse of illicit drugs, whether or not preceded by use of licit compounds [i.e., alcohol] may be more parsimoniously explained by their availability in the social environment and the level of the individual's liability that is common to all abusable substances [i.e., how prone the individual is to use all drugs].*[8]

5. **Which is the simplest explanation?** Note how the article makes reference to Occam's razor. These explanations are simpler because they utilize well-understood social and psychological theories about people's behaviour, and they do not require attributing to marijuana causal properties that have not been identified.

Evaluating Reason Explanations

The above account of explanations focused on causal explanations even though we said at the beginning that the method of justifying an explanatory claim, argument to the best explanation, also works for reason explanations. The following are the guiding questions for evaluating reason explanations:

1. Was the reason on the minds of the actors before they acted?

2. Is the reason the *real* reason?

3. Is there an intelligible link between the reason and the action?

4. Have plausible alternative explanations been addressed and eliminated?

5. Is this the most straightforward explanation?

As you can see, the pattern for evaluating a reason explanation is quite similar to that for a causal explanation. Unlike causal explanations, however, the actor is often the person giving the explanation, but the actor's explanation can be rejected if there are more plausible explanations available and if we have reason to think that the explanation offered is a rationalization rather than the true explanatory reason. Also, as with causal factors, people can have a number of reasons for their actions and the existence of one reason explanation does not necessarily refute the others. John could have gone to the store to get bread and visit his girlfriend. But the fact that there was no need to get bread tips the scale in favour of visiting his girlfriend as the *real* reason.

Keep in Mind

GUIDING QUESTIONS FOR EVALUATING CAUSAL CLAIMS

1. Is there a correlation between the supposed cause and effect? (for general causal claims only)

2. Does the cause occur before the effect?

3. Is there a credible causal link?

4. Are there other plausible alternative explanations that fit the facts? Can they be eliminated?

5. Is this the simplest explanation?

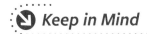

Keep in Mind

GUIDING QUESTIONS FOR EVALUATING REASON EXPLANATIONS

1. Was the reason on the minds of the actors before they acted?

2. Is the reason the *real* reason?

3. Is there an intelligible link between the reason and the action?

4. Have plausible alternative explanations been addressed and eliminated?

5. Is this the most straightforward explanation?

Apply Your Understanding
Exercises 3, 4

CHECK YOUR UNDERSTANDING

- *What is a* reductio ad absurdum? *Find an example in the dialogue.*
- *What is a precedent analogy? Give an example from the dialogue.*
- *What is a historical analogy? Give an example from the dialogue.*
- *What is a causal analogy? Give an example from the dialogue.*
- *Explain the concept of analogical distance.*
- *List four strategies for evaluating analogical arguments.*
- *What is a reason explanation? Give an example.*
- *What is a causal explanation? Give an example from the dialogue.*
- *Explain the term "argument to the best explanation."*
- *What is the difference between a particular explanation and a general explanation?*
- *List the five guiding questions for evaluating causal claims.*
- *What is the post hoc fallacy?*
- *Explain the principle of Occam's razor.*
- *Explain the following terms: i) correlation, ii) positive correlation, and iii) negative correlation.*
- *What is the questionable cause fallacy?*
- *List the guiding questions for evaluating reason explanations.*

EXERCISES

1. For each of the following arguments:

   i) State whether it is a legitimate *reductio* or whether it commits the slippery slope fallacy.

   ii) Explain your reasoning in each case.

   a) If you allow them to impose censorship on our school newspaper, they will soon censor the books and magazines in the library, our textbooks, and even the dictionaries and encyclopedias. Eventually, they will be telling the teachers what they can say and the students what they can think.

   b) We obviously cannot stop killing and eating farm animals and become vegetarians as some people recommend. For if we don't kill and eat farm animals, what are we supposed to do with them? Cows and pigs would roam all over the countryside, wrecking people's yards and causing danger on the highways. Obviously, it's better to kill the animals for food than to have them running loose and causing havoc.

   c) So, are you suggesting that we ban all dogs? This is the problem with you worrywarts when you get into government. You would have us all wearing seat belts at the dinner table because occasionally someone falls off a chair and gets hurt. I noted in the research that, while dog bites do represent an important source of injuries that show up in the emergency ward, dog bites are behind baseball as a source of emergency room injuries . . . Do you want to ban baseball?

   d) If an employer has to raise his operating costs—by raising the minimum wage, for example—he'll do other things to keep costs down, such as hiring fewer employees, spreading the work among existing staff, letting people go . . . Increasing the minimum wage leads to greater unemployment.

   e) Eight dollars an hour these days is only going to generate more and more poverty down the road. There are going to be a lot more homeless [people], and crimes will be on the rise since people aren't going to be able to afford to provide healthy environments for their children, with parents having to work two jobs, seven days a week, only going to leave their kids unparented and out on the streets meeting the wrong people and doing the wrong deeds.

2. For each of the following analogical arguments, work through the following process:

    i) State what type of analogy it is (precedent, historical, or causal).

    ii) Analyse the argument by using the table below (add more rows if needed).

Comparable Situation/Event or Precedent	Issue at Hand
Is like	
By analogy	

    iii) Evaluate the analogy using as many of the four recommended strategies (see page 87) as are applicable to the example.

        a) Not allowing women to go topless on beaches is gender discrimination. Men can go topless, so why not women?

        b) The U.S. should have realized that invading Iraq was a no-win proposition. You can't invade a foreign country to "liberate" them from what you see as political evils and expect to be thanked. Not everyone in the invaded country will see it that way, and you will end up with a war on your hands that you can't get out of. Didn't they learn anything from Vietnam?

        c) They laughed at Copernicus. They laughed at the Wright Brothers. They rejected Snow's theory of cholera, and now they laugh at homeopathy. But time will again prove them wrong.

        d) If an archaeologist finds a stone statue of a human figure in a field, he would rightly conclude that the statue was designed by an intelligent agent and was not a result of a random process. He would be justified in concluding this on the basis of the complexity of the statue and the purposive way in which the elements fit together. Similarly, living systems exhibit great complexity and the elements fit together in purposive ways in order to fulfill certain functions. Thus living systems must have been designed by an intelligent agent.[9]

        e) I don't understand all this teacher resistance to high stakes testing. Schools are like businesses: they produce a product—an educated student. Why shouldn't we expect schools to be efficient and accountable for the product they produce? If they're doing their job, then they shouldn't be afraid of comparisons and competition.

        f) People should not be critical of the new security measures. Some limitation of individual rights is justified in times of war, and this is a war on terror.

        g) Why shouldn't I believe that there are forces in the universe that control our destinies? So what if I can't see them? We can't see lots of things that scientists tell us about, like atoms and gravity and black holes, but scientists believe that they exist.

        h) This is daft. This is what leads to gun prohibition. People have perfectly good reasons for wanting to have guns—for hunting and sport, for example—but because guns are used by criminals, people like you claim that no one should have guns. People kill people with cars too; the problem is solved by prosecuting misuse, not the whole activity.

        i) My point was that we are anatomically capable of eating meat, so we do. Similarly, we are anatomically capable of having sex, so we do. It comes down to personal choice. Telling everyone to become vegetarian because a lot of animals are mistreated is like telling everyone to be celibate, because some women get raped.

        j) A fact that is conveniently overlooked by anti-capital punishment campaigners is that we are all ultimately going to die. In many cases, we will know of this in advance and suffer great pain and emotional anguish in the process. This is particularly true of those diagnosed as having terminal cancer. It is apparently acceptable to be "sentenced to death" by one's family doctor without having committed any crime at all, while it is totally unacceptable to be sentenced to death by a judge having been convicted of murder or drug trafficking (the crimes for which the majority of executions worldwide are carried out) after a fair and careful trial.[10]

3. Evaluate the following causal arguments using the guiding questions suggested in the chapter (see page 95):

   i) I was really lacking in energy. I read an article that said that carbohydrate consumption can make you feel sluggish, so I decided to reduce the carbs in my diet. I'm also exercising more and going to bed earlier. I'm now feeling much more energetic, so this low carb diet has obviously helped my problem.

   ii) Ever since I started wearing my lucky socks, I've been winning my tennis matches. I hope those socks never wear out!

   iii) Cities with large gay populations have the most thriving high tech industries.[11] So I guess gay people are good at technology.

   iv) I think that the reason that Phil doesn't eat broccoli is that he experienced some traumatic event while he was eating broccoli as a child and he unconsciously associates broccoli with unpleasant events.

   v) I was noticing that I was getting an upset stomach a lot after meals. I was wondering whether the cause might be all the milk I drink and cheese I eat. That made sense to me because my mother is intolerant to dairy products. So I cut out dairy completely and felt a lot better. Then I started to drink milk again and immediately felt worse. So I think that I'm probably intolerant to dairy as well.

   vi) Studies have shown that those who use hearing aids are more likely to have grey hair than brown or black. I hadn't realize before that hair colour is a causal factor in deafness.

4. Read the following scenario:

   All of a sudden Jack, your manager, who has never been very friendly, has taken to being very friendly at work with you and others. You know that he was seeing a counsellor, so perhaps that has helped to change his personality; or perhaps he has a new partner; or maybe he has won the lottery. Then you read a company directive from the human resources department that states that managers seeking promotion must be able to show that they have good and supportive relations with their staff.

   Describe the reasoning process you need to go through to determine which of the following is the best explanation of Jack's change of behaviour:

   i) Jack's therapy is working.

   ii) Jack has a new partner.

   iii) Jack has won the lottery.

   iv) Jack is reacting to the directive from human resources.

ENDNOTES

1. Doug Howard, "Letters to the editor," *The Globe and Mail*, Oct. 21, 2009, http://www.theglobeandmail.com/news/opinions/oct-22-letters-to-the-editor/article1332998/

2. The extent to which rats exposed to large amounts of a chemical for a short time is comparable to humans exposed to small amounts of a chemical for a long time is somewhat controversial, although the general use of what is called "animal models" is well accepted. For example, proving that a new drug is safe on rats is a usual prerequisite for experimenting on humans.

3. The Molotov cocktail is a generic name used for a variety of improvised incendiary weapons. Molotov cocktails

are frequently used by rioters due to the relative ease of production. *Wikipedia*, "Molotov Cocktail," http://en.wikipedia.org/wiki/Molotov_cocktail.

4. Shelley Fralic, "I'm a Big Loser Who Did Something about It; The Insidious Trend to Mollycoddle the Overweight Is Galling," The *Vancouver Sun*, Feb. 11, 2008 [Final Edition], http://o-www.proquest.com.library.capilanou.ca:80/ (accessed March 24, 2009).

5. It should be noted that in many circumstances causality can be circular. The recent collapse of the housing market in the U.S. started the recession but eventually caused the collapse in the financial sector which then caused an even

greater collapse of house prices, etc. Even if Nick's depression started before his use of marijuana, it is still possible that marijuana *now* contributes to the continuation of his depression.

6. There is another explanation not put forward in the dialogue; that is, that Nick has genetic tendencies to depression or drug dependency.

7. Michael J. Thun, et al., "Lung Cancer Occurrence in Never-Smokers: An Analysis of 13 Cohorts and 22 Cancer Registry Studies," *PLoS Medicine* 5, no. 9 (2008): e185.

8. Ralph E. Tarter, et al., "Predictors of Marijuana Use in Adolescents Before and After Licit Drug Use: Examination of the Gateway Hypothesis," *Am J Psychiatry* 163, no. 12 (2006): 2134-40.

9. *Wikipedia*, "Living Systems Theory," http://en.wikipedia.org/wiki/Living_systems_theory (accessed May 4, 2010).

10. Capital Punishment U.K., "Arguments For and Against Capital Punishment in the U.K.," http://www.capitalpunishmentuk.org/thoughts.html (accessed May 4, 2010).

11. Max Wyman, *The Defiant Imagination: Why Culture Matters* (Vancouver: Douglas & McIntyre, 2004), 40.

Chapter 6
Credible Sources and Appeals to Experts

Legalizing Marijuana II

Let's revisit the dialogue on marijuana from Chapter 5. As we mentioned in that chapter, one type of argument which Stephen uses is the appeal to authority. Stephen uses appeals to authority in these two arguments: 1) when he cites his school as a credible source of information on marijuana, and 2) when he cites his family doctor as a source for the claim that Nick is addicted to marijuana.

Stephen: *But marijuana is different. It's a gateway drug—it leads people on to harder drugs. We heard all about it in school last year.*

Phil: *I really doubt that…*

Stephen: *We also learned another good reason why marijuana is illegal. It's addictive and rots people's brains.*

Phil: *How do you know that? I bet that idea came from some anti drug-group—it's probably hopelessly biased. Besides, we all know people who use marijuana and seem perfectly sane and competent. Marijuana is actually safer than alcohol. For one thing, it doesn't make people aggressive the way alcohol often does.*

Stephen: *All you have to do is look at Sophia's cousin Nick to see the negative effects of marijuana. He's bombed all day and never gets anything done. He failed out of high school. He's a mess from the marijuana.*

Phil: *I'm not so sure—he was pretty messed up with his parents breaking up and his dad going to jail before he got into marijuana... His marijuana use is a sign he has a problem, but it's not the cause.*

Stephen: *I don't think you're right. I talked to my family doctor about Nick and he said that it's obvious that Nick is suffering from marijuana addiction.*

Both these arguments by Stephen illustrate a common way that we come to know things. Most of what we know, we know because someone else who should be knowledgeable told us. Our teachers and parents are a primary early source of knowledge. Books and other media quickly join in to supply us with what we believe is credible information. One of the great powers of culture and language is that very large amounts of knowledge and understanding can be passed on from person to person and from generation to generation. If we had to prove and discover everything for ourselves, we would know relatively little.

We need to realize, however, that the information that is passed on is not necessarily correct. The history of humanity records an enormous amount of intellectual and moral error. From the view that the world is flat and that the gods make lightning to the view that the oppression of women and members of various ethnic groups is justified, the history of human thought contains a vast collection of errors. In addition, not all of those who claim to know are credible. We rightly trust some sources of information more than others.

In this chapter, we discuss the criteria that determine the credibility of a source of information. Such sources are called *experts*, or more traditionally, *authorities*.

The dialogue continues.

Phil: Well, with all due respect to your school, I think that on the issue of drug information, they might not be that trustworthy. We know that schools are committed to telling students not to use drugs and giving them reasons for not doing it. And we know, rightly or wrongly, that most kids just ignore this stuff because they don't trust schools on this issue.

Stephen: Students are just being stupid and rebellious. They think that drugs, especially marijuana, are cool to use, and they don't want to know that they're harmful. Look at kids smoking cigarettes. Surely everyone knows that cigarettes are harmful. But they just ignore that information and smoke anyway.

Phil: I'm not saying that students are right to reject the information schools give them about drugs. I'm just saying that schools clearly have a bias, so we should do an inquiry before we just take their word for it.

Stephen: I suppose you have a point. Let's talk after you do some research.

What Do You Think ?

Why shouldn't we just trust Stephen's information?

As Stephen admits, we could check out the information provided by the school. But why not just trust it? There are three reasons. First, if a question is important to you, it is always good to dig deeper to check crucial information. You may hear that a particular hostel in Montreal is great, but if you are planning to visit Montreal, you would want to check the information. And now, because of the Web, the cost of checking claims has dropped significantly in terms of both time and money. There is seldom any reason not to check a claim of interest or importance. Second, it is widely believed that marijuana is a relatively harmless drug. The school's information has to go up against this popular view in the culture, so it bears a burden of proof. Third, we know that the government and the schools are committed to discouraging marijuana use. They may well have good reasons for doing so; but having committed themselves to this position, they have become interested parties and, as such, they could be a biased source of information. Remember, of course, that biased sources can be telling the truth; but it is wise to check carefully information from any sources which appear to be biased.

Stephen: Where are you going to get reliable information?

Checking sources is important if 1) the issue is important, 2) the claim is controversial and bears a burden of proof, or 3) there is reason to suspect bias in the source.

Phil: I don't know where your school got its information from, but when I went on the Web looking for information about drugs, I found one group that claims to supply information to schools. It's called The Addictive Drug Information Council. Here's a quotation from the council's 2003 paper against legalization:

The research evidence, contrary to what some say, does NOT suggest marijuana is in any way safe nor does it assure us we are not making a serious mistake if we increase our acceptance of and use of this substance. This is especially true given that marijuana today is quite a different substance than that experienced by many middle-aged Canadians. It is many times stronger due to deliberate cultivation to enhance the concentrations of the active ingredient, tetrahydrocannabinol (THC). The most recent and best-conducted research confirms that marijuana today is a powerful and potentially addictive drug.4,6,7[1]

Phil: That's a pretty powerful statement. And what's cool is that they have references.

Stephen: Did you check any of them out?

Phil: I did—I checked footnote 6 on the Web. Here's what I found. The study involved experiments on the withdrawal experience of a number of very serious users. They found people who had smoked on at least 5000 occasions—that's about 14 years of daily use! The researchers had the ex-users play a kind of game which was designed to measure aggressiveness. The aggressiveness was measured recording how many points a player subtracted from an opponent in response to the opponent's apparently subtracting points from the subject. As the researchers explained, when the experiment started, the people withdrawing from marijuana had the same tendency to subtract points as a group of people who weren't withdrawing. But when tested after seven days of withdrawal, the ex-users were more likely than the others to press the subtraction button. But here's the kicker: by the end of the month, ex-users were back to their original level of pressing the subtraction button and, therefore, their previous level of aggressiveness.

Stephen: So how does this prove anything?

Phil: It sure doesn't sound like even coming off a virtual lifetime of smoking marijuana has all that much of an effect. All I got out of it was that withdrawal from extremely long-term use can make people a bit nastier than they normally are for about a month.

Stephen: So that study doesn't seem to prove that marijuana is addictive. But don't you think that we should also look at the other studies?

Phil: Maybe. But before we do that, I think we should know a bit more about how to evaluate sources.

Even if we accept the report which Phil summarized above as a credible source, Phil discovered that the claim made by the Addictive Drug Information Council does not appear to be supported by this study. Phil only looked at one study, but his effort illustrates the benefit of checking sources which are supplied by groups with obvious biases. Note that what he discovered was not that the research was flawed; what he discovered was that the footnoted research did not provide support for the claim it was supposed to be supporting.

What we need to know is how to find and assess relevant and credible sources.

Evaluating the Credibility of Sources

Stephen: So we know now to watch out for bias, but that still leaves us with the problem of knowing where we can find credible sources of information.

Phil: Well, I certainly wouldn't go to your family doctor—not if we're looking for an opinion about Nick's marijuana use at any rate.

Stephen: What's wrong with my family doctor? I happen to think he's very fine, for your information. I trust him implicitly. Why, just the other day, my knee was acting up and . . .

Phil: I didn't mean to insult your doctor. I'm sure he's a wonderful physician. But he's never even seen Nick, for one thing. And I suspect he's never done research on the properties of marijuana, for another.

Stephen: So are you saying that we should go to researchers for our information? But they don't always agree. How do we know which one to trust?

Phil: I guess we can only really rely on their view when there's some agreement among the experts. Otherwise, all we know is that there are different views out there.

Stephen: But then we can try and find out their reasons. I'd be pretty suspicious of anyone who didn't give me their reasons—you know . . . "trust me . . ." We can look at the research the way you did to check out the school's information.

phil: Uh-huh—and we can check and see if it was published in a credible journal.

Stephen: Do you mean like *Maclean's?*

Phil: Not quite what I was thinking of. My dad was saying that some journals (the ones academics like to publish in) have this process for reviewing articles by other experts before they can get published. Peer review it's called. Known experts in the field decide whether the articles that are submitted meet the criteria of their area of study. So what appears should be reasonably credible.

Stephen: Wish I could have peer review for my exams before handing them in.

Phil: Right.

Stephen: And anyway, the one person I do trust in all this is my minister, and he says that using marijuana is morally wrong. It's abusing the body that God gave you to care for.

Phil: Forgive me if I don't defer to your minister on this issue. My rabbi wouldn't necessarily agree! But I don't take her as the expert here either. I think I have to come to my own judgment about moral issues, although I do take her views seriously since she's spent her life considering issues like this.

While using appropriate sources or authorities is the primary way we get our knowledge of the world, we should not be overly respectful or uncritical of scientific or other authorities.

While we generally have to trust appropriate sources or authorities because this is the primary way we get our knowledge of the world, we should not be overly respectful or uncritical of scientific or other authorities.

Why should we not be overly respectful or uncritical of authorities?

What Do You Think?

When we make an inquiry, we are almost always investigating claims in an area of controversy—perhaps one in which even experts disagree. To make a reasoned judgment in these situations, we need criteria for establishing what makes a source of information credible.

Guiding Questions for Evaluation of Sources

There are seven guiding questions you should ask in order to evaluate appeals to authority or expertise:

1. Is the claim from an appropriate domain of knowledge?
2. Is there consensus among the relevant experts supporting the claim?
3. Is the authority appealed to competent in the domain of the claim?
4. Has the expert had an opportunity to review relevant information before giving an opinion?
5. Is the expert trustworthy and free from bias?
6. Has the claim in question been subject to peer review or is it from a peer-reviewed source?
7. Does the expert supply plausible arguments or explanations for their point of view?

We will look at each of these questions in turn.

1. Is the claim from an appropriate domain of knowledge?

Expert-based claims must be in an area where such claims are appropriate. Certain kinds of claims are not appropriately settled or even supported by appeal to authority. One of the most significant of these types of claims is moral claims.

What Do You Think

Why do you think that moral claims are not appropriately supported by appeal to authority?

Moral claims cannot be defended by appeal to authority.

When people make moral decisions, they cannot say, as they often do about scientific claims, "I don't know, but they say you shouldn't." There are two reasons for this. As we will see below, a primary reason to trust expert judgment is that there is consensus among the experts. On those moral issues about which there is controversy, the experts themselves exhibit considerable disagreement. They disagree not only about a particular judgment, but also about what criteria to apply to make a particular judgment. This deep disagreement undermines any appeal to moral authorities to reliably adjudicate moral issues. Second, in a secular society such as ours, the responsibility for a moral judgment or decision stops with you. You can, of course, decide to obey the edicts of your church or government or even the advice of your friend; but it is still your decision and belief, and the responsibility rests with you. This is not to say that you should not listen to people who study ethical questions. They may well have insights to share. The crucial point is that you cannot appeal to their expertise to settle moral questions.

In aesthetic domains, where there is some degree of subjectivity (such as the discussion of Oscar-winning movies in Chapter 2), seeking expert opinion can also be helpful. But claims as to the quality of a movie cannot be *decided* by such an appeal. There is considerable consensus regarding some aspects of the arts; there is agreement, for example, that Bach, Mozart, Michelangelo, and Raphael were great artists, and that Picasso played a significant role in the history of modern art. There is not, however, the same degree of agreement regarding the assessment of contemporary work. Here there are often no clear and agreed-upon criteria nor, usually, sufficient consensus among experts to provide strong support for an appeal to expertise in this area. What interests practitioners in the field is often the inquiry itself and how it directs our attention to specific aspects of works and helps us to appreciate them. Arriving at a common judgment is a much less important goal in the aesthetic realm than it is in areas such as science or politics.

The physical sciences provide a broader basis for appeal to authority. If you want to know the speed of light or the molecular weight of oxygen, you can look them up in any textbook or ask any local physicist or chemist. There is virtual unanimity in these disciplines on these topics, and clear procedures and criteria for verifying the claims. But even these fields have their zones of dissensus, or disagreement. Astrophysicists can all tell you the speed of light and the approximate number of stars in our galaxy; but only recently have they reached consensus on the expanding nature of the universe, and at this point, they are unable to agree upon or even account for the particular rate of the universe's expansion. To take other areas of science, we know how old the earth is, although this question was settled only recently; and still more recently, there is a growing consensus that all *homo sapiens* emerged out of Africa. To the extent that experts in these fields agree, we, as laypeople, have good prima facie grounds to believe their claims.

We can also recognize, however, that, because of the challenges of doing research in certain fields, disciplines such as anthropology—even biological anthropology , the discipline that studies human origins—do not yield the same degree of certainty that a discipline like physics does. Non-experimental sciences will always be more subject to uncertainty. And sciences such as anthropology that are also vulnerable to the "luck" of finding fossils, tools, and other artifacts will never achieve the level of certainty that other observational sciences such as geology or ecology might achieve.

The characteristics of a domain of inquiry in which reliable appeals to authority can be made are these:

1. The domain is not an area characterized by moral autonomy.
2. The domain has widely agreed-upon procedures and criteria for establishing claims.
3. The domain is generally characterized by a significant degree of expert consensus.

2. Is there consensus among the relevant experts supporting the claim?

Even if the claim is from an appropriate domain of inquiry, if there is not a current consensus on a particular claim, then any appeal to expert authority is weakened.

Why do you think that a consensus among the relevant experts is important when appealing to expert authority on an issue?

What Do You Think ?

We are not saying that we should ignore or dismiss the claims of experts when there is expert disagreement. The point is that, when a claim is controversial within a discipline, support given by an appeal to any expert is weakened since one could also appeal to a counter-expert.

This observation illustrates a key idea about expert credibility: the credibility of experts is grounded on the credibility of the claim within their discipline. When there is no disciplinary agreement, a significant part of our basis for believing an expert is undercut.

Given expert disagreement, the most reasonable position for a layperson is to just admit, "I don't know because they don't know." But many of our inquiries will be driven by a need to make a decision on the best information we can get. On some occasions, this will mean taking a (fallibilist) position in areas where there is no reassuring consensus. The appropriate way to deal with such a situation is to study the competing arguments and do our best as laypeople to decide which view is most credible. Fortunately, on many matters, you do not need to make up your mind. You can leave the question about the existence of, for example, "dark matter" (which supposedly explains why the universe is expanding so slowly) to the experts to work out.

But as a citizen, you may need to make up your mind about the dangers and legality of marijuana use or the causes of climate change; and as an individual, you have to decide what to eat even if nutritionists disagree or exhibit a shifting consensus. Such decisions should not ignore expert views, but you will need to make them despite a lack of expert

The credibility of experts is grounded on the credibility of the claim within their discipline.

consensus. In these cases, you will need to make an inquiry and weigh the arguments pro and con, as we will demonstrate in Chapters 9 and 10.

Not only are disciplines not identical in their ability to generate consensus, but not all experts are equally credible as sources of knowledge.

3. Is the authority appealed to competent in the domain of the claim?

When considering the competence of an expert, we must also consider the kind of claim that is being made. As discussed in Chapter 5, the typical claims from science are general claims which form the basis of most scientific theories. In many cases, anyone competent in the field can give you the answer to your questions. So the criterion for expert appeals about general claims is that the expert is competent in the relevant domain of knowledge.

But when we turn to the *application* of general knowledge to specific cases, the kind of thing done by doctors and engineers, the particular expertise of the expert becomes far more important. Experienced doctors and engineers are widely sought because we know that the knowledge they have acquired over the years extends beyond whatever is contained in the scientific theories they are employing. Specialization is also relevant. We seek oncologists to treat our cancer (and ideally an oncologist who is a specialist in the particular cancer we have) because their greater level of specific expertise gives their claims and diagnoses more credibility. When building bridges, we seek engineers with bridge building experience, not experts in metal stress, although information about how metals handle stress is certainly relevant.

In summary, we seek experts with the most specific expertise and experience when dealing with particular problems such as these: Why does this car not work? Why am I experiencing this kind of pain? Where should we put the bridge? When dealing with general questions, however—How do motors work? or What is the function of the endocrine gland?—we can be confident if we get our information from a reliable source with the broadly relevant knowledge (e.g., a textbook).

We should also be careful of a phenomenon often associated with recipients of the Nobel Prize. Because of their renown, Nobel Prize winners' opinions are often sought on all sorts of topics for which they do not have the relevant expertise. Physicists' opinions on the safety of nuclear reactors may be better than yours and mine, but they are not as credible as those of nuclear engineers.

4. Has the expert had an opportunity to review relevant information before giving an opinion?

When seeking the judgment of an expert, we need to ensure that they have put their minds to the topic at hand. Especially in cases of particular and applied judgments, we need to know if they have done due diligence. Have they interviewed the relevant person or studied the relevant data? We should not rely on an expert's "off the top of their head" advice, as Phil points out with respect to the judgment of Stephen's family doctor regarding Nick's marijuana use. One could question whether Stephen's family doctor is an appropriate judge of whether any person is "addicted" to marijuana, as Phil, indeed, does. But in addition, it is clear that, without even meeting Nick, the doctor's opinion should not be given much weight.

5. Is the expert trustworthy and free from bias?

The expert sources should ideally be free from bias and self-interest in the issue. Depending on the issue and the integrity of the expert, the funding or ideological commitment of the expert may severely weaken his or her credibility. On the other hand, just because an expert has received funding or is on record as committed to a particular point of view does not mean that we can dismiss his or her opinion. (As we now know, that would be to commit the fallacy of circumstantial ad hominem.) But neither can we as readily rely on it.

When relying on the judgment of experts, we need to be confident that their judgment is not influenced by irrelevant considerations such as self-interest. It is disconcerting to hear that the advice on the appropriate vaccination regimen is coming from someone who is an owner of one of the vaccine patents. To claim that that person's advice should be ignored because of this is to indulge in the ad hominem fallacy; but to the extent that an expert is asking us to trust his or her judgment, raising issues of trustworthiness is not fallacious. Bias and self-interest are clearly crucial factors for assessing an expert judgment. In fact, for laypeople who know little about a field, assessing the trustworthiness of the source is one of the most important efforts we can make when evaluating the expert's claim. If the expert is trustworthy and free from bias, has the relevant expertise, and is informing us on an issue of disciplinary consensus, then it is reasonable to trust that expert's judgment.

6. Has the claim in question been subject to peer review, or is it from a peer-reviewed source?

We establish that experts have the relevant expertise in part by assessing their credentials. Peer review is crucial for establishing that someone is an appropriately well-informed expert, but it is also crucial in assessing individual claims. Expert consensus is a good basis for credibility in part because experts have the ability to evaluate the claims of their colleagues. While experimentation in science has contributed a considerable amount to its success, equally important is the role that scientific societies have served. Having to present one's views to one's colleagues is part of the process by which false claims and bad arguments are detected and rejected. It means that the consensus arrived at by experts is the result of successive review by peers.

This process, like any process, is far from foolproof. Sometimes even scandalously false evidence and claims escape initial detection by peer review. Peer review may also involve the rejection of true views. Nonetheless, as a layperson seeking credible and reliable sources of information, the best source is peer-reviewed information, in particular, information from peer-reviewed journals.

7. Does the expert supply plausible arguments or explanations for his or her point of view?

There is one more question we can ask. As the concept of informed consent in medicine suggests, even in the complex decision-making of medical practice, there is a level of patient understanding that the doctor must provide to enable the patient to give informed consent. This level may not be very high, but it is not the same as "I got the operation because the doctor said that was what I should do." It appears that many patients do make a decision on just such a basis, perhaps because of the deep psychological difficulties of dealing with their own health issues, or perhaps because they are not intellectually prepared to follow the doctor's argument. But equipped with the understanding of inquiry that you should have at the end of this text, you can and should attempt to ask for an adequate and plausible explanation.

Most scientific instruction in school is characterized by experts not only giving us the facts and theories but also showing how the theories can be used to explain how things work. The role of experiments in science education is to teach students to see how scientists verify claims and to see how scientific theories actually apply to the world. As students, our confidence in these presentations is very much dependent on our trust in the source; but when we complete such study, our understanding is not limited to merely quoting expert information. We should be able to go beyond saying, "I don't know, but experts say that..." We should also have a better understanding of the phenomenon in question and a

GUIDING QUESTIONS FOR ASSESSING APPEALS TO EXPERTISE

1. Is the claim from an appropriate domain of knowledge?
2. Is there consensus among the relevant experts supporting the claim?
3. Is the authority appealed to competent in the domain of the claim?
4. Has the expert had an opportunity to review relevant information before giving an opinion?
5. Is the expert trustworthy and free from bias?
6. Has the claim in question been subject to peer review, or is it from a peer-reviewed source?
7. Does the expert supply plausible arguments or explanations for his or her point of view?

Apply Your Understanding
Exercises 1, 2, 3, 4

better understanding of why the experts hold the views they do. The same is true for appeals to experts outside of school. If a doctor recommends a certain treatment, we can be told why: that it is more likely to succeed, that it has fewer side effects, and so on. If our car doesn't run properly, the mechanic can tell us that a break in the spark plug wire is causing the line to short to the engine, and that as a result the particular piston is not firing. You do not have to be a rocket scientist or even a car mechanic to understand that. And surely such an explanation is better than this: "I'll fix your car—trust me."

Those who argue that the climate is changing because of human activity do not simply make the claim but also present us with a plausible explanation consistent with current evidence: that CO_2 and other gases in the atmosphere trap and reflect heat emerging from the earth in a way similar to a greenhouse roof.[2]

The greenhouse model is a simplified but intelligible explanation. If we were to consider the theories of critics of this position, we would expect them to put forth an alternative explanation that is as plausible and consistent with the facts. As laypeople assessing information sources, we can and should take into account the explanation that experts provide. The failure of experts to supply an intelligible and plausible explanation weakens the credibility of their claims.

Fallacy: Improper Appeal to Authority

While the assessment of an appeal to expertise or authority cannot always be done superficially, we can often establish prima facie whether the appeal is extremely weak or even fallacious if any of the following is the case:

1. The appeal is not in an appropriate domain.
2. There is no expert consensus in a particular area. (In many cases, we would need to make further inquiry to establish the state of consensus in the particular domain or discipline.)
3. The expert appealed to does not have the appropriate expertise.
4. The expert has not had the appropriate opportunity to review relevant information.
5. The expert has obvious biases.

Failure of an expert appeal to meet the remaining criteria of an appeal to authority (see points 6 and 7 on page 107) weakens the appeal but does not necessarily make it fallacious. When we are doing an inquiry and looking for credible useful sources, we should seek out those sources that meet all seven criteria.

Fallacious Appeal to Expertise: An Example

SIXTY years ago, a Queensland farmer and amateur meteorologist, Inigo Owen Jones, produced long-range forecasts based on his observations of sunspot cycles. Many farmers in the state swore by his predictions, but he was discredited, even lampooned, by the scientific community. The Australian and New Zealand Association for the Advancement of Science, at its 1939 conference, totally rejected his ideas on cyclical variations. The Southern Oscillation Index and its El Nino effect were unknown then, but now we find science linking sunspots and the SOI ("Suns pulses point to drenching in the rain", 19/3).

Jones was no hayseed crackpot. He was descended from the famous English architect of that name; and on his mother's side, he was related to Daniel Bernoulli, the Swiss mathematician whose principle of fluids explains the high wind speed of cyclones.[3]

In what way does the story in the box illustrate an improper appeal to authority?

What Do
You Think ?

Finding Credible and Useful Sources

Phil: Let's try googling "marijuana addiction" and see what we come up with.

Stephen: My history prof says that we shouldn't be doing our research on the internet—that the Web isn't a credible source of information. We're supposed to go to the library and look in books.

Phil: Books are good, for sure. But it's so much faster and easier to do research with the internet, at least to get started. Then you can always follow up with the right books to go into more detail.

Stephen: Why should we believe what we find on the Web? Anyone can put up anything.

Phil: But there are some good websites. And besides, you can find books that say all kinds of crazy things, too.

Stephen: True. OK, let's have a go. Hey, have a look at this site—it's called *drugfreeworld.org*[4], and it has all kinds of information about different kinds of drugs and how bad they are for you. They list the long-term side effects of marijuana—things like psychotic symptoms, growth disorders, lung and heart damage, inability to learn, and reduction in male sex hormones. And there are a bunch of video clips of young people talking about how drugs, including marijuana, messed up their lives. It's a really cool website. You should check it out.

Phil: Sounds like anecdotal evidence to me. Who put up the site?

Stephen: A group called the Foundation for a Drug-Free World.

Phil: Do they look at any evidence or arguments that go against what they claim?

Stephen: Well, no.

Phil: What sources do they cite for their information?

Stephen: None that I can find.

Phil: I think I detect a credibility issue here. Not that some of the information might not be reliable and valuable. But I wouldn't rely on it without looking further.

Stephen: So what else have you found?

Phil: The article on cannabis (marijuana by another name) on *Wikipedia* says that studies on possible effects of marijuana have been mixed and that the long-term effects are not clear.

Stephen: *Wikipedia* . . . you've got to be kidding. I know that that's not a reliable site. We don't know anything about who's posted the information or whether they know anything about the subject. And other people can just go in and edit what's there.

Phil: That's what I used to think. But I read an article that claims that *Wikipedia* is as reliable as the *Encyclopedia Britannica* on lots of topics. Maybe that's because people have to use primary sources in their contributions.

Stephen: And, I guess, because there must be folks who keep an eagle eye on the articles and make sure nothing wrong or crazy gets in.

Phil: Anyway, *Wiki*'s only a first pass. We can always use the footnotes to check for credibility and find more information if we need it.

Stephen: Like you did with that information from the website of the Addictive Drug Information Council.

Phil: And besides, there are lots of reliable websites that publish credible material. Like the website of the CBC or other media outlets, for example.

Stephen: You keep talking about credible websites—but how can we know if they're credible?

Phil: I don't imagine it's all that different from how we know whether other sources are credible.

Using the Web

In the twenty-first century, the place where most people look for information first is on the Web. In fact, most begin their quest for information with the search engine *Google*.

What are some of the advantages and challenges of looking for information on the Web?

This is reasonable because of the great speed and ease with which one can use the Web and *Google*. But as we all know, there are no knowledge filters on the Web. The fact that a claim was found on the Web gives us no reason to think that it is credible.

But before we turn to the challenges of establishing authority on the Web, we need to ask what kind of sources of information are valuable to an inquiry. As the guiding questions for inquiry indicate, once we are clear on the issue, we need to look at the context for an overview of the controversy: its history and its social and political context (see Chapter 2). The sources most likely to provide such an overview, at least of popular contemporary issues, are responsible and credible media sources. While information from the media is never the last word on a topic, media often have articles that review the history and context of a controversy. Media such as the *CBC* or the *Globe and Mail* in Canada, *PBS* (Public Broadcasting) and the *New York Times* in the U.S., or the *BBC* and the *Guardian* in the U.K. frequently produce credible overview articles that can supply the kind of background we need to begin an inquiry. Popular science journals such as *New Scientist* and *Scientific American* can also be a useful preliminary source of context information and a doorway into primary research. On the issue of the decriminalization of marijuana, both the *CBC* and *PBS* have useful historical and contextual information available on the Web. These news sources are, at the moment, all free and often provide entry into an issue. One can access these news sources best by going straight to their sites. This is generally better than using *Google News* to search because that search will bring in information from a great variety of news sources of unknown credibility.

Another preliminary source of information is websites devoted to particular topics. Many of these are biased, and some are even designed for marketing purposes. But again, recognizing the bias of a site is important but is not a basis for rejection if the site contains useful and credible information.

On the topic of the decriminalization of drugs, there are innumerable sites advocating for such decriminalization and a few (often government based) arguing against. On this topic, it is very difficult to get clearly unbiased information (as the *PBS* site notes[5]). But that does not mean that these sites are without value. As noted earlier in the short inquiry into the claim that marijuana is addictive, the anti-marijuana site supplied useful footnotes to journal articles that one could then go to for further examination.

How do we evaluate information from a website? We evaluate it in a manner using guiding questions that are very similar to those we use to assess claims from supposedly expert sources:

1. Is the claim from an appropriate domain of knowledge?
2. Are the site authors or sources competent in the domain of the claim?
3. Is the site relatively free from bias? What effect does the site's bias have on the credibility of its arguments and information?
4. Does the site refer to peer-reviewed, ideally clickable sources for its claims?
5. Does the site supply plausible arguments or explanations for their point of view?

Another source of overview articles is scholarly **review articles** in peer-reviewed journals. These can help the inquirer not only establish the context and history of the issue, but also the state of expert consensus. In later chapters on science, we will discuss criteria for evaluating scientific articles. But as the discussion of the research used to support the claim that marijuana is addictive showed, we can sometimes make appropriate evaluations of scientific research just using basic critical thinking. In this case, the criticism was not that the research was in some way defective, but simply that it did not support the claim that marijuana is addictive.

Peer-reviewed articles are the "gold standard" (considered definitive) for research because their authors tend to meet most of the criteria for credible authority articulated in the guiding questions. The key issues when using such sources are 1) whether the arguments and evidence presented reflect a consensus of research, and 2) whether the argument presented is itself credible.

Unfortunately, access to most peer-reviewed journals is not free. But both public and post-secondary libraries will have access to many peer-reviewed journals; and using *Google Scholar,* you can often access at least the **abstracts** of the articles which will give you the basic idea of the information and arguments in the actual article.

In the box on the next page is an example of an abstract of a review article on the issue of marijuana addiction.[6] The abstract is free on the Web, and the complete article may be available at your university or college library site.

For some more superficial inquiries, the level of information found in an abstract may be sufficient. If you need to review the actual article, you will usually need access to the journal or a database that contains the journal.

✎ *Keep in Mind*

Guiding Questions for Evaluating Information from Websites

1. Is the claim from an appropriate domain of knowledge?
2. Are the site authors or sources competent in the domain of the claim?
3. Is the site relatively free from bias? What effect does the site's bias have on the credibility of its arguments and information?
4. Does the site refer to peer-reviewed, ideally clickable sources for its claims?
5. Does the site supply plausible arguments or explanations for the point of view being presented?

Review articles are articles that review the research.

An **abstract** is a brief summary of the information and arguments in a scholarly article.

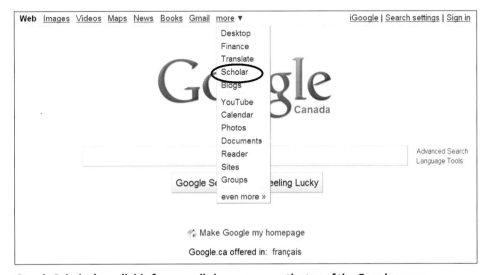

Google Scholar is available from a pull-down menu on the top of the ***Google*** screen (see screen shot). Once into ***Scholar,*** you enter your search terms as in ***Google.*** See your librarian for more details on this and the use of the databases and indexes at your institution to get access to peer-reviewed journals.

Example of an Abstract

Recent experimental papers have been published suggesting the appearance of withdrawal symptoms upon the cessation of cannabis use in human users and proposing the introduction of a diagnostic category for such symptoms. Research also continues to be published into the physiological effects of cannabis on animals via self-administration paradigms and the use of cannabinoid antagonists. Animal research does not provide a clear picture of a consistent withdrawal effect. The literature on withdrawal symptoms appearing in human users following the cessation of cannabis is investigated in this paper to clarify this issue further and enhance the scientific and lay debate on the status of the drug. Methodological weaknesses in the literature are highlighted. These include variable levels of drug-dose administered in laboratory conditions, lack of controlled studies and the absence of definitions of the withdrawal syndrome sought. It is suggested that the studies conducted to date do not provide a strong evidence base for the drawing of any conclusions as to the existence of a cannabis withdrawal syndrome in human users, or as to the cause of symptoms reported by those abstaining from the drug. On the basis of current research cannabis cannot be said to provide as clear a withdrawal pattern as other drugs of abuse, such as opiates. However, cannabis also highlights the need for a further defining of withdrawal, in particular the position that rebound effects occupy in this phenomenon. It is concluded that more controlled research might uncover a diagnosable withdrawal syndrome in human users and that there may be a precedent for the introduction of a cannabis withdrawal syndrome before the exact root of it is known.

Note that this is one expert's summary of the situation and it itself may be biased. A quick search of the medical research database PubMed *shows that this is an area of controversy among experts.*

Innumerable articles exist (on the Web, of course) explaining how to evaluate websites and Web information. But the Web presents no different a challenge than the library. While there is a vetting process used by some publishers, the mere fact that a book is published is little more reason to trust its information than that a text appears on the Web.

So how should we evaluate Web sources and websites? We can evaluate them by using the same questions that we reviewed above. Basically, a claim from a website is credible if the source successfully meets the criteria articulated in our questions about expert appeals and about credible claims generally. More specifically, we can ask the following:

Guiding Questions for Evaluating Websites

1. Who is supplying the argument or information?

- Is the supplier a *credible source* (government organization, academic institution, reputable publication)?

- Is there *bias* (obvious or not so obvious) because of financial support, commercial interest, or political bias (e.g., right wing, left wing, environmental group or opponent)?

- What seems to be the *motivation* for this site/study? (e.g., sell a product, push a particular viewpoint?)

- Does the site provide helpful information about its *sources/authors?*

- Does the knowledge of the source provide grounds for *confidence* or doubt?

- Does the source have the *relevant competencies* to support undocumented claims made on the site?

2. How is the argument or information presented?

- Is the tone of the presentation appropriate (e.g., not too many exclamation marks!!!)?

- Is the argument presented in an intelligible and reasonable form?

- Does the site depend on testimonials (fallacy of anecdotal evidence) to support its claims?

Wikipedia and Appeals to Authority

Our analysis of the criteria for appeals to authority can help explain the surprising success of *Wikipedia*. Most academics, the authors included, doubted that an open source wiki could supply reliable information. But thanks to *Wikipedia*'s insistence on claims being supported by primary research, and the remarkable willingness of informed people to monitor wiki pages, *Wikipedia* has proven as reliable on many topics as more traditional sources such as the *Encyclopedia Britannica*.

As we point out, when seeking information about general claims supported by disciplinary consensus, we do not need highly expert sources. What we need are *credible informants* who know the state of the disciplinary understanding. Our confidence in the source, then, is primarily based on our trust that the source is an appropriate informant. While it is true that it is virtually impossible to determine who the source of information is for a *Wikipedia* article, the reference to appropriate sources, the superficial credibility of the writing, and, at this point, the historic reliability of the wiki process provide considerable evidence that an article has been created by reasonably well-informed sources. But *Wikipedia* is still only a first place to go for most inquiries; it can be a good source of links to primary resources for more credible claims.[7]

- Are the conclusions/claims expressed with the appropriate level of confidence for the evidence supplied?

- In controversial areas, are a variety of positions reviewed and discussed?

- Does the site/author provide supporting references from credible sources (e.g., peer-reviewed journals), preferably with active links?

- Does the author/site help the reader get additional information, both pro and con? Is this easily accessed through links?

- Is the information current? Are dates given for the information?

One of the most famous information websites is *Wikipedia*. There remains considerable controversy about the status of *Wikipedia* as a source, especially in an academic situation. As you may have noted, we occasionally cite *Wikipedia* in this text. Used judiciously, *Wikipedia* is remarkably helpful for a certain limited kind of research. Since we do not know the authors of the *Wikipedia* article, we cannot assess the credibility of the article on the basis of author's expertise and trustworthiness. But we are usually given other information. We can make prima facie assessment of the argument/article quality and we can, as the editors of *Wikipedia* often do, check that there are appropriate footnotes which, in this circumstance especially, are the basis for accepting the claims in the encyclopedia entry.

Misleading or Untrustworthy Sites

An intentionally misleading and entertaining site is the site *Save the Endangered Northwest Tree Octopus* site at http://zapatopi.net/treeoctopus/pictured on page 115.[8] Besides common sense (tree octopuses?), the only way to detect its falsity is by noting the lack of references and the hokum way that "sightings" are "verified." But the site does demonstrate how easy it is to create a website that looks credible, but isn't. Check the footnotes.

The more typically non-credible website is one like the site about Cancer Fighting Strategies, pictured on the next page.

What problems do you detect in the Cancer Fighting Strategies website?

What Do You Think

Note the lack of footnotes despite the seeming precision of the numbers ("51 out of 65"). Note, as well, the air of conspiracy ("This is information your doctor can't tell you or doesn't know"), and finally, read the disclaimer in the fine print: "These statements have not been evaluated by the Food and Drug Administration. The products and information contained

Misleading Websites

Here's a description of just how misleading a site on the Web can be:

Imagine you're looking for information for your report about Martin Luther King Jr. You go online to *Google,* where you type "Martin Luther King." You notice that the fourth site listed is "Martin Luther King, Jr.: A True Historical Examination" (www.martinlutherking .org). You visit the site, and since you've never been taught to critically analyze Web sites for accuracy or bias, you have no reason to believe that what you're reading might be biased. The site claims to be "A True Historical Examination." Now an educated, sophisticated, and adult observer like yourself might notice that the homepage contains a few hints suggesting that this site isn't exactly what it claims to be. But these clues can be missed by a student looking for information. The site looks pretty legit and could easily be taken at face value by some…students. But to find out what it really is, go to the site, scroll down to the bottom of the page, and find the link to the site's host. Click on that link and see who put together this "True Historical Examination." You're in for a shock, as it's hosted by a white supremacy group. What better way for a hate group to get out their message than to disguise their agenda and masquerade their hate in a well-designed, albeit historically inaccurate, Web site. Keep in mind that anyone can put together a legitimate looking site.[9]

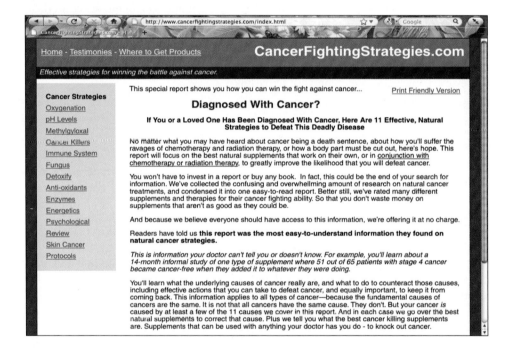

herein are not intended to diagnose, treat, cure, or prevent any diseases or medical problems. It is not intended to replace your doctor's recommendations."

One problem that especially plagues the Web is "link rot." Material, whether credible or not, can come and go on the Web with great ease. Links that are included on a site or in an article to provide support for a claim may turn out to be linked to non-existent pages. This is another reason to keep to peer-reviewed journals and credible media as sources. They will not disappear.[10]

Using Footnotes to Check Credibility

As a student, you may not be that fond of footnotes. Learning proper footnoting is a crucial task for academic writers which is why it is emphasized in most introductory writing courses. But while making footnotes may be a challenge and a bit tedious, using them is of

great value. The footnotes in *Wikipedia*, for example, not only provide the basis for credibility, but they also provide a doorway to further research.

As Phil showed above, however, the mere fact that a website or text has cited a footnote does not provide a basis for trust in a claim. Remember the guiding questions above. Presuming that we are in an appropriate domain for appeals to expertise, we still need to know if the expert cited and the disciplinary situation are such as to provide credibility. This often requires that we go to the cited article itself. This article will, of course, have footnotes which we may also want to check on. We can "drill down" as far as we wish in such a process, keeping in mind that as non-expert investigators, what we are looking for is mainly whether there is a reliable consensus among experts.

Phil: You know, Stephen, I realize now that what I need to do is to check out a review article. I found a pretty recent one, and in the abstract, the author states, "It is suggested that the studies conducted to date do not provide a strong evidence base for the drawing of any conclusions as to the existence of a cannabis withdrawal syndrome in human users, or as to the cause of symptoms reported by those abstaining from the drug. On the basis of current research cannabis cannot be said to provide as clear a withdrawal pattern as other drugs of abuse, such as opiates." Kind of a weird way of writing, but it seems that the evidence is just not there for a consensus on marijuana being addictive. When I looked for related articles, I found abstracts supporting all sorts of different positions. So I don't think we can be as confident as the Council is in believing that marijuana is addictive. But we can't just ignore the possibility either—you're right about that—though I do think that the Council's bias has led them to give a misleading impression of the research.

Stephen: Well, Sophia's cousin is a mess and I'm sure that the marijuana he uses isn't helping.

Phil : No one is saying the marijuana is helping or even that Sophia's cousin isn't suffering from using too much marijuana. The issue we started with was whether marijuana should be decriminalized and then you moved on to claiming that it's addictive. The evidence for that claim just isn't there. So it doesn't look like addiction can be a basis for arguing that marijuana shouldn't be decriminalized.

Apply Your Understanding Exercises 5, 6, 7

Using Books

We have focused on Web-based research because it is the most easily accessible and usually the most current research. However, depending on the topic and its importance, you may need to go to the library. Textbooks, although usually out of date in highly active fields, often provide the kind of overview that can give you a picture of the current understanding in the field. Just as there are key articles, there are key books; and if your research has revealed a particular book that many people refer to, then you probably need to look at that text.

Remember that the fact that a claim is in print, even in print in a textbook, does not make it true. You should note when reading scientific textbooks that they have ways of signalling the state of scientific uncertainty although they seldom emphasize it. When they say "Scientists currently believe…," they are giving you a hint that this is still an unsettled area of scientific controversy. This kind of introductory remark is in contrast to the more typical phrasing used to state claims that are uncontroversial: "The molecular weight of oxygen is…"

Getting credible information is a crucial part of any inquiry. It is also often a fascinating intellectual adventure. The Web has made this activity much easier than it once was. You no longer need easy access to a good library. Now that we have access to the Web, there is little need or excuse for just accepting what you have heard or read in the popular press. Checking on these claims, a form of inquiry itself, is something that you should be able to do with confidence once you have mastered the guidelines.

CHECK YOUR UNDERSTANDING

- *What are the questions you should ask of any appeal to an expert opinion?*
- *Why is appeal to experts not appropriate in moral issues?*
- *Can you find credible sources on the Web? How?*
- *Should you use* Wikipedia *for your research? Why? Why not?*
- *How does assessing a claim found on the Web differ from assessing claims made by experts?*
- *What makes an appeal to authority fallacious?*
- *Why should we care about footnotes?*
- *What is* Google Scholar?
- *What is an abstract?*

EXERCISES

1. Evaluate the appropriateness of the appeals to authority or expertise in the following arguments:

   i) Bill Gates has stated unequivocally that the new *Vista Windows* operating system will eliminate security issues and be the best operating system ever. As the inventor of Basic and former head of the largest software company in the world, he should know.

   ii) I'm against abortion because the Pope has decreed that it is immoral.

   iii) We have conducted an extensive review of studies claiming to have established the negative health effects of passive smoking. Our careful review has revealed some significant statistical anomalies and conceptual confusions in these studies. One should view with suspicion the correlational

and causal inferences regarding the connection between second-hand smoke and various alleged health risks which the authors have drawn from the research.*
(* Our thanks for the generous support from the tobacco coalition research fund for this important work.)

iv) I'm convinced that climate change is caused by human actions since I read an argument to that effect by the most recent winner of the Nobel Prize for literature.

v) I haven't had a chance to review the latest statistics, but as Vice-President of one of the largest corporations in the area, I would still maintain, as I have all along, that the current financial crisis is not severe and there will be an upturn in the near future.

vi) The cause of the problem in your heating system is rather technical and would be difficult for you to understand. But you can trust my professional judgment—I understand the problem and can repair it at a reasonable price.

vii) I realize that many of my colleagues disagree with my view, but my investigation has provided conclusive evidence that the rate of global warming is not increasing.

2. The following arguments are taken from dialogues in various chapters. For each argument, evaluate the appropriateness of the appeal to authority or expertise which is being made.

   i) **Nancy:** According to Pamela Anderson [a celebrity], who narrates the video, chickens are as intelligent as dogs and cats and, when they live in natural surroundings, they form friendships and lasting bonds with other birds, love their young, and enjoy a full life.

   ii) **Sophia:** I came across a really interesting article on animal welfare and factory farming, published by the Food and Agriculture Organization of the United Nations, written by a university professor who appears to have some expertise on the subject … He argues in this article that the situation is really more varied than many of the animal rights activists claim. There's actually very little research about how animals are treated in "factory farms," but what little there is shows a wide range of values and practices.

   iii) **Phil:** So now that we have all these views about the two films, what do we do with them? I mean, it's not like they all agree. That would make things easier.

   Sophia: But the majority of reviewers did like *Slumdog Millionaire* better.

   Phil: So I guess that decides it.

   iv) **McGregor:** Many dog groups claim that no dog or breed is inherently vicious—it all depends on training and environment. These groups point out that dogs that are poorly looked after and poorly trained (for example, dogs left outside on chains all the time) are particularly prone to attacking and that any breed can be trained to be aggressive.

   v) **Phil:** (in response to a newspaper article arguing for capital punishment) I'm thinking that the fact that the newspaper piece was written by a police chief is important. He does have a ton of experience dealing with murders and murderers, so he should know what he's talking about. He knows first hand the gritty reality of the crime world, and he certainly knows more about how murderers think and what motivates them than you or I do! So maybe we should take seriously what he has to say.

3. Suppose that you want to find out whether echinacea is helpful in preventing colds. Evaluate each of the following in terms of appropriateness as a source of this information, and explain your evaluation:

   i) your family physician

   ii) a spokesperson from a company which produces echinacea

   iii) a biologist doing research on the immune system

   iv) your best friend, who has told you that she has had excellent results with echinacea

   v) a prize-winning physicist

vi) an article by a journalist in a popular magazine

vii) a website entitled *Herbs for Healing*

4. Describe the kinds of sources (people and places) you would seek in order to get information or an opinion on each of the following (explain your choices):

    i) an explanation of how computers perform calculations

    ii) a diagnosis of a specific problem with your computer

    iii) an opinion on whether abortion should be allowed

    iv) background information on the war in Afghanistan

    v) whether the consumption of dietary fats is a factor in heart attacks

5. Evaluate the following website using the questions for evaluating websites. See exercise 6-5 on the textbook website.

    http://www.theantidrug.com/drug-information/marijuana-facts/default.aspx

6. Evaluate the following website on homeopathy. See exercise 6-6 on the textbook website.

    http://abchomeopathy.com/homeopathy.htm

7. Find three websites which deal with the issue of whether we should stop raising animals for meat, and evaluate each of these sites using the questions for evaluating websites.

ENDNOTES

1. The ADIC Website is no longer available, but the article by the Council is available online: Addictive Drug Information Council, "Proposed Marijuana Legislation Misguided," (May 27, 2003), http://www.boardoftrade.com/vbot_page.asp?pageID=910. The references within the quotation are listed below. Note that #7 is not primary research:

    4. M. Haney, A. S. Ward, S. D. Comer, R. W. Foltin, and M. W. Fischman. "Abstinence Symptoms Following Smoked Marijuana in Humans," *Psychopharmacology* 141, no. 4 (1998): 395–404.

    6. E. M. Kouri, H. G. Pope, and S. E. Lukas, "Changes in Aggressive Behavior During Withdrawal from Long-term Cannabis Use," *Psychopharmacology* 143 (1999): 302-308.

    7. "Marijuana's Adverse Effects," *Medical Information Bulletin* (2001), http://familydoctor.org/online/famdocen/home/common/addictions/drugs/485.html (accessed May 5, 2010).

2. A concise description of the greenhouse effect is given in the *Intergovernmental Panel on Climate Change Fourth Assessment Report*, "What is the Greenhouse Effect?" p. 115: "To balance the absorbed incoming [solar] energy, the Earth must, on average, radiate the same amount of energy back to space. Because the Earth is much colder than the Sun, it radiates at much longer wavelengths, primarily in the infrared part of the spectrum. Much of this thermal radiation emitted by the land and ocean is absorbed by the atmosphere, including clouds, and reradiated back to Earth. This is called the greenhouse effect."

3. Geoffrey Luck, *The Australian*, March 20, 2007 (accessed May 17, 2010, at http://pactiss.org:80/resources/media-articles-cartoons/meteorologistassociation.jpg/view).

4. Foundation for a Drug-Free World, http://www.drugfreeworld.org/ (accessed May 11, 2010).

5. *pbs.org*, "Busted: America's War on Marijuana," http://www.pbs.org/wgbh/pages/frontline/shows/dope/etc/synopsis.html (accessed May 11, 2010).

6. N. T. Smith, "A Review of the Published Literature into Cannabis Withdrawal Symptoms in Human Users," *Addiction* 97, no. 6 (2002): 621–32.

7. G. Giles, "Internet Encyclopaedias Go Head to Head," *Nature* 438, 7070 (2005), 900-901.

8. Zapato Productions, "Help Save the Endangered Pacific Northwest Tree Octopus, http://zapatopi.net/treeoctopus (accessed June 28, 2010).

9. Frank Westcott, "Intentionally Misleading Web Sites," Apr. 1, 2005, http://www.techlearning.com/article/3768

10. The University of California at Berkeley has one of the best sites on evaluating websites: http://www.lib.berkeley.edu/TeachingLib/Guides/Internet/Evaluate.html

Chapter 7
Identifying the Issue

Learning Objectives

After reading this chapter, you should be able to:

- identify the characteristics of an issue
- frame issues that are suitable for inquiry
- recognize problems of language use in how issues are framed
- distinguish factual, evaluative, and interpretive judgments
- identify the criteria according to which each type of judgment is evaluated

War?

Ravi and Winnie have run into each other in the corridor of their college.

Winnie: Hi, Ravi. Why so glum? You look like you lost your best friend.

Ravi: I have to write an essay on an issue of my choice for my history class. Trouble is, I can't decide what to write on.

Winnie: What issues are you considering?

Ravi: I'm thinking about war as a possibility.

Winnie: That's a pretty big topic!

Ravi: Yeah, I know. That way I won't run out of ideas.

What problems do you see with Ravi's idea of war as an issue for inquiry?

Winnie: I'll say. You'd have enough to keep you going for years! I really think that you need to narrow it down.

Ravi: I suppose. I could do the war in Afghanistan—that would be easy with so much information in the news. But we've been focusing on the Second World War in our course. Our prof says that World War II changed the course of world history in so many ways. Sounds pretty important. So maybe my issue could be World War II. That's a lot narrower.

Winnie: Well, it's a start. But that still covers an awful lot of ground. Why don't you choose some specific aspect or event that you learned about that interests you?

Ravi: Learning about the bombing of Hiroshima and Nagasaki at the end of the war really made an impression on me. It was such a major event—for the whole human race really. Why don't I focus on that?

Winnie: Good idea. But I think that an issue shouldn't just be a topic like "World War II" or even "the bombing of Hiroshima and Nagasaki." It has to be a question of some sort. What exactly do you want to know about the bombings?

Ravi: I'd like to know how many Japanese were killed. But I guess that's not really an issue. I can easily find the answer in my textbook or on the internet. It wouldn't make for much of an essay.

Winnie: Agreed. I think that an issue should be something that's controversial, something that people disagree about, not just a question where you can look up the answer—although I suppose that that question could be controversial if there's some disagreement about how the death count was arrived at.

Ravi: True. But I'm particularly interested in why the Americans decided to carry out the bombings, and whether that was the right thing to do. After all, they were the first ever (and so far only) attacks using nuclear weapons in history, and the targets were mostly civilians. How about this: "Is bombing innocent civilians wrong?"

Winnie: An ethical issue like that would be great. We discuss them all the time in our history class. And that's certainly an important one. But I think there's a problem with the issue as you've stated it . . .

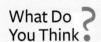

What do you think the problem is with Ravi's suggested issue?

Ravi: Yeah, I guess it is pretty general. It kind of gets away from the specific question of Hiroshima and Nagasaki.

Winnie: Not only that, Ravi, but do you honestly think that anyone would argue that it isn't wrong, given the way you've stated the question? An issue has to be a question that people actually do disagree about. There have to be genuine arguments on both sides, or it's not really a controversy.

Ravi: I've got it! "Were the Americans justified in committing a war crime by dropping atomic bombs on Hiroshima and Nagasaki in August 1945?" That's a lot more precise, it's a question, and it is controversial. Some people think that the bombings caused the Japanese to surrender and so prevented further mass casualties on both sides. Others argue that the bombings were unnecessary and immoral.

Winnie: Controversial it is. But the way you've stated the issue, you've already biased the answer before you start. The folks who argue that the bombing was justified don't think it's a war crime. They argue that it was necessary to "neutralize enemy non-combatants" in order to shorten the war and ensure an allied victory.

Ravi: That might be a good issue for my inquiry: Did the bombings, in fact, help bring about the end of the war? That would tell me whether or not the bombings were justified.

Winnie: Would it? I'm not so sure of that. Even if you found out that the bombings did help to end the war, that wouldn't necessarily mean that it was morally justifiable to use such a horrific weapon with such terrible consequences—and on civilians, too. That's a moral question.

Ravi: Yeah, I can see that. Well, back to my other idea. But I guess "war crime" has got to go?

Winnie: I think so.

Ravi: How about this: Were the Americans justified in dropping the atomic bomb on Hiroshima and Nagasaki in August 1945?

Winnie: Sounds pretty good to me. The only thing I'm wondering about now is treating the bombings of Hiroshima and of Nagasaki together: it could be that one was justified and the other wasn't. There are really two separate questions.

Ravi: Good point.

What Is the Issue?

At this point, we shall begin to work our way through the guidelines for inquiry, starting with the first guiding question: What is the issue? Although this may seem like a straightforward question, it takes some thought to identify a suitable issue for inquiry. Beginning with an issue which is clear, appropriate, focused, and well-framed is vital to the success of the whole inquiry process.

Beginning with an issue which is clear, appropriate, focused, and well-framed is vital to the success of the whole inquiry process.

Atomic Bombings of Hiroshima and Nagasaki[1]

In 1945, toward the end of World War II, the United States, at the executive order of the American President Harry S. Truman, took the momentous step of dropping atomic bombs on the Japanese cities of Hiroshima (August 6) and Nagasaki (August 9).

With the surrender of Germany on May 7, the war in Europe had ended; however, the war with Japan was still ongoing. The decision to drop the bombs was made after six months of intense fire-bombing of numerous other Japanese cities, and after an ultimatum to Japan yielded no results. These are the only attacks with nuclear weapons in the history of warfare.

It is estimated that the bombs killed more than 100,000 people by the end of 1945, with the five-year death total likely reaching or even exceeding 200,000, as cancer and other long-term effects took hold. In both cities, most of the dead were civilians.

On August 15, six days after the bombing of Nagasaki, Japan announced its surrender to the Allies, thereby officially ending the War in the Pacific and thus World War II.

What Is an Issue?

An **issue** is a matter which is unsettled, in dispute, or up for debate.

We might define an **issue** as a matter which is unsettled, in dispute, or up for debate. It may be a question about which people generally disagree or a challenge or puzzle of some sort. One kind of issue involves a disagreement over a claim—whether a certain claim is true or ought to be believed, or not. But issues may focus on other things besides claims; for example, interpretations of an artwork. We commonly deal with issues in politics or ethics, but issues exist in virtually any area of human thought and activity—in economics, environmental science, education, law, physics, the arts, and everyday life. So far in the text, we've come across issues focusing on such varied topics as vegetarianism, vicious dogs, films, the minimum wage, the legalization of marijuana, and war; and we will come across issues on many other topics as we work through the book.

Not just any question about which people disagree will constitute a suitable focus for inquiry, however. An issue for inquiry is one which can be examined through reason and argument. You and I may have very different views about whether chocolate ice cream tastes better than butter pecan, but this disagreement is based on individual taste and so cannot be settled through reason and argument (as we saw in Chapter 1). Thus, it cannot form the basis of an issue about which we can conduct an inquiry.

Issues generally arise naturally in the course of our activities when we are faced with conflicting views, challenges to our thinking, or questions which we want to investigate. The discovery that a classmate has become a vegetarian prompts the students to examine the issue of whether people should eat meat. The problem of vicious dog attacks forces the city councillors to consider the issue of what action should be taken to deal with dangerous dogs. The Academy Award results engage Sophia and Phil in an inquiry into the issue of which of two films is better. A news report involves Daimon and Nancy McGregor in debating the issue of whether the minimum wage should be raised. An issue potentially exists whenever there is some controversy, puzzle, challenge, or difference in point of view which can be examined in a reasoned manner.

The more we find out about a topic, the more potential issues present themselves, and the better we are able to refine the formulation of the issue.

The situation which Ravi faces in our dialogue is a little different. Rather than beginning with some pressing question, Ravi begins with the task of having to conduct an inquiry and faces the challenge of finding an issue on which to base the inquiry. Winnie wisely points out that he should let his own knowledge be his guide, as well as his interests and curiosity. We can only know what is controversial or unsettled about some topic when we know something about the topic; and the more we find out, the more potential issues present themselves, and the better we are able to refine the formulation of the issue.

Characteristics of an Issue

Given what an issue involves, there are certain features which characterize the kinds of issues which are suitable as a focus for inquiry.

Focus

An issue should not be too broad. If the issue is too encompassing, it will be difficult to deal with it in sufficient detail and do justice to its subtleties and complexities. It will also be difficult to address the various sides of the issue and examine the various aspects of context. An inquiry which focuses on an issue that is too broadly framed runs the risk of superficiality. It is, therefore, important to limit the scope of the issue by focusing on a specific aspect or aspects which are of particular relevance to the task and of particular interest to the person conducting the inquiry. Ravi's first attempt at an issue, war, is much too broad, and even his second attempt, World War II, is not much better in this respect.

Question versus Topic

An issue needs to be distinguished from a topic. A topic is a general subject such as the minimum wage, capital punishment, vegetarianism, or war. But such general formulations do not indicate what we want to find out about the topic. Do we want to know what causes wars? whether wars are correlated with subsequent economic prosperity? whether war can be avoided? whether war is ever justified? In order to get at what is under debate or at stake, an issue needs to be formulated as a question. Some examples of issues would be these: "Should the minimum wage be raised?", "Should there be capital punishment for murder?", or "Should we eat meat?" Ravi's first ideas for his essay (war, World War II, the bombing of Hiroshima and Nagasaki) are lacking on a number of grounds; but one of these is that they are not issues but rather topics.

Precision

In order to give rise to a productive inquiry, it is important that the statement of the issue not be overly vague; rather, it should be clear and precise. We need to know what exactly is the claim under discussion or the question at issue. If our issue is "Should the minimum wage be increased?", then this leaves open the question "by how much?" The inquiry might take a very different form if people are arguing for a ten cent increase rather than for a ten dollar increase. If the issue is "Should there be capital punishment?", then we want to ask, "for which crimes?" There are, after all, countries where there is capital punishment for adultery (as Sophie points out in Chapter 8). If we are inquiring into whether we should eat animals, then the inquiry may have different outcomes depending on which animals we are thinking of; for example, Nancy is opposed to eating meat but is not certain of her position regarding fish. And if we are focusing on the issue of whether the Americans were justified in bombing Hiroshima and Nagasaki, then it is important to separate the issue into two questions since each question may have a different answer.

Features that characterize an issue that is suitable for inquiry are that it is focused, precise, controversial, formulated as a question, and stated in neutral language.

Controversy

Because an issue is a matter which is unsettled or in dispute, an inquiry cannot be directed towards some information or state of affairs that is generally known or accepted. Questions such as "Does the earth revolve around the sun?", "Is smoking bad for your health?", or "When did Canada enter WWII?" are not appropriate issues for inquiry as these are not "live" questions but are considered settled according to current consensus (although the first two were controversial at one time). In addition, because issues are manifestations of controversy, there must be at least two plausible sides to any issue (usually more). Cases where people would not actually disagree or where there are no genuine arguments on one side—for example, "Is bombing innocent civilians wrong?"—do not make for real inquiry.

Neutrality

Ravi's proposed issue "Were the Americans justified in committing a war crime by dropping atomic bombs on Hiroshima and Nagasaki?" is problematic because the language he uses biases the nature of the inquiry from the beginning. **Framing** the issue in terms of a "war crime" implies that the action was not justifiable and so begs the question that is supposed to be under investigation. The use of particular language or concepts can slant an inquiry in a certain direction and inhibit a fair consideration of all sides of the question. Compare, for example, the following two formulations of the issue regarding what to do about vicious dog attacks: "Should we accept greater government control of private issues like dog ownership?" versus "Does government have an obligation to protect its citizens from inherently vicious dogs?" Each of these formulations is based on certain assumptions which would not

Framing an issue refers to setting up an issue in terms of a particular set of concepts which suggest a certain way of looking at the issue.

*Apply Your
Understanding
Exercises 1, 2, 3*

be accepted by those who hold the opposing view and so neither one constitutes a useful way to frame the issue. Instead, an issue should be framed in as neutral a manner as possible, in such a way that the various contending parties would agree to the formulation. (We'll look at this problem in more detail in the section on loaded language below.)

Problems with Language

Many of the examples above demonstrate the power of language in shaping our thoughts and point to the importance of being aware of the pitfalls and traps of language that we may fall into when attempting to frame an issue for inquiry. Such problematic use of language is often accidental, but it can also be the result of a deliberate attempt to mislead or confuse. We summarize some of the potential problems with language below.

Lack of Clarity

It is vitally important that an issue be stated clearly so that it is obvious what is at stake and what would count for and against various judgments. A lack of clarity may result in confusion and make it difficult to assess a claim or judgment. There are several common ways in which language may suffer from a lack of clarity.

Vagueness

Vagueness occurs when terms are imprecise so that the range of their application is not clear. Terms such as "bald" or "rich" are vague terms since it is not clear exactly how few hairs one has to have to be considered bald or exactly how much money one has to have to be considered rich. It is clear that Howie Mandel is bald and Céline Dion is not, but there are many borderline cases when it is not obvious whether the term applies. Similarly, we can assert with some confidence that Conrad Black is (or was) rich and the homeless person on the corner is not, but what about the many cases in between?

In addition, the appropriate range of a vague term is often determined by context: a person considered young in a seniors' home might be considered old in a college classroom. Although the preceding examples are not overly problematic, there are cases where there will be debate over the range of application of a term, as a great deal may hang on what is and is not encompassed by certain terms. For example, whether the term "person" extends to fetuses is at the centre of the abortion debate. And many legal debates focus on the appropriate range and application of terms such as "pre-meditated murder" or "rape."

> **What Do You Think?**
>
> *Can you think of some other examples where the vagueness of the language creates a problem in terms of the application of a term?*

Although some degree of vagueness is a normal aspect of language usage, problems occur when a term is too vague to do its job, and thus it becomes difficult to evaluate a claim. This type of problem of vagueness is particularly troublesome when framing an issue, as for example in these formulations: "Should the minimum wage be increased?", "Should there be capital punishment?", or "Should we eat animals?" In such cases, further specification of the issue is required in order to provide the starting point for a productive inquiry.

Generality

The less detailed or specific a term is, the more **general** we say it is. Thus "food" is a more general term than "vegetable," "vegetable" is more general than "root vegetable," and "root vegetable" is more general than "carrot." Generality becomes a problem when the term lacks sufficient detail for the purposes at hand and raises problems for evaluating

Vagueness occurs when terms are imprecise so that the range of their application is not clear.

Problems occur when a term is too vague to do its job, and it thus becomes difficult to evaluate a claim or judgment.

The less detailed or specific a term is, the more **general** we say it is.

claims. For example, if an issue is framed as "Should pets be allowed in apartments?", the term "pets" might be too general to make an appropriate evaluation as "pets" could include anything from a Labrador retriever to a tiny bird kept in a cage, and the arguments which apply to one (e.g., they're too large for apartments) might not apply to the other. Ravi's proposed issue, "Is bombing innocent civilians wrong?" is problematic for many reasons, but one of these is that, since he is interested in the specific case of the bombing of Hiroshima and Nagasaki, this framing is much too general.

Ambiguity

A term is **ambiguous** when it has multiple meanings or interpretations and it is not clear which interpretation is meant. Ambiguity can occur in a number of ways. Particular words or phrases can be ambiguous (**semantic ambiguity**). When the ambiguity is accidental, the resulting misunderstanding can be quite humourous. Take, for example, these headlines, all of which are examples of semantic ambiguity:

> *Defendant's speech ends in long sentence*
>
> *Hospitals are sued by 7 foot doctors*
>
> *Prostitutes appeal to Prime Minister*

Ambiguity can also result from problems in sentence structure (**syntactic ambiguity**), as, for example, in the headline "Two sisters reunited after 18 years at checkout counter," or the ad "Wanted: Man to take care of cow that does not smoke or drink."

In some cases, arguers may deliberately trade on an ambiguity to confuse or evade an issue. This deliberate use of ambiguity is called **equivocation.** A well-known example is the British Prime Minister Benjamin Disraeli's standard response when he received unsolicited manuscripts: "Many thanks; I shall lose no time in reading it." When used in an argument, equivocation is a fallacy because it involves changing the meaning of a term that is key to the validity of an argument (see Chapter 4).

Because of the possibility of misunderstanding regarding meanings, ambiguity can create problems when framing an issue. In the next part of the dialogue, Ravi mentions this as a possible issue: "How could good scientists have built the atom bomb?" The problem here is that the term "good" can have two different meanings, either good in the sense of proficient or good in the moral sense. The scientists who achieved the difficult tasks of building the bomb were clearly good in the sense of proficient; but we don't know beforehand whether they were (or were not) morally good—that itself is an issue we might want to inquire about. So the issue, as framed, takes advantage of that ambiguity.

Loaded Language

In addition to the literal meaning of words and expressions or what they refer to (their **denotation**), many words and expressions also have associations connected with them (their **connotations**) and may conjure up particular images or emotions. Thus it is often possible to use different words with different connotations to describe the same phenomenon, thereby evoking different reactions. Think of how different our reaction is to a location which is referred to as "colourful" rather than as "sleazy," or to a person who is called "interfering" as opposed to "concerned." The philosopher Bertrand Russell's well-known example makes this point nicely: "I am firm; you are stubborn; he is a pig-headed fool." In each of these cases, there are different value associations and emotional loadings connected with the various terms: some of the connotations have a positive force, either mild or strong; some have a negative association; and some terms may also be relatively neutral.

Because of the differing emotional connotations of words or expressions, the choice of language used to frame issues and arguments can affect and even slant the direction of inquiry, as we saw in our discussion of neutrality. Consider the differing effects of using

Generality becomes a problem when the term lacks sufficient detail for the purposes at hand and raises problems for evaluating claims.

A term is **ambiguous** when it has multiple meanings or interpretations and it is not clear which interpretation is meant:
- **Semantic ambiguity** occurs when particular words or phrases are ambiguous.
- **Syntactic ambiguity** occurs when the ambiguity is a result of the sentence structure.
- **Equivocation** is the deliberate use of ambiguity.

Because of the possibility of misunderstanding regarding meanings, ambiguity can create problems when framing an issue.

Denotation refers to the literal meaning of a word.

Connotation refers to the associations connected with a particular word.

Because of the differing emotional and value connotations of words or expressions, the choice of language used to frame issues and arguments can affect and even slant the direction of inquiry.

Euphemism refers to the use of emotionally neutral or positively charged words to substitute for highly charged negative ones.

Certain ways of framing an issue may prevent us from examining all sides of the issue since some positions are eliminated from consideration even before the inquiry begins.

Apply Your
Understanding
Exercises 4, 5, 6, 7

the terms "terrorists," "rebels," "guerillas," or "freedom fighters" when inquiring into the justification of a military action. In our dialogue, compare the value assumptions and emotional loading of describing the bombings of Hiroshima and Nagasaki as "bombing innocent civilians" versus "neutralizing enemy non-combatants."

In some cases, the strong positive or negative charge on language is entirely appropriate, as when referring to the mass murder of a large part of an ethnic group as a "genocide." But loaded language is problematic when used to raise emotional reactions in a way that is unjustifiable or controversial; for example, using "genocide" to refer to discrimination against a group of people.

On the other hand, emotionally neutral words or even positively charged words can be used to substitute for highly charged negative words or phrases which suggest something unpleasant. These are called **euphemisms.** Using euphemisms can take down the emotional level and encourage people to be less distressed about some distressing event or action or even to be positively disposed toward it. Many terms used by the military, for example, "collateral damage" (unintended killings) or "friendly fire" (firing on one's own troops) are attempts to make unacceptable actions sound innocuous. The phrase which Winnie refers to in the dialogue, "neutralize enemy non-combatants," is an example of a euphemism which is used to lessen one's negative reaction to the killing of civilians, thereby biasing the inquiry in a certain direction. Political talk and economic discourse are also fertile grounds for this type of language sleight-of-hand, with terms like "downsizing" and "economic correction" used to lessen the impact of what would normally be perceived as highly undesirable events.

These questions of language become particularly important in the framing of an issue as certain formulations will slant the inquiry in a particular direction. Compare, for example, the following formulations of the abortion issue:

> *Does an unborn child have a right to life?*
>
> *Does a fetus have rights?*
>
> *Should a woman have freedom of choice regarding her body?*

Each of these formulations contains assumptions that are controversial and would be the subject of debate in the inquiry, but these considerations are bypassed in each case because of the way the issue has been framed. Along the same line, compare these formulations of the issue regarding increasing the minimum wage: "Should we accept greater government interference in the economy?" versus "Should we pay people so little that they don't have enough to eat?" In both cases, some of the assumptions in question are built into the way the issue is framed. Thus such formulations may prevent us from examining all sides of an issue since some positions are eliminated from consideration even before the inquiry begins. We saw previously how Ravi's formulation of his issue as "Were the Americans justified in committing a war crime...?" suffers from a similar problem of framing since the term "war crime" prejudges the issue before the argumentation even begins.

Types of Judgments

The dialogue continues.

Ravi: I just had another idea for an issue I could write about. I'm thinking I could inquire into the role of the scientists who developed the bomb.

Winnie: Mmm...that sounds really interesting. What aspect would you like to focus on?

Ravi: Well, we learned in our class that some of the scientists who were working on the Manhattan Project—that's the project to build the bomb—started having qualms about participating, especially as it got later in the war and they started learning more about the effects of a nuclear explosion. I'd really be interested in looking into that.

Canada and the First Atomic Bombs[2]

Not many Canadians are aware of Canada's role in the Atomic Bomb project that led to the bombings of Hiroshima and Nagasaki at the end of the Second World War. The uranium for the bombs was contributed by Canada from its mine in Great Bear Lake. In addition, numerous Canadian scientists collaborated in the project. The most well-know of these, Louis Slotin, a young scientist from Winnipeg, died a year after the bombings due to a massive and fatal dose of radiation. Serious health consequences were also suffered by the Dene people who worked the mine. Canadians were not informed about Canadian participation until 1945, after the bombing of Hiroshima, when government Minister C.D. Howe, read a prepared statement for the press: "It is a distinct pleasure for me to announce... that Canadian scientists have played an intimate part, and have been associated in an effective way with this great scientific development."

What are some possible issues that Ravi could investigate on this topic?

What Do You Think ?

Winnie: What would your issue be?

Ravi: How about this: "Should scientists have continued to work on developing the atomic bomb after they became aware of its possible consequences?"

Winnie: Great idea! But I'm thinking that the word "should" is kind of ambiguous. Do you want to know whether continuing to work on the project was the right thing to do morally? Or are you interested in whether it was the best thing to do for practical reasons—for example, was it the best use of resources? I could imagine someone arguing that the scientists should not have continued to work on the bomb since it would have been more efficient to have them focus on some other aspect of the war effort. But this wouldn't get at the morality of the action.

Ravi: I'm definitely interested in the moral question. But now I have to figure out how to go about inquiring into that issue.

Winnie: Why don't you start by looking at the reasons the scientists gave for wanting to stop or to continue.

Ravi: People who supported building the bomb claimed that having the bomb would expedite the end of the war and save American lives. So I'll need to look into whether that's true. But the scientists who were opposed to continuing were very concerned about the possible consequences of nuclear weapons—like radiation hazards, the proliferation of weapons, and the potential for mass destruction. So I'll need to investigate what the risks actually were.

Winnie: Also, how likely were these risks? Might there have been ways to control these risks—for example, by controlling the spread of nuclear weapons? And how serious would the consequences be if they happened?

Ravi: After I look at all those issues, I'll need to see how all the reasons for and against stack up. I know that the scientists who were opposed to continuing believed that the risks of developing the bomb far outweighed any possible benefit, and I'll have to evaluate whether they were right.

Winnie: Exactly.

Ravi: And that should give me the answer to the question of whether the scientists should have continued working on the bomb.

Scientists and Responsibility[3]

Joseph Rotblatt, winner of the Nobel Peace Prize and the only scientist to withdraw from the Manhattan Project for reasons of conscience, has always been clear about the responsibility of the scientist:

"We scientists have to realise that what we are doing has an impact not only on the life of every individual, but also on the whole destiny of humankind.

All of us who want to preserve the human race owe an allegiance to humanity; and it's particularly the job of scientists, because most of the dangers to the world result from the work of scientists."

Winnie: Not so fast, Ravi. There's still a really important ethical issue that you haven't considered. I know that some scientists think that their job is strictly to focus on scientific matters and that it isn't their job to worry about how their discoveries are used. So I think you'll need to look at whether scientists have some moral responsibility for the work they do and what they find.

Ravi: I can see that. Obviously those who developed the bomb were good scientists, and I've been wondering how good scientists could have built something as destructive as the atomic bomb. Certainly the scientists who had qualms about continuing to work on the project believed that they did have some responsibilities for the results of their work. In fact, one of them, Joseph Rotblatt, went so far as to withdraw from the Manhattan Project in 1944 and put his efforts into organizing scientists worldwide to oppose nuclear weapons.

What Do You Think ?

Do you think that scientists have a moral responsibility for the results of their work?

It is important to understand what types of judgments are called for by the inquiry which we are undertaking because different types of judgments are supported by different types of reasons and arguments and are evaluated by different criteria.

Ravi has come up with a number of possible issues for his history essay. In the end, he has narrowed it down to two possibilities. In the first dialogue, he homes in on this issue: "Were the Americans justified in dropping the atomic bomb on Hiroshima and Nagasaki in August 1945?" In the second dialogue, he is considering focusing on a different issue: "Should scientists have continued to work on developing the atomic bomb after they became aware of its possible consequences?" But he realizes that he will need to consider a number of related issues when conducting either inquiry.

There are some differences among the issues which Ravi considers in terms of the kinds of judgments required in each case. The two issues mentioned above call for ethical judgments; but judgments focusing on factual description, scientific explanation, causal history, and political policy also feature in some of the related issues. It is important to understand what types of judgments are called for by the inquiry which we are undertaking because different types of judgments are supported by different types of reasons and arguments and are evaluated by different criteria.

Although there is a range of types of judgments, they can be categorized broadly into three types: factual judgments (including descriptive and explanatory judgments), evaluative judgments, and interpretive judgments.

Factual Judgments

Factual judgments (or judgments of fact) focus on describing or explaining some aspect of the way the world is.

As commonly used, the terms "fact" and "factual" are ambiguous. **Factual judgments** (or judgments of fact) are judgments which focus on describing or explaining some aspect of the way the world is. But to say that a claim is a fact is another way of saying that the claim is true; that is, that it expresses a correct description or explanation. Because of this ambiguity, the term "factual" may cause confusion: it may conjure up the idea of claims which are certain and beyond dispute.

It is important to keep in mind, however, that factual judgments, like all judgments, are fallible and subject to revision in the light of new evidence and arguments.

Descriptive Judgments

Descriptive judgments describe states of affairs.

Some factual judgments simply describe states of affairs. We shall refer to these as **descriptive judgments.** The assertion that approximately 160,000 people were killed by the bombing of Hiroshima is a descriptive judgment. In this example, the judgment is not particularly controversial (unless there is some question about how the statistics were gathered) and so the question "How many people were killed in the bombing of Hiroshima?" would likely not make for a good issue for inquiry, as Ravi quickly realizes. The answer to the question may, however, provide information that is necessary for addressing other issues such as whether the bombing was justified.

Descriptive judgments are generally arrived at through observation, but sometimes the observations involve the use of very sophisticated techniques and devices, like telescopes or particle accelerators. The main criterion used to evaluate descriptive judgments is that they are in accord with the evidence. What constitutes evidence varies somewhat from field to field. So, for example, the contents of documents is one type of evidence used in history. Observations of the results of experiments (e.g., readings on instruments) are an important type of evidence in physics. Systematically collected data on population characteristics or behaviours would constitute evidence in sociology.

The main criterion used to evaluate descriptive judgments is accord with the observational evidence.

Explanatory Judgments

Some factual judgments aim to explain how phenomena function (**explanatory judgments**). We looked at two types of explanatory judgments, **causal explanations** and **reason explanations** (also sometimes called purpose explanations), in Chapter 5. Many scientific judgments are of the causal type. The claims "Sugar causes hyperactivity" or "Playing violent video games causes violent behaviour in children" are explanatory judgments which go beyond demonstrating an observed connection between phenomena to posit a causal link between them. The issue regarding whether having the bomb helped shorten the war calls for a causal judgment. In explaining how phenomena function, causal explanations also tell us why certain events occurred—for example, Why was Jeffrey so out of control? Because he had just had a sweet treat.

A second type of explanatory judgment is the **reason explanation.** Reasons explanations are used all the time to understand human behaviour. The question "Why did the government not raise the minimum wage?" asks for the reasons for, rather than the cause(s) of, this decision. Was the government concerned about competitiveness? Did they want to satisfy their business supporters? Or did they have some other rationale in mind? Questions such as these do not ask for the cause of the decision but rather for the reasons for or purpose of the decision.

The issue which Ravi considers in the first dialogue concerning why the Americans decided to carry out the bombing of Hiroshima and Nagasaki calls for a judgment about their reasons; it is really asking what were the reasons that led the American leaders to use the atomic bomb. For any given reason explanation, we can always question whether it is merely a rationalization or the real reason (as we discussed in the Chapter 5). Thus if Ravi chose to inquire into this issue, it would not be sufficient to simply accept the reasons stated by the American government. Additional research into other types of historical evidence would be necessary in order to try to determine the real reasons (which may or may not be the same as the professed reasons). Such evidence could include documents of various sorts (e.g., reports, records of meetings, correspondence, testimonials) as well as interviews, photographs, and even physical evidence where available.

Explanatory judgments are based on observations but go beyond them to infer relationships among the phenomena observed. This form of reasoning, argument to the best explanation, is one we discussed in detail in the Chapter 5.

Explanatory judgments aim to explain how phenomena function.

Causal judgments are explanatory judgments which go beyond demonstrating an observed connection between phenomena to posit a causal link between them.

Reason explanations are explanatory judgments which identify the beliefs and purposes that motivated an action rather than the causes of the action.

Explanatory judgments are based on observations but go beyond them to infer relationships among the phenomena observed.

Evaluative Judgments

Evaluative judgments express an evaluation or assessment of an object, action, or phenomenon. Evaluative judgments occur in various areas and are of different types, the primary types being moral or ethical judgments (we shall use the terms interchangeably), aesthetic judgments, instrumental judgments, and comparative judgments of value.

Evaluative judgments express an evaluation or assessment of an object, action, or phenomenon.

Ethical Judgments

Ethical judgments deal with questions of what is right or wrong, good or bad, morally praiseworthy or blameworthy. Terms such as "justice," "fairness," "equity," "virtue," or "rights" indicate criteria according to which ethical judgments are made. Ethical judgments can apply to people ("Nancy is a person of integrity"), actions ("You should give more to charity," "Favouring Lester over Winnie wasn't fair"), or states of affairs ("The situation of the refugees is unjust").

The issue which Ravi ends up with in the first dialogue, "Were the Americans justified in dropping the atomic bomb on Hiroshima and Nagasaki in August 1945?" is an ethical issue since it is asking whether the Americans were *morally* justified in their action. "Is bombing innocent civilians wrong?" is also an ethical issue, although a rather flawed one in terms of its formulation. (A less loaded formulation would be "Is it wrong to target the civilian population in a war?") Similarly, the issue which he homes in on in the second dialogue, "Should scientists have continued to work on developing the atomic bomb after they became aware of its possible consequences?" is also an issue which calls for an ethical judgment since it is asking whether continuing to work on the atomic bomb was the best action to take from an ethical perspective. Winnie rightly points out that the ethical issue of whether scientists have a moral responsibility for their work and their findings would be an important one to consider in inquiring about the main issue.

Terms such as "justice," "fairness," "equity," "virtue," or "rights" indicate criteria according to which ethical judgments are made.

Aesthetic Judgments

Aesthetic judgments deal with questions having to do with the sensory, perceptual, or formal properties of objects and experiences; they arise most often in the realm of the arts. Whether the Henry Moore sculpture in front of Toronto City Hall is an example of good art, whether Celine Dion's performance of a particular song effectively captures the feeling of the piece, whether the buildings designed by Arthur Erickson harmonize or clash with their surroundings—these are examples of issues which call for aesthetic judgments.

Aesthetic judgments must be distinguished from other types of judgments which can be made about works of art. Whether a particular sculpture will provoke a lot of public protest, which singer's recording of a particular song will make the most money, whether a new building effectively serves the purpose for which it was designed—these issues call for monetary or practical judgments, not aesthetic judgments.

Terms such as "beautiful," "ugly," and "harmonious" are examples of criteria used for making aesthetic judgments. In some cases, aesthetic considerations and non-aesthetic considerations may conflict, as in the case of an elegant wine decanter which results in the spillage of wine. In other cases, aesthetic and non-aesthetic considerations may be in harmony, as in the case of the famous Nova Scotia sailing ship *Bluenose* (portrayed on the Canadian dime) which combines both grace and functionality. The issue which Sophia and Phil debate in Chapter 2, whether *Slumdog Millionaire* or *X-Men Origins: Wolverine* is a better film, is one which calls for an aesthetic judgment. We will also be coming across more aesthetic judgments in Chapter 14 when we deal with inquiry in the arts.

Instrumental Judgments

Instrumental judgments deal with questions having to do with reasoning about means to an end or goal. Is the screwdriver the best tool for the job? Is taking the highway the fastest way to get to our destination? These judgments involve assessing what action to take in a non-moral sense. Terms such as "practicality," "efficiency," and "cost-benefit" indicate instrumental issues and judgments.

Instrumental judgments generally have a factual component. For example, assessing cost-benefit requires knowledge of both the possible or likely costs and benefits of the policy under consideration. They generally involve evaluating what means will, in fact, enable us to achieve our ends, although determining what constitutes a cost or a benefit may not be simply a factual judgment. Several of the issues raised in the city council debate, including what policy would be most effective in curbing vicious dog attacks, and whether dog ban laws would be enforceable, are ones which call for instrumental judgments. The issue which Winnie alludes to regarding what policies might be put in place to control nuclear weapons also calls for an instrumental judgment. And interpreting Ravi's question regarding whether the scientists should have continued to work on the bomb in terms of efficiency rather than morality would call for an instrumental judgment as well. But this would not, of course, touch on the morality of the situation.

This kind of ambiguity brings up a crucial point: when inquiring into an issue, it is important to be clear about whether we are dealing with instrumental or with ethical issues since different criteria are used to evaluate each one. When inquiring into what action is best to take, both kinds of considerations can be involved. As a result, there is a common temptation to confuse the two. Thus, we may not realize that, even after dealing with instrumental considerations, ethical issues still need to be addressed, and vice versa. So even if the councillors were to determine that dog bans could be effective, they would still need to consider whether banning certain breeds of dogs violates the rights of dog owners. Even after considering whether the bombing of Hiroshima and Nagasaki would have been effective in helping to end the war, the Americans needed to consider whether it was an ethical action to take.

> It is important to be clear about whether we are dealing with instrumental or with ethical issues since different criteria are used to evaluate each one.

Comparative Judgments of Value

Comparative judgments of value deal with questions concerning what is of worth or value and the comparative importance of different values in making a judgment on an issue. In the vicious dog debate, the question of the relative importance of the rights of dog owners versus the safety of the public would be an issue calling for a comparative judgment of value. A judgment regarding whether the risks of developing the bomb outweighed any possible benefits would be another. And if someone made the claim that ethical considerations should have trumped practical considerations in the decision to drop the bomb, then this would be a comparative judgment of value as well. Some of the considerations which need to be weighed in making comparative judgments of value include ethical as compared to practical considerations, means as compared to ends, costs as compared to benefits, and conflicts among ethical values. We will be looking at how one can weigh these various considerations in Chapter 10.

> **Comparative judgments of value** deal with questions concerning what is of worth or value and the comparative importance of different values in making a judgment.

Distinguishing Between Factual and Evaluative Judgments

The distinction between factual judgments and evaluative judgments is a crucial one to recognize. Factual issues and evaluative issues call for different kinds of judgments which are supported by different kinds of arguments and are evaluated according to different kinds of criteria. Confusing the two, and in particular, trying to deal with evaluative issues as if they were factual, creates serious problems in our thinking.

Factual judgments are determined and supported by observing the way the world is. Evaluative judgments are not, however, determined and supported in this way. This fact has led some people to believe that value judgments are purely subjective and simply a matter of personal preference.

> Evaluative judgments can be justified by reasons and arguments, but they are of a different kind than those supporting factual judgments.

Do you think that value judgments are purely subjective and simply a matter of personal preference? Why or why not?

What Do You Think?

This is far from the case. Evaluative judgments can be justified by reasons and arguments, but they are of a different kind than those supporting factual judgments. Moreover,

Central criteria for evaluating ethical judgments concern 1) the moral quality of the act, 2) the duties and responsibility of the actor, and 3) the consequences of the act.

The criteria used to make aesthetic judgments relate largely to the perceptual or formal qualities of the object or experience and vary depending on the art in question.

Instrumental judgments appeal to criteria related to how well the action achieves the desired goals.

Comparative judgments of value appeal to criteria of worth and importance.

We commit the **naturalistic fallacy** when we try to come to a judgment on an issue which has an evaluative dimension purely on the basis of factual considerations.

in everyday life, people do not generally behave as if value judgments were subjective. Rather, we reason about evaluative issues all the time and tend to believe that our arguments are justified. Imagine, for example, that you disagree with the grade that your instructor has given you on an exam. You might make the argument that you merited a higher grade because your answers were correct according to the textbook and that her grading was unfair since a classmate who had given similar answers had received a higher grade. In other words, you offer her reasons for your evaluation and make reference to criteria such as merit and fairness. You would likely be unimpressed if the instructor said that grading was purely a subjective matter and that it was her preference to give you a failing grade. It is true that there can be some dimension of subjectivity in certain evaluative judgments, for example, in matters of taste (Phil hates broccoli, but Juanita loves it). And our response to the arts is subjective to some degree. But we can also make reasoned evaluations of artworks (as we saw in Chapter 2 and will see again in Chapter 14); and even in matters of taste, our palates can be educated. (Think of the wine connoisseur or the master chef.)

The kinds of criteria relevant to the assessment of evaluative judgments differ according to the type of judgment. While one can critically discuss what are the appropriate criteria for an ethical judgment, there are several that are clearly central:

- the moral quality of the act (e.g., Is it a lie?)

- the duties and responsibility of the actor (e.g., Teachers have special duties of fairness when marking their students' work.)

- the consequences of the act (e.g., Will it benefit many people?)

Suppose we are asked by our boss whether we know why a fellow employee is not at work. We happen to know he has gone skiing. If we tell the truth, the likely consequence is that he will be fired. In making our judgment about what to do, we need to consider our obligation to tell the truth, our responsibilities as an employee or manager, and the consequences of whatever action we take. The American president, for example, in his moral deliberations over bombing Hiroshima and Nagasaki, had to take into account the intrinsic moral horror of killing thousands of civilians, his duty to American citizens and soldiers, and the possible consequences of dropping or not dropping the bomb.

The criteria used to make aesthetic judgments relate largely to the perceptual or formal qualities of the object or experience and vary depending on the art in question. For film, evaluative criteria include aspects such as the quality of acting, dramatic tension, and effective use of cinematic techniques. For painting, formal criteria such as harmony and unity come into play. Many of the arts refer to criteria such as originality and a work's influence on the development of the art form.

Instrumental judgments appeal to criteria related to how well the action achieves the desired goals—for example, efficiency, cost-effectiveness, and satisfaction for stakeholders—and which action has the fewest downsides (although what counts as a downside may also be a matter for inquiry in some situations).

Comparative judgments of value appeal to criteria of worth and importance.

Our judgments often go wrong when we try to come to a judgment on an issue which has an evaluative dimension purely on the basis of factual considerations. Philosophers refer to this as the **naturalistic fallacy,** and the problem is particularly acute when dealing with ethical judgments. The problem is that simply describing the facts of any state of affairs cannot by itself tell us what we ought to do, or what the ethically right action is. For that, we also need some view of what is valuable or worthwhile (as well as what is unworthy or detrimental). In the first dialogue, we have an example of the naturalistic fallacy in action. Ravi thinks that if he answers the question "Did the bombings help to shorten the war?" then that will tell him whether or not the bombings were justified. But even if he found out that the bombings did help to shorten the war, he would not know whether the action was justifiable from an ethical perspective, as Winnie points out.

What are some of the additional issues which Ravi will have to consider in order to be able to address the issue of whether the bombings were justified?

What Do
You Think

To determine whether the bombings were justified, Ravi would also have to consider such issues as whether it was ethically permissible to target civilians and whether it was morally justifiable to use methods with such potentially devastating consequences for humanity. The answers to such questions cannot be based exclusively on factual considerations (although factual considerations will be relevant as well).

Some issues obviously call for evaluative judgments. But at times the evaluative dimension of an issue may be less obvious, with values assumptions implicit in the question or the way it is formulated and interwoven with factual considerations. So, for example, to address the issue of whether we should eat meat that comes from factory farms, it is true that we need information about the conditions of animals kept on these farms. But the issue cannot be addressed strictly by looking at farming practices since it also implicitly involves the question of whether humans have a moral obligation to animals. The debate over the raising of the minimum wage rests on differing assumptions about equity and merit and so cannot be resolved simply by looking at statistics, although some statistical information will be relevant to the deliberations. The issue of what action should be taken to prevent dog attacks hinges on differing views about the relative importance of values such as individual freedom and societal protection and how these values play out in the particular circumstances under discussion.

Thus it is extremely important to be able to distinguish issues which call for factual judgments from issues which call for evaluative judgments, and to recognize when there are values issues or assumptions embedded in other types of issues and interwoven with other types of considerations.

It is important to note, however, that some terms serve to describe and to evaluate at the same time. To call a person's utterance a lie is both to describe it as an instance of the person saying something that they know not to be true and to evaluate it in a negative way. Similarly, to call Nancy a compassionate person is both to describe certain of her qualities and actions (she cares about others, she feels empathy for their problems and hardships, etc.) and to make a positive evaluation of her character.

Interpretive Judgments

Interpretive judgments deal with questions of meaning. They involve making sense of data or phenomena within a particular framework. Interpretive judgments occur in many areas. We may offer interpretations of works of art; for example, Picasso's *Guernica* reflects the horrors of war. We may interpret the results of a scientific experiment; for example, the fact that the water came to a boil at 95 degrees Celsius means that we are higher than sea level. We may interpret the motives of a friend; Lester was so quiet because he didn't really want to be at Ahmed's party. When we standardize an argument, we are also offering an interpretation.

The criteria for evaluating an interpretative judgment include the following:

- correspondence with the data or evidence as well as with the interpretive framework of the discipline or area of study
- inclusiveness—the judgment accounts for all the evidence
- coherence—the judgment makes sense as a whole.

Interpretive judgments
deal with questions of
meaning.

Keep in Mind

TYPES OF JUDGMENTS

Factual
- Descriptive
- Explanatory
  - Causal
  - Reason

Evaluative
- Ethical
- Aesthetic
- Instrumental
- Comparative

Interpretive

*Apply Your
Understanding*
Exercises 8, 9, 10, 11

What these general criteria look like in practice will depend on the area in question. For example, the interpretation of the *Guernica* would have to fit with the details of the painting; it would have to be consistent with what is known about the artist, and it would have to take into account artistic and historical contexts as well as aesthetic criteria. The interpretation of the science experiment would have to fit with and provide the best explanation for the observations and be consistent with scientific principles. The interpretation of Lester's behaviour would have to be consistent with what we know about Lester's personality, with the context (e.g., he had another party that he wanted to attend), and with psychological theory.

The types of judgments we have been looking at occur in inquiries across a broad range of domains, including the sciences, the social sciences, the humanities, the arts, and daily life. It is important to recognize that there may be several different types of judgments that occur in any one domain. Science primarily involves judgments of a descriptive or causal nature, but can also involve ethical judgments, as we have seen in the dialogue. There may be causal, instrumental, and ethical judgments in the political realm. The study of history may involve factual, interpretive, or ethical judgments. Judgments in the arts might be interpretive, evaluative, or even ethical. The criteria, however, will differ to some extent according to the domain.

CHECK YOUR UNDERSTANDING

- *What are the characteristics of an issue which is appropriate for inquiry? Briefly explain each characteristic.*
- *What are three ways in which language can suffer from a lack of clarity? Explain in what way each one can be problematic.*
- *What is loaded language? Provide three examples of terms which have a negative loading.*
- *What is a euphemism? Give two examples of problematic euphemisms.*
- *What are the three principal types of judgments? Briefly describe each one.*
- *What are the main differences between factual and evaluative judgments?*
- *What is the naturalistic fallacy? Explain why it is fallacious.*

EXERCISES

1. Imagine that you have to write an essay to inquire into each of the topics listed below. For each topic, list three possible issues which could be the focus of your inquiry. Make sure that each issue you propose has the characteristics of a well-framed and appropriate issue for inquiry:

   i) substance abuse

   ii) gun control

   iii) climate change

   Get together with several classmates to share and discuss your list of issues.

2. In each of the examples below, there is some problem with the issue or how it is framed. For each example:

   i) Explain what the problem is.

   ii) Reframe the issue to avoid the problem, if possible. (For some examples, there may not be a salvageable issue.)

      a) Is the earth flat or round?
      b) Is it wrong to murder unborn babies?
      c) Unemployment
      d) How can we stop terrorism?
      e) Is euthanasia acceptable?
      f) Should CEOs be paid excessive salaries?
      g) Is war just?

3. Imagine that the following scene is taking place at a community meeting to discuss the topic of homeless people on local streets:

   Chair: Order please. We're ready to begin. Would someone please propose a wording for our agenda item for today?

   Omar Ali: Yes, I propose the following wording: "What action can be taken to reduce the blight of panhandlers on city streets?"

   Diego Alvarez: Now just a minute! I don't think that wording is very good at all! I propose the following wording instead: "What action can be taken to reduce the plight of panhandlers on city streets?" I think that captures the issue much better.

   Omar Ali: Now wait just a minute . . .

   Chair: Hmm . . . we seem to have a problem here.

   Work with a partner to continue the dialogue. Make sure that the dialogue you write accomplishes the following:

   i) It brings out the problems with both ways of framing the issue.

   ii) It ends with the suggestion of a more appropriate way to frame the issue.

4. Use Bertrand Russell's series of three phrases as a model ("I am firm; you are stubborn; he is a pig-headed fool") to accomplish the following:

   i) complete each of the following examples with terms that have a similar meaning (denotation) but different (and progressively more negative) connotations:

      a) I am brave; you are _____; he is _____.
      b) I am flexible; you are _____; he is _____.
      c) I am justifiably angry; you are _____; he is _____.

   ii) Make up three examples of your own.

5. Work in groups to complete these tasks:

    i) Make a list of all the euphemisms you can think of. (You can consult newspapers or magazines to add to your list.)

    ii) For five of the euphemisms, explain in what way they alter the emotional loading of what they describe.

    iii) Offer an alternative word or phrase which you think provides a more accurate connotation.

6. In each of the following examples, the issue is formulated in such a way as to contain assumptions which are controversial and slant the inquiry in a certain direction. For each issue, complete the following:

    i) Find the assumption(s).

    ii) Explain in what way they bias the inquiry.

    iii) Reframe the issue in a more neutral manner.

        a) How can distortions in the economy caused by government subsidies be avoided?
        b) What action can be taken to reduce the gross inequities in compensation between employers and workers?
        c) Why shouldn't the government legalize a harmless recreational drug like marijuana?
        d) How can we prevent the heartless massacre of innocent seal pups for fur coats for the rich?

7. Some environmentalists are trying to move from talking about the problem of global warming to talking about the problem of climate change. What reasons might they have for wanting to reframe the issue in this way? (Hint: Think about the assumptions built into each way of framing the issue and the impressions created by the different formulations.)

8. Read the piece on Canada's role in the invasion of Afghanistan, in Exercise 7-8 on the textbook website. Then do the following:

    i) Identify four issues which arise from this information which could be the basis for an inquiry. (Be sure that each one has the characteristics of a well-framed issue.)

    ii) Identify the type of judgment or judgments called for with respect to each issue you have identified.

9. Identify the type of judgment for each of the following (there may be more than one type of judgment involved):

    i) You shouldn't lie to your mother.

    ii) Banning vicious dogs would not be effective in reducing dog attacks.

    iii) Christopher Plummer's interpretation of King Lear was unparalleled.

    iv) The government should do more to help the poor.

    v) The French loss at the Battle of Quebec was a decisive event in the British conquest of New France.

    vi) There is no correlation between the consumption of dietary fats and the incidence of heart attacks.

    vii) Meiko deserves praise for returning the wallet she found.

    viii) Michelangelo's exaggeration of the proportions of the Madonna in the Pietà creates a sense of awe and pity.

    ix) "It is a far, far better thing that I do than I have ever done." (Sydney Carton, a character in Charles Dickens's novel *A Tale of Two Cities,* says this as he is about to sacrifice his life for another man.)

    x) One of the lessons of the novel *The English Patient* is how large a gap exists between the life we live and the story of it we prefer to tell.

    xi) It is unconscionable that Canada is now refusing to argue for clemency for Canadians held on death row in other countries.

xii) There's no point in taking antibiotics for a cold since colds are caused by viruses and not bacteria.

xiii) I can tell by the expression on his face that Ravi is upset.

xiv) We should focus on rehabilitation rather than on punishment when dealing with young people who break the law.

10. This assignment focuses on the dialogues on vegetarianism in Chapter 1:

   i) Re-read the dialogues.

   ii) Make a list of the various issues that come up in the dialogues.

   iii) For each issue, identify what type of judgment is called for.

   iv) Identify other possible issues in the debate over vegetarianism besides the ones explored by the students.

   v) For each issue you have proposed in Part iv), identify what type of judgment is called for.

11. Each of the following arguments rests on implicit assumptions of either a factual or an evaluative kind, or in some cases both. Identify the various assumptions which are implicit in each of the arguments and state whether they are factual or evaluative:

   i) This city suffers from serious traffic congestion. Therefore, we need more expressways to improve the transportation situation.

   ii) There is insufficient funding to maintain the current welfare system. Therefore, the government should put policies in place to eliminate the large-scale abuses of the welfare system.

   iii) Seventy-five percent of people think that those who commit premeditated murder should be put to death. So it's clear that we should have capital punishment.

   iv) Statistics show that females are more likely than males to drop out of top executive positions. Therefore, we should give priority to hiring males for such positions.

   v) Lester is unskilled. Therefore, he is lucky to be getting the pay he does.

ENDNOTES

1. www.ccnr.org/opinion_ge.html
   www.ccnr.org/opinion_ge.html
   www.cbc.ca/news/viewpoint/vp_rose/20050805.html
   www.user.dccnet.com/welcomewoods/Nuclear.../
   canada.htm
   http://www.dominionpaper.ca/original_peoples/2005/04/05/
   canada_rac.html

2. Gordon Edwards, "Canada and the Bomb: Past and Future," *Canadian Council for Nuclear Responsibility website,* http://www.ccnr.org/opinion_ge.html (accessed May 10, 2010).

3. Peace Pledge Union, "Joseph Rotblat," http://www.ppu.org.uk/learn/infodocs/people/pp-rotblat1.html#responsibility (accessed May 10, 2010).

Chapter 8
Understanding the Case: Reasons and Context

Learning Objectives

After reading this chapter, you should be able to:

- lay out the reasons on various sides of an issue
- identify the following aspects of context:
  - state of practice
  - history of the debate
  - intellectual, social, political, and historical contexts
- make appropriate use of contextual information when examining an issue

Capital Punishment

Our friend, Phil, has been reading an opinion piece in a newspaper in which the chief of police of his town is arguing for capital punishment for murder.

Phil: Hey, Sophia—let me read you something interesting:

Society has an obligation, first and foremost, to protect its citizens from harm. And the most serious form of harm is murder. Protecting citizens from murder involves ensuring that murderers don't repeat the offence. It also involves dissuading others from committing murder. Now I and other law enforcement officers know from a vast amount of first-hand experience with criminals that the only form of punishment that can effectively achieve both goals is the death penalty. Capital punishment involves taking the life of a person who has committed murder in order to save the lives of innocent people, and so is the best option under the circumstances.

> *What do you think of the argument that the police chief offers for capital punishment? What are its strengths? What problems to do you see?*

Phil: What he says makes a lot of sense. After all, society needs to do whatever it can to protect innocent people. And murderers have really given up their right to be protected because they've taken someone else's life. So killing them to save innocent people seems OK.

Sophia: Hold on a minute, Phil! Not so fast. You're leaping to conclusions again. You haven't even thought the issue through.

Phil: But what this guy says seems right.

Sophia: So are you just going to believe what he says without checking it out? What else would you expect a police chief to say?

Phil: Well, he does have a lot of experience with crime.

Sophia: But you haven't considered the other side. Your police chief certainly hasn't given us any of the arguments *against* capital punishment.

Phil: But what about his argument?

Sophia: I think that there's a lot more that we need to know before we can decide whether his argument is any good. We need more information. We need to know some facts about capital punishment. We need to look at all the arguments on both sides … We need to … I know. What we need to do is …

Sophia and Phil: … conduct an inquiry!

Sophia: Now the first step, if I remember right, is to be clear about what the issue is.

Phil: That's pretty easy. The issue is whether we should have capital punishment.

Sophia: For what crimes? We need to be specific. In some countries, there's the death penalty for adultery.

Phil: No, no … I wasn't suggesting that. I'm only thinking about cases of premeditated murder.

Sophia: I'm glad you're clear about that.

Phil: OK … next question—what kind of judgment does this involve?

Sophia: Well, since we're talking about what we "should" or "should not" do, then I guess it's an evaluative judgment. But I can see already that we'll also need to look at some factual claims on the way—like whether capital punishment really does help prevent murders.

Keep in Mind

GUIDING QUESTIONS FOR INQUIRY
- What is the issue?
- What kinds of claims or judgments are at issue?
- **What are the relevant reasons and arguments on various sides of the issue?**
- **What is the context of the issue?**
- How do we comparatively evaluate the various reasons and arguments to reach a reasoned judgment?

Relevant Reasons and Arguments on Various Sides of the Issue

The fact that an issue is controversial means that there is some debate around it. Thus, there will be a variety of positions or views on such an issue. But a debate involves more than just the statement of positions. It also means that arguments and evidence will have been brought forward to support these positions. And, in all likelihood, **objections** will have been raised to many of these arguments; **responses** will have been offered to some of these objections; and **alternative views** will have been put forth.

An **objection** is a reason or argument raised against a prior argument which casts the argument into doubt.

A **response** is an answer to or rebuttal of an objection.

An **alternative view** is a different view offered as an alternative to the argument in question.

In order to make a reasoned judgment, we will need to know the following:

- what various positions on the issue in question have been offered
- what evidence has been brought forward and what arguments have been made in defence of the various positions
- what objections have been levelled against the positions and what responses have been made to these
- what alternatives have been put forth

We will also need to know which positions and views are currently dominant, if any. If there is not one view which is dominant, we would be looking for the main competing views as well as the nature and extent of disagreement.

Making a reasoned judgment on an issue involves more than simply evaluating a particular argument. Rather, it involves making a comparative assessment of the relative strengths and weaknesses of the competing views. Being aware of the details of the current debate is, therefore, essential in order to come to a reasoned judgment.

Making a reasoned judgment on an issue involves making a comparative assessment of the relative strengths and weaknesses of the competing views. Being aware of the details of the current debate is essential in order to come to a reasoned judgment.

Context of the Issue

The kinds of issues which are the objects of our inquiries do not suddenly arise out of nowhere. They arise and are situated in a particular context, or particular contexts. Finding out about these contexts can help us in our inquiry. There are three aspects of context that we will focus on:

1. state of practice
2. history of the debate
3. intellectual, social, political, and historical contexts.

State of Practice

State of practice refers to how things stand at the moment with respect to the issue and its manifestations.

The **state of practice** is how things stand with respect to the issue and its manifestations. It is the current situation with respect to that practice. It can also be helpful to know something about the history of how we arrived at the current state of affairs. So, for example, if we are dealing with the issue of censorship, we would want to know what the current laws and practices are—what kind of material is prohibited or restricted, what the penalties are, to what extent there have been prosecutions, and so on. It might also be helpful to understand something of the history of how we arrived at our current laws. In the debate over whether people should eat meat, we would want to know about the actual treatment of animals on factory farms and what regulations exist to protect the welfare of the animals. In a debate about whether a particular film should win an Oscar, we would want to know what other films have been nominated, and perhaps information about the other works of the director in question.

Knowledge about the state of practice can provide us with information that may be relevant to evaluating claims and arguments. For one thing, it can help us understand why a particular issue is an issue—what is controversial or problematic about it, and why it is deserving of our attention.

Knowledge about the state of practice can provide us with information that may be relevant to evaluating claims and arguments.

Knowledge about the state of practice also lets us know where the force of current practice and opinion lie so that we can understand what any alternative views are up against, and whether and to what extent any of these views has the burden of proof (the responsibility for making the case and the degree of evidence required). As we saw in Chapter 4, a widely acknowledged guideline is that the burden of proof generally lies with those views which are in opposition to commonly accepted views or practices. Burden of proof in factual matters is strongest where there is good reason to believe that currently accepted beliefs are backed by research and reflection. So, for example, it would require a large amount of extremely credible evidence to put into question a well-established scientific theory.

Burden of proof in moral matters is much more controversial because appeal to common practice almost always begs the question and there is no legitimate appeal to expert knowledge. The pragmatic reality is, however, that whoever argues for a change in practice or moral view from the status quo will bear the argumentative burden of proof in a dialogue situation. So, for example, the burden of proof is on those who advocate change in laws.

Nonetheless, the determination of burden of proof is not always straightforward; and in many cases (e.g., debates over moral matters), there is no clear burden of proof. In addition, long-standing and firmly entrenched views and practices are in many cases overturned. Thus, it is of vital importance to fully lay out the arguments on all sides of an issue. The consideration of burden of proof will enter into the comparative evaluation and weighing of the various arguments, in determining how much evidence is necessary and when a case has been made. (We will examine this further in Chapter 10.)

Do you agree that the burden of proof should lie with those who are opposing commonly accepted views and practices?

What Do You Think?

History of the Debate

When an issue is controversial or has been contested, discussion and debate will likely have gone on over a period of time. Whether the issue is the nature of black holes or the acceptability of capital punishment, there is almost always a history of deliberation which has led to current practice or thinking about the issue. The current state of practice is a product of this debate; and, if the issue is still considered controversial, the debate is ongoing.

Learning about the history of the debate surrounding an issue can be very helpful, and in some cases essential, to understanding the issue and the various positions which are contesting for acceptance. There are cases when we can only really understand a position when we know something about where it came from. Views are often developed out of, as a reaction to, or as an alternative to existing views. Understanding such positions involves knowing what they were arguing against as well as what they were arguing for. So, for example, it is important to understand why certain scientific theories are accepted by understanding the nature of the problem which they were addressing, and by seeing what other theories they defeated and why. Only in this way will we understand why the dominant theory is seen as the best explanation and what issues still remain contested. Similarly, we cannot fully understand contemporary political debates without knowing something about the historical situation and the historical disagreements in which the contemporary debate has its roots. In addition, being aware of the argumentation used in past contexts might help us to avoid simply repeating past debates in our current situation when the contexts have changed.

Learning about the history of the debate surrounding an issue can be very helpful, and in some cases essential, to understanding the issue and the various positions which are contesting for acceptance.

Intellectual, Social, Political, and Historical Contexts

The roots of many issues can be found in certain ideas or philosophies about human nature, society, reality, and the world in general. These ideas may be philosophical, scientific, political, or religious; and they often affect how people will view certain issues and what kinds of positions they will take. For example, people's views on social issues such as gay marriage may arise from their religious beliefs, or their views on economic matters such as tax reform may be grounded in their political orientation.

Learning about the intellectual, social, political, and historical contexts in which an issue is situated can bring to light the assumptions which lie behind the various arguments. It can help us to understand where the proponents of the various arguments are coming from and it can give us insight into the world views which underlie the various positions.

Learning about the intellectual, social, political, and historical contexts in which an issue is situated can bring to light the assumptions and world views which lie behind the various arguments.

Mapping the Contexts

It might be helpful to think about these aspects of context in terms of concentric circles. In the centre is a circle representing the state of practice. This state of practice is embedded in a larger circle which represents the debate which has given rise to current thinking and practice. This circle is, in turn, embedded in an even larger circle representing the intellectual, social, political, and historical context which influences and grounds the debate.

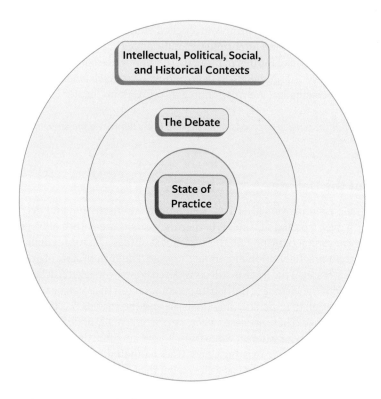

Laying out the contexts in which an issue is embedded is rather like creating an overview map of a territory which we are about to explore. It enables us to get the big picture of the issue and the factors and forces surrounding it. Later in the process, we will be able to zoom in and start to fill in the details. An example of mapping the context for the capital punishment debate is given later in the chapter (see page 153).

Laying Out the Current Debate

What Do You Think

List the arguments you can think of both for and against capital punishment.

Sophia: Our friend the police chief has presented one argument supporting capital punishment. But I suspect that he's only giving us one point of view. My guess is that, if we investigate further, we'll find lots of arguments supporting the other side.

Phil: So let's have a look at the internet . . . Let's see . . . Oh yeah. There are all kinds of references to articles and books that give arguments about capital punishment, both for and against.

Sophia: Why don't we try to list some of the arguments . . . Two of the main arguments offered for capital punishment are incapacitation—that it will prevent convicted murderers from murdering again—and deterrence—that it will discourage others from committing murders.

Phil: Those are exactly the arguments that our police chief uses! And I can see here that he's certainly not the first.

Sophia: Well, it's hard to argue with the fact that dead murderers can't commit more murders.

Phil: But there may be less drastic ways to achieve that.

Sophia: As for deterrence, lots of folks have objected to this idea, saying that there's considerable evidence that the death penalty does not, in fact, deter people from committing murders. (I sure would like to find out more about that evidence.)

Phil: But many upholders of deterrence still insist that experience tells them that it must be effective and that there are some studies that show that. Some also argue that there's a lack of evidence of deterrence in some contexts because there are so few actual executions, even where they have the death penalty.

Sophia: We'll need to check out that evidence, too.

Phil: The other main argument for capital punishment is retribution—that justice requires that offenders receive the punishment they deserve. And those who've committed murder deserve death.

Sophia: Ah . . . but here again, we have objections. Some folks argue that retribution is just a fancy word for revenge, and that revenge is not a morally defensible motive. And others claim that people who commit serious crimes such as murder are the products of their environment, and so they are not really responsible for their actions. It's also interesting that the main argument given in support of capital punishment these days seems to have changed from deterrence to retribution.

Phil: Another argument that comes up a lot has to do with cost—it's just too expensive to keep all those murderers in prison for their whole lives.

Sophia: But others object that cost shouldn't be a main issue here.

Phil: I'm also seeing arguments against capital punishment. One of the main ones is that taking a life is morally wrong, even if done by the state, and that the state should not descend to the level of the murderer. The supporters of capital punishment argue that the state is permitted to take actions that individuals can't—for example, locking people up and, in this case, killing people.

Sophia: Another argument is that punishment should serve to rehabilitate the offender, but clearly offenders can't be rehabilitated if they're dead.

Phil: But death penalty advocates argue that protecting innocent citizens is more important than rehabilitating criminals.

Sophia: And then some of the authors here point out that the legal system is not perfect and so innocent people will sometimes be executed. According to them, any practice that results in the killing of innocent people cannot be justified.

Phil: Yeah, I came across that one, too.

Sophia: Another argument that comes up is that criminals are often a product of a dysfunctional social environment and so should be treated accordingly. Although the pro capital punishment folks tend to criticize that argument for not acknowledging the personal responsibility of criminals for their actions.

Phil: Hmm . . . I'm noticing something interesting about many of these arguments: folks are arguing for or against capital punishment, but many of them don't even mention what alternative they're comparing it to. Are they comparing the merits of the death penalty to a 10- or 15-year prison sentence? Or are they comparing it to life imprisonment without parole?

Sophia: Good point, Phil! A person's view of capital punishment might be very different if the alternative is 10 years in prison or if it's life imprisonment without parole. People may not be happy about turning murderers loose after 10 years. But maybe life imprisonment without parole would be as good a deterrent as the death penalty. And it might even satisfy the people looking for retribution.

Phil: Well, I can certainly see now that there's a lot more to the issue of capital punishment than just the one argument from the police chief.[1]

Phil and Sophia are engaging in an essential step in the process of inquiry: laying out the arguments on various sides of the issue. They are not satisfied with looking at just one argument about capital punishment. They realize that there is more than one side to this issue and that the argument they have in front of them is part of a debate which is both historical and ongoing. In order to come to any reasoned position about capital punishment, they need to know what the arguments are on the various sides of the issue, what the objections to and criticisms of the various arguments have been, what responses have been put forth to these objections and criticisms, and which views are currently dominant.

This type of debate is not limited to areas in which there are issues which are obviously controversial—for example, issues of morality, social policy, or politics. Rather, it is a feature of virtually all areas of inquiry, including science and the arts. The process of science generally is and has been one of making reasoned judgments among competing theories and alternative explanations in the light of evidence and argument. Thus, there is debate with respect to scientific issues much as there is with respect to moral or political ones. Issues such as whether the universe is expanding or contracting, how birds navigate, and whether red wine has a beneficial effect on the heart are all the subject of ongoing debate; and it is possible to lay out the various arguments and objections that have led to the current consensus or the views which are currently competing for acceptance. (The nature of inquiry in science will be dealt with in detail in Chapter 12.)

The arts, too, are areas in which debate is the norm. Does rap qualify as "real music"? Should the sculpture *Meat Dress* (50 pounds of flank steak stitched together and hung on a plastic mannequin to rot) have been exhibited at the National Gallery of Canada? Which artist was really the first Renaissance artist? Are Glenn Gould's interpretations of the *Goldberg Variations* superior to all others? These are just a few examples of the kinds of debates which take place constantly in the arts.

Representing the Current Debate

A good way to represent the main features of the current debate is in a table which outlines the main arguments, objections, and responses (see Table of Arguments Pro and Con Capital Punishment on page 145). This type of table can provide a helpful overview of the main features of the **dialectic** (the argumentative exchange between various sides of an issue). It cannot lay out the arguments, objections, or responses in any detail; but at this stage, we are more interested in the overview than the details.

> In order to come to any reasoned position on an issue, one needs to know what the arguments are on the various sides of the issue, what the objections to and criticisms of the various arguments have been, what responses have been put forth to these objections and criticisms, and which views are currently dominant.

Dialectic refers to the argumentative exchange between various sides on an issue.

Table of Arguments Pro and Con Capital Punishment

Argument Name	Argument Summary	Objections	Responses
	PRO		
Incapacitation	CP prevents convicted murderers from committing more murders.	There are less drastic means to achieve this.	
Deterrence	CP will prevent or discourage people from committing murders.	There is evidence that CP doesn't work as a deterrent.	Experience attests to effectiveness. Some studies show a deterrent effect. There are few studies showing a deterrent effect due to so few executions.
Retribution	Justice requires that punishment be proportional to crime.	Revenge is not morally defensible. Individuals are products of their environment.	Murderers deserve to die. "An eye for an eye" is accepted in the Bible. Individuals are responsible and deserve what they get.
Cost	It is too expensive to keep people in prison.	Cost is not an appropriate consideration.	
	CON		
Morality	Taking a life is morally wrong.	Taking a life is justified if the person himself/herself took a life.	
Rehabilitation	Punishment should serve to rehabilitate but a person can't be rehabilitated if dead.	Protecting innocent citizens is more important than rehabilitating criminals.	
Executing the Innocent	Innocent people are sometimes executed.	The risk is small compared to the benefits.	Killing the innocent is never justified.
Social Causality	Criminals are often a product of a dysfunctional social environment and should be treated accordingly.	This argument fails to acknowledge the personal responsibility of criminals for their behaviour.	This is supported by statistical and psychological evidence. The argument is used only to mitigate the sentence, not to exonerate the criminal.

Apply Your Understanding Exercises 1, 2

Laying Out the Context

State of Practice

Sophia: I'm thinking that it would be a good idea to find out more about the current situation with respect to capital punishment. What do you know about the laws on capital punishment in various places?

Phil: Not very much, really. But I know how we can find out. Back to the internet.

List what you know about the laws on capital punishment where you live.

What Do You Think?

The Death Penalty in Canada: Twenty Years of Abolition [2]

From website for Amnesty International

Between 1892 and 1961, the penalty for all murders in Canada was death by hanging. In 1961, an act of Parliament divided murder into capital and non-capital categories.

The first private bill calling for abolition of the death penalty was introduced in 1914. In 1954, rape was removed from capital offenses. In 1956, a parliamentary committee recommended exempting juvenile offenders from the death penalty, providing expert counsel at all stages of the proceedings and the institution of mandatory appeals in capital cases.

Between 1954 and 1963, a private member's bill was introduced in each parliamentary session calling for abolition of the death penalty. The first major debate on the issue took place in the House of Commons in 1966. Following a lengthy and emotional debate, the government introduced and passed Bill C-168, which limited capital murder to the killing of on-duty police officers and prison guards.

On July 14, 1976, the House of Commons passed Bill C-84 on a free vote, abolishing capital punishment from the Canadian Criminal Code and replacing it with a mandatory life sentence without possibility of parole for 25 years for all first-degree murders.

Execution of Stanislaus Lacroix, March 21, 1902, said to be the last publicly viewed execution in Canada

Source: Library and Archives, C-014078/ MIKAN ID 3193849

Phil: Wow! There are so many sites about capital punishment. Here it is! I've found something about the practice of capital punishment in both Canada and the U.S. Execution by hanging for murder used to be a part of Canadian law; but from the late 1950s onward, its use was progressively restricted. Capital punishment was officially abolished in Canada in 1976. But even by 1963, all death sentences were being commuted, so there really hasn't been capital punishment in practice since 1963.[3]

Sophia: The debate's never really gone away, though. I think there's a deep concern among the public about what they see as the growing incidence of violent crime and the tendency for violent offenders to get off lightly because of plea bargains and all. Capital punishment's become hot again recently in Canada because of changes in government policy on the international front.

Phil: Yeah … I was reading something about new government policies on clemency appeals.

Sophia: What's the situation in the States?

Phil: There's still capital punishment in 35 of the states in the U.S.[4] Who would have thought that the situation in the U.S. and Canada would be so different!

Sophia: That's got me wondering about the rest of the world. How do things stand in other countries?

What Do You Think?

What percentage of the countries in the world would you estimate currently practise capital punishment?

No More Clemency Appeals for Canadians on Death Row in U.S.: Tories [5]

From CBC News website

The federal Conservatives will not intervene in the case of a Canadian on death row in the U.S., a move being blasted by some Opposition MPs as a government endorsement of capital punishment.

Public Safety Minister Stockwell Day said he won't ask American authorities to hand over Ronald Allen Smith, an Alberta man who has been on death row in Montana for more than 20 years.

"We will not actively pursue bringing back to Canada murderers who have been tried in a democratic country that supports the rule of law," Day told the House of Commons on Thursday. "It would send a wrong message. We want to preserve public safety here in Canada." ...

For years, it's been standard practice for Canada to lobby foreign governments to show mercy to its citizens when they face the death penalty. Ottawa would ask that their sentence be reduced to life in prison or request that the prisoner serve their term in a Canadian penitentiary.

But that policy has now officially changed.

Liberal Leader Stéphane Dion said Canadians should take this as a warning that if the Conservatives get a majority, the debate over capital punishment could be reopened.

"The fact that this government doesn't even want to try [asking for clemency] shows me what this government would try doing to Canada if they had a majority," Dion said.

NDP Leader Jack Layton said if the government won't even try to stop the execution of a Canadian citizen, it's in effect condoning capital punishment.

Phil: This is amazing! 139 countries around the world have either abolished the death penalty or no longer practise it even if it's still on the books, including all of Europe, Australia, Mexico, Russia, most of Central America, and parts of Africa.[6] There are only 64 countries that still practise capital punishment, and, except for the U.S., they're almost all in Africa, the Middle East, the Far East, and South Asia (countries like Afghanistan, China, Pakistan, Syria, Iran, Iraq, Malaysia, and Nigeria).[7]

Sophia: I have to admit I'm pretty surprised at the company that the U.S. is in—not exactly the staunchest defenders of human rights.

■ Abolitionist for All Crimes
   Abolitionist for Ordinary Crimes
■ Abolitionist in Practice
■ Retentionist Countries

Source: Death Penalty Information Center (www.deathpenaltyinfo.org).

Phil: That, in itself, doesn't make it wrong. Sounds like the fallacy of guilt by association to me. And besides, the minority is sometimes right.

Sophia: But it does make you wonder . . . Apparently, the United Nations General Assembly approved a worldwide moratorium on execution in 2007.[8] Why do you think capital punishment has been rejected in most places in the world? I think we're going to have to come back to this and think more about it when we get to the step of evaluating the reasons and arguments.

Phil: Here's something else we should really look at. Several of the websites give information about who gets the death sentence. They say that studies have consistently shown that, in the U.S., blacks are more likely to be charged with capital murder or receive a death sentence than whites, and that those who murder whites are more likely to be sentenced to death than those who murder blacks.[9]

Sophia: If that's true, it's pretty disturbing, and pretty important. We'll definitely want to investigate this further when we get to our evaluation.

Here Phil and Sophia are investigating the current situation with respect to capital punishment—not just locally but also globally. One of the aspects which their investigation reveals is that the debate about capital punishment takes a somewhat different form in different locations. In Canada and in some states in the U.S., it's a debate about reinstating a practice which has been abolished. In many of the U.S. states, it's a debate over abolishing a practice which currently exists. Since the burden of proof, from a pragmatic perspective, is generally on those who are opposing the status quo and advocating a change in what is the current practice, the onus in Canada and in U.S. abolitionist states is on those who argue for reinstatement. In most of the U.S., on the other hand, the onus is on those who are arguing for abolition. Knowing this can be helpful in understanding why certain arguments tend to be put forth, and why the debate has taken the form it has in each locale.

Knowledge about the current state of practice and its historical development can be helpful in understanding why certain arguments tend to be put forth, why the current debate takes the form it does, and where the burden of proof lies.

Knowledge of some of the precise details about the practice and its context can also shed a new light on an issue. For example, an awareness of the very small number of executions even in places that have the death penalty may be relevant to the debate over deterrence. Knowledge of actual sentencing practices may have implications for the assessment of the retribution argument. And an understanding of public perceptions of growing violence may help to shed light on the appeal of various arguments and positions.

As another example, the statistics regarding capital punishment and race in the U.S. can add an additional dimension to discussions about the desirability of the death penalty. It brings up the possible connection between capital punishment and racial prejudice, a consideration which may not be obvious from looking at the main arguments. This gives us an additional factor to consider in evaluating capital punishment.

Having some knowledge of how an issue has developed over time can also give us insights into some of its aspects. It seems helpful to know, for example, that there has been a gradual worldwide move toward the abolition of capital punishment. This fact does not, of course, imply that this is the correct position. Countries can sometimes become less enlightened, and the majority position is not necessarily the best one. Nonetheless, the fact that most countries of the world (and particularly those which have shown a concern for human rights) have arrived at the abolition view does give us an additional dimension to consider when evaluating capital punishment, as does the fact that the United Nations has called for a moratorium on executions.

History of the Debate

Phil: In doing this research, I'm discovering that some of these arguments go back a long way. For example, it looks like the retribution argument has a long history. In fact, the idea of "an eye for an eye" appears in the Bible way back in Leviticus 24:19–21, Exodus 21:23–27, and Deuteronomy 19:21.

Sophia: And also in Babylonian law in the Code of Hammurabi which dates way back to around 1800 to 1760 BCE.

Phil: So these are certainly not new ideas.

Sophia: Hey—look at this! In the Exodus passage, the phrase "an eye for an eye" is used in the context of instructing a person who has taken the eye of another person in a fight to give his own eye in compensation. So it's not really used here to say that a person has a right to retaliate if they've been harmed. Rather, it sets out a principle of compensation for loss, saying that a person owes another person compensation if they've done them harm.

Phil: That's kind of different from the way "an eye for an eye" tends to be used nowadays.

Sophia: Not only that, but the commentaries I'm reading here claim that these codes based on the idea of "an eye for an eye" were actually ways to refine and restrict the extent of retaliation.[10] Apparently, in the societies of the time, revenge, vendettas, and feuds were common, and often the retaliation would be a lot worse than the injury. So enacting codes based on "an eye for an eye" was a way of encouraging compensation for loss but regulating the punishment and making sure that it was fair and not overly harsh—that the punishment fit the crime, so to speak.

Phil: And I read that in the Jewish Torah, retribution is left to the realm of divine justice whereas earthly punishments are supposed to serve to remove dangerous offenders from society and to deter potential criminals[11] . So it's not really retribution here, but rather incapacitation and deterrence. Sound familiar? And the Torah also warns people against vengeance for the sake of vengeance and bearing a grudge against those who harm you.

Sophia: The Koran, although it allows retribution, encourages leniency and forgiveness.

Phil: Reminds me of "turning the other cheek."

Sophia: Wow! All this information puts the retribution argument into a new light, doesn't it?

Phil: And it shows the problems of taking things "out of context."

Sophia and Phil have discovered that debates about the appropriate punishment for crimes have a long history and that arguments based on incapacitation, deterrence, and retribution go back a long way. With respect to the retribution argument, in particular, they find that the notion of "an eye for an eye" came out of a context very different from today's and that it had a quite different meaning in its original context. So trying to draw unambiguous support for retribution from Biblical sources is rather problematic.

Issues which occupy us today have not popped out of nowhere. They have usually been discussed and debated over a period of time, in some cases over a very long period of time. And tracing this debate can prove enlightening for understanding the issue in its current form.

As another example, looking at the history of the debates over the control of firearms in Canada and the U.S. can help us to understand why these debates tend to take different forms in the two countries. In Canada, although the issue is still debated, there has been considerable acceptance of gun control legislation, whereas in the U.S., limitation on the ownership of firearms tends to be strongly resisted. U.S. resistance to gun control goes back to the American revolution. The American colonies justified their rebellion against the British Crown with the argument that the governed can legitimately "throw off" a government which violates individuals' inalienable rights. Thus the right to bear arms was seen as connected to the ability to resist a tyrannical government and became one of these inalienable rights which was enshrined in the U.S. Constitution.

Tracing the history of a debate can prove enlightening for understanding the issue in its current form.

Apply Your Understanding Exercises 3, 4

Canada, in contrast, was not engaged in an armed struggle for independence and so there are no parallel historical antecedents and ideas. Indeed, the phrase "Peace, order, and good government" [12] expresses the principles on which Canadian confederation was founded. The Canadian Charter of Rights makes no mention of a right to bear arms.

Understanding these differences in the history of the debate can make clear some of the fundamental assumptions which ground contemporary positions in the two countries.

Intellectual, Social, Political, and Historical Contexts

The combination of social and political forces at work at a particular time may also affect debates by bringing certain issues to popular attention and by exerting pressure in support of or opposition to certain positions.

Knowledge about the intellectual, social, political, and historical contexts which surround an issue can contribute to our understanding of the assumptions which lie behind various positions and why people might hold them. It can also help reveal to us why certain issues have surfaced (or resurfaced) at a particular time and place.

Phil: You know, looking at all these arguments, I'm starting to get the sense that the folks who hold these different positions are coming from different places.

Sophia: Yeah, I know what you mean.

Phil: The "pro" arguments all focus on a kind of "law and order" perspective. They're very concerned with the violence in society and are aiming for social order.

Sophia: Exactly. I was also thinking that the retribution argument, which many people think is related to the Biblical idea of "an eye for an eye," may be particularly attractive to those who subscribe to certain religious ideas.

Phil: Could be…

Sophia: The arguments against capital punishment seem to be much more focused on concerns about human rights, even for those who commit serious crimes.

Phil: And they also emphasize the role of the environment in shaping people. I'm thinking here of the idea that because people are products of their environment, they're not really entirely responsible for their actions.

Sophia: I agree. Whereas the folks on the "pro" side seem to have a different attitude about responsibility. The retribution argument seems to assume that people deserve what they get.

Phil: Uh-huh. Also, some of the arguments against capital punishment emphasize rehabilitation. The idea of rehabilitation is based on the belief that people can improve given the right environment. The proponents of capital punishment seem much less convinced of that.

Sophia: Yeah—I can see that. Some of the "con" arguments also seem to be based on concerns about unequal treatment, especially in the form of racism. So they apparently believe that society, the way it is now, may not be fair; and people may not, in fact, always deserve what they get.

Sophia and Phil have noticed that the arguments for and against capital punishment are based on rather different views about people and about societies. The ideas which underlie many of the "pro" arguments such as a primary concern for law and order, self-reliance, and individual responsibility can be seen as part of a world view which is usually characterized as conservative. The term "conservative" generally refers to views which put a central focus on stability and continuity within society and which emphasize social order, traditional values, individual responsibility, and a limited role for government in economic and social matters. The "con" arguments, on the other hand, form part of a perspective which

"Conservative" vs. "Liberal"

Issue	Conservative	Liberal
	Views that put a central focus on traditional values, individual responsibility, and a limited role for government in economic and social matters	Views that focus on social improvement and which emphasize equality, human rights, and an active role for government in the economy and in social improvement
Economy	The free market is key to economic well-being. It rewards hard work and the resultant distribution of wealth is basically fair.	Although playing a major role, the free market does not produce a fair distribution of wealth. Many major economic goods (e.g., health, power) are best supplied by government.
Taxes	Low taxes and a smaller government are supported on the theory that lower taxes create a climate for economic growth and that government is usually inefficient.	Taxes support public programs from health care and housing to infrastructure development. An appropriate level of taxation is crucial to collective well-being.
Role of government	Government's role is to protect private property, provide defence, and maintain basic liberties within the traditional value framework; e.g., support economic freedom, but keep recreational drugs illegal.	Government's role is to provide a means for achieving collective goods and protecting the individual. Government has a role in encouraging progressive attitudes and tolerance of differences; e.g., gender equality, gay marriage, anti-racism.
Crime and law and order	The death penalty is a punishment that fits the crime. Most criminals do not receive appropriately severe penalties.	The death penalty is inhumane punishment. It does not deter crime. Crime needs to be addressed primarily at the level of reducing social inequities and rehabilitating criminals.
The Environment	While we all desire clean water, clean air, and a clean planet, environmental policies extend the power of government and reduce economic growth. Conservatives suspect that there is a pro-government agenda behind most environmental theories.	The government must play an active role in environmental protection. Industrial growth must be shaped and controlled by governmental policies to avoid global warming and other environmental ills.

is often characterized as liberal. "Liberal" generally refers to views which focus on social change and which emphasize equality, human rights, social responsibility, and an active role for government in the economy and in social improvement.

Although the terms "liberal" and "conservative" are commonly used to refer to particular orientations to social or political issues, they do not refer to distinct, fixed bodies of belief. Rather, these are vague terms which are used in a number of different ways in different contexts with somewhat different meanings or emphases. Thus someone who is seen to be of a conservative orientation in Canada may be considered a liberal in the U.S. Nor are these categories mutually exclusive. We should not, for example, draw the conclusion that those espousing a conservative world view do not care about equality and human rights or that those of a liberal persuasion are unconcerned about law and order or social stability. Rather, these characterizations reflect basic orientations and emphases and a particular individual's views may lie somewhere on a continuum between the two. It is also possible that people could have a conservative perspective on some issues but hold a liberal view on others.

People's positions on issues are often grounded in underlying views of this kind. So, for example, in the issue related to the vicious dogs, Councillor McGregor seems to hold a libertarian view of the world, believing strongly in the priority of human liberty and taking positions that oppose government intervention: he opposes any kind of regulation of dog ownership. Councillor Onassis, on the other hand, supports the role of government

Liberal and Conservative versus liberal and conservative

It is important to distinguish the small "c" and small "l" sense of conservative and liberal, referring to the orientations outlined above, from the names of two major Canadian political parties, the Conservatives and the Liberals. The fact that the names of the political parties are the same as the names of these political orientations is not, of course, coincidental, as the members of each of these parties share elements of these political orientations. Nonetheless, the views of the members of each of these parties are not uniform and cover the whole range of possibilities described above.

In the context of our inquiry, it is interesting to note that the vote that resulted in the abolition of capital punishment in Canada in 1976 was a free vote which was supported by members of all political parties.

In most cases, a whole world view underlies people's views on individual issues, particularly in the case of controversial issues.

Knowing the intellectual, social, political, and historical context of the argument can help us to better understand the various positions on an issue and to understand the basis for the controversy.

Apply Your Understanding
Exercises 5, 6, 7

in regulating behaviour in order to protect citizens from harm. His advocacy of imposing regulations is consistent with this philosophy.

Examples abound. Critics of environmental legislation (e.g., a carbon tax) may come from a pro-business orientation which opposes limitations on the ability of corporations to make profits. Individuals opposed to stem cell research often come from a religious orientation which holds the fetus as inviolable. Equal pay legislation may be grounded in certain feminist concerns regarding gender equity. In most cases, a whole world view underlies people's views on individual issues, particularly in the case of controversial issues.

It would be a mistake, however, to judge an argument based on the social or political orientation of its source. (See the fallacy of guilt by association in Chapter 4.) A non-believer is not justified in making this argument: "Religious fundamentalists in North America support teaching children to read; since I am not a religious fundamentalist, I cannot accept teaching children to read." It is no more valid for someone of a conservative persuasion to argue this way: "Liberals support the abolition of capital punishment so the abolition of capital punishment can't be right." Dismissing an argument because of the political or social views of the source would be another example of the ad hominem fallacy which we've seen in Chapter 4. Instead, we have to look at the strengths and weaknesses of the individual argument.

Knowing the intellectual, social, political, and historical context of the argument can, however, help us to better understand the various positions on an issue and to understand the basis for the controversy. It can reveal the assumptions on which arguments are based, assumptions which may not be obvious or explicitly stated in the argument. This type of information will become relevant when we move on to the task of evaluating the various arguments and positions.

At this stage of our inquiry, we are gathering information which may be relevant to the understanding of the issue, to the evaluation of the various arguments and cases, and to arriving at a reasoned judgment. But some of this information may turn out to be irrelevant, or only marginally relevant. We will not really know until we begin to focus on the criteria for evaluation of reasons and arguments. But it is important, at this point, to investigate various aspects of context and not to ignore information which might turn out to be revealing or significant. Looking at context can give us a much deeper understanding of the intricacies and subtleties of an issue, and such understanding is indispensable for coming to a reasoned judgment.

Mapping the Context: Capital Punishment

Intellectual, Political, Social, and Historical Contexts
- pro arguments linked to conservative world view
- con arguments linked to liberal world view

The Debate:
- history of incapacitation, deterrence, and retribution arguments
- critiques of deterrence argument
- recent ascendancy of retribution argument

State of Practice:
- majority of countries in world have abolished or no longer practise captital punisment
- worldwide trend toward abolition
- public concern about violent crimes and leniency towards violent offenders

CHECK YOUR UNDERSTANDING

- *Why is it important to lay out the current debate on an issue?*
- *What are the various elements that need to be included when laying out the current debate?*
- *Name and briefly describe three arguments in favour of capital punishment.*
- *Name and briefly describe four arguments opposed to capital punishment.*
- *What are the three aspects of context identified in the chapter? Briefly describe each one.*
- *Why is it important to find out about each of these aspects of context?*
- *For each aspect, describe how knowing about it is helpful in inquiring about the issue of capital punishment.*

EXERCISES

1. Reread the debate over the banning of dangerous dogs in Chapter 2. Make a "Table of Arguments Pro and Con Banning Dangerous Dogs" to list the arguments, objections, and responses to the objections which you find in the dialogue. (See the model on page 145.)

2. Reread the dialogue at the beginning of Chapter 5 on legalizing marijuana. Make a "Table of Arguments Pro and Con Legalizing Marijuana" to list the arguments, objections, and responses to the objections which you find in the dialogue.

3. This assignment focuses on the issue of whether a person should eat meat. Do research to discover what you can about the history of the debate around this issue.

4. Choose one of the following issues:
   - Should women take a combat role in the army?
   - Should animals be used in medical testing?
   - Should daycare for all children be subsidized by the government?

   Do research to discover what you can about the history of the debate around the issue you have chosen.

5. This assignment focuses on the dialogue listed under exercise 8-5 on the textbook website.

   i) Pick out the reasons offered in the dialogue both for and against arranged marriages, the objections offered to the arguments, and the responses offered to the objections. Make a "Table of Arguments Pro and Con Arranged Marriages" to list the arguments, objections, and responses.

   ii) List any questions you can think of regarding aspects of context which would be helpful to know about in order to reach a reasoned judgment on the issue of arranged marriages. Categorize your questions under the following headings:
   a) state of practice
   b) history of the debate
   c) intellectual, social, political, and historical contexts
      (Try to come up with questions in all the categories.)

   iii) Go to the website http://debatepedia.idebate.org/en/index.php/Debate:_Arranged_marriage. Read the section on "Background and Context of Debate."

   a) Pick out the various pieces of information about context which are given in the section.
   b) Categorize the information under the same headings as in ii) above.

6. This assignment focuses on identifying the contexts surrounding the issue of whether condoms should be made available to students in schools. Read the article for exercise 8-6 on the textbook website. Do some research on the issue of condom distribution (the internet is a good resource) in order to respond to the following questions:

   i) laying out the current debate

   List briefly the main arguments you find on both sides of the issue of condom distribution. List any objections you find to the main arguments.

   ii) identifying the contexts

   a) state of practice: What is the current situation with respect to the availability and distribution of condoms in schools in your area?
   b) history of the debate: Have views about condom distribution changed in the last number of years (and if so, how)?
   c) intellectual, social, political, and historical contexts: What do you know or can you find out about the person or group making the argument in the question cited in the exercise? How might this information be relevant to the evaluation of the argument? What can you discover about the political or social views or the philosophical world views of the proponents of the various positions in the debate? What are the assumptions on which they are basing their arguments?

7. This assignment focuses on the topic of surrogate motherhood.

   i) Clarify precisely what the issue is that you will investigate. Consider any value assumptions which might be built into the term "surrogate motherhood" when framing your issue.

   ii) Do research (in books or on the internet) to identify arguments both for and against surrogate motherhood.

   iii) Make a "Table of Arguments Pro and Con Surrogate Motherhood" to list the arguments, objections, and responses which you find. Try to find arguments which deal with a range of concerns including ethical, legal, and health considerations.

   iv) Working with a partner, write a dialogue between two (or more) individuals debating the pros and cons of surrogate motherhood based on the arguments, objections, and responses which you have recorded in the table.

ENDNOTES

1. For a summary of some of the main arguments, see Death Penalty Information Centre website, http://www.deathpenaltyinfo.org/home.

2. Amnesty International, "The Death Penalty in Canada: Twenty Years of Abolition," http://www.amnesty.ca/deathpenalty/canada.php (accessed May 11, 2010).

3. *Wikipedia*, "Capital punishment in Canada," http://en.wikipedia.org/wiki/Capital_punishment_in_Canada (accessed May 11, 2010).

4. Death Penalty Information Center, "Facts about the Death Penalty," http://www.deathpenaltyinfo.org/FactSheet.pdf

5. CBC, "No more clemency appeals for Canadians on death row in U.S.: Tories," http://www.cbc.ca/canada/story/2007/11/01/death-penalty.html

6. Death Penalty Information Center, "Abolitionist and Retentionist Countries," http://www.deathpenaltyinfo.org/abolitionist-and-retentionist-countries (accessed May 11, 2010).

7. Ibid.

8. Amnesty International, "UN Adopts Landmark Decision on Global Moratorium on Executions," http://www.amnesty.org/en/library/info/IOR30/025/2007 (accessed May 16, 2010).

9. David Baldus, referenced in "Arbitrariness," *Death Penalty Information website*, http://www.deathpenaltyinfo.org/arbitrariness (accessed May 14, 2010).

10. Pursuing the Truth Ministries, "An Eye for an Eye," http://www.pursuingthetruth.org/studies/files/eyeforeye.htm.

11. *Wikipedia*, "Eye for an Eye," http://en.wikipedia.org/wiki/Eye_for_an_eye (accessed May 12, 2010).

12. The Canadian Encyclopedia, "Peace, Order, and Good Government," http://www.thecanadianencyclopedia.com/index.cfm?PgNm=TCE&Params=A1ARTA0006162.

Chapter 9
Evaluating the Arguments

Capital Punishment II

Sophia and Phil continue the discussion of capital punishment which they began in the previous chapter.

Phil: You know, Sophia, we've looked at a lot of information and arguments about capital punishment. And I can see now that the issue is much more complicated than you might believe just by looking at the police chief's argument. But even after all that, I still don't know what to think about capital punishment. Should I support it or not?

Sophia: You've got a point, Phil. We never got that far. We did manage to clarify the issue . . .

Phil: "Should there be capital punishment for pre-meditated murder?"

Sophia: . . . and we did figure out that inquiring into that issue would involve both factual judgments and value judgments.

Phil: Uh-huh. And we found out some important information about the context.

Sophia: But we still need to evaluate the arguments in order to decide what to believe.

Evaluating the Main Reasons and Arguments

Review the main arguments pro and con capital punishment that Phil and Sophia identified in Chapter 8.

What Do You Think ?

Phil: OK—maybe we should start by reviewing the arguments that we found. First, on the pro side, there's the incapacitation argument, the deterrence argument, the retribution argument, and the cost argument.

Sophia: And on the con side, there's the argument about the immorality of taking a life, the rehabilitation argument, the social causality argument, and the argument about executing the innocent.

Sophia: In that article that you were reading that got us started on the whole issue, the arguments that the police chief gives look like versions of the incapacitation and deterrence arguments. We discovered in our investigation that there's more to the issue than just what he says in the article, but we never really looked carefully at his arguments. So maybe that would be a good place to start. Why don't you read the article again?

Phil: (*reading aloud*)
"Society has an obligation, first and foremost, to protect its citizens from harm. And the most serious form of harm is murder. Protecting citizens from murder involves ensuring that murderers don't repeat the offence. It also involves dissuading others from committing murder. Now I and other law enforcement officers know from a vast amount of first-hand experience with criminals that the only form of punishment that can effectively achieve both goals is the death penalty. Capital punishment involves taking the life of a person who has committed murder in order to save the lives of innocent people, and so is the best option under the circumstances."

What problems do you see in the police chief's arguments?

What Do You Think ?

Keep in Mind

GUIDING QUESTIONS FOR INQUIRY
- What is the issue?
- What kinds of claims or judgments are at issue?
- What are the relevant reasons and arguments on various sides of the issue?
- What is the context of the issue?
- **How do we comparatively evaluate the various reasons and arguments to reach a reasoned judgment?**

Sophia: One thing that strikes me about his arguments is that he's basing his claims about the effectiveness of capital punishment solely on his own experience. He doesn't mention any research or statistics—just "a vast amount of first-hand experience with criminals."

Phil: He does have a ton of experience dealing with murders and murderers, though, so he should know what he's talking about. He knows first-hand the gritty reality of the crime world, and he certainly knows more about how murderers think and what motivates them than you or I do! So maybe we should take seriously what he has to say.

Sophia: But his particular experience doesn't provide a basis for making such a sweeping generalization. Claiming that it does is the fallacy of anecdotal evidence. He also claims that the death penalty is the best option under the circumstances; but he doesn't say what the other options are or on what basis he judges that capital punishment is the best.

Phil: I'm also thinking that, being a police chief, he's hardly an unbiased source of information. He likely has a very particular perspective on things, being concerned with law and order. I don't imagine that we should look to his arguments in order to get a balanced view.

Sophia: I also don't think that we should accept him as an authority on this issue. After all, capital punishment is essentially a moral issue, and he has no particular expertise in moral issues, police chief or not. I don't think that his pronouncements about society's obligations or what's morally acceptable have any special authority. I think that we'll have to puzzle those issues through ourselves.

Phil: Well, we're certainly not impressed with the arguments that the police chief offers in that article. I guess that means that the deterrence and incapacitation arguments don't hold water.

What Do You Think ?

Do you agree with Phil that the problems in the police chief's arguments indicate that the deterrence and incapacitation arguments are wrong?

Sophia: No, I don't think it means that at all. It only means that the police chief doesn't give us very good reasons for believing the incapacitation or deterrence views. But that doesn't mean that the views are wrong, only that his particular arguments don't provide much support for them.

Phil: So we still need to evaluate those arguments, as well as all the others?

Sophia: Yup. We have our work cut out for us! Why don't we start by seeing what we can find out about deterrence. There must be lots of studies that have been done to determine whether capital punishment works as a deterrent.

In the dialogue in Chapter 8, Phil and Sophia began to look at the issue of capital punishment. They started by identifying and clarifying the issue and determining what types of judgments would be involved in their inquiry. Laying out the reasons and arguments on the various sides of the debate was a centrally important aspect of the inquiry process, as was investigating aspects of context that may play a role in evaluation.

In the current dialogue, they go on to address the matter of evaluation. The process begins with an evaluation of the individual arguments. Phil and Sophia have a particular version of two of the arguments as a starting point, the arguments offered by the police chief in the newspaper article. Thus they are able to engage in the kind of prima facie evaluation of individual arguments that we learned about in Chapter 4, to see if there are any fallacies or obvious problems in the reasoning. They do, in fact, encounter fallacies of anecdotal evidence and improper appeal to authority, as well as possible bias in the argument.

Showing that an argument is poor or fallacious does not demonstrate that the conclusion is wrong.

The fact that there are fallacies in the arguments that the police chief offers does not, however, invalidate the views which he is defending. What it does demonstrate is that these particular arguments do not provide much, if any, support for these views. Thus the need for evaluation still remains. There are ways to evaluate these claims, but they will require going beyond a prima facie evaluation of the particular arguments offered.

What Do You Think ?

How can Phil and Sophia go about evaluating the factual claims and ethical arguments regarding capital punishment which they have found?

With respect to the factual claims (regarding, for example, the effectiveness of capital punishment as a deterrent), they will need to see what research has been done and what other evidence is available. With regard to the moral issues, the conflicting arguments will have to be assessed according to the criteria for evaluating ethical judgments (as discussed in Chapter 7).

Evaluating the Pro Arguments

Phil: You were certainly right that there's a lot of information about the effectiveness of the death penalty as a deterrent, and the material that I found was on the whole quite negative. That really amazed me because the idea of deterrence just seems to make so much sense. But in fact, there's lots of evidence that seems to indicate that there is no positive correlation between the abolition of the death penalty and an increase in the murder rate. Quite the opposite, in fact.

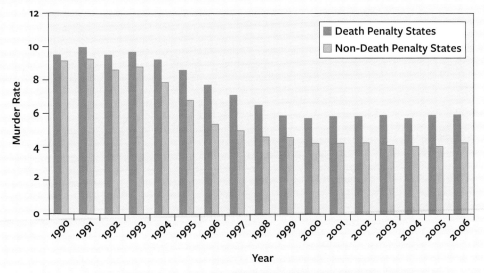

Murder Rates in Death Penalty States and Non-Death Penalty States

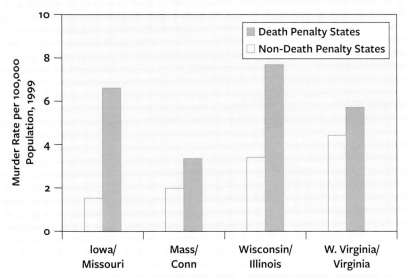

Death Penalty States Often Have a Higher Murder Rate than Their Neighbouring Non-Death Penalty States[1]

After the abolition of capital punishment in Canada, there was a general trend downward (after an initial rise). And in the U.S., the murder rate is highest in those states that have retained the death penalty. In fact, there's a striking similarity between the U.S. and Canada in the change of murder rates despite the U.S. having capital punishment.[2]

Sophia: You know, that actually makes sense once you think about it. I read that a large percentage of murders are by people who know their victims. They're often committed in the heat of passion, when folks aren't likely to be thinking through the possible consequences of their actions.

Phil: That's true. But some death penalty supporters argue that capital punishment might be effective with certain types of murderers—those who plan their crimes and can assess the risks. And I also came across the argument that the reason that so many of the studies don't show a deterrent effect is that there are so few actual executions that potential murderers

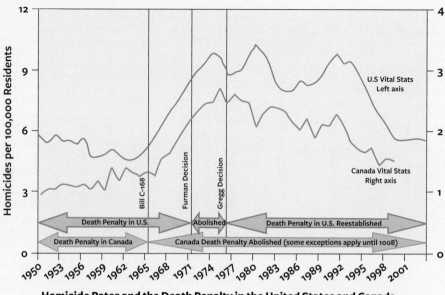

Homicide Rates and the Death Penalty in the United States and Canada

realize that the chances of being executed are quite small. The murder rate in a place like Singapore, where they carry out lots of executions, is very low.[3]

Sophia: That's pretty drastic, though.

Phil: Another interesting fact that I came across is that, in Canada, the overall conviction rate for first-degree murder doubled in the decade following abolition. Some folks argue that that's because juries became more willing to convict for murder once they weren't forced to make life and death decisions.[4] So it looks like abolition resulted in getting more murderers off the streets!

Sophia: The research I looked at showed some consensus among criminologists that the death penalty is not an effective deterrent. For example, in a recent survey, over 80% of the experts surveyed said that they believe the existing research does not support a deterrence justification for the death penalty. And even law enforcement personnel seem to agree that capital punishment is not effective as a deterrent,[5] though their views do not, in and of themselves, prove anything.

Phil: I did come across some recent studies, though, that claim a deterrent effect.[7] But there have been lots of criticisms of these studies by experts in the field who claim that they were filled with technical and conceptual errors, including using improper statistical analyses and leaving out important data and key variables.[8] The authors of the studies I'm referring to are also critical of the methods and findings of the research that claims to find no deterrent effect. There's obviously some debate around this question, but the research that claims that there's no deterrent effect seems to have the day.

Sophia: One thing I'm wondering about, though, is some of the sources we're using. A lot of our information has come from sources like the Death Penalty Information Center, which is clearly opposed to capital punishment, and from sources like The Criminal Justice Legal Foundation and a website called *Capital Punishment in the UK,* which are clearly for the death penalty. I'm worried that the information on these websites may be biased.

Phil: I had the same concerns. But the Death Penalty Information Center is a centre for the collection of information and resources about capital punishment and its Board of Directors

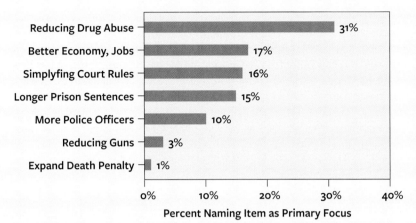

Police Chiefs Place Death Penalty Last in Reducing Violent Crime [6]

is made up of all kinds of extremely prominent experts in the area, like eminent law professors and attorneys who have been involved in important death penalty cases.

Sophia: Lawyers who've defended important death penalty cases would likely have a vested interest in being against capital punishment, though.

Phil: True. But the Center also gives lots of references to the actual studies and research which is the basis for the various claims, and the studies all seem to be from credible peer-reviewed sources like the *Ohio State Journal of Criminal Law*, the *Stanford Law Review*, and the *Annual Review of Law and Social Science*. The organization clearly has a point of view, but it seems to be well supported by research.

Sophia: Did you have a look at any of the original studies?

Phil: I did, and they corroborate the information presented on the website.

Sophia: What about the Criminal Justice Legal Foundation?

Phil: They say that their purpose is "to assure that people who are guilty of committing crimes receive swift and certain punishment in an orderly and constitutional manner." So they clearly have an agenda. The research they cite appears to be from refereed journals like the *Journal of Criminal Justice*, the *Journal of Law, Economics and Policy*, and the *American Journal of Economics and Sociology*; but the research is all supporting one side of the debate.

Sophia: What about the *Capital Punishment in the UK* website?

Phil: It seems to be run by an individual and not an organization. Though it cites a lot of "facts" and statistics, it doesn't provide any references. We learned that that's a reason for concern about credibility.

Sophia: When we were looking at the arguments for and against capital punishment, remember we noticed that deterrence is no longer the main argument offered in support of capital punishment. Now I understand why. If there is any evidence for a deterrent effect, it doesn't seem to be all that strong.

Phil and Sophia have begun their evaluation of the various pro and con arguments by checking out the evidence in support of the deterrence argument, an argument which focuses on the consequences of capital punishment. The claim that capital punishment is effective in deterring murder is a factual claim, so it can be evaluated by looking at the empirical evidence. Sophia and Phil find various kinds of evidence that is relevant to evaluating this claim.

One type of evidence has to do with the relationship between the existence of capital punishment and the murder rate. If capital punishment were an effective deterrent, then one would expect that the murder rate would be higher in jurisdictions that do not have the death penalty. This is not the case, however. In the U.S., abolitionist states have a consistently lower murder rate than retentionist states, and the Canadian experience is that abolition was accompanied by a generally declining rate of murder. To demonstrate a correlation is not, of course, to assert a causal connection (as we saw in Chapter 5), so one should not conclude that abolishing the death penalty causes lower murder rates. There are likely factors in the various jurisdictions that contribute to both the abolition of the death penalty and lower murder rates. What the finding does demonstrate, however, is that the prediction of higher murder rates accompanying abolition of the death penalty is not borne out.

This evidence is supported by the views of the majority of experts (criminologists and law officials) who argue that existing research does not support the deterrence position. Phil encountered a few studies claiming to find a deterrent effect, but the criticisms of the studies by experts puts the credibility of these studies into question. There is considerable expert consensus regarding the ineffectiveness of deterrence, although this position is not uncontested. Expert consensus plays a key role in establishing factual claims (as was discussed in Chapter 6).

The strength of the evidence against deterrence came as a considerable surprise to our inquirers because the idea that the death penalty would deter potential murderers from committing murder seems so intuitively plausible. This demonstrates that you should not mistake plausibility for strong evidence; rather, you should evaluate the actual evidence in support of key factual claims.

You should not mistake plausibility for strong evidence; rather, you should evaluate the actual evidence in support of key factual claims.

Phil: OK—so we've dealt with the deterrence argument. But there are still a bunch of other arguments to evaluate.

Sophia: The police chief also talks about capital punishment as a way to ensure that murderers don't repeat the offence—that's the incapacitation argument.

What Do You Think ?

How would you evaluate the incapacitation argument?

Phil: We do have to admit that it's pretty effective. A dead murderer can't murder again. But that seems like a pretty drastic way to keep murderers off the street. Keeping them in prison will accomplish the same thing, without raising all the moral issues about the government killing people.

Sophia: And if the Canadian experience about murder convictions increasing is any indication, it may be even more effective.

Phil: Right.

Sophia: I'd really like to have a look at the retribution argument. It seems to be the most common argument made these days for capital punishment, but it looks to me like simply a desire for revenge.

Phil: I don't agree. I think it's only right that a person who commits a murder pays for his or her crime. And if someone murders someone else, then the appropriate punishment is that the life of the murderer taken away. You know—an eye for an eye. The folks who support retribution are seeking justice, not revenge.

Sophia: But remember where the idea of "an eye for an eye" comes from? It was originally used in the Bible as a principle of compensation. It seems to me that the religious right have changed its meaning to use it as a justification for revenge.

Phil: Sophia, I think that the fact that the retribution argument is supported by the religious right might be clouding your judgment and preventing you from recognizing a legitimate desire for justice. Do you remember that fellow Ivan that my father used to work with? Did you know that his daughter was one of the victims of that mass murderer who was kidnapping and torturing young girls a few years ago? I think that parents like Ivan have every right to want that guy dead. It's not right that he gets to keep on living after what he did.

Sophia: Maybe you're right, Phil. People do have a right to want to see justice done. I guess I would too, under those circumstances.

Phil: But when you see what actually happens in the courts in sentencing, what with plea bargaining and all . . . It's like in this novel I read where a man's wife is brutally murdered and he's enraged by how the court system seems to be more weighted toward the offender than the victim.[9] That doesn't seem like justice.

Sophia: True. But on the other hand, I was reading about some of the folks who've committed murders. So many of them were raised in absolutely appalling, abusive conditions. I don't agree with those people who think that that somehow lessens their responsibility for what they've done. But it does make me feel at least a bit sympathetic towards them and reluctant to put them to death.

Phil: But not all murderers were raised in those types of conditions. Some come from what appear to be "good" homes.

Sophia: That's true too. But in any case, I think that justice can be served by other means besides the state putting someone to death. I certainly wouldn't want to see these murderers go free or get early parole. But keeping someone in jail for the rest of his or her life is a pretty severe punishment—for some, it might be even more cruel than being put to death. It may not satisfy the desire for revenge that people close to such events may sometimes experience. But then, maybe revenge is not the best motive for making these kinds of decisions.

Phil: You may be right about that. I have to admit that I'm pretty emotionally involved. Maybe life imprisonment can meet the demand for justice.

Sophia and Phil have moved on to evaluate the two other main arguments that they have identified on the pro side of the capital punishment debate, incapacitation and retribution. Unlike the deterrence argument, where the evaluation focused primarily on a factual claim regarding effectiveness, the evaluation of the incapacitation argument focuses largely on an evaluative judgment regarding the desirability of execution as a means of keeping murderers from reoffending. Both Sophia and Phil agree that the ends do not justify the means in this case. By evaluating the death penalty in comparison with its alternative, namely life imprisonment, they are able to see that there are less extreme and less morally problematic means to achieve the end advocated by the incapacitation argument.

There is, of course, also a factual claim implicit in this argument, namely that the death penalty is effective in preventing reoffending. That claim is self-evidently true ("Dead murderers can't murder again," as Phil notes); however, it may turn out, ironically, that the existence of capital punishment may result in fewer convictions and thus result in more murderers being left free. But this is a claim that would also need to be checked out.

The retribution argument is essentially an ethical argument which makes an appeal to justice. It does not focus on the consequences of capital punishment, as does the deterrence argument. Instead, it focuses on the moral import of the punishment itself: the death of the perpetrator satisfies the requirement for an appropriate punishment for murder and restores a kind of moral balance. The biblical concept of "an eye for an eye" is often evoked as a justification for retribution. Opponents of the retribution argument would argue that justice only requires the punishment of the murderer, not his or her death. They view the

An important aspect of evaluation of instrumental claims (claims about effective means to achieve a particular goal or end) involves evaluating a proposed action or policy in comparison with other alternatives.

It is important to be aware of one's initial views and leanings, and how they may be affecting how we frame an issue, in order to avoid possible biases. It is similarly important to be aware of the contextual factors which might be influencing and grounding the views of others.

desire for the death of the perpetrator as a matter of revenge, which they do not see as a morally defensible motivation.

How one evaluates arguments may be influenced by the kind of contextual (even personal) factors that we discussed in the previous chapter. For example, the point which Sophia makes regarding the sympathy due to many murderers because of the appalling social circumstances in which they were raised is grounded in a liberal world view which emphasizes social causation and social responsibility. As another example, Sophia's rejection of the retribution argument seems at least partly connected to her antipathy to the religious right, a group with whom this argument is often associated. And Phil's personal connection to a murder victim affects the way in which he views retribution.

This is not to say that they do not have valid reasons for their views. But it does point to the importance of being aware of our initial views and leanings, and how they may be affecting how we frame an issue. Being self-aware in this way is necessary to avoid possible biases. It is similarly important to be aware of the contextual factors which might be influencing and grounding the views of others. In this case, becoming aware about their own possible biases allows both Sophia and Phil to be more open to hearing the opposing arguments and acknowledging what might be acceptable in the other position. Thus Sophia could acknowledge that there might be some element of a morally legitimate desire for justice underlying retribution. And Phil is able to realize that the desire for justice could be satisfied through life imprisonment without resorting to the morally contested practice of the state killing some of its citizens.

Phil: Another argument that we should have a look at is that keeping people in prison rather than executing them is too expensive. And I have to agree. It's galling that we have to spend all that taxpayer money on prisons and guards—keeping these folks in food and shelter—after what they've done.

Sophia: I was surprised to discover, though, that in fact, the death penalty is much much more expensive than life imprisonment without parole. Every single study I came across agreed with that.[10]

Phil: That's amazing! I guess it shows again that we need to check out these facts that may seem so obvious at first.

Sophia: Of course, supporters of capital punishment point out that the reason the death penalty is more expensive is because of all the appeals and length of time on death row. They would tell you that if executions took place more quickly, then capital punishment would be cheaper.

Phil: So are they implying that we should execute people more quickly in order to save money?

Sophia: Even if it was less expensive to execute people, that still wouldn't be a reason to do it. I think it's morally wrong for all the reasons we've talked about, and anyone who would argue that costs are more important than morality simply has their priorities mixed up.

Phil: But it really galls people to have to pay taxes to keep some horrible criminal in jail for years.

Sophia: I'm sure you're right. But living in a just and humane society has a price.

Phil's perception that it is more expensive to keep people in prison for life than to execute them is a common one, and its initial plausibility might tempt one not to investigate further. But to cut short your investigation would be to mistake plausibility for strong evidence. This claim turns out to be false (at least in North America), as Sophia points out. In addition, Sophia makes an extremely important point when she notes that prioritizing costs over moral considerations is highly problematic. Note how she also frames the issue of cost within the greater idea of living in a just and humane society. In evaluating arguments, one must often make judgments of comparative value (see Chapter 7), and valuing expediency over morality will usually be a moral error.

Evaluating the Con Arguments

Phil: We've had a look at the main arguments in favour of capital punishment. We ought to have a go at the arguments against.

Sophia: One obvious argument is that taking a life is morally wrong, even if it's done by the state—or perhaps, especially if it's done by the state.

Phil: But the supporters of capital punishment argue that it's justified if the person in question took someone else's life. It's as if, by committing a murder, a person gives up the right to life.

Do you agree that a person gives up the right to life by committing a murder?

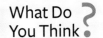

What Do
You Think ?

Sophia: But can people really give up their right to life? Is it the kind of thing that a person can give up? I mean, if it's an intrinsic value?

Phil: But don't rights imply responsibilities? I just can't see that we would want to say that a mass murderer still has the right to live, even after what he or she has done.

Sophia: I just don't know. It seems to me that taking a life is wrong, especially when it's done in a planned and premeditated way. It's possible that there may be a few exceptional cases when it's justified, but the reasons would have to be extremely compelling. And whether or not the reasons are strong enough is a pretty big moral question. But maybe we don't have to decide on that for our purposes.

Phil: Why not?

Sophia: Because there's another moral argument against capital punishment which I think is very strong and which doesn't depend on us agreeing about whether one can ever justify killing. It has to do with the risk of executing innocent people. We know that the justice system isn't perfect and that innocent people do get convicted. So if you have the death penalty, it's very likely that some innocent people will be executed. And that surely isn't right.

Phil: But the supporters of capital punishment argue that the risks are small in comparison to the benefits.

Sophia: Now I really have to disagree with that. First of all, I don't think that the risk is all that small. The information that I found indicates that the number if people convicted of murder and later found to be innocent is pretty significant. In the U.S., for example, 131 people on death row have been exonerated since 1973. Then there are others who were released or who had their sentences commuted due to probable innocence, and still others who were executed but where there are doubts about their guilt. And that's only the ones that we know about. Just recently I read that New Mexico has abolished the death penalty after four people who'd been executed were shown to be innocent through DNA evidence.[11]

There aren't similar stats for Canada since there is no death penalty, but there are quite a few well-known cases of wrongful convictions—people like David Milgaard, Donald Marshall, and Stephen Truscott. Truscott was sentenced to be hanged, but his sentence was later commuted. Milgaard and Marshall may well have been executed if capital punishment was still in effect.

Phil: I have to admit that these cases are pretty disturbing. But maybe they're justified by all the lives of innocent people that would be saved.

Sophia: Phil, you're forgetting what we found out about deterrence. There's no compelling evidence that capital punishment would save any lives. So in terms of benefits versus risks, it seems mostly risk and very little benefit.

Dennis Williams of Illinois spent 18 years on death row. His charges were later dropped due to new DNA evidence and he was released from prison in 1996.

Wrongfully Convicted: High-profile Cases Where the Courts Got It Wrong: Steven Truscott[12]

In 1959, Truscott was sentenced to be hanged at age 14 for a schoolmate's murder, becoming Canada's youngest death-row inmate.

After the original conviction, Steven Truscott spent four months in the shadow of the gallows until his death sentence was commuted to life imprisonment. Paroled in 1969, Truscott disappeared into an anonymous existence in a southern Ontario city.

On Aug. 28, 2007—48 years later—the Ontario Court of Appeal unanimously overturned Truscott's conviction and acquitted him, declaring the case "a miscarriage of justice" that "must be quashed."

The judges went on to say, however, that "the court is not satisfied that the appellant has been able to demonstrate his factual innocence."

In July 2008, the Ontario government announced it would pay Truscott $6.5 million in compensation for his ordeal.

Phil: I guess you're right.

Sophia: And besides, I don't know that risking executing the wrong people could ever be justified, even if there were some benefits. It just seems morally wrong.

Phil: I have to agree there.

Sophia: Anyway, killing seems to me to be especially wrong if it's done by the state.

Phil: What's that got to do with it? The state is allowed to do things that individuals aren't, like declaring wars or locking people up.

Sophia: The government is supposed to protect its citizens and their rights. It's bad enough when some individual murders a member of the society—but we know that there are immoral people out there. But the state is supposed to act for the good of its citizens, not kill innocent members of society.

The two arguments which Sophia and Phil examine next are both moral arguments. The first is a very general argument, that taking a life is morally wrong. The second is an argument more specific to the case at hand, that the risk of executing innocent people cannot be morally justified. Now certainly, if it were possible to establish that taking a life is always and under all circumstances morally wrong and can never be justified, then the second claim, that the risk of executing innocent people cannot be justified, would follow. There is widespread agreement that taking a life is morally wrong under most circumstances, and so a prima facie presumption against doing so also exists. But the question of whether and under what circumstances it can ever be justified is a huge moral question which would take our inquirers far beyond the scope of the issue in question.

Sophia comes to the realization, however, that they do not need to tackle this very general and very thorny moral claim which would be very difficult to establish (although an interesting issue for a philosophical inquiry). It is sufficient to deal with the issue which relates specifically to the capital punishment case. In other words, one does not have to establish the stronger claim that taking a life can never be justified in order to establish the weaker claim that the state taking the life of some of its innocent citizens cannot be justified. This type of narrowing of a question from very general claims that are difficult to establish to the more particular claims which relate specifically to the case at hand is an important strategy in attempting to reach a reasoned judgment on a complex issue.

The argument under discussion focuses on one of the likely consequences of capital punishment—that some innocent people will be executed. The argument is that this consequence is morally unacceptable because the killing of innocent people violates a fundamental value. The fact that the killing is committed by the state is seen as adding to its moral unacceptability because the role of the government is to protect its citizens from harm and not to do them

The narrowing of a question from very general claims that are difficult to establish to the more particular claims which relate specifically to the case at hand is an important strategy in attempting to reach a reasoned judgment on a complex issue.

harm. Thus we can see that all three criteria for evaluating ethical judgments—consequences, inherent value, and the role and responsibility of the actor—are present in this argument.

The question of comparative risks and benefits is also raised in the discussion and comes up often in debates regarding social policies. The risks involved in an action or policy are not easy to assess: risk has to do with the likelihood of some future negative consequence that might result from a current or proposed action; it is impossible to determine with certainty. But past events can give us some guidance. (Remember our discussion of historical analogies from Chapter 5.) Thus Sophia draws on the information about past cases of wrongful convictions to argue that the risk of executing innocent people is real and significant. Sophia also draws on factual evidence to support the argument that the benefits of capital punishment are negligible.

When assessing risks versus benefits, an important question is whether there are some risks that are never acceptable. Sophia wonders, for example, whether the risk of killing innocent people could ever be justified, even if it had some benefits.

Moreover, moral considerations have a special kind of priority over other types of considerations in our deliberations. Considerations of what is right, good, or just should usually override considerations of efficiency or instrumental effectiveness when assessing risks and benefits.[13] (The issue of risk versus benefit is one we will be discussing in more detail in the next chapter).

Sophia: One anti-capital punishment argument we haven't looked at yet is that punishment should involve attempting to rehabilitate the person who has committed a crime. And obviously capital punishment eliminates any possibility of rehabilitation.

Phil: It's true—you can't rehabilitate someone if they're dead. But isn't it more important to protect innocent citizens than to try to rehabilitate criminals?

Sophia: Phil, you're forgetting something…

What is Phil forgetting?

Phil: Oh yeah—there's no compelling evidence that capital punishment does anything to protect innocent citizens.

Sophia: You've got it.

Phil: But is there really any reason to believe that hardened murderers will change their stripes? Or do they simply behave themselves and fake being sorry in order to get out of jail and escape from the punishment they deserve? That doesn't seem right.

Sophia: Why shouldn't we believe that at least some people can change if they are given a chance and some help? Think about the environment many of them have grown up in.

The rehabilitation argument against capital punishment is based on the idea that even a murderer might repent, reform, and become a productive individual, and that it is not ethical to cut off this possibility and to discard a human life. Upholders of this view tend to hold a world view which emphasizes social causality and the role of the environment in shaping people, and thus tend to support reform efforts and to have a somewhat optimistic view of the possibilities for change. The detractors tend to put a great deal of emphasis on an individual's responsibility for his or her actions and to hold a less optimistic view about the possibility for reform.

There might be possibilities for gaining some insight into this issue through empirical investigation, for example with respect to rates of recidivism (reoffending) for convicted murderers; but this would be a complicated process involving a comparison of the results of various types of interventions aimed at rehabilitation, and it may not produce any definitive results.

Central criteria for evaluating ethical judgments relate to 1) the moral quality of the act, 2) the duties and responsibility of the actor, and 3) the consequences of the act.

Past events can give us some guidance in assessing future risks and benefits of an action or policy.

What Do You Think ?

Moral considerations should generally take priority over other types of considerations when assessing risks and benefits.

At the end of this part of the dialogue, Sophia and Phil have been unable to reach any agreed-upon conclusion about the possibility of rehabilitation. Nonetheless, they are still able to make a judgment about the argument: the argument against rehabilitation rests on the claim that it is more important to protect innocent people than to try to rehabilitate the guilty, and we've seen that capital punishment has not shown itself to be effective in protecting people. The argument against rehabilitation fails for this reason.

Apply Your Understanding Exercises 1, 2

Identifying and Evaluating Additional Arguments

Phil: It looks like we've covered the main arguments on both sides of the debate.

Sophia: But there are a few more arguments that we came across in our research. We should probably look at those as well just to be complete.

Phil: OK. One argument I found is that capital punishment constitutes a "cruel and unusual punishment."

Sophia: How unusual it is depends on where you are. In some places, like the state of Texas, it isn't all that unusual. But it certainly is cruel. Do you remember those photos and descriptions of executions we saw on the internet?[14]

Phil: And how. They turned my stomach.

Sophia: Especially the ones of the botched executions.

Phil: But then again, some of these folks did pretty horrible things to the people they murdered. I read some of those gruesome details as well.

Sophia: I know. But we're morally outraged by those acts. Having that kind of cruelty deliberately inflicted on people by the government, which is supposed to represent a civilized society, simply isn't acceptable.

Phil: I have to agree. Another argument that came up is that capital punishment discriminates against marginalized groups in society, like ethnic minorities or the poor.

Sophia: That seems particularly true of the blacks in the U.S. The stats seem to bear out the fact that blacks are much more likely to receive the death penalty than whites for similar crimes (38% higher in one study), and killers of white victims are much more likely to receive the death penalty than killers of black victims. In fact, most of the studies reviewing race and the death penalty have found a pattern of either race-of-victim or race-of-defendant discrimination or both.[15]

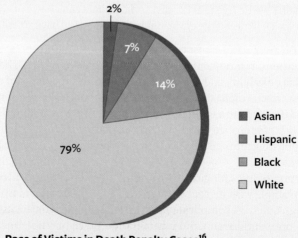

Race of Victims in Death Penalty Cases[16]

Phil: That's a horrible situation, and it does seem to indicate that there's some discrimination going on somewhere. But I'm wondering whether it's really an argument against capital punishment. It might just mean that efforts need to be made to get rid of the discrimination.

Sophia: But given the current state of society, inequalities in terms of race and wealth and power do exist and aren't likely to go away overnight. So capital punishment does turn out, in practice, to be discriminatory.

Phil: Another strike against it, I would say.

Sophia: Here's one last argument that came up: that the debate over the death penalty focuses exclusively on punishment as a way to prevent murders whereas we should be focusing our attention on crime prevention more broadly.

Phil: There's something to that. But I think the argument sets up a kind of false dilemma. It's not that we have to choose between focusing either on prevention or on punishment. We have to think about both. It may be that focusing on various means of prevention may help eventually reduce the number of crimes that need to be punished. But as long as there are crimes being committed, we have to think about what the appropriate kind of punishment is.

The consideration of additional or alternative arguments is necessary in order to ensure that all sides of an issue are taken into account.

Sophia: I agree that the argument doesn't really address the issue of whether or not we should have capital punishment. But it does point out something important about the context of the debate. The real underlying issue is how to prevent violence in society and make our communities safer places. But by focusing on the death penalty, the issue gets framed in terms of punishment, and the underlying question of how to make improvements in society in order to lessen crime gets sidestepped.

Phil: Look Sophia, I've made a table listing the pro and con arguments (without the objections and responses this time) and entered our evaluations of the main arguments onto it. I've also put the arguments and evaluation into a diagram. I think that helps make the big picture much clearer.

At this stage of their evaluation process, Sophia and Phil have turned to a consideration of some additional arguments sometimes offered in the capital punishment debate. The consideration of additional or alternative arguments is necessary in order to ensure that all sides of an issue are taken into account (See Phil's arguments table on page 170.).

Evaluating Individual Arguments: Summing Up

To this point, Sophia and Phil have been engaged in evaluating the various individual arguments offered on different sides of the capital punishment debate. The first step in the process was to conduct a prima facie evaluation of the argument which was the impetus for their inquiry, that of the local chief of police. In making a prima facie analysis, we look for obvious weakness and fallacies. In this case, Phil and Sophia concluded that, because there are a number of such problems with his arguments, the chief's arguments did not provide much support for his pro capital punishment position.

Evaluating the arguments in the capital punishment debate involves dealing with different kinds of issues which need to be evaluated in different ways.

The next step was to evaluate the various claims made on both sides of the debate. It is important to note that this process involves dealing with different kinds of claims which need to be evaluated in different ways.

Many of the arguments in the capital punishment debate rest on claims of a factual nature. Arguments regarding the effectiveness of deterrence, the known incidence of conviction for murder of innocent individuals, the relationship between race and capital convictions, or the costs of capital punishment can be evaluated by looking at factual evidence. In such cases, it is important not to be misled by what may seem initially plausible (e.g., that deterrence is effective or that the cost of the death penalty is higher than that of life imprisonment) and to investigate the evidence in support of these claims.

Evaluation of Arguments		
Argument Name	**Argument Summary**	**Evaluation**
	PRO	
Incapacitation	CP prevents convicted murderers from committing more murders.	Life imprisonment could achieve this.
Deterrence	CP will prevent or discourage people from committing murders.	Evidence does not support the deterrence effect.
Retribution	Justice requires that punishment be proportional to crime.	Justice could be satisfied by life imprisonment.
Cost	It is too expensive to keep people in prison for life.	There is evidence that CP is more expensive than imprisonment; it is a mistake to prioritize costs over morality.
	CON	
Morality	Taking a life is morally wrong.	Because of its prima facie value, this argument would require extremely strong reasons to override.
Rehabilitation	Punishment should serve to rehabilitate but a person can't be rehabilitated if dead.	The likelihood of rehabilitation is an unresolved issue.
Executing the innocent	Innocent people are sometimes executed, a situation which is morally unacceptable.	Risks are significant; risk of killing innocent people by the state is a strong objection.
Social Causality	Criminals are often a product of a dysfunctional social environment and should be treated accordingly.	This argument does not justify exonerating murderers but it may justify showing compassion.

Many of the issues involved in the capital punishment debate require moral judgments. Questions such as whether taking a life can ever be justified, whether murderers give up their right to life, or whether the risk of killing innocent individuals can ever be justified are moral issues which are at the heart of the debate. Moral judgments are justified not through factual evidence but rather through argumentation according to criteria: the moral quality of the act, the duties and responsibility of the actor, and the consequences of the act.

Many issues which Sophia and Phil have examined involve both factual and moral judgments. Such issues cannot be resolved solely through factual considerations, and to try to do so is to commit the naturalistic fallacy (see Chapter 7). So, for example, it would not be sufficient, in order to justify the incapacitation argument, to show (if one could) that capital punishment was an effective method for keeping murderers off the streets. We would still have to consider the morality of the state executing people despite the fact that other means are available for accomplishing the same goal.

Another important point with respect to evaluation is that arguments often need to be assessed in light of available alternatives. For example, Phil and Sophia realize that both the retribution and incapacitation arguments for capital punishment must be assessed in comparison to less morally problematic alternatives (e.g., life imprisonment) which could achieve the same goal. It is true that the

Keep in Mind 4

EVALUATING INDIVIDUAL ARGUMENTS

- Conduct a prima facie evaluation looking for fallacies and other obvious weaknesses.
- Assess the factual claims based on credible sources.
- Assess the evaluative arguments according to the relevant criteria.
- Assess the possibilities in light of the alternatives.

death penalty would prevent any murderer from committing more murders, but the recognition that life imprisonment could achieve the same end is an important aspect of evaluating the value of the incapacitation argument.

As we know, reaching a reasoned judgment involves more than the assessment of individual arguments. The dialogues between Sophia and Phil demonstrate the dialectical nature of inquiry. They do not simply evaluate the individual arguments for or against capital punishment in isolation from each other. They also deal with criticisms, objections, and counter-arguments, and they seek out alternative views and arguments. The evaluation of reasons and arguments required to come to a reasoned judgment is, in the end, a comparative enterprise. A full account of this will be presented in the next chapter.

Apply Your Understanding Exercises 3, 4

Graph of Argumentation on Capital Punishment

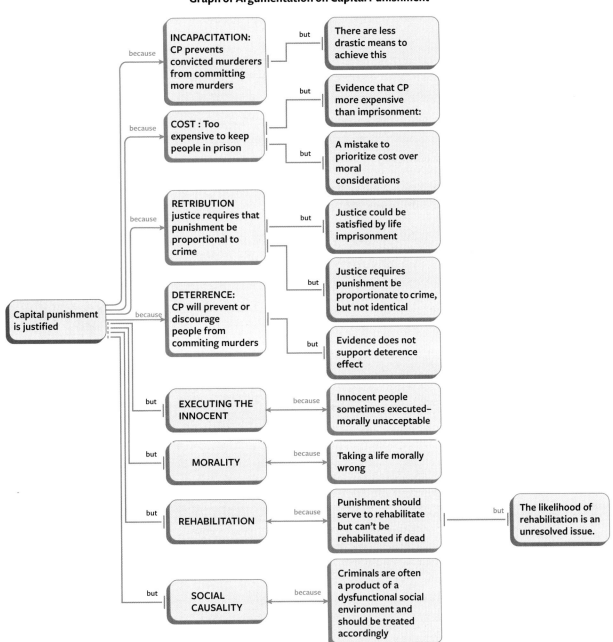

CHECK YOUR UNDERSTANDING

- *What are some of the problems in the police chief's arguments?*
- *What is the evidence with respect to the effectiveness of deterrence?*
- *What are the arguments for and against the incapacitation argument?*
- *What are the arguments for and against the retribution argument?*
- *Give two examples from the dialogue of how social and political views and personal experiences can affect how a person views an issue.*
- *Describe two problems with the cost argument.*
- *Describe the ethical arguments against capital punishment.*
- *What conclusion do Sophia and Phil come to with respect to the rehabilitation argument?*
- *List the additional arguments which Phil and Sophia address. Give a brief evaluation of each one.*

EXERCISES

1. For each of arguments listed below, complete the following steps:

    i) Identify what kinds of claims are involved (there may be more than one).

    ii) Describe briefly how you would go about evaluating them.

    a) I don't think that we should eat meat because of the horrible conditions in which animals raised for meat are kept.

    b) I don't think that we should eat meat because we humans have no right to kill other living creatures for our selfish purposes.

    c) I don't think that we should eat meat because it is not healthy to do so.

    d) Raising the minimum wage always results in the loss of minimum wage jobs. So I don't think that it's a good idea.

    e) Raising the minimum wage rewards the less skilled and less able. So I don't think that it's a good idea.

    f) We ought to ban pit bulls because they are exceptionally dangerous dogs.

    g) Marijuana is a gateway drug that leads to the use of more dangerous, addictive drugs. For that reason, it should not be legalized.

    h) Legalizing marijuana would amount to condoning the use of drugs, and drug use weakens the moral fibre of society. For that reason, marijuana should not be legalized.

    i) Marijuana should not be legalized because it is a dangerous drug with side effects such as psychotic symptoms, growth disorders, and lung and heart damage.

2. Read the opinion piece below. Then do the following:

    i) Perform a prima facie evaluation of the arguments.

    ii) Make a list of the main claims made in the piece.

    iii) Identify what kinds of claims they are.

    iv) Describe briefly how you would go about evaluating each one.

    I don't think there's anything wrong with copying CDs that my friends or I have bought. The record companies rip us off with their ridiculous prices so I don't see why we shouldn't rip them off a bit. Everyone I know does it. Besides, the record companies are pulling in huge profits so they're not going to suffer over a few copies more or less. And it's not bad for the artists since they get their music more widely distributed.

3. The following questions build on some of the assignments in Chapter 8:

    i) From Chapter 8, question 1: Using your "Table of Arguments Pro and Con Banning Dangerous Dogs," evaluate each of the arguments you have listed.

ii) From Chapter 8, question 2: Using your "Table of Arguments Pro and Con Legalizing Marijuana," evaluate each of the arguments you have listed.

iii) From Chapter 8, question 5: Using your "Table of Arguments Pro and Con Arranged Marriages," evaluate each of the arguments you have listed.

4. Look up each of the following debates on the internet (see also Exercise 9-4 on the text website). Read over the "Background and Context" section and all the pro and con arguments. For each one, do the following:

i) Pick out what you think are the three most important arguments on each of the pro and con sides.

ii) Evaluate these arguments.

a) Moral trade-offs: Is animal testing morally right if it reduces human suffering? (section of debate on animal testing).
http://debatepedia.idebate.org/index.php/Debate:_Animal_testing

b) Should prostitution be legal?
http://debatepedia.idebate.org/index.php/Debate:_Prostitution

c) In a democracy, is civil disobedience an appropriate weapon in the fight for justice?
http://debatepedia.idebate.org/index.php/Resolved:_In_a_democracy%2C_civil_disobedience_is_an_appropriate_weapon_in_the_fight_for_justice

d) Is torture ever justified?
http://debatepedia.idebate.org/index.php/Debate:_Torture

ENDNOTES

1. Death Penalty Information Center, "Deterrence," http://www.deathpenaltyinfo.org/deterrence-states-without-death-penalty-have-had-consistently-lower-murder-rates (accessed April 15, 2009).

2. John Donohue and Justin J. Wolfers, "Uses and Abuses of Empirical Evidence in the Death Penalty Debate," *Stanford Law Review* v. 58 (Dec. 2005): 791–850.

3. Capital Punishment U.K., "Arguments For and Against Capital Punishment," http://www.capitalpunishmentuk.org/thoughts.html (accessed May 14, 2010).

4. Amnesty International, "The Death Penalty in Canada: Twenty Years of Abolition," http://www.amnesty.ca/death-penalty/canada.php (accessed April 18, 2009).

5. M. Radelet and R. Akers, "Deterrence and the Death Penalty: The Views of the Experts," 1995, in http://www.deathpenaltyinfo.org/law-enforcement-views-deterrence#lawenforcement (accessed May 14, 2010).

6. Death Penalty Information Center, "Law Enforcement and the Death Penalty," http://www.deathpenaltyinfo.org/law-enforcement-views-deterrence (accessed April 15, 2009).

7. Criminal Justice Legal Foundation, "Articles on the Death Penalty," http://www.cjlf.org/deathpenalty/DPDeterrence.htm (accessed May 14, 2010).

8. Death Penalty Information Center, "Discussion of Recent Deterrence Studies," http://www.deathpenaltyinfo.org/discussion-recent-deterrence-studies (accessed May 14, 2010).

9. Mel Bradshaw, *Victim Impact* (Toronto: Napoleon Publishing, 2008).

10. Death Penalty Information Center, "Millions Misspent," http://www.deathpenaltyinfo.org/node/599 (accessed May 14, 2010).

11. CNN, "New Mexico Governor Repeals Death Penalty," http://edition.cnn.com/2009/CRIME/03/18/new.mexico.death.penalty/ (accessed May 7, 2009).

12. CBC, "Canada's Wrongful Convictions," Oct. 23, 2009, http://www.cbc.ca/canada/story/2009/08/06/f-wrongfully-convicted.html.

13. Under what circumstances effectiveness or even consequences can override legitimate prima facie moral principles is highly controversial and complex. While it might be acceptable to tell a "white lie" to avoid hurting someone's feelings (an example of "instrumental effectiveness"), there are cogent objections to actions such as a government deceiving its people by exaggerating the possibility of an epidemic in order to get them to take proper precautions. The complexity of these considerations goes beyond the reach of this text.

14. Death Penalty Information Center, "Descriptions of Execution Methods," http://www.deathpenaltyinfo.org/descriptions-execution-methods, (accessed May 14, 2010).

15. David Baldus, referenced in "Arbitrariness," http://www.deathpenaltyinfo.org/arbitrariness (accessed May 14, 2010).

16. Death Penalty Information Center, "Arbitrariness," http://www.deathpenaltyinfo.org/arbitrariness (accessed April 24, 2009).

Chapter 10
Making a Judgment and Making a Case

Learning Objectives

After reading this chapter, you should be able to:

- apply appropriate guidelines in coming to a reasoned judgment
- apportion judgment to the weight of evidence
- evaluate a given case
- make a reasonable case

Capital Punishment III

Sophia and Phil continue their inquiry into capital punishment.

Phil: You know, Sophia, we've looked at a lot of arguments and information on capital punishment. But I think that the conclusion is becoming obvious to me. The weight of arguments clearly points against capital punishment.

Sophia: What made you come to that conclusion?

Phil: Well, it's pretty clear that there's little evidence to support the deterrence argument.

Sophia: Agreed.

Phil: And the incapacitation argument is really "overkill" (sorry about that) since the same result can be achieved by less drastic means.

Sophia: Agreed again.

Phil: The cost issue is a red herring since it's simply not true given the current system of appeals.

Sophia: Right again.

Phil: I think that there is something legitimate to the retribution argument in terms of the desire for justice. But you've convinced me that with capital punishment, we risk an even greater injustice, that of possibly executing an innocent person. Besides, retribution can be achieved with life imprisonment.

Sophia: I'm with you.

Phil: So what we're left with are all the moral problems of the state killing some of its citizens and, in particular, some of its citizens who are innocent. That's a very strong argument against.

Sophia: Especially since there are alternatives to capital punishment available to us.

Phil: And also given the worldwide trend toward abolition, supported by important organizations like the U.N.—the arguments for capital punishment would have to be very strong to counter that.

Sophia: Which they're not.

Phil: So, all in all, I have to agree with the abolitionists—we should not have the death penalty.[1]

Do you agree with Phil's assessment of the arguments? Why or why not?

Reaching a Reasoned Judgment

In Chapter 8, Phil and Sophia identified the main arguments in the capital punishment debate, as well as the main objections and responses. Laying out the debate in a comprehensive manner is an indispensable prelude to evaluation. In the previous chapter, our inquirers were engaged in an evaluation of the various individual arguments for and against capital punishment. Doing a prima facie evaluation of the various arguments as well as investigating the various claims and arguments for their credibility is a necessary and essential aspect of the process of coming to a reasoned judgment. It is not sufficient, however.

In order to come to a reasoned judgment, we need to perform a comparative evaluation of the arguments in order to determine their weight in terms of the overall case, and then combine the various evaluations in order to make a final judgment. This process involves balancing the various considerations which have come to light. The various aspects of context which we have been looking at play an important role at this stage.

This is a process which Sophia and Phil began in the previous chapters and now continue to its culmination in a reasoned judgment about the capital punishment issue. There are a number of key moves they have made along the way in order to arrive at this point. These include the identification and evaluation of individual arguments as discussed in the previous chapters.

Review the main aspects involved in evaluating individual arguments.

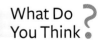

There are a number of moves related specifically to the comparative evaluation, weighing, and balancing of the various considerations and arguments:

• Establishing the burden of proof

Establishing whether there is a burden of proof and, if so, where it lies, as well as establishing the standard of proof demanded by it are all important in determining the weight of evidence that is required to make a case. The context, and, in particular, the current state of

Keep in Mind

GUIDING QUESTIONS FOR INQUIRY

- What is the issue?
- What kinds of claims or judgments are at issue?
- What are the relevant reasons and arguments on various sides of the issue?
- What is the context of the issue?
- **How do we comparatively evaluate the various reasons and arguments to reach a reasoned judgment?**

practice with respect to an issue, can help to establish the burden of proof as those arguing against the status quo generally have at least a pragmatic obligation to make their case (see Chapter 8). Thus Phil and Sophia recognize that there is a pragmatic burden of proof on those who argue for a change in the laws regarding capital punishment, which in the context of their discussion means those who argue for reinstatement. They also recognize that the growing consensus internationally for the elimination of capital punishment provides prima facie support for abolition and suggests that the burden of proof bears on those advocating retention. But since there is still sufficient international disagreement, a clear burden of proof likely cannot be established.[2]

• Assessing the possibilities in light of the alternatives

Arguments often need to be assessed in light of the alternatives that are available. So, for example, although the incapacitation argument is in some sense valid—it is the case that dead murderers cannot re-offend—Phil and Sophia realize that the goal of preventing re-offending can also be met by life imprisonment, which is less morally problematic. Similarly, although they recognize the legitimacy of the retribution argument, they recognize that it also must be assessed in comparison to a less morally troubling alternative such as life imprisonment.

• Considering differences in how the issue and arguments are framed

The kinds of arguments which are used in a debate will be largely determined by how the issue is framed (see Chapter 7). Recognizing differences in framing can help us to understand the assumptions underlying opposing arguments (which are often connected with social, political, or intellectual world views); in turn, we are then in a better position to comparatively evaluate them. This might include considering alternative, more inclusive frames. Thus Sophia and Phil recognize that an adherence to viewing capital punishment solely in terms of punishment or solely in terms of crime reduction may result in a lack of recognition of the validity in the opposing view; it may also cause them to ignore other possibilities—for example, they might not have addressed capital punishment in terms of the injustice of potentially killing innocent people.

• Recognizing points that may be valid in various views

Good reasons often do not reside entirely in one or other of the conflicting views. It is important, in arriving at a reasoned judgment, to recognize the valid points in each view. Thus Sophia, while continuing to disapprove of revenge as a rationale, comes to recognize the legitimacy of the desire for justice that is involved in the retribution position.

• Synthesizing the strengths of different views into your judgment

The evaluation of the arguments on various sides of an issue will likely reveal strong points in different views which can be incorporated into your judgment. In their inquiry, Phil and Sophia recognize the legitimacy of the desire for justice underlying the retribution argument for capital punishment but judge that it can be met by means other than capital punishment (e.g., life imprisonment).

• Weighing and balancing different considerations, values, and arguments

In coming to a reasoned judgment, it is often necessary to make comparative judgments of value (see Chapter 7), and to weigh the relative importance of different considerations, values, and arguments. In their inquiry, Sophia and Phil recognize that moral considerations should generally take priority over cost considerations; and they recognize that, whatever the justice of retribution, it is outweighed by the greater injustice of executing innocent people. Weighing and balancing various considerations is a crucial aspect involved in coming to a reasoned judgment and is discussed in greater detail below.

- **Considering whether your personal convictions and experiences may be colouring your judgment**

In coming to a reasoned judgment, evaluation of the arguments should not be unduly influenced by the evaluator's initial views and experiences. That does not mean that we should not have views, but it does mean that we should be aware of our initial views on the issues so that we can consider opposing arguments in a fair-minded way and make a more objective judgment. So, for example, Sophia recognizes that at least some of her antipathy to the idea of retribution may be related to its association with religious fundamentalist views. This allows her to give more fair-minded consideration to the valid aspects of the retribution argument. Similarly, once Phil recognizes that his attachment to retribution may be connected to his acquaintance with a murder victim, he is better able to consider the pros and cons of retribution and to consider alternatives in an open-minded manner.

Weighing Competing Considerations

Arriving at a reasoned judgment depends centrally on the weight given to the various reasons and arguments. In Phil and Sophia's capital punishment inquiry, some retentionist arguments were shown to be inadequate (e.g., the deterrence and cost arguments) on factual grounds. Other arguments depended more on moral considerations. The retentionist moral argument for retribution came out as having some weight, although it was shown that the demand for retribution could be satisfied by means other than capital punishment. On the other hand, at least one of the moral arguments against capital punishment came out as strong, indeed overriding—the moral arguments against an institution that executes the innocent. Thus the weakness of both the factual arguments and moral considerations in support of capital punishment compared to the moral significance of executing the innocent made the judgment reasonably clear. In many cases, however, arriving at a judgment will be more difficult. There are a number of concepts and considerations that are useful in making such judgments.

- **Comparative judgments of value**

This process of weighing, of deciding the strength of various reasons and considerations, involves making comparative judgments of value (see Chapter 7). Different values may pull in different directions, so the significance of the various considerations needs to be assessed.

What are some examples of comparative judgments of value that Phil and Sophia make in evaluating the arguments on capital punishment?

Sophia's argument that the cost of keeping murderers in prison is just the price we must pay for living in a humane world is an example of this type of comparative judgment. The judgment about the relative weight to be given to two moral arguments, the retribution argument and the killing of innocents argument, also involves (to some extent) a judgment regarding their comparative moral significance.

Keep in Mind

GUIDELINES FOR REACHING A REASONED JUDGMENT

- Ensure that the relevant arguments, objections, and responses have been identified.
- Evaluate the individual arguments.
- Establish, if possible, which view bears the burden of proof.
- Assess the possibilities in light of the alternatives.
- Consider differences in how the issues and arguments are framed.
- Recognize points that may be valid in various views.
- Synthesize the strengths of different views into the judgment.
- Weigh and balance different considerations, values, and arguments.
- Consider whether your own personal convictions and experiences may be colouring your judgment.

What Do You Think?

- ## Degree of certainty or likelihood regarding claims

In assigning weight to various considerations or arguments, it is not only their significance which must be considered, but also their degree of certainty or likelihood. As an example, the possibility of executing innocents has considerable moral weight as an argument against capital punishment, but one might argue that its overall weight would be lessened if it turned out that this were an extremely rare occurrence. In fact, however, the evidence as to the frequency of innocent people being executed adds to the weight of this argument. Similarly, if there were compelling evidence for a deterrent effect, then deterrence would likely be a very strong pro capital punishment argument, as preventing murders is generally considered to be very important. The fact that there is no compelling evidence, however, tips the balance in the other direction. (Sophia keeps reminding Phil of this point in the dialogue in Chapter 9.)

- ## Ethical considerations versus practical considerations

In making a judgment with respect to an action or proposal, it is important to focus on ethical as well as practical considerations (as discussed in Chapter 7). What is more, ethical considerations should generally have priority over considerations of efficiency or practicality.

- ## Means and ends

In evaluating an action or proposal, evaluators should keep in mind the ends or aims of the action as well as the means that may be used to achieve those ends. A common problem is to lose sight of an end by overly concentrating on the means. For example, in the capital punishment debate, if you focus on punishment as a means to reduce violent crime, you might lose sight of the overall goal of crime reduction. As Sophia's example of alternative ways of achieving incapacitation shows, there are often other, perhaps better, ways to achieve the same ends. You cannot adequately evaluate means without consideration of alternative ways of achieving the same end. It is also important to consider the ethical implications of any proposed means and to recognize that some ends don't justify some means (as Sophia recognizes with respect to the incapacitation argument or the cost reduction argument).

- ## Cost and benefit

Considerations of cost and benefit focus on the possible negative and positive consequences of some action or proposal. There can be both practical and ethical costs and benefits associated with actions, and it is important to consider both types. Considerations in assessing cost and benefit include both short-term and long-term consequences, benefits and costs, the likelihood of these outcomes, the magnitude of the outcomes, who would be affected, and the distribution of costs and benefits.

- ## Conflicts among ethical values

Ethical considerations may themselves at times conflict and pull in different directions. Thus, for example, considerations regarding the rights of criminals may conflict with considerations regarding the well-being of other citizens. And some ethical considerations, like the value of life, have priority over others, such as keeping promises. The state could, for example, throw every petty criminal in jail for life and undoubtedly reduce crime. But doing so would be a major transgression of the greater duty of the state to treat all its citizens, even criminals, fairly.

In some cases, this tension between ethical values takes the form of a conflict between principles—between saving a life and keeping a promise, for example. In other cases, it is a

conflict between principles and consequences, as, for example, between protecting citizens and treating people justly. One of the points which the conflict among ethical values highlights is the importance of considering a variety of ethical considerations and implications and not just one (e.g., Sophia and Phil should not be totally preoccupied with considerations of justice in the form of retribution and ignore the possible consequence of killing innocents).

Dealing with Differences in Weighting

There is no magic formula for weighing reasons; and in many cases, the weighing process will not lead to one uncontested outcome. Individuals may disagree about how to weigh various reasons and balance various considerations. Such a disagreement could be based on any of the factors listed above—differences in comparative judgments of value, differences in how likelihood or costs and benefits are assessed, or differences in how means and ends are balanced. This issue of disagreement in weighting is particularly challenging in cases where the differences are based on different philosophical, social, or political views. One example is the greater emphasis on individual responsibility behind some of the arguments in favour of capital punishment (e.g., the retribution argument) versus the emphasis on social causality behind some of the arguments against (e.g., the rehabilitation argument). Other examples are the libertarian versus the interventionist views of the role of government which lie behind McGregor's and Onassis's disagreement over dangerous dog legislation, or McGregor's neo-conservative versus Nancy's progressivist views on minimum wage.

Differences of weighting may also be a result of differences in priorities even among those who hold very similar world views. As an example, among people toward the left of the political spectrum, there are those who support a carbon tax because they believe that it would have a positive impact on the environment, while there are others who oppose it because they believe that it would have a negative impact on economically disadvantaged individuals. Although both groups value both the environment and economic equality, they prioritize these values differently with respect to this particular issue. Their differences in judgment may also be based to some extent on differences in how they assess the likelihood of the various possible outcomes or how they calculate the short-term versus the long-term costs and benefits of the different policies.

There may, however, be ways to come to an agreed-upon judgment even in the face of such differences. Arriving at a reasoned judgment is sometimes not a case of accepting one or another view in its totality, but rather of taking into consideration valid points from a number of views and dealing with the legitimate concerns of different positions. Thus, for example, the city council was able to agree upon a decision regarding dangerous dog legislation which accommodated both Onassis's concern for public safety and McGregor's concern for the rights of dog owners, without needing to resolve the underlying world view issues between them.

But even when such accommodation is not a possibility, there is room for some progress. We often simply accept our positions and priorities as given and fixed. But the possibility exists of taking the process of reason-giving and evaluation farther than we often do, by attempting to make explicit the considerations, values, and priorities which lie behind our weightings (including to ourselves).

What benefits can you think of in pursuing an inquiry dialogue in the face of differences in how you and your discussant weigh various considerations?

We do not always recognize the considerations that we are taking into account when making a judgment or the assumptions that underpin how we value objects, actions, or

Keep in Mind

CONSIDERATIONS IN WEIGHING

- Comparative judgments of value
- Degree of certainty or likelihood regarding claims
- Ethical considerations and practical considerations
- Means and ends
- Cost and benefit
- Conflicts among ethical values

Arriving at a reasoned judgment is sometimes not a case of accepting one or another view in its totality, but rather of taking into consideration valid points from a number of views and dealing with the legitimate concerns of different positions.

What Do You Think?

Making explicit the considerations that we are taking into account when making a judgment and the assumptions that underpin how we value objects, actions, or people, opens them up for conscious consideration and evaluation by others and by ourselves.

Apply Your Understanding Exercise 1

people. Making them explicit opens them up for conscious consideration and evaluation by others and by ourselves. And listening to how others justify their weightings may lead us to realize that there might be good reasons to broaden our considerations or alter our own priorities. Someone whose world view leads naturally to a focus on the rights of the accused might, for example, become convinced by hearing arguments about the need for proportion between a crime and its punishment and might see that an exclusive focus on the rights of the accused is excessive and should be reconsidered. Or, someone supporting the banning of certain dog breeds might become aware, through exchanging justifications with someone opposing the ban, that he or she had only considered the possible benefits in terms of public safety but had failed sufficiently to take into consideration the costs in terms of restrictions on individual freedom.

Attempting to justify our judgments and priorities may also reveal to us instances when we are relying on habit, authority, or ideology rather than on good reasons. In such cases, an attempt to overcome "ideological fixity" and remain open-minded can be helpful. (Strategies for overcoming ideological fixity are discussed in Chapter 11.)

At the end, there still may be no resolution and the parties may agree to disagree. But even in such cases, the process of attempting to justify our values and priorities can help us to understand where individuals who hold different views are "coming from."

Apportioning Judgment

Not all judgments will warrant an equal level of confidence. It is important to apportion one's judgment to the strength of the reasons. The judgment which Phil makes at the end regarding the unacceptability of capital punishment is a **reasonably confident judgment** ("the conclusion is becoming obvious to me"). He is justified in making a judgment with this level of confidence since the reasons he cites are strong and hold up well against objections and criticisms, and in light of arguments on the other side. (We need to remind ourselves, however, that all our judgments are fallible—see Chapter 1—and so, no matter how well justified our confidence is, there is always the possibility that we will be wrong.)

We can distinguish the level of confidence which is justified in the case of Phil's assessment of the capital punishment issue from that which would be justified regarding judgments which are relatively non-controversial. The judgments that smoking causes cancer or that killing innocent people is wrong are based on well-established reasons and evidence, and we would be justified in making **very confident judgments** on these matters. Although the reasons for Phil's judgment in the capital punishment case are strong, they are not conclusive. The issue is still deemed controversial, and others might (and do) evaluate the reasons differently. Thus a **very confident judgment** about capital punishment would not be justified.

It is not always the case that the reasons and arguments on one side of an issue are strong enough to justify a confident judgment. In some cases, there may be some strong reasons and some problems with each of the various positions in question. In such cases, we need to weigh the strengths and weaknesses and make a **judgment on balance.** Such judgments will of necessity be more tentative than when the weighting is more clear-cut.

There will also be cases in which the weight of reasons for different positions seems equally balanced, or where there is insufficient evidence in order to make a judgment. Sophia and Phil's discussion of the rehabilitation argument is an example. The appropriate response in such cases is not to carry on and make a judgment regardless but rather to **suspend judgment.**

Keep in Mind ✔

JUDGMENT AND CONFIDENCE

- A *very confident judgment* is warranted when the weight of reasons clearly supports the judgment and the issue is considered settled.
- A *reasonably confident judgment* is warranted when the weight of reasons strongly supports the judgment but the issue is still controversial.
- A *tentative judgment* is warranted when the weight of reasons is not overwhelming but is supportive of one position; we can make a *judgment on balance.*
- A *suspended judgment* is warranted when the reasons for different positions are closely balanced or when there is insufficient evidence to make a judgment.

LEVELS OF PROOF

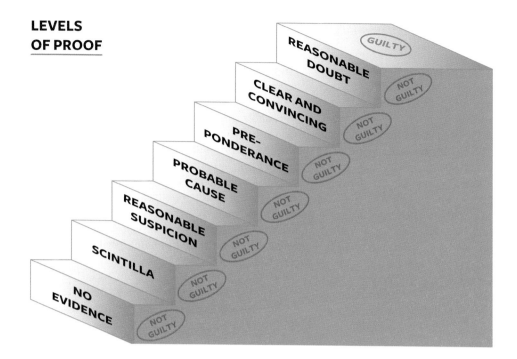

We are not talking about how confident a particular individual may happen to *feel* regarding their judgments. Some individuals tend to be overconfident and may feel a level of confidence in their judgments that is unwarranted, while others may generally lack confidence in their own views. And we may feel an unwarranted degree of confidence in our views if they are shared by those around us.

But the kind of confidence we are referring to here is *rational* confidence—the level of confidence that is justified by the strength of the reasons and evidence.

Clearly, the four-part distinction in judgments from "very confident" through to "suspended" allows for a range of possibilities in between. We can be more or less confident, more or less tentative, depending on the strength of the reasons and evidence which support the judgment. These four levels of judgment can be seen as marking positions along a continuum of judgment confidence.

The challenge comes when we are called to act on a judgment. The greater the consequences of action (or inaction), the greater the need for a level of evidence that would support a confident judgment. One would like always to be in a position to make a confident judgment based on well-established evidence, but that is not always possible. We are often required to make a judgment in conditions of uncertainty where not taking action may have as serious consequences as acting.

Here a comparison with the law can be instructive. In criminal matters, guilt depends on proof beyond a reasonable doubt. This test requires evidence sufficient to justify a very confident judgment. Such a high level of confidence is required in this case because so much is at stake (freedom versus imprisonment, or even life versus death). In civil matters, however, the criterion is balance of probabilities, that is, judgment is found in favour of the claimant if it is more likely that the claimant is right than wrong—a clear use of the idea of balancing the evidence. In this case, a somewhat lesser standard of evidence and thus a more tentative level of judgment are considered adequate because there is usually less at stake than in the criminal case. Issues of such great consequence as whether to have capital punishment would seem to demand a high level of evidence and require at least a reasonably confident judgment.

Apply Your Understanding Exercises 2, 3

Evaluating a Given Case

To this point, Phil and Sophia have been engaged in their own inquiry about capital punishment, working through the guiding questions in order to arrive at a reasoned judgment on the issue. Very often, however, we come across or are presented with cases made by others. These may be presented in anything from an opinion piece in the media (e.g., an editorial) to full-length books. Such cases differ from the short arguments that we studied in Chapters 4 and 5 in that they offer more than one argument in favour of their position and appear to be claiming that the arguments presented are adequate to support their judgment.

While conducting an inquiry involves attempting to reach a reasoned judgment on an issue, evaluating a given case involves trying to determine to what extent the author of the case has been successful in presenting a reasoned judgment. Determining this will involve, first, evaluating the individual arguments in terms of both a prima facie evaluation of the reasoning and an evaluation of the various claims for credibility. But it will also involve judging to what extent and how effectively the case deals with the relevant considerations for reaching a reasoned judgment.

One way to evaluate to what extent a given case does an effective job of coming to a reasoned judgment is by focusing on the errors or fallacies to be avoided. The following is a list of fallacies of judgment that can appear in the cases you are evaluating:

......
Keep in Mind ☑

**GUIDELINES FOR
EVALUATING A GIVEN
CASE**
Evaluate the individual
arguments:
• Prima facie evaluation
• Credibility
Check for fallacies of judgment:
• Failure to undertake a
comprehensive examination
of the various competing
arguments
• Failure to give appropriate
consideration to the burden
of proof
• Failure to consider the
uncertainty of claims
• Failure to consider ethical
arguments
• Failure to consider
alternative solutions or
possibilities
• Failure to consider relevant
objections
• Failure to consider
implications
• Biased framing
• "Either–or" fallacy
• Inappropriate weighting

Fallacies of Judgment

Failure to Undertake a Comprehensive Examination of the Various Competing Arguments

Since reaching a reasoned judgment involves a comparative evaluation of the various reasons and arguments on an issue, the failure to take into account any of the significant arguments on the issue constitutes a serious defect in a case.

Failure to Give Appropriate Consideration to the Burden of Proof

Failing to determine where the burden of proof lies or misplacing the burden of proof may result in an inappropriate determination of how much evidence is needed to make a case or of when a case has been made successfully.

Failure to Consider the Uncertainty of Claims

Taking claims as certain where the evidence in support of the claim is not, in fact, compelling may result in making an unjustified judgment or making a judgment with a greater degree of confidence than is warranted.

Failure to Consider Ethical Arguments

We have seen the importance of taking into consideration ethical as well as practical considerations when making a judgment. Judgments which fail to take into account ethical considerations are faulty for that reason.

Failure to Consider Alternative Solutions or Possibilities

Although individual arguments can be assessed to some extent on their own (e.g., prima facie), the strength of a case can only be evaluated in light of the alternatives available. Ignoring possible and plausible alternatives (e.g., ignoring life imprisonment as an alternative to the death penalty) would be a ground for criticism of a given case.

Failure to Consider Objections

Because argumentation is dialectical, involving not just particular arguments but also objections and responses to the objections, any reasoned case must do more than offer arguments. It must respond to any known and important objections. Failure to do so is a fallacy of judgment.

Failure to Consider Implications

Many views will have implications in the larger world. Failure to evaluate those implications constitutes a limitation of the view. For example, one might make a case that actually carrying out executions on virtually everyone who is sentenced to death (as they do, for example, in Singapore) would increase the deterrent effect of capital punishment. But it would be important also to evaluate the likely implications for the society as a whole of having such a strict and, some might say, inhumane policy.

Biased Framing

Too narrow framing of an issue or argument, or framing in a way that slants the discussion toward a particular perspective may exclude the consideration of other possibilities and thus bias the judgment. Ravi's framing of his issue regarding the bombing of Hiroshima (in Chapter 7) in terms of whether the bombing of innocent civilians was justified is an example of the fallacy of biased framing.

"Either–Or" Fallacy

Many issues have more than two sides. Moreover, there are often intermediate possibilities between two opposing positions. Therefore, viewing all issues in terms of "either–or"—as a choice between two opposing positions—can oversimplify issues and result in a failure to recognize other, possibly more reasonable possibilities. Arguing, for example, that because there are problems with traffic on some local streets, all parking on all local streets should be completely eliminated is an example of this fallacy. The argument fails to take into consideration such possibilities as eliminating parking on some local streets or limiting parking on all local streets.

Inappropriate Weighting

This fallacy consists in giving undue weight to certain aspects of an issue when making a judgment. As an example, prioritizing possible reductions in costs over moral issues such as the potential of executing innocent individuals would be an error of this sort.

Apply Your Understanding Exercises 4, 5, 6

Evaluate the case made by Warren Allmand against capital punishment in the feature box on the previous page.

What Do You Think?

Making a Reasonable Case

Phil: You know, Sophia, I'm remembering how convinced I was by the police chief's argument when I first read it. But that was before we'd done our investigation and thought the issues through. I imagine there must be lots of folks like me out there who might also be convinced because they don't understand the arguments and issues.

Sophia: I'm sure there are.

Phil: So what I think we ought to do is to write a letter to the editor to respond to the police chief's comments.

The following is an excerpt from the presentation by Warren Allmand (Solicitor General of Canada, 1972–1976) to the Canadian Parliament in the debate to abolish capital punishment (July 14, 1976):

Restoration of capital punishment is prompted by the fear that murders, particularly murders where police officers have been the victims, are increasing due to a failure to provide a sufficiently strong deterrent. It is evident that capital punishment may satisfy the strong sense of moral and emotional outrage that many of us experience when a murder is committed, and there is no doubt that the threat a particular individual has posed to society is terminated absolutely. There are, however, other crucial issues involved.

The paramount issue is one of morality. Are we justified in taking a human life through capital punishment? Execution does not erase the crime of murder. It takes away another life. The commandment "Thou shalt not kill" is part of our Judaeo-Christian heritage. It emphasizes the value of human life and should make us wonder whether we should take yet another life in retribution. Personally, I believe it is wrong to take the life of another person except as a last resort in self-defence. Before we had statistical evidence on the effectiveness of capital punishment, it was indeed considered as a last resort in the defence of society. However, evidence now available shows that this is not the case . . . An examination of the evidence, statistics and research in Canada, the United States and Europe, indeed indicates that capital punishment does not effectively lower the murder rate . . . It is my view that the burden of proving that capital punishment is a good deterrent against murder is on those who want to retain capital punishment. On the basis of the facts and data available, I do not believe that this is a burden that they can discharge . . .

In concluding, I feel it is important to present an accurate view of the extent to which violent crime is prevalent in our society and what its causes and its consequences are. Current debate seems to have focussed on the question of [the] capital punishment and left it at that. I think that the evidence I have put forward shows that this is not an effective means of combating violent crime . . . What, then, do I suggest in place of this? Some of the measures that I propose to prevent and reduce crime are the following: better trained, better deployed and better equipped policemen; effective gun control; proactive rather than reactive police work; more effective correctional programs for juveniles and adults; more effective social and economic programs to remove the causes of crime; improved treatment for alcoholics and drug addicts; improved education and recreation programs; possible restrictions on the showing of violence on television and through other media; measures to promote respect for legitimate authority in the home, the school, the church, community associations and government. If these and other measures were pursued with more vigour, we would do much more to lower our crime rate than we would if we merely emphasized the application of harsh penalties after the fact.[3]

Sophia: Good idea, Phil. But letters to the editors can't be very long—around 200 words, I'd say. How can we make a reasonable case in so few words?

Phil: That will certainly be hard. But let's give it a try.

What Do You Think?

How would you write a letter to the editor to respond to the chief's arguments in a maximum of 200 words? What would be most important to say with so few words?

Sophia: OK. So how should we start?

Phil: First off, we need to make it clear that we don't agree with the police chief. How does this sound?

In your recent opinion piece you stated that you "and other law enforcement officers know from a vast amount of first-hand experience with criminals that the only form of punishment that can effectively [protect citizens from murders] is the death penalty." But what makes you think you know? Have you studied the research on deterrence? If you had, you would know that there is no support for the claim that capital punishment deters murder. That's just a myth, and it is irresponsible of you to put forward such a myth and claim you have authority to do so.

Sophia: Hmm, I don't think it's too good an idea to attack the police chief personally. First of all, letters to the editor have to be written to the editor, not the person you're responding to. And attacking the chief sounds too "ad hominem." I think it will just make him mad and won't really persuade anyone else. After all, we know that lots of people believe that capital punishment does deter crime. Why should they believe you?

Phil: Good points. I'm not an expert. I need to think about how I can make a credible claim that others would believe. And we know it's never a good idea to get too personal in an argument. So what do you think we should do?

Sophia: Well, we could acknowledge the chief's opinion and how plausible the claim is, but then cite some credible source who says it just isn't so.

Phil: Appeal to a credible authority. Good idea.

Sophia: Maybe we could also point out how many people get involved in gangs which murder one another. The fact that you're likely to get murdered doesn't seem to deter the very kinds of people we're trying to deter from murdering others.

Phil: Good point, Sophia.

Sophia: We can also use the fact that a large number of murders are crimes of passion among people who know each other. They're hardly likely to be doing cost–benefit analysis.

Phil: In other words, we could appeal to some other aspects of "common sense" to show some of the problems with the deterrence argument.

Sophia: Exactly.

Phil: How's this?

> In a recent opinion piece, the police chief stated that ". . . law enforcement officers know from a vast amount of first-hand experience with criminals that the only form of punishment that can effectively [protect citizens from murders] is the death penalty." Such a position sounds plausible, but the evidence just doesn't add up. Since Canada eliminated the death penalty in 1976, the rate of homicide has declined. And in the U.S., the murder rate is highest in death penalty states. In addition, many of the chief's colleagues don't agree with him. A survey of police chiefs done in the U.S. in 1995 ranked the death penalty as the least relevant way to reduce violent crimes. Some may think it is just common sense to believe that execution will reduce murders, but if you think about who is involved in most violent crime, you realize that these are people (like gang members) who risk death all the time and still go on with their violent lifestyle.

Sophia: I think that's a lot better. But we still haven't brought up the other crucial point—that capital punishment results in innocent people being executed. And we've already used up most of our words.

Phil: You're right. People need to face the moral issue of the execution of innocent people. All the recent use of DNA to show that many innocent people have been convicted should bring that to people's attention. So what about this?

> In a recent opinion piece, the police chief stated that ". . . law enforcement officers know from a vast amount of first-hand experience with criminals that the only form of punishment that can effectively [protect citizens from murders] is the death penalty." Such a position sounds plausible, but the evidence just doesn't add up. Since Canada eliminated the death penalty in 1976, the rate of homicide has declined. And in the U.S., the murder rate is highest in death penalty states. In addition, many of the chief's colleagues don't agree. A survey of police chiefs done in the U.S. in 1995 found that 67% of the chiefs do not believe that the death penalty reduces violent crimes. Some may think it is just common sense to

believe that execution will reduce murders, but if you think about who is involved in most violent crimes, you realize that these are people (such as gang members) who risk death all the time and still go on with their violent lifestyle.

Not only does capital punishment fail to deter murderers from killing innocent people, it actually results in innocent people being killed. Recently, the state of New Mexico abolished the death penalty when the Governor, a former supporter of the death penalty, acknowledged that four innocent people had been executed in his state.

Sophia: Hey, Phil, that's pretty good. You've gotten rid of the attacks on the police chief but have still managed to use other police chiefs to support our position on deterrence. And you've added the huge objection that capital punishment results in innocent people being killed. I like the symmetry you've added at the end. But I think it needs a concluding sentence. Something with a bit of punch that summarizes the argument and might catch the eye of the editor so that the letter will get published.

Phil: I think we need to acknowledge the context of the police chief's piece. There's been another outbreak of gang violence and so there's been a call for stiffer penalties. Since we don't have capital punishment here, what about this: "We should not let the widespread demand for being tough on crime lead us to return to capital punishment, which is both ineffective and immoral."

Sophia: A bit long winded, I am afraid—and dull. What about this instead: " Sure, we all hate crime. But capital punishment won't stop it and it will kill innocent people."

Phil: Even more dramatic: "Capital punishment doesn't protect innocent people; it kills them."

Sophia: That may be a bit over the top.

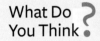
What Do You Think

How would you end the letter?

The following week . . .

Phil: Hey, I just got an email from the newspaper. They liked our letter and they want us to write a longer op-ed[4] piece. A sort of student perspective on capital punishment.

Sophia: That's great, Phil! Now we can take more considerations into account and make a better case. We also don't have to respond directly to the police chief.

A longer piece will allow Phil and Sophia to make a more thorough case by developing more arguments, considering more objections, and providing support for their claims. It allows for a more reasoned presentation to the reader. But even the longer piece will require them to be clear on what points are essential—both in the sense of essential for the case to be persuasive and essential in providing the rational basis for their position.

Phil: I know that you were always opposed but I wasn't, so I think it would be worthwhile to think about where I was coming from before we started our inquiry. If I can be persuaded by what I learned, so can others. I also know from English class that the first question you ask when you're writing is, "Who is the audience?" In this case, it's people like me: people who think capital punishment deters and who think that it's only fair that evil murderers are executed. It was hard for me to accept that capital punishment doesn't deter and that was key to changing my mind. But I also know that a lot of our friends think it would be cheaper to execute criminals than to keep them in jail for life. On reflection, it seems crazy to think you could justify killing someone to save money; but once people decide someone is a really bad criminal, they tend to lose sight of morality.

Sophia: It seems to me that the most important objection and one that no one can deny is that using capital punishment will result in innocent people being executed. No matter how much a person thinks murderers should be executed, I don't think anyone thinks that it's OK to execute people who didn't commit a crime.

Phil: So I guess the question is how to begin—with the strongest objection (innocents get executed) or the view most likely held by the supporters of capital punishment (that it deters).

Sophia: I think we should go with the deterrence issue because, even if someone acknowledges that capital punishment will result in the occasional innocent person being killed, they could argue that even more innocent people will be killed if we don't have capital punishment. So, if capital punishment was a significant deterrent, you might still try to justify it despite the objection about executing innocents.

Phil: So how do you think we should begin? We're not experts in criminology or anything. How can we get anyone to accept our arguments?

Sophia: First of all, we make sure that we take into account the opposing arguments so the reader can see that we know what we're talking about. We refer to experts to support any of our controversial or surprising claims. Don't forget that many of our arguments are moral arguments and they don't need expertise to have credibility. We also keep the tone of the writing reasonable.

Phil's Draft:

> Recent murders in our city have renewed the call for the death penalty, including a recent opinion piece by the chief of police calling for a return to capital punishment. Most of those murdered have been young gang members. As young people ourselves, we have become interested in seeing if the police chief's proposed solution is an appropriate way to deal with this problem.

> We have learned a number of things from our inquiry into this issue. The first is that there is no good evidence that reintroducing the death penalty will reduce the murder rate. At first, we found this surprising. Surely the fear of death is a powerful deterrent. But on reflection, we realized that the young people who are the current victims and perpetrators of this wave of violence know that gang involvement is dangerous and even life-threatening, and yet many of them voluntarily join gangs. We also learned that over half of all murders are committed by people who know their victim, suggesting that irrationality and emotion play a major role in many murders.

> When we looked at the statistical evidence, we saw the surprising fact that those places without the death penalty also have fewer murders. In Canada, for instance, the murder rate has declined since capital punishment was abolished. There is a great deal of research in this area and we are not, of course, experts; but even our initial review of the research shows that there is no strong proof that capital punishment actually deters. There is even some evidence that it may encourage homicide because in many neighbouring states in the U.S., those states that have capital punishment have higher rates of murder. To us, it seems clear that capital punishment will not make our streets safer.

> But some may think, "Well, it may not deter people, but a dead murderer will not murder again." Others may feel that we should have capital punishment because some people's crimes are so hideous that the perpetrators deserve to die. Adding to that, it seems outrageous that citizens should have to pay to keep such people alive.

> We have considered these arguments too, and while we have sympathy with them, we do not believe they can support a return to capital punishment. The claim that a dead murderer cannot murder again is hard to argue with, but sentencing someone to life imprisonment without parole could achieve the same end. The big problem is that any legal system will make errors and sentence the innocent. By sentencing people to life imprisonment,

we can both prevent reoffending and allow for correcting errors. In Canada just recently, a number of convictions of people who had been given life sentences have been reversed. In the U.S., a number of those on death row have also been found to be innocent. Even worse, we can see that in the U.S., black men are far more likely to be sentenced to death than white men for the same crime. So the problem is that any system designed to execute truly hideous criminals will almost certainly also execute innocent people. As to expense, it turns out that sentencing people to death with all the appropriate appeals allowed in an attempt to avoid mistakes costs more than just putting someone in jail for life. When you think about it, this isn't hard to understand. The death of the occasional criminal is hardly going to enable the penal system to close a prison or even a cell block.

Lastly, we noted from our research that most civilized countries, with the exception of the U.S., have abolished capital punishment. This seems to us a sign of moral progress. Do we really want our government to be in the business of executing its own citizens? Isn't this a practice that, like racism or sexism, we have moved beyond? As young people, we are proud to live in a country that has rejected the ineffective and morally repugnant practice of execution. We should never return to the barbarism of capital punishment.

Sophia: Not bad, Phil, though I think that talking about "civilized" countries is rather loaded. But I have a little trouble with the ending again. It just seems too heavy-handed even though I am, of course, in complete agreement. And comparing racism and capital punishment is, as you know, a pretty clear case of guilt by association.

Phil: Ending these pieces with enough "punch" without resorting to fallacious style arguments is hard. Do you have any ideas?

What Do You Think?

How would you end the opinion piece?

The goal of making a case is to provide an argument that succeeds at rational persuasion. As we know from watching some TV ads, a great many persuasive efforts ignore rationality. But our approach to inquiry and dialogue means respecting the rationality of one's audience or interlocutor. At the point of making a reasonable case, we should already have gone through the process of comparatively evaluating reasons and arguments to come to a reasoned judgment. Making a reasonable case is really presenting the results of an inquiry in such a manner that the audience will also come to see that the judgment is reasonable. It is a method of persuasion that will maintain mutual respect in the long run. No one should feel duped or manipulated as a result of our making our case.

Sophia has already articulated many of the key considerations involved in making a reasonable case:

Keep in Mind ✓

GUIDING QUESTIONS FOR MAKING A REASONABLE CASE:

1. Audience?
2. Goal?
3. Objections and replies?
4. Tone?
5. Facts vs. values?
6. Common ground?
7. Credible sources?

1. Audience

Who is your audience? Are you writing for people who more or less agree with you? for people who are unlikely to have an opinion already? or for people who you know disagree with you?

2. Goal

Is your goal to reinforce people's beliefs by giving them more reasons in support of the view? Are you trying to weaken people's conviction for a view? Or are you actually trying to change people's minds on an issue?

3. Objections and replies

Does your approach acknowledge and address the counter-arguments to your view? On controversial questions, showing that the counter-claims or counter-arguments are weak is often as crucial as justifying your own claims. This approach also shows respect for your audience and establishes your credibility.

4. Tone

Have you kept the tone of the writing reasonable? Remember you are often trying to persuade someone who does not already agree with you, not "rallying the troops."

5. Facts vs. values

Have you distinguished between factual claims—which, if controversial, need support from credible sources—and evaluative claims—which are supported by principled arguments and do not need to be (usually should not be) based on appeals to experts?

6. Common ground

Have you found common ground with your audience to serve as the basis of your case? Have you identified shared moral perspectives (such as "we all agree that the state should not execute innocent people") as common ground in moral arguments? Can you find analogies which have as their "case at hand" a shared example which can be used as a precedent to support your position?

7. Credible sources

Have you used credible sources to support any controversial or surprising factual claim?

In the dialogue, Phil and Sophia anticipate an audience who might disagree with their judgment. Thus they begin their argument with the objections that they anticipate such an audience might have. They have two problems: a lack of personal credibility on the topic and widespread views of their audience about the effectiveness and legitimacy of capital punishment. For these reasons, they start off their argument by addressing these counterarguments and claims.

But not every argument should start this way. If you anticipate that the audience is not particularly well informed or opinionated about the topic you are presenting, you may well start with a more positive approach, giving reasons why your view should be accepted and only later anticipating objections and responding.

Notice also that Phil does not argue that no criminal should be executed, no matter how awful his crime or how many people he has killed. This is a claim that is even more controversial than the general claim that capital punishment should be abolished. An argument based on the claim that no one deserves to die for their crimes is not necessary for making the case against capital punishment and violates the first rule of argument construction, that premises should be more plausible than the conclusion. Instead Phil acknowledges people's sense that some people's behaviour is so bad that they deserve to die, but shows that this view does not entail having capital punishment because of the strong countervailing consideration of legal errors resulting in innocent people being executed.

Phil also argues at the end that the desire to see people executed may be a belief left over from a more brutal and less morally progressive time, but he does not rest his argument on this claim. As Sophia points out, his strategy there might be described as "guilt by association" as he attempts to associate capital punishment with racism. We have left it to you to articulate an equally effective but more reasonable ending.

Apply Your Understanding Exercise 7

CHECK YOUR UNDERSTANDING

- *List the guidelines for coming to a reasoned judgment. Give an example of each from the dialogue.*
- *Under what circumstances is it appropriate to make each of the following kinds of judgments: a very confident judgment; a reasonably confident judgment; a tentative judgment; a suspended judgment?*
- *Describe six considerations or sets of concepts which are useful for weighing competing considerations.*
- *Why is it helpful to attempt to justify how one has weighed various considerations?*
- *List and give examples of the fallacies of judgment.*
- *What is the goal of making a case?*
- *Why is rational persuasion superior to other types of persuasion?*
- *What are the factors to be considered in trying to make a reasonable case?*

EXERCISES

1. In each of the following exchanges, there are differences in how the participants prioritize the various values involved in the issue under discussion.

    i) Outline the values that are in tension in each exchange.

    ii) Describe how each of the interlocutors weighs these values.

    iii) Discuss how you would weigh these values in this situation, and why.

    a) **Onassis:** Another pit bull attack. That's the third one this year! We've got to do something. Council has a responsibility to the people to protect them from these attacks.

    McGregor: Oh no! There you go again, Onassis, wanting to make another law and take away people's freedoms. Even dogs aren't safe from your rule mongering.

    b) **Phil:** I still think that *X-Men Origins* is an awesome film. It's suspenseful and fun and has some terrific acting.

    Sophia: But you have to admit that having a weak, incoherent plot is a pretty serious problem, and you can't make up for it with a few decent performances and some thrills.

    c) **McGregor:** People who are paid the minimum wage get it because that's what they're worth. No skill, low pay—that's only fair.

    Nancy: But I certainly don't think that it's fair to pay anyone so little that they barely have enough to eat when others are waltzing around with bulging pockets, no matter what their skill level.

    d) **Ravi:** The supporters of building the bomb claimed that having the bomb would expedite the end of the war and save American lives.

    Winnie: But the scientists who were opposed to continuing the project were very concerned about the possible consequences of nuclear weapons—like radiation hazards, the proliferation of weapons, and the potential for mass destruction.

    e) **Omar Ali:** I support the proposal to build the new factory. Our unemployment rate is high, and this factory will bring many new jobs to our region and improve the standard of living for the most economically disadvantaged.

    Diego Alvarez: I have to oppose the proposal. This type of factory is known for toxic emissions and will create an unacceptable environmental hazard.

2. The following questions follow from the assignments in Chapter 9, question #3:

    i) Comparatively evaluate the cases for and against banning dangerous dogs, using as a basis your evaluation of the individual arguments from part i).

ii) Comparatively evaluate the cases for and against legalizing marijuana using as a basis your evaluation of the individual arguments from part ii).

iii) Comparatively evaluate the cases for and against arranged marriages using as a basis your evaluation of the individual arguments from part iii).

3. At the end of the inquiry with Sophia, Phil makes the judgment that "we should not have capital punishment." We categorized this as a reasonably confident judgment. Respond to the following questions, justifying your response in each case:

i) Was Phil justified in making a reasonably confident judgment given the evidence and arguments that he and Sophia considered?

ii) Was Phil justified in the level of confidence of judgment he displayed in the context of writing a letter to the editor?

iii) Imagine that Phil was about to vote in a referendum on the reinstatement of capital punishment. What level of confidence of judgment would he be justified in making in this context?

4. Evaluate the case that Phil makes in his opinion piece for the newspaper to see if he commits any fallacies of judgment.

5. For each of the opinion pieces listed in Exercise 10-5 of the textbook website, complete the following tasks:

i) Do a prima facie evaluation of the arguments.

ii) Identify any fallacies of judgment which are committed.

iii) Explain why they are problematic.

iv) Give an overall evaluation of the case.

6. Comparatively evaluate the two cases on the issue of the legalization of drugs found in Exercise 10-6 on the textbook website.

7. The following assignments involve writing a letter to the editor in response to an opinion piece:

i) Choose one of the opinion pieces from question #5 above. Write a letter to the editor in response to the piece.

ii) Find three opinion pieces which interest you. (You can find them in newspapers or on the internet, often in blogs.) Choose one and write a letter to the editor in response to the piece.

ENDNOTES

1. The process of coming to a reasoned judgment which Phil and Sophia have engaged in has much in common with the well-known decision-making procedure described by Benjamin Franklin in a letter to John Priestley in 1772. See http://www.procon.org/viewbackgroundresource .asp?resourceID=1474.

2. Anyone advocating in Canada for the return of capital punishment would clearly bear both the pragmatic and moral burden of proof.

3. Warren Allmand, "Prevention and Control of Crime in Canada," in Wesley Cragg, ed., *Contemporary Moral Issues,* 2nd ed. (Toronto: McGraw-Hill Ryerson, 1987).

4. "Op-ed" is the term for the page opposite the editorial page of a newspaper. Opinion pieces from authors who do not work for the newspaper and letters to the editor are usually found there.

Chapter 11
Dialogue and the Spirit of Inquiry

Learning Objectives

After reading this chapter, you should be able to:

- recognize the obstacles to the spirit of inquiry
- apply the guiding questions for achieving the spirit of inquiry in order to overcome the obstacles
- conduct a dialogue in a productive and respectful manner
- respond appropriately to fallacies

Hate Speech

Members of the local community are assembled in the community hall to discuss the issue of whether a representative from a neo-Nazi group should be given permission to use the hall for a public speech. In attendance are our student friends as well as some of their various relatives.

Omar Ali: Madame Chair, this request is obviously outrageous and should have been refused at the council level. I really don't understand why we're all sitting here wasting our time.

Chair: This issue was clearly generating controversy within our community, and council felt that it should be discussed in a public forum.

Ali: There's no point. Our community won't stand for such a thing!

Daimon McGregor: Now just one moment, Ali. Don't claim to represent the community. I'm a member of the community just as much as you are. And I don't agree with you.

Ali: What! You mean to say that you think it's OK that some Nazi skinheads get up in our community hall and spread hateful lies about me, my family, and other members of the community? And we should just let them?

McGregor: I didn't say that I think what they say is OK. But I do think that everyone has a right to say what they want in a free society, and governments have no business trying to muzzle them. That's what "free" means. Otherwise we'll be like China.

Ali: I can't believe that a man like you, a prominent businessman and member of council, could support those Nazi thugs!

McGregor: How dare you imply such a thing!

Chair: Gentlemen, please! Let's keep to the topic and not get personal. Mr. Onassis.

Theo Onassis: I think that there's an important point that—

McGregor: My father died fighting Nazis in WW II, and . . .

Onassis: I think that there's an important point that—

McGregor: . . . I really resent your innuendo.

Chair: Mr. McGregor, please—Mr. Onassis has the floor.

Onassis: Thank you, Madame Chair. As I was saying (or trying to say), I think that there's an important point that's being missed here. What these groups say is repugnant, it's true; but we can't start censoring opinions we don't agree with, or we may all end up in danger of having our views censored some day. A democratic society has to allow for dissent and that sometimes means tolerating distasteful views.

Ravi: There's something I'd like to say, if that's OK.

Chair: Of course, Ravi.

Ravi: I can only speak from personal experience. But I understand what it's like to be singled out and picked on because of my race and because I look different. Taunts and bullying at school, sure—you kind of expect that. But I've even been physically attacked by a gang who called me all kinds of horrible names which I won't repeat. Luckily, someone came by or they might have beaten me to a pulp. It just doesn't seem right to me that we should let these Nazi guys spread hateful lies about us and use our own community hall to do it. I've experienced the results.

Nancy: Oh Ravi, how awful! I had no idea what terrible effects hate speech can have.

Onassis: It's very sad that that kind of thing happens. We ought to be doing a better job educating young people. But I still think we shouldn't lose sight of the principle of freedom of speech.

Sunita Singh: I would like to point out, with all due respect, Mr. Onassis and Mr. McGregor, that you cannot really understand the harm done by hate speech because you and your families are never the objects of this kind of racial attack.

McGregor: Are you implying that I am insensitive and racist? I resent that.

Singh: You know I wasn't implying any such thing, Mr. McGregor.

Ali: But you may want to consider the possibility . . .

Chair: Gentlemen!

Nancy: I think that Dr. Singh has a point. I had no idea what Ravi has gone through. And I don't and won't know what it's like to be subjected to that kind of treatment. It makes me realize how racist our society is.

Ali: How right you are.

Lester: Well, I understand what Ravi's experienced. I do know, Ravi. Being black around here's not exactly a smooth ride. I've been the brunt of racial slurs and attacks, too. And it's ugly.

But I see these guys as ignorant, hateful clowns. And I don't agree about censoring them. I don't want to let them win by letting them think they're so powerful and important that they scare us.

Agatha Chong: Who can or cannot understand what, seems to me beside the point.

Singh: I don't agree. I don't see how someone who hasn't experienced how profoundly undermining and destructive it can be to be the object of such racial attacks can properly evaluate the harm done by hate speech.

Chong: There may be something in what you say, or not. I'm not sure. Nonetheless, I do think we've gotten sidetracked and still haven't dealt with Onassis's argument. I have to agree that silencing views we find unpalatable is a slippery slope that can lead to the silencing of legitimate dissent.

Mona Gold: Of course, freedom of speech is important. No one here would deny that. But all freedoms have their limitations; all of us (well, most of us) would agree with that, too. And these kinds of racist ideas breed hatred, and ultimately violence. We have terrible examples throughout history of what can happen when such views are given voice in the society. We simply cannot take the chance. We are justified in placing reasonable limits on the expression of hatred.

Alvarez: Yes. It's well known that hate speech leads to violence.

Stephen: The Bible tells us, "Love your neighbour as yourself."

Chong: One of the problems with silencing these extremist views is that they go underground and are transmitted to people in a one-sided way as if they were the truth. The best way to counter them is to take them on in open public debate, counter their falsities and fallacious reasoning with evidence and good arguments, and demonstrate how irrational, deceptive, and hateful they really are.

Singh: We have to do something to counteract these hateful ideas. I hadn't really considered that it might be more effective to refute them openly rather than trying to silence them and

The Law and Hate Speech

Criminal Code of Canada

According to Sections 318 and 319 of the *Criminal Code*, it is a criminal offence to advocate genocide, to publicly incite hatred, and to wilfully promote hatred against an "identifiable group." An identifiable group is any group of people distinguished by colour, race, religion, ethnic origin, or sexual orientation. These *Criminal Code* provisions are intended to prohibit the public distribution of hate propaganda, and they do not cover private speech.

Canadian Charter of Rights and Freedoms[1]

Section 2 of the *Canadian Charter of Rights and Freedoms* guarantees freedom of thought, belief, opinion, and expression to all Canadians. All Charter rights are, however, subject to reasonable limits that can be demonstrably justified in a free and democratic society.

In 1990, the Supreme Court of Canada considered the constitutionality of Section 319 (2) of the *Criminal Code* (the crime of wilfully promoting hatred) in the context of charges laid against an Alberta high school teacher, James Keegstra. Keegstra taught his students that the Holocaust did not occur but was part of a Jewish conspiracy. The issue in question was whether Section 319 (2) violates the constitutional right to freedom of expression. The Court held that, although this section does limit free speech, it is a reasonable limit consistent with a democratic society, and is, therefore, constitutional.

ending up having them being spread underground without any opposition. If I had some good reason to think that that's the case, then I might be persuaded to change my mind about the request.

Winnie: We learned in history class that there were hate laws in Germany during the rise of Nazism. They certainly didn't seem to do much good.

Singh: Hmm…But what makes you think, Agatha, that people will believe us rather than them?

Chong: We have to have faith that the most reasonable view will prevail in the end.

Onassis: "Veritas omnia vincit."

Alvarez: In English please, Mr. Onassis. My Latin's a little rusty.

Onassis: Sorry. "Truth conquers all."

Gold: I think you have on overly optimistic view of human rationality, Agatha.

McGregor: Indeed—just look at Ali.

Chair: Mr. McGregor!

Chong: I have to concede that there are risks in giving these people a platform. But I believe that silencing unpopular views poses even great risks to a democratic society.

Alvarez: I believe that a society has a right to set moral standards. Ours is a society that says it values its multicultural dimension. We must send a clear message that these hateful racist views are simply not acceptable in a decent, tolerant, diverse society like ours.

Ali: It's about time someone said something sensible around here.

McGregor: My dear Ali, the day the government or you or anyone else starts to dictate to me what I ought to think about morality is the day I'll know I should start learning Chinese.

Ali: We've been going on about this long enough. Nothing anyone says has convinced me or could convince me that these Nazi thugs should be allowed to speak. Let's just make a decision and get on with it.

Onassis: I don't agree with cutting short our deliberations. We need to consider carefully the implications of any action we take. But I'm afraid that the chances of getting anywhere in this forum are small. Some of us have very different social and political ideas. For example, I'm a liberal while McGregor here has these peculiar libertarian ideas. I don't see how we could ever agree.

McGregor: The "peculiar" was unnecessary, Onassis; but otherwise I happen to agree with you.

Chong: So you believe, Theo, that there's no point in people who have different political or social orientations trying to come to some agreement on issues they disagree about? Is that a fair statement of your position?

Onassis: I guess that would be the implication of what I said. But now that I hear it, I'm not so sure. We have to do just that on city council, and somehow we manage. Although it isn't always easy.

Sophia: Madame Chair, is it all right if I make a suggestion?

Chair: Certainly, Sophia.

Sophia: It's pretty clear that there are lots of contentious issues here. But listening to everyone, it seems to me that there are also some points that everyone can agree on. I'm wondering whether looking for points of agreement might help us make some progress.

Chair: That's an excellent suggestion, Sophia. Thank you. Would you like to begin?

Sophia: OK . . . sure. I think that everyone here would agree that what these Nazi guys say is hateful and objectionable and that we'd all be a lot happier if they didn't say such things.

Chair: I think we would all agree. (*There are nods of agreement from around the room.*)

Singh: Would you all agree that this kind of hate speech is hurtful and harmful?

Ali: Most definitely. (*More nods.*)

McGregor: Well, I can understand that certain people would feel hurt and not like what they say. I don't like what they say. But harm? It's only words—as long as they don't explicitly incite people to violence. People should have thicker skins.

Gold: But we've seen throughout history how, when hatred toward certain groups is accepted in a society, violence isn't far behind.

McGregor: But even if there's the possibility of harm, I still don't think that that justifies repressive measures.

Singh: But you will grant the possibility of harm?

McGregor: Well . . . at least for argument's sake.

Chong: I imagine that we would also all agree that freedom of speech is an important value of a democratic society.

McGregor: You won't hear any disagreement from me.

Ali: In general. But there are limits.

Gold: Of course, there are limits. That's why we have laws against libel and defamation, and why you're not allowed to yell "fire" in a crowded theatre when there's no fire. I think that would be another point of agreement. (More nods.)

McGregor: I think that yelling "fire" in a theatre is different. In that case, the harm is much more immediate and obvious: people getting trampled.

Gold: Do you concede, though, that there have to be some limitations in certain circumstances?

McGregor: I do. But they should be kept to an absolute minimum. The less government interference in our lives, the better.

Chair: Perhaps I could try to summarize the points on which we have agreement. I believe that we all agree that what the group in question has to say is repugnant and hateful, and that this type of hate-mongering is harmful, or at least is potentially harmful. We also all agree that freedom of speech is an important value and should be protected to the extent possible.

Sophia: So it's not like people disagree on the basic values. But different people seem to be more concerned about one of these values than the other.

Phil: They weigh them differently!

Sophia: So I'm wondering whether it might be possible to find a solution that would take into account both these values and deal with everyone's concerns.

Ali: But either we give them the permit to speak or we don't. And I say we don't.

Lester: What about if we let them speak but also find ways to present some counter-arguments and different views, as Ms. Chong was suggesting.

Ravi: We could hand out flyers pointing out how crazy the things they say are.

Phil: A bunch of us could attend the presentation and raise objections and ask challenging questions.

Nancy: We could demonstrate outside with placards saying that our community does not condone racist views.

Stephen: Yeah. I could hold up a placard saying "Love Your Neighbour."

Winnie: Maybe we could even challenge them to a debate.

Gold: I'd be concerned about giving them that much attention and publicity. That's just what they want.

Ravi: Or maybe it would bring racism to people's attention. I don't think most people know what's going on out there.

Singh: I think that the solution of respecting freedom of speech by allowing them to speak but finding ways to counter their hateful message has some merit. I'd be interested in pursuing further some of the ideas that our younger generation of citizens has come up with. Would it be possible for a few of us to try and come up with a proposal about how to proceed along the lines that are being suggested? We could circulate it in the community to get feedback, then pass it on to the council for a decision.

Chair: Yes, that would be possible.

Chong: I'd be interested in working with you, Sunita.

Lester: So would I, Dr. Singh . . . if that's OK.

Singh: Absolutely!

Chair: Can I see a show of hands of those in favour of Sunita Singh's suggestion? . . . It appears that the group supports the idea. It's not unanimous, but it is a clear majority.

Ali: I could not support any proposal that would allow these thugs to speak. If that's what you decide, then I'll be out there protesting loud and clear.

McGregor: I think allowing them to speak is the right decision. Don't expect me to stand in the town square holding up a placard. But the rest of you can do what you want. It's still a free country—for the moment.

Achieving the Spirit of Inquiry

In Chapter 1, we pointed out that inquiry requires of its participants a certain orientation or attitude which we call the spirit of inquiry. At the most general level, the spirit of inquiry involves an appreciation of reason and a commitment to base beliefs and actions on inquiry. In particular, the spirit of inquiry embodies these two aspects:

1. open-mindedness, which involves being open to challenges to our arguments, counter-evidence, and views which oppose our own; and

2. fair-mindedness, which requires that we be fair in our portrayal of views with which we disagree. We must also be aware of our biases, and as objective as possible in our judgments.

Although we may recognize the value of these attitudes as ideals for engaging in inquiry, they are not always easy to achieve in practice. There are various factors which pose obstacles to achieving the spirit of inquiry, as our students recognize with respect to the hate speech discussion.

What Do You Think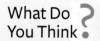

In what ways was the spirit of inquiry violated by the participants at the meeting?

Post Mortem

The students are assembled in a café after the community meeting.

Phil: What did you folks think of the meeting?

Winnie: I think that the issue's really important, and it's great that the whole community got together to talk about it.

Lester: But boy, things sure went off the rails more than once.

Nancy: Some people were really rude—my dad, for one.

Ahmed: My uncle wasn't exactly Mr. Nice either. I wonder why people act like that when they get into a debate?

What Do You Think

Why do you think that people sometimes violate the spirit of inquiry when they are involved in a debate?

Nancy: I know that my dad always gets so stuck in his own political views that he refuses to listen to any other positions. Nothing will make him change his mind. It's so maddening!

Ahmed: I get the feeling that some people, like my Uncle Omar, just don't want to hear any other views.

Sophia: Sometimes people just want to be right rather than trying to find the best view.

Ahmed: It's sort of like it's comforting to think you have the truth, and it's scary to have to doubt your views and be uncertain. I know I feel like that sometimes when you guys challenge my ideas in class. It's much easier when everyone agrees with you. Then you feel sure that you're right.

Phil: Yeah. When somebody criticizes your view, you feel kind of under attack, so you just want to defend yourself.

Nancy: My dad again. When Dr. Singh said that he wasn't really in a position to understand how harmful hate speech can be, he got very defensive and went way over the top. He didn't listen to her point at all. He just totally misconstrued it and then took offence at something she hadn't even said.

Stephen: There's also a lot of pressure when you're into a hot topic like this and everyone's disagreeing with everyone else. I think people often just react emotionally and say things off the tops of their heads.

Sophia: That's true. But that kind of pressure can also lead to people simply agreeing with what others say no matter what their own view is.

Nancy: I agree that that can be a problem. Though folks didn't seem to be having much trouble expressing their own views at this meeting!

Ravi: I also think that a person's own experiences can influence how they see an issue. I know that my horrible experience with that gang really affected me, and at first it was hard for me to see any other point of view.

Sophia: But I also thought that some of the participants were very open-minded and fair. Like your mother, Ravi. She was very willing to listen to other points of view and arguments.

Lester: And she even changed her mind by the end because of the arguments she heard. That's pretty impressive.

Winnie: Not to be biased or anything, but I thought that my mom made a good move when she recognized that there are dangers in giving those Nazi guys a platform. She was willing to acknowledge a weakness in her own position, which I think shows open-mindedness.

Obstacles to the Spirit of Inquiry

In reflecting on what happened at the meeting, the students begin to recognize instances where the inquiry went awry and where the appropriate attitudes were not in place, as well as examples when participants demonstrated a true spirit of inquiry. They also begin to reflect on what some of the obstacles might be to achieving the spirit of inquiry.

Ideological Fixity

One major obstacle to open-mindedness is inflexibility in our views. This may stem from an unwavering and unquestioning commitment to a political, social, or philosophical position, what we have called **ideological fixity.** It is the kind of unquestioning commitment which McGregor exhibits to his libertarian philosophy and which prevents him from ever considering positions or arguments which run contrary to this ideology. This is not to say that we should not have an orientation or hold a position. But to hold such a position rationally involves recognizing that we are fallible and that our position, or parts of it, could be overturned by the force of good reasons and evidence. Thus we should be open to consider views which oppose our own, and to take seriously evidence and arguments which tell against our position. In contrast, someone suffering from ideological fixity uses their ideology to insulate their position against challenges. Thus McGregor inevitably responds to others' arguments through a libertarian lens rather than truly attempting to consider the other position and whether it may have any merit.

> **Ideological fixity** is an unwavering and unquestioning commitment to a political, social, or philosophical position.

Ignorance of Other Views

Fixity can also occur when a person is not aware of other positions or points of view. This may simply be a case of not being willing to commit the time and energy necessary to seek out other views or of not understanding the importance of exploring other possibilities. But curiosity, a concern for truth, a willingness to follow reasoning where it leads, and a desire to act on the basis of reasons are all aspects of the spirit of inquiry, and these require commitment and effort.

The Need to Be Right

Sometimes blindness to other positions is a result of people simply not wanting to hear any views which run contrary to their own. This may be behind Omar Ali's fixity in his view. Ali begins with a very definite position on the issue at hand, declares on several occasions that nothing would make him change his mind, and does not even want the issue discussed. He is also hostile to other views and to the individuals who hold them. Such closed-mindedness is the very opposite of the spirit of inquiry.

The Desire for Certainty

Resistance to hearing other views may result, at least in part, from the desire for certainty, which appears to be a common human characteristic. It is comforting to feel that we know

John Dewey (1859–1952), an eminent philosopher, psychologist, educator, social critic, and political activist, emphasized the centrality of inquiry in acquiring knowledge as well as the importance of the appropriate attitudes for inquiry. In this passage, he described one of the obstacles to the spirit of inquiry:

"The path of least resistance and least trouble is a mental rut already made. It requires troublesome work to undertake the alternation of old beliefs. Self-conceit often regards it as a sign of weakness to admit that a belief to which we have once committed ourselves is wrong. We get so identified with an idea that it is literally a "pet" notion and we rise to its defense and stop our eyes and ears to anything different."[2]

where things stand and unsettling to be forced to doubt what we have previously taken as true, as Ravi points out. But given the fallible nature of our knowledge, an acceptance of some degree of uncertainty is a necessary aspect of inquiry.

Identification with Our Beliefs

Another cause of fixity is the tendency to identify with our beliefs or ideas. We may begin to feel that our beliefs constitute an essential part of who we are; as a result, we are reluctant to give them up. We may also derive a degree of self-satisfaction from being right and feel that it is a sign of weakness to admit that something we believed is not, in fact, worthy of belief.

Defensiveness

Identification with our beliefs can lead to another obstacle to the spirit of inquiry—defensiveness. When we see our beliefs as part of our identity and when we derive a sense of self-satisfaction from holding the right beliefs, then the criticism of our beliefs may seem like a personal attack. We can see this particularly in McGregor's reaction to Sunita Singh's comment. Both Ravi and Phil acknowledge similar feelings of defensiveness when their views are challenged.

Groupthink

In a group situation, a lack of open-minded consideration of other views may result from the influence of other members of the group. When a particular view is widely held and confidently expressed in the group, there is often pressure on all group members to share this position. If a participant already holds this position, then the reinforcement of the group may cause them to hold it with even greater confidence, a confidence that may not be warranted by the evidence and arguments. If they do not already hold the position, then pressure of an overt social kind, or a more subtle psychological kind, may make it very difficult to hold a contrary view. Although we did not see an example of this in the town hall meeting (indeed, the participants were very willing to express their individual views), it is a problem which Sophia points out in the "post mortem."

Keep in Mind 🔲

OBSTACLES TO THE SPIRIT OF INQUIRY

- Ideological fixity
- Ignorance of other views
- The need to be right
- The desire for certainty
- Identification with our beliefs
- Defensiveness
- Groupthink
- Preconceptions or biases
- Fallacious reasoning
- Rushing to response

Preconceptions or Biases

Another obstacle to the spirit of inquiry takes the form of initial preconceptions or personal biases. Much or most of the time, we will begin an inquiry with initial views on the issue at hand, and with knowledge and experiences that will affect how we view the issue. These initial views or past experiences can become problematic when we are unaware of their existence and unknowingly allow them to affect our evaluation of the issue. These views or experiences become biases when they blind us to other views and colour our judgment. Ali's biases on the issue of hate speech affect his ability to listen to opposing arguments. And Ravi recognizes that his personal experience with racial violence made it difficult for him to consider other points of view.

Fallacious Reasoning

The spirit of inquiry is also hampered by the use of fallacious reasoning. Fallacies are arguments which are logically weak but which have considerable persuasive power (see Chapter 4). Using rhetoric to illicitly persuade, rather than logic to rationally convince, violates the commitment to reason which characterizes the spirit of inquiry.[3] The use of the kind of ad hominems which both McGregor and Ali engage in or the creation of a straw person to mischaracterize a view (as McGregor does with Singh's comment) divert the inquiry from its rational course and can make for bad feelings, as we can see in the exchanges at the meeting.

Apply Your Understanding Exercise 1

Rushing to Response

Violations to the spirit of inquiry often occur in the heat of debate. There seems to be a common human tendency to react emotionally in pressure situations and to respond almost automatically, without taking the time to give the issue careful consideration and to measure one's responses.

Overcoming the Obstacles to Inquiry

The obstacles to inquiry which we have described represent common and widespread human tendencies. There are, however, some strategies that one can employ as a way of attempting to overcome or counteract these obstacles.

Know Your Initial Views and Biases

One strategy is to make ourselves explicitly aware of both our initial views on an issue and any possible biases we may have. When beginning an inquiry, we can make note of the position we are starting with and why, as well as any overarching perspective or world view we are bringing to the issue. Personal experiences or history which might affect our attitudes toward or evaluation of the issue can also be noted. As an example, before the community meeting, Ravi could have asked himself what his view was on the question of giving the neo-Nazi group permission to speak. He might have noted that he had a strong negative reaction to the idea and asked himself to what extent his experience of being attacked by a gang might affect his judgment and his ability to consider other views in a fair-minded way.

Monitor Your Process of Inquiry and Dialogue

The next strategy is to monitor our process of inquiry and dialogue as it proceeds to check for fixity, biases, or other obstacles to open-minded and fair-minded inquiry. We can ask ourselves these questions: "Are my preconceptions and initial perspectives biasing how I evaluate various arguments?" "Am I really listening to and seriously considering the other views and arguments?" "Am I fairly representing other positions?" "Am I being open to criticism?"

Another useful strategy is to take time to consider our response. Asking ourselves the question "Is my response measured and appropriate?" may help us to avoid violations to the spirit of inquiry. In addition, asking ourselves, "Am I being unduly influenced by the views of the group?" may help us to base our views on reasons and evidence and not to be subject to the pressure to conform.

Countering defensiveness involves understanding that criticism should not be taken personally and that critical interaction is a way of coming to a better view. If we succeed in cultivating a sense of self-satisfaction from being reasonable rather than from being right, then being willing to accept other arguments, acknowledge errors, and so on, all become part of our identity. Asking ourselves, "Am I identifying with being a reasonable person rather than with a particular view?" may help to remind us to maintain a spirit of inquiry.

Keep in Mind

GUIDING QUESTIONS FOR ACHIEVING THE SPIRIT OF INQUIRY

1. Know your initial views and biases:
   - What position on this issue am I starting with?
   - What perspectives am I bringing to the evaluation of this issue?
   - Am I bringing any personal experiences to this issue that might colour my judgment?

2. Monitor your process of inquiry and dialogue:
   - Are my preconceptions and initial perspectives biasing how I evaluate various arguments?
   - Am I really listening to and seriously considering all views and arguments?
   - Am I fairly representing other positions?
   - Am I being open to criticism?
   - Are my responses measured and appropriate?
   - Am I being unduly influenced by the views of the group?
   - Am I identifying with being a reasonable person rather than with a particular point of view?
   - Am I avoiding the use of fallacious reasoning?

3. Evaluate your own view:
   - What are the weaknesses in the view I favour?
   - What are likely criticisms and objections to this view?
   - What alternative arguments are there to this view?
   - What evidence or arguments would count against the view I favour?
   - What would make me change my mind about the issue?

We must also carefully monitor our arguments in order to avoid the use of fallacious reasoning. Being aware of common fallacies such as ad hominem, appeal to popularity, or hasty conclusion, and assiduously avoiding their use, can help to keep inquiry on its rational track and thus respect the commitment to reason which characterizes the spirit of inquiry.

It is especially important to avoid the straw person fallacy. This very common error of misdescribing contrary views may stem from inadvertently misunderstanding a view or from deliberately misdescribing it to make it an easier target for our criticisms. In either case, it is highly problematic as it deflects the discussion from the point at issue and often makes the opposing view sound ridiculous in the process. One strategy to avoid the straw person fallacy it to carefully and charitably understand the opposing argument before criticizing it. In a dialogue, one can carefully restate the opposing position in such a way that the other arguer will agree that that is their position.

Evaluate Your Own Views

A careful and critical evaluation of our own views is helpful in order to maintain open-mindedness in an inquiry. To this end, it is important to be aware of the weaknesses in our view. It is likely that no position, however well thought out, will be without flaws or weak points, and recognizing these weak points is a sign that we have considered our own views in a fair and open way. Moreover, acknowledging any weaknesses openly in the debate reflects an attitude of searching for the best views as opposed to wanting to win at all costs. We see a demonstration of this type of willingness to acknowledge weaknesses in Agatha Chong's admission that her position regarding allowing the group to speak does have dangers.

Another important and useful strategy is to deliberately seek out criticisms, objections, and alternative arguments. Avoiding criticism of our views and a consideration of alternatives is a sign of closed-mindedness. But it is not enough to deal with criticisms and alternatives that happen to come our way. Inquiry involves a comparative judgment among those views which have been proposed and which are vying for acceptance. Thus we are required to find out what these views are. Failure to do so leaves us in danger of succumbing to the kind of fixity that arises from being unaware of the problems in our own view and the merits of other views.

If we hold our views in an open-minded way and are aware of their weaknesses, then we should understand what sorts of reasons and arguments would count against these views. Moreover, open-mindedness implies a willingness to change our minds if the arguments warrant. In this regard, a helpful strategy is to ask ourselves what reasons and arguments would cause us to change our mind. A demonstration of this process is provided by Sunita Singh when she states that if she had some good reason to think that countering hate speech was more effective than silencing it, then she might be persuaded to change her mind about the group's request. And, in fact, when confronted with such arguments, she does change her mind.

Apply Your Understanding Exercise 2

The students continue their "post mortem" of the events at the meeting.

Ahmed: I'm still really bothered by how some people spoke to each other and treated each other at the meeting. It wasn't very nice.

Nancy: My dad was the worst. He kept interrupting poor Mr. Onassis and wouldn't let him speak. How rude!

Lester: And it wasn't very helpful either. In a community discussion like that, everyone should be able say their piece. When people interrupt each other, some folks may get cut out of the discussion.

Winnie: And it makes for bad feelings.

Phil: Also, certain people, not to mention any names, liked to hog the conversation and not leave much space for other folks to express their opinions.

Ahmed: I also didn't think it was very good when my Uncle Omar wanted to cut the discussion short. You need to give everyone the chance to talk it through. And we weren't anywhere near a resolution at that point.

Lester: I got the feeling that some people didn't really understand what a discussion like that is about. We were trying to come up with a reasonable solution to the issue by exchanging views and giving arguments. But some of them just wanted to have their own view win out.

Winnie: I also didn't like that a few people were so aggressive. They didn't want to listen; they just wanted to fight.

Phil: And fight they did. How about all those ad hominems flying around! A few people really got caught up in personal attacks and kept losing sight of the issue.

Nancy: And got defensive too. Good old Dad again. His reaction to Dr. Singh's comment was really uncalled for and created a negative atmosphere.

Juanita: I think the point about atmosphere's really important. Everyone should feel free to speak and not feel put down or intimidated or made to feel dumb.

Sophia: Are you referring by any chance to my father's pronouncement in Latin?

Juanita: Well...

Sophia: He does that sometimes. Mostly in Greek, though. Definitely not helpful to the discussion.

Winnie: Fortunately, though, most people were reasonable and willing to listen to other people's points.

Sophia: That's true. And there were some things that people did that really helped the process along. For instance, I thought it was great when your mother restated my father's point about liberals and libertarians and then said, "Is that a fair statement of your position?" She was being very careful not to misinterpret his position, but at the same time she made him see the implications of his view. Very neat.

Lester: I also was impressed by how a number of people conceded points that went against their own view. Like Mrs. Gold and Mrs. Chong.

Phil: And even Mr. McGregor was willing to grant the possibility that hate speech might be harmful—if only for argument's sake.

Lester: I thought that one of the most important moves in making the process work was trying to find out what points people share and not just what they disagree about.

Ravi: Way to go, Sophia! You really saved the day.

Ahmed: And then Lester came up with a solution that dealt with everyone's concerns.

Winnie: You two should run for town council!

Conducting a Dialogue

Although inquiries take many forms, some of which are written, they often take place in the form of actual verbal interactions among individuals. We have seen many examples of such dialogues throughout the text.

Not all dialogues between people are inquiry dialogues. The kind of dialogue involved in inquiry is distinctive since its goal is to come to a reasoned judgment through collective rational discussion. Because of this goal, inquiry dialogues have certain requirements: 1) that participants treat each other with respect, 2) that everyone concerned has the possibility to participate, and 3) that all concerned have a commitment to pursuing the dialogue in a productive manner.[4]

Keep in Mind

REQUIREMENTS FOR AN INQUIRY DIALOGUE

- Participants treat each other with respect.
- Everyone has the possibility to participate.
- All participants have a commitment to pursuing the dialogue in a productive manner.

....
Keep in Mind ☑:
....

GUIDELINES FOR CONDUCTING A DIALOGUE

Respectful Treatment
- Show respect for the contribution of other participants.
- Be minimally combative and attempt to maintain friendliness and dialogue.
- Do not engage in personal attacks or ad hominems.
- Do not "moralize" the opposing position.

Meaningful Participation
- Do not interrupt or prevent others from expressing their views or criticisms.
- Do not monopolize the conversation.
- Do not cut short the process of dialogue.
- Do not intimidate, manipulate, or otherwise discourage others from participating.

Productive Interaction
- Maintain the dialogue at the level of reasons and arguments.
- Stay relevant; do not use distraction ploys.
- Be clear and accurate; do not confuse or mislead.
- Seriously consider the arguments of others; do not listen to them only in order to find fault.
- Seriously consider criticisms; do not be defensive.
- Seek common ground.
- Restate others' views in such a way that they agree with your restatement.
- Be willing to concede points when faced with stronger arguments.
- Be willing to concede certain points for the sake of the argument.
- If you reach a real impasse, agree to disagree in an amicable manner.

What this means in practice is that, in addition to trying to cultivate the various aspects of the spirit of inquiry as described above, we also need to pay attention to the particulars of the interpersonal interaction involved in dialogue situations. This is especially important given that, in the heat of face-to-face debate over controversial issues, the possibility of intolerance, personal attacks, injured feelings, and the breakdown of the dialogue is ever-present. We witnessed clear examples of these challenges in the discussion at the meeting.

Respectful Treatment

One overarching principle in dialogical interactions (as, indeed, in any other civil interaction) is respect. This means giving respectful attention to the contributions of other participants in the dialogue and avoiding personal attacks and a combative posture. The kinds of personal attacks and ad hominems engaged in by both McGregor and Ali run counter to the spirit of inquiry and are destructive of the respectful relationship necessary to keep a dialogue moving forward. Maintaining friendliness in a dialogical situation is a much preferable option both in terms of producing a productive outcome and in terms of fostering positive relationships.

A negative variation on this problem takes place when an arguer puts a moralistic frame onto an opponent's position, so that the opposing point of view is cast not just as wrong, but also as bad or evil. This is a move which Ali makes a number of times at the beginning of the community discussion; for example, he is creating a moralistic frame when he calls the proposal outrageous, claims that the community would not stand for such a thing, and accuses McGregor of supporting the "Nazi thugs." Once a position is framed in this way, it becomes much more difficult and awkward to respond and maintain the position.

Meaningful Participation

Inquiry dialogues ideally involve the meaningful participation of all interested parties. This implies that everyone's contributions should be welcomed and encouraged, and no one should be excluded, discouraged from participating, or hindered in their participation. Participants should feel free to pose questions, make arguments, and offer criticisms and suggestions. Some of the moves which can exclude or discourage are the following:

1. interrupting or otherwise preventing others from expressing their view or criticisms (e.g., McGregor's interruption of Onassis)
2. monopolizing the conversation
3. intimidating other participants through exercise of power or authority, aggressive demeanor (e.g., Ali and McGregor), or use of jargon or other technical knowledge not accessible to others (e.g., Onassis's use of Latin)
4. cutting short the process of deliberation (e.g., Ali's attempt to end the discussion)

Productive Interaction

Ultimately the aim is to keep the dialogue productive and operating at the level of reasons and arguments. This means that participants should ensure that their arguments are relevant and not use moves that distract from the arguments at issue. The participants should state their points clearly and accurately, with no attempt to confuse or mislead. In this regard, Onassis's quotation in Latin, although probably innocent in intent, likely had the effect of confusing as well as excluding some of the other participants. Participants can also keep the dialogue productive by

Political debate is often criticized for its lack of decorum and respectful dialogue. In this excerpt from an interview, Elizabeth May, leader of the Green Party of Canada, speaks about her objectives to change the tone and substance of debate in the House of Commons:

"The most important thing is to revitalize Canadian democracy at a very basic level. Right now, certainly in the House of Commons, the behaviour of most parties . . . they're all badly behaved. . . . But there needs to be, I think, someone who raises the bar through their own behaviour, through an injunction to fellow parliamentarians not to . . . have behaviour that's disgraceful and the voters end up thinking, 'I hope my children don't see this.' That's not appropriate. So I will be a very strong voice for decorum and appropriate behaviour and for recognizing that the House of Commons should be a place where ideas of substance are debated, where we see more cooperation and less partisanship."[5]

seriously considering others' arguments, as opposed to listening to them in order to find fault, and by seriously considering their criticisms, as opposed to becoming defensive.

One very important strategy in conducting a productive dialogue is to seek points on which there is agreement as opposed to focusing solely on the areas of disagreement. In order for a dialogue even to get off the ground, there needs to be some common ground; finding points of agreement is often a key move in working toward resolution. This was clearly the case at the community meeting.

Restating another person's view in such a way that they acknowledge its accuracy is a helpful technique to avoid creating a straw person and thus keep the dialogue from getting side-tracked. Being willing to concede points when faced with a stronger argument is also important in moving a dialogue forward; conceding a strong point reflects an open-minded attitude. It can also be helpful at times to concede a point for the sake of argument even when one is not entirely convinced of the point. Such a move can keep a discussion going when it seems to have reached an impasse. This is the move that McGregor makes when he concedes the possibility of harm "for argument's sake," even though he is not fully convinced. This allows the group to build the common ground necessary to lead to a resolution. Acknowledging the possibility that another view may be correct does not necessarily imply changing one's mind. What it does involve is not dismissing the position out of hand in order to see where the dialogue can go.

Finally, if you reach a real impasse and resolution does not seem possible, then the appropriate action is to agree to disagree in an amicable manner.

Apply Your Understanding
Exercises 3, 4

Responding to Fallacies

Earlier in the chapter, we saw how fallacious reasoning is an obstacle to achieving the spirit of inquiry. Thus it is important to avoid its use when conducting dialogues. It may be the case, however, that other participants are not so enlightened. As a consequence, we need to consider how to respond when someone else uses fallacious reasoning with us.

This is especially an issue in a dialogue because, in the heat of the moment, it is easy to fall prey to the rhetorical ploys and not recognize the logical errors. So, for example, when Ali uses a combination of ad hominem and straw person against McGregor ("I can't believe that a man like you, a prominent businessman and member of our town council, could support those Nazi thugs!"), McGregor becomes offended. A more appropriate response would have been to point out that the comment was both irrelevant to the issue and misrepresented McGregor's position. As we saw in Chapter 4, fallacies tend to be convincing because they depend on certain rhetorical effects, while they are fallacious because they commit logical errors. The key to responding to fallacies is to notice the rhetorical effect and resist its temptation, and go on to recognize and address the logical error.

Let's examine several of the exchanges in the chapter dialogue, to compare how the participants actually responded to how they might have responded.

The key to responding to fallacies is to notice the rhetorical effect and resist its temptation, and go on to recognize and address the logical error.

Ad Hominem and Straw Person

Ali: I can't believe that a man like you, a prominent businessman and member of our town council, could support those Nazi thugs!

Response:

McGregor: How dare you imply such a thing!

Better response:

My professional roles are irrelevant to evaluating my position on this issue. And to say that I support Nazi thugs is a perversion of my view. I support free speech which sometimes involves having to tolerate repugnant views being aired in public.

Ad Hominem

The key in responding to an ad hominem is not to become offended by personal innuendos or distracted by engaging with whether or not the attribution is correct. Instead, point out that the personal comments are not relevant to evaluating the issue at hand.

Straw Person

In responding to a straw person, you should not respond to the misdescribed version of your argument, but rather point out the inaccuracy. This is precisely what Sunita Singh does in the following exchange.

McGregor: Are you implying that I am insensitive and racist? I resent that.

Good response:

Singh: You know I wasn't implying any such thing, Mr. McGregor.

Post Hoc (False Causal Claim)

Below are two examples of responses to the post hoc fallacy from the initial dialogue in this chapter:

Ravi: It just doesn't seem right to me that we should let these Nazi guys spread hateful lies about us and use our own community hall to do it. I've experienced the results.

Response:

Nancy: Oh Ravi, how awful! I had no idea what terrible effects hate speech can have.

Better response:

Oh Ravi, how awful! But we have no way of knowing whether hate speech contributed to the attack. There are also lots of other reasons why gang members might engage in this type of violence.

In the first response, Nancy simply accepts Ravi's implication of a causal connection; a better response would be to question whether there is any evidence of a causal link.

In the following excerpt, no one responds to Mona Gold's implication that hate speech contributes to violence, although it would have been appropriate for someone to question the implied connection.

Gold: But we've seen throughout history how, when hatred toward certain groups is accepted in a society, violence isn't far behind.

Response: none

Better response: But is there evidence that hate speech caused the violence? Maybe some other factors in those societies gave rise to both hate speech and violence.

Popularity

Ali: Yes. Everyone knows that hate speech leads to violence.

Response: none

Better response: That might be a widely held view, but do we really have evidence to support it?

The fallacy of appeal to popularity can be countered by refusing to engage in the issue of whether or not everyone does think this or that, and by pointing out that the popularity of the view or practice does not (generally) provide evidence for accepting it.

Faulty Analogy

Gold: Of course there are [limits]. That's why we have laws against libel and defamation, and why you're not allowed to yell "fire" in a crowded theatre when there's no fire . . .

Good response:

McGregor: I think that yelling "fire" in a theatre is different. In that case, the harm is much more immediate and obvious: people getting trampled.

A questionable analogy can be countered by demonstrating that the items being compared are not comparable in some way (as McGregor does), by offering a better analogy, or by offering an alternative analogy which is a *reductio* (see Chapter 5).

Problematic Premise

Ali: There's no point. Our community won't stand for such a thing!

Good Response:

McGregor: Now just one moment, Ali. Don't claim to represent the community. I'm a member of the community just as much as you are. And I don't agree with you.

McGregor's aggressive tone leaves something to be desired, but the move of responding to the questionable premise with a counter-example is an appropriate one. Another appropriate response would be to ask for evidence for the claim.

Irrelevant Reason

Sunita Singh: I would like to point out, with all due respect, Mr. Onassis and Mr. McGregor, that you cannot really understand the harm done by hate speech because you and your families are never the objects of this kind of racial attack.

Keep in Mind

Popularity
- I know that many (most) people think that, but let's look at the evidence . . .
- (Common practice) So what if everyone does it; that doesn't make it right. You wouldn't jump off a bridge just because everyone else was doing it.

Faulty Analogy
- I really don't think those things are comparable. For example, . . .
- A better analogy would be . . .
- That's like saying . . . (alternative analogy which is a *reductio*)
- Interesting analogy, but what principle are you defending?

Problematic Premise
- I don't know—that's a pretty controversial claim; what's your evidence for that?
- I'm not willing to accept that without more evidence.

Irrelevant Reason
- I really don't see the relevance of (his history, personality, previous associations) to the issue; the issue is . . .

Anecdotal Evidence
- Yes, well . . . That example may be true, but have you considered . . .?
- If I had had that experience, I would probably feel the same way; but one such experience is not really enough to support such a sweeping generalization.
- I think you are making too much of your one experience.

Hasty Conclusion
- I think that's a bit quick. I mean, that is only one case.
- So why do you think that? Do you have more evidence/ reasons than that?
- That seems a bit broad given your experience (evidence).

McGregor's Response: Are you implying that I am insensitive and racist? I resent that.

Better response: (by Agatha Chong) Who can or cannot understand what, seems to me beside the point . . . We've gotten sidetracked and still haven't dealt with Onassis's argument, which I think is a good one.

McGregor's negative reaction to Sunita Singh's comment is quite inappropriate. Agatha Chong makes the more pertinent point that Sunita's comment is not particularly relevant to assessing Onassis's argument (although Sunita later argues that her point is not irrelevant).

Anecdotal Evidence and Hasty Conclusion

Nancy: I had no idea what Ravi has gone through . . . It makes me realize how racist our society is.

Response:

Ali: How right you are.

Better response: I think that what Ravi had to endure is unconscionable. But we can't conclude that the whole society is racist based on one incident. That's something we'd have to investigate further.

*Apply Your
Understanding
Exercise 5*

Concluding solely on the basis of the attack which Ravi experienced that an entire society is racist is a case of both anecdotal evidence and hasty conclusion. The appropriate response involves pointing out that one cannot make such a generalization on the basis of one incident and requesting more evidence. One can also counter a hasty conclusion with counter-examples—for example, that a person of Haitian origin has been chosen the Governor General of Canada or that a black person has been elected President of the United States. Anecdotes can be used to reasonably refute a generalization although they cannot support one.

CHECK YOUR UNDERSTANDING

- *Describe the key attitudes and commitments which comprise the spirit of inquiry.*
- *List and briefly describe each of the obstacles to achieving the spirit of inquiry.*
- *List and briefly describe the strategies for overcoming the obstacles for each of the following categories:*
  - *Know your initial views and biases.*
  - *Monitor your process of inquiry and dialogue.*
  - *Evaluate your own view.*
- *What are the three main requirements for an inquiry dialogue? Describe the guidelines for conducting a dialogue which relate to each of the requirements.*
- *Why is it important to know how to respond to fallacies?*
- *Discuss the key strategy for responding to each of the following fallacies:*
  - *straw person*
  - *ad hominem*
  - *popularity*
  - *anecdotal evidence*

EXERCISES

1. Identify the obstacles to the spirit of inquiry which are exemplified in each of the following:

   i) I never read articles critical of the environmental movement. I'm a committed environmentalist after all.

   ii) No, I haven't considered arguments that others have made against the legalization of marijuana. I'm not aware that there are any.

   iii) I'm so happy I won that argument on the raising of the minimum wage. I knew I was right all along.

   iv) Why should we bother listening to the rest of his speech supporting capital punishment? We already know what the right position is on that issue.

   v) I'm going to have difficulty remaining friendly with Phil after he criticized my views about vegetarianism.

   vi) You're saying you see a flaw in my argument? Boy, are you ever a critical person!

2. Read the news report on the textbook website under Exercise 11-2. The assignment will involve working with a partner to write and present a dialogue representing your inquiry into this issue: "Should the authorities have taken the children away from the parents?"

   i) Working individually, respond to the first set of guiding questions (see page 201) for achieving the spirit of inquiry (under "Know your initial views and biases"). Make note of your responses.

   ii) Find a partner to work with who has a different initial view on the issue.

   iii) Working together, lay out the main arguments on each side of the issue. (You can find these in the news report.)

   iv) Conduct an oral dialogue with your partner in which you evaluate the arguments on each side of the issue.

   v) As individuals, go back and respond to the second and third sets of guiding questions for achieving the spirit of inquiry. (See "Monitor your process of inquiry and dialogue" and "Evaluate your own view" on page 201). Make note of your responses.

   vi) Work with your partner to write up your dialogue, refining it to reflect any changes you would like to make based on your answers to the guiding questions. Present the dialogue to the class.

3. Read the dialogue for assignment 11-3 on the textbook website.

   i) Note instances in which participants violate the guidelines for conducting a dialogue and explain in what way they are violations.

   ii) Note the positive dialogical moves which participants make and explain how they move the dialogue forward.

   iii) Rewrite the dialogue in a way that respects the principles for conducting a dialogue.

4. Listen to the political debates at the following websites:

   > http://www.youtube.com/watch?v=5xUy2inkGHQ&feature=related

   > http://www.youtube.com/watch?v=d3dl6ifRG-0&feature=related

   For each one, evaluate the debate in terms of the ways in which it meets or fails to meet the requirements of an inquiry dialogue as well as the ways in which it exemplifies or violates the spirit of inquiry.

5. For each of the following dialogue excerpts,

   i) identify the fallacy committed,

   ii) explain why the response given is inappropriate, and

   iii) provide an appropriate response.

   a) **Ahmed:** I wouldn't listen to Walter's views on vegetarianism. He's one of those animal rights extremists.

   Ravi: I don't really think he's all that extreme. I know people who have more extreme views.

b) **Juanita:** I'm going to get a tattoo! My mom says I'll regret it when I'm forty. But everyone I know has one.

   Nancy: I don't have one.

c) **Phil:** People from small towns are really honest. I dropped my wallet when I was visiting this town where my dad's family comes from, and someone found it and returned it to me.

   Ahmed: That's great. I'll remember that the next time I visit a small town.

d) **Onassis:** I'm thinking of supporting the green candidate in the election.

   McGregor: I'm really surprised that you'd be in favour of blocking logging roads and chaining yourself to trees.

   Onassis: Your views on the environment come out of the dark ages!

e) **Winnie:** I'm not surprised that you think that marijuana should be legalized. Wasn't your cousin Nick arrested for possession?

   Sophia: My cousin Nick's a good guy—he's just had some tough breaks.

f) **McGregor:** Financial success is the most important thing in people's lives. So we ought to support Wilbur Wright since he's most supportive of business interests.

   Alvarez: I don't much care for Wilbur Wright.

g) **Ravi:** Whenever the team eats at that burger joint before a game, we always lose.

   Ahmed: We'd better find another place to eat before our games.

ENDNOTES

1. Media Awareness Network, "Online Hate and the Law," http://www.media-awareness.ca/english/issues/online_hate/when_is_hate_a_crime.cfm (accessed Nov. 7, 2009).

2. John Dewey, *The Later Works of John Dewey, Volume 8, 1925–1953: Essays and How We Think*, rev. ed., ed. Jo Ann Boydston (Southern Illinois University, 2008), 136.

3. The idea that fallacies are obstacles to dialogue and to the resolution of disagreement is developed in detail by the proponents of Pragma-dialectics. See, for example, F. H. van Eemeren and R. Grootendorst, *A Systematic Theory of Argumentation: The Pragma-dialectical Approach* (Cambridge: Cambridge University Press, 2004).

4. For an elaboration of these requirements, see N. Burbules, *Dialogue in Teaching* (New York: Teachers College Press, 1993).

5. Elizabeth May, "Changing the Climate in Parliament," *YouTube.com*, http://www.youtube.com/watch?v=WKDbZDLjCs4 (accessed May 18, 2010).

Chapter 12
Inquiry in the Natural Sciences

I Hate Science!

Winnie, Juanita, and Stephen are sitting in the college cafeteria. Juanita has the college calendar open in front of her.

Juanita: I see here that we're required to take at least one science course. Ugh! Borrring!

Stephen: But there's no way round it. You have to take one.

Winnie: What do you mean, boring? Science is great. It's the main way we understand the world. And scientists make real progress in their investigations. Not only that, but what they learn is amazing. The details of the world are mind-boggling, and it's scientists who uncover them.

Stephen: Boy, I can see you're a real believer.

Juanita: Science is simply boring. There's nothing but a bunch of facts that you have to memorize. There's no discussion, no difference of opinions, no imagination. Just here's the way it is—memorize it and remember it for the final exam.

What Do You Think ?

Do you think that science is simply a matter of facts to be memorized? Why or why not?

Winnie: It sounds as if you didn't really learn about science in high school. Science requires a huge amount of imagination and insight. The mysteries that science uncovers are amazing. Science tells us how animals evolve, how mountains are built, how oceans are formed, how your body works.

Stephen: It makes you realize how complex and intricate the natural world is.

Winnie: What's boring is the way science is often taught. No one had any idea of the size and age of the universe until scientists figured it out. Have you seen those pictures from the Hubble telescope?

Stephen: They're incredible. Nature is awe-inspiring.

Winnie: And just think about it. These are pictures of stars that are millions of light years away. I mean, they may have exploded by the time we see them.

Juanita: But it's all so cut and dried. In my literature class, we can discuss what was motivating Hamlet or why *Catcher in the Rye* is a good book. In science class, you're just told stuff—and it's impossible to remember all the details.

Winnie: You've obviously had some bad learning experiences with science classes. I think one problem is that no one told you about the history of scientific discoveries. There's lots of debate in science, but what tends to be taught is the stuff that's been settled. If you look at history, though, you'll see that there were great debates. And if you do some inquiring, you'll see that there are still debates. Like the debates about "dark matter" or the cause of global warming.

Juanita: How could I do that? Science is so difficult to understand. All that math and stuff.

Winnie: Not all science is like that. You should try reading about how scientists make discoveries. A good introduction might be the history of geology. I have my prof's lecture notes right here if you want to have a look. One thing you'll see is that scientists follow the principles of inquiry.

This is a page from Winnie's geology notes:

Hutton

There are many stories from the history of science that illustrate how scientific inquiry takes place and exemplify its main features. One story begins with James Hutton (1726–1797), who is usually described as the founder of the science of geology. His work in the late eighteenth century is a good example of scientific practice and imagination.

At the time Hutton began his research, Biblical scholarship had determined that the earth was a mere 6000 years old. Hutton developed a dramatically different view.

Hutton noticed that there were two different kinds of rocks on his two farms and hypothesized that there must be a place where these two kinds meet. His inquiry was successful and he found what is now called an unconformity. *There were horizontal layers of gray shale piled on top of vertical layers of red sandstone, as shown in the photo.[1] In addition, he noted elsewhere that there were fingers of granite running into the sandstone. From these and other observations, he concluded the following:*

1. *The lower, upturned sandstone layers must have been deposited a long time ago, tilted and then eroded down.*
2. *These sandstone layers must then have been covered with new layers of sedimentation that had also eroded and created the upper layers.*

3. *The fingers of granite meant that the granite must have been molten at some time and, therefore, that there must be great heat in the earth where this process could occur. In addition, from observation of the current, almost undetectable rate of erosion and depositing of sand in the oceans, he reasoned that all these processes would involve enormous amounts of time.*

In 1788, he presented his theory in a paper submitted to the newly formed scientific organization, the Royal Society of Edinburgh. His insights required not merely keen observational ability, but a dramatic and imaginative break with the views of the day.[2]

Hutton's work illustrates some of the key aspects of scientific inquiry:

1. Hutton's reasoning was based on observation, and not, for example, Biblical scholarship.

2. His theory was offered as the best explanation available at the time for a number of observations. (See Chapter 5 on argument to the best explanation.)

3. His theory was fruitful, leading to many other insights; for example, it explained the location of fossils and eventually became part of the basis for Darwin's theory of evolution.

4. He brought these results to his expert peers for critical scrutiny.

Hutton's work also illustrates the role that an imaginative leap often plays in scientific discovery. Most science does not have quite this revolutionary character and involves primarily the careful application of general theories to specific problems. But occasionally great scientists such as Copernicus, Galileo, Newton, Hutton, Darwin, Einstein, and others make an imaginative breakthrough of this dramatic sort, which is called a "paradigm shift."[3]

In what way does Hutton's work exhibit an imaginative leap?

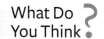

What Do You Think?

In science, context plays a key role. Context determines the burden of proof that a theory faces, and the available technology can facilitate or limit what can be investigated scientifically. While Hutton's story illustrates some general aspects of science, it leaves out the crucial role that technology can play. Hutton was able to make his observations with his own eyes; but much of scientific progress depends on the use of special tools which enable or facilitate observation, including telescopes for viewing the celestial world, microscopes

Technology in Science

The great observation of Galileo that there are moons revolving around Jupiter depended on his use of a telescope that he made himself. As Galileo states, "On the 7th day of January in the present year, 1610, in the first hour of the following night, when I was viewing the constellations of the heavons [sic] through a telescope, the planet Jupiter presented itself to my view, and as I had prepared for myself a very excellent instrument, I noticed a circumstance which I had never been able to notice before, namely that three little stars, small but very bright, were near the planet..."

Not only did optical technology enable early scientists to observe and generate new theories of the cosmic world; it also enabled them to peer into the micro-world of living organisms, such as bacteria, which are invisible to the naked eye. In the late eighteenth century, a Dutch lens grinder, Anthony van Leeuwenhoek (1632–1723), using an early microscope, observed algae in a rain barrel and bacteria in plaque taken from people's teeth—including from two old men who had never brushed their teeth in their lives![4]

for viewing the micro-world, and, more recently, particle colliders for examining the structure of subatomic particles, and DNA sequencing for investigating human origins and biological structure. The role that available technology plays in science is one important way in which historical context affects scientific discovery.

As noted above in the case of Hutton, great breakthroughs in science often require a significant revision of the current understanding of the world. The ease with which one can do this depends not only on the intellect, imagination, and character of the investigator, but also on the degree to which the view conflicts with well-established views. This illustrates another important influence of historical context on scientific inquiry.

The Basics of Scientific Reasoning: Arguments and Evaluation

The term "science" covers a wide range of endeavours, from archeology to zoology. It ranges in natural science from the study of basic particles of matter by physicists to the study of the vastness of the universe by astronomers and astrophysicists, and in social science from the study of how individuals make choices by psychologists to the study of complex social systems by sociologists, anthropologists, and economists. The range of scientific inquiry is vast.

Nonetheless, despite what you may have heard about the "scientific method," there is no well-defined common *method* to these various disciplines. What, then, distinguishes scientific inquiry from inquiry in other disciplines? One distinguishing feature relates to the kind of claims dealt with by scientific inquiry. Scientific inquiry deals with questions of fact and the explanation of facts.[5]

Another dominant characteristic of science is its approach to establishing its claims; that is, the nature of the reasons and arguments, and the kinds of criteria used to evaluate claims.

In principle, all scientific disciplines ground their claims on observation. That is why they are called *empirical* sciences (from the Greek word *empeirikos* which means "experience"). These observations can involve collecting data about single mother poverty, or collecting bits of carbon at an archeological dig. Observation can involve little white dots on a photographic plate or visual observations of star clusters. The range of relevant observations is very large. What distinguishes scientific observations from everyday observations is that they are done with systematic care and precision.

Scientific theories involve more than a summary of observations, however. Scientists use observations primarily as the basis for creating and testing theories. In our study of inquiry, we are interested in how scientists test and establish their theories. The basic method is the method we discussed in Chapter 5: argument to the best explanation.

What Do You Think?   *Explain the method of argument to the best explanation.*

Whether discussing the big bang theory or the causes of cancer, scientists will endeavour to show that the theory they favour provides the best available explanation of the phenomena being studied. Thus the history and the state of the controversy in which the scientific theory is put forward play a crucial role in the evaluation of scientific theories.

Another essential aspect of science is its approach to and method of criticism. Scientific claims must face not only the test of observation (as Galileo notes), but also the test of expert peer review. Scientists publish their findings in peer-reviewed journals in order that other experts can assess whether their data are credible and whether their theory constitutes *the best explanation*. Scientists understand that science progresses not only by amassing support for theories, but also crucially by eliminating false theories. This process of ongoing peer review is another central aspect of the context in which scientific inquiry is practised.

Dialogue in Science

The dialogical dimension of scientific inquiry is demonstrated very clearly in this dialogue written by Galileo Galilei, in which he argues for the Copernican view that the earth and other planets revolve around the sun. In order to make this argument, he must defend the Copernican view against the prevalent Aristotelian picture of the universe. In the excerpt of the dialogue below, Salviati argues that the existence of sun spots constitutes evidence that heavenly bodies can change, while Simplicius calls on the authority of Aristotelian teaching that the heavens are unchanging. This dialogue also demonstrates how the appeal to sensory evidence is beginning to be relied upon in early modern science in contrast to the previous appeal to abstract argument alone.

Galileo Galilei: "Dialogue Concerning the Two Chief World Systems" (1632)[6]

Simplicius: To tell the truth, I have not made such long and careful observations [of sun spots] that I can qualify as an authority on the facts of this matter; but certainly I wish to do so, and then to see whether I can once more succeed in reconciling what experience presents to us with what Aristotle teaches. For obviously two truths cannot contradict one another.

Salviati: Whenever you wish to reconcile what your senses show you with the soundest teachings of Aristotle, you will have no trouble at all. Does not Aristotle say that because of the great distance, celestial matters cannot be treated very definitely?

Simplicius: He does say so, quite clearly.

Salviati: Does he not also declare that what sensible experience shows ought to be preferred over any argument, even one that seems to be extremely well founded? And does he not say this positively and without a bit of hesitation?

Simplicius: He does.

Salviati: Then of the two propositions, both of them Aristotelian doctrines, the second—which says it is necessary to prefer the senses over arguments—is a more solid and definite doctrine than the other, which holds the heavens to be inalterable. Therefore it is better Aristotelian philosophy to say, "Heaven is alterable because my senses tell me so," than to say, "Heaven is inalterable because Aristotle was so persuaded by reasoning." Add to this that we possess a better basis for reasoning about celestial things than Aristotle did. He admitted such perceptions to be very difficult for him by reason of the distance from his senses, and conceded that one whose senses could better represent them would be able to philosophize about them with more certainty. Now we, thanks to the telescope, have brought the heavens thirty or forty times closer to us than they were to Aristotle, so that we can discern many things in them that he could not see; among other things these sunspots, which were absolutely invisible to him. Therefore we can treat of the heavens and the sun more confidently than Aristotle could.

While there are many similarities between how the social sciences and the natural sciences approach inquiry, there are enough differences that we will treat these two disciplinary categories in different chapters. This chapter will deal with inquiry in the natural sciences, and we will discuss inquiry in the social sciences in Chapter 13.

Argument to the Best Explanation in the Natural Sciences

As discussed in Chapter 5, argument to the best explanation is a method that we all use in a wide variety of situations. Whether we are trying to figure out what caused the First World War or what caused the water stains on the ceiling, we will usually review a number of candidate explanations. Take the water stain on the ceiling. Was there a leak in the roof? Was a pipe leaking? Did the ceiling always have this stain and we just never noticed it before? We would probably reason as follows: "I doubt that I failed to notice the stain. Also, when I touch it, it feels wet. The stain on the ceiling in the kitchen is under the bathroom so it could well be a pipe that is leaking. It is less likely that the roof over the bathroom is leaking

Apply Your Understanding Exercises 1, 2

and the water is somehow coming down to the kitchen." I can now go upstairs and check for leaks. If I find a leaky pipe, I can reasonably conclude that the best explanation of the water stain is the leaky pipe (although, of course, the roof and the pipe could both be leaking. Clearly, though, the first thing I should do is fix the pipe.)

This simple, practical example illustrates the reasoning process that characterizes scientific investigation: development of various hypotheses and a winnowing down to the best explanation. The history of geology provides a clear example of how scientific investigation employs this reasoning process.

The recent acceptance of the theory of plate tectonics as an explanation for a range of phenomena from earthquakes to mountain formation has brought geology to popular attention. The concepts that the earth is billions of years old and that continents move are both staggering insights into the workings of the earth. The process leading to their acceptance was a long and complex one that required careful observation, improved technology, and great collective efforts and sharing of information from a wide range of disciplines. The recent history of geology illustrates just such a process.

Here is another excerpt from Winnie's geology notes:

Hess

Until the 1960s, geologists did not accept what we have come to know as the theory of plate tectonics. Some earlier geologists speculated that there had been continental movement. However, there was no theoretical model that could explain how such enormous objects as continents could move around. So those ideas were not credited. Yet anyone who looked at a map of the earth could see that the continents seemed to be separated pieces of a large puzzle.

In 1912, Alfred Wegener proposed a theory of continental drift to account for the apparent fact that the continents such as Africa and South America appear to fit together. He is often credited as the father of plate tectonics; but there were earlier theorists, looking at the maps of the past, who also speculated that the continents fit together.[7]

What Wegener added to the theory was the observation that the rock formations and fossilized plants and animals showed appropriate similarities at matching continental margins. Because he was unable to give an account or model of how such enormous things as continents could "drift" around the world, his theories were largely rejected and even treated with derision. His theories explained some observations, but they were not credited because they could not be made coherent with what was then believed about the physical structure of the oceans and continents.

His theory was revived in the 1960s led by an American geologist, Harry Hess. Hess proposed that the recently discovered mid-oceanic ridges were spreading and that the continents were sitting on plates which were propelled by the slowly moving "currents" of the underlying mantle.[8, 9]

As Hess acknowledged in his seminal paper, this theory was initially speculative and contrary to current theories. But it did have the virtue of being the most reasonable inference from existing knowledge. As Hess states:

> *mantle convection is considered a radical hypothesis not widely accepted by geologists and geophysicists. If it were accepted, a rather reasonable story could be constructed to describe the evolution of ocean basins and the waters within them. Whole realms of previously unrelated facts fall into a regular pattern, which suggests that close approach to satisfactory theory is being attained.[10]*

Hess's theory provided a way to account for the observations of Wegener and also for an increasing collection of surprising **anomalies**—*data for which there was no satisfactory explanation according to accepted theories—about the magnetic orientation of rocks. It turns out that basalt (the kind of rock that is produced by volcanoes) contains magnetite which, as the name suggests, behaves as though composed of small compass needles that oriented themselves towards the North Pole when the basalt was hot before it solidified. For reasons*

Having an acceptable explanatory model is an important criterion for the acceptance of scientific claims.

An **anomaly** refers to data for which there is not a satisfactory explanation according to accepted theories.

How the Continents Previously Fit Together

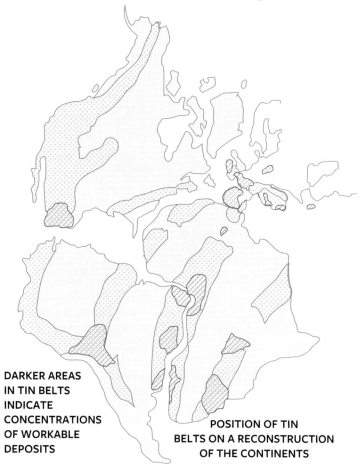

DARKER AREAS
IN TIN BELTS
INDICATE
CONCENTRATIONS
OF WORKABLE
DEPOSITS

POSITION OF TIN
BELTS ON A RECONSTRUCTION
OF THE CONTINENTS

Source: Roberts, The Macmillan Field Guide to Goelolgical Structures, 105

A Model for the Continents "Floating" on the Mantel

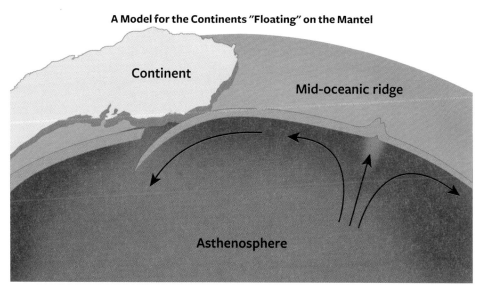

Continent

Mid-oceanic ridge

Asthenosphere

Image Courtesy of U.S. Geological Survey (USGS),

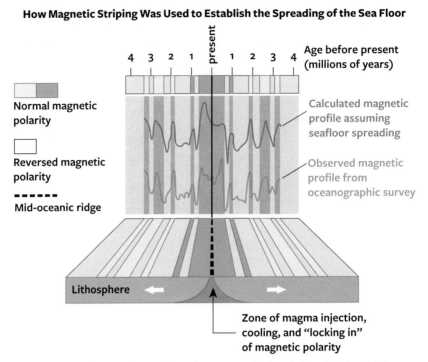

How Magnetic Striping Was Used to Establish the Spreading of the Sea Floor

Source: Copyright of Psychopharmacology is the property of Springer Science & Business Media

still not well understood, every few hundred thousand years, the North and South Poles switch positions so that a compass needle which had pointed north would, after the switch, point south. The magnetite in the basalt therefore reveals the location of the pole at its moment of solidification.[11]

In addition, the orientation of the magnetite is not only horizontal but vertical. The closer the basalt is to the poles when it solidifies, the more vertical the orientation of magnetite "compass needle" whether near the North or South Pole. At the time of Hess's writing, there were anomalies in the magnetic data. There was magnetic data accumulating that showed that rock near the equator had formed at locations much nearer the poles than their current locations. Since continental movement had been rejected, there was no adequate explanation for these observations. Hess sums up this way at the end of his paper:

> *In this chapter the writer has attempted to invent an evolution for ocean basins. It is hardly likely that all of the numerous assumptions made are correct. Nevertheless it appears to be a useful framework for testing various and sundry groups of hypotheses relating to the oceans. It is hoped that the framework with necessary patching and repair may eventually form the basis for a new and sounder structure.[12]*

What Do You Think

What were the reasons and evidence in support of Hess's theory of continental drift? What was the main reason counting against the view?

Hess's theory demonstrates important aspects of a successful new theoretical model:

1. *It should provide a more comprehensive explanation of current information including hitherto inexplicable observations.*

2. *It should be able to generate new predictions that can be tested.*

Hess's theory accomplished both; and within a year of the publication of Hess's paper, new magnetic readings at the spreading ridge in the middle of the Atlantic showed that the ocean floor was indeed moving (see illustration).

Hess's work is an example of paleogeology, the study of the geological history of the planet (from the Greek paleo *meaning "ancient"). Finding new evidence that supports the theory in a science like paleogeology is similar to successful predictions in a science such as physics. When Halley, using Newton's laws, correctly predicted the 1759 reappearance of the comet that is now named after him, the accuracy of his prediction provided a great boost to the credibility of Newton's theories.*[13]

Although theories about historical processes such as plate tectonics do not depend on predictions about future events for their support, a similar method of confirmation is used. In the case of plate tectonics, Hess's theory of sea floor spreading was quickly confirmed, not by successful predictions of future events but by the discovery of additional data that was supportive of his theory. In this case, new measurements of ocean floor changes in magnetism showed that the ocean floor was, indeed, moving away from the oceanic ridges. A U.S. Geological Services article about Hess's discovery summarizes in this way:

> *In 1962, Hess was well aware that solid evidence was still lacking to test his hypothesis and to convince a more receptive but still skeptical scientific community. But the Vine-Matthews explanation of magnetic striping [the change in magnetic orientation of the magnetite as one moved farther from the spreading ridge, as seen in the illustration on page 218] of the seafloor a year later and additional oceanic exploration during subsequent years ultimately provided the arguments to confirm Hess' model of seafloor spreading. The theory was strengthened further when dating studies showed that the seafloor becomes older with distance away from the ridge crests. Finally, improved seismic data confirmed that oceanic crust was indeed sinking into the trenches, fully proving Hess' hypothesis, which was based largely on intuitive geologic reasoning. His basic idea of seafloor spreading along mid-oceanic ridges has well withstood the test of time.*[14]

It should also be noted that not only did Hess's theory fit new data, but it has since demonstrated great explanatory power. Plate tectonics has yielded new explanations of earthquakes, mountain building, and volcanoes. As with Newton's and Darwin's great insights, a wealth of phenomena now became comprehensible. This aspect of the theory is often identified as "fruitfulness"—the capacity of a theory to support a wide variety of resarch possiblities and to provide a large range of explanatory insights.

The story of the work of Hess illustrates a number of aspects of scientific inquiry. It shows again that detailed and precise observation, powerful explanatory models, technology, peer review, and imagination all play an important role in scientific progress and theory confirmation.[15]

The Process of Inquiry in the Natural Sciences: An Example

Let's see how our structure of inquiry applies to the development and confirmation of the theory of plate tectonics.

What Is the Issue? What Kinds of Claims and Judgments Are at Issue?

There were two questions:

1. Had the continents moved over time? If they had, scientists could explain a considerable amount of the observational information (e.g., the matching of mineral deposits, the magnetic anomalies).

2. Was there a mechanism that could explain how the continents moved?

These are both factual questions. They are also questions about an explanation. This illustrates the fact that scientists want to know not only what happened (is happening, will happen) but why it is happening. What is the causal explanation?

 *Keep in Mind*

GUIDING QUESTIONS FOR INQUIRY

- What is the issue?
- What kinds of claims or judgments are at issue?
- What are the relevant aspects of context surrounding the issue?
- What are the relevant reasons and arguments on various sides of the issue?
- How do we comparatively evaluate the various reasons and arguments in order to reach a reasoned judgment?

Scientists create models to provide explanations. These models can be pictures or other physical models, or they can be complex mathematical models run on a computer.

While the answers to these questions will always be factual, they will often take the form of models (e.g., the model of the atom as a kind of solar system, or global warming as the product of a greenhouse-like phenomenon.) These models can be pictures or other physical models, or they can be complex mathematical models run on a computer; and they can provide the basis for understanding the phenomenon and also for suggesting other data (e.g., predictions) that would be the case if the model was correct.

In Hess's case, the key claim was that the continents were moved by a current in the viscous mantle under the earth's crust.

What Is the Context of the Issue?

The context was, first of all, an existing view that the continents could not have moved because there appeared to be no mechanism for such movement. There was, however, some theoretical tension because of the considerable as-yet-unexplained evidence that the continents had been together at some earlier time. Such a collection of dissonant information is a fertile situation for scientific progress.

Second, there was new information about the nature of the ocean floor and magnetic inconsistencies. The rapid acceptance of the theory resulted from both the unsatisfactory state of previous explanations and the almost immediate discovery of confirmatory data of the spreading of the ocean floor.

What Are the Relevant Reasons and Arguments on Various Sides of the Issue?

The two basic views were the floating continents view and the stationary continents view. The main argument for the stationary view was that there was no known physical model to account for any movement. The evidence that the continents had once been in a different position than they are now was considerable, but the acceptance of that idea was blocked by the lack of a feasible mechanism that could explain the movement.

The new evidence of ocean floor movement provided powerful support for the drift thesis. Additional evidence emerged rapidly showing that the oceanic plates were moving under the continental shelf. This information enabled the theory to provide additional explanations for how the majority of mountains were formed and earthquakes were generated. The powerful explanatory breadth of the theory added considerable support for the moving continents view.

How Do We Comparatively Evaluate the Various Reasons and Arguments in order to Reach a Reasoned Judgment?

Scientists evaluated the two competing theories (i.e., continents moved, continents didn't move) in terms of their explanatory power and their consistency with observations. The test of each theory was not simply that it fit with existing data, but that it generated new hypotheses that could be tested, such as the magnetic striping of the area around mid-ocean ridges. The ability of a new explanatory model both to explain numerous facts and to provide a basis for further inquiry makes it very attractive to scientific investigation.

During the period of development of the plate tectonic model, even non-scientists inquiring into this controversy might have been able to track the increasing success of the theory in the scientific literature. More likely, they would have had to seek the views of contemporary geologists. A look at the citation index[16] to see what geologists were saying about Hess's paper would also have helped. The rapidity with which his view received supporting evidence suggests that many recognized the power of his view and were willing to explore its implications. A review of the contemporary geological literature would have revealed this. This example demonstrates that a layperson can be in a position to inquire even into those scientific debates which are contemporary and controversial.

Apply Your Understanding Exercise 3

Reasoned Judgment and Scientific Inquiry

Now that we have looked at a few historical examples from science, we can identify some of the crucial elements of a scientific inquiry. But first, we should point out that not all scientific inquiries result in such grand theories as plate tectonics or the bacterial cause of disease (some aspects of which are reviewed below). Much of science is about establishing a very particular claim working within a well-established theoretical framework. As laypeople intent on making use of scientific information in our inquiries, we will usually be concerned with particular scientific claims—for example, whether a particular gene is responsible for a particular illness, whether vaccination is an effective public health policy, or whether cellphones cause brain cancer. Assessing these more common types of claims, claims which do not involve any dramatic change of theory, is similar to the assessment of the more theoretical and revolutionary claims that we have looked at so far, except that the assessment of these more common claims involves less emphasis on criteria that are more relevant to theory assessment, such as the criteria of fruitfulness (see page 222) discussed below.

Causal Explanations

In many ways, the scientific identification of cause is quite similar to the more commonsensical approach to identifying causes that we discussed in Chapter 5.

What are the criteria used to evaluate general causal claims?

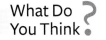
What Do You Think?

Scientists use basically the same criteria, but they have refined these commonsensical considerations. Science is not just about "facts." It is about making sense of the facts in a way that explains them and can then be further tested. One way in which scientific explanations tend to differ from more commonsensical explanations is in the presumption that observable phenomena can often be explained in terms of unobservable micro processes. Science tends to progress by providing explanations with an increasing level of detail. In biology, for example, the theory of genes added enormously to Darwin's theory of natural selection. Later, the discovery of DNA added a detailed chemical model for understanding the way that genes work. The tendency of scientific explanations to be based on increasingly small micro phenomena is sometimes identified as **reduction.** The idea of reduction in science is that observable processes, like illness or biological growth, can be explained in terms of more basic, often invisible processes at the cellular or chemical level. Successful reduction involves the increased understanding that is achieved by identifying the micro processes which explain the larger macro phenomena.

Reduction refers to the idea in science that observable processes, like illness or biological growth, can be explained in terms of more basic, often invisible processes at the cellular or chemical level.

What are some examples in science of micro processes being used to explain larger macro phenomena?

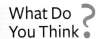
What Do You Think?

For example, we use the activity of microscopic bacteria to explain macro phenomena like a runny nose and a cough, or the movement of electrons to explain the macro phenomenon of lightning.

Testability

The first thing any theory must do, of course, is fit the known facts. But the second requirement for a theory is that it must be testable. Testability requires that a theory or claim must be able to identify the kind of observational evidence that will support it and the kind that will count against it. Thus a theory should provide a basis for inferring more possible claims that can be tested. Testing does not necessarily involve experiments, although experiments are a particularly good way to test a theory. Contrary to what you may have heard, not all science is based on the experimental method. As you

Testability requires that a theory or claim must be able to identify the kind of observational evidence that will support it and the kind that will count against it.

Early Experiments

One of the more famous early experiments in the history of science was conducted by an Italian poet, Francesco Redi, who was addressing the then popular view that living creatures could spontaneously emerge from matter. He used his experiment to prove that maggots in meat did not spontaneously develop in meat, but were the results of flies laying eggs. Here is how the Encyclopaedia Britannica *describes the experiment:*[17]

In 1668, in one of the first examples of a biological experiment with proper controls, Redi set up a series of flasks containing different meats, half of the flasks sealed, half open. He then repeated the experiment but, instead of sealing the flasks, covered half of them with gauze so that air could enter. Although the meat in all of the flasks putrefied, he found that only in the open and uncovered flasks, which flies had entered freely, did the meat contain maggots.

see from the history of geology, science can make great progress without necessarily using experiments. Nonetheless, experiments have played a crucial role in much scientific advance.

Experiments

Experiments involve testing a theory or claim by varying only one factor, the one that we hypothesize is the cause in question, and seeing if this results in predicted changes in the outcome.

A **confounding factor** is any factor other than the cause being studied that could be part of the explanation for the observed outcome.

What Do You Think ?

What are some of the advantages of using experiments to test a theory or claim?

Experiments are valuable because you can much more easily test a claim if you can control everything in the lab. Experiments enable us to minimize the problem of competing explanations for an outcome, what is often called in scientific studies the problem of **confounding factors.** A confounding factor is any factor other than the cause being studied that could be part of the explanation for the observed outcome.

A theory demonstrates fruitfulness when it does not just imply a few facts that can be tested, but when it suggests a whole research project filled with explanations of diverse phenomena.

But experiments are only applicable to a limited range of phenomena, so scientists use a variety of methods to test claims. The main method of testing that scientists use is attempting to identify the best explanation for the phenomena being studied (as was discussed in Chapter 5). This may involve making predictions based on the theory and seeing if they occur. Or it may involve making inferences about further information that we might find given a particular claim or theory. This method was illustrated in the example we just read: a test of Hess's theory was finding other evidence of the movement of the continents. What is crucial to the testing of a scientific theory is that there are implications which can be tested against additional observations. Often figuring out what these implications are and how to test them requires great ingenuity and imagination. But the best scientific insights provide the basis for many such inferences.

Fruitfulness

Keep in Mind ☑

CHARACTERISTICS OF SCIENTIFIC INQUIRY
- causal explanations
- testability
- fruitfulness
- peer review

Related to testability is a much broader concept, fruitfulness. This is a criterion especially applicable to theories. A theory is fruitful when it does not just imply a few facts that can be tested, but when it suggests a whole research project filled with explanations of diverse phenomena. Both Hutton's and Hess's hypotheses proved enormously fruitful in explaining a wide range of disparate phenomena. As mentioned, Hutton's work opened the way for another extremely fruitful insight, Darwin's theory of natural selection. The great insights of science result not only in a particular explanation, but in theories that suggest innumerable possibilities for further understanding and research.

Peer Review

Related to testability and argument to the best explanation is peer review. Scientists must publish peer-reviewed articles in professional journals, which are read by peers who examine the arguments and evidence further. These readers see whether the evidence adequately supports the claims, or whether there are other competing explanations that haven't been addressed. This willingness to subject claims to ongoing peer review is not unique to science, but it is crucial to the establishment of credible scientific claims. What is somewhat unique to science is that there is often a "convergence" among peers on the correctness of a claim as a result of explanatory success and repeated testing. Claims may be initially greeted by skepticism; but if they survive the peer review process and other investigations and research, their credibility is enhanced. Enduring claims that have survived extensive research enter the core of understanding used by scientists and are worthy of confident belief.

Apply Your Understanding Exercise 4

Evolution

. . . .

Winnie, Stephen, and Juanita continue their conversation about the study of science.

Juanita: I admit learning about the history of geology did teach me things about the world that I didn't know. And there wasn't any math. I had to look up a few things, but basically I could understand it. It really was amazing that they found those splits in the middle of the ocean— and that all this explains earthquakes and volcanoes. So OK, maybe science isn't all that bad.

Winnie: And if we study biology, we see a much more complex and beautiful world of plants and animals with all their remarkably developed abilities and intricate designs. It makes you feel in awe of nature.

Stephen: Right! And it provides clear proof of the existence of a creator, a magnificent creator who designed living things in all their complexity and intricacy.

Winnie: Now just a minute, Steve. Thanks to Darwin, science can now explain why the natural world is so full of the wonderful things that we see. Darwin showed that there was no need for the creator to explain the vast variety of species on earth.

Stephen: One thing I do know is that evolution is just a theory, and it's a theory with a lot of holes in it. Scientists try to cover up those holes, but they're there; and they show that there must be other forces at work to produce such an intricate and well-functioning entity as a human body. I mean, look at the eye. Do you really expect me to believe that humans were created by blind chance?

Juanita: You know the old story that millions of monkeys slaving away endlessly on computers would never write a play of Shakespeare?

Winnie: I agree—they wouldn't. But that's not Darwin's theory. I think we should make an inquiry into the theory of evolution and see just what the issues are, what the history of this debate is, and what the evidence is pro and con.

Stephen: Sure. I'm glad to take on evolution.

What Is the Issue? What Kinds of Claims and Judgments Are at Issue?

Winnie: OK. So let's get clear on the issue: the question is whether the natural world is the result of divine creation or the result of a process of evolution and natural selection as Darwin argued.

Stephen: Natural selection, whatever that is, versus God's creation as an explanation of the natural world.

Charles Darwin, 1809–1882, a British naturalist, is famous for his theories of evolution and natural selection. Like several scientists before him, Darwin believed that all the life on earth evolved (developed gradually) over millions of years from a few common ancestors. In 1831, Darwin set out on *H.M.S. Beagle* on a British science expedition around the world. In South America, Darwin found fossils of animals that were extinct but similar to modern species. On the Galapagos Islands in the Pacific Ocean, he noticed plants and animals of the same general type as those in South America. Darwin studied plants and animals everywhere he went, collecting specimens to study later. After returning to London in 1836, Darwin conducted thorough research of his notes and specimens. This study provided evidence for his theories of evolution and natural selection, which he published in his book *The Origin of the Species* in 1859.[18]

Winnie: Now you need to know that Darwin's theory is not that humans and other species were created by blind chance, some kind of cosmic fluke. That's not the theory of natural selection.

Juanita: It's not?

Winnie: No, it isn't. In his book, *The Origin of the Species,* he goes into the argument in depth, laying out his evidence in great detail and constantly addressing objections. It's really a fantastic study in argumentation. All I can give you now is a fairly crude summary of his argument. You should read the book.

Juanita: Sounds kind of heavy.

Stephen: You can just give us the short version.

What Are the Relevant Reasons and Arguments on Various Sides of the Issue?

Winnie: The first thing Darwin points out is how animal breeders are able to breed dramatically different creatures than what they start with. Look at the incredible variety of dogs which are all produced by human breeding, starting with wolves. Since there's such variability in offspring that breeders can modify breeds through "human selection," nature can do the same thing through "natural selection." A chance variation in new generations that gives a creature an advantage in a particular environment will tend to help that creature prosper and reproduce, and those that don't have the advantage will tend to die off. This is true of both plants and animals. So that's his theory: species change and are created by a slow incremental process of natural selection favouring some variations over others. The process involves literally billions of years.

Juanita: That's pretty amazing.

Winnie: Let me give you an analogy, though it isn't Darwin's. Think of the odds of getting four aces when you're dealt four cards. Assuming no one is cheating, the odds are pretty astronomical. But suppose you just keep getting dealt four cards over and over, and when you get an ace you keep it; then you're dealt four more cards, and when you get a second ace, you keep that too. Obviously by this process, it would be inevitable that you'd eventually get four aces in a reasonable number of deals. Four aces on one deal is a "miracle." Four aces after many deals and "ace selection" is just what you'd expect. And that's how evolution proceeds, by small modifications, keeping the successful ones, and getting rid of the unsuccessful.

Stephen: OK, I get the theory. Nice analogy, but why should I believe this is how it really happened?

What Is the Context of the Issue?

Winnie: Good question. I think we should look at the arguments and context. The concerns you're raising were ones that Darwin was quite aware of when he published his *Origins of the Species.* He knew that he was up against the belief in creationism, which was very strong at the

The Creation

Excerpts from the Judeo-Christian account in Genesis, Chapter 1(King James Version).

1 In the beginning God created the heaven and the earth.

3 And God said, Let there be light: and there was light.

11 And God said, Let the earth bring forth grass, the herb yielding seed, *and* the fruit tree yielding fruit after his kind, whose seed *is* in itself, upon the earth: and it was so.

14 And God said, Let there be lights in the firmament of the heaven to divide the day from the night; and let them be for signs, and for seasons, and for days, and years:

20 And God said, Let the waters bring forth abundantly the moving creature that hath life, and fowl *that* may fly above the earth in the open firmament of heaven.

21 And God created great whales, and every living creature that moveth, which the waters brought forth abundantly, after their kind, and every winged fowl after his kind: and God saw that *it was* good.

24 And God said, Let the earth bring forth the living creature after his kind, cattle, and creeping thing, and beast of the earth after his kind: and it was so.

26 And God said, Let us make man in our image, after our likeness: and let them have dominion over the fish of the sea, and over the fowl of the air, and over the cattle, and over all the earth, and over every creeping thing that creepeth upon the earth.

27 So God created man in his *own* image, in the image of God created he him; male and female created he them.

31 And God saw every thing that he had made, and, behold, *it was* very good.

time. In fact, you really can't understand his book if you don't know the creationist/Genesis theory that he was up against and how widely it was accepted among scientists of that time. One of the most striking aspects of *Origins of the Species* is how careful Darwin is to acknowledge and address objections to his theory.

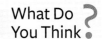

Why did Darwin's theory have to meet a strong burden of proof?

What Do You Think

Darwin's theory was put forth at a time when the creationist account (an excerpt of which is found above) was widely believed by both laypeople and scientists. Because it was a challenge to existing scientific views and dominant religious views, Darwin accepted that his theory had to meet a strong burden of proof.

How Do We Comparatively Evaluate the Various Reasons and Arguments in Order to Reach a Reasoned Judgment?

Winnie: Do you remember the concept of argument to the best explanation? Darwin's strategy was a clear case of that. He shows that the creationist accounts can't explain what we know about species and the fossil record, but that his theory can. In other words, his theory is the better of the competing explanations.

Juanita: I don't understand the bit about the fossil record.

Winnie: A big problem for the creationists even in Darwin's day was the evidence from fossils. The creationist theory required all species to have been created at once. But what the fossil record showed is that there were creatures deeper in the rocks—so, from an earlier time—which were different and quite a bit simpler than those further up the rocks. And, very important, the remains of humans didn't show up until quite high in the fossil record. Most of the earlier fossils also were not like anything currently living so they were species that had come and gone. In Darwin's time, no one knew how very old the earth was. But thanks to Hutton and the theory of sedimentation, which you were just reading about, Juanita, many people realized that the earth must be at least millions of years old. So it seemed that there would have been enough time for these species to change and to come and go. The creationist theory can't explain the fossil record, but Darwin can.

Note how Darwin uses argument to the best explanation. He indicates that he clearly sees all the objections to his theory and then goes on to reply to each one.

Stephen: Of course, I know a bit about Genesis. Not that I believe that it's literally true. I am more in favour of a view called "intelligent design," which is much more scientific. My view is simply that you can't explain the existence of the natural world merely by an appeal to evolution and natural selection. It's just too amazing. Lots of scientists agree with that as well. For instance, Michael Behe[19], as well as others, argues that at least some parts of the world are just too intricate and complex to be simply the result of chance and natural selection. It's not plausible that complex creatures like ourselves could have been produced by this slow incremental process.

Winnie: Again Darwin saw these objections coming. Let me read to you from Chapter 6, which Darwin called "Objections." You'll see how Darwin uses argument to the best explanation. He shows that he sees all the objections to his theory but then he replies to each one.

LONG before having arrived at this part of my work, a crowd of difficulties will have occurred to the reader. Some of them are so grave that to this day I can never reflect on them without being staggered; but, to the best of my judgment, the greater number are only apparent, and those that are real are not, I think, fatal to my theory.

These difficulties and objections may be classed under the following heads: -Firstly, why, if species have descended from other species by insensibly fine gradations, do we not everywhere see innumerable transitional forms? Why is not all nature in confusion instead of the species being, as we see them, well defined?

Secondly, is it possible that an animal having, for instance, the structure and habits of a bat, could have been formed by the modification of some animal with wholly different habits? Can we believe that natural selection could produce, on the one hand, organs of trifling importance, such as the tail of a giraffe, which serves as a fly-flapper, and, on the other hand, organs of such wonderful structure, as the eye, of which we hardly as yet fully understand the inimitable perfection?

Thirdly, can instincts be acquired and modified through natural selection? What shall we say to so marvellous an instinct as that which leads the bee to make cells, which have practically anticipated the discoveries of profound mathematicians?

Fourthly, how can we account for species, when crossed, being sterile and producing sterile offspring, whereas, when varieties are crossed, their fertility is unimpaired?

Organs of extreme perfection and complication. *To suppose that the eye, with all its inimitable contrivances for adjusting the focus to different distances, for admitting different amounts of light, and for the correction of spherical and chromatic aberration, could have been formed by natural selection, seems, I freely confess, absurd in the highest possible degree. Yet reason tells me, that if numerous gradations from a perfect and complex eye to one very imperfect and simple, each grade being useful to its possessor, can be shown to exist; if further, the eye does vary ever so slightly, and the variations be inherited, which is certainly the case; and if any variation or modification in the organ be ever useful to an animal under changing conditions of life, then the difficulty of believing that a perfect and complex eye could be formed by natural selection, though insuperable by our imagination, can hardly be considered real. How a nerve comes to be sensitive to light, hardly concerns us more than how life itself first originated; but I may remark that several facts make me suspect that any sensitive nerve may be rendered sensitive to light, and likewise to those coarser vibrations of the air which produce sound.[20]*

Problems and anomalies that cannot currently be explained by a theory are not sufficient to show that a theory should be rejected or that another explanation is the best explanation. There are an enormous number of phenomena that we cannot explain.[21] For example, we still don't have an adequate explanation of why cells become cancerous—but we would surely not want to credit this puzzle to a *bad designer*. The existence of currently inexplicable phenomena is part of the normal scientific process. There is an enormous burden of proof on anyone who wishes to reject a well-established and fruitful theory. Rejecting a theory like natural selection at this time in history would require a large set of conflicting observations *and* an alternative theory that had more explanatory and predictive power, before scientists would be justified in abandoning their current theory.

Stephen: But what about the problem that science is supposed to explain the underlying mechanisms for phenomena? Darwin didn't have any way of explaining how traits got changed or passed on or anything.

Winnie: You're right. That was a crucial weakness in Darwin's theory. But in the twentieth century, this problem was solved with Mendel's theory of genetics and the biochemistry of DNA. So now Darwin's theory has all the ingredients of a well-established scientific theory. It's been enormously fruitful, it explains a vast range of phenomena, and it's led to the discovery of underlying micro-explanations.

Stephen: OK, so Darwin's made some good arguments for his theory. And he's stuck to the basic strategy of argument to the best explanation. But that doesn't mean his theory isn't just a theory and that there aren't problems with the theory that no one can explain.

In what way is Stephen committing the fallacy of equivocation in his use of the term "theory"?

What Do You Think?

Winnie: You seem to be using the word "theory" in the sense of an unconfirmed or untested hypothesis. Like a detective who has a theory about the crime.

Stephen: Right. Is there anything wrong with that? I mean, we don't talk about Newton's theory of gravity—we talk about his *law* of gravity. Gravity isn't a theory.

Winnie: True, but to understand that you need to look at the history of science again. Newton talked about laws because he believed he was revealing God's laws—the laws which the celestial bodies obeyed. By the time we get to Darwin, Darwin knows he's not articulating God's laws. He's putting forward a powerful scientific theory. The distinction in science is between well-established theories and those that are not well established or even false. The word "theory" isn't used in science to put down a scientific claim or suggest it's not credible. Darwin's theory is extremely well established and enormously fruitful. It's a model of a highly successful account of the natural world.

Calling a scientific theory a "theory" is not to suggest that it is especially uncertain or unjustified. There are well-established theories and new and poorly established theories. In addition, theories of great fruitfulness such as natural selection or Newtonian mechanics, when confronted with problems and anomalies, are most likely to be adapted rather than replaced by a totally different theory. Abandoning evolutionary theory for a spiritual account of evolution is not like abandoning one theory in science and replacing it by another, such as we saw with Hess and plate tectonics. It means abandoning scientific explanation altogether.

Calling a scientific theory a "theory" is not to suggest that it is especially uncertain or unjustified.

Stephen: But not all scientists believe Darwin's theory.

Winnie: I'm sure you're right. And a few of those doubters have made great efforts to try and undermine confidence in evolutionary theory in favour of some kind of intelligent design version of creationism. But when they do that, they're not really doing science. They've taken a theological viewpoint.

Stephen: That sounds like a scientific prejudice to me. They're showing that evolutionary theory can't explain certain things and that the best explanation is an intelligent designer. Why isn't that science? Isn't that what scientists do—show problems with theories and offer better explanations?

Winnie: Yes and no. For example, some scientists disagree with the idea that evolution happens in a fairly uniform manner. They believe that evolution goes forward in fits and starts because the fossil record seems to reveal periods of relative species stability and then periods of dramatic increase and change in species. But none of these scientists doubts the basic causal processes of natural selection. Rather, they're trying to come up with a similar, physical, Darwinian account of these periods of relatively great change. That's quite different from saying that Darwin's theory can't explain something at this point in time, so we must abandon the search for physical causes and go with divine intervention.

Stephen: But what's wrong with that? If we couldn't explain the development of the eye without a designer, then it would just be good science to accept the designer explanation.

Winnie: Nice try, but notice that the designer theory isn't really an explanation. It doesn't tell us how the eye was made—just poof, the eye. It doesn't explain the variations of light-sensing creatures. It doesn't tell us why the eagle sees better than we do. It's the opposite of a fruitful theory. It's just this: "God did it. Now stop asking questions."

Stephen: So when there are problems with a scientific theory, one which is well established anyways, we just dismiss the problem?

Winnie: I didn't say that. Problems are what make science interesting. Figuring out how to explain things we don't currently understand is the business of science. But moving to intelligent design is to abandon the project. Even the intelligent design people don't deny the fossil record or that many species exhibit descent and modification. They just pick on a few examples that may pose a challenge and say that Darwin's theory can't explain that, so there must be divine intervention.

Stephen: OK, so maybe intelligent design has some problems. But I still like the idea of a divine creator.

(Apply Your Understanding Exercises 5, 6, 7)

Spiritual explanations lack the kind of fruitfulness we find in Darwin's approach. They do not yield new insights or predictions about other phenomena. Once we postulate the intelligent designer as an explanation, nothing else follows from it that enables us to make predictions or have insight into other aspects of the world. Naturalistic theories, in contrast, are fruitful, having models that lead to new explanations and predictions.

Science and Statistics

While the theories of plate tectonics and natural selection illustrate many aspects of inquiry in the physical sciences, there is at least one key aspect omitted: statistical methodology. Statistical methodology is seldom central in chemistry and physics although statistical modelling plays a key role in quantum theory in physics. Statistical methodology is, however, important in many other sciences. Statistics play a key role in an area like population biology which is currently one of the central domains for the application and advancement of the theory of natural selection. As we will see in the next chapter, statistics also play a key role in inquiry in the social sciences. Below, we introduce statistical reasoning by looking at the application of statistics to epidemics. This application of statistics grew into the discipline of epidemiology, and it is epidemiology that provides many of the studies on health now published so commonly in the media.

And I Really Hate Statistics!

Juanita: Well, that stuff on Darwin and geology was actually pretty interesting, but thank goodness there was no math. As I think about it now, it was the math in science class that really turned me off.

Early Medical Statisticians[22]

While there were many practitioners of medical statistics in the mid-nineteenth century, one of the most renowned was Florence Nightingale, who is remembered most for her work of professionalizing nursing. Nightingale also made brilliant use of statistics on the deaths of soldiers in the Crimean War, demonstrating that the English government's negligent treatment of their soldiers caused more deaths than the enemy did. By instituting improved hygiene among the soldiers in the hospital in Scutari, Turkey, she was able to reduce the mortality rate from 40% to 2% and, of course, prove it with statistics. Nightingale went on to use her statistical acumen to press successfully for significant changes in the treatment of British soldiers. As part of that effort, she created a whole new form of graphic presentation of statistics, making her the mother of "forensic graphing." As a leading statistician of the day, she worked with William Farr, another medical statistician. Farr, in turn, worked with John Snow, who is often credited as the father of epidemiology—originally the study of the spread of disease (epidemics), though now more generally the statistical study of health.

Winnie: I'm sorry you feel that way, Juanita, because math is central to a lot of science. Without precise calculations, scientists couldn't make the kinds of predictions they do and we wouldn't have the kind of technology we have. It took a lot of math to make that cellphone you're so fond of.

Juanita: But you just showed me two examples of science without any math.

Winnie: Good point. You can understand a great deal of science without any math. Maybe science courses should emphasize that. But math, and especially statistics, play a crucial role in many sciences, especially the social sciences.

Juanita: Statistics—ugh! They're impossible!

Winnie: You have my sympathy. Statistics can be boring and incomprehensible. But with even a little understanding, you can make a lot more sense of what scientists are saying. Have you ever heard of Florence Nightingale?

Juanita: Of course. She founded the nursing profession, didn't she?

Winnie: Yes, but she was also one of the first people to use statistics to change public policy. She used graphs to show how the British Army hospitals were killing more soldiers than were dying on the battlefield.

Juanita: How did she do that?

Winnie: Well, I've got some more notes for you to read about the early days of the use of statistics in science that will help you understand. And don't worry—there are no numbers or formulas.

Juanita: I'll give it try, but I don't know . . .

Here is another page from Winnie's notes.

SCIENCE AND STATISTICS

The statistical approach to studying phenomena such as the spread of disease was first developed in the mid-19th century. A striking example of the early use of statistics in studying health was John Snow's search for the cause of cholera. Snow is famous for identifying and statistically demonstrating that the terrifying plague of cholera in London was spread by the consumption of polluted water.

Snow: The Search for the Cause of Cholera

In the mid 1800s, there were two competing theories of the cause of cholera epidemics. This was at a time before the identification of the microbial cause of the disease, or even the acceptance of germs as the cause of illness. The dominant theory at the time was the miasma theory—that epidemics were caused by bad air. This theory, championed by many theorists including William Farr, had some statistical support in that those closer to the river seemed more prone to illness. This fit with the view that bad air descended from higher regions and was more concentrated at lower regions.

John Snow, an eminent London physician who had treated many cholera patients, noted that they first reported stomach pains and then diarrhea. This led him to suspect that ingestion, not air, was the source of the disease. He also observed that in one group of row houses, one side of the block had experienced widespread disease yet only one person on the other side had become ill. He noted that sewage on the infected side flowed into the well used by people on that side of the street but not into the well used by the other side.

Snow, with the help of Farr, collected and published statistical data from the 1849 cholera outbreak which supported his theory of water-borne illness, but he was unable to make any headway against the dominant miasma view. When the epidemic struck again in 1854, Snow and the Registrar's office (led by Farr) worked together to determine whether there was a relationship between certain sources of water (namely the Southwark and Vauxhall Water Company whose water contained London sewage) and cholera deaths. Snow was quickly able to establish that mortality among those consuming water from the Southwark and Vauxhall Company's water was 5 to 10 times that of those drinking water from other suppliers. Snow produced a famous map,[23] which graphically illustrated how the disease was focused around a particular well. The handle to the pump was immediately removed and the spread of the disease declined dramatically.

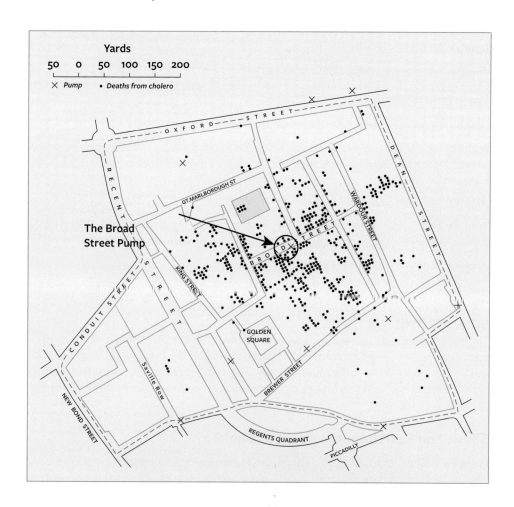

Snow's technique was to demonstrate many examples of a correlation between exposure to polluted water and the incidence of cholera. Not everyone who drank the water died and many people who did not drink from the polluted water did get cholera. Nevertheless, using the map, Snow was able to show a strong correlation between the polluted drinking water and the incidence of cholera. (As discussed in Chapter 5, a correlation exists when two factors such as polluted water and cholera vary together or co-vary.)

Unfortunately, Snow did not have a biological explanation of how the polluted water caused the spread of cholera because his work preceded that of Pasteur and the development of the germ theory of illness. Snow's polluted water theory was also up against the dominant and long standing theory of miasmas, noxious forms of "bad air." (The miasma theory has since, of course, been supplanted by the germ theory of disease.)

As a result, despite his continued effort to collect evidence of a causal link, his theory did not receive widespread acceptance until after his death. In 1866, eight years after Snow's death, Farr wrote a report supporting Snow's theory with extensive statistical information. Farr and others, informed by the development of the germ theory of disease, had come to see that Snow's theory was the best explanation for the spread of the disease. Snow is credited with being the father of modern epidemiology because of his pioneering work and the statistical and mapping methods he used.[24]

Inquiry and Statistics: An Example

What Is the Issue? What Kinds of Claims and Judgments Are at Issue?

This is a very useful question in the context of statistical research. Basically there are two possibilities: the researchers may only be claiming a correlation, or they may be making a causal claim based in part on evidence of a correlation. (See the section on causal arguments in Chapter 5, pages 93–95 for a discussion of causal explanations and correlation.)

Was Snow only claiming a correlation between cholera and the consumption of polluted water or was he making a causal claim?

What Do
You Think **?**

Snow believed that the correlation between cholera and the consumption of polluted water revealed that something in the polluted water was the cause of cholera.

What Are the Relevant Reasons and Arguments on Various Sides of the Issue?

Snow's pollution theory and the alternative miasma view have been reviewed above. In fairness to his critics, there were cases of the disease where the linkage to polluted waters did not appear to exist. In addition, the miasma theory did have some correlational evidence to support it, although it was weaker than the correlational evidence supporting the polluted water theory. Crucially, there was no biological explanation, no established theory of micro-organisms that could explain the linkage. Snow has been vindicated, but it was not obvious at first, because of the arguments and information of the day.

What Is the Context of the Issue?

In scientific inquiry, one important aspect of context is the history of inquiry of the question being investigated. In this regard, it is important to ask whether the current study is consistent with or contrary to previous studies. We also want to know whether this claim has been extensively or only minimally studied. For this reason, we need to know the context of Snow's research. In Snow's case, he had some evidence from the previous cholera epidemic that made him suspicious that polluted water was the source of the plague. He was prepared when the epidemic hit again and, therefore, he was able to collect very convincing data confirming the correlation between polluted water consumption and cholera.

He was also in a position to alter the situation by having the pump handle removed, and the immediate decline in the incidence of cholera gave him additional grounds for believing that the polluted water was the cause of cholera. Unfortunately for Snow, the context was one in which there was a dominant alternative view, and the germ theory of disease was not yet available.

How Do We Comparatively Evaluate the Various Reasons and Arguments in Order to Reach a Reasoned Judgment?

What Do You Think ?

How reasonable was it to accept Snow's theory?

Apply Your Understanding Exercises 8, 9

At the time, Snow had grounds for making a causal claim because of the decline in cholera resulting from the removal of the well handle. But his lack of an explanatory model was a reasonable limit to the acceptance of his view. His method of collecting data to establish a causal claim was, however, an insight of great fruitfulness and has become a backbone of most scientific inquiry.

Scientific Inquiry: A Final Note

You may have noted that we have not used traditional experimental sciences such as physics and chemistry to illustrate scientific inquiry. Rather, we have illustrated scientific inquiry by looking at geology and evolution theory, which exemplify the observational approach of science. Learning only about experimental sciences gives a limited impression of the breadth, complexity, and challenges of scientific evidence and argument. In experimental sciences such as physics and chemistry, researchers often have the enviable luxury of being able to control virtually every factor when doing their investigation. When these researchers manipulate something, by adding a chemical or increasing a force, for example, they can be reasonably confident that the result is caused by the factor they changed—not by some other confounding factor. Because experiments provide a high level of control, the experimental sciences usually have more straightforward arguments for what constitutes the best explanation of their results.

Observational sciences, on the other hand, face special challenges. In the sciences we have alluded to in this chapter, the observations are often very remote in time from the phenomena being investigated. As we saw, this creates an additional challenge for the task of identifying the best explanation. You should note that one way that this problem is addressed is by analogy. Geologists theorize about glacial activity in part by noticing how current glaciers behave. Biologists can run experiments to show how species, such as fruit flies, evolve in the lab; but then they must argue by analogy, as Darwin did, that this process is mimicked in the field.

We also do not wish to leave readers with the impression that all debate in science is about large and profound theories such as evolution or global warming. Most debates are about much more particular topics. Sometimes, the debates are about very esoteric topics such as the accuracy of carbon dating; and sometimes, scientists debate better-known topics such as what accounts for the disappearance of the dinosaurs and many other species some 65 million years ago. Science progresses because of debate and because scientists continue to search for new evidence and the best explanation for the phenomenon at issue.[25]

Apply Your Understanding Exercises 10, 11, 12

In the next chapter, we will study in more detail the use of statistics in science, with a focus on the social sciences. We will look at the scientific investigation of human behaviour and the special challenges human behaviour presents for inquiry.

CHECK YOUR UNDERSTANDING

- *What are the key aspects of scientific inquiry that are illustrated by Hutton's work in geology?*
- *Alfred Wegener, the early theorist of "continent drift," could not get his theory accepted. Why not?*
- *In what way was Wegener's inability to persuade his colleagues similar to Snow's inability to persuade his?*
- *What are the crucial elements of scientific inquiry?*
- *How did Florence Nightingale influence the British government?*
- *Darwin's theory came up against what ruling point of view at the time?*
- *Why is Darwin's theory of evolution a better explanation of biological phenomena than is that of the intelligent design theorists?*
- *What is the difference between a correlation and a causal relationship?*
- *What is the key difference between observational and experimental sciences?*

EXERCISES

1. Imagine that you are at home and can't find your critical thinking text. Keep in mind the following circumstances:

    i) You share a study space with your sister.

    ii) Your house has just had a spring cleaning by someone who has never cleaned your place before.

    iii) Your dog has a habit of collecting objects around the house.

    iv) You stopped by at your friend's place on the way home from classes.

    v) You have a tendency to be absent-minded.

    How might you go about finding the best explanation for the disappearance of your text (and perhaps find the text)?

2. Read the following scenario:

    Police decide to investigate the whereabouts of Jason Smithers after receiving a report from the ice-making plant where he works that he has not been in to work for several days. The officers break into the house, taking care to avoid the puddle of water on the floor, and find Mr. Smithers hanging from a rope in the centre of the room. There is a table and several chairs in the room but they are neatly stacked at the side of the room. There is no other furniture nearby, nor is there a ladder in the room. Scattered on the floor is a huge pile of overdue bills. The door is locked from the inside. One small window is unlocked, though it is not large enough to allow an adult to gain entry. The neighbours have not observed any activity at his house in several days.

    Choose which of the following you think is the best explanation of the Mr. Smithers' death. Explain your reasons for accepting one explanation and rejecting the others.

    i) A thief broke into the house, surprising Mr. Smithers, who was at home with a cold, and hanged him.

    ii) Mr. Smithers, bored with his job at the plant, hanged himself by standing on a chair, kicking the chair out of the way in the process.

    iii) One of Mr. Smithers' disgruntled colleagues (a person of small stature) entered the house through the window, had a loud fight with Mr. Smithers, hanged him, and exited through the window.

    iv) Mr. Smithers, depressed over his large debt, hanged himself by standing on a block of ice.

3. Write an imaginary dialogue between Hess and a skeptical scientific colleague. Imagine that the dialogue takes place in 1962, before there was solid evidence to test Hess's hypothesis. In the dialogue, Hess and the colleague debate the merits of Hess's theory as well as the problems with it.

4. Which of the following claims are testable? For each claim that you think is testable, describe how you might go about testing it.

   i) Water boils at a lower temperature at higher altitudes.

   ii) It's wrong to break your promises.

   iii) Thinking about things that you want will make them happen. If they don't happen, you haven't thought hard enough.

   iv) Dietary fat contributes to raised cholesterol levels.

   v) People with blond hair are more likely to develop skin cancer than people with black hair.

   vi) Water goes down the drain in a clockwise direction in the northern hemisphere and in a counter-clockwise direction in the southern hemisphere.

   vii) The lack of concrete evidence that John committed the robbery demonstrates how effectively he has covered his tracks.

5. One of the objections to Darwin's theory is the peacock's tail. The tail seemed not only useless but an actual liability for the male peacock. It makes it hard for him to fly and even harder to hide. How could such a thing have evolved? Darwin was aware of this objection, and had an answer which was controversial and still perhaps under-appreciated in its application. Find out his answer and assess how well supported and fruitful this theory is.

6. The evolution of the colouring of the peppered moth in England has often been cited as evidence for the speed of evolution. The theory was that the moth's colouring darkens in response to the level of soot that darkens the trees on which it rested. Theoretically, the colouring was camouflage; and darker moths, therefore, had an evolutionary advantage over lighter ones.

   Creationists have been particularly critical of these claims. Robert Matthews, for example, wrote an article for *The Sunday Telegraph,* March 14, 1999, claiming that "Evolution experts are quietly admitting that one of their most cherished examples of Darwin's theory, the rise and fall of the peppered moth, is based on a series of scientific blunders. Experiments using the moth in the Fifties and long believed to prove the truth of natural selection are now thought to be worthless, having been designed to come up with the 'right' answer."

   Inquire about Matthews's claim and what is the best explanation for the changes in the peppered moth.

7. How likely is an earthquake where you live? How would you find out? How confident should we be in the answer? How did the sources you found justify their answer?

8. *Heaven and Earth* was written by an Australian geologist, Ian Plimer. He apparently rejects the theory of anthropogenic global climate change (global climate change caused by human activity). Here are two URLs for popular articles discussing the book. The first reference is an interview with Plimer published in the British news magazine *Spectator,* and the second is a response published in the *Huffington Post.* Neither article is written by an expert, but there are arguments about expertise.

   Make a pro and con table of the arguments by Plimer and his critic's responses. Indicate which arguments you find more credible, and why.

   Spectator article by James Delingpole: "Meet the man who has exposed the great climate change con trick," available at http://www.spectator.co.uk/essays/all/3755623/meet-the-man-who-has-exposed-the-great-climate-change-con-trick.thtml.

   Huffington Post article by Alex Higgins: "The Spectator Is Hot for Global Warming Denial," available at http://www.huffingtonpost.com/alex-higgins/the-ispectatori-is-hot-fo_b_230873.html.

9. Listen to one of these debates on climate change. Then evaluate the presentations, and give your general assessment.

   a) This is an hour-long video version of a debate, but you could also work from the edited audio version below:

   VIDEO: "Global Warming Is Not a Crisis," *Intelligence*[2], available at http://intelligencesquaredus.org/index.php/past-debates/global-warming-is-not-a-crisis/

Here is an edited audio version of the *Intelligence²* debate:

AUDIO: http://www.npr.org/templates/story/story.php?storyId=9082151

b) Here is an alternative debate that is only about 12 minutes long which could also be used: "McNeil/Klimer Climate Change 'Debate'," *The Clean Industrial Revolution website,* available at http://www.thecleanrevolution.com.au/2009/11/video-of-mcneilplimer-climate-change-debate/.

10. There have been many comments in the news recently about the advantages of Vitamin D, especially for people living in the north. Do an inquiry to find out whether taking a Vitamin D supplement makes sense given the current state of research. Don't forget to consider the cons including cost and possible side effects.

11. There has been a lot of controversy about vaccination recently. Do an inquiry to develop an informed opinion about whether the following people should get vaccinated: yourself, your elderly relatives, young children.

12. There has been controversy over whether the radiation from cell towers or high-powered transmission lines—even the emissions from wireless modems—make people ill or increase the risk of cancer. Do a brief inquiry on one of these topics, and make and defend a reasoned judgment.

ENDNOTES

1. John L. Roberts, *The Macmillan Field Guide to Geological Structures* (Toronto: Macmillan, 1996), 105.

2. American Museum of Natural History, "James Hutton: The Founder of Modern Geology," http://www.amnh.org/education/resources/rfl/web/essaybooks/earth/p_hutton.html (accessed Dec 6, 2009).

3. Thomas Kuhn, *The Structure of Scientific Revolutions* (Chicago: University of Chicago Press, 1962, 1970, 1996). Thomas Kuhn introduced the idea of a paradigm shift in science to distinguish cases of dramatic and wholesale change in scientific theory such as Newton's work or Galileo's. A paradigm is an exemplary model, but Kuhn uses "paradigm" to describe a fundamentally different way of viewing the world.

4. University of California Museum of Paleontology, "Antony van Leeuwenhoek (1632–1723)," http://www.ucmp.berkeley.edu/history/leeuwenhoek.html (accessed May 25, 2010).

5. Susan Haack, *Defending Science: Within Reason Between Scientism and Cynicism* (Amherst, NY: Prometheus Books, 2007), 9–10. See also Peter Lipton, *Inference to the Best Explanation,* 2nd ed. (New York: Routledge, 2004).

6. Galileo Galilei, *Dialogue Concerning the Two Chief World Systems,* trans. Stillman Drake (Berkeley, CA: University of California Press, 1953; rev. 1967).

7. U.S. Geological Survey, "Developing the Theory," http://pubs.usgs.gov/gip/dynamic/developing.html (accessed May 20, 2010).

8. The theory was that these currents were created by convection in this way: "as a substance is heated its density

decreases and rises to the surface until it is cooled and sinks again. This repeated heating and cooling results in a current which may be enough to cause continents to move." (from University of California Museum of Paleontology, "Plate Tectonics: The Rocky History of an Idea," http://www.ucmp.berkeley.edu/geology/techist.html.)

9. University of California Museum of Paleontology, "Plate Tectonics: The Rocky History of an Idea," http://www.ucmp.berkeley.edu/geology/techist.html (accessed May 25, 2010).

10. Harry Hess, "History of Ocean Basins," in *Petrographic Studies: A Volume in Honor of A. F. Buddington* (New York: Geological Society of America, 1962), 599–820. Available at http://www.mantleplumes.org/WebDocuments/Hess1962.pdf.

11. U.S. Geological Survey, "Developing the Theory," http://pubs.usgs.gov/gip/dynamic/developing.html (accessed May 20, 2010).

12. Hess; see note 10 above.

13. A. J. Meadows, "Edmond Halley and Early Modern Astronomy," *Oxford Dictionary of National Biography,* http://oxforddnb.com/public/themes/92/92735.html.

14. U.S. Geological Survey, "Harry Hammond Hess: Spreading the Seafloor," http://pubs.usgs.gov/gip/dynamic/HHH.html (accessed Dec 6, 2009).

15. For a slightly different and more complex account of the history of plate tectonics which still emphasizes the role of context in scientific proof, see Naomi Oreskes, "Continental Drift," *University of California at San Diego*

History Department, http://history.ucsd.edu/_files/faculty/oreskes-naomi/Continentaldrift2002.pdf (accessed May 25, 2010).

16. A citation index lists the number of articles that refer to a particular article. *Google Scholar* provides such a measurement in its citations.

17. Encyclopedia Britannica, "Francesco Redi," *eb.com,* http://www.britannica.com/EBchecked/topic/494690/Francesco-Redi (accessed May 25, 2010).

18. Lucidcafe: Library, "Charles Darwin," http://www2.lucidcafe.com/lucidcafe/library/96feb/darwin.html (accessed May 19, 2010).

19. Michael J. Behe, *Darwin's Black Box* (New York: Free Press, 1996).

20. Charles Darwin, *On the Origin of the Species,* http://www.literature.org/authors/darwin-charles/the-origin-of-species/chapter-06.html.

21. The mistaken belief that a handful of unexplained anomalies can undermine a well-established theory also lies at the heart of all conspiratorial thinking; see Chapter 16.

22. University of Auckland Department of Statistics, "Florence Nightingale–Statistical Links," http://www.stat.auckland.ac.nz/~teachers/2007/S1UsingStatistics/florence-nightingale.doc.

23. Edward R.Tufte, *The Visual Display of Quantitative Information* (Cheshire, CT: Graphics Press, 1983).

24. David Vashon, "Father of Modern Epidemiology," *U.C.L.A.,* http://www.ph.ucla.edu/epi/snow/fatherofepidemiology.html (accessed May 20, 2010).

25. The following books are useful for further inquiry into the nature of scientific reasoning : Mark Battersby, *Is That a Fact? A Field Guide to Statistical and Scientific Information* (Peterborough, ON: Broadview Press, 2009); Stephen Carey, *A Beginner's Guide to Scientific Method,* 3rd Edition (Belmont, CA: Wadsworth, 2004); Ronald Giere, *Understanding Scientific Reasoning,* 5th ed. (Belmont CA: Wadsworth, 2005); Susan Haack, *Defending Science—Within Reason: Between Scientism and Cynicism* (Amherst, NY: Prometheus Books, 2007).

Chapter 13
Inquiry in the Social Sciences

Learning Objectives

After reading this chapter, you should be able to:

- understand and make reasonable evaluations of claims based on statistical inference using concepts such as these:
  - experimental versus observational studies
  - prospective and retrospective studies
  - sample and population
  - generalizability
- evaluate statistically based causal claims in terms of argument to the best explanation

Video Violence

Nancy comes across Phil in the lounge at their college. Phil is absorbed in what he's doing on his computer, and periodically shouts out things like "Bam!" and "Gotcha!" and "Take that!"

Nancy: What are you up to, Phil?

Phil: I just got the coolest new game. It's called *Resident Evil 4*. It's scary and gory and full of great challenges to blow away the enemy. It's spectacular. Body parts flying everywhere. Want to have a go?

Nancy: Ugh! I can't believe you play those games. They're going to make you even weirder than you are already.

Phil: Give me a break. All that stuff about video games making people violent is hogwash. I'm 20, and my brother Michael is 24 .We've played games since whenever and have never even been in a fight.

Nancy: Well, maybe they don't affect you as strongly. Just because some people can smoke cigarettes all their lives and die at 90, that doesn't mean cigarettes don't kill people. The fact that you and your brother survived violent video games doesn't prove anything either.

Phil: I agree that my brother and I don't prove anything. But neither do the Columbine shooters, and people are always talking about them. Most people are sane and can play video games without going off the deep end. Some people can go off the deep end for almost no reason, and maybe video games can help them get there. It's not the video game's fault. It's like saying driving cars leads to running people over. It isn't the car's fault.

Nancy: Not the cars themselves, but the way they're hyped in the culture. Ads emphasizing how fast they go; pictures of them racing around mountainous roads. The media portrayal of cars encourages speeding, especially among young men. You surely can't deny that. And the same thing is true with violent video games and the whole hyping of violence in the culture. Violent movies; extremely violent sports. I mean, we are on our way to Roman circuses and watching people being eaten by lions. It's barbaric.

Phil: As I recall, your Roman circus argument is called an argument by spectre. Violence, even youth violence, comes and goes with or without violent video games or movies like *Terminator II*. It's a very few people, if any, who go over the edge from seeing them.

Nancy: Well, I don't know how you know that. It seems obvious that being exposed to violence in the media will make people generally insensitive, even if only a few actually become violent.

Phil: So are you saying it's so obvious that we don't need to do any research to find out whether you're right? You rejected my appeal to me and my brother, and now you're appealing to what seems obvious to you? That's pretty lame.

Nancy: Point taken. We should find out what the experts say.

Phil: But wait a minute. Let's stick to the program before we go off and do our research. Let's make sure that we agree on the issue.

In the last chapter, we looked at how scientists go about making discoveries and claims in the natural world. In this chapter, we apply similar strategies for inquiry into the human world. But the scientific study of humans, whether focusing on physical health such as nutrition, or on mental health such as the influence of violent video games, presents many special challenges not present in the study of the natural world. For example, experimenting on humans is limited by many ethical and practical problems. Also, unlike rocks, humans are aware of being studied and may behave differently as a result. This chapter will focus on some of these challenges and provide guidance for assessing scientific claims about humans.

From a list of the 10 most violent games, in *Family Media Guide*[1]:

- *Resident Evil 4*—"Player is a Special Forces agent sent to recover the President's kidnapped daughter. During the first minutes of play, it's possible to find the corpse of a woman pinned up on a wall—by a pitchfork through her face."

- *Grand Theft Auto: San Andreas*—"Player is a young man working with gangs to gain respect. His mission includes murder, theft, and destruction on every imaginable level. Player recovers his health by visiting prostitutes then recovers funds by beating them to death and taking their money."

- *NARC*—"Player can choose between two narcotics agents attempting to take a dangerous drug off the streets and shut down the KRAK cartel while being subject to temptations including drugs and money. To enhance abilities, player takes drugs including pot, Quaaludes, ecstasy, LSD, and 'Liquid Soul'—which provides the ability to kick enemies' heads off."

Assessing Scientific Claims in the Social Sciences: An Example

What Is the Issue? What Kinds of Claims or Judgments Are at Issue?

What is the issue? What kind of claim does it involve?

What Do You Think?

Phil: As I see it, the issue is whether playing violent video games makes people violent.

Nancy: Hmm, that's a bit strong. I'm not expecting someone who plays a few games to go out and start attacking people. I think the issue is whether people who play violent video games will have a greater tendency to violence than those who don't.

Phil: That seems too vague because it could simply mean that people who like violent video games also tend to like to punch out their neighbour. That wouldn't put the blame on video games.

Nancy: OK. How's this? Does playing video games cause people to have an increased inclination to be aggressive?

Phil: You have to have violence in there. People can play an aggressive game of tennis. That's not the issue.

Nancy: Then how's this? The issue is whether playing violent video games increases a player's inclination to be physically aggressive.

Phil: I'm OK with that.

What Are the Reasons and Arguments on the Various Sides of the Issue?

Nancy: I suspect that video games have a big impact on aggressiveness because the players actually do the violent acts; they don't just watch them.

Phil: Wait a minute—games are games. Nobody is doing real violence.

Nancy: You know what I mean. I mean, they're interactive and so would make people feel more comfortable with initiating real violence.

List the arguments on various sides of the issue which Phil and Nancy have given.

What Do You Think?

Phil: Maybe, but you can't just say that. We need real evidence, not just your speculations and anecdotes of people crediting violence to video games.

Nancy: Right. So what should we do?

What sources could Phil and Nancy consult in order to help them evaluate the arguments?

What Do You Think?

Phil: We could go ask our psych prof, or we could go to the *Psychoinfo* database that we learned about in psych class. And, of course, there's always *Google* and *Wikipedia*.

Nancy: But I wonder whether there's any way to do experiments. I mean, you can't get people to play a lot of violent video games and then see if they attack people.

What Is the Context of the Issue?

What are the aspects of context which are relevant to the issue?

What Do You Think?

Phil: I agree, experimentation would be difficult, but let's remember the context. We're living in a world of increasing sales of violent video games. From time to time, there are calls by people like you to have them banned or controlled. That means that we're living in a kind of giant social experiment. But it also means that evidence on this topic is likely to be influenced by people's political views.

What Do You Think ?

What do you think is the "giant experiment" that Phil is referring to?

How Do We Comparatively Evaluate the Various Reasons and Arguments in Order to Reach a Reasoned Judgment?

Nancy: What do you mean by a giant social experiment?

Phil: Well, they've been selling video games by the millions for years. If video games contribute to violence, we should see an increase in violence correlated with the increase in video game use. When Sophia and I were looking into capital punishment, we found that there was no increase in murder when they got rid of capital punishment. That showed that capital punishment didn't act as a deterrent. If there's no increase in violence associated with the sale of violent video games, that would be a strong argument against their bad influence. On the other hand, if violence is up, especially among the game-playing generation, that would make a prima facie case for games contributing to violence.

Nancy: That's a good point, and it supports my point. The world has become incredibly more violent. All you hear about in the media is more and more violence and more and more of it done by young people. I can hardly believe how easy it was to prove my point.

Phil: Hold on. That's just your impression from the media. The media hypes violent crime just the way car manufacturers hype speed, and for the same reason: it sells. We need to do some inquiry before we can claim to know what's really going on.

Nancy: I suppose you're right. Where should we look for evidence?

Phil: Obviously the government keeps records on crimes. So we can start there. Finding out about video game sales might be a bit trickier, but let's see what we can find. I've got my computer here, so I'll get a coffee and we can check some things out.

Before following Phil on his research, a brief introduction to the complexity of research in the social sciences will help us assess what Phil finds.

Evaluation of Claims Based on Statistical Inference

The intent of any study or experiment is to study a relatively small group of subjects to see if a cause or at least a correlation can be found between those exposed to the supposed cause (in this case, violent video games) and the effect (e.g., violent tendencies). When we evaluate studies, one of the main questions we will be asking is whether these studies provide a good basis to generalize to a larger population.

There are two basic approaches to studying human behaviour, **observational** and **experimental.**

Observational Studies

In observational studies, the researchers study samples of individuals without intervening or experimenting. They just observe and collect data. There are two basic kinds of observational studies: **retrospective** and **prospective.**

Retrospective Studies

A **retrospective study** (often called a case-controlled study) typically identifies a group of people suffering from an illness or exhibiting a certain kind of behaviour (e.g., lung cancer, violent behaviour) and attempts to find factors in the history of this group that are different from those in a group of similar people who do not have the illness or effect (the "control group"). Scientists can perform retrospective studies examining any human phenomena. These studies start with people who have the relevant effect (e.g., violent tendencies) and look backward in time to see if something in their past is correlated with the current effect. The advantage of this kind of study is that it is relatively quick and inexpensive. By studying people with some behaviour pattern of interest and working back to the possible causes, we can study behaviour that is infrequent without studying hundreds of thousands of people.

Unfortunately, there are a number of problems with this type of study. One serious problem is that it usually relies on participants correctly remembering their relevant experiences. The second problem is finding controls who are representative of (and comparable to) the relevant population but who do not have the effect (illness or behaviour) in question. Remember that to establish a correlation we need a relevant comparison. Comparing violent people brought up in rough neighbourhoods to non-violent people who had a different background would result in the confounding factor of social background obscuring whether violent video games had anything to do with a person's violent tendencies. Because there is always the problem that the controls may differ from the studied group in more ways than the suspected causal factor and because data from the past may be inaccurate, retrospective studies are the most inconclusive type of study.

> A **retrospective study** (often called a case-controlled study) typically identifies a group of people suffering from an illness or exhibiting a certain kind of behaviour (e.g., lung cancer, violent behaviour) and attempts to find a factor or factors in the history of this group that are different from those in a group of similar people who do not have the illness or effect (the "control group").

Prospective Studies

Prospective studies isolate a group of subjects, often called a cohort (these studies are often called cohort studies) and follow the subjects over time looking for correlates to outcomes such as the occurrence of a disease or violent tendencies. Sometimes, these prospective studies are very large-scale studies that last years, even decades. Such studies are expensive and time consuming, but they provide a much more accurate picture of associations between behaviour and outcomes—for example, between education and wealth, or between exposure to violent media and violent behaviour.

Nonetheless, prospective studies are also plagued by confounding factors. For example, people who are careful about their diet are also likely to take care of themselves in other ways, and people who watch violent media may also hang out with criminals. This confounding makes it difficult to determine which of the factors is causally effective and to what degree. Even when there is credible evidence of a correlation, establishing the cause of this correlation is quite difficult.

> **Prospective studies** isolate a group of subjects, often called a cohort (these studies are often called cohort studies) and follow the subjects over time looking for correlates to outcomes such as the occurrence of a disease or violent tendencies.

Why isn't a correlation between violence and watching violent media sufficient to establish a causal connection between watching violent media and being violent?

What Do You Think ?

Experimental Studies

Because of the difficulty of eliminating confounding factors and establishing causal direction in observational studies, the best way to test a causal theory is to run an experiment. But experiments are not necessary to establish a causal claim. For example, the claim that smoking causes lung cancer has never been proven experimentally, but it is an extremely well-established causal connection. Nonetheless, if experiments are possible, they can often supply the best evidence for a causal claim.

An experiment is **double blind** if neither the subjects nor the experimenters know who has gotten the treatment, that is, who has been exposed to the cause in question.

The idea of **random sampling** is that the assignment of individuals into the two groups being studied should not be biased in some way; for example, one group should not be older or healthier or "meaner" than the other.

A **statistically significant difference** is a difference that is sufficiently large that we can show mathematically that the difference between the two groups is unlikely to be due to chance.

Calling a result "statistically significant" does not mean that it is significant in the sense of "really important."

Chance variation happens in the short run or with small groups, but underlying tendencies show up in the long run.

A **sample** is the group of people selected to provide a basis for making an inference about the target population that is the object of the researcher's inquiry.

A **sample of convenience** is a sample of subjects that researchers can get easy access to—for example, students, or people who respond to ads for volunteer subjects.

There are, however, two problems with experiments involving human behaviour. First, it is frequently not possible or ethical to run appropriate experiments on humans. Second, many experiments are only weakly representative of the actual behaviour that is the subject of the study. Nonetheless, credible experimental evidence can often add considerable weight to causal claims.

The best form of experimental method (sometimes called the "gold standard") is the **double blind** randomized control trial, or RCT. An experiment is double blind when neither the subjects nor the experimenters know who has gotten the treatment, that is, who has been exposed to the cause in question. The idea of **random sampling** is that the assignment of individuals into the two groups being studied should not be biased in some way; for example, one group should not be older or healthier or "meaner" than the other. The outcomes of the experiment are then observed to see if there is a **statistically significant difference** between the outcomes of the two groups. A statistically significant difference is a difference that is sufficiently large that we can show mathematically that the difference between the two groups is unlikely to be due to chance.

It is important to note that calling a result "statistically significant" does not mean that it is significant in the sense of "really important." To add to the confusion, many people, especially in the media, often refer to "statistically significant results" as simply "significant results."

Intuitively, we understand that if you want to know if there is a difference between the behaviour of two groups, you cannot just experiment on, say, six subjects. The differences between the two groups of three could just be the luck of the draw with such a small number. As the number in each group gets larger (provided they are randomly assigned), it becomes increasingly likely that any difference in behaviour from group to group is due to the causal factor, not to chance variability. Chance variation happens in the short run or with small groups, but underlying tendencies show up in the long run. Consider the weather. If you live in a temperate climate, you know that, by pure chance, the temperature of a day in January might be similar to that of a day in April. But it is extremely unlikely that the average temperature in the month of January will be anything like that of April.

While experiments provide strong support for a causal claim, even experiments are subject to confounding factors. One of the problems is that when studying humans, the subjects being studied (both the experimental and control groups) are not randomly selected from the target population. When sampling, the aim should be to select a **sample** that is representative of the target population and as a result provides a good basis for generalizing the results of the study to the target population at large. But many studies fail to address the fact that the samples being studied are not randomly selected from the population or arguably representative. In fact, most studies of humans are based on **samples of convenience**—basically volunteers who agree to be subjects of the study. As a result, we cannot be confident that the results of the experiment are generalizable to the target population.

Often these samples are clearly biased. For example, one of the most famous early cohort studies studied the health of male graduates of Harvard but became the basis for numerous recommendations about health. To what extent would we be warranted in inferring from this very special group to the larger population of (male and female) North Americans, to say nothing of human beings? The question about any study or experiment is whether the results found in the subject group are reasonably generalizable to the larger population.

Because of these considerations, no one study, not even an experimental study, should be seen as conclusive. Generally, in social science, having a variety of studies, done under varying conditions, that yield consistent results, is what gives weight to a claim. Because of the difficulties in studying humans and human behaviour, we do not expect the same degree of scientific consensus as we look for in the natural sciences. Non-scientists, concerned to get the best information in the shortest time, need to look for summaries of the studies to see if there is an emerging consensus or **convergence** in the research.

A little while later.

Phil: Well, I've come across some interesting stuff. One thing I found on a U.S. website is that while the sale of video games has more than doubled in the last ten years, murders and violent crimes are down. Not only is there no positive correlation between video sales and violent crime, if anything there's a negative correlation.

Nancy: OK, so there's no evidence from the "big social experiment." And I'm amazed that violent murder rates are down. So many things are changing along with the sale of violent video games. It's hard to tell if playing the games is adding to violence while something else like reduced drug use is reducing violence.

Phil: So how have you been researching the issue?

Nancy: I looked into the psychological research. People have been studying the effects of violent media on people for years, and they're pretty confident that exposure to violent media does make people more violent. The study of violent video games is still a bit new, but it points the same way. So combining the two results gives pretty good reason to think violent video games do contribute to violence. Have a look at this:

Violent Video Games: Myths, Facts, and Unanswered Questions

by Craig A. Anderson

A historical examination of the research on the effects of media violence reveals that debate concerning whether such exposure is a significant **risk factor** *for aggressive and violent behavior should have been over years ago (Bushman & Anderson, 2001). Four types of media violence studies provide converging evidence of such effects: laboratory experiments, field experiments, cross-sectional correlation studies, and longitudinal studies (Anderson & Bushman, 2002a; Bushman & Huesmann, 2000). But the development of a new genre— electronic video games—reinvigorated the debate.*

Two features of video games fuel renewed interest by researchers, public policy makers, and the general public. First, the active role required by video games is a double-edged sword. It helps educational video games be excellent teaching tools for motivational and learning process reasons. But, it also may make violent video games even more hazardous than violent television or cinema. Second, the arrival of a new generation of ultraviolent video games beginning in the early 1990s and continuing unabated to the present resulted in large numbers of children and youths actively participating in entertainment violence that went way beyond anything available to them on television or in movies. Recent video games reward players for killing innocent bystanders, police, and prostitutes, using a wide range of weapons including guns, knives, flame throwers, swords, baseball bats, cars, hands, and feet.[2]

Phil: Well, with all due respect to that Anderson fellow, this sounds more like speculation than research. All he's saying is that previous research showed some effect from violent media and, therefore, so much the worse for video games.

Nancy: You didn't let me finish. Notice how he refers to the context created by the history of relevant research. I think he's saying that the burden of proof is on those who deny that violent video games are going to make people violent. Further on in the website, he replies to a number of objections (he calls them "myths") just like we're learning to do in our critical thinking course. For example, read this:

Myth 1. *Violent video game research has yielded very mixed results.*

Convergence is an emerging consensus, when a majority of studies supports a particular theory.

In social science, a variety of studies, done under varying conditions, that yield consistent results, are what give weight to a claim.

A **risk factor** is any factor for which there is sufficient evidence to show that it is correlated with a particular (usually negative) outcome. Calling a factor a risk factor avoids making a claim that the relationship is causal.

Note the use of "significance" and "non-significance" without the word "statistical." It is, therefore, unclear as to whether the results are not due to chance (i.e., are statistically significant) or whether the results are of some importance (i.e., are significant).

Facts: *Some studies have yielded non-significant video game effects, just as some smoking studies failed to find a significant link to lung cancer.*

But when one combines all relevant empirical studies using **meta-analytic techniques,** *five separate effects emerge with considerable consistency. Violent video games are significantly associated with: increased aggressive behavior, thoughts, and affect; increased physiological arousal; and decreased prosocial (helping) behavior. Average effect sizes for experimental studies (which help establish causality) and correlational studies (which allow examination of serious violent behaviour) appear comparables.*[3]

Meta-analysis is a statistical method which involves sifting through all previous research and collecting the data from high-quality studies into one big sample and then doing statistical analysis on this new "sample." This method results in larger samples and, in principle, more reliable statistical conclusions.

Nancy: See—the results are converging, which we know is strong evidence for a scientific claim.

Phil: I don't get it. How can you do experiments that show people are made violent by playing video games?

Nancy: Researchers randomly assign subjects to two groups. One group of individuals, the control group, plays an ordinary video game; and the other group, the experimental group, plays a violent game. Then they're tested in some way for their aggressive or violent attitudes. In one case, the subjects played another game after the video games which supposedly involved them giving retaliatory blasts of a horn to their opponent. What Anderson found is that people who played the violent video game on average gave louder blasts than those who hadn't played the violent game. He claims that the difference was statistically significant and that, therefore, the researchers have good reason to believe that playing the violent video game increased the aggressiveness of video game players.

Phil: Well, now I can see how they do it, but I don't know how convincing those results are. The horn thing seems like a pretty dubious test of aggressiveness, to say nothing of violence. And anyway, maybe they were just a bit hyped up at that moment. Just like after seeing a football game or a good movie. It all passes pretty quick.

Nancy: But he also found that the group of people who played a lot of violent video games were quite a bit more violent than those who didn't.

Phil: I hate to point out the obvious, but some people are violent and those people will probably like playing violent video games. Anderson has got to show that the games lead to the violent personality and not the other way around.

Nancy: Anderson admits that's a problem. That's why he did the experiments.

Phil: You seem pretty impressed with this Anderson fellow, and I see that he is some kind of expert. But I think we should hear from some other people who are not so involved in the research. I'm going to check with some other experts to see if there are contrary opinions.

While acknowledging Anderson's expertise in this area, Phil realizes that it is also a good idea to check for a summary of the evidence by someone who is not so personally involved in the research. This is a good strategy for assessing expert evidence. Sometimes even the most eminent experts in a field are not the most reliable source of information because of their personal commitment to their own theories. It is useful to check their claims against more disinterested researchers.

Phil: Look at what the U.S. Surgeon General has to say:

Effect size is a measure of the difference of the behaviour of the experimental group compared to the control group.

A recent meta-analysis of these studies found that the overall **effect size** *for both randomized and correlational studies was small for physical aggression (r = .19) and moderate for aggressive thinking (r = .27)…. In separate analyses, the effect sizes for both randomized and cross-sectional studies was small (r = .18 and .19, respectively). The impact of video games on violent behaviour remains to be determined.*[4]

Effect size

The **effect size** referred to by both Anderson and the Surgeon General is a measure of the difference along various measures of the aggressiveness of the experimental (violent game playing) group compared to the control group. While "r" is not easily interpreted, it can be converted to a more intuitively understandable measure of effect size, namely **relative risk.** Relative risk is a measure of the impact a particular factor has on an outcome. For example, the effect of smoking on the incidence of lung cancer is a relative risk of 10; that is, 10 times more smokers get lung cancer than non-smokers. The effect size of exposure to second-hand smoke (or relative risk) appears to be about 1.2.[5] An "r" measure of .18 is equivalent to a relative risk of about 1.4; that is, those playing the violent video games were 1.4 times more likely to exhibit aggressive behaviour, however measured.

Phil: It doesn't look like the Surgeon General was very impressed. It seems to me that the evidence is far from conclusive and there's really no reason why I shouldn't have my fun.

Nancy: I think that's a little quick and self-serving. The Surgeon General's opinion is just one piece of evidence. Remember Anderson's argument that since there's strong evidence that exposure to violent video encourages violence, it's even more likely that playing violent video games will do the same.

Phil: But the fact is that the evidence at this point is weak. The experimental evidence has weak effects and dubious methods, the observational evidence can't determine the direction of the correlation, and frankly, the claim that exposure to violence is a "risk factor" for violent behaviour seems to me to be pretty vague. Even Anderson doesn't come out and say it "causes" people to be violent.

Nancy: You've made some good points, Phil. I agree that we should suspend judgment until there's more evidence. Though I still think it's a dreadful use of your time to play such revolting games.

Phil: You really should try before you make a judgment. Sure you don't want to have a go …? (Nancy rolls her eyes as she leaves.)

Relative risk is a measure of the impact of a particular factor on an outcome.

Have Phil and Nancy made a reasonable assessment of the evidence?

What Do You Think

In order to decide whether Phil and Nancy have made a reasonable assessment of the evidence, it will be helpful to look at the criteria for evaluating causal claims in statistical studies.

Evaluating Causal Claims in Statistical Research

Once a correlation is established, the evidence for best explanation in statistical research consists of the following:

Evidence of a "Dose Relationship"

Causal claims are strengthened when there is evidence showing that the more exposure to the factor in question (e.g., whether the exposure is to tobacco smoke or to violent media), the more frequent the outcome (lung cancer or violent behaviour).

Evidence of a Fit with Existing Causal Understanding

The causal claim being studied is more credible if it fits with existing understanding in the discipline. In the case of health issues, a plausible biological explanation is ideally supported by biological research such as research on animals or cells in

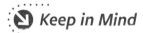
Keep in Mind

EVALUATING CAUSAL CLAIMS IN STATISTICAL RESEARCH
- Evidence of a "dose relationship"
- Evidence of a fit with existing causal understanding
- Demonstration that alternative explanations are less credible

Petri dishes. In many cases, however, we have to be careful that the plausibility of an explanation does not lead us to ignore the problems with the evidence. While it seems plausible that exposure to violent media and violent video games would make at least some people more violent, we have to look carefully at the scientific evidence before accepting this platitude.

Demonstration that Alternative Explanations are Less Credible

A causal claim is strengthened when it is shown that alternative explanations for the correlation (such as data collection error, experimental bias, or some other confounding factors) are not credible. In the case of violence and violent video games, there are at least two competing explanations:

- Social factors determine the level of violence and the level of interest in playing violent games.
- Individuals with violent tendencies will be drawn to violent video games.

Let us now review the case for the claim that playing violent video games increases the tendency to violence. First, we summarize the arguments in our table.

Claim: Playing violent video games increases a player's inclination to be physically aggressive.		
Argument Summary	**Objections**	**Evaluation**
PRO		
Common sense	Mere plausibility without studies is not real evidence: the fallacy of popularity	Weak evidence even though it is a common belief that the media influences people's behaviour
Anderson's research showing statistically significant effects if small effect size	Surgeon General's more negative assessment	Questionable experimental validity and small effect size weaken this support
Observational studies correlating a history of violence with playing violent video games	Difficulty in determining temporal order and, therefore, cause and effect direction	
Analogy with results from exposure to violent videos		This seems a strong argument although we haven't checked this research on videos
CON		
Lack of increase in violence generally despite increase in the sales of violent video games	Confounding factors could have obscured the effect of video games	Does suggest that the impact, if any, of video games on youth violence is small. Also argues against a "dose relationship"

Because of the limited research and problems noted above, Nancy and Phil's tentative negative judgment seems quite reasonable.

The issue of the relationship between playing violent video games and violence is clearly a factual question involving a causal claim, although exactly what the claim of interest is, is not easy to decide. This issue illustrates a complexity with the use of the concept of cause in scientific investigation involving statistics. In everyday reasoning and in much of scientific reasoning, a cause is identified as the sufficient condition for some event; that is, when the cause happens, the effect must happen. The broken pipe caused the leak, the corrupted print driver prevented the printing, and so on. But in statistically based research, researchers are looking for **causal factors,** of which there can be many. A factor is a causal factor for

A factor is a **causal factor** for an outcome if the factor is correlated with the outcome and if the best explanation for this correlation is that there is a causal relationship.

an outcome if the factor is correlated with the outcome and if the best explanation for this correlation is that there is a causal relationship.

We commonly use the concept of causal factors in health studies. Whether you get an illness, like cancer, is likely to be the result of many factors, including your genes, your lifestyle, your exposure to carcinogens, and so on. Since the causal mechanism is often not clear, researchers resort, as Anderson does, to talking about risk factors rather than causal factors. This means that they have good reason to believe a particular (risk) factor is associated with some negative outcome, but they do not have adequate evidence to claim that this factor is a causal factor in the outcome.

Considerations for Evaluating Causal Claims in the Social Sciences

The basic guidelines for evaluating claims in the social sciences are the same as those in the physical sciences, but having humans as the subject of inquiry presents a number of special challenges:

Generalizability

There are two issues here: experimental validity and sample generalizability. In the dialogue, Phil questions whether horn blasting is a credible measure of aggression. This is the question of **validity**—whether an experiment provides a good basis for generalizing to real world behaviour.

It should be noted that the problem of generalizability is not eliminated by randomly assigning the sample subjects into the experimental and control groups. Such random assignments ensure that if there are *statistically significant differences* at the end of the experiment, it is unlikely that these differences were due to chance. But such a procedure does not provide a mathematical basis for inferring from these results to the population at large. One can argue that the sample chosen was a good sample for generalizing, but this is not the same as a statistically based inference.

Many psychological experiments are based on studies of the convenient sample of college undergraduate students; obviously these samples are neither random nor even plausibly representative of the larger population. In most of these studies, the researchers even fail to indicate what they take to be the target population. Is the target population undergraduates? Undergraduates at their university? Or are the results meant to be a basis for making claims about the population of human beings in general (as is often implied)? Numerous studies of differing groups, including cross cultural studies, can enhance the generalizability of experimental results.

An experiment is said to have **validity** if it provides a good basis for generalizing to real world behaviour.

Order of Cause and Effect

Observational studies provide weak support for a causal claim when we cannot determine if the supposed cause actually precedes the effect. When doing observational studies of the effect of a factor (such as playing video games) on the attitudes and behaviour of the participants, it is often difficult to determine whether the factor of interest (the possible cause) preceded the effect.

Social Causation

Many explanations in sociology and other related disciplines are based on the view that some aspects of human behaviour can best be understood by studying the society in which they occur. From this perspective, an individual's or a group's behaviour is best explained by reference to the social environment in which it takes place. Consider the following explanations of someone being unemployed. If we ask why a particular person, say John, is poor and unemployed, we might focus on his personal characteristics such as his lack of

Keep in Mind ✔

CONSIDERATIONS FOR
EVALUATING CAUSAL
CLAIMS IN SOCIAL
SCIENCE
• Generalizability
• Order of cause and effect
• Social causation
• Prediction
• Explanatory and causal role of
  meaning

skills, or his addiction to television, perhaps even his poor childhood upbringing. In other words, we could offer to explain his situation in terms of facts about him.

But if the rate of unemployment rises in society due to an economic downturn, from 5% to 8%, for example, we know that the additional 3% are unemployed not because of bad habits, slothful personality, or an unfortunate childhood, but because they got caught in an economic downturn. So if John is laid off at work and cannot get another job because there are now so many newly laid-off people seeking work, the explanation for his unemployment is social, not personal. These two explanatory perspectives (explanation based on facts about the individual versus explanation in terms of greater social factors) influence which discipline we look to for explanations (psychology, sociology, or economics).[6]

Prediction

As in all sciences, explanations of human behaviour are established through argument to the best explanation. If an explanation leads to successful predictions, that is a powerful argument for it being the best explanation. But prediction often plays a smaller role in verification of claims in the social sciences than in the natural sciences. The great complexity of factors influencing human behaviour and the fact of human self-consciousness and free will make the prediction of human behaviour much more difficult than the prediction of natural phenomena. This is one reason that claims in the social sciences are generally more uncertain and tend not to be supported by the same level of consensus as we find in the natural sciences.

The Explanatory and Causal Role of Meaning

Understanding human behaviour means that we are dealing with phenomena in which meaning is crucial to explanation. The explanation of why McGregor insulted Ali at the public meeting depends first on the identification of the remark as an insult. The power of words is not physical. What makes words causally effective is their meaning. As a result, any study of humans cannot be merely a study of physical causes. Meaning, belief, and intention must all play a crucial role in an adequate explanation of human behaviour. These are very different kinds of explanatory concepts than concepts used in the natural sciences, such as force, which do not require the object being acted upon to have any understanding of what is happening.

Apply Your
Understanding
Exercises 1, 2, 3, 4

Studying Human Nature

In this section, we take a more multidisciplinary approach to looking at research. What is particularly interesting about studying human nature is that research from a wide range of disciplines is relevant and much of it is convergent.

The issue in question is one of the perennial questions about human behaviour: to what extent do humans have an inborn nature, and to what extent are we products of our environment and personal history? This debate has frequently been couched as the "nature/nurture debate."

Human Nature: Nasty or Nice?

Ravi, Nancy, Winnie, Phil, and Juanita are assembled in the lounge later in the afternoon after Phil's and Nancy's discussion of video games.

Ravi: You know, when I heard about your research on the influence of violent video games, I couldn't help thinking just how violent humans are. Look at the 20th century—millions dying in wars and now all over the world people blowing each other up. Human beings are so nasty.

Nancy: I think you're exaggerating. There are lots of good people out there. It's society that messes them up. People don't make wars; governments do.

Ravi: It's not just violence. People are so selfish. They steal your parking place; they butt ahead in line-ups. And greedy . . . look at the last financial meltdown that ruined so many people. And the very people that ruined everybody still thought they should be paid millions—I mean *millions*.

Nancy: They're no different from lots of others. The whole capitalist system is built on greed and makes people incredibly greedy.

Phil: The financial meltdown was unfortunate; but as my father points out, if you want to see a real economic mess, look at the Russians or Chinese before they abandoned communism. They lived in a permanent economic crisis. That's because they didn't respect people's basic selfishness. If you want people to do things, you have to provide incentives.

Juanita: I think that's a gross exaggeration. People often do nice things for others; some even sacrifice their lives for others. Look at the doctors who work for Médicin sans Frontières.[7] They could be working in wealthy countries and getting rich, and instead they're out there saving people's lives, working under awful conditions for virtually no financial reward. And look at the people who dedicate their lives to a spiritual quest. Humans have a lot of goodness in them if you give them a chance.

Ravi: Those are exceptions. Winnie, you're the one who understands Darwin. Doesn't evolution show that it's all competition right back to the beginning, and only the fittest have survived? So here we are—products of a long fight to survive. We're the meanest winners of the struggle.

Nancy: That's not Darwinism; that's social Darwinism.[8] We learned about that in our sociology classes. That's a view that a bunch of right wingers used to justify inequality and brutality at the beginning of the 20th century. I don't know what Darwin would say, but it's pretty clear that people are shaped by their society and their family. That's why some people are selfish and why some societies are more selfish than others. Humans are products of their environment and their culture. They're not just animals driven by instincts.

Phil: I think that's pretty naïve. Look at sex and hunger. Those are animal urges that no one has to learn about it and everyone has.

Nancy: Yes and no. Look at all the different foods that people eat. We wouldn't even think about eating dogs, for example, but in other cultures they're a delicacy. And look at all the different arrangements for marriage: single family, villages, harems. It's all social. What counts as being sexually attractive is clearly cultural. The focus on thinness in our culture is what drives some young women into anorexia. Anorexia proves that humans can even override whatever instinct they have for eating.

Phil: Are you saying that we're not really like other animals? That we're a kind of blank slate to be programmed by our parents and society?

Winnie: That seems pretty unscientific to me.

Phil: Of course, I agree that we're shaped by our upbringing at least to some extent. It's hard to completely deny that. But we still have a basic nature and that includes greed and selfishness. That's why the market economy works so well.

Nancy: There you go with that capitalist baloney again. Boy, you are living proof of how people can be programmed by their parents.

> Actually Nancy is wrong. The social Darwinist view is a "should" claim, not a claim about how, in fact, natural selection works. It is the view that society should allow the weak to die off and reward the strong in order for society to progress. It did not come from Darwin.[9]

Phil: Hey, watch the ad hominems. Are we trying to have a reasonable discussion or what?

Nancy: Point taken.

Winnie: But instead of just debating, I think we should make an effort to clarify the issue.

What Is the Issue? What Kinds of Claims or Judgments Are at Issue?

Winnie: There seem to me to be at least two issues: first, to what extent do humans have an inherited nature? Are we mainly a product of environment and conditioning, or do we have a basic nature in our genes like other animals? And second, if we have a "nature," what's it like? Are we basically selfish and aggressive, or are our instincts more social and kindly like Juanita thinks?

Phil: I think we should take just one aspect of human behaviour to look at. Why don't we look at selfishness?

Nancy: I'm good with that, but we need to also get clear on the concept of selfishness. Not everything everyone does for themselves is selfish. When I eat food and drink water, I'm not being selfish.

Ravi: Well, you could be. You could give the food away to the starving and save the water for others.

Nancy: Yeah, but then I'd be dead. Selfishness isn't just doing something for yourself; it's doing too much for yourself. Giving to the starving isn't just not being selfish; it's being really generous and kind. If what you mean by saying people are selfish is that they don't give away all their food and die, then I guess we're selfish. But that's a crazy definition of selfishness. If we're going to use words like "selfish" and "generous," they have to have some meaning. Every act can't be selfish.

Ravi: So what is selfishness?

Nancy: We call someone selfish when they ignore the needs of others when it's not appropriate. And selfish actions are actions that fall below the minimum that we would consider decent. Just like generous acts are those that are more than what decency requires.

Winnie: I agree with you about the idea of selfishness, but I don't see what you've proved. You seem to think that you can show humans aren't selfish by just making a few verbal distinctions. I don't think so. I think we should look into the science of this question and not just try to settle it on verbal grounds.

Ravi: Look, we are evolved from animals. Animals that look after themselves and their children are the ones that survive. Nice animals don't finish last—they simply don't survive.

Nancy: I think the distinctions I'm making are important, but I agree that there's also a scientific issue. I bet psychologists, sociologists, and biologists all have something to say about this. Why don't we go with our interests and each look into one discipline? I'd be willing to see what sociologists say about this issue.

Phil: I'm interested in looking at that as well. Why don't we work together?

Winnie: And I'd like to see what Darwin and others say from the evolutionary perspective.

Juanita: I think I'll look into the philosophical history of the issue. My guess is that this hasn't always been a scientific question, and I'm not sure it's a question that science can answer.

Ravi: I guess that leaves me to do psychology.

Phil: So we're all set. But are we are clear on the issue? Is this it? "Are humans innately inclined always to act in their own self-interest?"

Winnie: That won't do because, even if people are self-interested, they may by mistake act against their self-interest—like investing in a stock scam.

Nancy: Well, how's this: "Are humans innately inclined always to try to act in their own self-interest?"

Phil: That sounds pretty good.

Winnie: Yeah. It gets rid of the moralistic aspect of selfishness. It sounds like something that science might be able to address.

Juanita: I think that way of framing the issue misses the key thing about humans: we care about each other. We don't just act in the interest of others by accident as an animal might; we empathize.

Phil: You may be right, but I don't see how we can study what people are feeling scientifically.

Juanita: Well then, so much the worse for science.

Winnie: You'd be amazed at what science can do. Why don't we leave it an open question? The issue is whether people really do act in the interest of others; and if they do, what motivates them to do so?

Phil: Sounds good. Why don't we meet here again tomorrow—same time.

Nancy was right to object to the use of selfishness to describe all human behaviour. What she was doing was **conceptual analysis**—clarifying our understanding of our concepts and getting clear on how we actually use the words that refer to them.

People sometimes bend the meaning of words outside their normal meaning without realizing that when they do that, the words they are using no longer refer to the same concept. "Selfish" and "selfishness" are obviously normative words. They are used to negatively describe someone or someone's behaviour and to distinguish it from non-selfish acceptable behaviour. Any attempt to apply these words to all behaviour or all people would require that the meaning of the words change. Such a change would also change their moral significance. Just as everyone cannot be tall, everyone cannot be selfish in our ordinary sense of the word. Of course, if you redefine "tall" as over 10 cm., then indeed all adult humans are tall. But how confusing and misleading. Using "selfish" to describe all human behaviour involves a similar kind of error.

> **Conceptual analysis** involves clarifying our understanding of our concepts and getting clear on how we actually use the words that refer to them.

What Is the Context of the Issue?

Juanita, Ravi, Nancy, and Phil meet the next day to continue their discussion of human nature.

Juanita: Boy, have we ever got on to a big question! People have been debating this issue for millennia. But I did notice that until Darwin, it wasn't seen as a scientific issue. There was a lot of speculation by a lot of philosophers. But everyone seems to be writing in reaction to Thomas Hobbes, who was writing after the English civil war in the mid-1600s.

Ravi: What was his view?

Juanita: He had an idea that before governments, people lived in a "state of nature" that was pretty terrible—"nasty, brutish and short" is his famous description. But actually he didn't have a clue what the state of nature was really like. The idea of the state of nature was largely based on rumours and myths from early explorers. Anyway, Jean-Jacques Rousseau hated Hobbes's

Rousseau and Hobbes on Human Nature

Thomas Hobbes, Leviathan, *1651*

[The state of nature is that]...men live without other security, than what their own strength, and their own invention shall furnish them withall. In such condition, there is no place for Industry; because the fruit thereof is uncertain; and consequently no Culture of the Earth; no Navigation, nor use of the commodities that may be imported by Sea; no commodious Building; no Instruments of moving, and removing such things as require much force; no Knowledge of the face of the Earth; no account of Time; no Arts; no Letters; no Society; and which is worst of all, continuall feare, and danger of violent death; And the life of man, solitary, poore, nasty, brutish, and short.

Jean-Jacques Rousseau, Discourse on Inequality, *1754*

The first man who, having fenced in a piece of land, said "This is mine," and found people naive enough to believe him, that man was the true founder of civil society. From how many crimes, wars, and murders, from how many horrors and misfortunes might not any one have saved mankind, by pulling up the stakes, or filling up the ditch, and crying to his fellows: Beware of listening to this impostor; you are undone if you once forget that the fruits of the earth belong to us all, and the earth itself to nobody.

---

theory and he had his own idea about the state of nature: he saw it as idyllic. Rousseau thought people were basically good and got messed up by civilization.

Nancy: I heard that Hobbes was some kind of fascist or something.

Juanita: Well, I'm no fan of Hobbes, but that's not really right. He felt that we needed a strong state to keep us from fighting with one another, so in that way he was very authoritarian. John Locke, a philosopher who was writing in the mid-1700s, took exception to Hobbes's view and defended democracy and freedom. He was sort of the intellectual godfather for the American Revolution.

Ravi: What was his view about human nature?

Juanita: He argued that people were basically a blank state. Locke was mostly interested in showing that people did not have innate knowledge. But his idea has carried on as the view that basically humans have little or no "innate nature." In this view, we're totally a product of our environment. Anthropologists still tend to favour this view because they study a lot of different cultures and see just how differently people behave in those cultures.[10]

Phil: You sure can see where some contemporary ideas come from.

Winnie: Nice background, but it all sounds like just a lot of speculation, not science.

Laissez-faire capitalism refers to the economic theory that prosperity is best attained with the smallest number of government restrictions of the market. "Laissez-faire" means roughly "let it be." The early nineteenth century was characterized by widespread belief in this doctrine (especially in England and the U.S.) until the horrors of child labour and other injustices made it clear that the government needed to impose restrictions on the market if people were to benefit more generally.

Juanita: True enough, but these views had enormous impact. In the middle of the nineteenth century, there was a great divide. On the one side was Darwin, who argued that there's a strong evolutionary factor in human behaviour. He believed people have evolved a social nature but that we are also naturally competitive. On the other side, there was Karl Marx and others who pushed the idea that it is society, not biology, that shapes human behaviour. Both these points of view were all tied up with economics and politics. Darwin was influenced by the harsh "laissez-faire" capitalism of his day, which made him see how competition would lead to natural selection. Marx, on the other hand, was repulsed by capitalist society and the effect it had on people. In his view, the original hunter–gatherer societies were characterized by a kind of natural

Darwin on Generosity

Charles Darwin, The Descent of Man, *1882*

The aid which we feel impelled to give to the helpless is mainly an incidental result of the instinct of sympathy, which was originally acquired as part of the social instincts, but subsequently rendered, in the manner previously indicated, more tender and more widely diffused. Nor could we check our sympathy, even at the urging of hard reason, without deterioration in the noblest part of our nature. The surgeon may harden himself whilst performing an operation, for he knows that he is acting for the good of his patient; but if we were intentionally to neglect the weak and helpless, it could only be for a contingent benefit, with an overwhelming present evil.... We must therefore bear the undoubtedly bad effects of the weak surviving and propagating their kind.

communism. So once humans were freed from the shackles of capitalism, they would presumably return to a fair and more cooperative way of living.

Winnie: Actually Darwin was quite a kind and generous person. Definitely not a social Darwinist. But he was influenced by Malthus who thought that there would always be a large class of more or less starving poor—as soon as people had enough to eat, they would reproduce and again put pressure on the resources.

Juanita: The whole issue gets even more political in the twentieth century, when Darwin's theory was used to justify racism and eugenics. The Nazis claimed biological superiority over Jews and others, and used it as a justification for their atrocities. This gave biological explanations of human behaviour a really bad name.

Phil: But surely now we don't associate evolution with racism.

Juanita: Well, it looks like it's a very recent change if we don't. In the 1960s, a very eminent biologist, E. O. Wilson, argued that biological explanations could explain all behaviour and that there was a large amount of human behaviour that could be explained genetically. He called his view "sociobiology" and was there ever a strong reaction against it! People suspected that advocates of sociobiology were a bunch of reactionaries or racists trying to bring back social Darwinism, or worse. But that suspicion seems to have passed, and there's now considerable effort being made to explore the biological basis of human nature. I know Winnie's going to give us the Darwinian view, so I'll leave it at that.

Think about your own view of human nature. Is it just something you have accepted from common beliefs in your community, or is it based on a consideration of the evidence?

What Do You Think ?

Learning about the intellectual, social, political, and historical contexts in which an issue is situated can bring to light the assumptions and world views which lie behind the various arguments. This is especially true concerning issues such as theories of human nature which have obvious political significance.

What this long history of the debate about human nature and selfishness teaches us is that these theories of human nature were tightly linked to differing political philosophies. We need to remember that just because a theory serves to justify certain political institutions does not mean that it is right or wrong. Proposals for political and economic arrangements need to accommodate the facts of human nature—assuming we can actually discover and verify those facts. But as we do our inquiry, we need to keep in mind the extent to which political points of view are likely to have influenced the science.

What Are the Relevant Reasons and Arguments on Various Sides of the Issue?

Winnie: That was great work, Juanita. When I started looking at this issue, I wasn't sure I could ever get the big picture. There's just so much material. The first thing I found out, though, is that we really didn't ask the right question from the biologist's point of view. Biologists don't talk about animals being selfish, but rather about them being "altruistic." For them, altruistic behaviour is behaviour by an organism that benefits the recipient more than the actor. Darwin started the discussion when he tried to deal with worker ants, which were infertile and sacrificed for the ant hill. His theory was that individuals that contributed to a successful group would be selected for by natural selection. He made the same argument when it came to explaining why humans were moral and cooperative: it was good for the group, which in turn helped the individuals.

Juanita: So Darwin believed that we evolved to be cooperative?

Darwin on Group Selection

Charles Darwin, The Descent of Man, *1882*

It must not be forgotten that although a high standard of morality gives but a slight or no advantage to an individual man and his children over the other men in his tribe, yet that an advancement of morality and an increase in the number of well-endowed men will certainly give an immense advantage of one tribe over another.

Winnie: Sort of. He believed that we are altruistic, and that, while this looks like an argument against his theory, if you consider groups, it isn't. Groups that had more mutually supportive members could out-reproduce less cooperative groups. So on the basis of group selection, Darwin thought altruism could be produced by natural selection operating on groups.

Nancy: That makes a lot of sense to me. Societies that are more cooperative seem a lot more likely to survive than those characterized by selfishness and competition.

Winnie: I don't want to get too complicated, but most biologists reject Darwin's theory. They feel that selfish individuals inside the group would have an advantage over the others, so that inevitably they would dominate and eliminate the cooperators and, of course, the group's effectiveness.

The problem for Darwin of explaining altruism (especially in ants!) was a purely scientific question. While some took Darwin's theory to mean that all creatures must evolve to act only in their self-interest, Darwin saw that, as a matter of fact, such a theory would not fit the facts both of animal societies and human behaviour. But the problem of how to explain self-sacrificing behaviour by ants and other animals remained a problem for biology well into the twentieth century. Despite Darwin's view, it was widely believed that the theory of natural selection entailed the view that altruistic organisms would tend to die off.

Winnie: Since the 60s, two other theories have been developed to explain human altruism and sociality. They're based on mathematical modelling and computer simulation of what happens when creatures reproduce over time. One theory is kin-selection. Basically the idea is that when you help your relatives, say your sister, you are helping half of your genes make it to the next generation. So this kind of helping does give a reproductive advantage to your genes, though not to you. This would also explain why people are so partial to family. The other theory is reciprocal altruism, which points out that if the creatures involved can remember who helped them and reciprocate, it could be in both creatures' interest to help one another, even if there were no shared genes. That's why predator fish don't eat certain smaller fish who clean their teeth! So both Darwin and contemporary biologists all believe in the biological origin of altruism, even if they disagree a bit about how it works.

Juanita: OK. So we have a Darwinian explanation of a kind of animal altruism. But that doesn't really deal with true altruism—where people help others just because they care about them. Darwinism makes it all sound pretty self-serving, or at least gene-serving.

Juanita's observation is true, but it may miss the relationship between biological theories and human behaviour. We may have evolved to have "natural inclinations" to help others (or at least kin), but that does not mean that we help others intentionally to promote our genes. We can help others because we care about them, or because we have moral feelings, or sympathy. But our capacity for these feelings may be rooted in a background that selected kin-helping or group-helping genes, perhaps even in pre-human species from which we descended.

Ravi: Well, psychologists do talk about what they call "psychological altruism." It's real altruism and includes not only acting in a way that benefits others, but doing so with the genuine intention to help others, not to get some reward. I learned that up until the 80s, many, perhaps most, social scientists believed that underlying all altruistic actions were egoistic motives.[11] I couldn't figure out exactly what caused the change, but some authors I read call it a "paradigm shift." The central question now is whether altruism is primarily innate (part of our genetic heritage), or whether it's something that's produced by parents and society. The answer seems to be a bit of both. Genes generally equip us to become altruistic, but if we have a really miserable childhood, that impulse might not develop. One analogy that everyone uses is language. Humans have an innate ability to learn language, but whether we learn a language and, of course, what language we learn depends on the environment. And the extent to which we develop language also depends on our early environment. We all know how hard it is to learn a second language at 19. So by analogy with language, the capacity for altruism and empathy is innate, but how it develops is dependent on our experience.

Nancy: Sociologists don't seem as concerned about the innateness issue since they've traditionally focused on the influence of social norms on behaviour. But the idea that altruism is totally social or based solely on parental influence has more or less been abandoned. Many sociologists have noticed that much of human generosity involves giving to people who don't know you, people you'll never meet. This kind of giving doesn't appear to fit any of the biological models, so something else must be going on.

Ravi: How is this science? Anyone can observe that people help others. What makes this scientific?

Phil: It can be scientific in a number of ways. Social psychologists can run experiments and see under what conditions people act altruistically. Sociologists have identified some social conditions that tend to discourage concern for others and also conditions that tend (to a lesser extent) to encourage selflessness. One of the more interesting experiments is something called the "ultimatum game." The results appear to refute the claim that all human actions are self-interested.

Juanita: It's funny how games keep coming up in social science research.

Phil: True, but not surprising. To run social science experiments, you have to get people to do stuff that is similar to real life, but not too real. Games are like that. You have a life and death struggle, and then you shake hands and go and have a beer.

Ravi: So what about this ultimatum experiment?

Nancy: It goes like this: You give one person (the proposer) a sum of money, $10 for example, and ask her how she would like to allocate this money (in units of $1), between herself and another person in another room, whom she'll never meet. The other person (the responder) can accept the proposed division, and they both go home with some money; or the responder can reject it, and no one gets any money.[12]

Ravi: Obviously a responder will never reject any amount. Whatever they get, they're ahead of the game.

Nancy: Well, that shows you've been taking Economics 100. That's what economic theory says people should and would do. But they don't.

Winnie: So what usually happens?

Nancy: On average, people offer about 50%, and responders reject any offer under 20%.

Ravi: That's really interesting. But what does this show?

Nancy: That as usual economists' psychological theories are wrong.

Ravi: And as usual, you are fond of pointing that out. But what does it show?

Juanita: It seems to me that it shows that people have a natural tendency to fairness and an intolerance of being treated unfairly. Why else would the proposer share the money 50-50?

Nancy: That's what I thought at first. And when I read that they get the same results in Europe, Asia, and North America, I was impressed. Psychology seemed to be tapping into a universal human characteristic and proving it by doing cross-cultural studies, not just studies of North American college students.

Ravi: I think I here a "but" coming.

Nancy: You're right. One group of psychologists decided to try the game in really different cultures, and they showed that the offers and responses of people from these other cultures differed dramatically. The key factor appeared to be the extent to which people in the other cultures were integrated into a market economy. When they were, people tended to offer around 50%. When they weren't integrated into a market economy, the results depended on how "gifts" were viewed. In one culture, for example, to receive a gift kind of puts the giver in a superior position to the recipient. In that culture, proposers tended to make what we would call generous offers and responders rejected them.

The ultimatum game illustrates a very successful use of experimentation in social science research. It addresses many of the important considerations involved in such research.

Generalizability and Experimentation

As we noted above, there are two issues concerning generalizability from experiments:

1) Are the experiments valid? That is, do they provide a good basis for generalizing to real world behaviour?

2) Do the samples provide a good basis for generalizing to the target population?

By doing studies in different cultures, the researchers were able to make a cogent case that fairness was a common (if not universal) human concern, but that it was also significantly culturally based.

Argument to the Best Explanation

The results also showed that an egoistic account of motivation was not the best explanation for these experimental results—and probably many other phenomena. By refuting the predictions based on the egoistic theory, in these and other experiments, researchers were able to show that the egoism explanation was not adequate. This experiment shows that experiments in the social sciences are used in quite similar ways to experimentation in the natural sciences. It also demonstrates that such experiments can result in the kind of convergence of views that we usually find in the natural sciences.

The Role of Meaning

Meaning plays a crucial role in explanations in the social sciences. The results of the ultimatum game illustrate this. It was the meaning of the money and not the amount of the money offered (not the actual quantity) that influenced the responder's decision. If people thought the amount offered was unfair or a put-down, they rejected it.

Ravi: So generosity and fairness are all about culture?

Phil: Not quite. Culture has a great influence, but so do other factors. There's another neat experiment called the "dictator game." In this game, "dictators" are given money and they can share it with another person. This time the responder has no say but just gets whatever the dictator gives. Now you would think dictators would just keep all the money for themselves. That's certainly what I expected. And in truly anonymous situations, the dictators, who were all college students, do just that. So that seems to confirm that there is some basic selfish tendency.

Nancy: But if the dictators think they're being observed, or if they're given some information about the recipient, they usually give about 50% away. That really struck me. It seems to me that this shows that empathy, based on some sense of the other person, really does affect people's behaviour.

Ravi: College students, anyway.

Nancy: Point taken.

How Do We Comparatively Evaluate the Various Reasons and Arguments in Order to Reach a Reasoned Judgment?

Phil: So what are we to make of all of this?

Winnie: It sure looks like there's a cross-disciplinary consensus that people are motivated not only by self-interest but also by fairness and a concern for others. How this all plays out depends on the culture and childhood experiences.

Nancy: Hardly surprising stuff, but contrary to what economists have been assuming for years. It shows why you just can't build a theory like economics on a bunch of dubious assumptions about what really motivates people. Our feelings for others and our cultural context obviously influence people's behaviour.

Nancy is attacking the standard view of human behaviour that has been the basis for economic theorizing. This view, often called the "homo economicus" view, assumes that humans are always motivated by rational self-interest. On this assumption, economists were able to work out quite complex models of economic behaviour. Recent work in what is called "behavioural economics," such as Nancy has cited in the dialogue, has undermined the credibility of this view. Some economists are now working on revised theories using information from such experiments as the ultimatum game.[13]

Ravi: So here's how I see what we've learned. Blank slate and total social determinism are both out. Looking at animals and mathematical models shows that we have clearly inherited tendencies to help others. But these innate tendencies will obviously be influenced by our culture and the presence of others.

Nancy: None of this is too surprising except that this was all widely denied in certain disciplines until just recently.

Winnie: I guess that's scientific progress.

Nancy: One thing that follows is that the free market theory based on egoistic assumptions needs revision.

Winnie: Darwin triumphs again!

Juanita: And believing that people are basically good isn't so old fashioned or even "new agey." It's just good science!

Further Reflections on the Study of Human Behaviour

What more have we learned about studying human behaviour as a result of the inquiry into innateness and human selfishness?

Need for Conceptual Analysis

Getting clear on an issue sometimes requires some conceptual analysis, which can avoid some obvious misunderstandings and misleading claims. When we are studying human behaviour, we need to be careful to sort out the evaluative issues from the factual ones, and to make sure that words are not being used in odd and misleading ways. Studying whether people are selfish is not a purely factual inquiry.

Influence of Political Issues

This topic area, as well as many other areas in the social sciences, is loaded with political issues which have consistently influenced the research. It should also be noted that this works both ways. Scientific theories about human behaviour can also influence political views.

Use of Mathematical Models

Mathematical models can sometimes play a key role in understanding in the biological/psychological sciences, as they can in the physical sciences.

Cross-cultural Experimentation

Despite their many challenges, experiments can play an important role in social science research; but cross-cultural studies are necessary to support any broad psychological generalization.

Need for Fallibilistic Approach

Research into the biological basis of human behaviour is still quite new and controversial. There has been a "paradigm shift" in this area in the last thirty years. So we should remember to be fallibilistic in our acceptance of the current theories.

What Do You Think ?

How much confidence do you think our inquirers should have based on their research?

As with many judgments about explanations of human behaviour, the scientific evidence must also contend with popular belief which establishes the burden of proof. But on

Claim: Humans are innately inclined always to try to act in their own self-interest.

Argument Summary	Objections	Evaluation
PRO		
Common sense	Politically influenced and anecdotal	Common sense goes both ways on this question and is an unreliable source.
Economic theory assumes that people act only in their perceived rational self–interest.	This assumption has proved theoretically useful but is not grounded in psychological research.	Economics has created powerful theoretical structures based on this assumption, but it is arguable that various failures of application are a result of using this as a basis for prediction.
Natural selection seems to imply that only selfish organisms will survive and reproduce.	As Darwin and contemporary theorists note, natural selection does not preclude organisms being altruistic. There are a number of candidate explanations for the survival of "altruistic genes."	Egoism is no longer the consensus view in evolutionary theory.
CON		
Anecdotal evidence of generosity and altruism is available.	Anecdotal evidence is not scientific and, as stated above, common sense goes both ways on this issue.	An important common sense observation, but common sense is weak if there is strong scientific evidence to the contrary.
Experimental evidence in ultimatum and dictator games shows that people's decisions are influenced by a variety of non-egoistic considerations including fairness, pride, and concern for others.	These are recent experiments and may be later refuted.	There is now considerable cross-disciplinary consensus resulting from these experiments, which have considerable generalizability because of the variety of subjects and cultures studied.

this question of innate human selfishness, common sense has gone two ways. We have all heard people praised for their genuine generosity and selfless courage. At the same time, there is a widespread view in our culture that all human activity is self-motivated and even selfish. It seems likely that the widespread acceptance of this latter view is the result of the influence of the market society in which we live. This should remind us that our "common-sensical" psychological views are also a product of the social environment and cannot be taken as necessarily providing genuine insights into the nature of human behaviour.

Making evaluations of claims about human nature involves assessing a complex mix of intuition, popular understanding, and scientific efforts from a number of disciplines. Despite this complexity, in the case of human selfishness, there actually seems to be considerable convergence from conceptual analysis to observational and experimental studies. The significant consensus about altruism suggests that we could take a reasonably confident judgment on this view. But the fact that the acceptance of altruistic behaviour as scientifically grounded is relatively recent may temper our confident judgment.

Apply Your
Understanding
Exercises 5, 6, 7

CHECK YOUR UNDERSTANDING

- *What is a sample a sample of?*
- *What are the two basic approaches to studying human behaviour?*
- *What are the two basic kinds of observational studies?*
- *What is the role of a correlation in establishing a causal relationship?*
- *What is the gold standard form of experimental research?*
- *What does "statistically significant" mean?*
- *What is a sample of convenience?*
- *What is a meta-analysis?*
- *What evidence is sufficient to infer a causal relationship?*
- *What is a causal factor? How does it differ from a risk factor?*
- *What are the five special considerations for evaluating claims in the social sciences?*
- *What special considerations are involved in assessing experimental evidence in the social sciences?*
- *What is conceptual analysis?*

EXERCISES

1. Identify the methodological problems or limitations in the following study designs:

    i) examining attitudes to dating among young adults using a sample of 27 male college students

    ii) having physicians choose which of their patients will receive the placebo and which will receive the treatment

    iii) studying the effects of alcohol consumption on cancer rates by using a sample of drinkers some of whom are also smokers

    iv) trying to determine whether stress is a causal factor in marital breakdown by seeing if there is a correlation between increased stress levels and marital breakdown

2. Identify the problems with the following study and its conclusions:

    In order to study the cause of teenage smoking, the researchers talked to a large number of teenage smokers and noted that a large number of them had parents who smoked. On this basis, they concluded that parent smoking is a predominant cause in teenage smoking. The researchers also interviewed smoking parents and discovered that of those who had teenage children, about 30% of the children over 13 smoked at least occasionally. They concluded that this again shows that parental smoking is a causal factor for teenage smoking.

3. Abstracts for three studies that examine the relationship between exposure to pornography by males and aggressiveness toward females are given under Exercise 13-3 of the textbook website. For each abstract, complete the following:

    i) Identify the type of study.

    ii) Evaluate the strengths and weaknesses of this type of study.

4. Read the excerpt from the article from the *FDA Consumer* on "The Infamous Beer and Gonorrhea Story" at http://findarticles.com/p/articles/mi_m3469/is_19_51/ai_62967141/ (see Exercise 13-4 on the textbook website).

   What is the implicit causal claim? What other explanations might account for this decline? Which explanation is the best ?

5. **Science and Online Dating.** Online dating services are big business and many claim to be scientifically based. Do an inquiry on the science of dating and mating. Can science tell us anything about finding the right partner? See Alina Tugend, "Blinded by Science in the Online Dating Game," *New York Times*, http://www.nytimes.com/2009/07/18/technology/internet/18shortcuts.html (see Exercise 13-5 on the textbook website).

6. **The Study of Happiness.** What makes people happy? This is another area where philosophers have created many theories, where economists have made many assumptions, where common sense itself seems pretty clear, and yet there is interesting cross-cultural research being done on this topic. Inquire into the social science research on the basis and causes of happiness. What does the research tell us about what makes people happy? Is the basis of happiness the same across all cultures studied? Can we make any inferences from the results of these studies as to how people should live? Does this research support any of the previous philosophical theories? Some critics find the results of these studies mere "common sense." What do you think?

7. In the following assignment, try to answer the questions below on the basis of the article supplied in Exercise 13-7 on the textbook website. Then answer the additional questions identified in the assignment.

   i) What is the causal claim being made?

   ii) What is the context of the research?

   iii) What are the relevant reasons and arguments presented in support of the claim?

   iv) How confident a judgment of the claim can be made based on the reasons and arguments presented in the article?

   When making this judgment, given that you only have one article, be sure to consider what information is missing that would be helpful for assessing the claim.

ENDNOTES

1. Yahoo, "10 Most Violent Games Named," http://videogames. yahoo.com/newsarticle?eid =416427 (accessed May 26, 2010).

   Teambox: "Family Media Guide Identifies Top 10 Ultra Violent Games" http://news.teamxbox.com/xbox/9826/ Family-Media-Guide-Identifies-Top-10-Ultra-Violent-Games/

   Gamespot:10 Most Violent Games Named: http://www .gamespot.com/news/6140463.html

2. Craig A. Anderson, "Violent Video Games: Myths, Facts, and Unanswered Questions," *American Psychological Association,* available at http://www.apa.org/science/about/psa/2003/10/ anderson.aspx

3. Ibid.

4. "Youth Violence: A Report of the Surgeon General–Appendix 4-B," available at http://www.surgeongeneral. gov/library/youthviolence/chapter4/appendix4bsec2. html#ViolenceOtherMedia.

5. For more information about the effect size of smoking, see Mark Battersby, *Is That a Fact?* (Peterborough ON: Broadview, 2009).

6. For a detailed discussion of the complex issues of explanation in social sciences, see Stanford Encyclo-paedia of Philosophy, "Methodological Individualism," rev. Mar. 12, 2009, http://plato.stanford.edu/entries/ methodological-individualism.

7. To learn more about Médecins Sans Frontières, go to their website at http://www.msf.org/.

8. See *Wikipedia,* "Social Darwinism," http://en.wikipedia.org/ wiki/Social_Darwinism, for a description of the history of the idea.

9. Ibid.

10. Juanita's version of all these theories is quite simplified, but in the case of Locke especially so, since his theory of "blank slate" was really about how we didn't know anything at birth and learned everything from experience. But the phrase "blank slate" has come down to us as meaning that humans have little or no innate nature. See *The Blank Slate* by Steven Pinker (Toronto: Penguin, 2002).

11. Jane Allyn Piliavin and Hong-Wen Charng, "Altruism: A Review of Recent Theory and Research," *Annual Review of Sociology* 16 (1990): 27–65.

12. J. Henrich, R. Boyd, S. Bowles, H. Gintis, E. Fehr, and C. Camerer, *Foundations of Human Sociality: Ethnography and Experiments in 15 Small-scale Societies* (Toronto: Oxford University Press, 2004).

13. There is considerable work being done in "behavioural eco-nomics" in an attempt to ground economic theorizing in a more accurate view of human motivation and behaviour. For example, see Dan Ariely, *Predictably Irrational* (New York: HarperCollins, 2009) and Ariely's website at http://www.predictablyirrational.com. See also the references at *Wikipedia,* "Behavioral Economics," http:// en.wikipedia.org/wiki/Behavioral_economics#cite_note-16 (accessed Dec. 28, 2009).

Chapter 14
Inquiry in the Arts

Learning Objectives

After reading this chapter, you should be able to:

- apply the guiding questions to inquiries about works of art
- apply appropriate criteria to the interpretation of works of art
- make critical judgments about the value of works of art
- evaluate disputes regarding controversial works of public art

Guernica

Camillia Bell is taking a group of students through a new, and very special, travelling art exhibition. Present are Ahmed, Juanita, Lester, Winnie, Phil, and Stephen. The group comes across a painting, a very large canvass that takes up a whole wall (see next page).

Phil: This is the famous painting that we all came here to see? You've got to be kidding! It's just a bunch of weird sketchy shapes and figures.

Stephen: Yeah—they don't look at all like real people.

Ahmed: It looks a lot like my little brother's drawings, the ones that we have on the fridge.

Juanita: You guys just don't appreciate art. I love it!

Ahmed: Why?

Juanita: It blows me away! I can't explain why—you can't explain these things.

Winnie: I think that a painting either grabs you or it doesn't. Art's like that. It's all a matter of taste, just like food.

Phil: Well, for me this one goes in the category of broccoli.

Ahmed: Hey, guys, have a look at this one.

(Ahmed points to a painting on the opposite wall.)

Now this I can understand. It looks like a real scene with real people. I can see why folks think this is good. But I don't really understand why the other one is so famous. The guy can't even draw.

Lester : Well, I'm very struck by the painting, though I don't know enough about it to really judge. But experts who know a lot about art think it's pretty special.

Ahmed: But how can we make sense of it? How do we know if it's any good?

Camillia: You're all asking really great questions. It shows you're thinking about the artworks and reacting to them. Art should make you think and react. And your first reactions to the painting are important. But it is possible to go beyond your initial impressions, to try to make sense of the painting and consider its value.

Ahmed: Ah . . . so you're going to tell us what this painting means and why everyone thinks it's so great?

Camillia: Not quite. But what I can do, if you'd like, is give you some guidance and resources for investigating these questions yourself.

Winnie: You mean we're going to do an inquiry about this painting? I didn't think you could inquire about the arts—beauty in the eye of the beholder and all that.

Phil: Well, I'm sure game to try!

Others: Sure, let's have a go!

What Do You Think ?

What is your initial impression of the first painting?

The students have come across an artwork that is challenging. It is not representational in any obvious way and they are puzzled as to what to make of it. Why is it painted the way it is? What does it mean? Why do experts value it so highly? How can they know if it is any good?

Most of the students have strong reactions, either positive or negative; but they don't know how to get beyond their initial impressions. Some of them, in fact, believe that this is not possible, that art is purely subjective, that "beauty is in the eye of the beholder."

It is true that, in the case of works of art, our personal, subjective reactions are important and should not be overlooked. It is, however, also possible to investigate, to find out more about a work and its context, be it a painting, a play, a dance, or a piece of music, and to make reasoned judgments about the work. And our reactions to a work may change in the process. Art can be the subject of inquiry in much the same way as science, politics, or issues in daily life. Although there are important differences among these various sorts of inquiries, there are important similarities as well, as we shall see.

Applying the Guiding Questions to Inquiry about Works of Art

Phil: So how we do start?

Juanita: Since we're conducting an inquiry, why don't we see if we can use the "guiding questions for inquiry" that we've learned?

What Is the Issue? What Kinds of Claims or Judgments Are at Issue?

Ahmed: OK. So what's the issue? And what kinds of claims or judgments are we trying to make?

What is the issue? What kinds of claims or judgments are at issue?

What Do
You Think **?**

Winnie: I can see two main questions that we're wanting to answer: what does the painting mean, and is it any good?

Lester: Right. Now as to the kinds of judgments that we want to make ... For the first question, we're asking what the painting means, so I guess we'll need to make an interpretive judgment.

Winnie: And for the second question, we're going to try to evaluate whether the painting is any good, so we'll need to make an aesthetic judgment.

What Are the Relevant Reasons and Arguments on Various Sides of the Issue?

Juanita: And now we have the guiding question about the reasons on various sides of the issue.

Phil: This is the part where we go off to do research. So it's time to hit the library, folks.

Lester: Yeah, we need to see how the experts have interpreted the painting and why they think it's good—or not.

Camillia: For our inquiry about the painting, I'm going to ask you to begin with a different kind of research: observation. I would like you to start by examining the painting closely yourselves to see what *you* can see in the painting. Try to come up with some of your own hypotheses about what the painting means based on what you observe. At that point, we'll be ready to do external research about what others have said about the work.

Ahmed: So why shouldn't we just go straight to the experts right away? Why bother with this observation stuff? I mean, what do we know?

Camillia: It's a good idea to observe first because art is meant to be looked at and engaged with. Sometimes when viewers go directly to outside information, they never really look at the work closely or get involved with it. And they may never try to interpret the work themselves or make their own judgments; instead, they just depend on what others say. It is important to gather additional information to help you, but it's best to do so after you've had the chance to begin to interact with the painting on your own terms.

The students have discovered that they can use the same structure of inquiry as they have used to guide their inquiries in other areas. There is a slight difference in that Camillia has asked them to leave their outside research until later and to begin with more direct, observational research. Many teachers of art appreciation recommend this approach because it fosters an early and direct interaction with an artwork. The viewer is encouraged to observe the details of the work, to think, and to raise questions. It is important not to bypass this process of personal engagement by immediately depending on outside sources for one's interpretation and judgments, since you may then end up never really thinking about and engaging with the work. And ultimately, art is to be engaged with and appreciated by each individual viewer.

Camillia has also asked the students to generate hypotheses based on their observations. This process of observation and generating hypotheses based on the evidence is one we associate most commonly with science, but we can see that it also plays a role in art appreciation. The process is not limited to works of visual art but can also be applied to novels, poems, musical works—in fact, to works of any artistic genre.

The kinds of resources for inquiry we've seen before have been largely outside resources, from books and the internet. But as we can see in this case, a person can also be a resource. Someone with expertise in an area can act as a mentor to guide participants and direct them to various aspects and other resources, as Camillia is doing in this inquiry.

Observation

Camillia: Let's start with what's written on the sign beside the painting.

Juanita: *Guernica*, Pablo Picasso, 1937.

Phil: Picasso—I've certainly heard the name but can't say as I know anything about him. But the word "Guernica" doesn't really mean anything to me.

Camillia: We'll come back to that. But for now, let's turn to the painting itself. In order to really observe carefully, I would like you to try and describe exactly what you see in the painting in as much detail as possible.

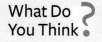
What Do You Think?

Describe the painting in as much detail as you can. Describe only what you see.

Phil: OK, I'll have a go. There's been this alien invasion, and all the people and animals are misshapen because of this invisible particle-melting gas that the aliens have sprayed over everything and they're running away from—

Juanita: You've been watching too many horror movies, Phil.

Camillia: You've come up with an interesting interpretation, Phil. But at this stage, let's leave interpretation aside and try to simply describe what we see. What objects can you identify?

Ahmed: Well, I can see some people—mostly women—a few animals, and what I think is a statue.

Camillia: Let's try to describe them in more detail.

Juanita: Well, on the left I see a woman with her head tilted back and her mouth open. It looks to me like she's screaming. She's holding a baby. The way it's lying with its head back makes me think it might be sick—or even dead.

Lester: Just behind the woman there's a large bull. It's in a strange position, with its body facing toward the centre, but its head facing the other away.

Ahmed: Oh yeah, so it is. I hadn't noticed that.

Winnie: In the centre, there's this horse. Its head is raised up and its mouth is open. It almost looks to me like it's screaming too.

Phil: And look! There's something sticking into the horse's body—looks like some kind of knife or dagger. So maybe that's why he's screaming.

Ahmed: Good eyes, Phil. I didn't even see the dagger.

Juanita: Above the horse's head, there's a light of some sort. A light bulb? Or maybe the sun?

Lester: And I see a bird to the right of the bull's head. I think he's flying toward the light.

Stephen: I thought he was sitting on a roof.

Ahmed: I didn't even see him!

Winnie: On the top toward the right, there's a woman holding a lamp leaning out of a window. And to the right of her, there's another woman. It looks like her clothes are burning; in fact, I would say that the whole building's on fire.

Juanita: Just below the woman with the lamp, there's another woman who seems to be rushing towards the left.

Phil: Along the bottom, below the bull, there's this figure, or at least its head and arms. It's like parts of a person—or maybe a statue. It has what looks like a broken sword in its hand, so maybe it's a statue of a warrior.

Winnie: I just noticed something else. There's a flower growing out of the warrior's sword.

Lester: Hey guys, have a look at this! If you look really closely at the horse's head, you can see a skull formed by the horse's nose and upper teeth.

Ahmed: No way! That's really cool! You know, I have to admit that I couldn't really see the point of all this observation stuff when we started. But others are pointing out things in the painting that I didn't notice. So now we know that we're all seeing the same thing, so to speak.

This process of describing a work in detail has an important point, as Ahmed has realized. It slows down the tendency to jump to conclusions (as Phil was beginning to do with his aliens interpretation) and allows viewers time to see as much as can be seen before deciding about meaning and worth. It also promotes agreement among the viewers as to what they are looking at and gives them a store of visual facts which will form the basis for interpretation and critical judgment.

Camillia: So far, we've been looking at the content of the painting—what objects and actions you're able to identify. But we have to remember that an artist chooses to paint the content in a certain way. He or she uses lines, shapes, colours, patterns, and relationships to create certain effects, and knowing something about those choices can also help us to understand the work.

What do you notice about the way that the artist uses colours, lines, shapes, and patterns in the painting?

What Do You Think ?

Camillia: Let's start with basic things like the size of the painting.

Ahmed: It's huge! I'd say about 3.5 metres high, and probably over 7 metres long.

Camillia: How is it made? What media are used?

Lester: Oil paint on canvass, as far as I can tell.

Camillia: What about colour?

Stephen: It doesn't really have any colour to speak of—only black and white, and shades of grey.

Camillia: What do you notice about the style of this painting?

Phil: The people and animals don't look like real people and animals. They're sort of…I don't know…weird and distorted—kind of like cartoon characters.

Camillia: Can you say more about how they're different?

Winnie: Well, the faces are just shapes, really. And everything looks kind of flat.

Lester: That's because there's no shading or perspective.

Camillia: Maybe you need to explain that, Lester.

Lester: Sure, Mom. Artists use perspective to give a realistic sense of space—the way objects look to the eye. Painters have known how to do this since the 1400s, so this painter must have chosen not to use it.

Winnie: Something else I'm noticing is that the painting seems very busy. The whole canvass seems to be filled up. There's hardly any blank space anywhere.

Phil: There's something that's kind of weird going on here. I know that this is just a painting and doesn't have any moving parts. But I get the feeling that everyone and everything's rushing toward the left.

Camillia: Why do you think that is? What is there in the painting that creates that impression?

Phil: Well, most of the people and animals are facing toward the left—even the bull, although his body faces right. And then there's that woman on the bottom right who seems to be running toward the left. And the woman with the light whose arm is stretched way out in that direction. They all seem to create a feeling of movement.

Juanita: You mentioned shapes and patterns, Ms. Bell. I can see some shapes that are repeated in the painting. Like the heads of the woman with the light and the woman below her, which are the same shape. And then there are the two women with their heads back, screaming, one on the far right and one on the far left.

Lester: They seem to frame the painting and give it balance.

Winnie: You know, I always just thought about art in terms of how it affects us and whether someone likes a painting or not. I never really thought very much about how an artist uses lines and shapes and colour and patterns to create those effects. It makes you look at the painting in a different way.

A work of art is more than its content, as Camillia points out. The artist makes deliberate choices in terms of materials and techniques to express what he or she wants to express in a particular form. And works of art will affect us because of the ways in which the artist has used the elements and principles of art to create the desired effects. In addition to subject matter, paintings have a style and an organization; and they make use of principles such as balance, repetition, and movement to do their work. Having some understanding of these elements, principles, and techniques can give the viewer another way into the artwork and another avenue for interpretation and judgment.

Apply Your Understanding Exercise 1

Interpretation

Ahmed: OK, we've done all this observation stuff—which I have to admit was pretty interesting. But when do we get to the part where we find out what it all means? What is this painting all about?

Camillia: What do you think it's about, now that you've had a good look at it?

Phil: So it's time to generate some hypotheses?

Camillia: Yes, indeed. Let's start with the mood or atmosphere.

Winnie: It's pretty bleak and horrible.

Camillia: Why do you say that?

Winnie: Well, the colours for one thing. It's very dark, all black and white and grey—not exactly your bright happy colours.

Lester: The use of black and white makes it very stark—and dramatic.

Winnie: And everything in the painting is so crammed together, with all the space used up. It feels very chaotic.

Camillia: What feelings or emotions do you see in the painting?

Juanita: Fear. And pain—terrible pain.

Ahmed: Violence and suffering.

Camillia: What do you see in the painting that makes you say that?

Juanita: The women on the far right and far left are both screaming in agony. And so is the horse. The other characters all have these anguished looks on their faces.

Winnie: And there's a woman on fire and an injured or dead baby.

Stephen: And a dagger and sword.

Lester: And don't forget the skull, which represents death.

Camillia: Is there a story being told in the painting?

Phil: There's been this alien invasion and all the people and animals—

Juanita: Oh Phil, there you go again.

Camillia: No, let's listen to Phil's interpretation. Phil, what do you see in the painting that makes you say that?

Phil: Well, you can see that something horrible and violent has happened because there are buildings on fire, people and animals have been injured or killed, and folks are scared and are screaming and crying—just like the others said. And I also think that the people are running away from something, probably something that's on the right because there's this sense of movement that we talked about.

Ahmed: I'm with you so far, Phil. But what about the aliens?

Phil: I'm getting to that. So I think, what are they running away from? And it reminded me of this horror movie I saw the other night where this band of extraterrestrials from the planet Zork landed on earth and—

Juanita: We get the idea, Phil.

Ahmed: Sorry Phil, but I don't think I buy it. First of all, I don't think that they knew anything about particle-melting gas in 1937.

Winnie: And besides, we can see things like flames and a sword and a dagger which would suggest some other explanations for the destruction and suffering, like a fire or a war. And these seem more likely explanations than the alien bit.

Juanita: I have to agree with the others, Phil. I don't see anything in the painting that would suggest an alien invasion.

Phil: But then why are all the people misshapen? I thought that the particle-melting gas was a great explanation.

Lester: It's my guess that the artist wasn't trying to make the figures look realistic. Not all art is realistic. I suspect that he had some reason to choose this particular style. I'm looking forward to finding out more about that when we do our research.

Ahmed : So we all seem to agree that the painting is about violence and suffering—probably war.

Stephen: If so, it's a pretty grim picture of war—none of those glorious war heroes.

Lester: The fact that the sword is broken and that there's a flower growing out of it would support the idea that the painting may be some kind of anti-war statement.

Juanita: Yeah, and the woman with the light might symbolize someone trying to find some hope in the situation.

Ahmed: But I'm wondering about the bull. What's he doing there, and why is he standing in that weird position?

Winnie: The bull makes me think of bullfights. And I know that Picasso was Spanish so that would fit.

Phil: But he doesn't look like one of those charging bulls about to stick it to the matador. In fact, he looks kind of sad to me.

Ahmed: But why is he folded over?

Juanita: It seems like he's turned away from the horrible scene—like he can't bear to look at it.

Lester: It looks to me like he's protecting the woman and baby.

Phil: I'm wondering about why the artist made the painting so enormous. It's sure not your average hang-over-the-sofa picture. I guess he thought he was making a statement about something big and important and that it deserved a lot of space.

Juanita: He must have wanted it to have a big impact (which it does).

Ahmed: OK, we've made all these hypotheses about what the painting means. Now do we get to find out if we're right?

Juanita: And if we are right that the painting expresses some sort of anti-war sentiment, then I'd like to know why the painter was moved to paint about this.

Phil: If Lester's right that Picasso chose to do the painting in this strange kind of style, then I would really like to know why.

Camillia: I think it's time now to move on to do some research about the artist and the context in which the painting was done so that you can try to answer those questions. There's an excellent resource collection on the main floor of the gallery with books, slides, videos, and internet resources. I think you'll find what you need there for your research.

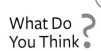

What do you think the students need to find out in order to answer their questions?

At this stage in the process, the students are beginning to apply what they learned from their observations to the task of interpretation—the task of trying to make sense of the painting and understand what it might mean. All artworks are about something, although what they are about may not always be immediately obvious. They may deal with subject matter or issues external to the work—for example, social issues in the culture such as war or poverty. They may have as their focus issues specific to the artist such as personal struggles or psychological traumas. But artworks can also be about form, about experimenting with colour or line or technique. Much modern abstract art would fall into this category. And art is sometimes about other art, reacting to or commenting on other artworks or types of art. Some artworks are immediately accessible to most people while others are highly intellectual and may require more external knowledge for their interpretation.

You may begin the process of interpretation with your initial impressions, forming hypotheses on the basis of observations, then checking the interpretations against the evidence to see which hypotheses provide the best explanation of the evidence. This is the process that the students are using, and it has aspects in common with scientific inquiry (argument to the best explanation).

It is important to recognize that there can be a number of reasonable interpretations of the same artwork. Art is complex and ambiguous by its nature, engaging us by giving us the opportunity to think and imagine. It is not the case that there is just one and only one correct interpretation of a work. There may be several interpretations that are equally supported by the evidence, both observational and contextual. Having multiple interpretations is, in fact, a positive aspect since it is likely that no one interpretation will be exhaustive of the meaning of an artwork. Thus there is a communal aspect to interpreting an artwork as a group of people observing and discussing a work together can pool and debate their interpretations, as our students do, in order to delve more deeply into the meaning of the work.

Nonetheless, not all interpretations are equally valid. Some are more reasonable, convincing, enlightening, or informative than others. The main criteria that are often used to judge the validity of an interpretation are correspondence, inclusiveness, and coherence. Correspondence means that the interpretation corresponds with or matches what we can see in the artwork and what we know about the context. Inclusiveness means that the interpretation accounts for all the evidence and doesn't leave out any troublesome aspects that don't fit the interpretation. Coherence refers to the idea that all aspects of the interpretation fit together and that the interpretation makes sense as a whole. We can see these criteria at work as the students generate various hypotheses about the meaning of *Guernica* and as they provide evidence to support their interpretations, encouraged by Camillia's constant refrain, "What do you see in the painting that makes you say that?"

Let's consider the interpretation which Phil offers for *Guernica* in order to illustrate in more detail how these criteria operate. First, it is important to note that many aspects of Phil's interpretation are justifiable according to the evidence in the painting. The idea that something violent has occurred, that people are suffering and frightened, and that they are running away from something all correspond to aspects that can be observed. Another point in favour of Phil's interpretation is that it does seem to be coherent in and of itself.

There are several ways in which Phil's interpretation goes off the rails, however. The most notable way is that his thesis that there has been an alien attack is not supported by any evidence whatsoever in the painting. His interpretation is not inclusive in that it leaves out aspects such as the dagger and the broken sword. In addition, his idea about particle-melting gas does not fit with what we know about the historical period nor does it take into

Keep in Mind

CRITERIA FOR JUDGING THE VALIDITY OF AN INTERPRETATION

- correspondence—interpretation corresponds with features of the artwork and with context
- inclusiveness—interpretation accounts for all the evidence
- coherence—aspects of interpretation fit together

account the fact that there may be a different and better explanation of the manner of portrayal in terms of a non-representational artistic style.

At this point, our students have come up with various interpretations of *Guernica*, both as a whole and in terms of individual elements, based on their observations of the painting itself, and they have supported them with evidence from the work. It is now time for them to do some outside research and gather information about the historical, political, and artistic contexts in order to take their inquiry further.

What Is the Context of the Issue?

Phil: Well, I now know what the title, *Guernica*, refers to. It seems that on April 26, 1937, during the Spanish Civil War, the Nazi air force bombed the Spanish town of Guernica. They say that the attack killed as many as 1600 people, and that lots more were injured.

Winnie: I read that Picasso had been commissioned to paint a mural for Spain's building at the Paris World Fair. He had some other ideas in mind for the mural; but when the attack happened, he changed his plans and painted the bombing of Guernica instead.

Ahmed: So we were right about the painting being about war.

Stephen: But we didn't know any details about the war or its context.

Juanita: The event was obviously very significant to him for it to be the inspiration for such an important mural. I wonder why. Did anyone find out anything more about the Spanish Civil War and Picasso's view of it?

Lester: I did. The Spanish Civil War was a major conflict that took place in Spain from 1936 to 1939. Nationalist rebels, led by General Francisco Franco, who was a fascist, were attempting to overthrow the Republican government. The German Nazis were Franco's allies. The Nationalists won in the end and founded a dictatorship led by Franco.

Winnie: Apparently, the bombing of Guernica was a particularly horrible act. The village didn't have any strategic value, but it did have historical significance and was the cultural capital of the Basque people. The Nazi air force devastated the town, dumping 100 000 pounds of high explosives and incendiary bombs on it. They massacred huge numbers of civilians. The bombing of Guernica was seen as a symbol of the brutality of Franco and his Nazi allies. Picasso was very much opposed to Franco and to the fascists.

Juanita: We can certainly see in the painting how strong his feelings were against the war and the bombing.

Phil: I read that Picasso was so much against the fascists that after Franco won, he loaned *Guernica* to the Museum of Modern Art in New York, and specified that the work could only go back to Spain if democracy returned. Spain became a democracy again in 1978, and the painting went back to Spain in 1981.

Ahmed: You know, I have to admit that looking at the painting really carefully and trying to come up with our own interpretations really got me into the painting. And I'm impressed with all the ideas we could come up with before we even knew anything about it. But now that I know all these details about when and why it was painted and what was going on at that time, I can get a lot more out of it.

Juanita: Yeah, it's like I can really understand now how awful the event was and how devastated Picasso must have felt about it.

Lester: But the painting's about more than the bombing of Guernica. I think that Picasso's also making a comment on the brutality and inhumanity of the fascists.

Winnie: It was really important to know something about the history and about Picasso's political views in order to understand that.

Ahmed: I was really wanting to find out more about this Picasso guy so I concentrated my research on him. Listen to this: Pablo Diego José Francisco de Paula Juan Nepomuceno María de los Remedios Cipriano de la Santísima Trinidad Martyr Patricio Clito Ruíz y Picasso (no, I'm not kidding) was born in 1881 in Malaga, Spain, and died in France in 1973. His father was a painter and young Pablo Diego José got a pretty heavy-duty and traditional art training from a very young age. In fact, he actually became a master of the realistic style. And—get this, folks—you know that painting of the communion scene we saw earlier on (with the girl in the white dress kneeling) that I thought was so good—*that* was actually painted by Picasso, too!

Phil: So he sure did know how to draw!

Ahmed: And how! He went through a number of different styles after his realistic period: the Blue Period (mostly gloomy paintings in blues and greens); the Rose Period (more cheery paintings in oranges and pinks); the African-influenced period, when his work was starting to get less realistic; and then cubism.

Lester: Ah, cubism. I've been reading a lot about that (and seeing a lot of slides). It seems that the artists of this period were moving away from the idea that art should be realistic and copy nature. They were starting to reject the traditional techniques of perspective that I was talking about before. Apparently, they were trying to emphasize the idea that a painting is a human construction and that a canvas really has only two dimensions. So, instead of trying to create an illusion of three dimensions, they broke objects up into geometric forms and re-assembled them in abstract ways. It's like they were focusing on what we know about objects rather than on how we perceive them. Cubist paintings let us see an object from several different angles all at the same time. *Guernica* wasn't strictly a cubist painting, though; it was done after Picasso's cubist period.

What are some of the cubist influences that you notice in Guernica?

What Do You Think ?

Winnie: But you can see elements that come from cubism. The painting's not done in a realistic style. There's certainly no illusion of copying nature. The people and animals are mostly shapes, as we said before; and their bodies seem to be made up of separate pieces.

Phil: So I guess Lester was right that Picasso was actually aiming to paint like this. But why? I would think that an artist would want to make things look realistic.

Can you think of any reason why some artists might not want their paintings to look realistic?

What Do You Think ?

Camillia: If you look at art throughout history and in other locales, it becomes evident that art hasn't always been focused on realistic representation. In medieval Europe, for example, paintings were made to inspire religious devotion and not to glorify the things of "this world," and so the placement and size of characters were determined by their importance in the religious hierarchy, not by how they would actually look. The kind of representational art that we're so used to seeing really only became prominent in the Italian Renaissance in the 1400s, and it started to change again in the late 1800s and early 1900s. Did anyone find anything out about why the arts were moving away from representation during Picasso's period?

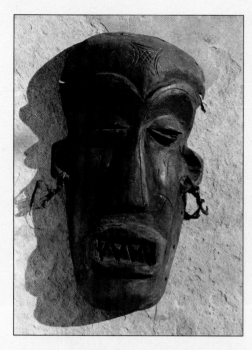

Lester: I did. I read in several places that a key factor was the rising importance of photography. After all, a photograph is a much better and more realistic representation of nature than any painting could be. So painting was left to find a different purpose.

Juanita: I also read that Picasso was very influenced by seeing Iberian sculptures and artifacts from Greece, Africa, and the South Pacific. Apparently the geometric features, the long noses and flattened, sunken faces in many of his paintings were inspired by these masks and sculptures which were very different from Western realistic sculptures. Have a look at this picture I found. The resemblance is pretty amazing.

Winnie: Well, I was interested to find out how the art critics interpreted the painting.

Ahmed: At last, we get to see if we were right!

Winnie: It's not quite that straightforward, Ahmed. Everyone seems to agree that the painting is a statement about the horrors of war, so we were right on that count. But they also see it as a symbol for the Spanish people of their liberation from oppression, and that's something that we couldn't know without knowing about the background of the painting. But there is some disagreement amongst the experts about some of symbolism in the painting. Some of them see the bull as representing aggression (in this case, the aggressive fascist state); and some see it as a victim of violence (here, the suffering Spanish people). And the horse with the dagger has been interpreted as either Franco's regime and its inevitable downfall, or as the Spanish people dying a senseless death. But both sides offer evidence from the painting for their interpretations, just as we did.

Ahmed: So we were doing what the critics do. How about that!

While the value of careful observation and initial reactions and interpretations has been evident in the dialogue, we have also seen that in the end it is difficult to interpret an artwork with any depth or accuracy without knowing about the context in which the work was developed. Knowledge of the historical and political circumstances surrounding a work can give us access to meaning in a way which is not possible without it. (This type of knowledge will be more important for some works than for others.) In the case of *Guernica*, for example, knowledge about the Spanish Civil War, the bombing of Guernica, and the fascist regime allows us to understand the events, emotions, and comments that are being expressed in this painting.

Knowledge about the artist, his or her personal and artistic history as well as social, political, and artistic views, can help us to understand what he or she is trying to express or accomplish in an artwork. In the case of *Guernica*, knowledge of Picasso's political views can give us insight into the meaning of the work. And an understanding of Picasso's cubist and post-cubist styles is indispensable in understanding why the painting is painted in the way that it is and in preventing misunderstandings of the type to which Phil fell victim.

Apply Your Understanding Exercise 2

Understanding a work of art also involves understanding something about where the work fits into the history of art. It is important to recognize that art has a history and that its aims as well as its styles have changed and developed over time. Art changes in response to what is going on in the world as well as in response to what has come before it artistically. Some works only make sense when seen in this context. In the case of *Guernica*, understanding the state of the visual arts at the time and the factors influencing its development (i.e., the development of photography, an exposure to non-Western art) can help us to understand the departure from realism that Picasso's work exemplified.

How Do We Comparatively Evaluate the Various Reasons and Arguments to Reach a Reasoned Judgment?

Phil: We've considered our first question—what does the painting mean? But what about our second question—is it any good?

Ahmed: So is this where we get to see what the experts say?

Juanita: I don't know if we should be relying totally on experts for our judgments. After all, why did we do all this inquiry if we're just going to end up repeating what others say?

Stephen: These are people who have spent their whole lives studying art, so they should know what they're talking about. It should be worth listening to what they have to say.

Lester: I think it's important to know what they have to say, but also why. Why do so many art critics value *Guernica* so highly? We need to know the reasons behind their judgments and what criteria they're using. Then we can evaluate their reasons plus our thoughts and reactions and come to our own judgments.

Camillia: What did you find out about the critical judgments of the art critics? What criteria were they using, and what criteria do you think are appropriate?

What criteria do you think are appropriate for evaluating works of art?

What Do You Think ?

Juanita: My mom judges a painting by whether it goes with the sofa. Somehow I don't think that's an appropriate criterion.

Phil: And anyway, *Guernica* wouldn't fit over anyone's sofa!

Lester: The influence that a work has on the arts was one criterion that quite a number of the critics I read used. In that context, they talked about the major influence that Picasso's work had on the history of art. It seems that it changed the direction of art, revolutionizing painting and sculpture all over Europe, America, and Russia. It also inspired related movements in architecture, literature, and music.

Phil: So *Guernica* certainly was original.

Winnie: Uh-huh. I read that one of the big accomplishments of the painting was that it took traditional themes which had been prominent in previous paintings but reworked them to make them modern and relevant to a new time and context.

Phil: I also found out that cubism has had a strong impact on the culture in general, beyond the arts. You can find cubist-type images all over the place—for example, in ads.

Ahmed: And Picasso's name is certainly well known (well, maybe not his whole name). For instance, my mom always says to my little brother when he does his drawings, "I think we have a little Picasso on our hands."

Juanita: The painting was certainly important for the people of Spain, as a kind of symbol of their culture and their liberation.

Lester: But it also has a wider significance. It's become an international symbol of the horrors of war.

Juanita: That's all very fine. But I think that an artwork has to affect people emotionally. *Guernica* blew me away from the first moment I saw it. That's got to be important when we're talking about whether a work of art is any good.

Phil: Well, I didn't like it at the beginning. But I am kind of warming to it now.

Lester: I don't think it's just a question of whether one person likes it or doesn't (although that obviously matters to the person). If a work of art is going to be considered good, then it needs to affect many people over a long period of time. And *Guernica* has certainly done that.

Winnie: I don't think that it's enough that people have an emotional reaction. We should also learn something from a painting or other artwork, something important for the culture or for humanity, like the horror of war. A really good artwork should get people to see things differently, and maybe want to change things.

Ahmed: From all the observing and discussion that we did, I can see that this painting really got us to exercise our imagination—Phil especially! We sure talked about the painting for a long time, and we came up with lots of interesting ideas.

Camillia: Perhaps we can summarize the criteria we've come up with and then see how *Guernica* fairs overall.

Lester: Well, there's the influence on the history of art.

Winnie: The impact on the culture.

Keep in Mind

CRITERIA FOR EVALUATING AN ARTWORK

- influence on the history of art
- impact on the culture
- originality
- eliciting an emotional reaction
- withstanding the "test of time"
- expressing important ideas or values
- encouraging imagination
- skilful execution

Phil: Originality.

Juanita: Whether it provokes an emotional reaction.

Lester: Whether a work withstands the "test of time."

Winnie: Expressing important ideas or values.

Ahmed: Encouraging imagination.

Phil: I have to admit that *Guernica* stacks up really well on all those counts.

Others: Agreed.

Phil: But I do have one negative. The painting is really hard to understand. Remember my first reaction? I wouldn't have given it a second glance if Ms. Bell hadn't encouraged us to inquire about it. You really need to look at the painting very carefully, to think a lot about it, and find out lots of information in order to be able to understand what it's all about and appreciate it.

Winnie: But is that really a negative? Why should we think that an artwork needs to be easy to understand at first glance to be any good? We learned so much from all the observation and research and discussion, and we were able to appreciate the painting in real depth. I don't think that "easy to understand" should be one of our criteria for the worth of an artwork.

Phil: You might be right. But what about if there was this painting that you couldn't understand even after doing all the observation and research? If it was so "way out there" that it was impossible to understand except by a few people in the know. I would think that that would be a negative.

Winnie: Maybe you have a point there. My dad always complains that contemporary "new" music is like that.

What Do You Think ?

Is the fact that an artwork is difficult to understand a negative point in evaluating the work?

Ahmed: While we're on the negatives, it doesn't seem to me that a painting like *Guernica* requires as much skill to paint as some of the other paintings in the gallery that actually resemble people and scenes. I was really surprised to find out that Picasso did that communion painting that we saw earlier. You would never know it from looking at *Guernica*. I would think that skill should be a factor for judging.

Lester: I agree that a painting that we consider good should be done with skill. But *Guernica* has a different purpose and is done in a different style than those paintings you're referring to, and it demonstrates skill in a different way.

Ahmed: OK, but I still think that it's somehow more impressive to be able to paint in that realistic style.

Camillia: Fair enough. So how do you think *Guernica* "stacks up" overall?

Ahmed: Well, I think that my complaint is a relatively minor one in the grand scheme of things. I have to agree that by all the other criteria, *Guernica* is a slam-dunk.

Phil: Yeah, I'll buy that.

Having explored the question of interpretation, the group now turns to the question of critical judgment: Is the painting any good? In their research, the students have discovered what art critics have had to say about *Guernica*. While the views of those who have a great deal of expertise should carry some weight, the students realize that they should not simply rely on the judgments of others. It is important to know their reasons, however, as Lester realizes. Laying out the various reasons is a prelude to making a reasoned judgment in light of the context. Another requirement for making a reasoned judgment is knowing what criteria are appropriate, and the reasons offered by the critics are a good source of appropriate criteria for judgments about artistic worth.

It is important to determine which criteria are most appropriate for judging the particular artwork under discussion.

The criteria suggested fall into different categories. Some of the criteria, such as provoking an emotional reaction, encouraging imagination, or accessibility, focus on the audience and its reception of the work. Other criteria, such as skilful execution or originality, relate primarily to features of the work itself. Still others, such as the influence on art history or impact on the culture, focus on the influence of the work on external circumstances.

Not all criteria are equally relevant for judging every work, however. The criteria used must be appropriate to the purposes and genre of the work. For example, it would be inappropriate to judge *Guernica* by the criteria of accurate representation which are appropriate for realistic works, as Lester points out to Ahmed. Nor is dealing with a socially significant theme a relevant criterion for judging abstract works since they tend to have as their purpose experimentation with form rather than the expression of an external theme. Thus it is important to determine which criteria are most appropriate for judging the particular artwork under discussion.

Apply Your Understanding Exercise 3

In order to come to a reasoned judgment about the quality of the artwork, you must determine what evidence there is in the work and in the information about context that relates to each criterion, and then you have to comparatively evaluate the various reasons and evidence. The *Guernica* case is not overly contentious because of the sheer weight of positive critical judgments supported by considerable compelling evidence, as compared with very few negative critical judgments.

Phil does raise a negative point regarding the accessibility of the painting, and the issue of whether and to what extent this is a problem was the subject of some debate. Thus the appropriateness of the criterion he is using is up for discussion. Ahmed also expresses a reservation, in this case regarding the level of skill exhibited by the painting. Ahmed is drawing on what is generally considered to be a legitimate and important criterion of artistic worth. Lester disagrees with Ahmed's judgment, however, arguing that it is based on a misunderstanding about the nature of the genre. Thus he is disagreeing, not with the criterion, but with the evidence offered related to the criterion.

It may also be the case that Ahmed's judgment is based, at least in part, on a personal preference—he may simply not like non-realistic painting. But liking is not the same as critical judgment (Juanita's mother may not want to hang a particular painting over her sofa, but she still might recognize that it's a good work). In the end, Ahmed does concede that, given the weight of evidence, his was a relatively minor consideration.

In order to come to a reasoned judgment about the quality of an artwork, you must determine what evidence there is in the work and in the information about context that relates to each criterion and then comparatively evaluate the various reasons and evidence.

"The Meat Dress"[1]

One particularly controversial artwork is the sculpture, *Vanitas: Flesh Dress for an Albino Anorectic,* which was acquired by the National Gallery of Canada in 1991. The sculpture consists of 50 pounds of salted, pounded raw steak stitched together in the form of a dress. The artist, Jana Sterbak, claims that the sculpture deals with issues of power, sexuality, control, and mortality; but the work has provoked outrage from politicians, food-aid agencies, and the general public, some of whom have sent food scraps to the Gallery in protest.

There is a great deal of consensus around the importance of *Guernica,* but judgments regarding other artworks may be more contentious. In order to come to a critical judgment in such cases, it will be especially important to lay out the reasons on various sides and be clear about the criteria appealed to by the various critics. It will also be important to determine which criteria are most appropriate to the particular work, and which of these criteria should be given the most weight given the specifics of the work. In this regard, a knowledge of the context of the debate surrounding the work and its artistic history may provide information relevant to its evaluation. Knowing something about the purpose of a work and the artistic background to which it is responding can put us in a better position to choose among competing judgments. For example, in trying to make a critical judgment about an artwork such as artist Jana Sterbak's *Vanitas: Flesh Dress for an Albino Anorectic* (see the feature box above), it is extremely helpful to understand something about the anti-aesthetic orientation, the rejection of traditional artistic materials and standards, and the blurring of the boundaries between art and life characteristic of much contemporary art.

Apply Your Understanding Exercise 4

The aspects of critical judgment we have looked at until now have relied largely on reasoned analysis, and one might well ask what role, if any, our own reactions to a work should play in critical judgment. What about Juanita's view that an artwork should affect people emotionally? Juanita is certainly right to some extent. A work that never elicited any kind of response from anyone at any time would likely not be very successful. Art should engage us emotionally in some way. (This may involve purely aesthetic emotions and/or emotions related to our life experiences.) So our own reactions are important, and can be a starting point for judgment.

Simply relying on our own initial reactions as a basis for judgment would be a mistake, however, since our reactions may be quite individual, depending on such factors as our background, knowledge, and state of mind. In addition, our reactions to a work can change on the basis of knowledge and exposure (as seemed to be happening with Phil). An appropriate way to think about the role of people's reactions might be in terms of Lester's point that if a work of art is going to be considered good, then it needs to affect many people over a long period of time.

Camillia: Now that you've had the chance to observe and inquire about *Guernica,* it might be interesting to look back at your initial reactions. Have your thoughts or feelings about the work changed? If so, how? What made you change your mind?

What Do You Think?   *Have your thoughts or feelings about the painting changed? If so, how? What made you change your mind?*

Lester: The painting struck me right away. I've seen pictures of it in books, but seeing it live is really different—it makes a much stronger impression. But I didn't know enough to really judge the work or understand it in depth. Now I can understand why it's considered important and I can appreciate it at a different level.

Phil: I have to say that, at first, I couldn't really believe that this was the famous painting that people were making such a fuss about. It just seemed like a bunch of scribbles to me. But with all our inquiring, I kind of got into it. I really got involved in the story that we see in the painting. And the history around the painting is amazing. I learned a lot and can see now what the painting's all about. And I even understand now why Picasso did the painting in this weird style. I'm even starting to warm to it—kind of.

Juanita: As for me, I was blown away when I first saw *Guernica* but I didn't think that you could explain those things. I'm still blown away by it, but now that I've found out more about the painting, I understand something about why it has the effect it does. And maybe I'm even more blown away now that I know all the awful facts about the fascists and the war and the attack on the village.

Winnie: I've sort of liked it all along, though I didn't really understand it at the beginning. But something really important that I've learned is that you can make critical judgments about art based on reasons and evidence. Art isn't just a matter of taste. Now I realize that I should take the time to really look at a work of art, and I know something about how to look and what to look for.

Ahmed: When we first looked at the painting, I really didn't understand what the big deal was either. But now I can see why people think it's important. And I have to admit that looking at it and talking about it was pretty interesting. I can even see why others might like it. But I have to say that I still don't like it very much myself. Maybe I should, but I don't.

Winnie: Is there any reason why we should all agree about the painting at the end, Ms. Bell?

Camillia: No, there's really no reason in this case. It's important that we all go through the inquiry process and share our ideas and judgments. But in the end, we may come to different judgments; and as long as they're based on relevant criteria and evidence, that's just fine. And whatever our critical judgments, we still may have different preferences about what we like and don't like. What matters is that our inquiry opens up new possibilities for appreciating the work.

The Nature of Inquiry in the Arts

Our *Guernica* case has shown us an example of an inquiry in one area of the arts. Contrary to Winnie's original view that art is all a matter of taste, we see here that art can be the subject of inquiry. Inquiry in the arts shares many features with other types of inquiries and the same guiding questions can be used.

There are some interesting similarities in the process of inquiry in the arts and in science. Both involve centrally the evaluation and weighing of reasons and arguments. Moreover, generating hypotheses based on observation, testing them against evidence, and seeking the best explanation of evidence all play some role in both endeavours.

There are also important differences, however. One of these has to do with the role of subjective factors in the inquiry process. In the arts case, the reactions of the students to the painting constituted an important starting point for inquiry as well as an important consideration at the end of the inquiry process. In addition, the collective reaction of people to an artwork was considered a relevant criterion of evaluation. This is the case because artworks are meant to be engaged with and appreciated by the individual viewers.

Engaging with artworks is not an entirely subjective process but also involves reasons and arguments, as we've seen throughout this inquiry. Critical judgment does not reduce to subjective impressions. Nonetheless, subjective reactions do have an important role to play; they interact with objective factors.

In the case of science, on the other hand, subjective factors are not considered desirable. Although it has been acknowledged by contemporary theorists that scientific practice is not totally free of values and the personal commitments of scientists, every effort is made to minimize subjective influences and make scientific inquiry as objective as possible.

The purpose of an inquiry in the arts may also be different from the purposes of other sorts of inquiries. In the case of the *Guernica* inquiry, it was not necessary for the participants to come to an agreement about either of the two questions. No decision rested on the results of the inquiry, which was undertaken for the sake of gaining understanding and opening up possibilities for appreciation. There are cases, though, where some decision or choice does rest on the outcome of an aesthetic inquiry; for example, whether you should go to see a certain film or whether an art gallery should buy a particular painting. In these cases, the issue is whether the work is worthy of the expenditure of resources (either time or money) and will repay one's serious attention and efforts to understand and appreciate it.

The example we've been examining involved an inquiry in the visual arts. But similar types of inquiries are also possible in other areas of the arts. Inquiries about meaning and interpretation are common in literature, drama, and film, but also occur in dance and music. Questions such as these all require interpretive judgments and can be addressed through the inquiry process: "What's the meaning of the phrase, 'Do not go gentle into that good night'?"; "What is the main theme of the novel, *Brave New World?*; "Why did Hamlet hesitate in killing Claudius?"; "What ideas are being expressed in the ballet *The Rite of Spring?*" Questions which require evaluative judgments also occur frequently in all the arts. Here are some examples: "Which is Margaret Atwood's best novel?", "Should *Slumdog Millionaire* have won the Oscar for Best Picture?" "Are Glenn Gould's interpretation of the *Goldberg Variations* superior to all others?"

Although many of us may not spend a great deal of time in art galleries or concert halls, one way in which we are all constantly exposed to aspects of the arts is through media. We are constantly surrounded by visual images and bombarded by musical and aural stimuli. In this context, many of the aspects of the arts which we have been investigating become relevant. It is possible to make critical judgments about visual and aural media through engaging in an inquiry of the type we've been looking at. One can ask questions of meaning and interpretation (e.g., "What meaning or message does this image convey?" and "What effects is this ad intended to have on the viewer?"). One can ask questions of evaluation ("Is this an effective ad?" or "Is this ad truthful? misleading?"). Or one can focus on questions of form ("How does this visual image create the desired effect?"). From these various perspectives, it is possible to gain a critical stance toward aspects of visual and aural media.

Apply Your Understanding Exercise 5, 6

A Public Art Controversy

In 1981, a sculpture 3.5 metres high and 36 metres long entitled *Tilted Arc*, by the American sculptor Richard Serra, was erected in Federal Plaza in New York City. The sculpture had been commissioned by a U.S. government body, the General Service Administration (GSA).

In March 1985, after a series of complaints and criticisms of the sculpture, the GSA undertook a public hearing to discuss whether the sculpture should be removed and relocated. The following excerpts are drawn from transcripts of the hearing.[2]

Tilted Arc

Joseph I. Liebman: My name is Joseph I. Liebman: I am the Attorney in Charge of the International Trade Office, Civil Division, U.S. Department of Justice, with offices located at 26 Federal Plaza... Those of us who work there probably spend more time in the vicinity of the plaza than any other place. Our working environment affects our creativity, productivity, and our physical and mental well-being, which impacts on our personal lives... While the plaza never fulfilled all my expectations, at least until 1980 I regarded it as a relaxing, reflective space where I could walk, sit, and contemplate in an unhurried manner... I remember the band concerts. I remember the musical sounds of neighborhood children playing on the plaza, while their mothers, sheltered under the courthouse, rocked baby carriages...

I remember walking freely in the plaza... undisturbed by the presence of other people engaged in conversation or young lovers holding hands... All those things are just memories now, ending with the installation of the *Tilted Arc*... The Arc has condemned us to lead emptier lives; the children, the bands, and I no longer visit the plaza... Whatever artistic value the Arc may have does not justify the disruption of the plaza and our lives... Relocate it on other land; reprieve us from our desolate condemnation.

Norman Steinlauf: My name is Norman Steinlauf, and I have been a tenant in this building since 1971... [F]ederal employees, and more important the residents of surrounding communities, were not consulted regarding the Arc. Granted, most of us may not be experts on judging art, but we know when someone or something intrudes upon our environment, and that is a cause for concern... No one asked those of us who "live" here for an opinion; that I believe is the democratic process—the missing element until this hearing.

Richard Serra: My name is Richard Serra, and I am an American sculptor, and American artist... I don't make portable objects. I don't make works that can be relocated or site adjusted. I make works that deal with the environmental components of given places... When a known space changes through the inclusion of a site-specific sculpture, one is called upon to relate to the space differently... When the government invited me to propose a sculpture for the plaza, it sought and asked for a "site-specific" sculpture. As this phrase implies, a site-specific sculpture is one which is conceived and created in relation to the particular conditions of a specific site, and only those conditions. To remove *Tilted Arc*, therefore, is to destroy it... It has also been suggested that the "public" did not choose to install the work in the first place. In fact, the choice of artist, approval of the sculpture, and decision to install it permanently in the plaza were made by a public entity, the GSA. Its determination proceeded on the basis of national standards, carefully formulated procedures, and a jury system to ensure impartiality and the selection of art of lasting value. The selection of the sculpture therefore was made by, and on behalf of, the public. The [Art-in-Architecture] program would have no meaning unless it effectuated, as well as signified and symbolized, freedom of creative expression. This implies that once the artist is selected, through objective procedures, the artist's work must be uncensored, respected, and tolerated, although deemed abhorrent, or perceived as challenging, or experienced as threatening.

Edward D. Re (Chief Judge, United States Court of International Trade): I want to emphasize that, personally and officially, I have never inhibited, and do not now wish to inhibit, artistic expression in any form...However, from the moment the *Tilted Arc* was installed, we at the court received phone calls and visits by members of the public or public servants who daily visit and work in the Federal Plaza area. All who spoke to me or other members of the court uniformly expressed questions and doubts as to the placement of the *Tilted Arc* in the simple and open plaza...What constitutes artistic expression is not the issue before us today. Rather, the issue is the governmental responsibility to the public when arriving at a decision to place art that is paid for with public funds in a public plaza or other public location...The public...should participate in the decision-making process to purchase art with public funds for a public place...My purpose is simply to highlight that the decision to place the steel wall was not made in accordance with due process and that the request for its removal stems from the public's desire that the plaza should not have been altered, dislocated and changed.

Virginia Kee: I am Virginia Kee, a resident of Chinatown. I am a member of Community Board #3. I am not here representing any group...but I am here as a person from the neighborhood...History has shown that what may be valued in one time, or beautiful in one time to one group of people may be an outrage or an offense to others. Genius and beauty is always perception and, though I may not fully appreciate the *Tilted Arc* at Federal Plaza or the sculpture at Police Plaza, I defend their right to be there...To remove a work of art based on perceived public pressure may be a dangerous precedent.

Representative Theodore Weiss: Imagine, if you will, this curved slab of welded steel, 12 feet high, 120 feet long, weighing over 73 tons [about 66 tonnes], bisecting the street in front of your house, and you can imagine the reaction of those who live and work in the area. Many who first viewed *Tilted Arc* regarded it as an abandoned piece of construction material, a relic perhaps too large and cumbersome to move...Mr. Serra argues that, because his work is site-specific, just to move it to another location would destroy it. It has, he maintains, a proprietary claim upon the plaza just as real as that of a painting to its canvas. But I suggest that there are other valid claims upon the plaza that conflict with Mr. Serra's, and that the scales tip in their favor. The community—those thousands of people who live and work in the area—have the right to reclaim this small oasis for the respite and relaxation for which it was intended...Many of those who fear the removal of the *Tilted Arc* openly admit that the sculpture in this plaza...was ill-conceived. But they say that...they are concerned that relocating the work itself may establish a bad precedent. Being concerned about what wrongful things may be done in the future is no justification for allowing a wrong to continue in the present...

Margo Jacobs: My name is Margo Jacobs. I am a physical anthropologist...I am also married to Robert Allen Jacobs, one of the architects of the Federal Office Building and International Court of Trade. However, today I speak to you...as an individual and as a member of the public. I have a bachelor of arts degree in art and architectural history from New York University...The plaza is a site-specific work of art incorporating a geometric pavement design, now disrupted...The function of the plaza or piazza or square has always been to encourage members of the public and workers from the surrounding areas to mingle, congregate, move freely back and forth...That is what we had in Foley Square until a 120-foot long, 12-foot high metal sculpture was placed in the center, cutting the plaza in half and reducing its effectiveness as a public place...Mr. Serra's work, according to him, was deliberately designed to change, alter, and dislocate someone else's artistic creation. This is wrong. The architects and landscape architects...consider themselves to be artists too. How would Mr. Serra feel if someone came in today and destroyed his design? From what I hear he would not like it.

Gustave Harrow: I speak as counsel to Richard Serra, and...I have a serious question to raise as to the legitimacy of the convening of this panel...The convening of the hearing may be illegal because it was called by an official to consider breaching a binding contract between the government and an individual...As to the due process: convening this hearing violates the meaning and spirit of due process, since it entails an effort to change the rules after the game has been played.

Rosalind Krauss: I am Rosalind Krauss, professor of art history at the City University of New York, and an art critic … [T]he presence of Richard Serra's *Tilted Arc* invests a major portion of its site with a use we must call aesthetic … The kind of vector *Tilted Arc* explores is that of vision, more specifically what it means for vision to be invested with a purpose, so that if we look out into space it is not just a vacant stare that we cast in front of us, but an act of looking that expects to find an object, a direction, a goal … In the beauty of its doing this, *Tilted Arc* establishes itself as a great work of art.

Jessie Gray: My name is Jessie Gray, and I am speaking as an artist who lives outside of New York City but exhibits here in New York City as well. [O]ur public money is being squandered so that a small group of artists can make a financial killing. These artists are part of a … clique of galleries, curators, and critics. They write about each other, recommend and promote each other, and, as in the case of the Serra sculpture, they sit on each other's boards and advise and give grants and monies to each other. They, the political camp that is in control now, I believe, personally, advocates a dehumanized and minimal art, and in some cases an art that is … just plain smart-aleckness … Now the way they intimidate you is to just give you a smoke screen of intellectual mumbo-jumbo about art … and they will do this to make you feel you know nothing, should have no opinion, and just generally get rid of you …

Clara Weyergraf-Serra: I am Clara Weyergraf-Serra. I am married to Richard Serra, and as his wife, have witnessed his involvement with the General Services Administration from 1979 up to today … In spite of my general mistrust in government … I cannot believe the manipulations and malicious tricks which have been used by governmental officials to achieve the goal of tearing down a work of art … To perform this show trial is in itself an act of lawlessness. Inquisition-like procedures are being instituted under the guise of democracy … A petition is circulating in the Federal Building asking those who work there to vote on the artistic merit of *Tilted Arc*. Are we really back to a situation where the "healthy instincts" of the people are going to decide what is art and what isn't? Book burning, I thought, was part of German history. The smell of burning books is in the air right here, right now.

Phil La Basi: I have been a federal employee for twenty-two years, about eleven years in this building. First of all, I would like to say that I really resent the implication that those of us who oppose this structure are cretins or some sort of reactionaries. It seems to be very typical of self-serving artists and so-called pseudointellectuals that when they disagree with something someone else has to say, they attack the person. So I am not going to attack the artist. What I see there is something that looks like a tank trap to prevent an armed attack from Chinatown in case of a Soviet invasion … I think we can call anything art if we call that art …

Joel Kovel: My name is Joel Kovel. I am a writer, a Professor at the Albert Einstein College of Medicine and at the New School for Social Research … The value of art can never be determined by popularity contests or immediate concerns of taste. Every lesson from the history of art tells us that. The *Tilted Arc* is … subversive, and this very hearing proves its subversiveness and hence its value … I would submit that it is the true measure of a free and democratic society that it permits opposition of this sort; and that, therefore it is essential for this hearing to result in the preservation of Serra's work as a measure of the value of opposition which this society can tolerate.

Roberta Smith: My name is Roberta Smith. I am an art critic … The piece he [Serra] has made for the Federal Plaza is an excellent example of Minimalism, which has already been watched by the influential … It is one of the two best public sculptures in New York City … This is a confrontational, aggressive piece in a confrontational, aggressive town.

Harry Watson: Gentlemen, my name is Harry Delaney Watson. I work for the Bureau of Investigations of the State of New York as a supervisor. I have lived in this area for the last twenty years and work in this area. Every time I pass this so-called sculpture, I just can't believe it …

[T]his goes beyond the realm of stupidity. This goes into even worse than insanity. I think that an insane person would say, "How crazy can you be to pay $175,000 for that rusted metal wall?"...I believe that it was a complete waste of money...I can't see where anybody would approve such a piece of nonsense or garbage in this day and age, and I hope that this can be resolved and that it be taken down.

William Rubin: My name is William Rubin and I am Director of the Department of Painting and Sculpture at the Museum of Modern Art...About a hundred years ago the Impressionist and Post-Impressionist artists...were being reviled as ridiculous by the public and the established press...By the end of the fifty-year period in 1939, however, the Impressionists and Post-Impressionists had long since been accepted by our culture as great voices of the Western tradition...I tell this story because it illustrates a truth that seems to me very relevant in the present situation: namely, that truly challenging works of art require a period of time before their artistic language can be understood by a broader public...I therefore propose that consideration of this issue be deferred for a period of at least ten years.

Holly Solomon: I have a gallery in SoHo and now I've moved to Fifty-seventh street...I can only tell you, gentlemen, that this is business, and to take down the piece is bad business...the bottom line is that this has financial value, and you really have to understand that you have a responsibility to the financial community. You cannot destroy property.

Betty St. Clair: My name is Betty St. Clair. I am associated with the law firm of Rabinowitz, Boudin, Standard, Krinsky and Liebman; and we represent the National Emergency Civil Liberties Committee...ECLC believes that artistic expression, no less than religious freedom or political expression, is entitled to full and complete constitutional protection, and that our critical judgments of the merit of a particular artistic piece cannot justify, in constitutional terms, the government's action with respect to a particular piece of art...The Constitution says that it is improper for government to decide, because a piece of artwork offends some people, that it cannot exist.

Public Art[3]

The term "public art" refers to works of art that have been created by an artist specifically to be sited in a public space and therefore accessible to a broad audience. Such works may be permanent, temporary, or ephemeral. Within the art world, the term often indicates a particular working practice which includes site specificity, community involvement, and collaboration. Public art is sometimes controversial due to many factors: a desire on the part of the artist to provoke, the diverse backgrounds of the viewing public, and the issues it raises regarding the appropriate use of public resources and spaces, and regarding civic oversight.

The public hearing over *Tilted Arc* constitutes an interesting case for our purposes for a number of reasons. First, it is an example of an actual inquiry that was conducted in order to make a decision about a controversial issue relating to the arts. The case is on historical record and the excerpts are based on actual testimony at the hearing. Focusing as it does on a work of public art, the case also provides an example of a number of issues in the arts which we have not looked at to this point—in particular, how artistic values interact with other types of values.

The case is somewhat different from other inquiries we've seen, however, because the speakers were simply offering reasons, but were not themselves engaged in the entire inquiry process. It was, rather, the judge who oversaw the hearing who evaluated the various reasons and arguments in order to come to a reasoned judgment on the issue. This process is similar in some ways to the type of inquiry we see in trials. The witnesses give evidence, and the judge or jury evaluates the evidence and makes a judgment. The tasks of offering reasons and of evaluating reasons are present, but they are conducted by different individuals.

The excerpts quoted above constitute only a part of all the testimony given at the hearing. There has also been a great deal written about this case. All of this, in conjunction with the additional documentation available, can provide a rich source of material on which to base your own inquiry. In what follows, we shall work through some of the guiding questions together in order that, at the end, you will be in a position to conduct your own inquiry on this issue.

What Is the Issue? What Kinds of Claims or Judgments Are at Issue?

Write down what you see as the main issue in this controversy. List as well some of the subsidiary issues which will need to be addressed in order to come to a judgment on the main issue. For each issue, specify the kind of judgment that is required. Compare your response to the analysis below.

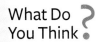

The primary issue is whether the sculpture should stay where it is or whether it should be removed and/or relocated. This issue requires an evaluative judgment. There are a number of subsidiary issues that arise which require different types of judgments:

- Is the *Tilted Arc* (good) art? (aesthetic judgment)
- Would removal constitute an infringement of the contract between Serra and the government? (legal judgment)
- Would removal constitute a violation of freedom of expression? (ethical judgment)
- Would removal constitute a violation of due process? (ethical/legal judgment)
- Does the sculpture interfere with the use of the space in the plaza? (factual judgment)
- Would removal of the sculpture be bad for business? (economic judgment)
- Who should make decisions about public art? (political judgment)
- How do we weigh artistic values versus other types of values? (comparative judgment of value)

What Are the Relevant Reasons and Arguments on Various Sides of the Issue?

Make a table of the arguments pro and con the removal of Tilted Arc *that you find in the testimony. Check your list against the list of arguments below. Add any arguments that you didn't include in your table, and make note of any arguments you found that are not listed below. Add to the table any objections to the arguments and responses to the objections that you find in the testimony.*

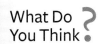

Arguments for relocation:

- It isn't art. It isn't good art.
- People who have to "live" with it dislike it.
- The plaza has become unusable for relaxation and for social functions and pleasure.
- It was a waste of public money.
- There was an absence of participation of the community in the selection process.
- It was an "in-group" with vested interests who decided on the sculpture.

Arguments against relocation:

- It is aesthetically good.
- Expert opinion should have priority over popular taste in decisions about art.
- Time is required for new or difficult art to be accepted.
- Relocating site-specific art amounts to destroying it.
- The hearing is a violation of due process.

- The removal of the sculpture would be a violation of freedom of expression.
- The removal of the sculpture would violate the contract between the artist and the government.
- The removal of the sculpture would set a dangerous precedent, leading to increased censorship of public art.
- Removal of the sculpture would be bad for business.

There are a number of objections and responses which focus on the usability of the plaza, the process for selection, the implications of site-specificity, and the issue of precedent, among others.

What Is the Context of the Issue?

What Do You Think?

There are nume rous contexts which are relevant to the evaluation of the Tilted Arc *controversy. List all the various contexts which you can think of that might be relevant. Check your response against the list below and add any contexts that you have not included.*

- the previous state and use of Federal Plaza
- the original selection process for the sculpture (including procedure, criteria, and composition of the selection committee)
- other critical opinion about the sculpture
- the nature, history, goals, and funding of public art
- the artistic context (in particular, the style in which Serra worked; site-specific art)
- legal context (regarding Serra's contract; constitutional regulations regarding freedom of expression)
- public opinion about the sculpture and the controversy (broader than just those testifying)
- the hearing (lead-up, procedures, politics, precedents)
- sources: the witnesses at the hearing (number, background, expertise, and representativeness of those on each side)
- the media coverage of the controversy
- the sculpture itself (to see it for oneself in order to evaluate claims)

How Do We Comparatively Evaluate the Various Reasons and Arguments to Reach a Reasoned Judgment?

In order to comparatively evaluate the reasons and arguments around this issue, it will first be necessary to evaluate the individual arguments. This will involve a prima facie evaluation, checking for fallacies and other problems in the reasoning (see Chapter 4). Conducting a comparative evaluation will also involve trying to think of alternative positions or additional arguments, then evaluating reasons and arguments on the different sides of the issue, and weighing and balancing conflicting considerations.

What Do You Think?

Make a list of the considerations or values which are in conflict in the controversy. Check your list against the list below.

- aesthetic values versus other types of values (social, legal, moral, political)
- rights of artists versus rights of the community
- proprietary claim of original design of the plaza versus of the sculpture

- relevance and weight of expert versus non-expert opinion
- how to weigh testimonies of various witnesses—number? representativeness? expertise? how to take into account possible vested interests?

Apply Your Understanding Exercise 7, 8, 9, 10, 11, 12

The case of the *Titled Arc* provides a very rich example of inquiry employed to resolve a real-life issue in the arts. Such controversies about public art are not uncommon. In the exercises that follow, you will have the opportunity to work through this case in more detail in order to reach your own judgment about the issue, and to inquire about other public art controversies.

Olympic Public Art to Light Up Vancouver[4]

Excerpt from article by Kevin Griffin in the Vancouver Sun, *September 17, 2008.*

The biggest public artwork initiative in the city's history is poised to transform several high-profile spots around Vancouver as part of the Olympic public art program....

Altogether, more than 15 public art works are expected to be going up around the city during the next 15 months. Total price tag works out to about $5.8 million....

Richard Newirth, the city official in charge of the public art program, said he doesn't mind if the new public art generates healthy controversy....

"That's what public art is meant to do—provoke controversy," he said in an interview. "Some people say that public art is not successful if everyone loves it because then it's not inspiring any debate or reaction. It's just bland. If you water it down to the lowest common denominator, you'll lose everything. Hopefully, some people will love some things and hate some things, but love that the city is doing it."

CHECK YOUR UNDERSTANDING

- *Why do teachers of art appreciation tend to recommend close observation of an artwork before looking at what others have said about the work?*
- *What are the main criteria for judging the validity of an interpretation in the arts?*
- *What are some of the strengths of Phil's aliens interpretation of Guernica? What are some of its problems?*
- *Why is it advantageous to have a group of people observing and discussing an artwork together?*
- *How did knowledge of the historical, political, and artistic contexts aid the students in interpreting Guernica?*
- *What are some criteria for evaluating works of art?*
- *What is the appropriate role of the views of critics in arriving at our own critical judgments of a work?*
- *In what ways is inquiry in the arts similar to inquiry in science? In what ways is it different?*
- *Describe the Tilted Arc.*
- *What was the purpose of the hearing held by the GSA in March 1985?*
- *What were the main complaints of the tenants of the buildings in Federal Plaza?*
- *What were the main arguments by Serra in defence of the sculpture?*
- *What makes this case interesting for us when studying inquiry in the arts?*
- *How is the Tilted Arc case different from other inquiries we've looked at?*

EXERCISES

1. i) Look at the painting at this website: http://www.artchive.com/artchive/M/monet/adresse.jpg.html.
       (See Exercise 14-1 on the textbook website.) Write a description of this painting in as much detail
       as you can. Include details of formal aspects (line, colour, style, etc.) as well as details of content.
       Then compare your descriptions with a partner to see to what extent your descriptions are similar,
       and what is missed in each one.

    ii) Find a painting which strikes you as visually interesting. Describe it to a partner who cannot see
       it. The other person will try to make a drawing of the painting based on the description. See how
       closely the drawing resembles the painting.

2. Listen to the song "The Sound of Silence" by Simon & Garfunkel (you can listen to it on *YouTube*). You
    can view the lyrics at http://sglyrics.myrmid.com/sounds.htm#track01 (or google "Sound of Silence
    lyrics").

    The task is to develop and argue for an interpretation of the song/poem which is appropriate and
    plausible. Use the following steps:

     i) Carefully analyze the language and images in the poem, considering possible meanings.

     ii) Generate possible interpretations of the poem based on the above.

     iii) Research the context in which the poem was developed, including historical and social context and
        information about the writers' style and ideas.

     iv) Develop and argue for an interpretation of the poem which meets the criteria for a valid
        interpretation.

3. Think of some piece of music that you think is good. List reasons why you like it. Compare it to a piece
    of the same genre which you don't think is as good. Give reasons why you judge one to be better than
    the other. What are the criteria that you are using?

4. Is it art?

     i) In 1952, the composer John Cage wrote the composition 4'33". The composition consists of 4
        minutes and 33 seconds of silence. Its three movements are performed without a single note being
        played. You can see it being performed here: http://www.youtube.com/watch?v=hUJagb7hL0E.

        Is it music? This question has been extremely controversial in musical circles. Conduct an inquiry
        into the question of whether 4´33˝ is music. Give the reasons that have been offered both for
        and against. Determine what criteria have been used. Investigate the aspects of context which
        are relevant to deciding the issue. Evaluate the various reasons in order to come to a reasoned
        judgment on the question.

     ii) Conduct an inquiry into whether Jana Sterbak's *Vanitas: Flesh Dress for an Albino Anorectic*
        (see p. 278) is art.

5. Look carefully at the ad at http://consumerist.com/2008/04/is-this-absolut-ad-cheeky-or-distasteful
    .html. (See Exercise 14-5 on the textbook website.) Note: This ad was designed specifically to be shown
    in Mexico.

    Respond to the following questions using the guiding questions for inquiry as a guide:

     i) What meaning or message does this advertisement convey?

        (Use the strategies for arriving at an interpretation and the criteria for evaluating an interpretation
        used in the *Guernica* example. Pay special attention to the political and historical contexts.)

     ii) How does the visual image in this ad convey the message?

        (Look for use of colour, line, shape and pattern; how images are connected and juxtaposed; and
        juxtaposition of images and written text.)

     iii) Evaluate the accuracy and truthfulness of the message.

(Think about what criteria you would use to evaluate the truthfulness of an ad. Look out for some of the fallacies which you learned about in Chapter 4.)

6. Write a review of a film that you have seen recently. Use the structure of inquiry and process used in the *Guernica* example to evaluate the film. (See "The Great Film Debate" in Chapter 2 for more guidance with respect to possible criteria.)

7. Conduct your own inquiry on the issue of the relocation of the *Tilted Arc*. Follow the guiding questions for inquiry. Make use of the work you have done when working through the guiding questions in the *Titled Arc* section.

    i) What is the issue? What kinds of claims or judgments are at issue?

    ii) What are the reasons and arguments on various sides of the issue?

      (Insert your pro and con table.)

    iii) What is the context of the issue?

      Choose two of the contexts from your list from the context question in the *Titled Arc* section; select those you think are most important. Conduct research on these aspects of context, and show how they are relevant to making a judgments on the issue.

    iv) How do we comparatively evaluate the reasons and arguments to reach a reasoned judgment?

      (a) Evaluate the individual arguments in the testimony: Identify the main fallacies or problems in reasoning which you find.

      (b) Compare and weigh the reasons and arguments on both sides; try to think of any additional arguments or alternative points of view which were not represented in the testimony; take into consideration the various conflicting values and considerations you listed previously.

    On the basis of your inquiry, what would you decide about the relocation of *Tilted Arc*?

8. The philosopher of art, Arthur Danto, made the following observation with respect to the *Tilted Arc* controversy: "*Tilted Arc* made vivid the truth that something may succeed as a work of art but fail as a work of public art."[5]

    The purpose of the assignment is to evaluate Danto's claim by going through the following steps:

    i) List some of the ways in which a work of public art shares the features of other types of works of art.

    ii) List some of the ways in which a work of public art is different from other types of works of art. (Think of issues such as purpose, location, nature of audience, nature of interaction with audience, and funding.)

    iii) List some of the criteria for success of an artwork (see the *Guernica* discussion for assistance).

    iv) List some of the criteria for success of a work of public art (your answers to (i) and (ii) should be helpful here).

    v) On the basis of the preceding analysis, evaluate Danto's statement.

9. As a result of the *Tilted Arc* controversy, the GSA decided to provide for consultation with local groups before a work of art is commissioned. Lawyer Alvin Lane wrote the following in an article for the *New York Times* in response to the move:

    This plan will mitigate dissension, but it may have the distasteful side-effect of corrupting the selection panel's freedom. If we leave the selection of public art to the residents of a community—or even permit their strong influence on the process—we will end up with an esthetic common denominator of sterile, benign and conventional art that will neither offend nor stimulate anyone. The purpose of Government-sponsored art is to elevate the public's appreciation of all art ... Selection, therefore, cannot be left to a popular vote. Only a panel of recognized art experts ... can properly choose the high caliber of public art that justifies the expenditure of public funds.[6]

    Evaluate Mr. Lane's argument.

10. Shakespeare's play, *The Taming of the Shrew*, is the tale of the courtship between Petruchio, a gentleman from Verona, and Katherine, his stubborn and wilful bride-to-be (the shrew of the title). At first, Katherine wants nothing to do with the relationship and resists Petruchio's advances, but he "tames" her with a variety of psychological "tortures" until she eventually succumbs and becomes an obedient wife. The play has been severely criticized because it is said to represent the subjugation of women and to contain damaging stereotypes of women as subservient to men. Many have argued that it should not be taught in schools or even that it should be banned from the school system.

    For this assignment, imagine that a local school board will be meeting to decide on whether *The Taming of the Shrew* should be banned from the local secondary schools.

    i) Work in groups of three to list all the arguments you can, both in favour of and against the ban. (You may do research to find additional arguments.) Include objections to arguments and responses to the objections where relevant.

    ii) As a group, write a dialogue between a parent who is in favour of banning the play, a secondary school student who is against banning it, and a member of the school board who is undecided on the issue but will have to vote on the question at the school board meeting.

11. Inquire into a local public art controversy using the guiding questions for inquiry. Follow the example of the *Tilted Arc* inquiry (hint: internet search under "public art controversies + your city; or local newspaper archives).

12. Imagine that your college is having a competition to design a piece of public art to be placed at the entrance to the college and that a call has been put out for designs.

    Work in groups to do the following:

    i) Decide what process you would you use to choose which design to accept; give your reasoning for choosing this process. (Include the arguments against as well as in favour of the process you choose, and your evaluation of these arguments.)

    ii) Describe the criteria you would use to choose the design as well as a justification for those criteria.

    iii) Describe and/or create a design for a piece of public art for the competition; describe why it is an appropriate design for the location.

ENDNOTES

1. Snopes.com, "The Meat Dress," www.snopes.com/politics/arts/meatdress.asp (accessed July 26, 2010); National Gallery of Canada, "The Meat Dress and Other Tales," http://www.gallery.ca/english/2141.htm (accessed July 26, 2010); Walker Art Center, "So, Why Is This Art?" http://schools.walkerart.org/swita/all2.html?ref=all:31 (accessed July 26, 2010).

2. [Source of *Tilted Arc* inquiry: to come from permissions]

3. *Wikipedia.org*, "Public Art," http://en.wikipedia.org/wiki/Public_art (accessed May 28, 2010); Newport News Public Art Foundation, "What is Public Art?" http://nnpaf.org/what_is_art.html (accessed July 26, 2010); Planning Portal, "Glossary," http://www.planningportal.gov.uk/england/government/glossary/p (accessed July 26, 2010); Arts SA, "What Is Public Art?" http://www.arts.sa.gov.au/site/page.cfm?u=291 (accessed July 26, 2010).

4. Kevin Griffin, "Olympic Public Art to Light Up Vancouver," *Vancouver Sun*, Sept. 17, 2008. html?id=a343e287-fa48-4ae1-bf2e-ca817b718ae9.

5. Harriet F. Senie, *The Tilted Arc Controversy: Dangerous Precedent?* (Minneapolis: University of Minnesota Press, 2002), 73.

6. M. Battin et al., *Puzzles About Art* (Bedford / St. Martin's, 1989), 196.

Chapter 15
Inquiry in Philosophy: Ethics

Learning Objectives

After reading this chapter, you should be able to:

- understand a way to approach ethical issues
- understand the issues surrounding the idea of ethical relativism
- articulate some of the primary arguments for and against ethical relativism
- inquire with some competence into other ethical issues

It's All Relative

Sophia has just finished reading a piece in the newspaper when Ravi joins her in the cafeteria.

Sophia: How disgusting!

Ravi: I don't think the food's that bad.

Sophia: No—I'm talking about an article in the paper.

Ravi: So what's so disgusting?

Sophia: Polygamy! I've been reading about this case in a small community not far from here. It's really awful the way those men have so many wives. There's even a photo of the "big happy family"!

B.C. Religious Leaders Charged with Polygamy[1]

Excerpt from cbc.ca

Two rival leaders of a religious community in Bountiful, B.C., were released from custody Wednesday night after being charged with practising polygamy.

Winston Blackmore and James Oler were charged with one count each on Tuesday of breaching Section 293 of the Criminal Code—which bans polygamy —by entering into a conjugal relationship with more than one individual at a time.

The charges against Blackmore, 52, are linked to his alleged marriages to 19 women, dating back to May 2005. The charges against Oler, 44, are linked to his marriages to two women, dating back to November 2004 . . .

The RCMP investigation into allegations of polygamy in the isolated, rural community in southeastern B.C. began in 2005 and included interviews with 90 people in B.C., Utah, Idaho and Nevada.

But following the conclusion of the investigation, B.C.'s Crown prosecutors remained reluctant to lay polygamy charges for fear they would be declared unconstitutional on the basis of religious freedom.

Source: Jonathan Hayward/Canadian Press

Ravi: Why is it so awful? I don't really see the problem. Lots of different cultures have polygamy.

Sophia: Well, that doesn't make it right.

Ravi: That's just your point of view. I mean, who are we to say what's right? We were brought up in a particular culture with a particular point of view which we think is right, and they were brought up differently.

Sophia: Are you saying that if you were brought up to think the world is flat, that would be right?

Ravi: I would think it was right.

Sophia: Yeah, but you would be wrong. And with some luck, you might learn that.

Ravi: Well, I might be wrong about that because there's a world out there. And if you can get a good look at it from out in the solar system or find some other objective evidence, you can find out that the world is round. But for issues like who you can marry, you can't go somewhere and see that they're "right" or "wrong." They're just society's rules.

Sophia: Surely you're not saying that morality is a matter of opinion.

Ravi: Of course it is. That's why there's so much disagreement.

Sophia: I agree there's a lot of disagreement, but there's also a lot of agreement. Nobody thinks slavery is OK. And what about Nazism? Is thinking it's right to commit genocide just a matter of opinion?

Ravi: Well, of course, I don't think the Nazis were right. But if you and I had been brought up in Germany at that time, we might have thought so.

Sophia: I hope not. But whether we did or not, we would have been wrong.

Ravi: I agree that genocide is wrong, horribly wrong. But I don't see how you can prove that. Isn't it just what someone's been taught? But since there's no way to measure right and wrong, how do we know who's right?

Sophia: That's a very good question, and I don't really know the answer. But I do know that at least some horrible things like genocide are clearly wrong. And I also know that while cultures have held revolting views, as the Nazis did, even in those cultures there was disagreement. So claiming that "this is right in this culture because this culture says so" isn't so simple either.

Ravi: I still don't see it. If you take how people should dress or which side of the road to drive on, I'm pretty sure that those are totally cultural. But when you take something like polygamy, I don't know how you can be so sure.

Sophia: Which side of the road you drive on and proper dress are totally social, but they're not the same kind of thing as saying something is morally wrong.

Ravi: I'm not so sure about that.

Sophia: You know…I'm thinking it might be helpful to sort this out using an inquiry.

Do you think that polygamy is morally wrong? Why or why not?

What Do
You Think

Ethical Inquiry

There are many areas of philosophical inquiry:

- ethics (the question of how we should act and why)
- metaphysics (the question of what there is; e.g., God, minds, matter?)
- epistemology (the question of what the basis of our knowledge of the world is)
- political philosophy (the question of how our collective lives should be organized and on what principles)
- aesthetics (the questions of what is art, its significance, and how we should judge it)

The inquiry which Ravi and Sophia are about to undertake is a philosophical inquiry in the realm of ethics.

Unlike most academic disciplines, philosophy is concerned not only with getting the facts of the world correct, but also with finding out what is the right thing to do; that is, philosophy is concerned with ethical issues. Many of the issues addressed in this text (for example, whether capital punishment is justified) are ethical issues. The issue which Sophia and Ravi are beginning to address is just such an issue.

Inquiry on Ethical Relativism

What Is the Issue? What Kinds of Claims or Judgments Are at Issue?

Sophia: The first question, of course, is what exactly is the issue we're discussing.

Ravi: Well, it seems to me that the question is whether there's an absolute universal morality that everyone should adhere to.

Sophia: Hmm…"absolute" makes it sound a bit stronger than I want. I just want to say that there is a right and wrong about some issues. Ethics is not all relative to the culture, like which side to drive on. But it's also not all a matter of personal opinion, like me liking hot fudge sundaes or you thinking that nose-piercing is gross.

Ravi: So how would you frame the issue?

Sophia: I would want to argue that there are some moral truths, some things that are just wrong. Slavery was wrong in ancient Greece and in the U.S. south even if in the past it was an accepted practice in those cultures. And I'd also want to say that the increased acceptance of universal human rights is an example of moral progress. I admit that I don't know how I know these things, but they seem to me to be clearly true. I would like to get some help from Dr. Weise when we get to philosophy class.

Do you agree with Sophia that there really are some moral truths? Are some things just wrong?

Ethical (or cultural) **relativism** is the view that right and wrong are determined by the customs and practices of a particular culture.

The issue which Sophia and Ravi are addressing—whether we can ever say that a practice in another culture is (or was) morally wrong—is a version of a well-known issue in philosophy, the issue of **ethical relativism.** There are actually two related issues. One is about the descriptive judgment that different cultures have different values and ethical views. While this may seem true to most of us, some philosophers have argued that there are widespread shared ethical values. The other issue concerns the evaluative judgment that what makes an act right or wrong is determined by local cultural norms. In this view, there are no universal ethical rules and values; rather, right and wrong are determined by the customs and practices of a particular culture. It is the evaluative issue that Ravi and Sophia are investigating. This view, also known as **cultural relativism,** was strongly supported by anthropologists in the late nineteenth and early twentieth centuries.

Ethnocentrism is the tendency to view one's own culture as more important than and morally and intellectually superior to any other culture.

The anthropologists argued against the long-standing assumptions of Europeans that the practices in other societies were morally (and intellectually) inferior. These assumptions had helped support the Europeans' sense of righteousness as they moved to control other cultures. It was appropriate to criticize the Europeans for being **ethnocentric,** and many anthropologists attacked this ethnocentrism on the basis that there was no moral right and wrong. They claimed that neither European culture nor any other culture had a moral basis for disagreeing with the practices of other cultures.[2] They argued that moral views were fundamentally cultural and what made a practice right or wrong were the standards of the culture.

What Are the Reasons and Arguments on Various Sides of the Issue?

The next day, Ravi and Sophia are in Dr. Weise's philosophy class.

Ravi: Dr. Weise, Sophia and I were discussing a case of polygamy we heard about, and that led us to disagree about whether you can criticize other cultures' ways of doing things. I argued that you can't. Each culture has its own standards. If we criticize other cultures, we're pretending that somehow we know the truth but they don't. Sophia feels that she knows that some things are just wrong. And I have to admit that things like slavery do seem to me to be wrong. But neither of us could see how we could know whether something was really wrong.

Dr. Weise: Well, you've raised a really deep and important question known as the question of relativism. This is actually the subject of a long debate in philosophy. I'm glad to see that you already realize that it's difficult to really be a consistent relativist. Philosophers, as early as Plato, showed that relativism led to inconsistency.

Ravi: In what way?

Dr. Weise: Let's take as an example the anthropologists who believed that culture determined right and wrong. They claimed that it was morally wrong for European cultures to treat non-European cultures in a patronizing and critical manner. Can you see how this led them into a contradiction?

Sophia: Well…if they were arguing that it was wrong for European cultures to treat non-European cultures in a certain way, they had to be assuming that there was a right way and a wrong way to relate to other cultures.

Moral Progress

The fact that we can judge historical cultures such as ancient Greece or the slave-owning southern U.S. illustrates another aspect of non-relativism—moral progress. To the extent to which we can judge that current moral judgments are wiser and more sensitive to the rights of all people, we judge that there has been moral progress. One of the most striking examples of that progress has been the increased acceptance of equal human rights through the twentieth century, despite, and in fact partly because of, the genocidal atrocities that occurred in it. Such blatant evil helped underline the moral horror of viewing fellow humans as not possessing equal human rights. If you are a cynic and do not think that humans have made moral progress, you are still thinking like a non-relativist. Both the judgment of progress and that of non-progress require standards that can be applied across cultures and over time.

Dr. Weise: Exactly! If they could reject the views of their own culture as being wrong, then it could not be true that what made an action right or wrong was what the culture dictated.

Sophia: That seems like a pretty strong argument.

Dr. Weise: And yet relativism keeps being put forward as a reasonable position—even more so now because we are so aware of the practices of other cultures. And, of course, it sounds so decent to say that you shouldn't judge others, and it can sound arrogant or racist when you're critical. The anthropologists and others who supported relativism were, of course, well intentioned; but they obviously had strong views about how cultures should treat one another, and these couldn't be just "their" rules. They believed cultural intolerance was wrong wherever it occurred.

Believing that one holds a morally correct view does not justify imposing that moral perspective on others.

Ravi: Well, I'm a lot more comfortable with a rule that says, "Mind your own business and don't go around telling other people what's right and wrong," than I am with some absolutist view that claims to know what's right and what's wrong.

Dr. Weise: I sympathize with your concern, but you've confused a couple of things. For example, because I believe I hold a morally correct view does not mean that I have to go around correcting everyone. And it certainly does not mean that I have a right to invade another country and try to shove my views down their throats. In fact, I think you could argue that trying to impose your moral views is usually morally wrong.

Ravi: Hah, "usually wrong," not "always wrong." That sounds like relativism to me.

Dr. Weise: Time for another distinction. The debate about relativism is not a debate in ethics. It's a debate in the field of **meta-ethics.** Meta-ethics is the study of the basis of ethics and the logic of moral terms. It is contrasted with **normative ethics,** which looks at which rules and judgments express correct moral views. While normative ethics addresses questions like "What should we do?", meta-ethics considers questions like "What is goodness?" or "How can we tell right from wrong?"

Meta-ethics is the study of the basis of ethics and the logic of moral terms. **Normative ethics** looks at which rules and judgments express correct moral views.

When we discuss cultural relativism or what we would call meta-ethical relativism, we are actually not having an ethical discussion, but a discussion about the basis, if any, of moral judgments When we turn to the issue of when it is morally appropriate to intervene in another culture, then we are having a moral argument. In the domain of moral argument, the facts of a situation are crucial to deciding what is the morally correct thing to do.

Sophia: But I've heard people argue that morality involves following the correct moral rules.

Dr. Weise: Consider this example. Take the rule that you should return things you've borrowed. And say you've borrowed a knife from someone, and he shows up in a state of self-destructive depression and asks for the knife back. Should you give him the knife?

Table of Arguments Pro and Con Relativism

Name of Theory	Description	Pro Argument	Con Argument	Responses
Ethical (or cultural) relativism	What is right and wrong is determined by the culture; therefore, you cannot use the norms of one culture to judge another.	We learn our moral point of view from our culture.	We learn almost everything from our culture, but that doesn't make what we know only true for our culture.	True, but many claims can be proved by science or observation. Moral claims can't be proven.
		Cultures differ in their moral judgments and rules. There is no objective measure to decide between cultures.	Widespread difference in belief does not justify the notion that there are no correct beliefs.	We should be careful of ethnocentrism which is a great danger if we adopt objectivism.
		People have used moral objectivism to oppress less powerful cultures.	Relativism is not consistent with a requirement to tolerate other cultures.	We need also at least to acknowledge that it is very difficult to fully understand a cultural practice from the outside. Thus, judgment of other cultures' practices is easily flawed.
			Believing in relativism means that there cannot be moral progress, only change.	Moral progress is a western idea.
			Impossible to apply consistently.	
Objectivism/ Universalism	There is a right and wrong. Moral rules apply universally in time and place.	We all find certain acts such as genocide morally repugnant. No one really believes that opposing genocide is "just a matter of opinion." Clearly some moral judgments can be right or wrong.	There is no way to objectively prove moral claims as you can do in science.	Since we do resolve moral issues by arguing and using criteria, the situation of moral reasoning is not that different from evaluating claims in the sciences.
		We recognize that some rules are local rules, and some issues are issues of personal opinion (e.g., clothing styles), but we make a distinction between these and the more profound rules such as rules against killing, which we do not see as either a local rule or a mere personal opinion. That's why we call them moral rules.	Calling moral rules universal rules just begs the question. There is no clear standard, no way to "measure" right and wrong to adjudicate disagreement. Moral rules are just rules of cultural order.	Moral judgments can be rationally defended—by comparable weighting of alternatives against such criteria as harmful consequences, violation of rights, moral duties, etc.
		Objectivism fits with the judgment that many cultures have made moral progress by; for example, recognizing universal human rights.	Believing in objective moral views means that people will try to impose these views on others.	Believing that a practice is morally wrong does not mean that one is justified in intervening in the culture. Many judgments of right and wrong are about earlier cultures: e.g., slavery.

Ravi: Clearly not.

Dr. Weise: Of course. This is the kind of counter-example that philosophers use to show the limits of a narrowly rule-governed morality and why circumstances and consequences are often morally relevant. A key approach in evaluating moral reasoning is to consider whether there are counter-examples to a claim. So if you're considering the issue of whether to use violence in a particular case to prevent some moral outrage like genocide, obviously you must consider the particular situation. In a sense, yes, my judgment is relative, but in a good sense. I make my moral decisions based on the facts of the situation. But what I don't do is simply ask what some culture thinks.

Ravi: OK, so you consider the situation, but then how do you decide what's right and wrong?

Dr. Weise: I'll try to answer that, but first let me point out that if you're not a relativist, you should recognize just how complex it can be to figure out what's right or wrong in a particular situation. Taking the relativist position and just asking what's accepted in the culture may be much easier.

Ravi: With all due respect, Dr. Weise, you haven't really answered Sophia's and my question. Once we give up relativism, then what do we do?

Dr. Weise: Good point. Let me give you the really simple answer: we reason. People justify their ethical positions by giving moral reasons, not by saying "That's how we do it here." "That's how we do it here" is a reason for rules about manners and which side of the road to drive on. And that's a good enough reason in these cases because we recognize that these are local rules or customs and not issues that have moral significance.

Ravi: It seems to me that some people view issues about politeness as moral issues. They get mad at you if aren't properly respectful and stuff.

Sophia: Being inconsiderate and impolite can hurt people's feelings, and we would tell someone that they shouldn't have done that if it hurt the person's feelings.

Dr. Weise: These are all good points. But notice that the moral issue doesn't concern not saying thank you or how you dress. It's about being inconsiderate and hurting the feelings of others. Hurting others does raise moral issues. We believe that generally people should not harm others; in fact, we believe that generally people should be kind to one another. But how kindness and respect are displayed differs from culture to culture. We all believe it is grossly wrong to drive on the wrong side of road since you might kill someone. But which side of the road is the correct side to drive on differs from country to country.

Ravi: But sometimes you do need to hurt someone; for example, by telling them the truth, you could hurt their feelings. Or maybe you need to put someone in jail because they're a menace.

Sophia: But don't you see what Dr. Weise is saying? It's a moral rule that you need to have a justification for harming others. The default view is "don't do harm," but it can be overridden by other moral considerations like protecting others from harm.

Dr. Weise: Thanks, Sophia. You're right that the model of burden of proof and prima facie judgment fits ethical reasoning as well as it does scientific reasoning. Moral reasoning also shares with scientific reasoning an attempt to evaluate from an unbiased and objective perspective. Of course, we are always a bit limited by our culture and current understandings, but striving to get beyond that, whether it's in physics or moral reasoning, is part of the challenge.

Ravi has raised the issue of how we can know what is right or wrong given that right and wrong are not "out there" to be observed the way we can observe phenomena in science. But remember that scientific judgments are not based simply on observation. Observation is part of the scientific process, but the credibility of a claim is still based on argument.

A key move in evaluating moral reasoning is to consider whether there are counter-examples to a claim.

People justify their ethical positions by giving moral reasons.

The process of moral reasoning involves reflecting on and critically evaluating our moral intuitions and the moral positions of others in the light of moral principles in an attempt to arrive at a consistent, balanced, and reasoned judgment.

Apply Your Understanding Exercises 1, 2

In ethics, it is true that we do have to ground our claims in part in an appeal to moral intuitions, and these can, of course, be a product of cultural influence. But we have a process for reflecting on these, for becoming aware of our own cultural biases (see Chapter 11). We can consider and critically evaluate our moral intuitions and the moral positions of others in the light of moral principles in an attempt to arrive at a consistent, balanced, and reasoned judgment about what is morally correct. One primary concern is to achieve a reasonable and moral consistency. We cannot claim to be acting morally if we judge our own case differently than others (e.g., it's acceptable for me to lie, but it's an outrage for him to lie to me).

We also recognize that, as different as people are in various cultures, we have underlying similarities. Similarities in biology and in the conditions of human life give rise to similar challenges and experiences. All humans need to eat and organize the production or gathering of food. We all need to raise our young and deal somehow with the grief of death. We also suffer in much the same way and experience joy in much the same way. Such commonalities provide some common ground for moral ideas and practices.

Moreover, language, which is fundamental to all human cultures, is central to our ability to reason about morality. We can tell one another that an act is wrong, and people's behaviour is influenced by this statement. We can give one another reasons for doing or not doing things, and all cultures do this.

Inquiry into Polygamy

Ravi: So, Dr. Weise, now that we've seen that we can argue about moral matters, I was wondering what you think about the polygamy issue.

Dr. Weise: It doesn't really matter what I think. But it's a good question for an ethical inquiry. Of course, we'll need to begin by clarifying the issue.

What Is the Issue? What Kinds of Claims or Judgments Are at Issue?

Sophia: The issue is whether polygamy is morally wrong.

Ravi: And whether it should be prohibited or legally tolerated. I know that polygamy is currently against the law in both Canada and the U.S. But since it's practised within certain religious groups, it's possible that polygamy laws violate the right to religious freedom.

Dr. Weise: Notice that these two questions raise the issue that we discussed earlier about relativism. Even when we have a moral view which we think is right, we can still ask whether it would be appropriate to try to push or enforce our moral view on others. So here we have both those questions up for grabs. Let's start with the question "Is polygamy morally wrong?" What do you think?

Sophia: I hate it that women are treated that way.

Ravi: That's not a reason; that's just your opinion.

Dr. Weise: I have to agree with Ravi here. The kinds of reasons that justify our moral judgments have to appeal to widely held values, such as equality of all humans or our duties of kindness. They can't just be about what we like or don't like. I call these widely held values "public reasons." As you know from your understanding of inquiry, some reasons are stronger than others, and some reasons people give aren't even relevant. So saying that you hate that women are treated that way may satisfy you, but it couldn't be a reason for anyone else.

Moral judgments should be justified by public (shared) reasons as opposed to personal feelings of approval or dislike.

Our inquirers have determined that we can reason about moral matters much as we do about scientific and other matters, and that we do this through the use of public reasons;

that is, we use reasons that appeal to considerations or criteria which are available to all. We have come across the three basic kinds of considerations involved in assessing the morality of an act or situation previously (See Chapter 7, page 132, and Chapter 9, page 167). We should note, however, that there has been considerable philosophical debate on the issue of justifying moral judgments. There have, historically, been various philosophical theories, each of which has given rise to a different principle for grounding ethical judgments. Although some philosophers may argue about which principle is primary, a widely accepted view is that each of the three main principles furnishes an important consideration, and that all three are required for complete moral deliberation.

The first consideration when deciding what to do is the moral quality of the act itself. Some actions seem to be inherently wrong. Lying, being cruel to people, and killing people are wrong. The wrongness of such actions is often seen as grounded in the principle of "respect for persons." This is a principle, developed by the eighteenth century philosopher Immanuel Kant, which captures the idea that all human beings are deserving of basic respect as human beings regardless of their particular situation and characteristics. All persons have basic rights and responsibilities simply by virtue of being human. This means that we ought to treat people not merely as means to achieving our own ends, but as ends in themselves.

The principle of "respect for persons" is the idea that all human beings are deserving of basic respect as human beings. This means that we ought to treat people not merely as means to achieving our own ends, but as ends in themselves.

Many people who talk about the quality of an act invoke a rule to express this quality, such as "lying is wrong" or "you should respect your parents." But whether talking about moral qualities or rules, the underlying idea is similar: the moral focus is on the act itself or the rule that applies, not on the consequences of doing the act or following the rule. But this approach has limitations. The judgment of the moral quality of an act will often involve reference to more than one rule. Sometimes violating one moral rule is required because a more important rule overrides that one. To take a simple case, if you promised to have dinner at someone's house, then you have a duty to keep that promise. But if a close relative falls ill and needs to be rushed to the hospital, then the duty to support your sick relative overrides your previous promise.

The second consideration is what our duties are—whether we have special responsibilities associated with our position or relationships over and above the basic responsibilities which Kant saw as part of being human. We have duties to our children and friends, but we also have duties in our role as teacher, employer, public servant, and so on. For example, my duty as a teacher requires me to be fair in marking and that duty overrides any general obligation to be kind or nice.

A well-known version of consequentialism is **utilitarianism,** a view developed by Jeremy Bentham (1748–1832) and John Stuart Mill (1806–1873), which holds that the best action is the one which results in the greatest benefit for the greatest number.

The third consideration relates to the consequences of the action. The consequentialist position holds that the morality of an action is determined by the consequences of the action. This position has been criticized on the grounds that it would justify violating the rights of individuals or groups if that would result in better consequences for the majority. This criticism underscores the point that considering consequences in and of themselves is not sufficient. We also need to consider the moral quality of the act.

But the reverse is also true. We usually cannot justify an act simply by referring to the moral quality of the act without also considering the consequences of our action, especially if the consequences are harmful to others. There is a general moral injunction to avoid acts that do harm to others. If as a teacher I am given personal information by a student that reveals that the student is planning to hurt other students, then I should reveal the information because my general duty to confidentiality is overridden by the possibility of harmful consequences.

The three considerations in making a moral judgment are these: 1) the moral quality of the act, 2) our duties or responsibilities, and 3) the consequences of the act.

What all this means is that in moral judgment as in other controversies, coming to a reasoned judgment does not involve relying solely on one type of consideration. It involves, rather, weighing a number of competing and, in some cases, even contradictory considerations.

And last, there is what we might call the **generalizability principle** which is expressed in the famous golden rule: "Do unto others as you would have them do unto you." In other words, the rules you follow and judgments you make when relating to others are rules and judgments you think everyone should make in a similar situation when relating to you. Presumably you, too, would agree that a health crisis overrides a dinner invitation, even if it was you who had made the dinner.

Two of these considerations apply to the polygamy issue. The first consideration is the moral quality of the act often invoked by reference to a moral rule. If the women are forced to marry, this would involve violating the moral rule against coercion. Sometimes, as in imprisonment, coercion can be justified by some other value, like justice or protection of the public; but intrinsically coercion is a bad thing.

Second, we should look at the consequences of the polygamy arrangement. Are the women made deeply unhappy, or do they lead deprived and diminished lives, as a result of polygamy? This question, like the question of whether they are coerced, is a more or less factual question. We would need to know the details of the arrangements before we could evaluate the situation.

Sophia: I can see now that my previous reason was just an opinion. So let me say instead that it's wrong for a man to have more than one wife.

Ravi: That doesn't seem any better than your other reason. How is that an argument?

Dr. Weise: Ravi has a point. But there are some acts that we just see as wrong. We already talked about harming people being prima facie wrong. And why is harming people wrong? Well, it just is. There are basic beliefs that we cannot justify but which provide the basis for justifying other beliefs. But I don't think that the wrongness of having more than one wife is in the category of a basic belief.

Ravi: Why couldn't one test for whether a belief is basic by universality? If most cultures share the same judgment, then we can say that it is a known moral fact. But with polygamy, there are many cultures that have it, so we can't say that we know that it's wrong.

Sophia: But most cultures oppress women. We've only moved to some real enlightenment about the equality of women in the twentieth century—and only in some places. So are you going to say that the lack of universal respect for women is an argument against the principle of equality of women?

Ravi: That's a good point. The fact that so many cultures believe it's OK to oppress women is just that old fallacy of popularity. I can see that I still don't understand how we can justify a moral belief.

Dr. Weise: Let me help out a bit here. I think that there's an almost universal basic belief that equals should be treated equally. What we have seen over the centuries, in relation to both women and other cultures, is that the dominant male group tried to argue that the other cultures and women were not really equals to them: they were seen as not rational or as animals. So it wasn't so much that people didn't recognize the principle of equality; rather, they came up with self-serving theories that justified limiting its application.

Sophia: So are you saying that I could base my argument on human equality? That polygamy violates the principle of equal treatment for all?

Dr. Weise: I think that could be a way to go. At least then, you'd be grounding your argument in a widely shared belief.

Sophia: Well then, I'd have to say that the issue boils down to exploitation. Polygamy is wrong because it involves the exploitation of women. Women don't want to be one of a bunch of sexual servants for some old guy. They would only do that if they were forced. And forcing people to have sex is clearly wrong.

Ravi: Just to be clear, I'm not suggesting it's OK for women to be forced to have sex. But how do we know those women are being forced into these relationships? There's a long tradition in certain cultures of this kind of arrangement. How can you assume that they must be forced? Marriage arrangements differ from culture to culture. This is an area where we might easily be guilty of ethnocentrism.

Sophia: I've read stories about 14-year-old girls being married off to men in their 40s. Surely, that is not voluntary.

Ravi: Agreed. That's child abuse. In fact, in most places in the world, the age of consent to sexual relationships is 16, and many places require anyone under 18 to get permission to marry. But that's an issue for another inquiry. Our issue is whether there's anything wrong with adults being married voluntarily to more than one person.

Sophia: I agree that that's the issue, though we shouldn't ignore what really goes on.

Ravi: But before we get feeling too righteous, we should remember that many people in our culture have more than one spouse—just not at the same time. We accept people getting divorced or breaking up and going into a relationship with another person.

Sophia: I don't think that's a fair comparison. Of course, you can divorce and go to be with another person. That's a kind of recognition of women's (and men's) legitimate rights.

Ravi: Well then, what about people having affairs? People who do that are not married to more than one person, but they are having sex with more than one person. Why is that OK?

Sophia: It isn't OK. We know that it's morally wrong and terribly hurtful to many people.

Ravi: But it isn't against the law. Men who marry more than one woman seem somehow morally better than those who just have sex with more than one person.

Reasoning by analogy is common in ethics as we try to decide what to do in a controversial case by drawing analogies with other cases that are not controversial.

Is polygamy morally superior to adultery?

Note Ravi's analogical reasoning. Reasoning by analogy is common in ethics as we try to decide what to do in a controversial case by drawing analogies with other cases that are not controversial. In this case, we do not have laws against adultery even though we morally disapprove of it. Polygamy is like adultery in that a person has more than one sexual partner; but unlike adultery, polygamy is not secretive. At the same time, being married to a person provides moral protection and duties to that person that affairs do not provide. Thus the analogy suggests that polygamy is morally superior to being married and having an affair.

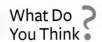

What Do You Think ?

Apply Your Understanding Exercises 3, 4

Sophia: I think the key difference is that polygamy is an institution that does not respect women. Women may accept it because they are brainwashed but that doesn't make it right. No self-respecting women would let herself be wife number three. Come on.

Ravi: We agree with you, but how can we know that for sure? We can believe that our marriage arrangements are right, that they're the ones that most respect women and are the only ones that any woman would choose. But that doesn't mean that people might not willingly opt for some other arrangement. Look how our view of marriage has changed. Now people live together before marriage, sometimes without ever marrying. And we have legalized gay marriages, which many people in our culture still find morally upsetting. Ideas about marriage can change.

Sophia: That's true. But those newer practices like living together and gay marriage can be defended on moral grounds. They don't violate people's right to equality. In fact, gay marriage is a legal recognition of the equal rights of gay people. Polygamy's different.

Key philosophical tools for ethical reasoning:

- arguments
- conceptual analysis (see Chapter 13, p. 251)
- analogies
- counter-examples

Ravi: We haven't settled whether polygamy violates women's equality, but we seem to have moved on to the legal question.

Sophia: Well, maybe the legal issue is more important. I still think it's wrong for women, but as long as there isn't child abuse, I guess we have to tolerate it. But you know, if these women could get an education, I'm sure most of them would reject the arrangement.

Ravi: You could be right, but now we're up against issues of religious freedom for sure. We let parents educate their kids as they choose as long as they meet certain minimal academic standards. And we do that because of a whole history of freedom of religion.

Sophia: That's true.

Ravi: And what about arranged marriages? That's still practised a lot in my cultural tradition. In fact, my cousin Anil had an arranged marriage. She consented to the arrangement; in fact, she was very happy about it. Although I suspect you would argue that it's not real consent (just like Winnie did when we discussed the issue). But whether or not you believe there's real consent, you have to recognize that we're up against a different cultural tradition. Interfering doesn't seem very wise even if we think the practice is misguided.

Sophia: So there are different kinds of marriage arrangements that you think we should tolerate or that the law must tolerate because of the issue of religious freedom, or whatever the principle is that allows people to maintain their marriage traditions and to raise their kids as they see fit.

The Mormon sect in British Columbia that engages in polygamy argues that its practices are protected by freedom of religion. Freedom of religion is one of the doctrines that enables many different sub-cultures to live more or less peacefully together and it may well provide legal protection for the practice. Of course, if there is child abuse, that is a different question, and that practice would not be protected by freedom of religion. This illustrates also how the law draws its limits of involvement. The basic principle that we have in North America is that if adults are freely consenting to an activity and not harming others, the state should not get involved regardless of what the majority may think of the practice. This principle is only partly honoured so that we have laws which restrict activities that are disapproved of but that do not involve direct harm to others. The laws against prostitution and drug usage are good examples.

Sophia: But then what about clitorectomy?

Ravi: What about what?

Sophia: The cutting of a young girl's clitoris so that she can't enjoy sex.

Ravi: That's horrible. Now that is too much.

Sophia: But it is a cultural practice of some people. Many young girls seek out the operation even in countries where it's prohibited because they think they need it in order to be able to marry. It happens in some countries in Africa and the Middle East mostly. But most crucially for my point, it's also practised here in North America. Surely we don't have to tolerate that?

Ravi: Agreed. That's more than our society should tolerate. This is different from polygamy in that it involves very young girls, right? And also it involves irrevocable harm. It is a real form of child abuse and we have a duty to prohibit it.

Sophia: So there are certain practices in certain subcultures in our society that you wouldn't tolerate?

Ravi: Clearly. And I don't think I'm being inconsistent. Remember Dr. Weise's point. You have to ask, given your moral view, whether intervening will work and make things better. I think this is probably the case, though I suspect that efforts to prosecute will result in the practice going even more underground. Clearly education should play a crucial role here. Still, as a society, we have to say this practice cannot be accepted.

Sophia: I'm glad you see my point.

Ravi: In this case, I do.

Sophia: Though I think we need to be careful not to start feeling too self-righteous; we mustn't ignore all the moral problems here at home. Like all those children who live in poverty while others have so much. It's not fair.

Ravi: So what is fair?

Sophia: Sounds like another challenging inquiry to me.

Table of Arguments Pro and Con Polygamy

Name of View	Description	Pro Argument	Con Argument	Responses
Polygamy	Polygamy (having more than one spouse) is morally acceptable.	Polygamy is widely practised in many countries.	There are many sexist practices that are widespread; that does not make them acceptable.	This is a very ethnocentric attitude which presumes that the model of relationships in the west should be the model for all cultures.
		There is nothing obviously wrong with it as long as participants are consenting adults.	Polygamy fundamentally involves the exploitation of women even if they are "consenting." Real consent requires that people have real choices; these marriages occur either in sects or closed societies where real choices are limited.	
		Polygamy is better than the common practice of many people to be married and have affairs.	Better doesn't make it right—both practices could be wrong.	
		Consistent with serial monogamy.	Completely different than serial monogamy in that one has only one spouse at a time.	
Legal Tolerance	The law should not interfere with the practice of polygamy as long as there is no child abuse involved.	If consenting adults, then there is no reason to intervene, whatever we think of the practice.	It is a gross form of sexual inequality that is no longer acceptable in this society. It almost certainly involves child abuse; legalizing or even tolerating it will perpetuate this abuse.	Child exploitation is a valid issue, but should not be confused with the issue of tolerance for alternative religious practices.

Moral inquiry is an ongoing process. We are constantly faced with moral challenges in both our personal and our community lives. People's views on moral matters differ a great deal. You may think that an inquiry considering the alternative views may not change other people's minds. But it might. Considering what can be said in support of alternative points of views remains one of the best ways to avoid not only ethnocentrism, but more generally, dogmatic and self-satisfied thinking.

Apply Your
Understanding
Exercises 5, 6, 7

CHECK YOUR UNDERSTANDING

- *What is ethical relativism?*
- *What is ethnocentrism? Give an example of an ethnocentric belief or practice.*
- *Explain how relativism leads to an inconsistency.*
- *Explain the difference between meta-ethics and normative ethics.*
- *Give an example where considering the facts of the situation is relevant to making a moral judgment.*
- *How do people generally justify their moral judgments?*
- *List some common features of human beings across cultures which can provide some common basis for moral ideas and practices.*
- *Identify the two different issues that are involved in the polygamy case.*
- *What are the three principal considerations in making a moral judgment?*
- *What are the two considerations which apply in the polygamy case? Explain how they apply.*

EXERCISES

1. Analyze and evaluate the following arguments:

    i) It's OK for me to have sex with someone other than my partner as long as my partner doesn't know about it, because that way no one is hurt and so no harm is done.

    ii) Abortion is wrong because it is wrong to kill unborn babies.

    iii) Imagine that a crazed killer invades a corporation board meeting looking for the corporate officer who rejected a grievance against the company. The intruder threatens to kill each person in the room one by one if the group doesn't identify the officer being targeted. The right thing for the group to do would be to give up the corporate officer in order to save all the others.

    iv) We ought to accept the beliefs and practices of other cultures for two reasons. One reason is that there are not grounds for asserting that the beliefs and practices of one culture are superior to those of another culture and thus we must accept the legitimacy of all cultures' beliefs and practices alongside our own. The other reason is that we might learn something from the beliefs and practices of other cultures.

    v) Copying DVDs may be right for you, but it's not right for me. Values are relative, after all.

    vi) We have no right to criticize societies that do not grant equal rights to women. The belief in gender equality is widely held in our culture, but it is not a part of some other cultural traditions.

2. Try to find counter-examples to the following claims:

    i) The best action is the one that results in the greatest benefit for the greatest number.

    ii) We have a special duty to our family and so should give them priority in moral matters.

    iii) It is wrong to lie.

    iv) Thou shalt not steal.

    v) The best society is one governed by the will of the majority.

    vi) True equality exists when everyone is treated exactly the same way.

3. Do an inquiry into whether euthanasia is ethically justifiable. What are the strongest arguments pro and con? How confident a judgment can you make?

4. Evaluate the following ethical analogies:

    i) Male circumcision is just like female circumcision—a barbaric practice supported by cultural prejudice.

ii) If we accept polygamy on the grounds of cultural relativism, then we would also have to accept clitorectomy. But we do not accept clitorectomy as a morally acceptable practice.

iii) European colonization of North America is like a home invasion: the residents are not asked, and they are forcefully moved. The land should be returned to the natives.

iv) Since the medical profession is opposed to doctors conducting death-by-injection executions of convicted murderers, they should also be opposed to doctors performing abortions. Any other position is ethically inconceivable.

v) Outlawing speech that promotes hatred toward a group of people is a legitimate limitation on freedom of speech. We do allow limitations when public well-being is concerned; for example, we do not allow someone to shout "fire" in a crowded theatre when there is no fire and people might get trampled to death.

vi) If we agree that polygamy should be illegal, then we should also make adultery illegal, as it also involves having sex with more than one partner.

vii) Thinking that it is justified to try to resolve an international problem by using a bomb attack is just as ridiculous as thinking that it would be justified to try to resolve a neighbourhood problem by blowing up someone's house.

5. Polyamory refers to having more than one sexual partner at a time.

i) Conduct an inquiry on the morality of polyamory.

ii) Write a dialogue representing the inquiry.

6. Read the dialogue on the textbook website under Exercise 15-6. Then do the following:

i) Inquire into the issue raised in the dialogue.

ii) Continue the dialogue to some resolution of the issue.

7. Evaluate the following brief essay on the topic of relativism as an example of a philosophical inquiry in ethics.

Since the very dawn of time, the problem of relativism has been considered by many of the greatest and deepest thinkers in history. There are lots of philosophers who have supported relativism, such as Jaina Anekantavada, Protagoras, Spinoza, Hume, Nietzsche, and the anthropologists Ruth Benedict and Edward Westermarck. So relativism must be well supported. For example, Protagoras said, "Man is the measure of all things."

As for my own opinion, I believe that relativism is true. But that's just my opinion. The question of relativism is, after all, a subjective one. So it can be seen from the above arguments that there are many different points of view about the relativism problem.

ENDNOTES

1. CBC.ca, "B.C. Religious Leaders Charged with Polygamy," http://www.cbc.ca/canada/british-columbia/story/2009/01/07/bc-blackmore-polygamy-charges.html (accessed Jan. 6, 2010).

2. John Webber Cook, *Morality and Cultural Differences* (New York: Oxford University Press, 1999)

Chapter 16
Inquiry into the Extraordinary

The Secret

Juanita and Winnie have gotten together a few days before their midterm math exam. Winnie is pouring over her textbook while Juanita is staring resolutely into space.

Winnie: I thought you were having trouble in math. Aren't you going to prepare for the exam?

Juanita: I am preparing for the exam.

Winnie: Then why aren't you looking at your book?

Juanita: I've discovered a better way to prepare. I've found The Secret.

Winnie: I thought that the secret to doing well on an exam was to study.

Juanita: No, I mean *The Secret*.[1] It's this amazing book that tells you how to get the things you want just by thinking about them.

Winnie: Juanita, tell me you're not serious.

Juanita: No, really. You think positive thoughts about what you want, and your thoughts attract those things to you. It's called the law of attraction. So I'm thinking really hard about doing well on the exam, and my thoughts will make it happen.

Winnie: Yeah, right.

Juanita: But I have to feel it and really believe that it will happen. If I just visualize myself getting an A on the exam, then I will!

Winnie: Look, Juanita, I've actually read the book—I thought it was a hoot. But I didn't expect any of my friends to actually buy that bunk.

Juanita: Winnie, you are such a skeptic!

Winnie: I'll take that as a compliment.

Juanita: I mean, there's all kinds of evidence that this works.

Winnie: Like what?

Juanita: Well, there are lots of quotes from experts who talk about how powerful The Secret is and explain how it works. And then there are stories from people whose lives have been changed by using it. And another really important point is that lots of famous people throughout history—like Shakespeare, Beethoven, Newton, and Jesus—have known about The Secret.

Winnie: Right…

Juanita: Then, another point—you'll really like this one, Winnie—it's been proven scientifically! The Secret is based on natural laws and scientific principles.

Winnie: Scientific—give me a break!

Juanita: Don't be so negative, Winnie. It makes perfect sense. Everyone talks about the power of positive thinking. It's worked for me when I've tried it! Me and lots of other people. The book's a bestseller, and they've even made a movie of it. All those people must know something.

Winnie: That "evidence" has more holes in it than a Swiss cheese. I don't know where to start. Didn't you learn anything in our critical thinking course?

Juanita: One thing I did learn is that it's important to be open-minded and seriously consider other views. I don't think you're being very open-minded, Winnie.

Winnie: OK, point taken. So what we ought to do is to look at the evidence more closely and evaluate whether there's anything to it.

Juanita: That's fine by me.

What initial problems do you see in the evidence that Juanita offers?

What Do
You Think

In this dialogue, Juanita is impressed with and influenced by a book that has gained many adherents. The book makes extraordinary claims about how we can get what we want in life; in the process, it makes extraordinary claims about how the world functions.[2] While Juanita is caught up in the vision the book portrays and believes it without reservation, Winnie takes a more critical attitude.

The focus of this chapter is inquiry about the extraordinary. By "the extraordinary," we are referring to phenomena which seem to fall outside our ordinary explanatory schemes. These include phenomena that seem mysterious or puzzling, phenomena for which there does not appear to be an adequate explanation in "ordinary" terms. Examples include the alleged mysterious disappearance of ships in the Bermuda triangle or the phenomenon of crop circles.

The explanations offered for such phenomena frequently involve claims which are themselves extraordinary: the suspension of the laws of physics for the Bermuda triangle disappearances or the work of extraterrestrial beings for the crop circles, for example. In addition, extraordinary explanations are sometimes offered for "ordinary" or everyday phenomena; for example, astrological theories about the positions of planets are sometimes suggested to explain human behaviour, which we normally explain by means of psychological theories.

Extraordinary beliefs are often popular and widely held. Take, for example, the ubiquity of beliefs in astrology, reincarnation, ESP, alien abductions, and conspiracies of all kinds.

It is, however, the very extraordinariness of the claims that should put us on our guard. This is not to suggest that all extraordinary claims are unsubstantiated. Some very well established claims in science may seem, or have initially seemed, strange and counterintuitive. What it does mean is that we cannot take such claims at face value. We need to be skeptics, as Winnie is, and to examine them with a critical eye. Extraordinary claims call for inquiry.

What Is the Issue? What Kinds of Claims or Judgments Are at Issue?

Winnie: OK then, the first step is to identify the issue.

Juanita: I guess the issue is whether I should believe what they say in *The Secret*.

Winnie: That's pretty broad. They say a lot of things.

Juanita: You're right. How about whether my thinking about doing well on the exam will make it happen?

Winnie: We might want to make it a little more general. How about this: "Can thinking about something bring it into being or make it happen?"

Juanita: Sounds good.

Do Americans Believe in the Paranormal?

Gallup News Service, June 16, 2005[4]

PRINCETON, NJ—About three in four Americans profess at least one paranormal belief, according to a recent Gallup survey. The most popular is extrasensory perception (ESP), mentioned by 41%, followed closely by belief in haunted houses (37%). A special analysis of the data shows that 73% of Americans believe in at least one of the 10 items listed, while 27% believe in none of them. A Gallup survey in 2001 provided similar results—76% professed belief in at least one of the 10 items. The full list of items includes:

	% Believe in
Extrasensory perception, or ESP	41
That houses can be haunted	37
Ghosts/that spirits of dead people can come back in certain places/situations	32
Telepathy/communication between minds without using traditional senses	31
Clairvoyance/the power of the mind to know the past and predict the future	26
Astrology, or that the position of the stars and planets can affect people's lives	25
That people can communicate mentally with someone who has died	21
Witches	21
Reincarnation, that is, the rebirth of the soul in a new body after death	20
Channeling/allowing a 'spirit-being' to temporarily assume control of body	9

Bigfoot and Other Beasts: A Field Guide to Unproven Animals[3]

From cbc.ca

Throughout the last century, there have been many reported sightings in the Pacific Northwest of a tall, hairy, ape-like creature that walks on two legs. Some reports describe groups of Sasquatches foraging for berries, some say it knows how to swim, whistle, verbalize, even scream. Invariably, it is described as "shy."

According to one account, the term "Sasquatch" comes from a Chehalis word meaning "wild man" and was coined by a teacher in British Columbia in the 1920s. The Sasquatch name is usually applied to sightings in Canada, especially B.C.—but Bigfoot/Sasquatch researchers often use the terms interchangeably.

Bigfoot researchers have analysed feces and hair samples supposedly left by the mysterious creatures. Giant footprints yield calculations about the creature's weight and size (almost three metres tall and 150 to 325 kg)...

In December 2006, a Sasquatch-like creature was apparently spotted by a woman driving near the northern Saskatchewan community of Deschambault Lake.

In April 2005, a car ferry operator in Norway House, Man., shot three minutes of video of a "big, black figure" moving on the opposite side of the river. He said the creature was massive. The video is, to say the least, indistinct.

Source: AP Photo/Sasquatch Research Project, Roger Patterson and Bob Gimlin.

Winnie: I think we need to be clear here that the claim is that just thinking positive thoughts about something can, all on its own, literally bring some event or object into being. We're not talking about a metaphor or about our thoughts indirectly bringing something about because we have some idea that we act on. The thoughts literally attract the event or object. Is that right?

Juanita: Yes.

Winnie: So, in that case, what kind of judgment are we trying to make?

Juanita: Factual, I would say.

Winnie: Agreed.

Becoming clear about the exact nature of the claim is an important step for Juanita's and Winnie's inquiry. While the question, "Can thinking about something bring it into being or make it happen?" may seem straightforward, it is, in fact, ambiguous. It could mean that thinking can literally and directly bring something into being, or it could be used metaphorically in the sense that having a thought can be a prelude to taking action to make something happen. Thus my having an idea for a new way to prepare chicken cacciatore can be a prelude to buying the ingredients and doing all the preparation necessary to make the new recipe. So my idea is an indirect cause of the chicken cacciatore coming into being. This is quite different from the claim that my simply thinking about the chicken cacciatore will bring it into being.

What Are the Relevant Reasons and Arguments on Various Sides of the Issue?

Winnie: Why don't we start by you quickly going through the reasons why you believe the claim, and I'll make a note of each reason on a pro and con table. Then we can look at each one in more detail when we're doing the evaluation.

Juanita: OK. Well, when I first heard about the book, I knew that it was a bestseller. So I thought there must be something to it if so many people believe it.

Winnie: "Bestseller." What else?

Juanita: There are lots of experts quoted in the book who support this idea, and there's a consensus among them.

Winnie: "Experts." Go on.

Juanita: I think that a really strong reason is that lots of important people throughout history knew about The Secret and that it's in all the world's great religions.

Winnie: "Famous people." Next?

Juanita: The fact that the law of attraction works is supported by testimonials by all kinds of different people.

Winnie: "Testimonials." What else?

Juanita: The law of attraction has been scientifically proven.

Winnie: "Scientific." Right. Next reason.

Juanita: The law of attraction goes along with what lots of people say about the power of positive thinking.

Winnie: "Power of positive thinking." Uh-huh.

Juanita: And—this is the clincher — I've been trying it out, and it works.

Winnie: "Personal experience." Got it.

What Is the Context of the Issue?

Winnie: Next is context.

Juanita: I think that this book really speaks to a need that folks have these days. Lots of people feel that they don't have control in their lives and are looking for some way to improve how things are going.

Winnie: I think you're right. That's probably why self-help books are so popular. I also think that the fact that we live in a very consumer-oriented society is important. People always want more and more, so they would be happy to find some way of getting more of whatever it is that they want.

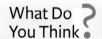

List any other contextual factors you can think of that might be relevant in assessing the claim.

How Do We Comparatively Evaluate the Various Reasons and Arguments in Order to Reach a Reasoned Judgment?

Prime Facie Evaluation

Winnie: Now on to the evaluation. Why don't we work our way through the various reasons?

Conduct a prima facie evaluation of the reasons offered by Juanita, identifying any informal fallacies that you spot.

Juanita: OK. My first reason was that so many people seem to believe it so there must be something to it. Everyone has been reading it since it first came out, and it's even been endorsed by Oprah.

Winnie: Juanita, do you remember when we learned about prima facie evaluation of arguments and about the fallacy of popularity?

Juanita: I think so. Isn't that when you try to justify a belief on the basis that lots of people believe it? But we know that lots of people have held silly and even immoral beliefs, so … Oh, I see the problem … But that in itself doesn't mean that the belief is wrong.

Winnie: No, it doesn't. But it does mean that we need to keep looking at other reasons.

Juanita: OK. So what about the fact that the law of attraction that *The Secret* is based on is supported by so many experts? Not only do they testify to how well it works, they also give explanations for how it operates—through the principle that like attracts like. So thoughts about love will attract love and thoughts about money will attract money. Or thoughts about succeeding on an exam will attract success on the exam. But negative thoughts will also attract their like, so thoughts about failure on an exam will attract failure on the exam. I remember we learned that if an expert can give you a plausible argument for their claim, that's all the more reason to trust what they say.

Winnie: But we need to ask who these "experts" are and what they're experts in. Since the claim about the law of attraction is a factual, scientific claim, then the appropriate domain of expertise would be science. But the people cited are mostly authors, spiritual teachers, entrepreneurs, wealth consultants (quite a few of those), healers, and personal empowerment trainers. Only two of the 29 are scientists, both quantum physicists.

Juanita: But there is a consensus among those experts, which we learned is important for evaluating expertise.

Winnie: A consensus is only meaningful if they really are experts in the relevant field, which these people are not. And anyway, the choice of who is cited in the book is very selective. It's by no means a representative sample of scientists who are knowledgeable in the area, to say the least. I think it's fair to say that the vast majority of scientists would say that the law of attraction is nonsense since it doesn't make any sense scientifically (but we'll get to that).

Juanita: Good.

Winnie: And another thing. Did you notice that almost all the individuals cited give talks or workshops on *The Secret* or related themes or have published books or developed programs in the area?

Juanita: I hadn't noticed that before. I hadn't considered the possibility before that they might stand to profit if people believe in the ideas of *The Secret*. Hmm … they don't sound much like unbiased sources, do they?

Winnie: Agreed.

Juanita: But what about the fact that all those very famous people throughout history, including poets like Shakespeare and Browning, musicians like Beethoven, artists like Leonardo da Vinci, and great thinkers like Socrates, Newton, and Victor Hugo have expressed the law of attraction in their works? And religions such as Christianity, Judaism, Islam, Hinduism, and Buddhism have revealed The Secret in their writings and stories. The Secret was even recorded in 3000 BCE in stone!

Winnie: And what exactly is the evidence for that rather sweeping claim?

Juanita: I … hmm … well … The author of the book says so. That's not much of a ground for believing it, is it?

Winnie: And besides, what exactly could it mean to say that Shakespeare or Newton, or— what is most absurd—Beethoven, expressed the law of attraction in their work? The claim is so vague that it would be completely impossible to verify.

Juanita: I guess so. But there are all those testimonials from people whose lives were changed by the law of attraction. For example, there's a man who started receiving cheques in the mail as soon as he started visualizing cheques coming in the mail. Another one always gets a parking spot by visualizing one exactly where he wants it. There's a woman who found her perfect part- ner when she started acting as if she'd already found him. Another woman talks about how she healed herself from breast cancer without any radiation or chemotherapy by imagining herself as already healed and by watching funny movies. And there's one man who now lives in a four- and-a-half million dollar mansion, has a wife who he says is "to die for," travels to fantastic places, and has had all kinds of adventures, all since he started applying The Secret to his life! And, get this—a Belize oil team discovered an abundant supply of high quality oil where other companies couldn't, once they developed a mental picture of Belize being a successful oil-producing coun- try. There are lots more stories, and they're all very compelling. That's got to count for something.

Winnie: We'll see.

Juanita: And then there are my own personal experiences using the law of attraction. Like the other day, I was realizing that I hadn't heard from my friend Carlos for a long time. So I kept thinking about Carlos and imagining hearing from him, and the next day—guess what? I got an email from him! And yesterday my wrist was really hurting me from playing volleyball. So I con- centrated hard on feeling good and imagined myself spiking the ball with no pain in my wrist. And when I woke up this morning, my wrist was fine!

Winnie: Time for another fallacy review. Do you remember the fallacy of anecdotal evidence?

Juanita: Yeah. That's when you try to base a strong generalization on stories or anecdotes. Hmm … I guess that's exactly what's going on here, isn't it? I'm making a claim about how the entire universe functions based on a few stories. So even though the stories are compelling, they can't provide enough evidence to support such a vast generalization.

Winnie: Exactly. And the stories don't provide any evidence whatsoever unless they're accurate. But we know that the author of the book and the "experts" who are quoted have something to gain by our belief—

Juanita: So we have a reason to be a bit skeptical about the accounts of these people's experi- ences that we're being told?

Winnie: Right. But you know, even if all the accounts were perfectly sincere, there's another issue that I think is relevant. Our psych prof was telling us about the problem of **confirmation bias**. That's the tendency to focus on the events or facts that confirm our ideas and not notice the ones that contradict them. So if people have the idea that thinking about something is going to make it happen, they will be more likely to notice when something they were thinking about happens, and less likely to notice all the times when it doesn't. Are you aware of all the times you may have thought about Carlos without hearing from him?

Juanita: No. But I have to admit that that's likely since I do think about him a lot.

Winnie: Or all the times you thought about feeling better when you were sick but still felt awful? Or had a feeling that you were going to do well on a test, but you didn't since you hadn't studied enough? Or …

Juanita: OK, Winnie, I think you've made the point.

Confirmation bias is the tendency to look for and notice evidence that con- firms our beliefs, and not look for, ignore, or under- value evidence that contra- dicts our beliefs.

Winnie and Juanita have begun evaluating the reasons offered in support of the law of attraction espoused by *The Secret* by conducting a prima facie evaluation, examining the arguments to detect any fallacies or problems in reasoning. Among the fallacies and problems they detect are the fallacy of popularity, improper appeal to authority, vagueness, hasty generalization, anecdotal evidence, problematic premise, biased sources, and confirmation bias. Finding so many problems even before getting to the evaluation of the substance of claims will in some cases provide sufficient reason for dismissing the view in question; it might not be worth your time or intellectual efforts to pursue it further. But because there are important issues at stake about the nature of science and of inquiry in general, our intrepid pair will carry on with the evaluation.

Evaluation of Scientific Claims and Causal Reasoning

Juanita: OK, so I can see that there are some problems in the reasoning. But still the law of attraction has been scientifically proven. It's a law of nature, just like gravity. We all know about magnetism, that like attracts like. But what I didn't know before is that thoughts are magnetic and have a frequency. When you think a thought, it goes out into the universe and attracts things that are on the same frequency. It's an idea supported by quantum physics, which tells us that the entire universe emerged from thought. You've got to be impressed by that, with your scientific bent.

What do you think about the claim that the law of attraction is scientific?

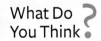
What Do You Think?

Winnie: Science is a subject I do know something about. And the claim that the law of attraction, or anything else in the book, is scientific is far-fetched, to say the least.

Juanita: Why do you say that?

Winnie: Remember we learned that one of the main characteristics of science is that its theories can be tested and counter-evidence will count against and even sometimes contribute to refuting the theory. But the law of attraction doesn't work like that. The theory states that if you think positive thoughts about what you want, those things will come to you. But if the things you want don't come to you, then you're not thinking positive thoughts (or not enough or not with enough feeling or belief or not for long enough . . .). So no evidence, even evidence that looks like counter-evidence, can count against the theory. It's a circular argument—the very opposite of true science.

Juanita: But what about magnetism and thoughts having frequencies and like attracting like and all those scientific principles that are behind the law of attraction?

Winnie: The law of attraction makes a causal claim—that thinking about something can bring it into being. So why don't we test it according to the criteria we learned for evaluating causal claims and then see what we think about those "scientific" principles?

Juanita: OK. I have my notes on causal reasoning right here.

As a review, write down the criteria for evaluating causal claims.

What Do You Think?

Juanita: Here's the first one: is there a correlation between the supposed cause and effect?

Winnie: How could we establish if all instances (or even most instances) of people getting what they want are correlated with thinking positive thoughts, or if all instances (or even most) of people not getting what they want correlate with thinking negative thoughts?

Juanita: Gee, I guess there really is no way to know that.

Winnie: And it's especially a problem because the claim is that people are having these thoughts whether they are aware of it or not. We have no reason to believe this except that it says so in the theory which we're trying to test.

Juanita: Sounds circular to me.

Winnie: Indeed. Next criterion.

Juanita: Did the claimed cause occur before the effect?

Winnie: Again, we have no way of knowing. It looks to me like there's a lot of post hoc reasoning going on—a good thing happened so the person must have thought positive thoughts about it.

Juanita: That's a problem. Next criterion: is there a credible causal link?

Winnie: What do you think, Juanita?

Juanita: I think that there is. The law of attraction works on the scientific principle that like attracts like. Thoughts have frequencies which go into the universe and attract things that are on the same frequency. That explains how thinking about something can bring it into being.

Winnie: But the key word is "credible," Juanita. That explanation runs contrary to everything we know about science. One giant mistake is that, with magnetism, it's not the like poles that attract each other but rather the opposite poles.

Juanita: Are you sure about that? Like attracting like sounds right to me. I'm going to check it out on the internet. Magnetism. "Magnets have two poles, called the north (N) and south (S) poles. Two magnets will be attracted by their opposite poles, and each will repel the like pole of the other magnet."[5] Here's another one: "Like poles repel, unlike poles attract."[6] Wow! So the whole theory rests on a major scientific misconception.

Winnie: Right. And other ideas basic to the theory, for example, that thoughts have frequencies, that thoughts are somehow broadcast outside our bodies (into the whole universe, no less), or that thoughts by themselves could somehow bring things into being, also have absolutely no basis in scientific fact. You don't need to trust me—check it out on a decent science website or in any basic science text. There are all kinds of claims throughout the book that are just as erroneous. For example, "food doesn't make you fat but thoughts about food do."

Juanita: Don't I wish!

Winnie: How about these claims from the book? "Our physiology creates disease to let us know we have an imbalanced perspective or we're not being loving and grateful." "We have enough energy in our bodies to illuminate a whole city for a week." It would require an extraordinary amount of extraordinarily strong evidence to substantiate claims that go so much against widely accepted scientific theories. But the book provides no evidence at all.

Juanita: I can see that now.

Winnie: Instead of providing scientific evidence from systematic observations or experiments, they argue through analogy, such as that our thoughts are like magnets or we are like TV transmitters. But these are not very good analogies.

Juanita: Right—because the things they're comparing are not alike in the ways they say. We just saw that.

Winnie: But what makes this way of reasoning an even bigger problem is that they interpret the analogies as if they were scientific facts! So then they have these claims that they pass off as scientific but that go against all our established scientific theories.

Juanita: But what about quantum theory? It says in the book that quantum theory tells us that the universe emerges from thought. That seems to support the law of attraction.

Winnie: Don't get me started on popular misinterpretations of quantum theory. It drives me mad! Quantum physics is all about very very small phenomena and what happens when you try to measure them. It's not about parking spots suddenly appearing or finding oil in Belize. You can't go making a whole theory of the world that completely conflicts with how we know things work based on some very specialized scientific theory. Even the leading physicists are not clear on what the implications might be for how the world works at the level of large objects, if there are any.

Juanita: Why don't we move on to the next criterion, or maybe even the next two since they're related? Are there other plausible alternative explanations that fit the facts and can they be eliminated? And which is the simplest explanation?

Winnie: We've seen already that there are very well established scientific theories to explain how the world works and the causal connections between things. They've been well tested, they're elegant, and they've allowed us to do tremendous things, like building amazing computers and travelling in space and curing diseases. Wouldn't you agree that these theories provide much better explanations than a theory like the law of attraction which is completely unsubstantiated, makes scientifically dubious causal claims, and requires a lot of unproven assumptions?

In this part of their evaluation, Juanita and Winnie are focussing on the claim that the law of attraction—that is, the theory that thinking about something will bring it into being—is scientific. There are two aspects to their evaluation. One deals with whether the theory qualifies as a scientific theory, and the other with whether what the theory claims is justified. In conducting this evaluation, they use many of the concepts and guidelines regarding the nature of scientific inquiry (Chapter 12), the evaluation of scientific claims (Chapter 12), and the evaluation of causal reasoning (Chapter 5) that we've learned about previously.

The issue of whether the theory is scientific is an extremely important one. A main feature of science is that its theories are testable, as Winnie points out. Theories must be supported by evidence, but it must also be possible for evidence to count against a theory and at times even contribute to its elimination in favour of a more-justified alternative (see Chapter 12). Theories which are constructed in such a way that any counter-evidence is automatically explained away by the theory do not qualify as scientific.

The criteria for evaluating causal reasoning play a crucial role in Winnie's and Juanita's assessment of the law of attraction. They determine that no correlation between the claimed cause and effect can be established, that much of the reasoning is post hoc, and that alleged causal links are scientifically dubious. In addition, and importantly, there are existing scientific theories which explain the phenomena in question which are very well justified and have the virtue of simplicity. It is important to keep in mind that, when a proposed explanation is extraordinary—that is, when it runs counter to the body of accepted scientific theory—the burden of proof is on the extraordinary explanation. The burden of proof is very far from being discharged in this case.

Finally, one must exercise caution in the face of an assertion that a particular, otherwise contentious claim is supported by some major scientific theory. It is not uncommon that theories such as the theory of relativity or quantum theory are used as support for certain non-scientific claims about the nature of the world. For example, the theory of relativity is sometimes taken to imply that all claims, including moral claims, are relative; or quantum theory is taken to imply that our perceptions create phenomena (as is the case here). Scientific theories are, however, developed in the context of specific scientific problems and tend to be complex in their implications, even for scientists. Attempting to draw such implications from scientific theories is a dubious enterprise at best and often represents a misuse of scientific theory.

It must be possible for evidence to count against a theory and at times even contribute to its elimination in favour of a better justified alternative. Theories which are constructed in such a way that any counter-evidence is automatically explained away by the theory do not qualify as scientific.

When a proposed explanation is extraordinary—that is, when it runs counter to the body of accepted scientific theory—there is a heavy burden of proof on the extraordinary explanation.

Attempting to draw non-scientific implications about the nature of the world from complex scientific theories often represents a misuse of scientific theory.

Juanita: But you're forgetting something really important, Winnie, and that's how well the law of attraction goes along with what lots of people say about the power of positive thinking. Like, if I keep thinking that I'm going to fail the math exam, I probably will—even my math teacher says that and tells me that I need to think positively. And when I'm doing my ski lessons, my instructor tells me to visualize myself skiing down the hill without a hitch. He says that if I think I'm going to fall, then I probably will. It's the same thing with relationships. I know that if I keep thinking about all the things that bug me about my little brother, he just seems to do more of those things. But if I focus on how sweet he can be, then he seems to just keep acting sweeter. The law of attraction explains why these kinds of things happen. How can you explain these things otherwise?

Winnie: First off, let me say that I agree that there's something to the power of positive thinking. I think it's true that people are often more successful in what they do if they have a positive attitude than if they don't believe they're going to succeed. Like you with your math tests and your skiing. And I agree that other people will tend to respond better to us when we're upbeat and happy than when we're grouchy and negative. And they'll often respond according to our expectations of them, whether they're positive or negative. Like what happens with your little brother.

Juanita: Oh, Winnie, I'm so glad that you agree! I didn't think you would, being the skeptic that you are.

Winnie: But the question is whether there's a better explanation for all this than that our thoughts are bringing these things into being.

Juanita: Like what?

Winnie: Can you think of any reasons why you might tend to do better on your math tests when you believe that you will?

Juanita: I guess that it gives me more confidence. When I don't think I understand the material and am worried that I'm going to fail, I get discouraged when I come across a hard question. I get into a kind of panic and can't concentrate. But when I feel more confident, then I don't give up so easily. I think I focus better and try harder because I believe I can do it.

Winnie: And what about skiing?

Juanita: I think it's a question of confidence again. When I'm at the top of a really challenging hill and I worry about falling, then I get nervous. I think I actually sit down (at least that's what my instructor says).

Winnie: We learned in our psychology class that there's been a lot of research on this topic, which they call self-efficacy. And it basically confirms what you're saying—that a strong belief that you can accomplish something makes it more likely that you'll be able to, and a strong sense that you can't will do the opposite.[7]

Juanita: Wow! I didn't realize that there's actually been research on this. So the *Secret* folks didn't invent this idea. But what about visualization? I do find that visualizing doing a perfect ski run really does help. Why would that be if it's not that my visualization is making it happen?

Winnie: I was reading something about the use of visualization in training athletes. Apparently, there's research that shows that it can really help, just as you describe. The explanation that's given is that it acts as a kind of mental rehearsal that can help in skill acquisition. It also causes the athletes to focus on the physical moves. And it can boost confidence.[8] I didn't see anything about the law of attraction.

Juanita: And is there also an alternative explanation for why my little brother is nastier when I focus on his annoying habits and sweeter when I focus on his good qualities?

Winnie: I'll bet that when you're focusing on what annoys you, you let him know that the things he's doing are driving you crazy.

Juanita: How could I help it?

Winnie: And when he's being co-operative, do you praise him and tell him how sweet he is?

Juanita: Definitely.

Winnie: You're doing what's known in psychology as positive reinforcement. You're giving him attention for certain behaviours. So it's not surprising that he continues with the behaviours you're reinforcing. It's how you're acting towards him that accounts for his behaviour, not just your thoughts on their own.[9]

Juanita: I have to admit that what you're saying makes sense. So in other words, I can accept what they say in the book about the power of positive thinking without accepting the idea that it's thoughts on their own that make things happen, which we've seen is pretty sketchy. There are explanations that make a lot more sense when you think about them. And they're even confirmed by psychological research.

Clearly much of the appeal for Juanita of the law of attraction lies in the fact that it seems to provide an account of the power of positive thinking. Although Winnie clearly does not believe the law of attraction, she does acknowledge those aspects that seem to be correct or plausible in the theory. She also demonstrates, however, that there are better explanations for the kinds of phenomena which Juanita cites, explanations which are supported by psychological research and which conform to common sense. It is often the case, when dealing with what seem like inexplicable phenomena, that there are simple and plausible explanations for them if only you look.

It is often the case, when dealing with what seem like inexplicable phenomena, that there are simple and plausible explanations for them if only you look.

Comparative Evaluation

Winnie: We've looked at a lot of reasons. Maybe it would be helpful to add an evaluation to our table of the arguments in order to see where we are.

Winnie and Juanita work together to record the arguments in support of and against the law of attraction. (See the table on page 318.)

Juanita: Well, that's pretty telling, isn't it? The arguments in support of the law of attraction are full of fallacies and problems in reasoning. And the claim that the theory is scientific seems pretty lame. There does seem to be something to what they say about the power of positive thinking but there are other more credible explanations for that. All in all, the law of attraction doesn't stand up very well, does it?

Winnie: You can say that again. Especially since we have tons of evidence that the world doesn't work the way the law of attraction says. And there are reasonable causal explanations for why people get or don't get what they want, usually some combination of effort, attitude, ability, and chance.

Juanita: Something that really strikes me when looking at the table is that the *Secret* folks don't offer any responses to these criticisms. In fact, they don't even acknowledge that there might be criticisms of their theory or alternative views. We learned that acknowledging and responding to criticisms and alternative views is a central aspect of real inquiry. But they just write as if everything they say is the unquestionable truth. I guess that should have put me on my guard right from the start.

Winnie: That's a really good point, Juanita.

Juanita: Something else that strikes me when I think about the whole process is how important it is to be aware of alternative views and explanations. Otherwise it's too easy to believe the views you read or hear about. They can seem to make so much sense until you realize that there might be explanations for things that are a lot better than the ones being offered.

Acknowledging and responding to criticisms and alternative views is a central aspect of inquiry.

Evaluation of the Arguments Pro and Con the Law of Attraction

Argument Name	Argument Summary	Evaluation
PRO		
Bestseller	Popularity of *The Secret*; there must be something to it	Fallacy of popularity; alternative explanations for popularity
Experts	Lots of experts quoted who support idea	Improper appeal to authority; biased sources; selectivity of sources
Famous people	Expressed by many famous people throughout history	Vagueness—impossible to verify
Testimonials	Many testimonials that the law works	Fallacy of anecdotal evidence; issue of trustworthiness of accounts
Scientific	Ideas have frequencies and attract their like; supported by quantum theory	Untestable; fails all criteria for a causal claim; contradicts well-established scientific theories; unjustified implications from quantum theory
Positive thinking	Confirmed by experiences of the power of positive thinking	Real phenomenon, but more credible alternative explanations exist
Personal experience	Confirmed by personal experiences	Confirmation bias
CON		
Accepted scientific theories	Well-established scientific theories to explain causal connections	
Alternative theories	Credible psychological theories to explain power of positive thinking	

Knowledge of alternative views and arguments is centrally important in helping to point out the problems in the view under consideration.

In comparatively evaluating the arguments for and against the law of attraction, Winnie and Juanita find the weight of evidence to be overwhelmingly against the theory and to be strong enough to warrant a very confident judgment. In addition to the problems with the specific arguments, Juanita also notices that the promoters of the law of attraction fail to respond to criticisms or acknowledge alternative views. Such a failure to acknowledge alternatives and respond to criticisms constitutes an additional reason counting against the view in question. In reflecting on the inquiry process, Juanita recognizes the crucial importance of the knowledge of alternatives in pointing out the problems in the view under consideration.

Juanita: There's something that's still bothering me, Winnie. If the law of attraction is so obviously full of holes, why do so many people believe it?

Winnie: That's a great question, Juanita. I keep asking myself the same thing. Do you have any ideas?

Juanita: Well, as I was saying before, I think that lots of people aren't happy with the way their lives are going. They're under financial pressure or their relationships aren't going so well or they're having problems in their jobs or in their studies. And they don't feel that they can change things. The message of *The Secret* might give people a sense that there is something they can do—that they can have control over their lives.

Winnie: I can see that. It makes people believe that they can get whatever they want—money, cars, love, money, parking spots, money, health, money … You must have noticed that money figures in the book a lot.

Juanita: Now that you mention it …

Winnie: I think that the idea appeals to people's desire to always have more. It's about getting what you want without putting in the necessary effort.

Juanita: You see that a lot—like people believing all those promises that they can lose weight without dieting.

Winnie: Or get an A without studying.

Juanita: Yeah, yeah. But the book does have some positive messages, like you should think positive thoughts, express gratitude for what you have (or will get), feel joy, show love towards others. These are all great and really appeal to people—maybe they just ignore the rest.

Winnie: I'm also thinking that framing the book in terms of an ancient "secret" rather than just an interesting idea appeals to people's desire for mystery. Folks seem to love things that are mysterious or mystical, like astrology or UFOs.

Juanita: Or the Da Vinci code (I have to admit I really loved that). It's like you're being let into something special and magical. The book is even made to look kind of like an old manuscript, with yellowed pages and fonts that look like handwriting.

Winnie: But they also try to make the idea more credible by claiming that it's scientific. People think of science as being some kind of ultimate authority, so claiming that the law of attraction has been scientifically proven makes people accept it without question.

Juanita: They explain the science part in a way that's very accessible. I think that lots of people are intimidated by science. But they have heard of magnetism and frequencies and TV transmitters, and so the explanations seem to make sense.

Winnie: Only problem is they're wrong. I guess they count on most people's lack of a real understanding of science.

Juanita: Yeah. You know, doing this inquiry I started to realize that my own knowledge of science is pretty sketchy so it's easy to convince me of things that aren't correct. I really do need to check things out. For instance, it wasn't that hard to find out that opposite poles attract and not like poles—a few minutes on the internet did the trick.

Winnie: It really is too bad that so many folks seem to be afraid of science or don't like it. If you want mystery and wonder, you have plenty of that in science—like black holes and quarks and other strange-seeming phenomena. The secrets of the universe that scientists uncover are much more exciting and awesome than any "secret" that this book claims to reveal.

Juanita: Maybe there's just not enough critical spirit around. Lots of people can't be bothered to think critically about what they read or hear, or maybe they don't know how. So they don't see all the fallacies and problems, and they fall for all the rhetorical strategies.

Winnie: And we can't forget media. This book has been so hyped, with movies and videos and websites and TV shows and workshops. Marketing counts for a lot these days.

Once the lack of support for the law of attraction becomes clear, the issue of the popularity of the view again comes to the fore. Winnie and Juanita have determined that the popularity of the view cannot serve as a reason in its support since people often believe untenable views. But Juanita is prompted to wonder why so many people believe it given its lack of credibility. The two speculate that the appeal of the view lies in certain features of the book, such as its positive messages, its sense of mystery, its scientific aura, and its rhetorical strategies. The book is also popular because it appeals to common qualities in the society such as people's discontent with their lives, their sense of acquisitiveness, their desire to get something for nothing. It also shows people's lack of scientific knowledge and a lack of ability and willingness to think critically. The fact that there are plausible alternative explanations for the popularity of the view provides a further objection to the popularity argument.

Juanita: Well, Winnie, I have to admit that there's a lot wrong with what they say in *The Secret*. But I am wondering what's the harm of people believing it if it gets them to think positive thoughts and feel gratitude and joy and love, even if it's not all strictly true.

Winnie: I agree that some of the messages are constructive. Positive thinking, and feeling love and gratitude and joy, are all good things. But these are not exactly new ideas. They've been expressed in many philosophies and religions for a long time. I bet your mother and your priest and probably your first grade teacher told you that you should be grateful for what you have in life and that you should love your family. And some of these ideas have been well supported by psychological research, as we've seen. You don't need this half-baked theory to tell you that it's better to be positive and loving than negative and nasty.

Juanita: But it seems like this is all news for lots of people. So what's so wrong if the book gets these messages out to more people?

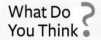
What Do You Think?

What's so wrong with believing things that are false if they might do some good?

Winnie: Where do I start? First of all, it's just plain bad to believe things that are false. Being a responsible, thinking human being implies having a respect for reason and truth. That's pretty basic.

Juanita: The spirit of inquiry means being committed to base what we think and do on good reasons—I remember that. Otherwise, we can be easily manipulated and we're likely to make bad decisions and bad judgments.

Winnie: I think that believing in the law of attraction can also promote self-centredness. Remember how they keep saying that the universe is like a giant catalogue—you just flip through it and order the experiences and products that you want? Talk about catering to consumerism and greed. And even positive feelings like gratitude and love are for the wrong reasons. You're supposed to feel them in order to get things back. I always thought they were good just for their own sake.

Juanita: The catalogue business is a bit much.

Winnie: Another major problem is that the theory can lead to inaction. If you really believe that it's your thoughts alone that make things happen, then you may not do what you really need to do in order to achieve things—for instance, working hard and improving your skills, or really working at having a good relationship.

Juanita: Or studying for an exam rather than just thinking about getting an A.

Winnie: Or trying to do something about all the problems in the world. Like one guy they quote who says he doesn't watch the news because it makes him feel bad. In fact, some people in the book seem to actually be suggesting that we shouldn't even try to deal with the world's problems. They say it's not our job to change the world and that by fighting against the things we don't want, like cancer or poverty or war, we just bring more of that thing into being.

Juanita: That's pretty scary.

Winnie: It gets worse. If you really believe that the good things that happen to people are a result of their thinking positive thoughts and the bad things are a result of their negative thoughts, then you would have to believe that all the tragedies and bad things that happen to people are their own fault. Tell that to Holocaust victims, or children starving to death in Africa, or people suffering from cancer. I frankly find that morally repulsive.

Juanita: I guess it's not so harmless after all.

Here Juanita and Winnie tackle an issue which is of critical importance: what is the harm of believing things that are not true? This question goes to the heart of the whole enterprise of inquiry. Inquiry is based on a commitment to truth, and to finding the best justified views as the best way to try to arrive at the truth. If we give up this commitment, we give up our best hope of making good decisions, of making sound judgments, of improving our lives and the lives of the others around us. We also give up our autonomy as individuals and give over our power to those who would manipulate us and take advantage of our credulity.

Apply Your Understanding Exercises 1, 2, 3

W. K. Clifford, "The Ethics of Belief"[10]

"The danger to society is not merely that it should believe wrong things, though that is great enough; but that it should become credulous, and lose the habit of testing things and inquiring into them, for then it must sink back into savagery... It may matter little to me, in my cloud-castle of sweet illusions and darling lies; but it matters much to Man that I have made my neighbors ready to deceive. The credulous man is father to the liar and the cheat."

Conspiracy Theories

9/11 Conspiracy?

Lester has just returned from a trip to visit his uncle.

Lester: What a nuisance. Ever since those planes brought down the World Trade Center, plane travel has become such a hassle.

Ahmed: (*quietly*) Planes didn't bring down the World Trade Center.

Lester: What did you say?

Ahmed: I said, planes didn't bring down the World Trade Center. Or crash into the Pentagon.

Lester: What are you talking about, Ahmed?

Ahmed: I saw this video on *YouTube* that Walter was sending around. It tells the true story of 9/11.

Lester: What do you mean by "the true story"?

Ahmed: The story that the officials tell about 9/11 is not what really happened. The video shows all the evidence that it wasn't planes that brought down the twin towers, that no plane crashed into the Pentagon, and that the official story about the fourth plane is wrong as well. I've learned, though, not to just take things on trust and that we should inquire. So I've been doing my own investigation. And it's true! There are lots of discrepancies in the official account—lots of eye-witness accounts and evidence of all kinds that conflict with the plane story. After you see all that, you just can't believe the "official" version any more.

Lester: But we know what really happened. Two planes were deliberately crashed into the twin towers and one into the Pentagon by a group of Al Qaeda terrorists led by Osama bin Laden. And one more was hijacked but brought down by a passenger revolt. There've been official investigations, and there's all kinds of evidence...

Ahmed: (*looking over his shoulder*) The true information's been hidden from us. It's all part of a giant conspiracy.

Lester: By who?

Ahmed: By the U.S. government, in order to justify invading Iraq.

Lester: Ahmed, this is absolutely ridiculous.

Ahmed: No, it's not. It actually makes a lot of sense when you think about it. It explains a lot of unexplained details and coincidences, and shows how different events are connected in an overall plan.

Lester: Far-fetched doesn't begin to describe this.

Ahmed: That's exactly what they want you to believe. See how well the cover-up works!

Lester: How exactly did you do this investigation?

Ahmed: I found lots of evidence on different websites and *YouTube* videos. I looked at a lot of different sites, not just one.

Lester: And did you look at the official reports and results of the various investigations? Or at criticisms of the claims or alternative explanations for the "data"?

Ahmed: No, but . . .

Lester: I think that your "inquiry" was somewhat limited, Ahmed. What we need to do is evaluate the arguments and sources, and look at alternative arguments. Then we can see what we think.

Ahmed: Sure—I'd love to do more inquiring into this. It's exciting, like one of those spy movies!

What Do You Think ?   *What is your reaction to the conspiracy theory that Ahmed is proposing regarding the events of 9/11?*

Conspiracy theories enjoy a great deal of popularity in contemporary society. The theories that Elvis faked his own death, that the Apollo moon landing was a hoax, that Princess Diana was murdered, that the Canadian government has been covering up the sighting of a UFO at Shag Harbour, Nova Scotia, in 1967, and other theories of a similar kind, have gained many adherents; websites purporting to prove such theories abound. The view that the official version of the events of 9/11 has been fabricated and the truth covered up is such a theory and is one of the most popular.[11]

What Do You Think ?   *Make a list of other conspiracy theories that you can think of.*

The claims of conspiracy regarding 9/11 are controversial, at the very least; and as with all controversial issues or questionable claims, we need to inquire and not just accept the claims at face value. This is particularly the case for conspiracy theories. A **conspiracy** can be defined as "a secret plan on the part of a group to influence events partly by covert action"[12], and a **conspiracy theory** is a proposed explanation of some historical event or events in terms of such a conspiracy.[13]

It is the case, of course, that real conspiracies exist. It is by now well established that the staff of then U.S. President Richard Nixon conspired to break into the Democratic National Committee headquarters and that Nixon himself conspired to cover up the Watergate burglary. Numerous plots by the CIA to assassinate Cuban president Fidel Castro are well documented.[14] And the official version of the events of 9/11, that a small group of Al Qaeda

A **conspiracy** is a secret plan on the part of a group to influence events partly by covert action. A **conspiracy theory** is a proposed explanation of some historical event or events in terms of such a conspiracy.

terrorists conspired to plan and carry out the attack, is itself a conspiracy theory. These are just a few examples.

What makes conspiracy theories potentially problematic, however, is that they frequently go against the accepted or official explanations of the events in question. They are usually explanations which are extraordinary in nature. For example, the theory that Elvis faked his death goes against the obvious and straightforward explanation that his death was just what it appeared to be—a natural death. And the theory that the Apollo moon landing was a hoax contradicts the obvious and simple explanation for all the data and evidence —that the moon landing happened. Of course, some events are appropriately explained as conspiracies, and a conspiracy theory may at times constitute the official explanation, as, for example, in the Al Qaeda case. But when they go against accepted theories and abundant credible evidence, when they constitute explanations which are extraordinary, then they carry the burden of proof—and a heavy one at that.

An additional noteworthy aspect of conspiracy theories is that it is part of the theory that the conspirators are taking measures to hide the truth. This gives conspiracy theories a particular logic which provides challenges to evaluation, as we shall see.

It is important to be able to recognize conspiracies when there is real evidence of their existence, but seeing a conspiracy behind every event is problematic. The issue is how to distinguish false from real conspiracies. Ahmed and Lester have been busy investigating this issue with respect to the events of 9/11.

> What makes conspiracy theories potentially problematic is that they often go against the accepted or official explanations of the events in question.

What Is the Issue? What Kinds of Claims or Judgments Are at Issue?

Lester: Let's start by trying to be clear about the issue.

Ahmed: I think the issue is whether planes brought down the twin towers and whether a plane struck the Pentagon.

Lester: That's part of it. But the claim that those things didn't happen is very much tied in with a broader claim—that the whole thing was part of a conspiracy. That seems to me to be the issue that we should focus on. The question about the planes will come into that.

Ahmed: OK. How about this: was there a conspiracy to commit the deeds of 9/11 and then cover them up?

Lester: No one is denying that there was a conspiracy to commit the actions, but the official story is that it was by Al Qaeda.

Ahmed: True. How about this: was there a conspiracy on the part of the U.S. government to commit the deeds of 9/11 and then cover them up?

Lester: Sounds good. And do we agree that it involves a factual judgment?

Ahmed: Agreed.

What Are the Relevant Reasons and Arguments on Various Side of the Issue?

Lester: Maybe we should start by summarizing the evidence and arguments for the official story—that the attacks were orchestrated and carried out by a group of Al Qaeda terrorists. First, there are all those eyewitnesses to the planes flying into the World Trade Center, including photos and video footage. Then there's all the physical evidence of both attacks—the wreckage of the planes, the bodies of the victims, the physical evidence of the damage to the buildings. There were commissioned reports, most notably the *9/11 Report,* which investigated the events, and also scientific investigations by experts of how the buildings collapsed, like the report by the National Institute of Standards and Technology (NIST) and the Federal

Emergency Management Agency (FEMA) Report. Then there were intercepted communications and documents linking Al Qaeda to the attacks as well as FBI investigations which confirmed their responsibility. Al Qaeda itself claimed responsibility for the attacks.

Ahmed: Those who believe in the conspiracy theory can poke holes in most of that so-called evidence. First of all, there's lots of evidence that the twin towers were brought down by controlled demolitions and not by the impact of the planes (though most conspiracy theorists don't deny that planes did hit the towers). The impact of planes couldn't have caused the kind of extensive damage to the buildings or fires hot enough to melt steel. Also, the way the buildings collapsed straight down and the ejection of dust are indicators of explosions.

Lester: And what about the Pentagon?

Ahmed: It was a missile and not a plane that hit the Pentagon. For one thing, the holes in the building were too small to be made by a plane. The bigger one was only 23 metres wide, but the wingspan of a Boeing 757 is about 38 metres. And authorities confiscated or destroyed the physical evidence.

Lester: Why would they do that?

Ahmed: This is where the conspiracy comes in. The evidence for that is pretty overwhelming. First of all, only "insiders" would have had the opportunity to plant the explosives. What's more, there's no hard evidence that any of alleged hijackers were on any of the flights; in fact, there's evidence that some of them weren't. And it's incredible that none of the flight crew was able to stop them.

Lester: Uh-huh.

Ahmed: Then there's all the evidence that at least some folks knew about the attacks in advance. Like the fact that government officials avoided the target areas on September 11. And stock trades on the two airlines involved reflected foreknowledge that the stocks would fall. What's even harder to believe is the lack of a military response to the attacks. It's truly inconceivable that the planes weren't intercepted by the air force. But what's most telling is the continual efforts of investigating officials to suppress evidence, for example, by removing and recycling the steel from Ground Zero, removing evidence and destroying documents, and offering conflicting and inconsistent accounts of events.

Lester: But what about the bin Laden tapes?

Ahmed: Those are clearly fakes.

Lester: So these folks are asking us to believe that the U.S. government would actually carry out attacks on its own citizens. Why on earth would they do such a thing?

Ahmed: The attacks made the American people so fearful of terrorists that the government could have free reign to do whatever it wanted. The attacks provided a justification for invading Iraq (which was really about gaining control of Middle Eastern oil), for increasing military spending, and for suppressing individual rights and liberties.

Lester: It sounds like they've got it all figured out.

Ahmed: Yup. The theory explains it all.

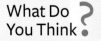
What Do You Think?

List the various arguments which are given in the dialogue on both sides of the 9/11 conspiracy issue on a table of pro and con arguments.

In laying out the reasons and arguments, our inquirers take care to look at evidence both for and against the official account. With respect to the conspiracy construal of the events,

Ahmed and Lester are faced with two kinds of evidence: evidence for the factual claims about the events, for example, how the buildings were destroyed; and evidence for the conspiracy, for example, questions of opportunity, foreknowledge, response, cover-up, and motivation.

What Is the Context of the Issue?

Lester: I think it's important to remember that the 9/11 attacks were a major, traumatic event for the U.S. and the western world. For the first time in our history, people from the North American continent felt under threat from foreign terrorist attacks. It created a great deal of fear, anger, and confusion, and I think that has something to do with how people have reacted.

Ahmed: The political context is also central here: the imperialistic ideology underlying American foreign policy, for example, and, in particular, the expressed intention of the U.S. administration to overthrow Saddam Hussein even prior to 9/11. Then there's also the internal political situation in the U.S. and the unpopularity of the Bush administration prior to 9/11.

Lester: It also seems to me that the theory of a 9/11 conspiracy became more popular in the context of growing criticism of the Iraq War and of President Bush, and also unhappiness with the government's new security measures, which many people saw as limiting their rights and freedoms.

Ahmed: In addition, the U.S government has been less than forthright on other occasions—for example, about the existence of weapons of mass destruction in Iraq—and has engaged in conspiracies before—like the Iran-Contra scandal.[15] Those facts give more credibility to the conspiracy view.

In the case of an event like 9/11, the context is highly emotionally charged and ideologically laden. This is an important factor in how events unfold and are perceived. The political context in which the events unfold also plays a key role in understanding and evaluating the issue.

How Do We Comparatively Evaluate the Various Reasons and Arguments in order to Reach a Reasoned Judgment?

Ahmed: OK. Let's start on the evaluation. What can you say about all that evidence that the World Trade Center was destroyed by a controlled demolition and not by the planes?

Lester: It's contradicted by the NIST and FEMA reports which were compiled by engineering experts, as well as by investigations by non-government organizations like the National Fire Protection Association and by scientists at Purdue University and Northwestern University.[16] The Purdue folks even did a computer simulation of the collapse which confirms the accepted account. I also found a couple of relevant articles in refereed journals. One, by an engineering professor at MIT, in the *Journal of the Minerals, Metals, and Materials Society*,[17] explains how the burning of the jet fuel together with other combustible material would generate sufficient heat to weaken the steel and how temperature differentials could cause the steel to sag and the trusses to fail, creating a pancaking effect when the floors collapsed one on top of the other. Another article, in the *Journal of Engineering Mechanics*,[18] showed that "if prolonged heating causes the majority of columns of a single floor to lose their load carrying capacity, the whole tower is doomed." I also found some more popular articles aimed at "debunking the conspiracy myths," such as in *Popular Mechanics, Scientific American,* and *Time* magazine. They generally

In the case of events that are highly significant for the society and emotionally charged, such as 9/11, the social and political contexts play a key role in understanding and evaluating the issue.

reiterate the arguments of the reports. The conspiracy folks accuse them of the straw person fallacy (attacking the silliest versions of the arguments). I agree to a point, but they still do offer some sound objections to the most prominent arguments.

Ahmed: Both NIST and FEMA are government agencies, so I would be skeptical of their reports, what with the conspiracy and all. But I have to admit that the others look like credible and unbiased sources.

Lester: What were the sources for the arguments you found?

Ahmed: Most of them were from the websites *911Truth.org, 9-11Research.com, abovetop-secret.com,* and *Architects and Engineers for 9/11 Truth.* They were also the main sources for the arguments I found about the plane crashing into the Pentagon and about what happened to the fourth plane.

Lester: Do you see any problems with these sources, Ahmed?

Ahmed: Well, I guess they all do have a pro-conspiracy theory agenda, now that I think about it.

Lester: Do you know anything about the background of the contributors?

Ahmed: I've had a glance at some of their bios. It seems like most of them aren't scientists but rather "independent researchers." Many are political activists who are critical of the government.

Lester: Do you think they have the relevant expertise to pose serious challenges to the scientific consensus?

Ahmed: Probably not. But there are some articles by scientists, which have been published in a refereed publication, the *Journal of 9/11 Studies.*

Lester: The *Journal of 9/11 Studies*—a refereed journal?

Ahmed: Well, they say it's refereed. Its mandate is to publish research that might not otherwise be published due to the resistance of other institutions. They also say that they believe that the case for the falsity of the official explanation is well established and demonstrated.

Lester: It hardly seems like an unbiased academic publication.

Ahmed: Another thing I'm noticing is that the same authors appear over and over again in many, or even most, of the articles

Lester: Another reason for skepticism.

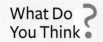
What Do You Think

How credible are the sources for the pro and con arguments?

Ahmed: You know, there are just so many conflicting claims and arguments out there. You'd think that they could just figure out who's right. This is science, after all.

Lester: There's one thing we have to remember. This event is unprecedented. So it's not like the scientists can say with confidence, "This is what happens to a building of this type that's been hit by a plane of this type going at this speed..." Nothing like this has ever happened before. So the best the scientists can do is to work with what they know about engineering and physics and apply this knowledge to everything they know about the details of the case to make reasoned judgments and come up with the best explanation. When any of the conspiracy theorists state categorically that the building could not have collapsed in this way or could only have collapsed in this other way, we should view those claims with suspicion.

Ahmed: I don't know. There are so many complex scientific arguments that are given on both sides. How can I possibly evaluate who's right? I don't know all that much about science.

Lester: It's true that we're not in a position to comparatively evaluate the details of the scientific claims. We don't have the relevant expertise. So our best guide is to try to find credible, unbiased sources and to go with the consensus of the experts.

Ahmed: But sometimes the experts are wrong. We've seen throughout history how the accepted view is often overturned. So we can't just dismiss views which go against the current consensus.

Lester: That's very true. But there need to be very strong arguments and evidence for the new view. Don't forget that a view which goes against the accepted one has a major burden of proof. Do you think that the conspiracy folks have met that burden of proof when it comes to the reason for the collapse of the World Trade Center?

Ahmed: It doesn't look like it, does it?

Lester: Something else: think about those actual conspiracies that we do know about, like Watergate or the CIA plots to assassinate Castro. How did we find out about them? Was it through the "revelations" of conspiracy theorists?

Ahmed: No. It was through investigative reporting and uncovering documents and things like that.

Lester: In other words, through the more traditional, credible methods of inquiry.

Investigating the reason for the destruction of the World Trade Center involves assessing claims which are scientific in nature, and the support offered for the various theories is complex and voluminous. Arguments are countered with objections, objections with responses, responses with counter-arguments, in a seemingly unending chain of increasing detail. Finding one's way through this mass of complex scientific detail poses a particular challenge for laypeople who are trying to evaluate the conspiracy theorists' arguments. The complexity and sophistication of the scientific questions involved make this an issue which is not easily evaluated by non-experts, which includes most of the individuals posting on the websites cited by Ahmed. The best guideline, one we have encountered frequently before, is expert consensus. Relying on expert consensus makes the evaluation of the credibility of sources paramount. Refereed journals constitute one clearly credible source; but even here, you must check out credibility, as the case of the *Journal of 9/11 Studies* demonstrates.

The best guideline when trying to evaluate complex and sophisticated scientific questions is expert consensus.

The point that Lester makes regarding the plane crash and subsequent building collapse being unprecedented is a significant one, and one which reveals an important aspect of scientific inquiry. Science does not prove theories right or wrong. Rather, it works through argument to the best explanation. Thus the lack of definite proof of a claim does not constitute evidence against the claim, and any claim that a certain theory has been proven beyond question must be viewed with suspicion.

Ahmed: But what about the evidence that it wasn't a plane that crashed into the Pentagon—like the fact that the holes in the building were too small to have been made by the plane?

Lester: Ahmed, what do you think happens to the wings of a plane when it crashes into a concrete building? Do you think they would punch holes in the building?

Ahmed: Hmm... probably not. I guess they would be destroyed.

Lester: So how big would the hole in the building be?

Ahmed: The width of the fuselage? Which is... let me guess— 23 metres wide?

Lester: Right you are. And tell me something: if it wasn't the plane that hit the Pentagon, then what exactly happened to American Airlines flight 77?

The lack of definite proof of a claim does not constitute evidence against the claim.

Ahmed: One theory is that the plane was destroyed and the passengers murdered by government agents.

Lester: Even you have to admit that that's pretty far-fetched.

Ahmed: Not if you understand about the conspiracy.

Lester: OK. Time to tackle the conspiracy arguments.

Ahmed: Now we'll get somewhere. After all, there's all that evidence.

Lester: Most of that "evidence" looks to me like a piecemeal collection of bits of data, and lots of it is problematic. For example, the claim that only insiders could have planted the explosives is beside the point if there were no explosives. It's just speculation to think that the flight crew should have been able to stop the hijackers. And lots of the claims are unsubstantiated. How do we know that government officials avoided travelling on September 11, that there's no hard evidence that the hijackers were on the flights, or that the bin Laden tapes are fakes?

Ahmed: But what about the fact that there was insider trading on the stock market that seems to indicate that some people had advance knowledge of the attacks?

Lester: I read that the 9/11 Commission did, in fact, find evidence of some unusual trading activity, but concluded that it could be attributed to reasons other than foreknowledge of the attacks. It seems to me that this kind of thing is the case for much of the alleged evidence—that there are other, more plausible explanations. For example, investigators attribute the lack of an immediate military response to the attacks to communication failures, to inefficiency, or to simple incompetence.

Ahmed: But there is clear evidence of government suppression of evidence and obstruction of investigations, like Bush asking the senate majority leader to limit congressional investigations[19] and opposing the establishment of a special commission to probe how the government dealt with terror warnings before September 11.[20] There were also complaints of FBI obstruction of the investigation.[21] And those are only a few examples.

Lester: The material I found suggests the same sorts of things.

Ahmed: Ah-hah! Now we've got something!

Lester: The question, though, is what that all means, and whether it's evidence that the government knew about and orchestrated the attacks.

Ahmed: What else could it mean?

What Do You Think?

Can you think of an alternative explanation for the evidence of government suppression of evidence?

Lester: Business as usual for that government, I would say. They haven't exactly had a history of openness. And problems in national security and government effectiveness are certainly not things that they would want revealed.

Ahmed: You've got to agree, though, that the Bush administration had all kinds of motives for orchestrating the attacks.

Lester: I do agree that there are reasons why the events suited their agenda, and they certainly managed to capitalize on them. But that doesn't in itself justify the claim that they were responsible for the events. You may not have been entirely unhappy when our philosophy prof lost our last essays—you told me that you didn't think you did well on it—but that doesn't mean that you "caused" the essays to disappear.

Ahmed: Well, maybe there are some problems with a few of the pieces of evidence. But there are still lots of facts that you can't explain away so easily. The conspiracy theory makes sense of all the unexplained pieces of evidence; otherwise, there's no way to explain them.

Lester: Remember that science doesn't offer proofs, only the best explanation of the data. Scientific inquiry is an ongoing quest to offer better, richer explanations. But at any particular time, there will always be data that can't be explained by even the best theory. And so scientific inquiry continues. We should be suspicious of any theory that claims to explain all the data.

Ahmed: Hmm…I'll have to think about that. I'm also not too happy about how you dismissed so much of the evidence. I thought that was a bit quick. Of course, all the government-sponsored reports and all the experts support the official position. What else would you expect from a conspiracy? Cover-up is what it's all about.

Lester: Ahmed, think about what you just said. If you find evidence for what the theory claims, then that supports the conspiracy theory. But if you don't find any evidence, then that's taken as evidence of a cover-up, and so that supports the conspiracy theory as well. Do you see any problems with that logic?

Ahmed: Well, I guess that it would be pretty hard to come up with any evidence that would count against the conspiracy theory.

Lester: Exactly.

Evaluating conspiracy theories involves assessing evidence and arguments in all the ways which we have learned for other sorts of claims. Conspiracy theories tend to make use of selective bits of data, often circumstantial and frequently unsubstantiated. Alternative explanations are often not considered. These sorts of problems can be discovered by evaluating the particular claims, as Lester is doing.

There are, however, certain features of how conspiracy theories are constructed which pose particular problems. One such feature is that they are often built upon discrepant or **anomalous data**. This refers to data for which there is not (or not yet) a satisfactory explanation according to accepted theories. It is in the nature of inquiry that there will always be such data. This is due to the complex and ambiguous nature of events and circumstances, as well as the fallible and incomplete nature of human inquiry. Anomalies are ever present and furnish the material for further inquiry. The mistake that conspiracy theories rest on is the belief that a handful of such anomalies can undermine a well-established theory.

> An **anomaly** refers to data for which there is not a satisfactory explanation according to accepted theories.

Scientific theories are not built on isolated pieces of data (as we saw in Chapter 12). Rather, they are built on evidence from many lines of inquiry coming together to form the best explanation for the event in question.

The circularity of conspiracy theory arguments is another common feature which raises issues for their evaluation. Because of the premise of secrecy and cover-up upon which conspiracy theories rest, a lack of evidence is also seen as constituting evidence. This renders conspiracy theories untestable, as Lester points out. A common strategy is to gather all the bits of data that seem to support the theory, ignore or explain away all data that does not fit the theory, then offer the theory as the only possible explanation for the events.

Because of the use of conspiracy as an overarching explanatory device to explain all data, even counter-examples and counter-arguments can be explained by the theory. Thus conspiracy theories appear to possess great explanatory power. They generally appear to have amassed more evidence than the official view since they pull together all the facts marshalled by the official account in terms of a cover-up, plus all the anomalies which the official view cannot account for. Thus they appear to explain all possible data. As we have just seen, however, it is exceedingly unlikely that any one theory can explain all the data. Conspiracy

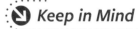

Keep in Mind

COMMON FEATURES OF CONSPIRACY THEORIES

- foundation of discrepant or anomalous data
- circularity: no evidence is also evidence
- misleading appearance of great explanatory power

Is Elvis Alive?[22]

Steve Clarke, in "Conspiracy Theories and Conspiratorial Theorizing"

The conventional explanation of the death of Elvis Presley, in 1977 at the age of 42, has a meagre evidential base, referring to Elvis' heart condition which is explained by appealing to facts about his lifestyle. The conspiratorial rival theory that Brewer-Giorgio[23] mounts is rich in detail, explaining, *inter alia*, why Elvis' middle name is misspelt on a tombstone (Elvis was superstitious and wouldn't want his name correctly spelt on a tombstone when he was in fact alive), and why Elvis' casket was unusually heavy (it contained a wax dummy and an air conditioning unit to stop the wax dummy from melting). Brewer-Giorgio can also explain away the apparent plausibility of the conventional explanation of Elvis' death. Given that Elvis wished to fake his own death it would have suited him to appear to be in poor health, so as to add plausibility to his cover story.

theories give the appearance of doing so because they explain away the data that does not fit their theory as being the result of the conspiracy. Thus the appearance of great explanatory power is misleading.

Ahmed: OK, so we've gone through this whole evaluation. Where does it leave us?

Lester: We're trying to find the best explanation of the events of 9/11. So why don't we summarize what our evaluation turned up and then see which side provides a better explanation?

Ahmed: Sounds good. What do we have?

Lester: First, there's the scientific evidence about what actually happened in the attacks. I would certainly say that the evidence supporting the official version is a lot stronger. Would you agree?

Ahmed: It does look like it. Unless, of course, there's a conspiracy . . .

Lester: About the alleged conspiracy, it seems to me that we didn't come across any credible evidence to suggest that the government executed the attacks, although the conspiracy theorists will argue that no evidence is also evidence. But we did find some evidence that seems to suggest an attempt by government to cover up exactly what happened, or at least be obstructionist to the investigations.

Ahmed: The conspiracy theory's also supported by all the actions that the government took after 9/11, which they probably wouldn't have been able to get away with without the excuse of a terrorist attack—like the invasion of Iraq and all the new security measures and limitations on individual freedoms.

Lester: Not everyone would agree with you about that, Ahmed. A number of people I know, including Stephen, think that the invasion of Iraq and the security measures were justified. But those are issues for another time. The point is that, even if one were to agree with you about the government actions after 9/11, there are two competing explanations for all of this. It could indicate a conspiracy on the part of the government to commit and then cover up the attacks. Or it could be a case of major ineffectiveness, incompetence, or even criminal negligence on the part of government agencies, plus an attempt to cover this up—this combined with opportunism in taking political advantage of the events.

Ahmed: How do we figure out which is the better explanation?

Lester: Why don't we list what we would have to believe for each version if it were true? First, the official version.

Ahmed: OK. We would have to believe that the scientific consensus is credible and not politically motivated. We'd have to believe that the government and its agencies were colossally incompetent or negligent, or both, and that they tried to cover up their incompetence. We'd also have to believe that the government was highly opportunistic and used the events to its political advantage.

Lester: Now for the conspiracy theory. We'd have to believe that non-scientists and non-engineers, most of whom appear politically motivated, can give a more credible technical analysis than appropriately trained experts. We'd also have to believe that many of the experts are lying and that the majority of evidence is false or has been misrepresented. We'd have to believe that none of the thousands of people who would need to have been involved in such a conspiracy would have come forward, even though they could become famous and probably make a fortune. And we'd also have to believe that the U.S. government would deliberately murder its own citizens. Here—I've made a summary on an argument evaluation table:

Evaluation of the Arguments Pro and Con 9/11 Conspiracy Theory		
Argument Name	**Argument Summary**	**Evaluation**
	PRO	
Scientific evidence	Scientific evidence that WTC not destroyed by plane	Sources not credible
Conspiracy	Anomalies in official story	Many are unsubstantiated; misuse of anomalies
	Evidence of advance knowledge	Alternative more plausible explanations
	Evidence of suppression of evidence and obstruction of investigation	More plausible explanation in terms of hiding inefficiency or incompetence
	Suited government agenda	Only implies government was opportunistic, not that they were responsible
		Argument for conspiracy circular
		Implausibility of mass misrepresentation of evidence by experts
		Implausibility of government deliberately murdering its citizens
	CON	
Scientific evidence	Scientific evidence that WTC destroyed by plane	Credible sources; consensus of experts
	Evidence of conspiracy by Al Qaeda	They claimed responsibility; tapes; intercepted communications

Which explanation do you think is more plausible?

Ahmed: Well, when you lay it out like that . . .

Lester and Ahmed have now come to the last phase in their inquiry, weighing the various arguments in order to arrive at an overall judgment. The process of evaluating all the arguments can sometimes be a bit overwhelming in terms of assimilating all the wealth of detail. This is particularly a problem as conspiracy theories tend to be built on a large accumulation of pieces of anomalous data, and the marshalling of such an overwhelming quantity of data is one of the rhetorical strategies employed by conspiracy theories. Thus summarizing the main findings of the evaluation can be helpful in clarifying what are the salient (most significant and important) points that need to be considered in making the judgment. The process of summarizing what would have to be the case in order for each account to be true is also an important step in helping Ahmed and Lester to see what are the assumptions and implications of each account and thus to decide which account provides the better, more plausible explanation.

Summarizing the main findings of an evaluation is helpful in clarifying what are the salient points that need to be considered in making a judgment.

Ahmed: I'm starting to see the problems in the 9/11 conspiracy theory. But so many people seem to believe it. That and other conspiracy theories, like Elvis faking his own death or the moon landing being a hoax. Why are conspiracy theories so popular when they're clearly so full of problems?

Lester: The 9/11 attacks were a huge, traumatic event. I think that people want to believe that huge, traumatic events must have huge, significant causes. Maybe thinking that such a major event was the work of a handful of people isn't emotionally satisfying. But a conspiracy on the part of the government is big. It's significant.

Ahmed: That makes sense.

Lester: I'm also thinking that an event like 9/11 makes people feel helpless, and it may give them a sense of power to feel that they can know what happened. Why do you think you found the conspiracy theory so appealing?

Ahmed: I think that I felt like I wasn't just being a patsy and accepting what the authorities wanted me to believe. I was thinking for myself. Finding out the real truth. Being a rebel. Though I guess I wasn't thinking for myself as well as I might have.

What is the appropriate attitude in the face of conspiracy theories? On the one hand, conspiracy theories are often plagued with the kinds of problems we have seen in the 9/11 case, and accepting them uncritically would be a mistake. On the other hand, there are real conspiracies and it would also be a mistake to always be tied uncritically to the official version of events. Erring in the one direction amounts to paranoia or excessive skepticism. Erring in the other direction becomes naïveté and excessive gullibility. As with other kinds of issues, we must always ask, what are the reasons and arguments on the various sides? In the process of comparative evaluation, it is, however, important to keep in mind the particular challenges which conspiracy theories pose.

Apply Your Understanding Exercises 4, 5, 6

CHECK YOUR UNDERSTANDING

- *List and explain the fallacies that Winnie and Juanita find in their prima facie evaluation of the arguments for the law of attraction.*
- *In what way does the argument for the law of attraction violate scientific principles?*
- *Evaluate the law of attraction according to the criteria for a causal claim.*
- *What are some of the alternative theories for explaining the power of positive thinking besides the law of attraction?*
- *Why do you think the ideas in The Secret are so popular?*
- *What is the harm of people believing things that are false?*
- *How would you define a conspiracy? a conspiracy theory?*
- *Why are conspiracy theories potentially problematic?*
- *What aspects of context surrounding the events of 9/11 are particularly important for understanding and evaluating the various explanations of the events?*
- *What problems are there with the sources for the pro conspiracy arguments that Ahmed found?*

- *What is the best guideline for a non-expert in evaluating complex, technical scientific arguments?*
- *List three common features of conspiracy theories.*
- *What are some of the reasons why the conspiracy theory of 9/11 might be so popular?*

EXERCISES

1. Choose two of the following extraordinary claims. Conduct an inquiry to investigate the claim:

   i) Former Canadian Prime Minister William Lyon Mackenzie King communed with the spirits of his dead dogs.

   ii) The Nazca lines, which are enormous "drawings" in the earth located on a plain in the Andes mountains, were the work of ancient "astronauts" who visited the earth in the distant past.

   iii) A person's horoscope can provide reliable information about his or her future.

   iv) The actor Shirley MacLaine was the lover of the Emperor Charlemagne in a past life.

   v) Shark cartilage can cure cancer.

   vi) Sasquatches exist.

2. Henry Ford, the American businessman and creator of modern assembly line production, was convinced that he had lived before. He describes his beliefs in a quotation on the textbook website under Exercise 16-2. After reading the quotation, list and evaluate the reasons Ford offers for believing in reincarnation.

3. There are some theorists who are critical of the idea that positive thinking will lead to success. In this regard, Dr. James Hill, Professor of Pediatrics at the University of Colorado, recommends that, instead of believing that one will succeed, one should be guided by the idea: "Expect failure but keep trying."

   i) Read the article "Positively Misguided: The Myths & Mistakes of the Positive Thinking Movement" by Steve Salerno (*eskeptic*, Jan.–June 2009, http://www.skeptic.com/eskeptic/09-04-15#feature). See textbook website under Exercise 3 i.

   ii) Inquire into the issue of whether positive thinking is likely to lead to success.

4. The following assignments relate to claims regarding UFOs.

   i) Read the is a summary of a report of an alleged encounter with a UFO indicated on the textbook website for Exercise 4 i.

   Conduct an inquiry to investigate the credibility of this report.

   (The full report is available at http://www.ufoevidence.org/cases/case376.htm)

   ii) The following two websites offer conflicting arguments regarding alleged government cover-ups of UFO sightings and alien contact:

   http://www.ufoevidence.org/documents/doc98.htm

   http://www.ufoevidence.org/documents/doc2027.htm

   Comparatively evaluate the two arguments.

   iii) Jimmy Carter is one of two U.S. Presidents who have reported seeing a UFO before becoming the President. Read his account at http://www.ufoevidence.org/cases/case297.htm (see textbook website).

   a) Evaluate Carter's report as evidence for the existence of UFOs.

   b) Evaluate Carter's report as evidence for the existence of extraterrestrial life.

   iv) The Roper report, conducted in the U.S. in 1992, claimed that 3.7 million Americans had been abducted by aliens.

   i) Read the account of the poll under Exercise 16-4iv on the textbook website.

   ii) Evaluate its claims regarding alien abductions.

5. View the video on "The Baloney Detection Kit" by Michael Shermer:

   http://www.youtube.com/watch?v=eUB4j0n2UDU&eurl

   Choose one of the extraordinary claims from question #1 above which you have not yet inquired about. Evaluate the claim according to the ten points of the Baloney Detection Kit which Shermer outlines.

6. Choose one of the following popular conspiracy theories, and complete the assignments.

   a) Elvis Presley faked his own death.

   b) The Apollo moon landing was a hoax.

   c) There is a conspiracy by the Illuminati, a powerful and secretive group, to rule mankind with a single world government and create the New World Order. They make use of political finance, social engineering, mind control, and fear-based propaganda to achieve their ends.

   d) Diana, Princess of Wales, was murdered.

   e) Paul McCartney died in a car crash in 1966 and was replaced in the Beatles by a look-alike and sound-alike.

   f) Government health officials, backed by the pharmaceutical industry, are systematically hiding information about the dangerous effects of vaccinations from the public.

      i) Inquire into one of these theories, paying attention to the special challenges of evaluating conspiracy theories.

      ii) Find your own example of a conspiracy theory and conduct an inquiry into it.

ENDNOTES

1. Rhonda Byrne, *The Secret* (New York: Atrium Books, 2006).

2. A video containing the main claims made in the book, *The Secret,* can be viewed at http://www.youtube.com/watch?v=_b1GKGWJbE8.

3. CBC.ca, "Bigfoot and Other Beasts: A Field Guide to Unproven Animals," Dec. 14, 2006, http://www.cbc.ca/news/background/fact_or_fiction/.

4. Gallup.com, "Three in Four Americans Believe in Paranormal," June 16, 2005, http://www.gallup.com/poll/16915/three-four-americans-believe-paranormal.aspx.

5. Ron Kurtus, "Basics of Magnetism," *School for Champions,* Oct. 6, 1006, http://www.school-for-champions.com/science/magnetism.htm.

6. Magnet Man, "Ten Facts about Magnets," http://www.coolmagnetman.com/magbasic.htm (accessed June 3, 2010).

7. Albert Bandura, *Self-efficacy: The Exercise of Control* (New York: Freeman, 1997).

8. Anees A. Sheikh and Errol R. Korn, eds., *Imagery in Sports and Physical Performance.* Amityville, NY: Baywood Publishing Company, Inc., 1994.

9. B.F. Skinner, *Science and Human Behavior* (New York: Macmillan, 1953); John E. R. Staddon and Yael Niv, "Operant Conditioning," *Scholarpedia.org* (2008), 3(9):2318.

10. W.K. Clifford, *Lectures and Essays* (London: Macmillan and Co., 1879), 2:185–186.

11. In 2008, 9/11 conspiracy theories topped a "greatest conspiracy theory" list compiled by the *Daily Telegraph*: see *wikipedia.org,* "9/11 Conspiracy Theories," http://en.wikipedia.org/wiki/9/11_conspiracy_theories. According to an estimate in *Popular Mechanics* published in March 2005, there were approximately 628,000 websites.

12. Charles Pidgen, "Popper Revisited, or What Is Wrong With Conspiracy Theories?" *Philosophy of the Social Sciences,* 25 (1995): 5.

13. Brian Keeley, "Of Conspiracy Theories," *The Journal of Philosophy,* 96, no. 3 (1999): 116.

14. The National Security Archive, "The CIA's Family Jewels," http://www.gwu.edu/~nsarchiv/NSAEBB/NSAEBB222/index.htm (accessed June 8, 2010).

15. "The Iran-Contra affair was a political scandal in the United States which came to light in November 1986. During the Reagan administration, in which senior U.S. figures, including President Ronald Reagan, agreed to facilitate the sale of arms to Iran, the subject of an arms embargo . . . [to] secure the release of hostages and . . . to fund Nicaraguan contras." See *wikipedia. com,* "Iran–Contra Affair," http://en.wikipedia.org/wiki/Iran-Contra_affair.

16. Larry Dignan, "Behind Purdue's computing simulation on the 2001 World Trade Center attack," *ZDNet*, June 20, 2007.

17. Thomas Eagar and Christopher Musso, "Why Did the World Trade Center Collapse: Science, Engineering, and Speculation," *Journal of the Minerals, Metals, and Materials Society*, 52, no. 12 (Dec. 2001).

18. Zdenˇek P. Baˇzant1 and Yong Zhou, "Why Did World Trade Center Collapse?—Simple Analysis," *Archive of Applied Mechanics* 71, no. 12 (Dec. 2001): 802–806.

19. CNN.com, "Bush asks Daschle to limit Sept. 11 probes." Jan. 29, 2002.

20. CBSNews.com, "Bush Opposes 9/11 Query Panel," May 23, 2002.

21. FOXNews.com, "Whistleblower Complains of FBI Obstruction," May 30, 2002.

22. Steve Clarke, "Conspiracy Theories and Conspiracy Theorizing," in David Coady, ed., *Conspiracy Theories: The Philosophical Debate* (Hampshire, U.K.: Ashgate Publishing Ltd., 2006).

23. Gail Brewer-Giorgio, *Elvis Alive?* (New York: Tudor, 1988).

Glossary

A

Abstract: An abstract is a brief summary of the information and arguments in a scholarly article. (6)

Abusive ad hominem: An abusive ad hominem is a malicious attack on an author used to reject the author's argument or position. (4)

Acceptability: A premise is acceptable to a particular person or audience if they believe it to be true. (4)

Ad hominem: Arguers commit the fallacy of ad hominem if they reject a proponent's argument on the basis of critical remarks about the proponent rather than the proponent's argument. (4)

Acceptable premise: A premise is acceptable to a particular person or audience if they believe it to be true. (4)

Aesthetic judgments: Aesthetic judgments deal with questions having to do with the sensory, perceptual, or formal properties of objects and experiences; they arise most often in the realm of the arts. (7)

Alternative view: An alternative view is a different view offered as an alternative to the argument in question. (8)

Ambiguity: A term is ambiguous when it has multiple meanings or interpretations and it is not clear which interpretation is meant. See also *semantic ambiguity, syntactic ambiguity, equivocation.* (7)

Analogical distance: Analogical distance is a metaphor to express the degree of difference between the two things being compared. (5)

Analogue: Two cases that are compared are called analogues. The analogue can be either the case at issue or the comparable precedent or event. (5)

Anecdotal evidence: The fallacy of anecdotal evidence occurs when an arguer uses an anecdote as strong evidence for a broad generalization. (4)

Anomaly: An anomaly refers to data for which there is not a satisfactory explanation according to accepted theories. (12; 16)

Appeal to tradition: An appeal to tradition is fallacious when the tradition itself is morally or intellectually questionable. (4)

Argument: An argument is a set of claims, one of which, the conclusion, is supported by one or more other claims, called premises. (3)

Argument from ignorance: A proponent is guilty of the fallacy of argument from ignorance when that proponent

concludes that his or her position is correct on the basis of a lack of evidence refuting her position. (4)

Argument to the best explanation: This is a method of reasoning that is used to establish a causal claim. It involves showing that a particular explanation is better than any other hypothesis. This usually involves showing that other hypotheses do not fit all the facts. (5)

Assumption: An assumption is an unstated but necessary part of an argument. (3)

Autonomous: Autonomous means self-directed, not forced. (1)

B

Begging the question: Arguers commit the fallacy of begging the question when they use a premise that is identical to their conclusion or assume the truth of the claim that is central to the controversy. (4)

Bias: Bias refers to the tendency to favour one perspective uncritically. (1)

Burden of proof: Burden of proof (also called *onus*) refers to the responsibility for making the case and the degree of evidence required. (4; 8)

C

Case: A case is a collection of arguments (pro and con) marshalled to support a position on an issue. (4)

Causal analogy: A causal analogy is an argument which suggests that because two phenomena (or entities) share relevant qualities, the causal properties of one will be like the causal properties of the other. (5)

Causal explanation: A causal explanation is an explanation in terms of antecedent events that made something happen. (5)

Causal factor: A factor is a causal factor for an outcome if the factor is correlated with the outcome and the best explanation for this correlation is that there is a causal relationship. (13)

Causal judgment: Causal judgments are explanatory judgments which go beyond demonstrating an observed connection between phenomena to posit a causal link between them. (7)

Circumstantial ad hominem: A circumstantial ad hominem is committed when facts about the background or loyalties of the author are used to dismiss the author's arguments and claims without actual reference to these arguments and claims. (4)

Cogent inductive argument: A cogent inductive argument is a strong inductive argument with credible premises. (4)

Comparative judgments of value: Comparative judgments of value deal with questions concerning what is of worth or value and the comparative importance of different values in making a judgment. (7)

Conceptual analysis: Conceptual analysis involves clarifying our understanding of our concepts and getting clear on how we actually use the words that refer to them. (13)

Conclusion: An argument is a set of claims, one of which, the conclusion, is supported by one or more other claims, called premises. (3)

Confirmation bias: Confirmation bias is the tendency to look for and notice evidence that confirms our beliefs and not look for, ignore, or undervalue evidence that contradicts our beliefs. (16)

Confounding factor: A confounding factor is any factor other than the cause being studied that could be part of the explanation for the observed outcome. (12)

Connotation: Connotation refers to the associations connected with a particular word. (7)

Conspiracy: A conspiracy is a secret plan on the part of a group to influence events partly by covert action. (16)

Conspiracy theory: A conspiracy theory is a proposed explanation of some historical event (or events) in terms of such a conspiracy. (16)

Convergence: There is convergence in research when a majority of studies tend to support a particular theory. (13)

Convergent argument: In a convergent argument, each premise independently provides support for the conclusion. (3)

Correlation: There is a correlation between two things when they co-vary. (5)

Counter-example: A counter-example is an example or instance which is an exception to a claim. (1)

Credibility: A claim is credible if it would be believed by any well-informed and reasonable person. (4)

Criteria: Criteria specify the relevant considerations that provide the basis for making a judgment. (1)

Critical evaluation: A critical evaluation is an assessment of the reasons and arguments on various sides of an issue. (1)

Cultural relativism: Cultural relativism is the view that right and wrong are determined by the customs and practices of a particular culture (also known as *ethical relativism*). (15)

D

Deductive argument: An argument is deductive if it is a linked argument and it appears that the author intended the truth of the premises to guarantee the truth of the conclusion. (3)

Denotation: Denotation refers to the literal meaning of a word. (7)

Descriptive judgments: Descriptive judgments describe states of affairs. (7)

Dialectic: This term refers to the argumentative exchange between various sides of an issue. (8)

Double Blind: An experiment is double blind if neither the subjects nor the experimenters know who has gotten the treatment; that is, who has been exposed to the cause in question. (13)

Dubious assumption: A dubious assumption is a claim that is necessary for the argument but that is itself quite doubtful. (3)

E

Effect size: Effect size is a measure of the difference of the behaviour of the experimental group compared to the control group. (13)

Entailment: A claim X entails another claim Y, when if X is true, then Y must be true. (3)

Equivocation: Equivocation is the deliberate use of ambiguity. Equivocation in argument occurs when there is an intentionally misleading use of a word in two different senses. (4; 7)

Ethical judgments: Ethical judgments deal with questions of what is right or wrong, good or bad, morally praiseworthy or blameworthy. (7)

Ethical relativism: Ethical relativism is the view that right and wrong are determined by the customs and practices of a particular culture (also known as *cultural relativism*). (15)

Ethnocentrism: Ethnocentrism is the tendency to view one's own culture as more important than and morally and intellectually superior to any other culture. (15)

Euphemism: Euphemism refers to the use of emotionally neutral or positively charged words to substitute for highly charged negative ones. (7)

Evaluative judgments: Evaluative judgments express an evaluation or assessment of an object, action, or phenomenon. (7)

Explanatory judgments: Explanatory judgments aim to explain how phenomena function. (7)

F

Factual judgments: Factual judgments (or judgments of fact) focus on describing or explaining some aspect of the way the world is. (7)

Fair-mindedness: Fair-mindedness requires us to be as unbiased and impartial as we can when making a judgment. (1)

Fallacy: A fallacy is a common type of weak argument that has considerable persuasive power; an argument pattern whose persuasive power greatly exceeds its probative value (i.e., evidential worth). (1; 4)

Fallibilism: Fallibilism is the recognition that any claim to knowledge could be mistaken. (1)

False dilemma: False dilemma is an attempt to force people to consider only two choices, one of which is usually repugnant. If they accept the dilemma, they must choose the other as the conclusion. (4)

Framing: Framing an issue refers to setting up an issue in terms of a particular set of concepts that suggest a certain way of looking at the issue. (5; 7)

G

Generality: The less detailed or specific a term is, the more general we say it is. (7)

General explanations: General explanations are not directed at an individual or a particular event, but rather at more general tendencies. (5)

Generalizability principle: The generalizability principle means that the rules you follow and judgments you make when relating to others are rules and judgments you think everyone should make in a similar situation. (15)

Guilt by association: Guilt by association is a fallacy in which a person argues for rejecting a claim because it is a position which is also held by people who are viewed unfavourably. (4)

H

Hasty generalization: Arguers commit the fallacy of hasty generalization when they generalize from only a few (or sometimes no) cases. (4)

Historical analogy: A historical analogy is one in which we try to use an understanding of previous events to predict what would happen now if we took similar action. (5)

I

Ideological fixity: Ideological fixity is an unwavering and unquestioning commitment to a political, social, or philosophical position. (11)

Improper appeal to common practice: Improper appeal to common practice is committed when a proponent attempts to defend a position by merely claiming that a practice is widespread. (4)

Inductive argument: In an inductive argument, the premises provide support for but do not entail the conclusion. (3)

Inquiry: Inquiry is the process of carefully examining an issue in order to come to a reasoned judgment. (1)

Instrumental judgments: Instrumental judgments deal with questions having to do with reasoning about means to an end or goal. (7)

Interpretive judgments: Interpretive judgments deal with questions of meaning. (7)

Irrelevance: A premise is irrelevant to a conclusion when its truth or falsity does not influence the truth or falsity of the conclusion. (4)

Irrelevant standard: Arguers commit the fallacy of irrelevant standard when they criticize a policy or program for not achieving goals which the program never expected to achieve. (4)

Issue: An issue is a challenge, controversy, or difference in point of view that can be the focus for inquiry; a matter which is unsettled, in dispute, or up for debate. (1; 7)

J

Justification: Justification means having good reasons for one's belief or action. (1)

L

Libertarianism: Someone who holds a libertarian view of the world believes strongly in the priority of human liberty and takes positions that oppose government intervention. (2)

Linked argument: In a linked argument, the premises do not provide direct, independent support for the conclusion, but work together like links of a chain. Linked arguments are only as strong as the weakest premise. (3)

M

Meta-analysis: Meta-analysis is a method statisticians have developed to bring together and use data from a multitude of studies. It is a statistical method which involves sifting through all previous research and collecting the data from high-quality studies into one big sample and then doing statistical analysis on this new "sample." This method results in larger samples and, in principle, more reliable statistical conclusions. (13)

Meta-ethics: Meta-ethics is the study of the basis of ethics and the logic of moral terms. (15)

N

Naturalistic fallacy: Proponents commit the naturalistic fallacy when they try to come to a judgment on an issue which has an evaluative dimension purely on the basis of factual considerations. (7)

Necessary condition: To say that X is a necessary condition for Y is to say that it is impossible to have Y without X. (3)

Negative correlation: There is a negative correlation between two things when as one thing increases the other decreases. (5)

Normative ethics: Normative ethics looks at which rules and judgments express correct moral views. (15)

O

Objection: An objection is a reason or argument raised against a prior argument which casts the argument into doubt. (8)

Occam's razor: Occam's razor, as it is applied in contemporary practice, can be stated as "all things being equal, choose the simplest explanation." (5)

Onus: This term refers to the responsibility for making the case (see *burden of proof*). (4)

Open-mindedness: Open-mindedness refers to the willingness to consider evidence and views that are contrary to our own. (1)

P

Particular explanations: Particular explanations focus on the question of why particular persons or things behave in a certain way. (5)

Popularity fallacy: The fallacy of popularity involves attempting to justify a belief on the basis that most people believe it or to justify an action on the basis that most people do it. (4)

Positive correlation: There is a positive correlation between two things if when one thing increases so does the other. (5)

Post hoc fallacy: The post hoc fallacy is the erroneous leap to the conclusion that one event has caused another from the fact that one event occurred before the other. (5)

Precedent analogy: A precedent analogy is an argument which attempts to establish a conclusion on the basis that the circumstances of the case at issue are like those of another case. (5)

Premise: An argument is a set of claims, one of which, the conclusion, is supported by one or more other claims, called premises. (3)

Prima facie: A prima facie judgment is a preliminary judgment made with the knowledge that it is tentative and open to revision in light of subsequent information or other considerations. (4; 5)

Principle of charity: The principle of charity states that one should choose the most favourable interpretation of the argument consistent with the actual argument content. (3)

Probative value: In law, probative value is the legal weight or evidential worth that a piece of evidence should be given when making a finding. (4)

Problematic premise: A premise that is neither credible nor acceptable is called a problematic premise. (4)

Prospective study: Prospective studies isolate a group of subjects, often called a cohort, and follow the subjects over time, looking for correlates to outcomes such as the occurrence of a disease or certain behavioural tendencies. (13)

Q

Questionable cause fallacy: The questionable cause fallacy is committed by any argument for a causal explanation that does not provide prima facie adequate evidence for the claim. (5)

R

Random sample: The idea of random sampling is that the assignment of individuals into the two groups being studied should not be biased in some way; for example, one group should not be older or healthier or "meaner" than the other. (13)

Reasons explanation: Reasons explanations are explanatory judgments which identify the beliefs and purposes that motivated an action rather than the causes of the action. (5; 7)

Reasoned judgment: A reasoned judgment is a judgment based on a critical evaluation of relevant information and arguments. (1)

Red herring: Arguers commit the fallacy of red herring when they introduce an irrelevant issue which has the effect of distracting from (or shifting the focus from) the question at hand. (4)

Reductio ad absurdum: *Reductio ad absurdum* is an argumentative strategy that argues that a particular position should be rejected because accepting it would justify absurd outcomes. (5)

Reduction: Reduction refers to the idea in science that observable processes like illness or biological growth can be explained in terms of more basic, often invisible processes at the cellular or chemical level. (12)

Relative risk: Relative risk is a measure of the impact of a particular factor on an outcome. (13)

Response: A response is an answer to or rebuttal of an objection. (8)

Retrospective study: A retrospective study typically identifies a group of people suffering from an illness or effect and attempts to find a factor or factors in the history of this group that are different than those in a group of similar people who do not have the illness or effect (the control group). (13)

Review article: Review articles are articles that review the research. (6)

Rhetorical effect: The rhetorical effect of an argument is its persuasive power. (4)

Risk factor: A risk factor is any factor for which there is sufficient evidence to show that it is correlated with a particular (usually negative) outcome. (13)

S

Sample: A sample is the group of people selected to provide a basis for making an inference about the target population that is the object of the researcher's inquiry. (13)

Sample of convenience: A sample of convenience is a sample of subjects that researchers can get easy access to; for example, students, or people who respond to ads for volunteer subjects. (13)

Semantic ambiguity: Semantic ambiguity occurs when particular words or phrases are ambiguous. (7)

Sound argument: A valid deductive argument with true premises is called a sound argument. (3)

Spectre: Arguers commit the fallacy of argument by spectre (often called the slippery slope fallacy) when they argue against an action on the grounds that the long run consequences of such an action will be disastrous, without supplying sufficient evidence to show that the supposed consequences are likely to follow. (4)

Standardizing an argument: Standardizing an argument is the process of outlining an argument to reveal its structure. (3)

State of practice: State of practice refers to how things stand at the moment with respect to the issue and its manifestations. (8)

Statistical significance: A statistically significant difference is a difference that is sufficiently large that we can show mathematically that the difference between the two groups is unlikely to be due to chance. (13)

Straw person: Arguers commit the fallacy of straw person when they attribute to a proponent a view the proponent does not hold; they pretend to refute the opposing view by attacking the misrepresented position. (4)

Strong inductive argument: With strong inductive arguments, if the premises are true, then it is *likely* that the conclusion is true. (3)

Sub-argument: The support for premises of an argument are called sub-arguments. (3)

Sufficient condition: To say that X is a sufficient condition for Y is to say that if X is present, then Y must also be present. (3)

Syntactic ambiguity: Syntactic ambiguity occurs when the ambiguity is a result of the sentence structure. (7)

T

Two wrongs fallacy: The two wrongs fallacy consists of trying to justify your wrongdoing on the basis that you were wronged, or claiming that you should get away with some wrong because others have gotten away with it. (4)

V

Vagueness: Vagueness occurs when terms are imprecise so that the range of their application is not clear. (7)

Validity (experimental): An experiment is said to have validity if it provides a good basis for generalizing to real-world behaviour. (13)

Valid argument form: An argument form is valid when, if true statements are substituted into the premises, the conclusion must be true. (3)

Photo Credits

p. 6	© Matteo De Stefano/istock
p. 25	Archives du 7eme Art/GetStock
p. 31	Getty Images
p. 49	© copyright 1997 by Randy Glasbergen www.glasbergen.com
p. 76	http://graphicalx.com/blog/2008/08/ad-hominem/
p. 111	Google.com
p. 114	http://www.cancerfightingstrategies.com/index.html
p. 115	http://zapatopi.net/treeoctopus/
p. 121	US Air Force
p. 146	Library and Archives Canada C-014078
p. 165	http://www.deathpenaltyinfo.org/
p. 212	© Copyright Anne Burgess and licensed for reuse under this Creative Commons Licence. www.geograph.org.uk
p. 230	Published by C.F. Cheffins, Lith, Southhampton Buildings, London, England, 1854 in Snow, John. On the Mode of Communication of Cholera, 2nd Ed, John Churchill, New Burlington Street, London, England, 1855.
p. 258	http://wiki.dickinson.edu/images/1/1b/Comic2-1368.pngwww.qwantz.com
p. 264	© Art Media / Heritage-Images / Imagestate (both images)
p. 267	Philip Game/GetStock.com
p. 273	© Art Media / Heritage-Images / Imagestate
p. 274	Royalty-Free/CORBIS/DAL
p. 278	© JANA STERBAK (b.1955 in Prague); Vanitas—Flesh dress for albino anorexic, 1987; collection of MNAM Centre Pompidou
p. 281	© 1985 David Aschkenas.
p. 292	Jonathan Hayward/Canadian Press
p. 322	AP Photo/Chao Soi Cheong
p. 325	Courtesy of www.911sharethetruth.com

Index

A

Abstracts, 111, 112
Abusive ad hominem, 65
Acceptable premise, 75–76
Ad hominem, 65–66, 206. *See also* Red herring
Aesthetic judgment, 21–22, 104, 130
Aesthetics, 293
Affirming the consequent, 50
Alexander the Great, 41
Allmand, Warren, 184
Alternative solutions, failure to consider, 182
Alternative views, 139, 140, 176, 316–317, 328–329
Altruism, 254–255
Ambiguity, 125
Analogical arguments, 46, 83–88
    evaluating, 85–88
    historical analogy, 84–85
    precedent analogies, 83–84
Analogical distance, 85–86
Analogical reasoning, 301
Analogues, 85
Anecdotal evidence, 63, 70–71, 208
Animal-control bylaw, 34
Anomalies, 216, 329
Anomalous data, 329
Appeal to authority. *See also* Sources
    claims lacking consensus among experts, 105–106
    competence of expert, 106
    domain of knowledge and, 104–105
    improper, 108
    physical sciences, 104–105
Appeal to tradition, 69–70
Argument
    analogical, 46, 83–88
    to best explanation, 215–220, 248, 256, 327, 329–330
    causal analogies, 84–85
    cogent inductive, 61
    convergent, 43–44
    defined, 41
    diagrammed, 42–45
    evaluated, 157–171
    and explanation, 88–91
    historical analogy, 84–85
    inductive, 46, 61–62
    and inquiry, 40
    key function of, 61
    linked, 42, 43, 44
    Modus Ponens (MP), 50, 51
    Modus Tolles (MT), 51
    narrowing a question, 166
    precedent analogies, 83–84
    principle of charity, 41–42
    probative value of, 63
    reductio, 82–83, 86, 87
    sound, 47
    standardizing the, 41–42
    strong inductive, 46, 61
    structure, 41–45
    sub-arguments, 44–45
    valid deductive, 45–50
    valid form, 47–48
Argumentation
    capital punishment, 171
    in reasoned judgment, 5–6, 9
Argument by spectre, 73–74
Argument from ignorance, 72–73
Aristotle, 41, 215
Arts, the
    context of issue, 272–274, 286
    debate in, 144
    evaluating artwork, 275–279, 286–287
    examination of issue, 265–266, 285–286
    interpretation, 268–272
    nature of inquiry in, 279–280
    observation, 265, 266–268
    public art controversy, 280–287
    structure of inquiry, 265–279
Assumptions, 53–54
Atomic bomb, 121, 127
Autonomous, 14

B

Banks, Russell, 27
Begging the question, 71–72, 329
Bentham, Jeremy, 299
Bernoulli, Daniel, 108
Best explanation, argument to, 215–220, 248, 256, 327, 329

Bias, 9, 66, 106–107, 110, 160–161
    as obstacle to inquiry, 200
    in sampling, 242
    self-awareness of personal, 164, 201
    sources, 61, 106–107, 160–161, 326
Biased framing, 183
Blackmore, Winston, 292
Braidwood Commission, 11
Burden of proof, 72–73, 140–141, 175–176
    conspiracy theories, 323
    extraordinary explanations, 315
    failure to give appropriate consideration to, 182
    scientific inquiry, 213

C

Campbell, Gordon, 60
Canadian Charter of Rights and Freedoms, 194
Capital punishment, 138–151
    appeals for clemency, 147
    in Canada, 146, 184
    "con" argument, 150, 165–168
    conservation *vs.* liberal view of, 151
    context, 145–153
    cost issue, 143, 164
    as "cruel and unusual punishment," 168
    current debate, 142–145
    deterrence argument, 143, 158–162
    discrimination issue, 166–167
    history of debate, 148–150
    incapacitation argument, 142–144, 162, 163
    moral issue, 143, 165, 166–167
    "pro" argument, 150, 158–164
    rehabilitation argument, 143, 167–168
    retribution argument, 143, 148–149
    risks and. benefits assessment, 167
    state of practice, 145–148
Case, 61
    evaluating a given, 182–183
    reasonable, 183–189
Case-controlled studies. *See* Retrospective studies
Castro, Fidel, 322
Causal claims, evaluating, 95, 245–248
Causal explanations, 90–95
    causal link, 91–92
    evaluating, 91–95
    general, 93–95
    Occam's razor, 93
    particular, 91–93
    and scientific inquiry, 221
Causal factor, 246
Certainty, desire for, 199–200
Charity, principle of, 41–42
Cholera, 229–232
Churchill, Winston, 127
Circular reasoning. *See* Begging the question
Circumstantial ad hominem, 66

Claims, 21–22, 29–30
    causal, 95, 245–248
    credible, 75
    evaluating, 61–62
    factual, 161–162, 169
    instrumental, 163
    lacking consensus among experts, 105–106
    weighing certainty or likelihood of, 178
Clifford, W.K., 317–321
Cogent inductive argument, 61
Cohort studies. *See* Prospective studies
Comparative judgements of value, 131, 164, 177, 220, 232, 317–322
Competing arguments, failure to examine, 182
Conceptual analysis, 251
Conclusion, 41
Confirmation bias, 312
Confounding factor, 222
Connotation, 125
Consequentialism, 299
Conservative orientation, 150–151, 152
Conspiracy, defined, 322
Conspiracy theories, 321–332
    alternative explanations, 328–329
    argument to best explanation, 329–330
    burden of proof, 323
    circularity of arguments in, 329
    context of issue, 325
    credibility of sources, 325–326
    defined, 322
    examination of issue, 323–325
    features of, 329–330
    selective data, use of, 329
    weighing claims, problem of, 331–332
Context of issues, 24–25, 31–32, 140–153
    in the arts, 272–274
    current debate laid out, 142–144
    extraordinary claims, 310, 325
    history of a debate, 141, 148–150
    intellectual, social, political and historical contexts, 141–144
    mapped, 142–153
    in science, 213, 220
    state of practice, 140–141, 145–148
    statistical research, 231–232
Continental drift, 216
Convergence, 243
Convergent argument, 43–44
Correlation, 93–94
Counter-example, 9, 49–50, 297
Creationism, 223–227
Credibility. *See also* Appeal to authority; Sources
    argument, 61
    of biased source, 61
    claims, 75, 77–78
    as concept, 62
    media sources, 110
    sources, 325–326

Criteria
  cogent inductive argument, 61
  critical evaluation, 5–6
Critical evaluation
  defined, 5
  of reasoning, 5–6. 9
  sources of information, 6–9, 100–118
Critical inquiry. *See* Inquiry
Cubism, 273, 275
Cultural relativism, 294

D

Darwin, Charles, 223–228, 249, 253, 254
Day, Stockwell, 147
Death penalty. *See* Capital punishment
Debate
  alternative views, 139–140
  in the arts, 144
  capital punishment, 142–153
  in critical inquiry, 11–13
  features of, 144–145
  history of a, 141, 148–150
  laid out, 143–144
  objections, 139–140
  responses, 139–140
  in scientific inquiry, 144
Deductive arguments, 45–46
Defensiveness, 200
Denotation, 125
Descent of Man (Darwin), 254
Descriptive judgments, 128–129
Dewey, John, 200
Dialectic, 144
Dialogue
  conducting, 203–208
  inquiry and, 13
  meaningful participation, 204
  productive interaction, 204–205
  respectful treatment, 204
  responding to fallacies, 205–208
  in science, 215
  self-monitoring of, 201
Dictator game, 257
Dion, Stéphane, 147
Discourse on Inequality (Rousseau), 252
Disraeli, Benjamin, 125
Double blind experiment, 242
Dubious assumptions, 54
Dziekanski, Robert, 11

E

Effect size, 244, 245
Egoyan, Atom, 27
"Either–or" fallacy, 183
Empirical sciences, 214

Enlightenment, 14
Entailment, 46
Epistemology, 293
Equivocation, 74–75, 125
Ethical arguments, failure to consider, 182
Ethical judgments, 30, 130
Ethical relativism, 293–298, 294
Ethics
  analogical reasoning, 301
  ethical relativism, 293–298
  examination of issue, 292–298
  generalizability principle, 300
  moral reasoning, 297–302
  "respect for persons," principle of, 299
  utilitarianism, 299
Ethnocentrism, 294
Euler, Leonhard, 49
Euler circles, 49
Euphemisms, 126
Evaluative judgments, 30, 129–133
Evolution, 223–228
Experiment, 222
Experimental studies, 241–243
Experimental validity, 247
Experts. *See also* Sources
  consensus among, 327
  evaluating, 104–108
Explanation
  argument *vs.*, 89
  causal, 90–95
  causal claims, 95
  general, 91
  general causal, 93–95
  particular, 91
  particular causal, 91–93
  reason, 89–90, 95
Explanatory judgments, 129
Extraordinary, the
  alternative explanations, 316–317, 328–329
  argument to best explanation, 327, 329–330
  burden of proof, 315
  causal reasoning, 313–317
  comparative evaluation, 317–321, 325–332
  context of issue, 310, 325
  defined, 307
  Elvis Presley, death of, 330
  examination of issue, 310, 323–325
  nature of claims, 307–309
  9/11 conspiracy theory, 321–332
  paranormal, 308
  prima facie evaluation, 310–313
  Sasquatch, 309

F

Factual claims, 161–162, 169
Factual judgments, 22, 30, 128–129, 131–133

Fair-mindedness, 15, 197
Fallacies, 62–78
    abusive ad hominem, 65
    ad hominem, 65–66, 206
    affirming the consequent, 50
    alternative solutions, failure to
        consider, 182
    anecdotal evidence, 63, 70–71, 208
    appeal to tradition, 69–70
    argument by spectre, 73–74
    argument from ignorance, 72–73
    begging the question, 71–72
    biased framing, 183
    burden of proof, failure to give appropriate consideration
        to, 182
    circumstantial ad hominem, 66
    competing arguments, failure of examine, 182
    defined, 9, 63
    "either–or," 183
    equivocation, 74–75
    false dilemma, 78
    faulty analogy, 207
    guilt by association, 67, 86–87, 87
    hasty conclusion, 208
    hasty generalization, 70
    illusory support, fallacies of, 64–75
    implications, failure to consider, 183
    improper appeal to authority, 108
    irrelevant reasons, 207–208
    irrelevant standard, 68
    of judgment, 182–183
    naturalistic, 132–133
    objections, failure to consider, 183
    popularity, 69–70, 207, 318–320
    post hoc, 91, 206–207
    problematic premise, 207
    questionable cause, 94
    red herring, 64–65
    responding to, 205–208
    rhetorical effect, 63–64
    similar fact evidence, 63
    straw person, 42, 67–68, 83
    two wrongs, 68–69
    unacceptability, fallacies of, 75–78
    uncertainty of claims, failure to consider, 182
Fallacious reasoning, 200–201
Fallibilism, 12, 105
False dilemma, 78
Farr, William, 229, 230
Faulty analogy, 207
Footnotes, 114–115
Framing an issue, 123, 176
Franco, General Francisco, 272
Freedom of religion, 302
Fruitfulness, 222, 229

G

Galileo, 213, 215
General causal explanations, 93–95
General explanation, 91
Generality, 124–125
Generalizability, 247, 256
Generalizability principle, 300
Google Scholar, 111
Grand Theft Auto, 238
Gray, Jessie, 283
Griffin, Kevin, 287
Groupthink, 200
Guernica, 263–279
Guilt by association, 67, 86–87, 87
Gun control, 149–150

H

Halley's Comet, 219
Harrow, Gustave, 282
Hasty conclusion, 208
Hasty generalization, 70
Hate speech, 194
Hess, Harry, 215–219
Historical analogy, 84–85
Hobbes, Thomas, 251–252
"Homo economicus" view, 257
Howe, C.D., 127
Human nature, 248–259
Hutton, James, 212–213

I

Identification with own beliefs, 200
Ideological fixity, 199–200
Ignorance, of other views, 199
Illusory support, fallacies of, 64–75
Implications, failure to consider, 183
Improper appeal to common practice, 69. *See also* Popularity,
    fallacy of
Inappropriate weighting, 183
Inductive argument, 46, 61–62
Inquiry
    argument and, 40
    critical evaluation, 5–9
    defined, 4, 122
    and dialogue, 13
    features of, 4–10
    guidelines for, 19–38
    guiding questions, 139
    issue, 4–5, 20–25, 29–32, 140–153
    nature of, 11–12
    occasions for, 10–11
    ongoing process of, 12–13
    overcoming to obstacles to, 201–203
    reasoned judgment, 5–10

self-monitoring of process of, 201–202
spirit of, 14–15, 197–203, 321
sprit of, 197–201
value of, 13–14
Inquiry dialogue. *See* Dialogue
Instrumental claims, 163
Instrumental judgments, 30, 130–131
Interpretive judgments, 30, 133–134, 280
Irrelevant premise, 64
Irrelevant reasons, 207–208
Irrelevant standard, 68
Issue
    characteristics, 122–124
    claims or judgments at, 21–22, 29–30
    context of, 24–25, 31–32, 140–153
    controversy, 123
    defined, 4
    examination of, 4–5, 22–24
    focus, 122
    as focus of critical inquiry, 4
    formulation, 20–21, 29
    frame, 123 (*see also* Issue, formulation)
    guiding questions, 28–29
    identifying the, 121–124
    neutrality, 123–124
    precision, 123
    question *vs.* topic, 123
    relevant reasons and arguments, 22–24, 30–31

J

Jacobs, Margo, 282
Jacobs, Robert Allen, 282
Jones, Inigo Owen, 108
Judgments
    aesthetic, 21–22, 130
    comparative judgements of value, 131, 164, 177, 220, 232, 317–321, 325–332
    descriptive, 128–129
    ethical, 30, 130
    evaluative, 30, 61–62, 129–133
    explanatory, 129
    factual, 22, 30, 128–129, 131–133
    instrumental, 30, 130–131
    interpretive, 30, 133–134, 280
    moral, 104, 141
    prima facie, 61–62
    reasonably confident, 180
    reasoned, 5–10, 25–28, 32–35, 177–183, 220, 221–228
    suspended, 180
    tentative, 180
    types of, 30, 126–134
    very confident, 180
Justification, 13

K

Kant, Immanuel, 14, 299
Kee, Virginia, 282
Keegstra, James, 194
Kin-selection, 254
Kovel, Joel, 283
Krauss, Rosalind, 283

L

Language
    ambiguity, 125
    euphemisms, 126
    generality, 124–125
    loaded, 125–126
    problematic use of, 124–126
    vagueness, 124
Layton, Jack, 147
Le Basi, Phil, 283
Leeuwenhoek, Anthony van, 213
Leviathan (Hobbes), 252
Liberal orientation, 151–152
Libertarian view, 32
Liebman, Joseph I., 281
Linked argument, 42, 43, 44
Loaded language, 125–126

M

Malthus, Thomas, 252
Marshall, Donald, 165
Marx, Karl, 252
Meaning, role of, 248, 257
Meta-analysis, 244
Meta-ethics, 295
Metaphysics, 293
Microscope, 213
Milgaard, Donald, 165
Minimum wage, 60
Modus Ponens (MP), 50, 51
Modus Tolles (MT), 51
Moral judgment, 104, 141, 299–301
Moral progress, 294, 295
Moral reasoning, 297–302

N

Narc, 238
Naturalistic fallacy, 132–133
Natural sciences
    argument to best explanation, 215–219
    process of inquiry, 219–220
Natural selection, 223, 250, 252
Necessary and sufficient condition, 50–53
Need to be right, 199
Negative correlation, 94

Newirth, Richard, 287
Nightingale, Florence, 229
9/11 Conspiracy. *See* Conspiracy theories
Nixon, Richard, 322
Normative ethics, 295

O

Objections, 139–140
    failure to consider, 183
Objectivism, 293–294, 296
Observation, 129
    in the arts, 265, 266–268
    in scientific inquiry, 214
Observational studies, 240–241
Occam's razor, 93
Oler, James, 292
Onus. *See* Burden of proof
Open-mindedness, 15, 197
Origins of the Species (Darwin), 224

P

Paranormal, 308
Particular causal explanation, 91–93
Particular explanation, 91
Peer review, 214, 223
Peer-reviewed sources, 107, 111
Personal convictions, See Self-awareness,
    of personal bias
Personal preferences, 6
Philosophical inquiry, 293
Picasso, 272–274
Plate tectonics, 215–219
Plato, 41
Political parties, orientation of, 152
Political philosophy, 293
Polygamy, 292, 298–303
Popularity, fallacy of, 69–70, 207, 318–320
Positive correlation, 94
Post hoc fallacy, 91, 206–207
Precedent analogies, 83–84
Preconceptions, 200
Prediction, 248
Premises, 41, 64. *See also* Claims
    acceptability criteria, 77–78
    acceptable, 75–76
    problematic, 75
    unacceptable, 78
Presley, Elvis, 330
Prima facie doubt, 76
Prima facie judgment, 61–62
Probative value, 63
Problematic premise, 75, 207
Prospective studies, 241
Psychological altruism, 255
Public art controversy, 280–287

"Public reasons," 298–299
Purpose explanations. *See* Causal explanations

Q

Quebec Agreement, 127
Question, *vs.* topic, 123
Questionable cause fallacy, 94

R

Racism, 252
Random sampling, 242
Re, Edward D., 281–282
Reasonable case, making a, 183–189
Reasonably confident judgments, 180
Reasoned judgment
    apportioning judgment, 180–181
    burden of proof, establishing, 175–176
    conflicting ethical values, 178
    cost and benefits, evaluation of, 178
    critical evaluation, 5–10
    defined, 5
    differences in weighting, 179–180
    ethical *vs.* practical considerations, 178
    evaluating reasons and arguments, 25–28, 32–35
    guidelines for reaching, 175–177
    maintaining objectivity, 177
    means and ends, 178
    in science, 220, 221–228
    synthesizing different views, 176
    weighing certainty or likelihood of claims, 178
    weighing different considerations, 176, 177–180
Reason explanations, 89–90, 95
Reasoning. *See* Argumentation; Moral reasoning;
    Scientific reasoning
Reciprocal altruism, 254
Red herring, 64–65. *See also* Ad hominem
Redi, Francesco, 221
Reductio argument, 82–83, 86, 87
Reduction, 221
Relative risk, 245
Resident Evil 4, 238
Respect, in inquiry dialogue, 204
"Respect for persons," principle of, 299
Responses, 139–140
Retrospective studies, 241
Review articles, 111
Rhetorical effect, 63–64
Risk factor, 243
Roosevelt, Franklin, 127
Rotblatt, Joseph, 127
Rousseau, Jean-Jacques, 251–252
Rubin, William, 284
Rushing to response, 201
Russell, Bertrand, 125

S

St. Clair, Betty, 284
Sample, 242
Sample generalizability, 247
Sample of convenience, 242
Sampling, 242
Sasquatch, 309
Scientific inquiry, 211–232
     anomalies, 216
     argument to best explanation, 215–220
     context of issues, 213, 220
     experiments, 222
     fruitfulness, 222, 229
     key aspects, 213
     in natural sciences, 219–220
     observation, 214
     peer review, 214
     reasoned judgment and, 220, 221–228
     statistical research, 231–232
     statistics, 228–232
     testability, 221–222, 315
     theories, 214–228
Scientific questions, evaluating, 327
Scientific reasoning, 214–215
Self-awareness, of personal
     bias, 164, 177, 201
Self-evaluation, of personal views, 202
Self-monitoring, of dialogue, 201–202
Semantic ambiguity, 125
Serra, Richard, 280, 281
Similar fact evidence, 63
Sinclair, Jim, 60
Slippery slope fallacy. *See* Argument
     by spectre
Smith, Roberta, 283
Smith, Ronald Allen, 147
Snow, John, 229
Social Darwinism, 249
Social sciences
     argument to best explanation, 248, 258
     assessing scientific claims in, 239–240
     causal claims, 245–248
     cause and effect, 247
     conceptual analysis, 251
     convergence, 243
     double blind experiment, 242
     effect size, 244, 245
     experimental studies, 241–243
     experimental validity, 247
     human nature, studying, 248–259
     inquiry in, 237–262
     meaning, role of, 248, 257
     meta-analysis, 244
     observational studies, 240–241
     prospective studies, 241
     random sampling, 242

     relative risk, 245
     retrospective studies, 241
     sample generalizability, 247
     sampling, 242
     social causation, 247
     statistical inferences in, 240–248
     statistically significance difference, 242
Sociobiology, 252
Socrates, 15, 41
Solomon, Holly, 284
Sound argument, 47
Sources, 6–9, 100–118
     biased, 61, 106–107, 160–161, 326
     books as, 116
     competence of expert, 106
     credible, 77, 325–326
     credible media sources, 110
     evaluating, 100–108
     finding credible, 109–116
     footnotes, 114–115
     peer-reviewed, 107, 111
     plausible explanations, 107–108
     review articles, 111
     textbooks as, 116
     Websites as, 110–115
     Wikipedia, 113
Spanish Civil War, 272
Specialization (expertise), 106
Spirit of Inquiry, 14–15, 197–203, 321
     achieving, 197–199
     ethics of belief, 321
     fair-mindedness, 15, 197
     obstacles to, 199–201
     open-mindedness, 15, 197
     overcoming obstacles to inquiry, 201–203
     responding to fallacies, 205–208
Standardizing the argument
     defined, 41
     and principle of charity, 41–42
Statistically significance difference, 242
Statistics
     causal claims, evaluating, 245–248
     in scientific inquiry, 228–232
     in social science inquiry, 240–248
Steinlauf, Norman, 281
Sterbak, Jana, 278
Straw person fallacy, 42, 67–68, 83
Strong inductive argument, 46, 61
Sub-arguments, 44–45
Sufficient condition, 51. *See also* Necessary
     and sufficient condition
Summarizing, 331–332
Suspended judgments, 180
Sweet Hereafter, The, 27
Syntactic ambiguity, 125

T

Technology, in science, 213
Teleological explanations. *See* Causal explanations
Telescope, 213
Tentative judgments, 180
Testability, 221–222, 315
Theory, scientific, 214–228
    causal explanations, 221
    confounding factor, 222
    experiments, 222
    fruitfulness, 222, 229
    testability, 221–222, 315
    vs. law, 227
Tilted Arc (Serra), 280–287
Topic, *vs.* question, 123
Truscott, Steven, 165, 166
Truth, concept, 62
Two wrongs, 68–69

U

Ultimatum game, 255–256
Unacceptability, fallacies of, 75–78
Uncertainty of claims, failure to consider, 182
Universal generalizations, 49–50
Universalism. *See* Objectivism
Untrustworthy websites, 113–114
Utilitarianism, 299

V

Vagueness, 124
Valid argument form, 47–48
Valid deductive arguments, 45–50

Validity, 247
Vancouver public art program, 287
Vanitas (Sterbak), 278
Venn, John, 49
Venn diagrams, 49
Very confident judgments, 180
"Vicious" dogs. *See* Animal-control bylaw
Video games, violent, 237–240
Vine-Matthews explanation of magnetic stripping, 219

W

Walker, D.C., 86
Watergate, 322
Watson, Harry, 283–284
Websites, 110–115
    bias, 110
    evaluating, 111, 112–113
    peer-reviewed articles, 111
    preliminary sources of
        information, 110–112
    untrustworthy, 113–114
    Wikipedia, 113
Wegener, Alfred, 216
Weiss, Theodore, 282
Weyergraf-Serra, Clara, 283
Wikipedia, 113
William of Occam, 93
Wilson, E.O., 252
Winter, John, 60